Olivier Urbain is Director of the Toda  Research. He is the author of *Daisak* *Transformation and Global Citizenship* *Conflict Transformation: Harmonies and Dissonances in Geopolitics* (2008, *Daisaku Ikeda and Dialogue for Peace* (2013), all published by I.B.Tauris.

A FORUM FOR PEACE

Daisaku Ikeda's Proposals to the UN

Edited by Olivier Urbain

in association with
THE TODA INSTITUTE FOR GLOBAL PEACE AND POLICY RESEARCH

Published in 2014 by I.B.Tauris & Co Ltd
6 Salem Road, London W2 4BU
175 Fifth Avenue, New York NY 10010
www.ibtauris.com

Distributed in the United States and Canada Exclusively by Palgrave Macmillan
175 Fifth Avenue, New York NY 10010

ISBN: 978 1 78076 840 3 (pb)
ISBN: 978 1 78076 839 7 (hb)

A full CIP record for this book is available from the British Library
A full CIP record is available from the Library of Congress

Library of Congress Catalog Card Number: available

Typeset in Garamond by Initial Typesetting Services, Edinburgh

Printed and bound in Great Britain by T.J. International, Padstow, Cornwall

Contents

Foreword

*Ambassador Anwarul K. Chowdhury**

It is a distinct pleasure for me to write this foreword of a very special publication on the contribution of a very special person for the cause of sustainable peace and development.

An apostle of peace and an esteemed humanist, Daisaku Ikeda, President of the Soka Gakkai International (SGI), has been issuing a peace proposal presented to the people of the world on 26 January every year since 1983, the year when the SGI was accredited as a nongovernmental organization (NGO) by the Economic and Social Council of the United Nations.

These annual peace proposals are well-conceived, well-thought-out and well-articulated, and focus on four areas of great importance and relevance to our world. Those relate to building the Culture of Peace, highlighting the contribution and participation of women, advancing reforms and promoting the relevance of the United Nations, and emphasizing humanism as the basis of global civilization.

2012 marked the thirtieth anniversary of Ikeda's sustained efforts to make the world a better place and the UN a better organization through his worthwhile recommendations and proposals. To mark the occasion, this publication concentrates on the United Nations and related areas as reflected in each of the peace proposals.

I recall Ikeda's unshakable belief in the UN, expressed to me in our dialogues and communications over the years, underscoring that to protect the United Nations is to protect our nations, ourselves, our children and our future. I know of no one who has highlighted the role and responsibility of the world body so consistently, relentlessly and substantively for such a long period of

* Under-Secretary-General and High Representative of the United Nations (2002–2007) and Ambassador of Bangladesh to the UN (1996–2001).

time. Some UN functionaries and scholars have addressed similar issues, but none for as long and as consistently as he has done. More significantly, he has evolved a consistent philosophy of support and encouragement for multilateralism with the UN system at its core. We feel truly proud of that.

Here I would like to reiterate what I said in 2003 on the occasion of the twentieth anniversary: "The unique worth of President Ikeda's proposals stands out when we find that they relate to humanity as a whole but, at the same time, are relevant for the welfare and well-being of every individual person." These proposals have contained brilliant ideas and suggestions for the betterment of our world. I recall with great honor and appreciation when in 2006 on behalf of the United Nations Secretary-General I received in Tokyo from President Ikeda his concrete proposals on the reform of the United Nations to make the organization more effective.

By their very nomenclature, President Ikeda's proposals relate to peace in general. He particularly emphasizes the positive, active pursuit of peace as opposed to the absence of war that he calls "passive peace." He has been emphasizing that the Culture of Peace—peace through dialogue; peace through nonviolence—should be the foundation of the new global society. I believe this focus on the Culture of Peace is very essential if the world is to become a peaceful and secure place for us and our future generations. He very appropriately underscores that peace is not something distant but is something which can be pursued through day-to-day efforts.

I notice with great satisfaction that in his proposals, he has highlighted empowerment of people as a major element in building the Culture of Peace and very eloquently emphasized the emergence of women in leading the way as active agents in creating peace. The 2001 peace proposal focused on the emergence of women in the twenty-first century, eloquently emphasizing that the emergence of women would have the potential of turning society toward the benefits of peace and prosperity.

Noting that 2010 is the tenth anniversary of UN Security Council Resolution 1325, which asks for equal participation of women at all decision-making levels, in his peace proposal that year, Ikeda urged a renewal of efforts to ensure gender equality in education and called for women's concerns and perspectives to be put at the center of human development initiatives. He also calls for schools to function as centers for fostering among young people a vibrant Culture of Peace.

President Ikeda's belief in human capacity and potential ability, particularly those of young people, to overcome the most insurmountable obstacles continues to inspire me immensely. He encourages the youth to further exert themselves in order to contribute to global peace and solidarity. Very meaningfully, he asserts that "In writing these proposals, my greatest hope, my determination and commitment is to sow the seeds of change in young people's hearts."

I particularly recall the emphasis President Ikeda put on human rights education, ecological integrity and infrastructure for peace in his 2008 peace proposal. This focus earned the deep admiration of the international community. His call for broadening grassroots engagement and empowerment of people through learning toward collective action and his initiative for the UN Decade of Education for Sustainable Development has been crucially remarkable.

Ikeda's editorial in the Inter Press Service (IPS) Journal in December 2008 with the title "There's No Law That Says People Have to Suffer" articulated wonderfully what needs to be done for the global realization of human rights. In this context, I also believe strongly that the time is now ripe for the United Nations to recognize the human right to peace as an independent, self-standing human right alongside the right to development.

President Ikeda's championship of the cause of disarmament, in particular the elimination of nuclear weapons, has been outstanding as the abolition of nuclear weapons has assumed new urgency in view of the uncertainty and insecurity that the world is passing through at the present time. He called for a "world without war" in his 1984 peace proposal and a "world without nuclear weapons" in his 2003 and 2010 peace proposals.

The world should respond to his call for intensive efforts over the coming years to achieve these objectives, culminating in a nuclear abolition summit to be held in Hiroshima and Nagasaki in 2015, which would symbolically mark the end of the era of nuclear weapons within the lifetimes of survivors of the nuclear bombings of those cities. By creating "expanding circles of physical and psychological security," President Ikeda believes such efforts could draw in countries whose nuclear intentions are unclear or which stand outside of existing nonproliferation regimes. His profound reiteration that "the use of the hard power of military force never produces real stability" is truly inspiring to all of us and should invariably be kept in focus by the world powers.

I also value tremendously the special attention Ikeda has given to highlighting the involvement of civil society in the activities of the UN. His proposals for a people's assembly and a global people's council are forward-looking and merit serious consideration by the international community.

In the 2010 peace proposal titled "Toward a New Era of Value Creation," Ikeda urges concrete steps toward generating meaningful employment opportunities—what the International Labour Organization (ILO) calls "decent work"—in the current economic downturn and making investment in education for girls a priority development objective.

I believe that the special attention which President Ikeda has given to reform of the United Nations in his peace proposals, particularly during the last few years, gives him a unique distinction in the international community. Recognizing the universal role of the UN, he emphasizes that to be effective the world body should be an organization of the people, by the people and for the people. He advocates that the focus of the programmes and activities of the United Nations should be on human security. In this context, his proposals relating to the rehabilitation of child soldiers and the banning of land mines have been remarkable. He has even looked into the future of the resource needs for UN activities and proposed a people's fund for additional funding sources for the organization so that it can avoid the current over-dependence on the contributions of member states.

Finally, I believe that the true foundation of all the peace proposals of President Ikeda has been the reawakening of the human spirit—a spirit that should energize and empower each and every individual belonging to our planet with love and concern for each other for the greater good of humanity. He talks about a human revolution which will bring out the best in everybody and which should be the ultimate objective of every individual and every nation.

It has been an honor for me to know President Ikeda from close quarters and to be appreciative of his unflinching commitment to peace. My meetings with him over the years have strengthened again and again my belief that our world is in need of the wisdom, dedication, compassion and guidance of a personality like him to spread the message of the Culture of Peace and human development for the benefit of humankind. I continue to cherish a wish to see him warmly welcomed at the United Nations so that representatives of the nations of the world and civil society have the opportunity to appreciate his genuine and powerful message for world peace and global development.

I strongly hope that this publication will be read by all those interested in the goals and objectives of the United Nations and its effectiveness, particularly by today's youth, encouraging all to contribute positively to the strengthening of what President Ikeda calls the "Parliament of Humanity."

List of Proposals

Peace Proposals

Nuclear Abolition Proposal

United Nations Proposal

Environment Proposals

CHAPTER 1

A UN Living Up to Its Mission

Fulfilling the Mission: Empowering the UN to Live Up to the World's Expectations

2006 United Nations Proposal (Full Text)
August 30, 2006

The structure of world peace cannot be the work of one man, or one party, or one Nation. . . . It must be a peace which rests on the cooperative effort of the whole world.[1]

These were the words with which US President Franklin D. Roosevelt[2]— one of the parents of the United Nations, and indeed, the man who gave the organization its name—addressed the US Congress in March 1945. Roosevelt didn't live to see the birth of the international organization dedicated to world peace of which he had dreamed. He passed away in April 1945, just one month after speaking these words and a few weeks before the United Nations Conference on International Organization convened to draft the United Nations Charter.

At the San Francisco Conference, attended by representatives of fifty nations, there was a surging sense of joy and hope that the birth of this international organization would help humankind break the vicious cycles of war and tragedy and move the world toward peace and security. The conference was described as a "landmark" and a "milestone in the long march of man to

---

1   Roosevelt, Franklin D. 1945. *The War Messages of Franklin D. Roosevelt: December 8, 1941, to April 13, 1945.* Washington: United States of America, p. 192.
2   Franklin D. Roosevelt (1882–1945), 32nd President of the United States (1933–45).

a better future,"[3] indicative of the world's great hope and expectation on the birth of the United Nations.

The United Nations Charter was adopted after three months of intensive debate and discussions, and was the culmination of the vow "to save succeeding generations from the scourge of war, which twice in our lifetime has brought untold sorrow to mankind. . . ."[4] These words in the Preamble of the Charter were not written merely as a reflection of the mistakes of the past, but were informed by a sense of responsibility for the generations to come.

A universal forum

Thirteen years ago (1993), I had occasion to visit the Opera House in San Francisco where the Charter was adopted. Reflecting on the dramatic moment in world history when the United Nations was born to serve as the parliament of humanity, I could not suppress a renewed sense of the immensity of the mission with which the UN has been entrusted.

That mission, to prevent the world from experiencing the scourge of yet another world war, has subsequently been constantly challenged; at times it seemed that the organization would fail in this most crucial task. This was certainly the case during the crises of the Cold War, when the world was split into rival blocs.

A variety of conflicts and tensions continue to plague the world, and the situation at the start of the twenty-first century has become further aggravated with the emerging crisis of international terrorism. Furthermore, global issues such as poverty, hunger, environmental degradation and refugee crises continue to pose fundamental threats to human dignity.

The difficult realities confronting the UN sixty years after its birth were expressed quite explicitly in the words of UN Secretary-General Kofi Annan[5] in his address to the 2005 World Summit: "deep divisions among Member States, and the underperformance of our collective institutions, were

---

3   Lauren, Paul Gordon. 1996. *Power and Prejudice: The Politics and Diplomacy of Racial Discrimination.* Boulder, Colorado: Westview Press, p. 161.

4   UN (United Nations). 1945. "Preamble" in the "Charter of the United Nations."

5   Kofi Annan (1938–), Ghanaian statesman, 7th Secretary-General of the United Nations (1997–2006).

preventing us from coming together to meet the threats we face and seize the opportunities before us."[6]

Given that the UN is an intergovernmental organization whose constituent members are sovereign states, innovative reform ideas and efforts will inevitably face the impediments of conflicting national interests. This is the disempowering reality that has confronted the UN for many years. People's disappointment in the UN has led to escalating criticism of the powerlessness of the international organization.

In certain respects, the UN has failed to keep pace with the changing realities of our times, and there are certainly many major hurdles and criticisms that the UN has yet to overcome. Nevertheless, as long as there are people in this world who suffer, who live under threats and crises, we absolutely cannot afford to dismiss the great value and mission of the UN.

With a membership of 192 states, the UN is the most universal forum available; the UN alone is capable of promoting international cooperation and conferring legitimacy to such efforts and actions. Therefore, I believe that there is no other realistic solution than to provide effective support to the UN and work for its revitalization. We must start from the recognition that the UN has, for sixty years, provided humanitarian assistance to regions in need and acted as a forum for global dialogue where international consensus could be reached on issues of importance.

As I engage in dialogue with the world's political, cultural and intellectual leaders, we often exchange thoughts on the future of the UN. If I were to distill and summarize their views, most of these leaders, while admitting the problems and challenges that the organization faces, subscribe to the view that the UN needs to be supported and empowered.

Many have pointed out that even if UN-centered initiatives are agreed on and ready to be implemented, there will always be national leaders who, to protect national interest or position, distance themselves from commitment to specific action. In my conversations with successive UN Secretaries-General, including Javier Pérez de Cuéllar[7] and Boutros Boutros-Ghali,[8] they have

---

6   Annan, Kofi. 2005. "Address to the 2005 World Summit." Press Release. September 14.

7   Javier Pérez de Cuéllar (1920–), Peruvian diplomat, 5th UN Secretary-General (1982–91), Prime Minister of Peru (2000–01).

8   Boutros Boutros-Ghali (1922–), Egyptian statesman, 6th UN Secretary-General (1992–96).

consistently pointed out the irony that while the world places the maximum expectations on the UN, it provides only minimal support.

The critical question, therefore, is how can this situation be resolved? First of all, we must constantly recall that a core purpose of the UN is to be the parliament of humanity, a venue where all voices can be heard and all perspectives represented. However seriously national interests clash and crises deepen, I believe that the answer lies in the commitment to a relentless process of dialogue, steadily creating the foundations for common efforts to resolve the challenges that face us.

Without dialogue, the world will continue to stumble through the confusion of darkness and division. Just as, in Greek mythology, Ariadne's thread made possible a safe exit from the Minotaur's labyrinth, dialogue can help us find our way out of the baffling maze of crises that surround us.

The continued process of dialogue fosters the ethos of coexistence and tolerance that our times demand. It is my firm belief that this will give birth to a "culture of peace"—the advent of which represents a critical transition in human history.

Today, the world faces mounting crises including the deadlock in Iraq and the Middle East as a whole, the possible development of nuclear weapons capabilities by North Korea and Iran, the deteriorating state of affairs in Afghanistan and ongoing regional conflicts in Africa and elsewhere. But the complexity of these challenging problems is precisely the reason why it is crucial to patiently and persistently seek out paths to resolution, making maximum use of the channels for global dialogue that are both the UN's most particular strength and the very well-springs of soft power.

The advancing processes of globalization worldwide have been accompanied by deepening divisions and conflicts—both within and between societies. We see around us a spreading "culture of war" that justifies the use of war and violent means to realize desired ends.

It is absolutely vital that we dismantle this culture of war. We must use dialogue to advance resolutely toward the creation of a truly peaceful global society in which there is genuine respect for differences of position and outlook and where there is a shared reverence for the human dignity of all.

I wish to urge again that the UN play a focal role in the grand project of constructing a civilization imbued with the spirit of dialogue.

Dag Hammarskjöld's commitment to dialogue

As we strive to envision the direction the UN should take in the twenty-first century, I believe there is much we can learn from the life and example of Dag Hammarskjöld,[9] the second Secretary-General of the organization. His achievements shine in the annals of UN history and his moral force and integrity as the "conscience of the United Nations" command wide respect to this day.

Dag Hammarskjöld was a statesman and economist born in Sweden just over a century ago. In the midst of the mounting tensions of the Cold War, Hammarskjöld took the lead in expanding the UN's responsibilities beyond a passive role of merely responding to crises, to a more proactive role in the promotion of peace in the world.

His talents were particularly visible in his efforts to resolve the Suez Crisis, as well as conflicts in Lebanon, Laos and elsewhere. His active pursuit of "quiet diplomacy," as he personally led missions to different regions in order to mediate conflicts, remains as his enduring legacy.

There were voices critical of this style of proactive diplomacy on the part of the UN and its Secretary-General. Hammarskjöld's actions were denounced, for example, by the Soviet Premier Nikita Khrushchev,[10] who demanded his resignation. Hammarskjöld refused to succumb to this pressure and continued to promote UN leadership for the resolution of international crises.

Hammarskjöld expressed his unwavering resolve in his book *Markings,* published after his death:

> "The Uncarved Block"—remain at the Center, which is yours and that of all humanity. For those goals which it gives to your life, do the utmost which, at each moment, is possible for you. Also, act without thinking of the consequences, or seeking anything for yourself.[11]

---

9   Dag Hammarskjöld (1905–61), Swedish economist and statesman, 2nd UN Secretary-General (1953–61), posthumous recipient of the Nobel Prize for Peace in 1961.

10 Nikita Khrushchev (1894–1971), Premier of the Soviet Union (1958–64).

11 Hammarskjöld, Dag. 1964. *Markings.* Trans. by Leif Sjoberg and W. H. Auden. New York: Alfred A. Knopf, p. 159.

Driven by a sense of moral, even religious, mission, he continued to strive until the last moment of his life to empower the UN to respond to the world's expectations.

In September 1961, en route to a meeting with President Moise Tshombe[12] of Katanga in an effort to resolve the Congo Crisis, Hammarskjöld's plane crashed in Northern Rhodesia (now Zambia), causing his death. He was fifty-six. For his outstanding achievements, Hammarskjöld was posthumously awarded the Nobel Peace Prize for 1961.

At the time of his death, Hammarskjöld was engaged not only in attempting to resolve the conflict in Congo, but in another important task. Hammarskjöld had profound respect for the "philosopher of dialogue," Martin Buber,[13] and was planning to translate his classic work *I and Thou* into Swedish.

Their friendship began in 1952, a year before Hammarskjöld became Secretary-General. As their exchanges and mutual respect deepened, a strong desire arose in Hammarskjöld to translate Buber's works. When he shared that wish with the philosopher, Buber suggested he translate *I and Thou*. This exchange took place just a few weeks before Hammarskjöld's fatal mission to Congo.

Hammarskjöld immediately contacted a publisher in Sweden and wrote a letter to Buber telling him agreement had been obtained. As he left New York for Congo, he had with him the German-language edition of *I and Thou*, which had been personally given to him by the author. He found the time amidst his demanding schedule, in flight and during his short stay in Leopoldville (now Kinshasa), to work on the translation of Buber's book. Later, after the plane crash, the first twelve pages of the Secretary-General's manuscript translation were found among his personal effects.

Buber received Hammarskjöld's final letter just one hour after he heard the news of the plane crash on the radio. Buber deeply lamented the death of this man of passion and goodwill who had given everything, including his life, for his mission.

Hammarskjöld shared a deep conviction with Buber, which he fervently wished to convey through the translation of Buber's work. This was the

---

12   Moise Tshombe (1919–69), President of the state of Katanga (1960–63), Premier of the united Congo Republic (now known as the Democratic Republic of the Congo) (1964–65).

13   Martin Buber (1878–1965), German-Jewish philosopher.

firm belief that no matter how dire and challenging the situation may be, humans must engage in sincere dialogue with others; that through this kind of genuine and sincere dialogue it is always possible to bridge the gaps of distrust that divide the world.

One well-known episode illustrates how Hammarskjöld put this conviction into practice. In 1955, in an attempt to secure the release of American prisoners of war captured during the Korean War, Hammarskjöld flew to China—then without a seat at the UN—and tried to meet with Premier Zhou Enlai.[14] People around him strongly advised him against the visit. Face-to-face with Zhou, without an official entourage and unable to use his own interpreter, Hammarskjöld stated the following during one of their private sessions:

> [I]t does not mean that I *appeal* to you or that I *ask you* for their release. It means that—inspired also by my faith in your wisdom and in your wish to promote peace—I have considered it my duty as forcefully as I can, and with deep conviction, to draw attention to the vital importance of their fate to the cause of peace. . . . Their fate may well decide the direction in which we will all be moving in the near future—towards peace, or away from peace. . . . [A]gainst all odds, [this case] has brought me around the world in order to put before you, in great frankness and trusting that we see eye to eye on the desperate need to avoid adding to existing frictions, my deep concern both as Secretary-General and as a man.[15]

I recall my own encounter with Premier Zhou Enlai in December 1974, a year before his death. Several years earlier, in September 1968, at a time when there were no official diplomatic relations between China and Japan as no formal peace had been concluded between them, I had called for the normalization of relations and urged that China be represented in the UN. Zhou Enlai was aware of my efforts, and despite ill health, insisted on meeting with me at his hospital in Beijing. With intense passion, Premier Zhou shared his thoughts with me: "In this critical period in the history of the world, all nations must stand as equals and help each other." He expressed his strong desire for enduring friendship between China and Japan.

---

14   Zhou Enlai (1898–1976), Premier of the People's Republic of China (1949–76).

15   (qtd. in) Urquhart, Brian. 1972. *Hammarskjöld*. New York: Norton, p. 106.

Based on this personal experience, I can easily imagine the kind of intent dialogue, the earnest soul-to-soul exchange, that unfolded between Zhou and Hammarskjöld. The meeting created a bond of trust between the two men which later led to the release of the eleven American airmen.

Whether it be intergovernmental relations or relations between the UN and member states, the most essential element is always encounter and dialogue between individual human beings. No matter how impossible a deadlock may seem, a breakthrough can always be found if we meet face-to-face and engage in genuine dialogue: I believe this was the conviction that motivated Hammarskjöld throughout his extensive travels as Secretary-General, meeting with and mediating between the parties to conflicts.

Hammarskjöld's passionate and relentless efforts to advance the peace process in the world embody the principles that should guide the UN in fulfilling its mission to build a new human civilization imbued with the spirit of dialogue. His legacy is one that must be passed on to the people of the twenty-first century.

Building grassroots support

Looking at the world today, the Middle East is just one of the regions where tensions remain high, and there is a strong need for the parties involved or affected by these tensions to communicate and engage in dialogue through the UN. This is critical to finding a breakthrough to persistent conflicts and bringing stability to the region.

After violent military clashes that continued for a month, a cease-fire in Lebanon was finally realized following a UN Security Council resolution calling for an immediate cessation of hostilities [Resolution 1701, passed on August 11, 2006, brought about a cease-fire halting hostilities between Israel and Lebanon].[16] But the underlying instability remains, as does the possibility that fighting may reignite at any time. This points to the urgent need to move proactively to the next step of rebuilding a stable and peaceful order in the region. It is my sincere hope that all parties will work through the UN to develop new channels for dialogue that will substantively further this process.

As I think about the profound mission the UN bears, I recall the words of Secretary-General Kofi Annan when he addressed the 2005 World Summit

---

16 United Nations (UN). 2006. "Resolution 1701 (2006)." S/RES/1701. Resolution adopted by the Secretary Council. August 11.

on September 14, 2005, attended by the leaders of 170 states: "We must find what President Franklin Roosevelt once called 'the courage to fulfill our responsibilities in an admittedly imperfect world.'"[17] The raison d'être of the UN, still entirely valid after sixty years, is encapsulated in this spirit of responsibility and courage.

It was the lifelong wish of my mentor, Josei Toda,[18] second president of the Soka Gakkai, to forge a global solidarity of ordinary citizens committed to support the UN. Along with the founding president of the Soka Gakkai, Tsunesaburo Makiguchi,[19] Josei Toda was imprisoned for nearly two years during World War II because his uncompromising convictions, rooted in his religious faith, led him to a direct confrontation with Japan's militarist fascism. He was released from prison immediately before the war ended, on July 3, 1945, just a few days after the UN Charter was adopted by the San Francisco Conference.

Toda's philosophy of peace was expressed in his call for the abolition of nuclear weapons and his ideal of "global nationalism" (Jp. *chikyu minzokushugi*),[20] which in today's terms could be interpreted as a global citizenship that transcends all distinctions of nationality, ethnicity and ideology.

Toda believed that the UN represented the distillation of wisdom of twentieth-century humankind. He was convinced of the need to protect and develop this embodiment of the world's hopes into the next century.

It was Toda's deepest desire to eliminate needless suffering from this planet by expanding the global solidarity of awakened and empowered individuals.

In my own family, four of my brothers were drafted into the war. My eldest brother died in battle. The grief experienced by my elderly parents was indescribably profound.

Nothing is more cruel than war, nothing more miserable. This was the reality engraved into my youthful life and consciousness.

Soon after the war, I encountered Toda and determined that I would join my mentor in the lifelong struggle to break the unending cycles of war and violence, and to contribute to the realization of a world of peace.

---

17   Annan, Kofi. 2005. "Address to the 2005 World Summit." Press Release. September 14.

18   Josei Toda (1900–58), second president of the Soka Gakkai (1951–58).

19   Tsunesaburo Makiguchi (1871–1944), founding president of the Soka Kyoiku Gakkai (forerunner of the Soka Gakkai) (1930–44).

20   Toda, Josei. 1981–90. *Toda Josei zenshu* [The Complete Works of Josei Toda]. 9 vols. Tokyo: Seikyo Shimbunsha. Vol. 3, p. 460.

Immediately after my inauguration as the third president of the Soka Gakkai, as heir to my mentor's will, I took the first step in this effort when I traveled to the United States. My choice of the United States was motivated in part by my awareness that this was the country where the United Nations Headquarters, the focal point of efforts for global peace, was located.

I still recall with vivid clarity my first visit to the UN Headquarters in New York in October 1960. Dag Hammarskjöld was Secretary-General and the 15th General Assembly was in session with the attendance of many of the world's leaders, including US President Dwight D. Eisenhower[21] and Soviet Premier Nikita Khrushchev.

As I observed the General Assembly and committee meetings, what left an indelible impression on me was the power and vibrancy emanating from the representatives of the newly independent African states participating in the debates. At this General Assembly, seventeen nations, including Cameroon, Togo and Madagascar, were welcomed as member states of the UN. All of these new states, with the exception of Cyprus, were from the African continent.

It was deeply inspiring to witness the passion of the African representatives brimming with fresh energy, determined to contribute to the making of a better world through the UN. Every time I think about the important mission of the UN, I cannot help but recall this scene.

Traveling to various different parts of the world, I have often sensed people's strong hopes and expectations for the UN. My efforts to engage in dialogue with political, intellectual and cultural leaders throughout the world stem from this desire to expand the network of like-minded people thinking beyond national, ethnic and religious differences, committed to supporting the UN.

While promoting dialogue among civilizations and among religions, I have at the same time felt the need to make concrete proposals for action. Every year since 1983, I have issued peace proposals in which I have set out ideas on ways to reinforce and revitalize the UN, stressing the importance of encouraging grassroots support.

The SGI has carried out a wide range of activities in support of the UN. As Cold War tensions mounted, we organized the exhibition "Nuclear Arms: Threat to Our World" in 1982, in support of the UN's World Disarmament

---

21   Dwight D. Eisenhower (1890–1969), 34th President of the United States (1953–61).

Campaign. This exhibition, which opened at the UN Headquarters in New York, toured twenty-five cities in sixteen countries, including the Soviet Union and China and other nuclear weapons states. In total it was viewed by some 1.2 million visitors.

After the end of the Cold War, the SGI organized the exhibition "War and Peace: From a Century of War to a Century of Hope" and updated the antinuclear exhibit, renaming it "Nuclear Arms: Threat to Humanity," in an effort to bring people together in their shared desire for peace and to generate a momentum toward realizing a world without war.

In the area of human rights education, the SGI organized the exhibition "Toward a Century of Humanity: An Overview of Human Rights in Today's World" in support of the UN Decade for Human Rights Education (1995–2004). With the end of the Decade, the SGI collaborated with other UN agencies and nongovernmental organizations (NGOs) to promote the creation of a new international framework to follow up the work of the Decade. These efforts culminated in the formal adoption of the World Programme for Human Rights Education.

In the area of ecological integrity and sustainability, the SGI, together with other NGOs, proposed the UN Decade of Education for Sustainable Development. This was later adopted by the General Assembly, with the United Nations Educational, Scientific and Cultural Organization (UNESCO) designated as the lead agency to promote the Decade, which began in 2005.

The SGI has long supported refugee relief activities through the United Nations High Commissioner for Refugees (UNHCR). In 1992, the SGI organized the Voice Aid campaign in response to the United Nations Transitional Authority in Cambodia's (UNTAC) request and donated about 300,000 second-hand radios to support the smooth organization and administration of free and fair elections in Cambodia.

Buddhist values and philosophy

The SGI's grassroots network of ordinary citizens in support of the UN has now expanded to include 190 countries and territories. These efforts are compelled by Buddhist values and philosophy, which uphold the inviolable dignity of life. The core principles that guide the UN are cognate with the principles of Buddhist humanism—peace, equality and compassion.

Motivated by these values, it is perhaps inevitable that SGI members feel compelled to support the UN.

In this context it is relevant to introduce the example of a contemporary of Shakyamuni[22]—a woman by the name of Srimala[23]—which appears in the Buddhist canon. Her vow is recorded as follows:

> If I see lonely people, people who have been jailed unjustly and have lost their freedom, people who are suffering from illness, disaster or poverty, I will not abandon them. I will bring them spiritual and material comfort.[24]

Srimala lived true to her vow and devoted her life to helping the suffering.

The teachings of the Buddhist reformer Nichiren,[25] which constitute the philosophical basis of the SGI's activities, are deeply imbued with the spirit of Mahayana Buddhism. Our efforts to support the UN as it strives to protect human dignity in our modern world are a natural consequence of putting into practice the bodhisattva way represented by Srimala's compassionate vow and actions.

In recent years, the UN has focused its efforts on the promotion of human rights, human security, human development, culture of peace and dialogue among civilizations. These are all undertakings that strike a chord with the philosophy of peace expounded in Buddhism.

The philosophical basis of our activities and thinking is elucidated in the treatise "On Establishing the Correct Teaching for the Peace of the Land" (Jp. *Rissho ankoku ron*), written by Nichiren in 1260 as he witnessed the sufferings of the ordinary people caught up in the incessant war and natural disasters that wracked thirteenth-century Japanese society.

In this treatise, instead of using either of the standard Chinese characters for "country," which have in their center elements that signify "sovereign" or "weapon," in the majority of cases Nichiren uses a character in which the

---

22   Shakyamuni (Gautama Siddartha) (*c.* 560–480 BCE), the founder of Buddhism.

23   Srimala, also known as Lady Shrimala or Queen Shrimala. A daughter of King Prasenajit of Kosala in India and his consort Mallika, in the time of Shakyamuni.

24   Wayman, Alex and Hideko Wayman, trans. 1974. *The Lion's Roar of Queen Srimala: A Buddhist Scripture on the Tathagata-garbha Theory.* New York: Columbia University Press, p. 65.

25   Nichiren (1222–82), Buddhist monk, founder of Nichiren Buddhism.

element signifying "ordinary people" is central. For Nichiren, the heart of the nation is neither the authorities nor the territory, but the ordinary people who inhabit it. This same spirit animates the modern concept of human security— where the foremost aim is to realize the peace and happiness of citizens.

Throughout this treatise, Nichiren critiqued the dominant philosophies of his times; he considered that their emphasis on introverted reflection encouraged an escapist attitude and made people feel incapable of effectively engaging in or transforming society. Instead, he promoted the belief that inherent in each individual is a robust power and potential; that each individual can become the protagonist and initiator of societal transformation. This belief shares much with the contemporary concept of empowerment that constitutes the core of human development.

Nichiren's treatise contains the following passage: "If you care anything about your personal security, you should first of all pray for order and tranquillity throughout the four quarters of the land. . . ."[26] This is a powerful call for the creation of a culture of peace, which is not limited to the security of the individual but seeks the security of the entire human race.

The ultimate inspiration underlying the SGI's promotion of consciousness-raising at the grassroots level through exhibitions and seminars, as well as our support for UN activities for education in the fields of disarmament, human rights and the environment, lies in this desire to realize the security of the entire human race.

Furthermore, the treatise unfolds as a dialogue between two individuals, the host and the guest, who have completely differing perspectives and views but who are both pained by the tragic realities tormenting their society. The host tells the guest, "I have been brooding alone upon this matter, indignant in my heart, but now that you have come, we can lament together. Let us discuss the question at length."[27] An earnest dialogue takes place as the two exchange their views on the causes of people's suffering, means to alleviate this suffering and what can be done to this end. At the conclusion of the dialogue, the host and guest vow to unite their efforts and work together toward a common goal.

---

26 Nichiren. 1999–2006. *The Writings of Nichiren Daishonin.* 2 vols. Ed. and trans. by The Gosho Translation Committee. Tokyo: Soka Gakkai. Vol. 1, p. 24.

27 Ibid., p. 7.

Dialogue has the power to inspire inner change in people and leads to positive action to transform society. This is the approach found in the wisdom of the Buddhist tradition since the days of Shakyamuni.

In the SGI Charter, adopted in 1995, this spirit is reflected thus: "SGI shall, based on the Buddhist spirit of tolerance, respect other religions, engage in dialogue and work together with them toward the resolution of fundamental issues concerning humanity."[28] Based on this spirit, the SGI has engaged in an open dialogue with people of diverse religious and cultural backgrounds in the hope of expanding the solidarity of awakened individuals committed to seeking ways to resolve the challenges facing our planet.

The soft power mission of the United Nations

As mentioned at the outset, I am convinced that the mission of the UN in the twenty-first century must be to defuse tensions and generate momentum toward peaceful coexistence through the power of dialogue. By centering on the processes of global dialogue it will best fulfill its function as a body for deliberation and action. In this way, it will lay the foundation for concerted action in such critical areas as human rights, human security and human development—the absolute prerequisites for the peace and happiness of the world's people.

In working toward these objectives, it is essential we remember that the core strength of the UN is its "soft power," the power of dialogue and international cooperation. This is true even in the field of global peace and security. While the UN Charter clearly recognizes the possibility of the exercise of "hard power," including military action, Chapter VI, on the pacific settlement of disputes, details those measures which are to be taken before the application of the enforcement measures set out in Chapter VII. Precedence is thus firmly placed on Chapter VI, with the use of hard power reserved for crisis situations as a means of last resort.

The Spanish philosopher José Ortega y Gasset[29] defined civilization as "the attempt to reduce force to being the *ultima ratio* [last resort]."[30] When we

---

28   SGI (Soka Gakkai International). 1995. "SGI Charter." http://www.sgi.org/resource-center/introductory-materials/sgi-charter.html (accessed April 2, 2013).

29   José Ortega y Gasset (1883–1955), Spanish philosopher.

30   Ortega y Gasset, José. 1932. *The Revolt of the Masses*. Authorized trans. Reprinted 1993. New York: Norton, p. 75.

think how the UN came into being as a reflection of the bitter lessons of two world wars, it is clear that this principle needs to be adamantly observed. I would like to reaffirm that the UN must continue to develop and enhance its soft power capacities. It should continue to focus on confidence-building and preventive measures and not be drawn into a reactive approach that attempts to solve problems through military force or other forms of hard power.

In the Eastern tradition, the sixtieth year marks the end of a cycle and the beginning of a new one. In that sense, I believe the UN's sixtieth anniversary, celebrated last year, provides a significant opportunity for the UN to renew its commitment to the noble mission with which it has been entrusted and make a new departure toward its fulfillment.

Here I would like to suggest that one axial theme around which the UN could develop is that of "humanitarian competition."

The idea of humanitarian competition was proposed by the founding president of the Soka Gakkai, Tsunesaburo Makiguchi, in his 1903 work *Jinsei chirigaku* (The Geography of Human Life).[31] Writing in an era when the forces of imperialism and colonialism were dominant throughout the world, Makiguchi criticized a state of affairs in which the crucial question of individual human happiness was being overshadowed by intense competition in the military, political and economic spheres. Reviewing the evolution of competition through its military, political and economic modes, he called for a transition from these predatory forms of competition to what he described as humanitarian competition—in which we strive, based on an ethos of coexistence, for the happiness of both ourselves and others.

Makiguchi described the key elements of this transformation as follows:

> Traditionally, military or political power has been used to expand territory and bring more people under one's control. Economic power, which may assume a different appearance or form, has been employed to the same effect as that realized through the exercise of military or political power. Humanitarian competition consists in using the invisible power of moral suasion to influence people. In other words, in place of submission exacted by the exercise of

---

31   Makiguchi, Tsunesaburo. [1903]. *Jinsei chirigaku* [The Geography of Human Life] in *Makiguchi Tsunesaburo zenshu* [The Complete Works of Tsunesaburo Makiguchi]. Tokyo: Daisanbunmei-sha. Vols. 1–2.

authority, we seek to gain the heartfelt respect [and cooperation] of others.[32]

This process of supplanting the exercise of authority with the earning of heartfelt respect could be expressed in contemporary terms as the transition away from the competition of hard power—where societies seek to dominate each other through military and political strength or overwhelming economic might. Rather, each country should compete in the realm of soft power—vying to accrue trust and friendship by manifesting diplomatic and cultural strengths and through contributions in the field of international cooperation that deploy the full range of human resources, technology and experience. This, I believe, is the essence of Makiguchi's proposal.

If such humanitarian competition—a competition for extended influence based on soft power—firmly takes root, we will see the last of conventional zero-sum competition in which winners prevail through the victimization and suffering of losers. It will open a way for a win-win era where the dignity of everyone on the globe is honored, with each country competing constructively to make the greatest contribution to humanity.

Sadly, the world is still dominated by ruthless competition for advantage with no thought given to the price paid by others. Such modes of competition, played out on an ever-expanding global scale, have made for steadily growing gaps between the rich and the poor. Moreover, as threats to human dignity— the crisis of the global environment is emblematic—become borderless, we need to bear in mind that no individual state acting in isolation can mount a truly effective response. UN Secretary-General Kofi Annan expressed this reality succinctly when he stated:

> I believe that in the twenty-first century [different perceptions of what is a threat] should not be allowed to lead the world's govern-ments to pursue very different priorities or to work at cross-purposes. . . . States working together can achieve things that are beyond what even the most powerful state can accomplish by itself.[33]

32   (trans. from) Makiguchi, Tsunesaburo. 1981–97. *Makiguchi Tsunesaburo zenshu* [The Complete Works of Tsunesaburo Makiguchi]. 10 vols. Tokyo: Daisanbunmei-sha. Vol. 2, p. 399.

33   Annan, Kofi. 2005. "'In Larger Freedom': Decision Time at the UN." *Foreign Affairs*. Vol. 84. Issue 3. May/June.

It is therefore essential that the UN function to effectively concentrate and coordinate the capacities of individual states and prevent them from becoming diluted or dispersed. It could be said that the success of efforts to develop the international organization—humanity's common asset—into a body fully and genuinely dedicated to the people of the world, depends on this process. Each state naturally desires to take an honorable position as a respected member of the international community. To tap this potential and channel competitive energies, not toward violence, but into humanitarian objectives—herein lies, I believe, the mission of the UN as the focal center of humanitarian competition. This is the course it should take in the twenty-first century.

To generate momentum in this direction and set benchmarks for firmly establishing the ideal of humanitarian competition at the core of the UN's activities, I would like to stress the importance of the following three shared elements: *a shared sense of purpose, a shared sense of responsibility* and *shared fields of action.* Based on this I would like to set out what I view to be the UN's core challenges and to suggest plans for reform.

Sharing purpose

As *a shared sense of purpose* I wish to propose the building of a culture of peace dedicated to the dignity and happiness of all people on the planet and based on the awareness that peace is much more than the mere absence of conflict. In this respect, poverty, a daily affront to human dignity, is the foremost issue to be tackled. According to the United Nations Development Programme (UNDP), in today's world as many as 2.5 billion people subsist on less than US$2 per day.[34]

Noting that the targets of the Millennium Development Goals, including halving the proportion of people living in extreme poverty by 2015, will not be achieved at the current rate, UNDP Administrator Kemal Derviş[35] warns:

> That would be a tragedy above all for the world's poor—but rich countries would not be immune to the consequences of failure. In an

---

34   See UNDP (United Nations Development Programme). 2006. "UNDP Annual Report 2006: Global Partnership for Development." New York: UNDP, p. 8.

35   Kemal Derviş (1949–), Turkish politician, head of the United Nations Development Programme (UNDP) (2005–09).

interdependent world our shared prosperity and collective security
depend critically on success in the war against poverty.[36]

In the shadow of a handful of countries that consume enormous resources
and boast affluent lifestyles, a vast portion of the world's inhabitants are
condemned to seemingly endless poverty; life in inhuman and degrading
conditions that persist for generation after generation. It is an overriding
humanitarian imperative to correct this gross distortion within the global
community. Nor is this an impossible task. The cost of eradicating poverty
has been estimated to be about one percent of global income. If even a portion
of the resources currently allocated to military spending could be directed to
poverty reduction, considerable progress could be made toward alleviating
the problem.

I strongly urge each country to seriously reconsider its spending priorities
and to actively support international cooperation for human development
focused on the empowerment of all individuals afflicted with poverty—
UNESCO's "Education for All" campaign in particular.

Together with poverty alleviation, disarmament, specifically nuclear disarmament, is vital if we are to put paid to the culture of war.

If the ideal of humanitarian competition is to take root in the international
community, we must firmly establish the awareness that no society can found
its security and well-being upon the terror and misery of another; we must
create a new set of global ethics.

The theory of nuclear deterrence, in seeking to ensure the security of one
state by threatening others with overwhelming destructive power, is diametrically opposed to the global ethics the new era demands.

The UN hosts an associated forum for multilateral talks on disarmament,
the Geneva-based Conference on Disarmament (CD). It is distressing, however, that disagreement among parties has kept it virtually nonfunctional for
almost ten years since its last achievement, the adoption of the Comprehensive
Nuclear Test Ban Treaty (CTBT) in 1996.

The stalemate persisted through last year (2005), the sixtieth anniversary of the atomic bombing of Hiroshima and Nagasaki, whose symbolic
significance could have been expected to provide impetus to disarmament

---

36 (qtd. in) UNDP (United Nations Development Programme). 2005. "More
Aid, Pro-Poor Trade Reform, and Long-Term Peace-Building Vital to Ending
Extreme Poverty." Press Release. September 7.

efforts. The Nuclear Non-Proliferation Treaty (NPT) Review Conference in May closed without producing any concrete results. Then, in September, the World Summit at the UN General Assembly issued an outcome document from which all mention of nuclear weapons had been deleted, to the great disappointment of all those who seek global peace.

It was against this backdrop that, in June 2006, the Weapons of Mass Destruction Commission, an independent group of international experts chaired by Hans Blix,[37] the former chief UN arms inspector for Iraq, submitted a proposal on nuclear disarmament and nonproliferation to Secretary-General Annan.

This document calls for a World Summit to be held at the UN to address the issues of disarmament, nonproliferation and terrorist use of weapons of mass destruction. To break the present deadlock at the Conference on Disarmament in Geneva, it proposes that only a two-thirds majority, instead of unanimity, be required to place issues on the agenda. "All states possessing nuclear weapons," it also recommends, "should commence planning for security without nuclear weapons. They should start preparing for the outlawing of nuclear weapons. . . ."[38]

These proposals are in line with the direction I have consistently asserted, and it is thus very easy for me to support them. I earnestly hope that all states will take the Commission's carefully considered recommendations seriously and promptly launch diplomatic efforts to break the impasse that is blocking progress toward disarmament.

Ten years have passed since, in 1996, the International Court of Justice issued an advisory opinion on the legality of nuclear weapons. In that opinion, the Court stated that "the threat or use of nuclear weapons would generally be contrary to international law,"[39] and that "[t]here exists an obligation to pursue in good faith and bring to a conclusion negotiations leading to nuclear disarmament in all its aspects under strict and effective international

---

37 Hans Blix (1928–), Swedish diplomat, Director General of the International Atomic Energy Agency (IAEA) (1981–2007).

38 WMDC (Weapons of Mass Destruction Commission). 2006. "Weapons of Terror: Freeing the World of Nuclear, Biological, and Chemical Arms." Stockholm, Sweden: WMDC, p. 109.

39 ICJ (International Court of Justice). 1996. "Legality of the Threat or Use of Nuclear Weapons, Advisory Opinion." *I.C.J. Reports.* July 8, p. 266.

control."[40] I think we should once again urge governments to recall the gravity of this opinion as we continue to build a committed international consensus for nuclear disarmament.

As the report of the Blix Commission points out, "Over the past decade, there has been a serious, and dangerous, loss of momentum and direction in disarmament and non-proliferation efforts." What is required is the political will for nuclear abolition. "And with that will, even the eventual elimination of nuclear weapons is not beyond the world's reach."[41] It is thus all the more important now that the people of the world raise their voices.

Toward this end I would like to propose a UN "decade of action by the world's people for nuclear abolition."

With nuclear weapons proliferation continuing unabated, the first step in challenging the harsh reality must be to bring more people to the awareness that the nuclear threat is both relevant to their lives and something they can take action about. Such a decade of action, jointly promoted by the UN and NGOs, would be vital in promoting this awareness.

I likewise support the early convening of a World Summit as called for by the Blix Commission or, alternatively, a Special Session of the UN General Assembly dedicated to intensive deliberation of disarmament issues. Such actions on the part of states would both reflect and support an emerging international consensus for disarmament.

The importance of working progressively toward the creation of a world without war through relentlessly pressing for nuclear disarmament and, ulti- mately, abolition: This was one of the points on which I strongly agreed with the late Sir Joseph Rotblat,[42] emeritus president of the Pugwash Conferences on Science and World Affairs, who passed away last year.

If we are to bring down the curtain, once and for all, on an era lived under the threat of nuclear destruction, we must rethink the understanding of national interest that would justify nuclear weapons as a "necessary evil" essential for deterrence. Both the Russell–Einstein Manifesto (1955),

---

40   Ibid., p. 267.

41   WMDC (Weapons of Mass Destruction Commission). 2006. "Weapons of Terror: Freeing the World of Nuclear, Biological, and Chemical Arms." Stockholm, Sweden: WMDC, p. 17.

42   Sir Joseph Rotblat (1908–2005), British physicist and philanthropist, founding member (1957), Secretary-General (1957–73), President (1988–97) of the Pugwash Conferences on Sciences and World Affairs.

cosigned by Dr. Rotblat, and my mentor Josei Toda's "Declaration Calling for the Abolition of Nuclear Weapons"[43] (1957) refuted the theory of deterrence and adamantly refused to acknowledge the use of nuclear arms under any circumstances.

As Toda strikingly phrased it, nuclear weapons threaten humanity's right to existence and are therefore an "absolute evil"; their abolition is humanity's common duty. The central goal of the decade of action by the world's people for nuclear abolition that I am proposing would be to elevate this concept into one of the central tenets of our age.

Here I have examined the challenges of poverty alleviation and disarmament from the perspective of a shared sense of purpose. There are, of course, many other issues that weigh heavily upon humankind. Among these is the global environmental crisis, the particular complexity of which lies in the fact that its resolution requires a fundamental reexamination of human civilization. My own sense of crisis has prompted me to call, in my annual peace proposals, for accelerated efforts to create an institutional framework that will bring together the wisdom of humankind toward the resolution of environmental challenges, including giving them dramatically greater centrality at the UN.

The issues of poverty, disarmament and the environment all demand the concerted efforts of international society based on a sense of belonging to humanity and a sense of responsibility toward the future. It is for these reasons that it is absolutely essential to establish a shared sense of purpose through the United Nations.

Sharing responsibility

I next wish to focus on the need to foster *a shared sense of responsibility,* specifically by establishing frameworks that encourage the youthful members of the rising generations to actively engage in various deliberations at the UN and in its agencies' local activities.

In February of 2006, the Toda Institute for Global Peace and Policy Research, which I founded ten years ago, held an international conference in Los Angeles on the theme of reforming and strengthening the UN. I was

---

43   Toda, Josei. 1981–90. *Toda Josei zenshu* [The Complete Works of Josei Toda]. 9 vols. Tokyo: Seikyo Shimbunsha. Vol. 4, pp. 564–66. (English text at http://www.joseitoda.org/vision/declaration.)

particularly struck by the vision statement presented by UN Under-Secretary-General Anwarul K. Chowdhury,[44] which included these words:

> In future, the United Nations should be an organization that inter-acts more closely and substantially with the young people to benefit from their ideas and enthusiasm in shaping the future of the world.[45]

Gaining the understanding and unwavering support of as many of the world's citizens as possible is essential if the UN is to fully realize its poten-tial. At the same time, the prerequisite for solving global problems is to supplant the prevailing mind-set, which places highest priority upon national interest, with a broad, shared sense of responsibility for the best interests of humankind and of the entire planet. Young people must be the protagonists in this endeavor.

I believe that the UN, having entered its sixty-first year, should make promoting young people's active engagement the central focus of its new departure. Archimedes[46] is quoted as saying, "Give me a place to stand and with a lever I will move the whole world," and it is in this spirit that we must ensure that young people have "a place to stand" within the UN process.

It is said that about half of countries emerging from conflict find themselves enmeshed in it again within five years. In societies that have experienced con-flict and the tragedy of cycles of recurring violence, it is extremely difficult for members of the generation in power to disentangle themselves from the cycle of hatred and violence. Thus, it is important to focus on the next generation, who are less bound up in the past, and to find ways to enable youth to explore new ideas, avenues and approaches to establishing peace and shared prosperity.

The same formula applies to the challenges of poverty alleviation, dis-armament and environmental degradation. Significant breakthroughs will only come about as the seeds of change planted in the hearts of the next generation through persistent, untiring efforts in the fields of education and

---

44   Anwarul K. Chowdhury (1943–), Bangladeshi diplomat, Under-Secretary-General and High Representative of the United Nations (2002–07).

45   Chowdhury, Anwarul K. 2006. "Vision Statement." Presented at the intern-ational conference on Transforming the United Nations: Human Development, Regional Conflicts, and Global Governance in a Post-Westphalian World sponsored by Toda Institute for Global Peace and Policy Research, February 4–5, in Los Angeles, USA.

46   Archimedes (c. 290–212 BCE), Greek mathematician.

awareness-raising come to fruition. My mentor's declaration against nuclear weapons, in entrusting the abolition of nuclear arms to young people, was based on just this kind of far-reaching future vision.

Along these lines, it would be worth considering holding a gathering of youth representatives from around the world every year prior to the annual UN General Assembly, giving world leaders an opportunity to listen to the views of the next generation. It would also be desirable to create means for students and young people to participate in local activities of UN agencies for a period of one or two years, positioning them to gain firsthand experience of the significance of the UN's activities as well as the challenges it faces. This would enable them to learn directly about the impact of global issues on people's lives, as well as participate in the search for solutions.

About five thousand people are currently dispatched to different parts of the world every year through the United Nations Volunteer (UNV) program. However, the average age of participants is thirty-nine years old, and they are recruited principally from among experts with professional experience in specialized areas.[47] I believe it would be helpful to enhance these activities with an additional framework providing hands-on experience for students and young people in their twenties.

Another area worth examining is improving the system of UN internship programs. These should accept not only graduate students but also undergraduates and young NGO staff members, providing them with the opportunity to support actual policymaking by preparing briefing papers for UN deliberations. Such a system would strengthen the framework by which young people can be involved in various aspects of the international organization. Graduates of Soka University of America are already active participants in the UN internship program.

Here I am reminded of a dialogue I conducted with the peace scholar Dr. Elise Boulding[48] in which she maintained the importance of providing future generations with arenas where they can fully express their abilities, stressing that we need to create more opportunities for young people to grow into their role as global citizens. She told me she used to recommend the students in her international peace studies class to spend a semester working

---

47   See UNV (United Nations Volunteers). 2006. "UN Volunteers for Peace and Development." http://www.unvolunteers.org (accessed April 2, 2013).

48   Elise Boulding (1920–2010), American peace scholar and activist.

as interns at a local chapter of an international NGO and actually experience its activities.

By implementing ideas such as these, I would hope that the structure of the UN as a whole could develop a sharper focus upon youth, actively planning for greater participation of young people. In that sense, I would like to suggest that consideration be given to the creation of an agency dedicated to activities for the youth of the world or a department of youth within the UN administration.

Such efforts would parallel the growing calls among NGOs for the establishment of an agency dedicated to developing more effective and coordinated policies for empowering women, who are, after all, half the world's population. The UN must strive to promote the empowerment of young people and women living in difficult conditions in various parts of the world. If the UN can at the same time ensure the active participation of young people and women in its activities, reflecting an ever-greater diversity of opinions in the full range of its policy initiatives, this would go far toward bringing about a more promising era for all.

I would also like to call on the world's universities and institutions of higher learning to actively support the work of the UN as an integral part of their social mission. Some universities already have systems in place whereby researchers and research institutes provide academic support to various UN activities. While expanding this type of program, universities should take the initiative in actively offering classes on UN activities with the aim of becoming consistent centers for awareness-raising among students and the general public.

At the same time, I would like to emphasize the key importance of building a student-centered network to support the UN.

I have in the past proposed the creation of a global network of citizens to protect and support the UN. I believe that fostering a new generation of people of talent and capacity, people whose commitment is to the whole of humankind rather than the interest of a specific state or ethnicity, is the only way to provide the UN with the long-term infusion of support it so seriously requires.

Students are the key to this. There are already NGOs dedicated to developing the network of UN support among students around the world. Further strengthening these, it should be possible to move toward a scenario in which individual students and universities connect with one another to form a web of networks supporting the UN, eventually permeating the entire globe. This is the future I envisage for renewed linkages between the UN, students and universities.

With respect to developing a shared sense of responsibility I would like to make one other proposal: To help resolve the UN's long-term challenge of securing stable sources of funding, a separate framework, parallel to the contributions of member states, might be initiated to solicit direct support from the world's citizens.

Securing a stable budget is essential if the UN is to fulfill its responsibilities to effectively respond to global issues. Delayed and overdue payment of assessed and pledged contributions undermines the UN's capacities. Financial restrictions often prevent it from engaging in urgent projects and important activities. To overcome these challenges, I would like to repeat my call that a people's fund for the UN be created to accept broad-based donations from civil society, making this an additional funding source to sustain the UN.

In point of fact, UNICEF's operating budget comes both from governmental contributions and private fundraising, with approximately one third of funds coming from the private sector.[49] This example demonstrates the potential for creating a new system whereby funds raised from individuals, organizations and globally active transnational corporations are used to support UN activities, primarily in humanitarian areas.

Sharing action

Finally, I would like to discuss the importance of *shared fields of action*. To this end, I would like to propose the establishment of regional UN offices, whose role would be to further deepen relationships between member states and the UN and coordinate various UN agencies' activities in each region.

It takes considerable time and effort to set UN activities in motion. In particular, when a society has fallen into crisis, the understanding and continuous support of the surrounding countries is essential.

Global issues are complex and inextricably intertwined in a way that makes separate, isolated efforts to resolve them unlikely to succeed. This is symbolized by the "PPE spiral" in which cycles of poverty, population growth and environmental degradation have set up a negative synergy. Global issues differ from area to area, demanding responses that are truly appropriate to the individual circumstances.

---

49   See UNICEF (United Nations Children's Fund). 2002. "2002 UNICEF Annual Report." New York: UNICEF, p. 30.

In light of these factors, I am convinced that establishing coordinating UN centers in each region could enhance responsiveness to the exigencies of *continuity, complexity and regionality*. Such centers could be of great importance in the more comprehensive promotion of human rights, human security and human development through approaches focused on individual people's peace and happiness.

Having said that, I do not think it is necessary to restructure existing agencies. The thrust of my proposal is to bring the UN and member states closer and to build a positive synergy among UN agencies in each region. This would enable them to establish shared fields of action and tackle regional issues in a more coordinated manner.

Specifically, existing bodies that might assume the functions of UN regional centers would include the five commissions under the Economic and Social Council (ECOSOC): the Economic and Social Commissions for Asia and the Pacific, for West Asia, for Africa, for Europe and for Latin America and the Caribbean.

Currently, as exemplified by the European Union and the African Union, regional integration and cooperation are progressing in different parts of the world. I believe there would be value in establishing UN regional centers that could act as a bridge between these organizations and the UN Headquarters, as well as providing pivotal points to sustain UN-centered global governance.

Lastly, I would like to emphasize, in addition to this plan, the need to strengthen partnership between the UN and civil society as the essential key to developing shared fields of action.

Civil society's participation in the UN dramatically increased through the series of UN conferences held in the 1990s. Partnerships of like-minded governments and NGOs brought about epoch-making achievements such as the conclusion of the Anti-Personnel Mines Convention and the adoption of the Rome Statute of the International Criminal Court (ICC).

The Panel of Eminent Persons on United Nations–Civil Society Relations was set up in 2003 and issued its report "We the Peoples: Civil Society, the United Nations and Global Governance"[50] (the Cardoso Report) the following year. The work of the panel has been important in raising awareness of civil society's role in supporting the work of the UN.

---

50   UNGA (United Nations General Assembly). 2004. "We the Peoples: Civil Society, the United Nations and Global Governance." A/58/817. Report of the Panel of Eminent Persons on United Nations–Civil Society Relations. June 11.

The Committee of Religious NGOs at the UN, whose chair is currently the SGI's representative to the UN, together with UN organizations and agencies and governments, organized the Conference on Interfaith Cooperation for Peace in June 2005. That these three parties—civil society, governments and the UN—collaborated in this way to hold an interfaith conference at the UN was seen as a truly groundbreaking event.

For the UN's revitalization and to ensure that it fulfills the expectations of the world's peoples, it is indispensable that the UN, member states and NGOs and other representatives of civil society appreciate one another's unique qualities and roles and deepen their partnership. I earnestly hope that the three parties will continue to sit at the same table to discuss the challenges facing humanity and develop creative new modalities of joint action in the spirit of dialogue and cooperation.

It is my sincere belief that these themes—a shared sense of purpose, a shared sense of responsibility and shared fields of action—are key to the development of the UN of the twenty-first century.

The League of Nations was created as a response to World War I; the United Nations was born out of the determination never to repeat the horrors of World War II. As members of the human race, we must put into action our determination to save our planet from the repetition of this kind of tragedy. We must further strengthen the UN in order to enhance global governance for the sake of all the planet's inhabitants.

We are compelled to take the courageous first step toward this goal. To this end, it is essential to build momentum for reform from the bottom up, bringing together the voices of the people in support of the UN. We cannot afford to wait passively for top-down reform to emerge from intergovernmental deliberations.

If we truly heed the warnings of the twentieth century, so plagued by tragedy, we can see that action and solidarity hold the keys to the twenty-first century. To the degree that people grasp this spirit and determine to forge widespread solidarity for change, we will be able to build a culture of peace throughout the globe. This, I am convinced, is the central challenge facing humanity in the twenty-first century.

The protagonists in this endeavor are none other than individual human beings—citizens, and above all, young people.

The motivating vision of the SGI is a world of peace and mutual flourishing in humanity's new millennium. To this end we will continue to join our efforts with those of people of goodwill the world over, striving to enable the UN to fulfill the noble mission with which it has been entrusted.

The Parliament of Humanity

From National Interest to the Interest of Humanity (1987)[51]

In the article "Peace Guidelines toward the Twenty-First Century"[52] which I contributed to the inaugural edition of the journal *Soka University Peace Research,* I listed the following six elements that I think are important in building lasting peace:

1. Upholding Japan's Peace Constitution;
2. Developing an understanding of the North–South problem;
3. Focusing on the role of the United Nations and developing an integrating system for a new world order;
4. Revitalizing communities;
5. Emphasizing peace education;
6. Establishing the dignity of the individual.

Regarding the third of these points, I believe that at present the key challenge in the effort to create a new order for our world is to develop and strengthen the functions of the United Nations, centering on its security functions. [. . .]

I am fully aware of the persistent criticisms of the inefficacy of the UN in the international political arena. Nevertheless, there is no effective alternative to replace it as an institutional framework for bringing the world together, and if these criticisms persist and people's indifference toward the UN is left unabated the world will be in danger of relapsing into a state of chaos.

---

51 From 1987 Peace Proposal, "Spreading the Brilliance of Peace toward the Century of the People."

52 Ikeda, Daisaku. 1979. "Peace Guidelines toward the Twenty-First Century" in *Soka University Peace Research.* No. 1. February, pp. 3–20.

Rather, I would like to place value on the fact that the UN—as an international organization dedicated to peace with a membership covering most of the world—has continued to exist for over four decades since the end of World War II. This is all the more remarkable in light of the short-lived fragility of the League of Nations.

The UN is not without dysfunctions, as evidenced in the crucial area of maintaining security. But the significance of its continued existence as humanity's forum for discussion is immeasurable no matter how divided opinions may be: to a greater extent than we imagine, it is a source of reassurance for the people of the world.

In the area of security, the UN's initiatives toward the resolution of such issues as the Suez crisis, the Cuban missile crisis and the Cyprus dispute must not be disregarded. I would not be the only one who shudders to imagine the possible consequences of these and other crises were it not for the United Nations.

In light also of its great contributions in social, economic and humanitarian areas—represented by the wide-ranging activities of the Economic and Social Council—it is impossible to envision the international community without the United Nations.

The significance of the Charter of the United Nations, the foundation treaty of the organization, must be emphasized in particular. The process that led from the Atlantic Charter of 1941 to the Charter of the United Nations of 1945 is deeply rooted in the peaceful ideals expressed in *Zum Ewigen Frieden* (Perpetual Peace) by Immanuel Kant,[53] from which US President Woodrow Wilson[54] is said to have derived his ideas, as well as the works of Jean-Jacques Rousseau,[55] Henri Bernardin de Saint-Pierre[56] and Desiderius Erasmus.[57]

The idealistic, humanitarian and universalist principles set forth in the Charter of the United Nations represent the prime point to which we must all return. It is the crystallization of the aspirations for peace and wisdom of

---

53   Immanuel Kant (1724–1804), German philosopher.

54   Thomas Woodrow Wilson (1856–1924), 28th President of the United States (1913–21).

55   Jean-Jacques Rousseau (1712–78), Swiss-born French philosopher.

56   Henri Bernardin de Saint-Pierre (1737–1814), French writer.

57   Desiderius Erasmus (1469–1536), Dutch humanist and scholar.

humanity following the experience of the devastation of two world wars. Even if at times during the course of its history the UN's actions have not always been consistent with those ideals, they will continue to serve as our guiding principles in the effort to develop a more integrated global system.

Throughout history, sovereign states have claimed the unconditional ability to use armed force and resort to war to protect their own interests as a natural right. Military establishments were considered a vital component of sovereign rights. The escalation of the scale of warfare in the twentieth century, however, has rendered inappropriate this attitude that was once taken for granted in international law. The exponential expansion of the ravages of modern warfare, which causes the destruction of resources and ruination of the land without discrimination between the victorious and the defeated, made it essential that restrictions be placed on what had formerly been considered the unconditional exercise of national sovereign rights. The idea of establishing structures to ensure universal security—in the form of the League of Nations and subsequently the United Nations—arose from this need.

The advent of nuclear weapons has made this change irreversible. Living under the nuclear shadow where the exercise of national sovereignty can directly lead to total annihilation, we have no choice but to shift our paradigm from national interests to the interests of humanity, transcending national borders, and from national sovereign rights to the sovereign rights of humanity. Otherwise, we will bring catastrophic destruction upon ourselves sooner or later.

In addition to the need for a radical transformation in our way of thinking, the key question is how to limit the exercise of national sovereignty and delegate authority to a transnational organization. I do not intend to discuss the methodology here. But I believe it is important to stress that this limitation and delegation of national sovereignty must be voluntary. Under present circumstances, any attempt at enforcing such changes on a powerful state could lead to war, and similar attempts against a smaller nation could easily become oppression. Either way, compulsion sows the seeds of future calamity.

The fourth of the six points I listed above is the revitalization of communities. Within the framework of individual nations, the term community refers to local communities and local areas, and from an international viewpoint it refers to ethnic groups. In order to explore a new world order based on the United Nations, ethnic groups must be revitalized even with much of their authority delegated to a transnational organization.

Here, the restriction and delegation of sovereign rights must be absolutely voluntary. If it is not, it can only bring about adverse effects. Though the task at hand is challenging, I hope that the UN will continue to place precedence on dialogue and persuasion over force, and abide by this principle.

The concept of nation-states tends to conjure a negative image, both in general and within the UN. Viewed from a historical perspective, however, it should be understood that nation-states have both positive and negative aspects. In the course of history, sovereign states developed their current reputation of aggressiveness as the colonialism and imperialism of the advanced great powers of the West began to dominate the world. But during their formative period, the nation-state was, to a greater or lesser degree, a defensive and self-reliant entity. This is why both Rousseau and Kant were extremely cautious against the infringement of sovereign rights by international institutions even in their enthusiastic search for a systematic structure for the sake of world peace.

Questioning "how far the right of confederation can be extended without jeopardizing that of sovereignty,"[58] Rousseau advocated the idea of an alliance of states, an intermediate between loosely combined leagues, which have little power to effect peace, and tightly united confederate states, which run the danger of infringing on sovereign rights. It was a delicate choice resulting from the evaluation of the competing advantages and disadvantages.

Kant believed that the goal of international unions should be limited to maintaining peace in order to protect sovereign rights. He wrote, "a federative association of states whose sole intention is to eliminate war is the only *lawful* arrangement which can be reconciled with their freedom."[59]

Clearly, both Rousseau and Kant considered sovereign states as defensive, self-reliant entities that deserve protection. It should be noted that the sovereign state as they saw it was not necessarily oppressive and had much in common with the sovereign power of the people.

---

58   Rousseau, Jean-Jacques. 1971. *Emile: Or On Education*. New York: Basic Books, p. 466.

59   Kant, Immanuel. 1970. "Perpetual Peace" in *Kant's Political Writings*. Ed. by Hans Reiss. Trans. by H. B. Nisbet. Cambridge: Cambridge University Press, p. 129.

This image of sovereign states is still alive today, and even holds life-and-death importance for the smaller states, especially those that emerged from colonialism in Asia and Africa after World War II.

For the people of the Third World, the spirit of the Bandung Conference—primarily underpinned by the following principles—is much more than a relic of the past:

1. Mutual respect for territorial integrity and sovereignty;
2. Mutual nonaggression;
3. Abstention from intervention in the internal affairs of another country;
4. Equality and reciprocity;
5. Peaceful coexistence.

It is solely to the credit of the United Nations that the principle of self-determination of peoples has been advanced in connection with the work of the UN Trusteeship Council after World War II. It is essential that efforts toward the next step, restrictions on sovereignty, not ruin such past achievements. I have repeatedly urged that the restriction and delegation of sovereign rights be on a voluntary basis because a delicate issue such as this requires time and a careful, gradual approach.

***

If the voluntary restriction and delegation of national sovereignty were to be likened to an automobile, the development of international public opinion to support the United Nations in its work for lasting peace would be analogous to the road maintenance and traffic control systems that are essential for its smooth operation.

Transnational exchanges among people, transcending ethnic and national boundaries, are rapidly increasing with the development of transportation. In addition to international relations among state-level institutions, grassroots relations among the people are undeniably generating momentum toward the creation of a new world order in this age of global interdependence.

Nongovernmental organizations (NGOs) represent one herald of the global surge of the power of the people. The SGI is one such NGO.

At present, there are an estimated 10,000 NGOs in the world working in areas such as the environment, human rights and disarmament. Approximately 800 of these NGOs are officially involved, albeit with considerable restrictions, in the activities of the United Nations, reflecting the voices of grassroots citizens. Broader participation of civil organizations in the UN would revitalize it with fresh energy by promoting civil participation and enabling the will of the people to be heard more. Strengthening cooperation and mutual exchange among civil organizations would further develop a solidarity among ordinary people that transcends national boundaries.

At the present stage, the participation and authority of such civil organizations in the UN is limited. There is no functional mechanism for coordinating diverse civil groups. These factors, plus the tendency for NGOs to arise mostly in developed countries, present numerous challenges. But the fostering of international public opinion is not an easy task. It requires conviction and perseverance, as seen in the Chinese fable of the foolish old man who removed the mountains.

This task could be summarized as the fostering of world citizens. Toward this goal, I would like to put forth a specific proposal here as a private citizen supporting the United Nations: The designation of the decade from 1991 to 2000 as a "United Nations Decade of Education for World Citizenship."

The United Nations has engaged in numerous long-term campaigns: numerous United Nations Development Decades (the first being 1961–70), through which development aid and cooperation for developing countries have been vigorously promoted, and the United Nations Decade for Women (1976–85), which contributed significantly to the promotion of women's rights and the position of women in society. In a similar way, efforts to foster world citizens will be increasingly important for the future, as the need for a global perspective will only become greater in the twenty-first century.

When asked his nationality, Socrates[60] is said to have replied that he was neither Athenian nor Greek, but a citizen of the world. The love of humanity through which one sees the entire world as one's home, transcending the narrow confines of state, ethnicity and territory, should be at the heart of education for fostering world citizens.

In more concrete terms, the curriculum should encompass the most crucial challenges facing humanity today, such as the environment, development, peace and human rights.

In the area of peace education, the cruelty of war, the threat of nuclear weapons and the necessity of disarmament need to be addressed. On the theme of development, the eradication of hunger and poverty would naturally be the focus. Attention needs to be directed to the reality of the world—a

---

60   Socrates (*c.* 470–399 BCE), Greek philosopher.

world where two countries in three are in poverty and some 500 million people suffer from malnutrition—to explore ways to ensure the economic welfare of humanity. The central theme of environmental education would be how people and nature can coexist harmoniously. For example, it would be important to learn the extent to which nuclear explosions seriously affect the ecosystem. Human rights education would instill in the learner the dignity of the individual.

All four of these categories pursue universal values that transcend national boundaries—an essential quality of world citizenship. They are mutually interrelated, with each one indispensable to realizing the goal of peace for humanity. Thus, education for world citizenship should also include these themes as a comprehensive curriculum focused on peace.

Since these four themes are central to the work of the United Nations, developing an awareness of its importance should naturally be one of the pillars in education for fostering world citizens.

Needless to say, education is a time-consuming process that requires perseverance. The fostering of world citizens is a new challenge, and we will need to bring our wisdom together to tackle it. To this end, I suggest that the United Nations University (UNU) be entrusted with the development of an educational curriculum to foster world citizenship, examining the contents and methodology of learning for the proposed Decade.

This work is consistent with the original mission of the UNU, a global university dedicated to realizing a peaceful world. Scholars, experts and peace research institutions could conduct research in the areas of the environment, development, peace and human rights, and the results could be used as part of the curriculum for education for world citizenship.

The wisdom of experts around the world is eagerly expected in this regard. The Soka University Peace Research Institute, which I founded, is prepared to make a full contribution to this cause.

Study materials appropriate for a world citizenship education curriculum would also need to be discussed. At the International Textbook Exhibition sponsored by the SGI and supported by the United Nations Department of Public Information (in 1985), many visitors expressed the need for textbooks written from a global perspective to cultivate a consciousness as members of humanity. Textbooks and a curriculum developed by bringing together the wisdom of experts from around the world in forums such as the UNU would certainly stimulate enthusiasm for fostering world citizens in many countries.

The next four years before the launch of this proposed Decade need to be used for preparations to make it successful, developing a firm vision and methodology. In addition to the efforts of the United Nations, grassroots efforts to galvanize public support would be essential to make the endeavor of fostering world citizens truly worthy of its name. NGOs should also help raise a broad awareness of the significance of the Decade throughout the world.

I hope that the participation of civil organizations will be made possible in the Decade campaign itself. They could contribute in their respective areas of expertise through research, exhibitions and publications.

The Soka Gakkai has been striving to raise awareness about peace issues through its antiwar exhibitions and publications, several of which have been translated into other languages. Linking such awareness-raising efforts at the grassroots level would also be an effective way of supporting the proposed Decade.

I believe that the development of international public opinion through such efforts will help advance the process of voluntary restriction and delegation of national sovereignty, powerfully revitalizing the United Nations and even shaping a new world order.

Choose a "Human Face" rather than a "National Face" (1989)[61]

In a little more than a decade, the twenty-first century will be upon us. We must make the best use of the remaining years of this century to prepare ourselves for the next. More than anything else, we must now cultivate, as the present century reaches its close, the kind of dynamic and flexible thinking that transcends the established paradigm.

A great transition is taking place today because of the weakening of the Yalta System—the US–Soviet bipolar structure that has been pivotal in postwar world politics for over four decades. It is giving way to a deepening chaos in a multipolarized world.

More than ten years ago, former US Secretary of State Henry A. Kissinger[62] observed that the world had two great military powers (the United States and the Soviet Union), the world economy had five major centers (the United States, the Soviet Union, China, Japan and Western Europe) and that global

---

61 From 1989 Peace Proposal, "Toward a New Globalism."

62 Henry Kissinger (1923–), US Secretary of State (1973–77), recipient of the Nobel Prize for Peace in 1973.

politics were becoming ever more multipolarized.[63] In his book *The Rise and Fall of the Great Powers*, Professor Paul M. Kennedy[64] of Yale University developed his own theory based on Dr. Kissinger's concept of the five major centers.[65]

As the trend toward disarmament gains momentum, there will certainly be an acceleration in the pace of multipolarization. It is important to recognize both the positive and negative potentials of this trend. On the one hand, it might lead to the formation of a new world order, but on the other, an inappropriate response could invite chaos that might become inextricable. If we simply allow these seismic shifts to take their course, our world might lapse into an anarchic chaos, a state Thomas Hobbes[66] described as a war of each against all.

What we need now is a vision for a new world order based on an understanding of our interdependence that transcends the conventional East–West and North–South frameworks. This is the most crucial challenge humanity is facing.

***

Today's seismic shifts have not only brought about the collapse of the US–Soviet structure. They are also responsible for the fundamental questioning of the system of nation-states, which have been considered the most important actors in the international community since their inception in mid-seventeenth-century Europe.

It would be unrealistic to expect the nation-state to disappear overnight. That does not mean, however, that we should adhere to established concepts. In the mid-nineteenth century, for example, who in Japan would have imagined that the Tokugawa shogunate (1603–1867) could be toppled so easily after almost 300 years of tight control of the country?

We should also remember that historically the nation-state is a relatively recent phenomenon, which reached its peak in the nineteenth century and

---

63   See Kissinger, Henry A. 1974. "The Nature of the National Dialogue," in *American Foreign Policy*. New York: Norton, pp. 128–29.

64   Paul M. Kennedy (1945–), British historian and author.

65   See Kennedy, Paul M. 1987. *The Rise and Fall of the Great Powers: Economic Change and Military Conflict from 1500 to 2000*. New York: Random House.

66   Thomas Hobbes (1588–1679), British philosopher.

began to show signs of weakening and decline around the end of World War I.

Further, with the advent of nuclear weapons, many began to question the capacity of states to wage war, a right that had long been taken for granted. Clearly, we are entering an era when the nation-state can no longer be considered the only effective unit of action or integration.

There is a growing awareness in the world that the solution to such global challenges as the threat of nuclear weapons and of environmental destruction requires new approaches that transcend national boundaries. We cannot think in terms of the future of humanity with our minds bound to the narrow confines of the sovereign state. We are living in an era where such a narrow mind-set can undermine the very basis of our survival.

Our times are calling for a new way of thinking based on a global vision. Attention should be paid to these new signs of change, in addition to economic and other factors, which are underlying an emerging emphasis on dialogue in the world.

***

As I have repeatedly emphasized, we must not forget the existence of NGOs in planning a world order centered on the United Nations. The General Assembly is often referred to as the parliament of humanity. It would not be worthy of the name if it continued to be just a showcase of sovereign states putting priority on national interests to the exclusion of others, overshadowed by the egotism of superpowers.

We need to remind ourselves that the Preamble of the Charter of the United Nations begins with the words "We the Peoples of the United Nations. . . ." If the UN is to function as a truly democratic organization as well as an effective peacekeeping force, the support of the citizens of the member states is intrinsic.

One important role of the United Nations that has emerged recently is its function as a forum for discussing the survival of the planet. In this, it is integrating the will of humanity as a borderless community instead of viewing the world from the standpoint of sovereign states. This task would not be achieved if left in the hands of sovereign states, with their intricate web of entangled interests.

What is needed today is to emphasize the human face rather than the national face, on which so much importance has been placed in the past. If the UN is more effectively to become a parliament of humanity in the true sense and function, it must strive above all to spotlight this human face. It is under these circumstances that the activities of NGOs are drawing greater attention and their importance is growing.

In support of the UN, the SGI sponsored the exhibition "Nuclear Arms: Threat to Our World" in twenty-five cities in sixteen countries between 1982 and 1988. We concentrated our efforts on the showing of this exhibition because the threat of nuclear weapons was hanging so heavily over humanity.

The threat has not disappeared. As the twenty-first century draws near, however, we feel the need for a more comprehensive vision for a new era without war: an approach that is not limited to nuclear weapons but also provides an overview of the history of war and weaponry of the twentieth century, including highly advanced weapons based on rapidly advancing technology.

We are now planning an updated version of the exhibition encompassing challenges for humanity in the twenty-first century such as environmental problems and human rights issues. We aim to show a new "War and Peace" exhibition throughout the world in the coming years, working in collaboration with like-minded NGOs.

Needless to say, the support of international public opinion is indispensable in establishing a new world order centered on the UN. The wisdom and power of NGOs must be brought together toward this end.

Here, I would like to propose the holding of an "NGO Peace Summit" as a way of focusing the power of civil society on discussing how to build such an order from multiple perspectives. This could be an international conference of NGOs, peace researchers and peace activists from around the world. The SGI is prepared to extend our full cooperation in close consultation with other NGOs toward the realization of such a meeting.

The Spirit of the UN Charter: "We the peoples. . ." (1991)[67]

The 1990s dawned with a kind of brightness that gave people a sense of hope for the future, heralding historic change, the arrival of an era of the people's will. The recent drastic changes in international affairs, however, have

---

67   From 1991 Peace Proposal, "Dawn of the Century of Humanity."

reminded us anew that the path to a new, post-Cold War world order will not be an easy one.

The world had just emerged from the long tunnel of the Cold War when Iraq invaded Kuwait in the summer of 1990; the ensuing conflict has plunged us again into darkness. [A deadline (January 15) was set for Iraq to withdraw from Kuwait; the deadline passed and at the time of writing the destruction and pollution of war was unfolding in the Gulf between Iraq and a multi-national force.]

Prior to the deadline, I joined in presenting an urgent personal appeal to Iraqi President Saddam Hussein[68] together with Soviet writer Chingiz Aitmatov,[69] British physicist Bernard Benson,[70] Club of Rome President Ricardo Díez Hochleitner,[71] Director-General of UNESCO Federico Mayor Zaragoza[72] and Nigerian playwright and winner of the Nobel Prize for Literature Wole Soyinka.[73] We called upon President Hussein to take the brave step of withdrawing from Kuwait and holding an international confer-ence to discuss the problems in the Middle East.

As a Buddhist upholding the dignity of life, I felt compelled to make this appeal. That war has nevertheless erupted fills me with profound sadness. I earnestly pray that it will end as soon as possible.

Here, I strongly urge the soonest possible cease-fire and the holding of an international conference under the leadership of the United Nations to open the way for a comprehensive peace in the Middle East.

The Cold War may have come to an end, but a new world order to replace the old will not take shape on its own. The value placed on military might has begun to diminish, primarily in Europe. But in other parts of the world, dic-tatorships relying on armed force still prevail. Ethnic, religious and economic confrontations are intensifying, signaling the increase of regional conflicts. The prospects for the peaceful development of a global society remain dim.

---

68   Saddam Hussein (1937–2006), President of Iraq (1979–2003).

69   Chingiz Aitmatov (1928–2008), Kyrgyz author.

70   Bernard S. Benson (1922–), British physicist and children's author.

71   Ricardo Díez Hochleitner (1953–), Spanish educationalist and economist, President of the Club of Rome (1991–2000).

72   Federico Mayor Zaragoza (1934–), Spanish statesman, Director-General of UNESCO (1987–99).

73   Wole Soyinka (1934–), Nigerian playwright and political activist, recipient of the Nobel Prize for Literature in 1986.

The outbreak of the Gulf War demonstrates how futile it is to formulate plans for a new world order without settling the North–South problem. The international community is in urgent need of bringing together people's wisdom to create a new vision for world peace, including the prevention of regional conflicts. This pressing need, combined with the increasing gravity of environmental problems, makes more apparent than ever the fact that protecting our one and only Earth is the shared challenge of humanity.

Today what is urgently needed is the power to conceive a new vision for world peace and above all, people's commitment to actively carry it out.

With this century drawing to its close, there is much speculation—both pessimistic and optimistic—about the future. But recent years have witnessed a gigantic surge toward democracy and an era of the will of the people. In order to ensure that this takes firm root, we need to remind ourselves of a passage from one of the classic speeches of John F. Kennedy[74]: "[M]an can be as big as he wants. No problem of human destiny is beyond human beings."[75] People of the world must join forces in pursuit of peace to turn back the reversal to chaos, opening the door to a new century.

***

The outbreak of the Gulf War has dampened the positive atmosphere inspired by the end of the Cold War and crushed the hopes of people who had begun to look forward to "a peace dividend." As Karl Jaspers[76] has written, however, there is no situation that is absolutely hopeless.[77] The important thing is what lessons the world will learn from the Gulf War. Viewed from a long-term perspective, this could be summarized as the reform and strengthening of the United Nations—the creation of a security and crisis management framework and a new world order centered on the UN.

The United Nations, under the leadership of Secretary-General Javier Pérez de Cuéllar,[78] made desperate efforts to mediate a peaceful resolution. When

---

74   John F. Kennedy (1917–63), 35th President of the United States (1960–63).

75   Kennedy, John F. 1963. "Commencement Address at American University, June 10, 1963."

76   Karl Jaspers (1883–1969), German philosopher.

77   See Jaspers, Karl. 1961. *The Future of Mankind.* Chicago, Illinois: University of Chicago Press, p. 167.

78   Javier Pérez de Cuéllar (1920–), Peruvian diplomat, 5th UN Secretary-General (1982–91), Prime Minister of Peru (2000–01).

the deadline passed, the US-led multinational force attacked Iraq. Secretary-General Pérez de Cuéllar expressed sorrow over the war, and it was indeed a sad occurrence for the UN. But it was not necessarily a disgrace, since the UN is not almighty. It was significant that as the situation grew critical, the world turned to the UN as the only remaining source of a solution to the conflict.

The power of the UN was paradoxically proven by the fact that the United States did not feel able to use force without the authorization of UN Security Council resolutions. The Gulf crisis has clearly demonstrated that international opinion can achieve such a binding effect only when expressed through the UN—this is the great weight the UN carries in the international community today.

The United Nations has been revitalized by the cooperation between the United States and the Soviet Union with emphasis on UN diplomacy. This is clearly shown in the fact that more than ten resolutions concerning the Gulf crisis were passed in the Security Council with no use of the veto.

At the same time, we must face the reality that the UN as it is today is not capable of exercising sufficient power to maintain world peace, as we have recently seen. In that sense, the challenge that lies before us is how to reform and strengthen the UN to create a new world order. This is the foremost challenge that each one of us must take upon ourselves as a personal concern—a challenge that humanity as a whole must face with all earnestness, rising above the Gulf War.

The world situation today is fundamentally different from what it was at the time of the founding of the United Nations. Multipolarized and complex changes have brought about a qualitative depth. International organizations have to be able to respond flexibly to such changes.

There is no doubt that the Charter of the United Nations is an outstanding set of guiding principles for the international community. But nearly half a century has passed since its inception. The time has come to consider modifications to correspond to our age.

Last year (1990), I had an in-depth discussion with Mr. Norman Cousins[79] on the issue of the reform and strengthening of the United Nations. "The aim of a revised United Nations," he said, "would be to have its own actual and potential forces, large enough to prevent aggression or to cope with it

---

79   Norman Cousins (1912–90), American author, President of the World Federalist Association (1976–91).

instantly if it should occur."[80] He also said, "The United Nations Charter anticipates the need for change in its own structure."[81]

Viewed in terms of a history of international organizations, the League of Nations represented a first phase and the United Nations represents a second phase. With the fiftieth anniversary of the United Nations four years away, it would be timely to make plans for a third-phase international organization refined and tailored to the needs of the twenty-first century. We should take this opportunity to map out a long-term UN reform program building on the original spirit that guided the founding of the United Nations.

The UN is made up of sovereign states. But we must seek the means to overcome the inevitable limitations imposed by its nature to create a third-phase organization. With all its achievements in the postwar years, it has suffered many frustrations and failures primarily because of its very nature as an organization of sovereign states: Member states have tended to put their own national interests first, crippling efforts to make decisions in the interests of humanity as a whole.

***

To break through the current limitations of the United Nations, precedence must be placed upon the "human face" over the state in its overall structure and operations. This has been my long-standing belief. The human face I refer to has, in fact, two aspects: one reflecting the people and the other humanity as a whole.

It is imperative today that the power of the people be activated and organized as the principal actors not only in the UN but throughout the international community. The UN, from its outset, had the two aspects of "the governments" and "the peoples," the subjects identified in the Preamble to the Charter: "We the peoples of the United Nations" and "our respective Governments."[82] In reality, however, the UN has always acted as an organization of governments. All its decisions have been made by those governments, and the people have been relegated to the backstage.

---

80   (trans. from) Cousins, Norman and Daisaku Ikeda. 1991. *Sekai shimin no taiwa* [Dialogue Between Citizens of the World]. Tokyo: Mainichi Shimbunsha, p. 158.

81   Ibid., p. 155.

82   UN (United Nations). 1945. "Preamble," in the "Charter of the United Nations."

I urge the UN to place more emphasis on the human face because the role of grassroots power, that of NGOs in particular, is growing extremely important today. There are greater expectations for them as effective actors to break through problems that might be difficult to solve in the hands of sovereign states.

Presently, the relationship between the United Nations and the NGOs is stipulated in Article 71 of the UN Charter as consisting of consultations exclusively with the Economic and Social Council.[83] But in reality, their cooperative relations have grown far beyond that. Especially noteworthy is the considerable influence NGOs have been exerting on interstate diplomacy through their active involvement in efforts to solve global problems by participating in UN conferences on the environment and disarmament. NGO activities are indispensable as their approach to seeking solutions to global problems is based on the standpoint of the interests of humankind, transcending national boundaries.

The fundamental purpose of a democratic organization is to check on government actions and keep them on the right course. The time is ripe to devise a mechanism to directly reflect more NGO input on the debates at the United Nations. I earnestly hope that the wisdom of the people will be brought together for the reform and strengthening of the UN system with a human face.

Some Keys to Strengthening the United Nations (1993)[84]

The United Nations as it stands today is an association of member states. Its agencies and organizations consist of the permanent delegations of the member states. Their structures do not allow non-state actors or NGOs to operate to the full extent of their potential.

Democracy is based on the idea that legitimacy derives from the sovereignty of the people. The key, therefore, to UN reform, in which democratization is a central issue, is to find ways in which the will of the people can be more accurately reflected in the operation of the international organization. It has been my contention for many years that the UN should bring to the fore its human, as opposed to its nation-state, aspect in terms of both its organization

---

83   See UN (United Nations). 1945. "Charter of the United Nations."
84   From 1993 Peace Proposal, "Toward a More Humane World in the Coming Century."

and operations. To make the faces of human beings more prominent, we must approach UN reform from two perspectives, namely, that of people as individuals and humanity as a whole.

One way to give the UN a human face would be to use the particular strengths of NGOs, which have been remarkably active players in international society in recent years, to reinforce UN activities. The United Nations Charter specifies that NGOs' relationships with the United Nations be restricted to consultation with the Economic and Social Council.[85] However, in light of the dynamic growth and activities of NGOs in the international community, as well as the scale of the cooperative relationships that already exist between NGOs and the UN, I believe these restrictions are unnatural. A mechanism should be put in place that enables the opinions of NGOs to be reflected not only in the Economic and Social Council, but also in the Security Council and the General Assembly.

I understand that experts are suggesting as part of UN reform that the Security Council be divided into four councils, each responsible for one of the following four areas: 1) peace and disarmament; 2) human rights and humanitarian concerns; 3) population, resources, environment and development; and 4) technology, information, communication and education. We have entered an era in which the cooperation of NGOs is essential in all four of these areas.

Last year (1992), Soka Gakkai youth members in Japan initiated the Voice Aid campaign (collecting used radios to send to Cambodia to raise awareness toward the general election to be held in July this year) in cooperation with the United Nations Transitional Authority in Cambodia (UNTAC) as part of its efforts to support the work of the United Nations. The campaign elicited a strong and positive response. Some 110,000 radios donated by Japanese citizens have already been delivered to Cambodia and the total number is forecast to exceed 280,000.

Civil organizations are capable of prompt action and are thus better suited to situations such as this that require quick response. With a mechanism that allows NGOs to participate in and work to their full potential in various fields of UN activity, the overall effectiveness of the UN could be enhanced significantly.

Recently, the concept of early warning is gaining increasing emphasis in UN activities. The UN has been developing a system designed to collect

---

85   See UN (United Nations). 1945. "Charter of the United Nations," Article 71.

information on signs of hazards concerning environmental destruction, natural disasters, famine, population movements, epidemics and nuclear accidents. The purpose is to make sure the people concerned are cautioned and to help provide solutions for problems before they reach crisis proportion. The system is an important component of the United Nations' attempts to engage in preventive diplomacy. The NGOs' strong capabilities in information gathering for early warning have been proven. If cooperative relations between NGOs and the UN are further developed, the system is sure to be even more effective.

To strengthen the UN, emphasis should be placed on creating a mechanism through which the Security Council, the General Assembly and the Secretary-General can mobilize all the resources of the various UN agencies toward the solution of a given problem. The weakness of the current UN is said to reflect the lack of such an organic, horizontally linked mechanism. In addition, the potential of NGOs could be fully utilized to enhance the overall effectiveness of the United Nations. For this reason I propose that, as a provisional measure, some kind of forum be established for regular consultations between the Secretary-General and representatives of NGOs.

***

Next, I would like to discuss the democratization of the General Assembly as a way to emphasize the interests of humanity as a whole over those of the nation-state. At present, most discussion concerning the reform and strengthening of the United Nations is focused on reforming the Security Council. While this is an important goal, I feel we should also give serious attention to reform of the General Assembly, since this is where the will of humankind is expressed through the consensus of the member states.

I am currently engaged in a dialogue with the internationally known scholar of peace studies, Dr. Johan Galtung,[86] the results of which are slated for publication. One of the important issues we have covered in our discussions is UN reform. In the course of our talks, Dr. Galtung presented his proposal that a new UN Peoples' Assembly be established alongside the existing General Assembly.[87]

---

86   Johan Galtung (1930–), Norwegian peace scholar.
87   See Galtung, Johan and Daisaku Ikeda. 1995. *Choose Peace*. London: Pluto Press, p. 137.

Although more thought must be given to the actual nature of such a body, he conceives it as a forum where issues can be discussed from a transnational (transcending ethnic and national boundaries) viewpoint, as opposed to the international (between nation-states) perspective that inevitably characterizes government-led globalism. I agree with Dr. Galtung's basic idea that, through the combined efforts of governments and private citizens, we can indeed build a better world.

I am fully aware that it is much easier to propose such a body than it is to actually create one. Fundamental reforms such as this could require revising the UN Charter, which is in itself a daunting task. One of the most pressing challenges facing us today, however, is to create, through a worldwide process of consensus-building, a system of global governance that will better reflect the realities of our modern world and will continue to function effectively into the twenty-first century.

On January 8, Mr. Peter Hansen,[88] the executive director of the Commission on Global Governance, paid a visit to the Soka Gakkai's headquarters, affording the opportunity for an exchange of opinions on various subjects. The latest report of the Commission makes the following statement, with which I am very much in sympathy:

> The nations of the world have created, over the past half century, an extensive system of international cooperation. In the centre stands the United Nations, with its Charter and its huge potential. In specific regions and areas, there exists further an array of important organizations. However, the institutions of global governance fall severely short of the demand of a new era.[89]

In 1990, Mr. Norman Cousins[90] and I published our dialogue, *Dialogue Between Citizens of the World*. Mr. Cousins, who since has sadly passed away,

---

88   Peter Hansen (1941–), Danish diplomat, UN Under-Secretary-General for Humanitarian Affairs and Emergency Relief Coordinator (1994–96), Commissioner-General of United Nations Relief and Works Agency (UNRWA) (1996–2005).

89   New World Commission on Global Democracy and Common Responsibility. 1992. "Terms of Reference, 2nd Draft." Geneva, p. 5.

90   Norman Cousins (1912–90), American author, President of the World Federalist Association (1976–91).

served as honorary president of the World Federalist Association[91] and was well known for his dedication to the strengthening of the United Nations. His insistence in our discussion on the need for a plenary conference to be held to discuss a new situation that could fundamentally affect the future of the UN remains unforgettable.[92]

It is true that, in the UN Charter, provision is made for such a review conference among member states when it is deemed necessary to open discussion concerning revision of the Charter.[93] Although such a review conference has in fact never been held, I believe that we now have ample reason to do so.

The celebration of the United Nations' fiftieth anniversary in 1995 would be an ideal opportunity for such a conference. I understand that the Commission on Global Governance will issue its report in 1994, the year before that anniversary, with suggestions for the establishment of a new organization for world governance.

I propose that the United Nations bring together the many wise ideas contained in reports such as this and take the initiative in holding a world summit meeting in 1995 to discuss UN reform. At the same time, we should consider holding a World NGO Summit that would rally the voices of all the world's citizens.

Participation of Civil Society

A Global People's Council (2000)[94]

Humanity needs to leave behind the era of war and division. Looking far into the future, we must embark on the challenge of removing the causes of war. We must abolish the institution of war itself and make the twenty-first century the start of an era where war is renounced throughout the world.

Globalization has brought to the surface problems that easily cross state borders, such as environmental destruction, poverty and a distressing increase

---

91 Subsequently renamed Citizens for Global Solutions.

92 See Cousins, Norman and Daisaku Ikeda. 1991. *Sekai shimin no taiwa* [Dialogue Between Citizens of the World]. Tokyo: Mainichi Shimbunsha, p. 155.

93 See UN (United Nations). 1945. "Chapter XVIII: Amendments, Article 109–1" in "Charter of the United Nations."

94 From 2000 Peace Proposal, "Peace through Dialogue: A Time to Talk."

in the numbers of refugees and displaced persons. Likewise, with greater travel, infectious diseases are spreading in new and disturbing patterns. We urgently need to come up with measures to deal with these issues.

Within the framework of the sovereign state system, crises have long been defined as territorial issues, and many states therefore have concentrated their efforts on military buildup. But the global issues now confronting us cannot be addressed using conventional approaches. In fact, it is these problems that, when left to fester, are causing internal conflicts and wars in many regions.

Faced as we are today with an escalation of global crises, what we need is an outlook that is focused not on the supremacy of national interest and security but on the interests of all humanity, and encourages us to face our common problems. In 1999, the United Nations Development Programme (UNDP), famous for its advocacy of the concept of human security as an alternative to state-centered security, issued a report entitled *Global Public Goods: International Cooperation in the 21st Century*.[95]

The term "global public goods" is the application to the global level of the standard economic term "public goods," which refers to goods that benefit all, such as a legal framework, justice system, healthy environment or education. Global public goods have benefits that are shared across nations, generations and population groups. In other words, they indicate the direction of a completely new international community that will not exclude any state, social stratum or individual, or harm future generations.

The UNDP report points out three problems to be resolved in realizing global public goods: a jurisdictional gap, a participation gap and an incentive gap. The jurisdictional gap refers to the gap between the global boundaries of today's major policy concerns and the national boundaries within which policymakers operate. The participation gap points to the fact that international cooperation is still primarily limited to an intergovernmental process even though there are numerous nongovernmental actors in the world. The incentive gap means that moral justifications alone are insufficient to persuade concerned states to change their policies and build cooperative relationships.

I believe that the United Nations is the only body capable of bridging these three gaps and laying the foundations for a framework of concerted action based upon the interests of humankind. As we stand at the threshold

---

95   UNDP (United Nations Development Programme). 1999. *Global Public Goods: International Cooperation in the 21st Century*. New York: Oxford University Press.

of a new millennium, we must draw up a grand design worthy of the advent of a global era and begin to take action toward realizing it. The most crucial challenge is therefore to strengthen the UN, so it may serve as the rallying point of humankind's joint struggle.

***

I believe that the driving force for bridging the jurisdictional gap, the participation gap and the incentive gap consists of grassroots solidarity in support of the UN and broad and multidimensional NGO activities. It has already been proven that NGOs' united efforts to broadly stir up public opinion can give rise to a force that can move the international community forward. NGOs have taken up themes that are often neglected within the framework of a state-centered international system, and have been pioneers in addressing ways to solve such problems—their achievements are truly great. I see tremendous promise in the way NGOs can channel the people's power to overcome the gaps that states alone cannot bridge. NGOs have won greater prominence thanks to their role in a series of world conferences starting with the Earth Summit of 1992.

In September 1994, then UN Secretary-General Boutros Boutros-Ghali[96] noted that "Nongovernmental organizations are now considered full participants in international life,"[97] and "are an essential part of the legitimacy without which no international activity can be meaningful."[98] Recently, NGOs are frequently referred to as civil society organizations (CSOs). Instead of the conventional name, which focuses on what they are *not,* the new name emphasizes their active role as sustainers of the global community. Although the significance of NGOs is growing in this way, their officially recognized interaction with the UN is limited to certain specified channels such as consultative status with the Economic and Social Council.

I have previously suggested plans for the establishment of a UN people's assembly consisting of representatives of civil society. Reform of the UN requires that it listen to the voices of ordinary citizens and work with ordinary citizens. Although creating such a people's assembly will of course be difficult,

---

96   Boutros Boutros-Ghali (1922–), Egyptian statesman, 6th UN Secretary-General (1992–96).

97   Willetts, Peter, ed. 1996. *"The Conscience of the World": The Influence of Non-Governmental Organisations in the UN System.* London: C. Hurst & Co., p. 311.

98   Ibid., p. 316.

I believe it is essential to establish some means whereby the people's voices reach the UN. I would therefore like to propose on this occasion the creation of a global people's council that will function as a consultative body to the General Assembly.

This council would be mandated to advise the General Assembly on themes for deliberation from the standpoint of realizing global public goods, and also call its attention to potential threats. Taking full advantage of NGOs' expertise in information gathering and firsthand experience in their fields of activity, such a council could contribute to the General Assembly's deliberations by promoting advance discussion of key issues.

With the completion of the cycle of UN-sponsored world conferences on critical global issues, the focus has now shifted to the follow-up of past conferences at five- or ten-year intervals. In light of this, I believe that it would be very significant for such a council to consistently monitor the implementation status of past agreements. Another important contribution could be to serve as the focus for networking among NGOs and member states and as a venue for sustained discussion toward enhancing global cooperation.

One of the subthemes for the NGO Millennium Forum scheduled to be held in May as a lead-up to the UN Millennium Assembly is "strengthening and democratizing the United Nations and other international organizations."[99] I sincerely hope that the Forum will deliberate and discuss meaningful plans for strengthening and reforming the UN from a people's perspective.

A People's Fund for the UN (2001)[100]

Crucial to the work of strengthening the soft power orientation of the United Nations is the task of enhancing cooperative relations between the UN and civil society, the broad spectrum of nongovernmental and volunteer movements. This is vital if we are to ensure that the UN is genuinely of the people, by the people and for the people.

The UN will be disempowered and marginalized if it is overtaken by the logic of confrontation and exclusion, the negative legacy of a twentieth

---

99   UN (United Nations). 2000. "Themes of the Millennium Forum." The Subthemes adopted by the Millennium Forum Steering Committee on June 29, 1999 and slightly revised on December 15, 1999.

100 From 2001 Peace Proposal, "Creating and Sustaining a Century of Life: Challenges for a New Era."

century that was dominated by competing national interests. If the UN gives in to the temptation to rely on pressure and coercion, this will create sources of further conflict, and it will lose credibility and trust. Therefore, it is essential to strengthen its identity as an organization dedicated to the well-being of all humankind and fundamentally supported by the people.

It is not too much to say that the destiny of humanity in the twenty-first century will be determined by the success of efforts to empower the UN and assure the people a central role in its workings.

This new imperative is clearly reflected in the Millennium Declaration. The section on strengthening the UN defines civil society as an indispensable partner and voices the resolve to "give greater opportunities to the private sector, nongovernmental organizations and civil society, in general, to contribute to the realization of the Organization's goals and programmes."[101]

This is a highly significant statement that explicitly aims at enabling the UN to grow beyond its current framework as a gathering of sovereign states. People's participation is the best way to revitalize the UN. Even more centrally, however, this is necessary if the UN is to transcend its present limitations and evolve into a pivotal focus for the activities of global civil society. By bringing together the wide-ranging talents and capacities of ordinary citizens, the UN will be able to enrich and strengthen the humanistic quality that should be its essence. This, I am convinced, is the path it should pursue as it moves into the future. Now is the time to take effective steps to implement and realize this vision.

In this regard, the proposals made at the We the Peoples Millennium Forum, a gathering of global civil society held in May 2000 as a lead-up to the Millennium Summit, are a rich source of ideas for concrete action. In one of the adopted papers, the Forum urges the creation of a global civil society forum. It calls for the extension of the NGOs' consultative rights of access and their participation in the General Assembly and other principal organs of the UN.[102]

---

101 UNGA (United Nations General Assembly). 2000. "United Nations Millennium Declaration." A/RES/55/2. Resolution adopted by the General Assembly. September 8.

102 See UNGA (United Nations General Assembly). 2000. "Strengthening the United Nations for the Twenty-first century." A/54/959. We the Peoples Millennium Forum Declaration and Agenda for Action. August 8.

These initiatives are consistent with ideas I have proposed in the past, and I call for them to be realized promptly. Last year, the Toda Institute for Global Peace and Policy Research published *Reimagining the Future,*[103] a report of the Global Governance Reform Project. This is a product of research conducted in collaboration with La Trobe University, Melbourne, and Focus on the Global South at Chulalongkorn University, Bangkok. Specifically, it reflects the work of two expert panels that included such leading thinkers as former UN Secretary-General Boutros Boutros-Ghali.[104]

Calling for democratized global governance as one of the keys to strengthening the UN, the report presents specific initiatives for bold reform, such as the creation of a people's assembly that will make the organization more open and accessible to civil society.

Some years ago, I had the opportunity to share views with Johan Galtung,[105] a pioneer of the field of peace studies. At that time, he offered this comment on the special value of a people's assembly: "Perhaps I believe more in long-lasting dialogues leading to new ideas and consensus than in short debates entailing few ideas and ending in decisions reached by means of voting, in which there are winners and losers."[106]

New institutional means must be developed that fully integrate people's participation in a process of dialogue. This is the most certain way of developing the kind of long-term vision that leaves no one behind and takes the interests and concerns of all parties into consideration. Plans along these lines are being proposed by various organizations, and I believe strongly that the time has come to take meaningful steps toward their realization.

NGOs should not simply be seen as playing a supporting role to that of governments; they, in fact, are the key actors in building a new international order based on an ethos of creative coexistence and autonomy. The UN will be effective in guarding the dignity and security of each individual to the degree that it incorporates people's energies and efforts.

103　Camilleri, Joseph A., Kamal Malhotra, Majid Tehranian, et al., eds. 2000. *Reimagining the Future: Towards Democratic Governance.* Bundoora, Australia. The Department of Politics, La Trobe UP.

104　Boutros Boutros-Ghali (1922–), Egyptian statesman, 6th UN Secretary-General (1992–96).

105　Johan Galtung (1930–), Norwegian peace scholar.

106　Galtung, Johan and Daisaku Ikeda. 1995. *Choose Peace.* London: Pluto Press, p. 140.

Similarly, one key to resolving the UN's long-standing challenge of securing stable sources of financing may lie in enlisting the support of the world's people. The current dependence on member states' contributions hinders the ability of the organization to engage in emergency responses to crises or to address issues in a focused and sustained manner. Stabilizing UN finances by including an additional funding stream would help alleviate these problems.

In this connection I would like to suggest the creation of a people's fund for the UN, learning from the examples of independent fund-raising implemented so successfully, for example, by UNICEF. This new body would be actively engaged in fund-raising, accepting donations from individuals, organizations and corporations. The funds collected would be used primarily to support the humanitarian activities of the UN.

The Security Council and NGOs (2005)[107]

In conjunction with restructuring designed to bring forth the UN's soft power capacities, I should like to propose reforms aimed at strengthening the partnership between the UN and civil society. In this connection, many thought-provoking concepts are set out in the report of the Panel of Eminent Persons chaired by former Brazilian president Fernando Henrique Cardoso,[108] "We the Peoples: Civil Society, the United Nations and Global Governance."[109]

The report calls upon the UN to mobilize and coordinate external cooperation rather than tackling problems alone; to this end, the UN must become an "outward-looking Organization" that is capable of bringing together the many actors relevant to different issues. A prerequisite for any such effort must surely be to build closer partnerships between the UN and civil society, in particular with NGOs.

Comparing the world in 1945 when the UN was founded to the world today, we note a great increase in the number of problems of global scale, as well as a plethora of NGOs mobilized to tackle them. We cannot ignore these momentous changes; confining discussion solely to internal reform of the UN would severely limit the benefit of any restructuring.

---

107 From 2005 Peace Proposal, "Toward a New Era of Dialogue: Humanism Explored."

108 Fernando Henrique Cardoso (1931–), President of Brazil (1995–2003).

109 UNGA (United Nations General Assembly). 2004. "We the Peoples: Civil Society, the United Nations and Global Governance." A/58/817. Report of the Panel of Eminent Persons on United Nations–Civil Society Relations. June 11.

This being the case, efforts should be made to ensure that the voices of the world's people are more clearly heard at the UN. For example, the other major organs of the UN could adopt the system of accrediting NGOs with consultative status that is presently used by ECOSOC. NGOs have for many years been able to observe UN General Assembly (UNGA) sessions and access relevant documents, but have not been able to make statements there.

At the series of Special Sessions of the UNGA convened during the 1990s, NGO representatives were able to address the Assembly and take part in intergovernmental discussions at the ministerial level. At the Security Council, too, since 1992 a practice known as the Arria Formula has been in place whereby a member of the Council may invite, among others, representatives of NGOs to address an informal gathering of members of the Council on issues of shared concern.

On the basis of these experiences, moves should be made to guarantee that the right to participate in debates as nonvoting observers and to propose agenda items that NGOs currently have relative to ECOSOC be extended to their relations with the UNGA and the Security Council. In 1963, President John F. Kennedy[110] addressed the UNGA as follows: "My fellow inhabitants of this planet: Let us take a stand here in this Assembly of nations. And let us see if we, in our own time, can move the world to a just and lasting peace."[111]

On the occasion of the UN's sixtieth anniversary, let us recall Kennedy's words as we reaffirm our commitment to uphold the underlying spirit of the UN Charter, which opens with the stirring phrase "We the peoples. . . ." For the good of our planet, for the good of humankind, let us make the most of this opportunity, bringing all our intelligence and conviction to bear on the challenges of reforming and strengthening the United Nations.

The General Assembly and NGOs (2006)[112]

I would like to discuss specific areas in which ordinary citizens—robust, engaged people acting as individuals and in solidarity—can work to build a global society of peace and creative coexistence. The United Nations must

110 John F. Kennedy (1917–63), 35th President of the United States (1960–63).

111 Kennedy, John F. 1963. "Address before the 18th General Assembly of the United Nations." John F. Kennedy Library and Museum. September 20.

112 From 2006 Peace Proposal, "A New Era of the People: Forging a Global Network of Robust Individuals."

serve as the key venue and focus for our efforts. Humanity faces a range of complex issues that show no regard for national borders—threats such as terrorism, armed conflict, poverty, environmental degradation, hunger and disease. A reformed and strengthened UN is essential to mustering effective responses to the global challenges of the new era.

As we search for the kind of UN reform that will reflect the perspectives and concerns of ordinary citizens, I would like to focus on a revitalization of the General Assembly (UNGA). While it goes without saying that the Security Council will continue to play a central role in maintaining global peace and security, the UNGA is crucially important as the only universal forum for dialogue where all member states can participate and develop responses to global challenges. I am convinced that efforts to increase the accessibility of this assembly of humankind would lead to a strengthening of the entire UN system.

"In Larger Freedom," a report by UN Secretary-General Kofi Annan[113] clarifies the direction of UNGA reform as follows: "It should concentrate on the major substantive issues of the day, *and establish mechanisms to engage fully and systematically with civil society*"[114] (emphasis added). While it is again truly disappointing that no specific measures were agreed upon at the 2005 World Summit, this approach undoubtedly holds the key to re-empowerment of the UNGA. Thus I would suggest that, to further establish effective collaborative relationships with civil society, frequent opportunities be created for the UNGA President and the members of each of its committees to closely consult with NGOs.

In June 2005, the General Assembly organized two days of informal hearings with civil society, creating an opportunity for NGO representatives and experts from around the world to express a broad range of opinions toward the 2005 World Summit. The first such attempt in the UN's history, and one that was later welcomed by the summit participants as a step toward an interactive engagement between civil society and member states, this was indeed a groundbreaking development.

At the same time, NGOs have undertaken the bold initiative of organizing the Millennium+5 NGO Network. This informal grouping of NGOs

---

113 Kofi Annan (1938–), Ghanaian statesman, 7th Secretary-General of the United Nations (1997–2006).

114 UN (United Nations). 2005. "Executive Summary" in "In Larger Freedom: Towards Development, Security and Human Rights for All."

active at the UN will bring together the input of civil society and liaise with the UN. I believe that such efforts to establish forums of dialogue between the world's ordinary citizens and the UN will help consolidate the UN's foundations as an international body that is underpinned by the twin pillars of its member states and civil society.

Based on the philosophy of Buddhist humanism, the SGI has consistently supported the activities of the UN. As an NGO, we have been active in a wide variety of ways, one recent example being the election of our representative as president of the Committee of Religious NGOs at the UN in June of last year.

Also, in February this year, in commemoration of its tenth anniversary, the Toda Institute for Global Peace and Policy Research will host an international conference in Los Angeles focused on reform and strengthening of the UN. Building on the success of the institute's research projects in such areas as human security and global governance and dialogue among civilizations, the conference will explore initiatives toward transforming the UN into an organization that is truly of, for and by the people.

An Under-Secretary-General for Civil Society Relations (2009)[115]

I would like to make some proposals for strengthening the United Nations, which was created out of the experience of two world wars and must serve as the hub of humanity's common struggle to address the global problems I have been discussing.

The Parliament of Man: The Past, Present, and Future of the United Nations by the historian Paul Kennedy[116] is a remarkable work that depicts what the world organization really stands for, illuminating its six decades of history. I was particularly struck by the fact that the history of the UN is narrated not just as one facet of international politics, but as "a story of human beings groping toward a common end, a future of mutual dignity, prosperity, and tolerance through shared control of international instruments."[117]

---

115 From 2009 Peace Proposal, "Toward Humanitarian Competition: A New Current in History."

116 Paul M. Kennedy (1945–), British historian and author.

117 Kennedy, Paul M. 2007. *The Parliament of Man: The Past, Present, and Future of the United Nations.* New York: Vintage Books, p. xv.

In other words, what Kennedy offers is a contemporary history of human-kind with the UN as the pivot. I would go even further and say that this can be understood as a history of humanitarian competition—with all its challenges and tribulations—in pursuit of the realization of the ideals of the UN Charter.

The key question facing the UN as it seeks to fulfill the mission mandated in its Charter is, according to Kennedy: "Can we modify our fears and egoisms to the common good and our own long-term advantage? Much of the history of the twenty-first century may depend on our collective response to that challenge."[118] When we consider the future of the UN from this perspective, the key issue is to build a robust partnership with civil society which would be a source of support and empowerment for generations to come.

As a step toward that goal, I would like to call for the creation of a post of under-secretary-general for civil society relations. This should be a permanent post specifically dedicated to enhancing the standing of NGOs within the UN system and the promotion of partnership with them. The under-secretary-general could, for example, participate in deliberations on primary UN themes such as peace and security, economic and social affairs, development and cooperation, humanitarian affairs and human rights to ensure that the views and concerns of civil society are represented.

A similar proposal was made by the Panel of Eminent Persons on United Nations–Civil Society Relations chaired by the former Brazilian president Fernando Henrique Cardoso[119] in 2004. As the panel's report stressed, "Civil society is now so vital to the United Nations that engaging with it well is a necessity, not an option."[120] It is crucial that NGOs not be confined to the role of observers, but be recognized as indispensable partners in the work of the UN. The importance of their contributions is likely only to grow as the twenty-first century progresses.

We cannot allow the opening words of the UN Charter "We, the peo-ples. . ." to be a mere rhetorical flourish but must work to bring about a UN in which the concerns and lives of real people are always central. These reforms would constitute a step toward that goal.

---

118 Ibid., p. xvii.

119 Fernando Henrique Cardoso (1931–), President of Brazil (1995–2003).

120 UNGA (United Nations General Assembly). 2004. "We the Peoples: Civil Society, the United Nations and Global Governance." A/58/817. Report of the Panel of Eminent Persons on United Nations–Civil Society Relations." June 11.

Soft Power

The Security Council and the Economic and Social Council (1994)[121]

In January 1994, United Nations Secretary-General Boutros Boutros-Ghali[122] submitted a report to the Security Council concerning the United Nations Operation in Somalia II (UNOSOM II), the UN's first peacekeeping operation, which has been deployed in Somalia. In the report, he recommended that the use of military power to force the Somalis to disarm be abandoned, and urged that the operation assume the mission of conventional peacekeeping operations focused on protecting supply routes used for humanitarian aid and goods.[123] This is one example that demonstrates how the impetuous use of force is not necessarily effective.

The single case of Somalia is not a sufficient basis upon which to judge the proper role of UN peacekeeping operations, however, because the UN will no doubt be required to respond in a flexible manner to a wide variety of circumstances in the future. Even so, if military force is considered a kind of "hard power," then we must not forget that the very foundation of the UN rests on the concept of "soft power," which means working to reconcile nations and harmonize their actions.

***

In the modern world, the complex interaction of various factors results in the eruption of many regional conflicts. However, the UN does not become involved until the situation has grown serious. One important issue that must be addressed, therefore, is what measures it can take to prevent such hostilities from arising in the first place. Many problems related to the political, economic and cultural structure of society lie behind these conflicts, including poverty, hunger, oppression and discrimination. Finding solutions to economic problems in particular can go a long way toward achieving resolution

---

121 From 1994 Peace Proposal, "Light of the Global Spirit: A New Dawn in Human History."

122 Boutros Boutros-Ghali (1922–), Egyptian statesman, 6th UN Secretary-General (1992–96).

123 See UNSC (United Nations Security Council). 1994. "Further Report of the Secretary-General Submitted in Pursuance of Paragraph 4 of Resolution 886 (1993)." S/1994/12. January 6.

in an armed conflict. Actions that depend on military force and ignore the underlying root factors cannot provide a true solution to the problem.

The challenge of solving the various social problems confronting different regions and improving and stabilizing the lives of all of the world's people can be more appropriately handled by the UN Economic and Social Council. To be effective, it would be vital for the Economic and Social Council to work closely with the Security Council.

Considering the crucial nature of its mission, the strengthening of the Economic and Social Council is an important aspect of UN reform. The key challenge for the United Nations from now on will be to enable departments within the UN Headquarters and organizations within the UN system to work efficiently with one another.

Human Security (1995)[124]

This year marks the fiftieth anniversary of the founding of the United Nations, an important milestone. Under normal circumstances, this would be an event worthy of heartfelt celebration, but in fact the environment in which the UN operates has grown increasingly difficult.

Plagued by the frequent regional conflicts that have erupted since the end of the Cold War, the international community looked to UN peacekeeping operations for a solution. However, expectations have been frustrated by the ineffectiveness of the UN's first peacekeeping operation in Somalia and the stalemate in the Bosnia situation. UN Secretary-General Boutros Boutros-Ghali[125] announced at the beginning of this year in his paper to the Security Council, "Supplement to an Agenda for Peace," that he would not take enforcement action for the foreseeable future.[126] This is symbolic of the failure of the UN peacekeeping framework as it presently stands.

Mr. Boutros-Ghali's statement represents his personal revision of a policy previously adopted by the UN for bolstering its peacekeeping operations with military strength and reflects the tough recognition of the fact that the

---

124 From 1995 Peace Proposal, "Creating a Century without War through Human Solidarity."

125 Boutros Boutros-Ghali (1922–), Egyptian statesman, 6th UN Secretary-General (1992–96).

126 See UNGA (United Nations General Assembly). 1995. "Supplement to an Agenda for Peace." A/50/60-S/1995/1. Position Paper of the Secretary-General on the Occasion of the Fiftieth Anniversary of the United Nations. January 3.

deployment of peacekeepers with the authority to use force is beyond the capacity of the United Nations. Given the inefficacy of peace enforcement efforts and an unpredictable future of continually expanding operations, Mr. Boutros-Ghali's change of direction was probably a wise one.

If the UN were to become embroiled in a conflict without the assent of the combatants and were to impose its will by force, it would simply become one of the combatants itself. As a neutral organization, the UN must be extremely careful in this regard. Mr. Boutros-Ghali's revision of policy does not mean, however, that the importance of the UN's role in maintaining and creating peace will diminish in any way.

It is imperative to break out of the narrow framework defined by peace-keeping operations and adopt a wider perspective that will enable us to comprehensively reassess the mission of the UN as it relates to peace and security. Since the principal function of the organization is to apply "soft power" to encourage cooperation among nations, harmonize their actions and construct systems and rules dedicated to peace, we must seek ways to optimize its efficacy. For its member states, as well as for NGOs supporting the international body, its fiftieth anniversary provides a good opportunity to give serious consideration to this issue.

Since its founding, the United Nations has depended primarily on the Security Council to preserve peace. Composed of five permanent members with veto powers, the council did not function effectively during the period of intense Cold War rivalry. Once the confrontation between East and West eased, however, there were surging expectations that the UN would fulfill more of its role in world affairs. Unfortunately, it would seem that the world body is at a loss as to how to fulfill these renewed expectations.

It is clear that the current system centered on a handful of major powers in the Security Council has reached its limit in terms of meeting the wide-ranging security needs of the world. This problem will not be solved through such simple reforms as permitting Japan and Germany to join the council's inner circle.

The crux of the problem is that the Security Council has failed to respond to the changing times, which demand a radical transformation of our concep-tion of security. Recently, there have been attempts to formulate a concept of "human security" (see, for example, the activities of the Commission on Global Governance) that transcends the old, limited interpretation of security as something achieved by and for the state. In today's world with many forms of humanitarian and human rights crises, this concept places top priority on human—rather than institutional—factors. It also ties in with the new movement to bring a personal face, the face of humanity, into prominence at the UN, which until now has been dominated by the interests of sovereign states.

Security cannot be achieved without taking into account the survival and well-being of the people affected and issues of justice and freedom. We live in a time when the basic rights that enable people to live in peace are threatened in many ways. Undeniably, these rights have been neglected because of the excessive priority given to the interests of states. The old security system, which openly uses hard power, or military strength, is growing increasingly obsolete. We must now focus all our wisdom on the task of establishing, as quickly as possible, a new "human security" framework centered around the UN that will comprehensively address threats to humanity.

The broad concept of human security cannot be realized on the basis of narrowly proscribed perceptions of peace. Rather, it is intimately linked to the idea of development. In 1994, Mr. Boutros-Ghali submitted his "Agenda for Development" to the UN General Assembly. In it, he presents a comprehensive outline of the five interrelated forces that propel sustainable development: peace, economic progress, environmental protection, social justice and democracy.[127] This report will no doubt be a focus at the World Summit for Social Development to be held this March in Copenhagen.

Building on these basic principles expounded in the Secretary-General's agenda, the UN should assume the leadership for world peace with a new vision. In cases of ethnic strife, for example, the UN's old method of intervening only after a conflict has entered an impossible quagmire has clearly reached its limits. Instead, each country should work to prevent ethnic conflicts from arising in the first place by vigorously promoting the above-mentioned five developmental forces within their borders.

To achieve this, the mandate and authority of the Economic and Social Council, responsible for development issues, must be fundamentally expanded and strengthened. A reinforced Economic and Social Council working in tandem with the Security Council with a renewed vision will be the only way for the UN to effectively ensure security in a way that properly corresponds to the changes in the international community.

---

127 See UNGA (United Nations General Assembly). 1994. "An Agenda for Development." A/48/935. Report of the Secretary-General. May 4, p. 39.

"Prevention" and "Stability" (2001)[128]

We have at last entered a new century. It is natural at such a time that there should be large measures of both hope and anxiety. Compared with the intellectual currents in vogue at the start of the twentieth century, what is starkly lacking today is the sense of optimism that was present then. Naturally there are great expectations regarding advances in science and technology—particularly in fields such as information and biotechnology—but there is also great foreboding, especially in Japan, about the political and economic fronts.

So what will the new century bring? I think that many people today harbor a profound sense of disillusionment that makes them question whether the twentieth century was really a period of advancement for humankind. This is because, while the remarkable progress of science and technology brought with it many blessings, the ceaseless occurrence of war and the unprecedented horrors of the age have cast an indelible shadow over people's hearts.

How can we dispel this dark shadow? What should be the core values on which to base human endeavors in the twenty-first century?

When I ponder these questions, I am reminded of my discussions with Linus Pauling,[129] hailed as the father of modern chemistry. In our discussions, later published in book form, I shared my long-standing belief that we must make the twenty-first century a "century of life." Dr. Pauling extended his full support to this concept, which he described as "a century in which greater attention will be paid to human beings and their happiness and health."[130]

Born in 1901, Dr. Pauling's life spanned the whole of the turbulent twentieth century. As a scientist and a peace activist, he never, right up until his death at age ninety-three, ceased to interrogate human and social realities. For this reason, perhaps, I sensed a unique weight in his words.

Our decision to title the Japanese edition of our dialogue "In Quest of a Century of Life" was likewise spurred by the conviction that unless humanity grapples with the fundamental questions of life and death, we will not be able to identify the challenges we must overcome or the direction in which to advance.

---

128 From 2001 Peace Proposal, "Creating and Sustaining a Century of Life: Challenges for a New Era."

129 Linus Pauling (1901–94), American scientist, recipient of the Nobel Prize in Chemistry in 1954 and the Nobel Prize for Peace in 1962.

130 Pauling, Linus and Daisaku Ikeda. 1992. *A Lifelong Quest for Peace*. Trans. and ed. by Richard L. Gage. Boston: Jones and Bartlett Publishers, p. 45.

How will history judge the twentieth century? *The Age of Extremes: The Short Twentieth Century, 1914–1991* by Eric Hobsbawm[131] is filled with valuable insights into this question. The introductory chapter of the book, "The Century: A Bird's Eye View," comprises the analyses of twelve thinkers of global standing. Reading this, one is struck by the consistency with which these views convey a sense of pained anguish.

René Dumont[132] (agronomist, ecologist, France):
"I see it only as a century of massacres and wars."

William Golding[133] (Nobel laureate, writer, Britain):
"I can't help thinking that this has been the most violent century in human history."[134]

Hobsbawm then asks: "Why, as the epigraphs to this chapter show, did so many reflective minds look back upon [the twentieth century] without satisfaction, and certainly without confidence in the future?" His answer is as follows: "Not only because it was without doubt the most murderous century of which we have record, both by the scale, frequency and length of the warfare which filled it, . . . but also by the unparalleled scale of the human catastrophes it produced, from the greatest famines in history to systematic genocide."[135]

It may not be entirely fair to focus exclusively on the darker sides of recent history. There are certainly aspects of the twentieth century that deserve to be recognized as genuine progress and advancement.

First and foremost, perhaps, is the fact that overt imperialism and colonialism are no longer acceptable. Likewise, the United Nations has, despite its many failings, continued to function as a global political organization for the past half-century, far longer than its short-lived predecessor, the League of Nations.

There are far fewer people who openly question democratic values. And while there is still a long way to go, the advances made by women, their

---

131 Eric Hobsbawm (1917–2012), British historian.

132 René Dumont (1904–2001), French agronomist.

133 William Golding (1911–93), British novelist, recipient of the Nobel Prize for Literature in 1983.

134 Hobsbawm, Eric. 1994. *The Age of Extremes: The Short Twentieth Century, 1914–1991*. London: Michael Joseph, p. 1.

135 Ibid., p. 13.

emergence in all realms of society over the course of the past century, have been truly remarkable. While science and technology have produced a distinctly mixed record, on the positive side must be counted material affluence (however grossly maldistributed) as well as progress in the fields of transport, communications, medical treatment and hygiene. These are all contributions whose importance I think no one would deny. And if we look at the degree to which humanity as a whole has access to human rights, there is a vast difference between the legal and institutional structures that existed 100 years ago and those that pertain today.

Despite these achievements, the undeniable fact is that the twentieth century was an era stained by an unconscionable amount of bloodshed. One analyst's estimate is that twice as many people were killed in wars during the twentieth century as in the preceding four centuries put together. The past century was indeed an era of mass slaughter—of megadeath—without parallel in history.[136]

***

To realize peace in the coming century, it is absolutely essential that we replace the traditional ascendancy of competing national interests—the cause of so much war and tragedy—with an international community dedicated to the welfare of the whole of humankind and Earth.

The UN can and must play a pivotal role in this transformation. The challenges facing humanity—promoting peace and disarmament, protecting the environment, eradicating poverty—clearly require that we cooperate and harmonize our efforts across national boundaries. Indeed, we must unite as one humanity engaged in a common struggle.

In this sense, we really have no choice but to turn to the UN. For half a century, it has been actively building international consensus as a forum for global dialogue; it has consistently engaged in humanitarian relief and assistance programs in different parts of the world. It is my belief that only the UN, for all its limitations and problems, can play the axial role in uniting humankind.

The United Nations Millennium Declaration adopted by the unprecedented gathering of heads of state and government at the Millennium Summit

---

136 See Sakurai, Tetsuo. 1999. *Senso no seiki—Dai-ichiji sekai taisen to seishin no kiki* [The Century of War—World War I and the Crisis of the Mind]. Tokyo: Heibonsha, p. 9.

of September 2000 has a profound significance in this regard. Calling on the countries of the world to share responsibility for managing global issues, the declaration clearly states: "As the most universal and most representative organization in the world, the United Nations must play the central role."[137]

The lofty objective and founding spirit of the UN are powerfully expressed in the Preamble of the Charter: "We the peoples of the United Nations, determined to save succeeding generations from the scourge of war, which twice in our lifetime has brought untold sorrow to mankind. . . ."[138] It is time to move forward with the effort to create a framework that genuinely engages all of humankind in a shared struggle to abolish the scourge of war from the face of Earth.

Discussion about the future direction of the UN inevitably focuses on such questions as: "What kind of world do we seek?" and "How will we respond to the various challenges that confront us?" As we ponder these questions, we must bear in mind above all that the UN's essential nature is to be found in "soft power"—the power of dialogue and cooperation.

While the UN Charter clearly accepts the possibility of the exercise of "hard power," including military action—Chapter VI, on the pacific settlement of disputes, is followed by Chapter VII, stipulating enforcement measures—precedence is firmly placed on the peaceful resolution of conflict; the use of hard power is reserved for crisis situations that absolutely necessitate it.[139] To realize international peace and security through soft power is the unchanging, foremost mission of the UN.

This is evident in the origins of the UN—the bitter lessons of two world wars. If we are to make the twenty-first century a century of life built on the ethos of creative coexistence and autonomy, it is vital that we never lose sight of this fundamental principle.

While the legitimate functions of the UN Security Council must be acknowledged, it is clear that the UN of the twenty-first century must be centered on a soft power approach that emphasizes conflict prevention and stabilization of potential crisis situations. This requires the promotion of

---

137 UNGA (United Nations General Assembly). 2000. "United Nations Millennium Declaration." A/RES/55/2. Resolution adopted by the General Assembly. September 18.

138 UN (United Nations). 1945. "Preamble," in the "Charter of the United Nations."

139 See UN (United Nations). 1945. "Charter of the United Nations."

human security—the safety and well-being of human beings rather than simply the integrity of national borders.

To this end, we should fully incorporate the invaluable lessons and experiences of the past fifty years to enable the Economic and Social Council and humanitarian agencies to assume ever more constructive and active roles. In that regard, I sincerely hope that meaningful results will emerge from an earnest debate on what we as humankind can do for future generations at the General Assembly Special Session on Children in September 2001.

A Global Governance Coordinating Panel (2005)[140]

Last year (2004), two bodies appointed by United Nations Secretary-General Kofi Annan[141] submitted their recommendations for reforming the UN. These were the High-level Panel on Threats, Challenges and Change, chaired by former prime minister Anand Panyarachun[142] of Thailand, and the Panel of Eminent Persons on Civil Society and UN Relationships, chaired by former president Fernando Henrique Cardoso[143] of Brazil.

The High-level Panel's report, "A More Secure World: Our Shared Responsibility," makes concrete recommendations that include enlargement of the Security Council and establishing a new Peacebuilding Commission. It also calls for measures to enhance the legal and institutional environment within which the UN responds to new threats. These proposed measures include: the rapid completion of negotiations on a comprehensive convention on terrorism; greater and more effective utilization of the International Criminal Court (ICC); and clearer criteria for the use of force.[144] Of these, the need for a body to assist in post-conflict peacebuilding is something I emphasized in last year's proposal, and I hope the panel's recommendation will be realized.

---

140 From 2005 Peace Proposal, "Toward a New Era of Dialogue: Humanism Explored."

141 Kofi Annan (1938–), Ghanaian statesman, 7th Secretary-General of the United Nations (1997–2006).

142 Anand Panyarachun (1932–), Prime Minister of Thailand (1991–92).

143 Fernando Henrique Cardoso (1931–), President of Brazil (1995–2003).

144 See United Nations High-Level Panel on Threats, Challenges, and Change. 2004. "A More Secure World: Our Shared Responsibility." New York: United Nations Publications.

The proposed overhaul of the Security Council that forms the main focus of the report would see the Council enlarged to better reflect such factors as regional representation and level of contribution to the UN. It is praiseworthy in its attempt to facilitate a wider sharing of responsibility and development of the Council into a deliberative body with a more global viewpoint.

Secretary-General Annan has stated that the UN's aim should be "to create a world that both has fewer threats and greater ability to meet those threats which nevertheless arise."[145] In addition to enhanced problem-solving capabilities, this will require a renewed emphasis on preventive measures.

When viewed in the context of these comments by the Secretary-General, the report's recommendations for enlarging the Security Council and establishing a new peacebuilding commission are perhaps more weighted toward problem solving.

I would like to emphasize a preventive engagement with global problems—the goal of creating a world with fewer threats cited by the Secretary-General—in my ideas on how the UN might be reformed to meet the needs of the twenty-first century. My reason is that I believe that the soft power of dialogue and cooperation lies at the heart of the UN, and soft power functions most effectively at the preventive end of the spectrum; namely, defining paradigms for addressing global problems, creating collaborative frameworks aimed at prevention and so forth.

I would first like to propose a greater role for the UN's Economic and Social Council (ECOSOC).

In addition to supporting development cooperation via debate and policy advisories on international economic and social issues, in recent years ECOSOC has played a key role in setting the agenda for priority UN action, channeling energies into issues such as the fight against poverty and managing the effects of globalization.

Drawing upon the experience of ECOSOC to date, I would hope that any UN restructuring and reform will place central emphasis on enhancing the following four soft power roles:

1. Identifying and prioritizing the issues the international community must address;

---

145 (trans. from) Annan, Kofi. 2004. "Shinseiki ni okeru aratana Kokuren [A New United Nations for a New Century]." Trans. by Mari Tomita. *International Affairs*. No. 534. Tokyo: The Japan Institute of International Affairs. September, p. 5.

2. Setting standards and targets for international cooperation;
3. Coordinating and enhancing the effectiveness of the UN's various activities;
4. Collecting and sharing information and best practices among UN agencies.

Part of my reason for stressing these roles is that in many instances the UN has moved to address such global problems as poverty and the environment only after they have reached crisis proportions. To move away from this ex post facto approach and reinvent itself as a prevention-focused body creating a world with fewer threats, the UN will need to strengthen its soft power capacities.

As part of restructuring in 1997, the various UN agencies were grouped by mission—peace and security; economic and social affairs; humanitarian affairs; and development—with executive committees for each. Above these is the Senior Management Group, which includes the conveners of each executive committee and meets regularly as the Secretary-General's cabinet.

To build on such efforts and enable the UN to fulfill the four soft power roles I identified above, there is a need for what might be termed a global governance coordinating panel, whose work would be closely linked to ECOSOC deliberations and decision-making. A working group of NGOs with relevant expertise could support the activities of this panel; input from and collaboration with these NGOs would help generate a common awareness of problems and raise the public profile of the relevant issues. By further enhancing system-wide information sharing and activity coordination, the panel would reflect the interrelated and complex nature of global problems.

The priority objective of such structural reforms should be achieving the Millennium Development Goals (MDGs), tackling those issues that endanger their realization by the target date of 2015. Research by the World Bank shows that the proportion of people living in extreme poverty (less than US$1 a day) fell by almost half between 1981 and 2001, from 40 percent to 21 percent of the world's population, an absolute decline of as many as 400 million despite rapid population growth.[146] As this statistic shows, realizing the MDGs may

---

146 World Bank. 2004. "Global Poverty Down by Half since 1981 but Progress Uneven as Economic Growth Eludes Many Countries." 2004/309/S. Press Release. April 23.

be difficult, but it is by no means impossible. What is required quite simply is a strong determination on the part of the international community.

A high-level plenary meeting of the UN General Assembly to comprehensively review the implementation of the Millennium Declaration and progress toward achieving the MDGs is scheduled for September. I appeal to the world's heads of state and government who gather at that time to reaffirm their commitment to the goal of ridding our world of unnecessary suffering.

An Office of Global Visioning (2009)[147]

I would like to propose the creation of an office of global visioning within the United Nations Secretariat in order to enable the international body to project and anticipate future trends and developments and focus its energies on these.

Commenting on a lecture I delivered on the theme of soft power at Harvard University in 1991, economist Dr. Kenneth E. Boulding[148] noted the power of legitimacy in realizing integration. Elsewhere he observed that while nation-states derive their legitimacy from past glories, the UN must seek legitimacy in the vision it offers for humanity's future.

Constrained in part by its nature as an intergovernmental body, the UN has tended to react only after problems have arisen. Former UN Under-Secretary-General Anwarul K. Chowdhury,[149] with whom I am currently engaged in a dialogue, has also expressed his concern that the UN lacks a section dedicated to anticipating the challenges that will confront humankind in the future.

I fully concur. It is essential that the UN be equipped with an organizational unit with think-tank functions capable of offering future-oriented vision and action strategies based on what the world will look like fifty or a hundred years from now. I would like to stress that ample attention should be paid to reflecting women's perspectives and the voices of young people in the operations of such a unit, and discussions should always have a focus on the empowerment of youth and children.

---

147 From 2009 Peace Proposal, "Toward Humanitarian Competition: A New Current in History."

148 Kenneth E. Boulding (1910–93), British-born American economist.

149 Anwarul K. Chowdhury (1943–), Bangladeshi diplomat, Under-Secretary-General and High Representative of the United Nations (2002–07).

Strengthening of the UN has been one of the consistent research themes of the Toda Institute for Global Peace and Policy Research since I established it in 1996, the year after the fiftieth anniversary of the founding of the UN. The Toda Institute will continue to develop research programs and activities that support the UN in this key function of identifying trends and developing a clear outlook for the human future.

Similarly, the Boston Research Center for the 21st Century[150] and the Institute of Oriental Philosophy will continue their efforts to pool the wisdom of humanity through active promotion of dialogue among religions and civilizations toward the resolution of issues that rank high on the UN's agenda.

Even when the challenges confronting us seem overwhelmingly difficult, the first step must be dialogue. Grounded in a faith in our shared humanity, frank discourse can transcend all differences of background, values and perspectives.

Dialogue has been at the very heart of the UN since its inception. According to Paul Kennedy,[151] the UN was from the start likened to a three-legged stool: the first leg represented measures to guarantee international security; the second leg improvement of economic conditions globally; and the third leg enhancement of understanding among the world's peoples. He stresses, "[H]owever strongly the first two legs were constructed, the system would fold—would collapse—if it did not produce ways of improving political and cultural understandings among peoples."[152]

Enhancing mutual understanding remains an urgent challenge today. The UN designated this year (2009) as the International Year of Reconciliation, and 2010 the International Year for the Rapprochement of Cultures. This attests to the degree to which the UN values tolerance and dialogue as indispensable to truth and justice.

Such efforts are needed now more than ever, given the number of critical problems the world is facing. In addition to the recent bloodshed in Gaza and other complex conflicts such as those in Sudan and the Democratic Republic of the Congo, globally the numbers of refugees and internally displaced persons (IDPs) continue to rise, and the threat of terror remains undiminished.

---

150 Subsequently renamed the Ikeda Center for Peace, Learning, and Dialogue.

151 Paul M. Kennedy (1945–), British historian and author.

152 Kennedy, Paul M. 2007. *The Parliament of Man: The Past, Present, and Future of the United Nations.* New York: Vintage Books, pp. 31–32.

While the UN must play a leading role in tackling these entrenched problems, cooperation among states and tenacious diplomatic efforts are also crucial.

At the most fundamental level, we must take initiatives to disrupt the cycle of violence and hatred and, in its place, build a robust and pervasive culture of peace. We must ensure that every individual can enjoy in full the right to live in peace and dignity. For only this will serve as a solid safeguard for the world of the twenty-first century.

Dialogue presents infinite possibilities; it is a challenge that can be taken up by anyone—any time—in order to realize the transformation from a culture of violence to a culture of peace.

It was based on this belief in the power of dialogue that, during the period 1974–75, as Cold War hostilities were intensifying, I made successive trips to China, the Soviet Union and the United States. As a concerned private citizen, I met with top-level leaders in each country in an effort to reduce and defuse tensions. Since that time, I have sought to counteract the forces of division by building bridges of friendship and trust around the world.

Dr. Arnold J. Toynbee[153] warmly encouraged me to pursue dialogue when I met with him in 1972 and 1973. Viewing human history in terms of "challenge and response" with a perspective spanning centuries or millennia, he focused on the possibilities of dialogue rooted in our shared humanity as the driving force for creating a new era.

Dr. Toynbee discussed the problem of human freedom in a lecture titled "Uniqueness and Recurrence in History" which he delivered in Japan in 1956. He noted that there appear to be laws governing the repetitive patterns in human history and extended this observation to the idea that civilizations have a life-cycle of approximately 800 years. However, he also emphatically asserted that certain human phenomena do not conform to such fixed patterns, concluding:

> Of all human phenomena, the one for which no set pattern in fact exists is the field of encounter and contact between one personality and another. It is from such encounter and contact that truly new creativity arises.[154]

---

153 Arnold J. Toynbee (1889–1975), British historian.

154 (trans. from) Toynbee, Arnold J. 1957. *Rekishi no kyokun* [The Lessons of History]. Tokyo: Iwanami Shoten, pp. 79–80.

If we allow ourselves to become confined within a certain ideology, ethnicity or religion, we will find ourselves at the mercy of the ebb and flow, stranded in the shallows of history, unable to make progress. In contrast, if we search beyond the arbitrary, surface labels and engage with each other as individuals in dialogue, generating spontaneous and intense interactions of heart and mind, we will be able to give rise to the "deeper, slower movements"[155] which Toynbee considered to ultimately shape human history.

With this conviction, I have actively pursued dialogue with leaders and thinkers in various fields. Refusing to be deterred by the barriers dividing people, I have traveled between sometimes antagonistic societies, seeking to open lines of dialogue and communication where none had existed. Out of the desire to share the lessons learned through these dialogues as widely as possible, many of them have been published in book form (fifty thus far, with another twenty in preparation).

The Soka Gakkai was born in 1930, in the midst of global crisis. The SGI was launched in 1975, also a time of crisis. Since then, we have consistently promoted initiatives to support the UN and have engaged in steadfast efforts, as contributing members of our respective societies, to build a culture of peace through grassroots dialogue. These efforts draw inspiration from Tsunesaburo Makiguchi's[156] vision of humanitarian competition and Josei Toda's[157] frequently voiced call to eliminate misery from the face of the planet.

Bound by a shared commitment to humanism and the greater good, our citizens' network has now expanded to 192 countries and territories around the world. The prospect Josei Toda shared with me in the course of our interactions—that the Soka Gakkai would develop into a magnificent vehicle for nurturing and empowering people—is steadily becoming a reality. Aiming toward the eightieth anniversary of the Soka Gakkai and the thirty-fifth anniversary of the SGI in 2010, we are determined to continue working in solidarity with people of goodwill everywhere toward the goal of a new era of peace and human flourishing.

---

155 Toynbee, Arnold J. 1948. *Civilization on Trial.* New York: Oxford University Press, p. 213.

156 Tsunesaburo Makiguchi (1871–1944), founding president of the Soka Kyoiku Gakkai (forerunner of the Soka Gakkai) (1930–44).

157 Josei Toda (1900–58), second president of the Soka Gakkai (1951–58).

A New Legal Framework for Conflict Resolution

International Law for Peace (1995)[158]

Although the end of the Cold War brought down the wall that divided East and West, humankind is still far from drafting a reliable blueprint for peace. Ethnic strife and regional conflicts are unceasing; the Earth's environment continues to deteriorate; refugees in great numbers flee suffering and hardship on several continents. The path before us is shadowed by these and other global problems.

The twenty-first century is just around the corner. Humankind has arrived at an important crossroads. We must decide whether we will merely stand still, resigned to our end-of-century dilemmas, or undauntedly address the issues we confront in order to open the door to the new century. Can the human race turn its fate around 180 degrees, putting behind us the century of war and brutality and raising the curtain confidently on a new century of hope and peace? We are being put to the test.

The year 1995 marks an important juncture because it is the fiftieth anniversary of the end of World War II. Various endeavors to look back critically at the past half century are being undertaken, and we should take this opportunity to refresh our memories of those years. We should remember how, amid the terrible ravages of war, we craved peace as a person craves water to quench desperate thirst.

We must sincerely aspire to attain the blessings of peace, to gain a fresh appreciation for the preciousness of life, and to bring about a lasting peace, fully aware that it is now possible. We need to be filled with burning idealism in the best sense of the term. Our crucial task is to reflect upon the past, define what has to be done in the present, and pool our wisdom to formulate a clear vision for the future. Indeed, this fiftieth anniversary offers the ideal chance to do so.

At the same time, we should remind ourselves that the horror of nuclear weapons was first known fifty years ago, in 1945. Over the past half century, rapid scientific and technological development has gone hand in hand with the threat of annihilation of the human race. Immense stockpiles of nuclear weapons hung like the Sword of Damocles over our heads while the East

---

158 From 1995 Peace Proposal, "Creating a Century without War through Human Solidarity."

and West persisted in their intense confrontation. The end of the Cold War seemed to ensure that the dark cloud of imminent nuclear holocaust might be cleared away, and for a while we were given the hope that a brighter future might actually break through. The intransigence of ethnic strife and the frequent outbreaks of regional warfare, however, have belied those hopes.

Humankind has faced the challenge of eradicating war since earliest times, and the sages of antiquity earnestly sought the solution to this difficult problem. The greater the destructive power of the weapons humans created, the exponentially more devastating the damage left in the wake of war. Thus peace is no longer an issue that can be ignored by any person of good conscience.

Coincidentally, this year also marks the 200th anniversary since the philosopher Immanuel Kant[159] wrote his famous *Perpetual Peace: A Philosophical Sketch*. Kant lived at a time of constant warfare, and in this essay he offers the world a prescription intended to end, once and for all, the wars that had been repeated over the centuries. He also warns that unless governments stop basing their policies on war, humankind is destined for eventual extinction. Unfortunately, Kant's warning has gone unheeded these past two centuries. We have yet to realize his ideal of permanent peace.

The present day can be considered a transitional period from the old era to a new one. Such periods have their characteristic confusion, but there is certainly no reason to be completely pessimistic. Rather, our future depends on whether or not we can muster enough hope to take advantage of opportunities as they present themselves.

It is now time for us to put the bitter lessons of this century to good use and ready ourselves for the leap forward into the third millennium. Now, more than ever, we require a vision backed by a solid philosophy, and we have to work to realize that vision through actions rooted in a strong and dynamic optimism. We may draw courage from the words of the French philosopher Alain,[160] who observed, "Pessimism comes from our passions; optimism from the will."[161] We must never abandon our confidence that, no matter what difficulties arise, humankind has the capacity to overcome them and forge

---

159 Immanuel Kant (1724–1804), German philosopher.
160 Alain, pseudonym of Émile-Auguste Chartier (1868–1951), French philosopher.
161 Alain. *Alain on Happiness*. 1989. Trans. by Robert D. and Jane E. Cottrell. Evanston, Illinois: Northwestern University Press, p. 250.

ahead. We also need clearly defined priorities that will help us prepare for the twenty-first century in the short time that remains. In this sense, the next five years are crucial.

In retrospect, we may wonder how well prepared people of the late nineteenth century were for the twentieth. One of the few notable movements at that time was the first Hague Conference of 1899, but arms reduction was never seriously discussed, and eventually the world fell into the cataclysm of World War I. In the decades that followed, the human race suffered through two indescribably tragic world wars.

At the end of the twentieth century, we have a different set of circumstances. First of all, we have the United Nations, which provides a forum for the global debates of the international community. We have also seen the development of several important movements since the 1990s began. With the UN playing a central role, conferences have already been held on such global concerns as the environment and development, human rights and population. This year (1995), the World Summit for Social Development and the Fourth World Conference on Women will be held. The major problems these conferences address will no doubt still be with us in the twenty-first century, but at least we are beginning the search for solutions. In these efforts, I sense a strong positive force of will that is different from the fin-de-siècle mentality of the nineteenth century. The question now is whether or not the conclusions reached will be put to productive use.

Now that the twenty-first century is upon us, we must ask ourselves what kind of century we ultimately want it to be. Above all, we want it to be a century without war, in which people no longer take up arms against each other. To that end, we must begin to build a global cooperative system for peace. The greatest tragedy of the twentieth century has been the loss of countless human lives in war. Including civilians, it is estimated that 22 million people died in World War I, and 60 million in World War II. One scholar called our era the "century of war dead."[162] This folly must not be repeated in the third millennium.

After witnessing the twentieth century's two world wars, Dutch historian Johan Huizinga[163] passed harsh judgment on war-hungry militarism, calling

---

162 (trans. from) Inoguchi, Kuniko. 1994. "Sekai no choryu to Kempo eno hyoka" [Evaluation of World Trends and the Constitution]. *Asahi Shimbun.* May 1.

163 Johan Huizinga (1872–1945), Dutch historian.

it the most harmful form of chronic cultural destruction. States that fall under the sway of militarism, he contended, not only degrade the citizens of the weaker countries they conquer, but force their own into slavery regardless of how rich their attainments or culture might be. Huizinga placed his hope in future generations, saying it is up to the next era to demonstrate whether or not the world is able to keep itself out of reach of what he described as the fearsome arms of the colossal monster.[164]

Huizinga himself died in February 1945, before World War II ended, and thus never saw the next era of which he spoke. In the half-century since, we have fortunately avoided another war engulfing the entire world, but count-less lives have still been claimed by the colossal monster.

In recent years, a growing number of military regimes have given way to democratic forms of government, a trend that brings new hope to many people. But the threat of war remains undiminished because there has been no dominant movement in the world toward disarmament and no progress yet made in ensuring the abolition of war as an institution. Now is the time for us to clearly define our vision and ask how we can create a cooperative system for peace that will enable us to realize a world without war.

To many, I may seem preoccupied with the problem of war. Why do I return to this topic every year, issuing one call for world peace after another? Why have I continued to demand that nations abolish their ministries of the army, navy and defense, and replace them with ministries of peace? Why have I insisted that a Universal Declaration Renouncing War be adopted as a UN resolution that will eventually develop into a "Global No-War Agreement" with binding power?

The answer to these questions is that war has held humankind in its irrev-ocable grip throughout history; it is the root source of all evil. War normalizes insanity—the kind that does not hesitate to destroy human beings as if they were mere insects, and tears all that is human and humane to shreds, pro-ducing an unending stream of refugees. It also cruelly damages our natural environment.

In 1994, the UN Children's Fund (UNICEF) published its annual report "The State of the World's Children," which tells us that over the past ten years, approximately two million children have been killed in wars. This far

---

164 See Huizinga, Johan. 1948. *Schriften zur Zeitkritik: Im Schatten von morgen* [Writings on Contemporary Criticism: In the Shadow of Tomorrow]. Zürich: Occident-Verlag.

exceeds the number of military personnel who lost their lives over the same period. Another four to five million children have been disabled, maimed, blinded or brain-damaged in war.[165] There is nothing more tragic than to see the children who represent the future of the world, injured or dying.

As a Buddhist, I deeply believe that no individual can experience true happiness or tranquillity until we turn humankind away from its obsession with war. We have already paid a heavy price for the lesson that nothing is more tragic and cruel than war. I believe we have as our first priority an obligation to our children to open a clear and reliable path to peace in the next century.

When contemplating internal factors that can help us abolish the misery and cruelty of war, we must not forget the doctrine so famously described in the Preamble of the UNESCO Constitution: "Since wars begin in the minds of men, it is in the minds of men that the defenses of peace must be constructed."[166]

Mahayana Buddhism, the basis of the practice of the members of the SGI, describes ten potential conditions of life inherent in a human being, known as the Ten Worlds. It is the four lowest worlds of Hell, Hunger, Animality and Anger, known together as the "four evil paths," that compel people to start wars. Controlled directly by instinct and desire, their thoughts and actions are inevitably foolish and barbaric. Therefore, from the Buddhist point of view, the issue of how to build the "defenses of peace" within the hearts of individuals takes precedence over any external institutional factors, and represents both the wellspring and the core of any attempt to build world peace.

***

To abolish armed conflict from the world, it is essential to find a way to protect disadvantaged minority populations within the borders of sovereign states, and to help guarantee their human rights and well-being. Economic development alone is not enough to satisfy the desires of these people, and it is important that their silent appeal be heard. One of the United Nations agencies is the Trusteeship Council, which is charged with improving the welfare and promoting the self-governance and independence of people

---

165 See Grant, James P. 1994. "The State of the World's Children." New York: Oxford University Press, p. 13.

166 UNESCO (United Nations Educational, Scientific and Cultural Organization). 1945. "Preamble" in "UNESCO Constitution."

living in UN trust territories (mostly colonies). Now that most colonies have achieved independence, the Trusteeship Council's mission is generally thought to be completed. I propose that this body be given a new mandate: to preserve cultural and ethnic diversity (particularly in war-ravaged areas like the former Yugoslavia) and to seek comprehensive solutions to the problems that accompany such diversity. I also suggest that the Trusteeship Council work in close conjunction with the UN High Commissioner for Refugees and the UN High Commissioner for Human Rights.

The first section of Article 1 of the UN Charter states that the purpose of the United Nations is to "maintain international peace and security" by resolving armed conflict "in conformity with the principles of justice and international law."[167] As is evident from the course of events since World War II, however, the Security Council, which is primarily responsible for fulfilling this mandate, has been unable to adequately do so.

In contemplating what international society will be like in the twenty-first century, I believe it is crucial to clarify and strengthen international law regarding peace. This could be accomplished through the further development and reinforcement of current international humanitarian law (the Hague and Geneva Conventions), and through the creation of a binding system that will encourage greater compliance.

For all its problems, the United Nations already exists, and nearly all the world's sovereign states belong to it. This is significant. Not even at the height of tensions during the Cold War did either the United States or the Soviet Union withdraw from membership. Now we must establish a closer relationship between this organization and international law, and promote the further codification of interaction among nations.

In December 1994, the UN General Assembly formally adopted a nuclear disarmament resolution proposed by Japan for the total abolition of nuclear weapons. The resolution notes that the potential for creating a world free from the threat of nuclear war has increased with the end of the Cold War, and calls on all nations that have not yet signed the Treaty on the Non-Proliferation of Nuclear Weapons (NPT) to do so as quickly as possible. It also urges nations that already possess nuclear weapons to work harder toward disarmament, with the ultimate goal of their complete abolishment. Finally, it asks all

---

167   UN (United Nations). 1945. "Charter of the United Nations."

nations to implement disarmament and nonproliferation agreements for weapons of mass destruction.[168]

Concerning whether or not the use or threatened use of nuclear weapons violates international law, the General Assembly also adopted a resolution requesting an advisory opinion from the International Court of Justice (ICJ). Of course, since General Assembly resolutions are nonbinding, some parties do not place importance upon them. I do not share this view, however. Nuclear weapons are capable of destroying all human and other life on Earth, so the question of how to deal with them is of universal concern to international society and calls for sound, humane, moral judgments. Whether or not a resolution is legally binding should not be of primary concern.

In strengthening international law regarding peace, it is best to appeal to people's consciences and gradually build up an atmosphere conducive to peace. Even though the resolutions adopted by the General Assembly lack binding power, we must still strive to create a world in which they are respected as expressions of the general will of humankind. This is because it is ultimately impossible to build up international law as a detailed body of penal provisions stipulated one law at a time.

Similarly, we must conclude that the current state of the United Nations—with the Security Council in a position of preeminence and the General Assembly playing a subordinate role—is undesirable. If we are to enhance the qualities of what should become a parliament of humanity, I believe we should do all we can to strengthen and further empower the General Assembly. With the end of the Cold War and progress of the peace process in the Middle East, world tensions are easing. Discussions conducted at the General Assembly are therefore moving away from confrontation and toward cooperation, with increasingly fruitful results. The time is ripe.

If we hope to maintain peace according to the principles of justice and international law, we must also strengthen the ICJ. In addition, we need a new international tribunal for trying war crimes. In this respect, the UN's adoption of a resolution to establish an international criminal court can be considered a step in the right direction. In light of the many ethnic conflicts that have erupted, there is an urgent need for such an institution. One of the most important issues in the twenty-first century will be the buttressing of

---

168 UNGA (United Nations General Assembly). 1995. "General and Complete Disarmament." A/RES/49/75. Resolution adopted by the General Assembly. January 9.

international legislative, executive and judiciary functions, with the United Nations as the pivotal point.

The International Criminal Court (1999)[169]

Transforming the culture of war requires severing the chain of vengeance. How can we accomplish this when, as is dramatized in the Aeschylus *Oresteia* trilogy, human fate appears to be an endless cycle of crime triggered by crime and violence triggered by violence?

In *Philosophy of Rights,* the German philosopher Georg Hegel[170] writes: "Thus revenge, as the positive action of a *particular* will, becomes *a new infringement*; because of this contradiction, it becomes part of an infinite progression and is inherited indefinitely from generation to generation."[171]

Hegel proceeds to show that a subsuming justice can halt the process. This must be a justice that, though capable of imposing sanction, is not vengeful.

In July 1998, at long last, there was an international agreement to create an International Criminal Court (ICC) establishing a venue for the kind of justice that can break the chain of revenge referred to above. First proposed more than half a century ago, the ICC is to be a standing court to try grievous assaults on international society such as genocide and war crimes.

Whereas the International Court of Justice (ICJ) adjudicates legal disputes between and among states, the ICC is to pursue individual criminal responsibility. International courts of the past—the Nuremberg Military Tribunal and the International Military Tribunal for the Far East following World War II, and international criminal tribunals established by the United Nations Security Council in connection with the former Yugoslavia and Rwanda—have been ad hoc and limited in jurisdiction to specific conflicts. In addition, they have often been criticized as examples of victors' justice.

Spurred by the intensifying violence of local conflicts, the desire for a permanently standing court to cope with a broader range of crimes and criminal procedures led to the agreement to create the ICC. Its provisions place within the court's competence: (1) genocide, (2) crimes against humanity, (3) war crimes, and (4) the crime of aggression. Even acts committed in the context

---

169 From 1999 Peace Proposal, "Toward a Culture of Peace: A Cosmic View."

170 Georg Wilhelm Friedrich Hegel (1770–1831), German philosopher.

171 Hegel, Georg W. F. 1991. *Elements of the Philosophy of Rights*. Trans. by H. B. Nisbet. New York: Cambridge University Press, p. 130.

of internal conflicts—previously considered outside the scope of international law—may be tried as war crimes. Maximum punishment stops short of the death penalty. This is especially noteworthy because, as is demonstrated in rising worldwide opposition to its use, the death penalty is unacceptable from a humanitarian and human rights perspective, or as a means of severing the chain of vengeance.

To be sure, there are still many details to be worked out regarding the ICC's jurisdiction, relations with the UN Security Council and enforcement powers. Nonetheless it has great significance as a key part of the systemic framework for overcoming the culture of war on the threshold of the twenty-first century.

Unfortunately, the use of nuclear and other weapons of mass destruction is outside the current competence of the court. I sincerely hope that this issue will be reexamined to improve the court's effectiveness.

Establishing Legal Systems for the Prevention of Terrorism (2002)[172]

Humanity last year (2001) was confronted with an extremely grave challenge to the effort to embark in an entirely new direction—the quest to part ways with the war and violence of the previous century. The September 11 terrorist attacks in the United States were a truly unprecedented act of mass murder, robbing thousands of innocent people of their lives. No cause or grievance can possibly justify such wanton destruction of human life.

It was particularly bitter that 2001, the first year of the new century, designated by the United Nations as the Year of Dialogue among Civilizations, should be marred by an incident diametrically opposed to the spirit of dialogue, of tolerance and coexistence. Further, despite the magnitude of the damage inflicted, no statement has ever been issued acknowledging guilt for the crime. The anonymous and cowardly nature of this act threatens to undermine humanity at its core. It is an assault and affront that tramples the world's aspirations to dialogue among civilizations.

***

---

172 From 2002 Peace Proposal, "The Humanism of the Middle Way: Dawn of a Global Civilization."

The noble intent behind the Year of Dialogue among Civilizations has been cruelly mocked by this heinous crime. To keep the attack from becoming the cause for a clash or even war between civilizations, we must never lose sight of the fact that it was, first and finally, a criminal act. I have consistently urged that the International Criminal Court (ICC), whose role and merits I deal with later in this proposal, be established and commence functioning at the earliest possible date. Terrorism is a crime that must be judged and punished before the law, and it is imperative that we take all measures to enhance the rule of law globally.

Such countermeasures alone are obviously not enough. Preventing and deterring future terrorist attacks requires strengthening international law and developing an effective international system of law enforcement.

***

I would like to emphasize that, as a prerequisite for the prevention of terrorism, we must make the principle of "punishment before the law" the firm and united stance of the international community. Similarly, it is vital that any response to terror be based on a universal set of principles and rules that impartially judge and punish any such act regardless of its nature or motivation.

With regard to the military actions led by the US and the UK, UN Secretary-General Kofi Annan[173] stated that this action should be viewed in light of the UN Security Council's reaffirmation of the right of individual and collective self-defense in accordance with the UN Charter.[174] Even acknowledging this view, we must be aware of the fact that military action leaves important problems unresolved, creating new ones that must be dealt with in the future.

I believe that it is crucial to aim for the creation of a transparent system that is universal in its application to suppress acts of terror, regardless of the political or ideological motives of the perpetrators. Even in the case of police action (entailing the minimum use of force necessary to restrain and

---

173 Kofi Annan (1938–), Ghanaian statesman, 7th Secretary-General of the United Nations (1997–2006).

174 See UN (United Nations). 2001. "'To Defeat Terrorism, We Need a Sustained Effort and Broad Strategy That Unite All Nations,' Says Secretary-General." SG/SM/7985 AFG/149. Press Release. October 8.

apprehend the criminals), locating such action within the context of a comprehensive system can prevent the situation from escalating.

It is therefore important to strengthen the structures and systems of international law, international law enforcement and the international judiciary. Together, these constitute the institutional basis for a comprehensive and coordinated response to terrorism.

The UN must play a central role in this effort. As Secretary-General Annan has stressed, the UN is uniquely positioned to help develop a broad and sustained strategy to eradicate terrorism.[175]

First, to strengthen international law, it is urgent that the comprehensive treaty for the prevention of international terrorism be completed and adopted. To date, twelve different international treaties and protocols against terrorism have been adopted, starting with the 1963 Tokyo Convention for the prevention of hijacking. Typically, these were drafted in response to specific crimes of terrorism, but over the years, terrorist organizations have developed increasingly broad international networks and adopted ever more sophisticated methods, so there is now a clear need for a convention that will support more comprehensive efforts to counter terrorism.

Each of the individual antiterrorism conventions is significant as a cornerstone of international cooperation to deter and prevent such grave criminal acts. Further efforts to ensure the widest possible ratification of these treaties are important, as has been stressed at various summit meetings to date. Complementing existing conventions, the comprehensive treaty for the prevention of terrorism would be a signal of international solidarity never to permit a repeat of the recent tragic events.

Second, regarding law enforcement, I would like to promote the idea of establishing a specialized standing organization within the UN to combat international crime as the core of an international law enforcement network. This new body would carefully coordinate its efforts with those of the International Criminal Police Organization (ICPO), or Interpol, and the domestic law enforcement agencies of each country.

Further, consideration should be given to the future possibility of establishing a constabulary force under direct UN control to respond in cases when national law enforcement agencies are inadequate to the task of identifying or

---

175 See UN (United Nations). 2001. "Secretary-General, Addressing Assembly on Terrorism, Calls for 'Immediate, Far-reaching Changes' in UN Response to Terror." SG/SM/7977 GA/9920. Press Release. October 1.

arresting members of criminal terrorist organizations. Police action through international cooperation would thus become established as an option to be exercised in lieu of either the use of force authorized by the Security Council (under Chapter VII of the UN Charter) or actions taken as an exercise of the right of individual or collective self-defense. As such, this would contribute to a more robust and flexible system to prevent and respond to terrorism.

Third, to strengthen the international judiciary, it is vital that the International Criminal Court (ICC) be established with all possible haste. The Rome Statute to establish a permanent international court for the purpose of trying individuals who have committed genocide, crimes against humanity, war crimes, etc., was adopted in 1998. But it has yet to be ratified by the necessary sixty signatory states and has therefore not become binding. As a result, the court has yet to be established and begin functioning.

I have repeatedly called for the early establishment of the ICC as a means to begin supplanting the rule of force with the rule of law. This would help break the interlocking chain reactions of hatred and retribution that have brought such suffering to humankind. As such, it has the potential to effect a qualitative transformation in the way we human beings have conducted our collective affairs to date. At present, such movements as the NGO Coalition for an ICC (CICC) are working to encourage ratification, an effort to which the SGI will offer active support.

In the meantime, we should consider an ad hoc tribunal to try terrorist crimes, similar to those created by the UN Security Council for crimes of genocide and other grave offenses committed in Rwanda and the former Yugoslavia. It is crucial that we make last year's terror attacks the occasion for establishing the principle that the crime of terrorism be brought to justice before an international judiciary.

Looking now at longer-term measures to prevent the recurrence of terrorism, I would like to discuss the role that Japan can play in the reconstruction of Afghanistan. In December of 2001, an interim government was established in Afghanistan. However, as a result of twenty-three years of war, some four million people have been forced to flee their homes, and most of the infrastructure that supported people's lives has been destroyed.[176] The international community is called on to provide timely humanitarian assistance and

---

176 See United Nations High Commissioner for Refugees. 2001. "Refugees by Numbers 2001." July 1.

sustained support for the reconstruction effort. I believe that this is an area in which Japan should play an active and contributory role.

Historically, Japan is not burdened by a military or diplomatic legacy of colonization or invasion in the region. It has developed relations of trust with many of Afghanistan's Central Asian neighbors, under the banner of its "Eurasian Diplomacy" and "Silk Road Diplomacy."

Concretely, prior to the terrorist attacks, Japan brought representatives of both the Taliban and the Northern Coalition to Tokyo for talks. Japan has also played a constructive role in providing humanitarian assistance to the people of Afghanistan. Most recently (January 21–22, 2002), Japan hosted the Ministerial Level Conference on Reconstruction Assistance to Afghanistan and made strong efforts to support the development of a reconstruction plan. In these and other ways, Japan has energetically engaged with the issue. While I certainly applaud such efforts, at the same time I hope they will be ongoing, persistent and guided by a long-term vision.

One of the tragic hallmarks of the twentieth century was the large-scale uprooting of people from their homes, their uncertain flight as refugees. It is now crucial to develop comprehensive strategies to prevent and resolve the regional and ethnic conflicts that have displaced people. We must also support post-conflict reconstruction to enable people to return to their homes and live normal lives.

Many of the conflicts of recent years have resulted in what are called complex emergencies, marked by the simultaneous occurrence of armed conflict, refugee movements, famine and destruction of the natural environment.

Responding to complex emergencies requires the careful coordination of multifaceted, multilevel actions. In concrete terms, Japan should become actively engaged in the UN's peacebuilding initiatives that support the efforts of societies to recover from destruction and build the foundations for a stable peace. Among the many aspects of peacebuilding are: promoting reconciliation among ethnic groups; encouraging respect for human rights; disarming and facilitating the social reintegration of the members of armed groups; establishing order under the rule of law; supporting the development of democratic institutions; and rebuilding basic infrastructure. The UN has opened, on a pilot basis, peacebuilding offices in the Central African Republic and elsewhere.

Japan has to date engaged in such efforts as the Azra and Tizin project to support the return and resettlement of Afghan refugees. Japan should strengthen its institutional capacity to cooperate with different UN agencies in support of such projects. It should work toward establishing a system that trains people with specialized skills who can be dispatched at any time as required. Demining is an especially urgent focus at present, and this is one area in which Japan can make a substantial contribution, providing technical cooperation and assistance.

Further, as a first step toward demonstrating that we have truly learned the bitter lesson of the world's abandonment of Afghanistan, I would like to propose that an Afghanistan peace center be established in Japan. This center would be engaged in providing up-to-date information to the world community regarding the progress of efforts toward peace and reconstruction. At the same time, it would seek to promote widespread understanding and appreciation of Afghanistan's unique cultural heritage.

Counter-Terrorism Strategies (2004)[177]

In the opening years of the twenty-first century, international society has been convulsed by the emergence of new threats and by divisive debate over how best to respond to them. Since the September 11, 2001, terror attacks in the United States, there has been an ongoing incidence of indiscriminate violence, which has devastated the lives of large numbers of ordinary citizens around the world. At the same time, there is growing anxiety over the proliferation of nuclear, chemical and other weapons of mass destruction.

The issue of inspections to determine the extent, if any, of Iraq's possession of such weapons was a major focus of global concern and controversy last year. In March, with world opinion divided over the rights and wrongs of the use of force against Iraq, whose government had for twelve years failed to implement in good faith the numerous resolutions of the United Nations Security Council, the United States and the United Kingdom made the decision to launch a military invasion. The overwhelming superiority of the coalition forces brought about the collapse of the Hussein regime after only twenty-one days of formal engagement. Since then, however, the United States and allied forces occupying and administering Iraq have come under constant attack, as have the offices of the United Nations. This has raised doubts about the prospects for rebuilding Iraq and bringing stability to the Middle East.

---

177 From 2004 Peace Proposal, "Inner Transformation: Creating a Global Groundswell for Peace."

A similar state of disorder is evident in Afghanistan, which was the scene of military action designed to extirpate the Al Qaeda terror organization. While a constitution was finally adopted in January of this year, attacks from what are thought to be the remnants of the Taliban regime persist, and there is danger that the security situation will further deteriorate.

The international community cannot and must not turn a blind eye to these new threats. Although it must demonstrate a firm resolve, recent events make it evident that an exclusive reliance on military force will not bring about a fundamental solution.

***

The Counter-Terrorism Committee (CTC) was brought into being within the United Nations on the basis of Security Council Resolution 1373,[178] adopted in September 2001, and the Counter-Terrorism Action Group was created for the purpose of aiding the CTC's activities during the G8 Summit held in Evian, France, in June 2003.

The prevention of terrorism requires improving the function and efficacy of the judicial systems of each country. Committed international cooperation is essential in supporting national efforts, and the bodies described above can play a key role. It is crucially important to create, through an international network of cooperation and with an emphasis on preventive measures, the conditions in which terrorism is forestalled and eliminated.

The International Criminal Court (ICC) needs to be central to this process. Officially launched by the swearing-in of its judges in March 2003, the ICC is the first permanent international criminal court established to try individuals for war crimes, genocide or crimes against humanity.

It is important to increase the number of states participating in the ICC and encourage its effective functioning. The ICC can help sever the cycles of hatred and violence that drive conflict and terror. It can contribute to establishing a culture of resolving conflicts through recourse to law rather than resort to force. Universality and credibility are crucial to the effectiveness of the court, and in this sense also the broadest possible participation is called for. In our capacity as an NGO, the SGI will strive to develop broad-based global support for the ICC through various activities to raise public awareness of its existence and the potential it offers.

---

178 UN (United Nations). 2001. "Resolution 1373 (2001)." S/RES/1373 (2001). Resolution adopted by the Security Council. September 28.

In the wake of the shocking August 2003 terrorist attack on the UN head-quarters in Baghdad, the Security Council adopted a resolution expressing strong condemnation of terror against UN personnel and humanitarian relief workers in zones of conflict, identifying these acts as war crimes.[179] The principle should be established for trying heinous crimes of terrorism in an international judicial venue such as the ICC. We should not underestimate the deterrent potential of such measures.

Also in this connection it is necessary to reinforce international humanitarian law, which was developed to define the legally acceptable behavior of combatants in wartime. This is needed to respond to new types of conflict, such as civil wars that spill over international borders, and to ensure that counter-terrorism measures are conducted in accord with the spirit of humanitarian law.

Peacebuilding

A UN Conflict Prevention Center (1989)[180]

When we cast our gaze at international affairs, which seem to be changing as rapidly as the waves of the ocean, we begin to see a steady current beneath the surface, heralding the dawn of a new era of dialogue.

The Joint Statement issued at the US–Soviet summit held in Moscow last year states as follows:

> The two leaders are convinced that the expanding political dialogue they have established represents an increasingly effective means of resolving issues of mutual interest and concern. They do not mini-mize the real differences of history, tradition and ideology which will continue to characterize the US–Soviet relationship. But they believe that the dialogue will endure, because it is based on realism and focused on the achievement of concrete results. It can serve as a constructive basis for addressing not only the problems of the present, but of tomorrow and the next century.[181]

---

179 UN (United Nations). 2003. "Resolution 1502 (2003)." S/RES/1502 (2003). Resolution adopted by the Security Council. August 26.

180 From 1989 Peace Proposal, "Toward a New Globalism."

181 Gorbachev, Mikhail and Ronald Reagan. 1988. "Joint Statement Following the Soviet–United States Summit Meeting in Moscow, June 1, 1988."

The key to resolving issues and building a constructive foundation of peace for the twenty-first century lies in dialogue—open conversations between top leaders that transcend differences in ideology and social system and leave preconceptions behind. This is something I have advocated for years.

US–Soviet summit talks between President George Bush[182] and General Secretary Mikhail Gorbachev[183] are expected to continue this year. Also, a Sino–Soviet summit is scheduled for May, the first such meeting China and the Soviet Union will have had in thirty years, drawing the attention of the entire world. As I have long emphasized the importance of meetings among the world's top leaders, I earnestly hope that this series of summit meetings will further accelerate the global trend toward the easing of tensions.

I emphasize the importance of dialogue because I believe the ability to use words and conduct dialogue is proof of one's humanity. In other words, only when we are immersed in an ocean of language do we become truly human. In *Phaedo,* Plato[184] associates hatred of language (*misologos*) with hatred of man (*misanthropos*).[185]

To give up on dialogue and words will lead to giving up on being human. The moment we abandon our humanity, we will cease to be the protagonist of history, only to have that position taken over by something base, rooted in animality. Indeed, throughout history, we have witnessed countless tragedies in which animality—under the disguise of ideology, a cause or dogma— tramples upon people with brute force and violence that utterly reject the possibility of dialogue.

Writing about the American Revolution, Hannah Arendt[186] stated, "[t]he end of rebellion is liberation, while the end of revolution is the foundation of freedom."[187] E. H. Carr[188] evaluated the Russian Revolution as "the first great

---

182 George H. W. Bush (1924–), 41st President of the United States (1989–93).

183 Mikhail Gorbachev (1931–), General Secretary of the Communist Party of the Soviet Union (1985–91), President of the Soviet Union (1990–91), recipient of the Nobel Prize for Peace in 1990.

184 Plato (*c.* 428–347 BCE), Greek philosopher. Student of Socrates and teacher of Aristotle.

185 See Plato. 1973. "Phaedo" in *The Portable Plato.* Trans. by Benjamin Jowett. Ed. by Scott Buchanan. New York: Viking Press, p. 238.

186 Hannah Arendt (1906–75), German-born American political scientist and philosopher.

187 Arendt, Hannah. 2006. *On Revolution.* London: Penguin Books, p. 133.

188 Edward Hallett Carr (1892–1982), British historian.

revolution in history to be deliberately planned and made."[189] Underlying these appraisals is a focus on humanity's ability to achieve domination, based on words and dialogue, over the impulse to give in to animality. To what extent the two revolutions realized their intended objectives is, of course, another story.

In this sense, an era of dialogue is synonymous with an era of humanity. The significance of revitalizing dialogue among world leaders, as well as on a grassroots level, cannot be emphasized too much.

***

The US and Soviet leaders exchanged New Year's messages this year. Mr. Gorbachev said: "[A]ll of us, however different, are really one family. I am sure we will find enough wisdom and goodwill to establish together a true period of peace for all humankind."[190] President Ronald Reagan[191] applauded the improvement in US–Soviet relations, saying that through their talks the two nations have found common ground.

Such a global way of thinking may be described as common sense from the standpoint of we, the people. But this has not been the case in the realm of international politics. It is therefore extremely significant that statements of this kind were made by political leaders, particularly the leaders of the two superpowers confronting each other with massive nuclear arsenals at hand. Self-identification as members of the global community indicates a new direction transcending the Cold War doctrine.

Today, no one would deny the enormous waves of change affecting the ideological confrontation between the United States and the Soviet Union, the superpowers that have ruled the postwar world. With the network of Pax Russo–Americana covering every corner of the world, the change will have an extremely profound impact not only on US–Soviet relations but also on the international community at large.

---

189 Carr, E. H. 1969. *1917: Before and After.* London: Macmillan, pp. 8–9.

190 Gorbachev, Mikhail and Ronald Reagan. 1989. "New Year's Messages of President Reagan and President Mikhail Gorbachev of the Soviet Union. January 1, 1989."

191 Ronald Reagan (1911–2004), 40th President of the United States (1981–89).

Almost thirty years have passed since Daniel Bell[192] first coined the phrase, "the end of ideology."[193] I believe that we are witnessing for the first time in the postwar years the potential for the creation of a world community regardless of differences of ideology or social system. Through their summit meetings, both the US and Soviet leaders have confirmed that they share common interests that are more important than ideology: the conclusion that they have no choice but to ensure mutual survival and work together to find a peaceful path to prosperity.

It is said that President Franklin D. Roosevelt[194] upheld the words of Ralph Waldo Emerson[195] as his guiding principle when he attended the Yalta Conference: "The only way to have a friend is to be one."[196] In light of the ensuing course of history, this may have only been subject to bitter cynicism.

Would it be too optimistic, or even sentimental to say that President Roosevelt's idealism is finally becoming a reality after more than four decades of the Yalta System, a time either short or long depending on who views it? In any event, I believe that the world of politics is bound to degenerate into a world ruled by what Plato described as "a mighty strong beast"[197] if we lack the rich poetic heart of Emerson.

At the same time, we must maintain a practical perception, as the Reagan–Gorbachev Joint Statement points out, that dialogue must be based on realism. If we look at the current cooperative mood between the United States and the Soviet Union and simply expect the world situation to improve, we will lose sight of reality. The new current of history has only begun, and the world is still facing a number of grave challenges.

It is essential for individuals to strive to take self-motivated action to make this current more powerful and broader. In other words, what is truly needed is active involvement and sustained effort, not the cold critique of a detached observer.

---

192 Daniel Bell (1919–2011), American sociologist.

193 Bell, Daniel. 1960. *The End of Ideology: On the Exhaustion of Political Ideas in the Fifties.* New York: Free Press, p. xii.

194 Franklin D. Roosevelt (1882–1945), 32nd President of the United States (1933–45).

195 Ralph Waldo Emerson (1803–82), American author.

196 (qtd. in) Roosevelt, Franklin D. 1945. "Fourth Inaugural Address." January 20.

197 Plato. 1892. *Dialogues, vol. 3 – Republic, Timaeus, Critias.* Trans. by B. Jowett. Oxford: Oxford University Press, p. 493.

In this connection, it is noteworthy that active efforts were made over the past year toward the peaceful resolution of various regional conflicts, reflecting the US–Soviet détente. These include the withdrawal of Soviet troops from Afghanistan, the cease-fire in the Iran–Iraq War and progress toward the settlement of the Western Sahara War and the Angolan Civil War. In the Middle East, the Palestine Liberation Organization (PLO) recognized Israel's right to existence and held talks with the United States, raising new hopes for the resolution of the conflicts in the region.

The United Nations played a crucial role last year in cultivating this global trend toward peace. As is well known, mediation efforts led by the UN and Secretary-General Javier Pérez de Cuéllar[198] had concrete effects particularly in achieving peace in Afghanistan and the cease-fire in the Iran–Iraq War.

It is also highly significant that the United Nations Peacekeeping Forces were awarded the Nobel Prize for Peace last year (1988), heightening the world's recognition of the UN's peacekeeping activities.

Needless to say, the UN was established to prevent war and ensure that humanity would never again suffer its ravages. Its underlying principle was to build a lasting, peaceful order upon the foundation of the voluntary cooperation of sovereign states. The vision of collective security as laid out in the Charter of the United Nations, however, remained unfulfilled in the postwar years in the face of the severe East–West confrontation. The ensuing history of the UN has been marked by struggle, frustration and trial and error caused by its inability to function effectively as a peacekeeper. Thus, many of the international disputes submitted to the Security Council or the General Assembly for arbitration have not been successfully resolved.

On the other hand, the UN has accomplished much, and its effectiveness has been recognized in such areas as economic development, the protection of human rights and humanitarian relief programs. Looking back over some forty years of its history, one would inevitably come to the realization that its effectiveness in peace, development or other issues only reflected the limited capacities to solve problems of the sovereign states that compose it. Indeed, although the UN was originally created as a medium to realize peace and the well-being of humanity, the truth is that the member states have not been able to fully bring out its potential.

---

198 Javier Pérez de Cuéllar (1920–), Peruvian diplomat, 5th UN Secretary-General (1982–91), Prime Minister of Peru (2000–01).

Last year, the role of the UN in solving regional conflicts began to draw renewed attention. Its capacity for diplomatic mediation and the potential of the UN Peacekeeping Forces were reconfirmed in that process. The world finally has a renewed awareness of the UN as an indispensable organization for maintaining global peace. United Nations experts predict that the pursuit and exploration of peace and security through the international body will be institutionalized and strengthened on a global scale from this year.

In his address last December to the United Nations General Assembly, General Secretary Gorbachev expressed his high expectations regarding the UN's role:

> We feel that States must to some extent review their attitude to the United Nations—this unique instrument without which world politics would be inconceivable today. The recent reinvigoration of its peacemaking role has again demonstrated the ability of the United Nations to assist its members in coping with the daunting challenges of our time. . . . It is the only Organization capable of merging into a single current their bilateral, regional and global efforts.[199]

Likewise, at the end of last year (1988), Chinese Foreign Minister Qian Qichen[200] stressed as one of China's diplomatic goals the establishment of a new order in international politics and the world economy centered on the United Nations.

I have consistently urged the strengthening of the authority of the UN, aiming for a new system of global integration centered upon it. Although we cannot afford to be entirely optimistic, the prospects for the twenty-first century would be bright if the UN were designated as the central organization responsible for maintaining world peace, and the global structure of military confrontation were replaced by a peaceful mechanism for the prevention of war.

In an increasingly multipolarized world, I think that the most practical approach is to focus on the UN as a means to build a new economic and political order. The original purpose of the UN was not to establish a world

---

199 Gorbachev, Mikhail. 2006. "From the Address to the 43rd Session of the United Nations General Assembly," in *The Road We Travelled, The Challenges We Face*. Moscow: Gorbachev Foundation, p. 35.

200 Qian Qichen (1928–), Chinese diplomat, Minister of Foreign Affairs (1988–98), Vice Premier (1993–2003).

order dominated by a few great powers: its founding spirit aimed to create an organization in which all nations—large and small—would work together to build a peaceful world.

It is widely known that prior to the inception of the United Nations, the United States, the United Kingdom and the Soviet Union had intertwined agendas concerning the nature of a postwar international organization for peace. Sir Winston Churchill[201] was firmly committed to a balance of power led by the great powers. Joseph Stalin[202] is also said to have asserted that leadership be taken by the great powers of the United States, the United Kingdom and the Soviet Union.

US Secretary of State Cordell Hull[203] played a crucial role in reversing their agendas. He believed, based on universalism, that all states should be represented regardless of size in a postwar organization for peace.

The Moscow Declaration issued at the conclusion of the October 1943 meeting of the foreign ministers of the United States, the United Kingdom and the Soviet Union, which Hull attended, called for the creation of a general international organization, based on the principle of the sovereign equality of all peace-loving states.[204] This was the first time the great powers formally acknowledged that this postwar international organization would be open to all states, irrespective of size and strength.

Hull's universalism was underpinned by globalism, the intention to forestall the danger of the world breaking up into antagonistic blocs under regionalism. It is said that Hull's passionate commitment to these ideals influenced President Roosevelt to shift from his position in favor of a world centered on the great powers and regionalism, ultimately leading to the inception of the United Nations with its basis in universalism.

Despite the complex web of agendas put forward by the great powers, the UN was made possible by the strong determination to never repeat the tragedy of war and the earnest desire to create an international organization to secure lasting peace.

---

201 Winston Churchill (1874–1965), British Prime Minister (1940–45, 1951–55).
202 Joseph Stalin (1879–1953), Premier of the Soviet Union (1941–53).
203 Cordell Hull (1871–1955), US Secretary of State (1933–44), recipient of the Nobel Prize for Peace in 1945.
204 Molotov, Vyacheslav, Anthony Eden, Cordell Hull and Foo Ping-sheung. 1943. "Declaration of the Four Nations on General Security (Moscow Declaration)." Signed by the governments of the Soviet Union, the United Kingdom, the United States of America, and China. October 30.

Today, as the Cold War structure begins to fall apart in the face of the new currents of history, it is both inevitable and profoundly significant that we return to the founding spirit of the UN and seek ways to build a global order for peace. We could remind ourselves that global multilateral diplomacy centered on the UN is essential in enhancing bilateral diplomacy and shaping an international order for peace. We must bring together wisdom from around the world to explore ways to further strengthen this original function of the United Nations.

In my annual peace proposal six years ago (1983), I called for the establishment of a nuclear war prevention center that would mediate between the United States and the Soviet Union. The two countries have since agreed to create the Nuclear Risk Reduction Center to prevent the accidental occurrence of nuclear war. This is a profoundly significant development, and I wish to express my full support.

At this time of heightened value placed on the UN, I urge that its original function to prevent conflicts be strengthened in some way. The Office for Research and the Collection of Information was launched in March 1987 as part of the Offices of the Secretary-General. The Office collects and analyzes information on a global scale to detect signs of possible conflict, to enable the Secretary-General to act proactively. I suggest that this function be further expanded and strengthened in the form of a more general UN conflict prevention center.

In response to the pressing needs of our era, various programs designed to promote disarmament are being implemented in different parts of the world. The UN has already established Regional Centres for Peace and Disarmament in Nepal, Togo and Peru to promote peace and disarmament in their respective regions. A conflict prevention center could work in close coordination with these initiatives.

A UN High Commissioner for Indigenous People and National Minorities (1993)[205]

The exhilarating winds of liberation and change experienced only a few years ago, with perestroika and the democratization of Eastern Europe, have dissipated. The end of the century approaches, and a sense of impending gloom

---

205 From 1993 Peace Proposal, "Toward a More Humane World in the Coming Century."

seems to grow more threatening. When the upheaval was at its height, I observed that the most important task confronting us was to find a way to channel the energy released by the new liberating forces in the world into a constructive direction. Unfortunately, this task is proving extremely difficult.

The long-standing mistrust and enmity engendered by ideological confrontation that gripped the world in the decades following World War II have largely dissolved, and we have arrived in the post-Cold War era. But the prospects for the creation of a new world order still look very dim. A number of regions torn by deep-rooted ethnic or religious strife present volatile situations which, if appropriate measures for their resolution are not taken, could lead to truly catastrophic consequences.

Ethnic conflicts in the former Soviet Union and Yugoslavia in particular seem only to grow more intense, with no signs of resolution. This is exactly why it is now said that conventional world maps are no longer sufficient to analyze today's international affairs and that we need a second map that shows the ethnic constituents of countries and regions. In the West also, strained ethnic and racial relations have become more pronounced, as evidenced by the 1992 Los Angeles riots and the rise of neo-Nazism in European countries. It will be hard for Japan to remain unaffected by these tensions.

**

A self-righteous and close-minded attitude, together with a resolutely inflexible response, will only result in the situation worsening. It makes dialogue impossible, and the inevitable consequence is an utter rejection of the possibility of dialogue and appeal to violence. History is filled with lessons of this kind.

The main reason ethnic problems degenerate into the kind of atrocity symbolized by "ethnic cleansing" is to be found in closed thinking and narrow-mindedness. Economic hardship may have acted as a trigger, but it does not provide explanation as to why the situation has to escalate into killing. I think that the true cause lies in a deeper pathology of close-mindedness that must be considered in terms of the history of civilization.

It is my belief that the essence of goodness is to be found in unity, and the essence of evil in division. The true nature of evil seeks to cause division in everything. It seeks to cause fissures in the human heart, severing the bonds among family members, allies, friends and acquaintances, and engendering enmity between countries as well as ethnic groups. It will further destroy the human sense of unity with nature and the universe. Where divisiveness reigns, human beings become isolated, only to bring misery and sorrow upon themselves.

**

It was not long after World War II (in 1952) that the second president of the Soka Gakkai, Josei Toda,[206] advocated the idea of "global nationalism" (Jp. *chikyu minzokushugi*).[207] With the intensifying tensions of the Cold War, few paid any attention to his vision, and it was dismissed as unrealistic or a fantasy at best at the time. But today, the term "transnational" (transcending ethnic and national boundaries)—the same concept in a contemporary expression— is drawing increasing attention as a key to comprehending and predicting the future direction of international politics.

**

Last year (1992) Guatemalan human rights activist Rigoberta Menchú Tum[208] was awarded the Nobel Peace Prize for her efforts championing the cause of the indigenous Mayan people. In Guatemala, where indigenous people constitute approximately 40 percent of the population, they remain confined to the lower strata of the socio-economic order. The prize was a recognition of the leadership Menchú Tum took in urging respect for the linguistic and cultural autonomy of the indigenous people.

This year is a momentous one for human rights; it has been designated the International Year of the World's Indigenous People, and the World Conference on Human Rights is to be held in Vienna this June. The issues involved here are compelling enough, I believe, to justify the establishment of a UN High Commissioner for Indigenous Peoples and National Minorities. Already last year (1992), the Conference on Security and Co-operation in Europe (CSCE)[209] moved in that direction by establishing its own High Commissioner on National Minorities. This should be expanded into a global scale as part of the UN system.

---

206 Josei Toda (1900–58), second president of the Soka Gakkai (1951–58).

207 Toda, Josei. 1981–90. *Toda Josei zenshu* [The Complete Works of Josei Toda]. 9 vols. Tokyo: Seikyo Shimbunsha. Vol. 3, p. 460.

208 Rigoberta Menchú Tum (1959–), Guatemalan activist, recipient of the Nobel Prize for Peace in 1992.

209 The forerunner of the Organization for Security and Co-operation in Europe (OSCE).

The office of a new High Commissioner, working in conjunction with the UN High Commissioner for Refugees, could become a powerful force protecting the rights of indigenous peoples and minorities throughout the world. It would be a groundbreaking step forward in efforts to bring the concerns of ordinary citizens to the forefront of the UN's activities.

A Conflict Prevention Committee (2000)[210]

It is my belief that peace and security must be considered, as United Nations Secretary-General Kofi Annan[211] urged in his annual report last year, from a standpoint of the transition from a "culture of reaction" to a "culture of prevention."[212] A culture of prevention is an approach that accords utmost importance to preventing problems before they happen and thereby minimizing consequent damage, rather than reacting to them after they have taken place.

The United Nations Office for the Coordination of Humanitarian Affairs (OCHA) is engaged in advocating, coordinating and promoting humanitarian assistance in crises and emergencies such as famine caused or complicated by internal war or international conflict, as well as natural disasters such as earthquakes and floods. OCHA is acting in close cooperation with other international agencies and NGOs in numerous countries and regions including, so far, the Democratic Republic of the Congo and Rwanda, the site of intense conflict, and disaster-stricken Bangladesh and the Democratic People's Republic of Korea.

Nevertheless, the reaction to an already present and severe emergency is inevitably limited in terms of the area that can be covered and the range of available measures. Such interventions must be highly focused and are extremely expensive in terms of time and effort. The UN has played a primary role in coordinating humanitarian assistance, but it must become more involved in preventing conditions that lead to emergencies.

---

210 From 2000 Peace Proposal, "Peace through Dialogue: A Time to Talk."

211 Kofi Annan (1938–), Ghanaian statesman, 7th Secretary-General of the United Nations (1997–2006).

212 UNGA (United Nations General Assembly). 1999. "Report of the Secretary-General on the Work of the Organization." A/54/1. Official Records Fifty-fourth Session Supplement No. 1. August 31.

It is therefore essential to reexamine the role that the UN can and should play in the prevention of conflict. The settlement of disputes is one of the UN's central functions as specifically provided for in the Charter, but it is becoming increasingly difficult to respond to the growing number of internal conflicts in the post-Cold War era.

In fact, during the Kosovo crisis, the UN's inability to prevent the situation from worsening was followed by an aerial bombardment by NATO, waged in the name of humanitarian intervention and without the endorsement of a Security Council resolution.

After this, the principles to govern a cease-fire were discussed at the G8 Cologne Summit. The summit welcomed the deployment in Kosovo of international civil and security presences in accordance with the UN Security Council resolution[213] of June 10, 1999. Although the Security Council's adoption of this resolution enabled the UN to coordinate the resolution of the conflict in its final stages, the issues surrounding military action undertaken without the sanction of the Security Council and the criteria for humanitarian intervention remain unresolved.

Against this backdrop, the Cologne Communiqué stressed the need to "recognize the important role the United Nations plays in crisis prevention and [to] seek to strengthen its capacity in this area."[214] We must remember the fact that under the Charter of the United Nations military action can only be used as a last resort, and this makes it all the more critical that the UN build a preventive system based on what is known as "soft power."

That leads me to join my voice in support of proposals to establish a conflict prevention committee as a subsidiary organ of the General Assembly with a mandate to continuously monitor regions threatened with conflict or war, provide preventive recommendations and, further, to afford protection to noncombatants.

To prevent a situation from worsening, the function of early warning is crucial, for it is impossible to take effective measures without a system capable of discerning potential triggers for conflict and indications of escalating confrontation. It will also be essential to create a system for sharing with the public the information and analysis accumulated through these ongoing monitoring activities. The sharing of information is a prerequisite for encouraging more

---

213 UN (United Nations). 1999. "Resolution 1244 (1999)." S/RES/1244 (1999). Resolution adopted by Security Council. June 10.
214 G8 Information Centre. 1999. "G8 Communiqué Köln 1999 Final." June 20.

states—including those that are not members of the Security Council—and NGOs to become concerned and participate in generating a solution, and to offer ideas for promoting peace.

Another role for such a conflict prevention committee to play would be to take exhaustive measures to protect noncombatants in order to minimize suffering. Under the current framework of international law, human rights are secured by international human rights law in peacetime and by international humanitarian law in times of armed conflict, with both legal regimes mutually complementing each other.

But conflicts of recent years have been characterized by the targeting of civilians, as seen in genocide and "ethnic cleansing." Acts which violate humanitarian law have become the objective of war rather than the outcome.

During a period of protracted social disorder as is found with an internal conflict, it is difficult to accurately designate when a state of war has emerged. This tends to engender a vacuum in which both human rights law and humanitarian law are disregarded. As a result, many citizens fall victim to open violation of the human rights that should be protected at all times.

In order to stop conflict areas from being reduced to anarchy where basic human rights are violated with impunity, it is essential to maintain surveillance to ensure a prompt transition from protection by human rights law to protection by humanitarian law, and to call for steps to guard noncombatants against attack. To achieve this, a conflict prevention committee—as a neutral observer body—could be responsible for officially determining whether or not the area in question has entered a state of war triggering the application of humanitarian law, and thus seek to ensure that human rights are safeguarded at all times.

This committee should be mandated to dispatch fact-finding missions to determine the realities of a conflict, to receive and consider appeals from individuals affected by conflicts, and to hold public hearings to air the grievances of all parties. I find public hearings to be particularly critical. Once an armed conflict has escalated, it is not easy for the parties concerned to sit down at the same table, even if areas for discussion still exist. It would be very meaningful for the UN to provide a forum for the mutual exchange of views before the situation deteriorates that far. If they have voiced their opinions and assertions to the international community in this way, the concerned parties' subsequent actions might be more restrained.

The Toda Institute for Global Peace and Policy Research is considering holding an international conference, in cooperation with other NGOs, to discuss basic outlines of such systems as a conflict prevention committee. If such a conference were held in Africa or other parts of the world which have been plagued by conflict, it would be able to incorporate into its discussions the voices of people experiencing actual conflict, thus beginning to fulfill the function of public hearings as discussed above.

A Peace Rehabilitation Council (2004)[215]

In addition to the challenges of reconstructing Iraq and Afghanistan, the question of peace between the Israelis and Palestinians remains a paramount concern, as does that of North Korea's nuclear weapons development program. The outlook for all of these issues is clouded in uncertainty.

Parallel with the concrete threat of war and conflict, we need to focus on the equally critical issue of the impact this state of affairs is having on the hearts and minds of people worldwide. The signal failure of military action to produce a clear prospect for peace has left many people with suffocating feelings of powerlessness and dread.

It may sometimes be possible to break an impasse through the use of military force or other forms of "hard power." At best, however, such action can only respond to the symptoms of conflict; to the degree it plants further seeds of hatred in regions already torn by strife, it can deepen and entrench antagonisms. This is a concern I share with many people of conscience and indeed, this dire possibility is becoming manifest in many places around the globe.

***

In addition to the debate over the use of military force, the Iraq crisis highlighted the UN's inability to function adequately when there is serious division among the Security Council members. Amidst deepening concern about this situation, the High-Level Panel on Threats, Challenges and Change was launched at the initiative of UN Secretary-General Kofi Annan,[216] and its first meeting was held in December 2003. It is mandated to: examine the current challenges to peace and security; consider the contribution that col-

---

215 From 2004 Peace Proposal, "Inner Transformation: Creating a Global Groundswell for Peace."

216 Kofi Annan (1938–), Ghanaian statesman, 7th Secretary-General of the United Nations (1997–2006).

lective action can make in addressing these challenges; review the functioning of the major organs of the UN and the relationship between them; and recommend ways of strengthening the UN through reform of its institutions and processes. The results of its deliberations are to be reported back to the Secretary-General in December before the end of the UN General Assembly's regular session.

The chairperson of the panel is the former prime minister of Thailand, Anand Panyarachun.[217] In October 2000, we met in Tokyo and discussed the prospects for the UN in the twenty-first century. Pointing out its inevitable limitations as a collective body of sovereign states, he observed that the organization was effective to the exact degree that its member states wished it to be so. He stressed, however, that its existence should be welcomed as a source of hope as it was undeniably making the world a better place. I fully share his view.

There are, in certain quarters, persistent questions about the effectiveness or even necessity of the UN. Some aspects of the organization as it stands may indeed be incompatible with the realities of today's world. But with 191 member states, there is no organization more universal than the UN; it is the only body that can truly serve as a foundation for and give legitimacy to international cooperation. In the absence of a realistic alternative, the best course is to strengthen it and make it more effective. The SGI has sought to do this by generating grassroots support for the UN on a global scale.

In order fully to learn and reflect the lessons of the Iraq crisis, it will be necessary to develop new systems and procedures that can be invoked when the international community again faces difficult decisions. But whatever form these take, it is clear that the UN must continue to be the pivot for international solidarity.

I would like to put forward two proposals for institutional reform of the UN along with ideas for creating a more positive environment for its effective functioning. First, the authority of the General Assembly needs to be enhanced as the focus of efforts to strengthen the UN.

In the UN Charter, the Security Council is given primary responsibility for the maintenance of international peace and security; it is the only organ whose decisions are legally binding on member states. In actuality, however, the veto

---

217 Anand Panyarachun (1932–), Prime Minister of Thailand (1991–92).

power granted only to the five permanent members prevents the Council from fulfilling its function when agreement cannot be reached.

In order to overcome the Security Council's limitations, it is essential to empower the General Assembly through strengthening both its structures and practices. The UN Charter stipulates that the General Assembly's responsibility for the maintenance of international peace and security is subordinate to that of the Security Council. But as a global forum for dialogue open to all member states, the General Assembly is uniquely representative of the members' views.

There is a body of precedent for the General Assembly meeting in emergency special session and making recommendations to member states when the Security Council fails to fulfill its primary responsibility due, for example, to the exercise of the veto. This process was established by the "Uniting for Peace" resolution adopted by the General Assembly in 1950, which enables emergency special sessions to be called by a vote of any nine members of the Security Council, or by a majority of the UN member states.

In the twenty-first century, the UN must be capable of fully representing and reflecting the views of the international community in searching for the most appropriate means of resolving problems. The practice of holding emergency special sessions of the General Assembly should be encouraged, and routes established by which their deliberations can be fed back to the Security Council—particularly when it is deadlocked on a matter involving coercive measures. This will provide a broader basis for making the difficult decisions needed to meet the new types of threat to peace that have emerged in recent years. In December 2003, the General Assembly unanimously adopted a resolution calling for steps to "increase the body's efficiency and effectiveness and to raise the level of its visibility, so that its decisions might have greater impact."[218]

The strength and authority of the UN lie in its ability to build consensus within the international community. While measures to counter threats to peace and security must be effective, even more crucially they must be seen as having legitimacy, which is in turn the basis for soft power.

My second proposal for institutional reform concerns the need to coordinate and integrate the strategies and activities of the UN agencies that

---

218 UNGA (United Nations General Assembly). 2003. "Revitalization of the Work of the General Assembly." A/RES/58/126. Resolution adopted by the General Assembly. December 19.

provide different forms of support for people and societies caught up in violent conflict. This must cover the entire process from the start of conflict to post-conflict peacebuilding activities.

Recently, the lack of continuity of relief activities in conflict situations has been identified as a serious problem. The need to eliminate such gaps is stressed in *Human Security Now,* the final report of the Commission on Human Security issued in May 2003. It states, "With a focus on protecting people rather than adhering to institutional mandates, the current compartmentalization among the numerous uncoordinated actors should be overcome."[219]

This report also maintains that all actors must work under a unified leadership and focus on the needs of people and societies afflicted by the ravages of conflict. "The responsibility to protect people in conflict should be complemented by a responsibility to rebuild, particularly after an international military intervention. The measure of success is not the cessation of conflict—it is the quality of the peace that is left behind."[220]

There is an increasingly urgent need to develop a comprehensive framework for relief activities to respond to conflicts of an ever more complex nature. I believe that a body should be created within the UN to take effective international leadership for this particular challenge.

Specifically, the Trusteeship Council, which has suspended operations, could be reconstituted as a "peace rehabilitation council" to assume this responsibility. This builds on an idea I discussed in my 1995 proposal, where I suggested that the Trusteeship Council be given a new role in protecting cultural and ethnic diversity in areas of conflict, working closely with the UN High Commissioner for Refugees and the High Commissioner for Human Rights.

Incorporating some of those functions, this peace rehabilitation council could assume primary responsibility for promoting and coordinating the whole range of activities from humanitarian relief to post-conflict peacebuilding. As it carries out its mandate, it should maintain continuous communication with all affected countries. Also, to ensure a high level of transparency and credibility, regular progress reports should be made to all concerned parties.

---

219 CHS (Commission on Human Security). 2003. *Human Security Now.* New York: CHS, p. 134.
220 Ibid., p. 136.

The Peacebuilding Commission (2006)[221]

The year 2005 was a historic one, marking the sixtieth anniversary of the end of World War II. It was also a year in which a variety of severe threats, each capable of thrusting people's daily lives into crisis, became manifest.

Nowhere was this more shockingly visible than in the series of natural disasters that struck different parts of the world. Before the wounds of the calamitous Sumatra earthquake and tsunami had begun to heal, India was hit in July 2005 by widespread flooding and, at the end of August, hurricanes inflicted enormous damage on the southern Gulf Coast of the United States. Large parts of Western Africa continue to suffer from severe food shortages and famine resulting from drought and locust infestations, and in October a massive earthquake in northern Kashmir left more than 73,000 dead and approximately 3 million people homeless.

The impact of Hurricane Katrina in the United States, the sight of a major American city paralyzed by the effects of flooding and its citizens left to fend for themselves in the most appalling conditions, brought into painfully sharp relief the vulnerability of even advanced industrial societies to natural disaster.

Likewise, continued terror attacks throughout the world—attacks which have killed and injured large numbers of innocent civilians—projected a deep insecurity into people's lives throughout 2005. In July, suicide bombings on London's public transport system killed dozens and injured hundreds of people. The shocking impact of these attacks was compounded by the fact that they were perpetrated in the face of heightened security measures in place for the G8 Summit. As part of a disturbing trend, increasingly indiscriminate violence—in Egypt, Indonesia, Iraq and elsewhere—claimed the lives of many ordinary citizens.

In addition, intolerance based on ethnic or national differences, often aggravated by international movements of population, has been the cause of conflict and criminal violence, and many societies are experiencing severe divisions. In the Darfur region of western Sudan, attacks by the so-called Janjaweed militia against the local population have claimed tens of thousands of lives and displaced some 1.9 million people. Conditions there, which UN

---

221 From 2006 Peace Proposal, "A New Era of the People: Forging a Global Network of Robust Individuals."

investigators have termed "the world's worst humanitarian crisis,"[222] have not improved, nor have the underlying causes been resolved.

Hate crimes have increased in the wake of the September 2001 terror attacks, in particular with a growing incidence of violence and discrimination against Muslims. Meanwhile, in October and November of last year (2005), disaffected young people took to the streets as riots broke out throughout France, leading to the imposition of curfews in many cities and towns.

Further, the rapidly advancing pace of globalization has increased the risk of infectious diseases spreading to epidemic proportion. The ongoing AIDS pandemic continues to strike sub-Saharan Africa particularly hard. Worldwide, AIDS is said to have claimed more than 25 million lives and left behind some 15 million orphans. Currently, approximately 40 million people are infected with the HIV virus that causes AIDS.

There are also strong concerns about the emergence of new and virulent forms of influenza. The mutation of animal influenza viruses to permit human-to-human transmission could inflict casualties on the scale of the Spanish Influenza, the great influenza pandemic of 1918–19.

The examples cited above are all representative of global issues that, directly or indirectly, affect us all. In no instance can we afford to regard them as unrelated to us, a fire on the other bank of the river as the Japanese expression has it. And, like global warming and the continued poverty that can serve as a breeding ground for terrorism, these issues are organically linked with the processes of globalization. They should be seen as its intrinsic products, just as much as the revolutionary changes on the economic, financial and information technology (IT) fronts with which it is more commonly associated. A holistic response that deals with both the positive and negative aspects of globalization is urgently required.

***

Following sustained debate of the Secretary-General's and other proposals, the High-level Plenary Meeting of the General Assembly held in September (2005) adopted the 2005 World Summit outcome document. It is truly regrettable that difficult and protracted negotiations over its contents resulted in deletion of all mention of nuclear disarmament and nuclear nonproliferation and saw only a most general agreement on a number of issues.

---

222   UN (United Nations). 2004. "Press Briefing on Humanitarian Crisis in Darfur, Sudan." April 2.

Despite these deficiencies, the summit saw progress in other areas. Most notable were agreements on measures to establish a United Nations Human Rights Council to replace the present Commission on Human Rights, to create a new Peacebuilding Commission, and to revamp the Central Emergency Revolving Fund to enable more effective rapid-response to humanitarian crises.

It is the sad reality of the UN, as an intergovernmental organization, that innovative reform ideas and undertakings will inevitably face the stubborn impediments of conflicting national interests. Nevertheless, pessimism accomplishes nothing, and we should instead focus on how best to implement the agreed-on plans and establish effective mechanisms to protect and improve the lives of the vulnerable members of the human family.

**

The new Peacebuilding Commission will provide advice and recommendations to both the General Assembly and the Security Council to support a sustained, coordinated and integrated approach to international assistance for all stages of recovery from violent conflict—from post-conflict peacebuilding to reconstruction.

I thoroughly welcome the creation of the Peacebuilding Commission, which will assume functions similar to those of the peace rehabilitation council I outlined in my 2004 proposal.

The UN has charged the Peacebuilding Commission with a variety of tasks. I believe the following three roles are of particular importance, and I hope all efforts will be made to realize these aims:

1. To engage not only the leaders of the governments or groups involved in a conflict but also the men and women living in afflicted areas, and to focus on removing the threats and fears they face.
2. To consult and coordinate with civil society and NGOs in order to secure sustained assistance from the international community for the full length of time required for the peacebuilding process.
3. To open the door for people from countries with experience of post-conflict recovery and peacebuilding to make a contribution to people in other countries suffering in the aftermath of conflict.

Post-conflict peacebuilding and rehabilitation tends to be considered in terms of the headline aspects of national reconstruction such as holding elections, forming a new government or drafting a constitution. But the experience of the twentieth century attests to the fact that the tragic noose of history can never be loosened unless the recovery process is grounded in the perspectives and concerns of ordinary people. With this lesson in mind, I think the Peacebuilding Commission should see its role as ensuring that international cooperation has bolder goals—that it embraces the rebuilding of people's daily lives, the reconstruction of their happiness.

Regional Governance

An Asia-Pacific Organization for Peace and Culture (1986)[223]

As interdependent relations among states grow deeper, it is becoming gradually more difficult for large-scale wars to break out. We must realize that nothing is more wasteful than war with its adverse effects and impacts on the economy, and nothing more destructive to the environment.

It may be impossible to eradicate all conflicts in the world at once. The important thing, however, is to create a regional framework for securing peace wherever possible and to spread this throughout the world. Taking into consideration the current state of the world, I believe the Asia-Pacific region has the potential for such a framework. Although there are potential causes for war in the region, no large-scale war is taking place at the moment.

The Middle East and Central America are mired in conflict and face situations so volatile that the slightest misjudgment could cause them to escalate into a global catastrophe. Viewed from the standpoint of structural violence, the problem of starvation in Africa is another challenge that must be addressed. It is not my intention to look away from these problems.

Nevertheless, when we consider the question of world peace, it is inevitable that we focus on the Asia-Pacific region, which requires a deeper look both at direct confrontations and at plights such as war and hunger, and also demands a comprehensive understanding of political, economic, cultural, educational and other factors. If we are to create lasting peace—refusing to see peace as a mere interlude between wars as has been the case throughout history—the Asia-Pacific region inevitably becomes a focal point. There is also an obvious geopolitical reason that I stress this region: Japan is deeply involved in the region both in terms of time and space, and must play an important role in it.

223 From 1986 Peace Proposal, "Dialogue for Lasting Peace."

As I stated in my proposal last year (1985), the Asia-Pacific region possesses multidimensional elements that distinguish it from Europe, where the North Atlantic Treaty Organization (NATO) and the Warsaw Pact confront each other. Those elements include: the two superpowers of the United States and the Soviet Union; Japan, one of the world's largest economies, with its Peace Constitution providing for the renunciation of war; Canada with its immense natural resources; China, which is making strides in modernization toward the twenty-first century; the Association of Southeast Asian Nations (ASEAN) with their growing influence; the rapidly growing Newly Industrialized Countries (NICs) of South Korea, Taiwan and Hong Kong; and Australia and New Zealand, which are leading the effort to establish a South Pacific Nuclear Free Zone. These are some of the multidimensional activities that are noteworthy in the region.

I met with Prime Minister Rajiv Gandhi[224] of India during his visit to Japan in November last year as part of my effort to help create peace in the Asia-Pacific region and the world, a goal that has been constantly on my mind.

India is actively engaged in diplomacy for peace with a focus on nuclear disarmament. India chaired the Six-Nation Initiative, joining with Sweden, Greece, Mexico, Tanzania and Argentina in calling for an end to the extension of the arms race into space and the conclusion of a Comprehensive Nuclear Test Ban Treaty (CTBT), stressing the significance of Hiroshima and Nagasaki in nuclear disarmament.

I have been paying much attention to the direction of Indian diplomacy, as well as that of China. The SGI has shown the exhibition "Nuclear Arms: Threat to Our World" in a total of twelve cities in ten countries, starting at the United Nations Headquarters in New York. We are aiming to show it in India (scheduled for January 1986) and Canada (scheduled for April 1986), and in China this fall. Our aim is to help nurture antiwar and antinuclear currents throughout the world and to lay the foundations for an Asia-Pacific era. I will continue to do my utmost to support this effort.

That the region is multidimensional means it is still in a chaotic state, entailing both risks and possibilities, and there is always the possibility that if the US–Soviet military confrontation in the region intensifies any further it could trigger a third world war.

---

224 Rajiv Gandhi (1944–91), Prime Minister of India (1984–89).

In May 1974, I met with Mr. André Malraux,[225] who was visiting Japan as a special representative of the French government. One of the statements he made on that occasion made an indelible impression on me. He maintained that if there were to be another world war, it would certainly break out in the Pacific region.[226] Japan must do its utmost to prevent such a catastrophe from happening.

At the same time, I believe that focusing intensely on the possibilities and potential role during the twenty-first century of the seemingly chaotic Asia-Pacific region will enable us to truly see the future course of history.

The French critic Paul Valéry[227] characterized European civilization as essentially consisting of the Mediterranean civilization—with Roman law, Christianity and the Greek spirit as its three major components—and observed that the European is defined "not by race, or language, or customs, but by his aims and the amplitude of his will."[228] It is through this that European civilization has gained its universality, for better or for worse.

Needless to say, European civilization has both positive and negative aspects. On one hand, the "aims and the amplitude of the will" have created many material benefits. But they also aggravated the ferocious nature of colonialism and imperialism. I believe that it is possible to co-opt the positive qualities of European and Mediterranean civilization and open new horizons for a new Asia-Pacific civilization.

As I have mentioned elsewhere, the late British historian Arnold J. Toynbee[229] emphasized the role of East Asia in the coming century. In our dialogue *Choose Life,* he enumerated the following eight reasons for this belief:

1. The Chinese people's experience, during the last twenty-one centuries, of maintaining an empire that is a regional model for a literally worldwide world-state;

---

225 André Malraux (1901–76), French writer, Minister of Cultural Affairs (1958–69).

226 See Malraux, André and Daisaku Ikeda. 1976. *Ningen kakumei to ningen no joken* [Changes Within: Human Revolution vs. Human Condition]. Tokyo: Seikyo Shimbunsha, p. 32.

227 Paul Valéry (1871–1945), French critic and poet.

228 Valéry, Paul. 1971. *The Collected Works of Paul Valéry: History and Politics.* Trans. by D. Folliot and J. Mathews. New Jersey: Princeton University Press, p. 323.

229 Arnold J. Toynbee (1889–1975), British historian.

2. The ecumenical spirit with which the Chinese have been imbued during this long chapter of Chinese history;

3. The humanism of the Confucian *Weltanschauung*;

4. The rationalism of both Confucianism and Buddhism;

5. The sense of the mystery of the universe and the recognition that human attempts to dominate the universe are self-defeating;

6. The conviction that, far from trying to dominate non-human nature, man's aim should be to live in harmony with it;

7. The demonstration, by the Japanese people, that it is possible for East Asian peoples to beat the Western peoples at the Westerners' own modern game of applying science to both civilian and military technology; and

8. The courage shown by both the Japanese and the Vietnamese in daring to challenge the West.[230]

It is not my intention to discuss his analysis here, and I am fully aware that there are other views on the subject. But I must say that in our far-sighted challenge and struggle to create a new civilization, we need to constantly ensure that it is based on a new humanism that places value on human dignity and the shared interests of humanity.

As the case of Japan illustrates, the world's attention is primarily directed toward the economic aspect of the Asia-Pacific region. While it is important to address immediate problems, economic competition should not be over-emphasized. They should be approached with an expansive vision for world peace whereby an Asia-Pacific civilization would be truly imbued with new meaning for the history of humanity, in accordance with the spirit of the Russell–Einstein Manifesto: "We appeal, as human beings, to human beings: Remember your humanity, and forget the rest."[231]

As a first step toward such a vision, I propose the establishment of an Asia-Pacific Organization for Peace and Culture as a center for the development of cooperative relations of equality and mutual benefit among the countries in the region.

---

230 See Toynbee, Arnold J. and Daisaku Ikeda. 1976. *Choose Life: A Dialogue*. Oxford: Oxford University Press, pp. 231–32.

231 Russell, Bertrand and Albert Einstein. 1955. "The Russell–Einstein Manifesto, issued in London, 9 July 1955."

Rather than being directly under the jurisdiction of the United Nations, an Asia-Pacific Organization for Peace and Culture would be more loosely affiliated with the organization. It could also work in some way with the United Nations Economic and Social Commission for Asia and the Pacific, which reports to the Economic and Social Council, to help and reinforce its work in areas of peace, culture and disarmament.

When I met with Dr. Richard Coudenhove-Kalergi[232] in 1967, we discussed my idea for the establishment of a United Nations Asia and Far East Regional Office in Tokyo.[233] Based on subsequent developments around the world, this idea has now evolved into an Asia-Pacific Organization for Peace and Culture, which would aim to provide a permanent forum of equal discussion to address regional issues, sustain peace, achieve disarmament and develop the economy.

It goes without saying that I will continue to promote the ideals of the Charter of the United Nations toward their fuller blossoming. With a membership of 159 countries, the UN, headquartered in New York, is a parliament of humanity for world peace, seeking solutions for various problems facing the international community. I have consistently engaged in efforts to support it in every way I can.

It is well known, however, that the UN has many inadequacies in areas such as its security function. Encompassing the entire world, its global nature makes it difficult to deal effectively with regional problems.

The time has come to create an organization that corresponds to the needs of the era with a completely new approach. I suggest that a policy of decentralization with a focus on regions be adopted.

An Asia-Pacific Organization for Peace and Culture would also explore a new role for NGOs in line with the needs of a new era. In the contemporary world, the private sector is tremendously active and its role is increasingly more important. But the participation of the people and NGOs in the UN remains inadequate.

An Asia-Pacific Organization for Peace and Culture would urge active civil participation, and NGOs should explore means by which they can contribute

232 Count Richard Nikolaus von Coudenhove-Kalergi (1894–1972), Austrian thinker and founder of the first Pan-European movement.

233 See Coudenhove-Kalergi, Richard and Ikeda Daisaku. 1972. *Bunmei–nishi to higashi* [Civilization, East and West]. Tokyo: Sankei Shimbunsha, p. 67.

to it. Together, they can open new horizons through close coordination of their activities. As an NGO, the SGI will give our utmost support to the realization of such a vision.

When I look toward the twenty-first century, I believe that we need to bring together the wisdom of the peoples to create a system of global integration. But this cannot be achieved overnight. Sustained efforts with a regional focus are essential if we are to achieve results on a global scale.

Cooperation in the Asia-Pacific region has been discussed in various ways, resulting in a variety of detailed plans. Ideas for economic organizations have been advocated as a means to promote interdependence and create formal structures for regional economic cooperation. But there have been no concrete moves toward implementation of these plans—partly because the region is vast, multidimensional and highly diverse. Differences in social systems, ethnic, religious and cultural diversity and the variety of stages of economic development make it difficult to form cooperative relations.

It has been suggested that, compared to the cultural and historical commonality that made it possible for European countries to create the European Communities, the nations of the Asia-Pacific region are too diverse politically, economically and culturally to be united. It must be remembered that any plan that places an excessive emphasis on politics (security) and the economy would be fragile and easily invite friction and resistance.

I therefore suggest that the vision for an Asia-Pacific Organization for Peace and Culture be based on peace, disarmament, development and culture. The most important point here is to respect the diversity and multidimensional nature of the cultural traditions in the region, adamantly refusing uniform policies that prefer or impose a particular culture on others. Mutual understanding can be cultivated only where there is respect for indigenous cultures.

Creating a new organization requires sustained efforts. It would not have to be launched as a perfect entity with the participation of all nations in the region from the outset. Its development could be gradual, starting with any area that appears promising. What matters is to create a permanent forum of discussion based on mutual trust with a flexible spirit, advancing one step at a time. As a preliminary stage, a loosely organized consultative body would suffice.

I would like to suggest that, as a trial, the leaders of the nations in the region meet for an Asia-Pacific summit. There have been summit meetings of developed countries, but no such meeting has been held in the region. I hope that an Asia-Pacific Organization for Peace and Culture would eventually serve as a model of international organizations that can truly meet the needs of the twenty-first century, steadily building upon such efforts.

A UN Asia Office (1994)[234]

Eight years ago (1986), in my annual proposal commemorating SGI Day, I presented a vision for an Asia-Pacific Organization for Peace and Culture that would properly reflect the dawning of the Asia-Pacific era. I also suggested an Asia-Pacific summit, in which all leaders of the region would participate.

My proposal was based on the hope to create a permanent forum for Asia-Pacific countries to talk on an equal footing about such regional issues as the protection of peace and human rights, disarmament, economic development and the promotion of cultural and academic exchange. I felt it was essential to establish a base that permits the development of equal and mutually beneficial cooperative relations among Asia-Pacific countries.

To that end, I suggested that we adopt a flexible, gradual approach, beginning with the tasks that are already within our grasp, and slowly building up an organization based on mutual trust that would provide a regular forum for consultation. I also pointed out that a loose conference format might be suitable at the start.

At the time, I had in mind the image of the Conference on Security and Co-operation in Europe (CSCE),[235] which was established in an attempt to create a new framework for Europe. I believed that Asia-Pacific countries also need such a forum of dialogue. The CSCE was not conceived of as a permanent regional organization, but rather as a series of conferences where leaders from all member nations could meet together, with the results of each meeting building incrementally on the achievements of past sessions.

In calling for the creation of an Asia-Pacific Organization for Peace and Culture, I was hoping to see a similarly flexible forum of discussion in the Asia-Pacific region. I suggested that the organization be linked with NGOs and focus on peace, disarmament, development and culture as central

---

234 From 1994 Peace Proposal, "Light of the Global Spirit: A New Dawn in Human History."

235 The forerunner of the Organization for Security and Co-operation in Europe (OSCE).

themes to make sure that the voices of ordinary people are both heard and reflected.

One of the reasons I proposed a framework that went beyond Asia to include other Pacific countries was that I believe the Asia-Pacific region has the potential to create a new kind of civilization that encompasses tremendous diversity. I cannot forget the views expressed by Count Richard Coudenhove-Kalergi,[236] one of the first to advocate pan-Europeanism, and the historian Arnold J. Toynbee[237] in our past discussions. With their unique insights into world history, both placed great hope in the advent of an Asia-Pacific civilization.

Another reason I specified the Asia-Pacific was because it would be unrealistic to create a forum without the participation of the United States, which has deep connections with Asia. The question that is constantly on my mind is how to create harmonious cooperation among the United States, China, Japan and, possibly, Russia. Viewed from a broad perspective, this challenge constitutes a massive experiment in harmonizing and reconciling the civilizations of such countries as the United States, China and Japan, which differ greatly in terms of history, culture, ethnic roots and social structure.

The Asia-Pacific Economic Cooperation (APEC) summit in Seattle last year (1993) held out signs of progress toward the realization of such a vision. My attention was particularly drawn to the fact that the Vision Statement stressed the spirit of community. I applaud the forward-looking stance of this document, which, for the first time in this century, described the Asia-Pacific region as a single community.[238]

It was eight years ago that I stressed the need for an Asia-Pacific summit, and it is of great significance that the leaders of the APEC countries met at the summit meeting last year. They have begun to move toward stronger ties of friendship and mutual understanding under open regionalism with respect for the differences that exist among their countries. While seeking to continue with a loosely organized structure, APEC plans to hold another summit this year (1994), a sign implying future progress toward institutionalization.

---

236 Count Richard Nikolaus von Coudenhove-Kalergi (1894–1972), Austrian thinker, founder of the first Pan-European movement.

237 Arnold J. Toynbee (1889–1975), British historian.

238 APEC (Asia-Pacific Economic Cooperation). 1993. "Leaders' Declaration: Seattle Declaration – APEC Leaders Economic Vision Statement." November 20.

There is another move that deserves special attention: Japan reportedly intends to take the initiative in establishing an Asia-Pacific cultural exchange and cooperation council that would function as the cultural counterpart of APEC. Tokyo will also propose the creation of a network for the promotion of intellectual exchange in the Asia-Pacific region in the private sector, drawing on the strength of NGOs. I have long urged that emphasis be placed not only on economic and security issues but also on educational and cultural perspectives. I welcome these developments with open arms.

Last September (1993), I delivered a lecture at Harvard University ("Mahayana Buddhism and Twenty-first-Century Civilization"). One topic everyone seemed to be talking about there was the thesis "The Clash of Civilizations?"[239] by Samuel Huntington,[240] which discusses post-Cold War problems and conflicts arising from the collision of seven major civilizations: Western, Confucian, Japanese, Islamic, Hindu, Slavic-Orthodox and Latin American (or eight, adding African civilization). Of these, the clashes in greatest danger of culminating in violent conflict are, according to Huntington, those between Western and non-Western civilizations.

Certainly, there are civilizations in the world that have been shaped by various cultural and religious traditions. These cultural and religious differences, however, do not necessarily have to lead to confrontations or clashes. We can find numerous cases in history of ethnic groups with different cultural and religious traditions coexisting amicably.

Our challenge is to learn what conditions can lead to confrontation and explore ways to prevent this happening. The key lies in building multilayered structures of restraint based on the principle of cooperation that prevents confrontation and crisis from escalating into conflict. The key words here are cooperation and the principle of restraint, that which creates and maintains order.

To borrow a phrase from Mr. Joseph Nye,[241] "soft power is not competitive power, but rather cooperative power."[242] We must avoid the divisiveness

---

239 Huntington, Samuel. 1993. "The Clash of Civilizations?" in *Foreign Affairs.* Summer 1993 issue. Florida: Council of Foreign Relations. Vol. 72. No. 3.

240 Samuel P. Huntington (1927–2008), American political scientist.

241 Joseph S. Nye Jr. (1937–), American political scientist, US Assistant Secretary of Defense for International Security Affairs (1994–95).

242 (trans. from) Nye, Joseph S. Jr. 1991. "Remarks" quoted in the *Seikyo Shimbun.* September 28, p. 2.

caused by competition, and replace it with soft power, which engenders cooperation and unity. To accomplish this, we must see how far we can go in establishing self-control and restraint as the guiding principles of international behavior, and work to incorporate those principles in our community structures.

I have in the past pointed out the need for a United Nations regional headquarters in Asia. The UN already has a number of organizations in the region, including the UN Economic and Social Commission for Asia and the Pacific (ESCAP) in Bangkok and the United Nations University (UNU) in Tokyo. Asia has a huge population, including 1.2 billion in China and 800 million in India; it has long suffered the devastation of war even after World War II in the form of the Korean and Vietnam Wars, and its peace continues to be threatened by regional conflicts and by partition and confrontation in Northeast Asia. Problems in such areas as human rights and the environment are also intensifying. With all of these difficulties confronting the region, I think it is time the UN established a regional headquarters in Asia.

Europe has the Conference on Security and Co-operation in Europe, contributing to the emergence of a new European order, and the UN Office at Geneva, home for many UN agencies. Similarly, Asia would need two pillars: an Asia-Pacific Organization for Peace and Culture and an Asian Office of the United Nations.

As to the location for the latter, the first place that comes to mind is India, the great land of spirituality that gave birth to the peace philosophy of Shakyamuni[243] and King Ashoka,[244] and in this century Mahatma Gandhi[245] and Prime Minister Jawaharlal Nehru,[246] the pioneer of the Non-aligned Movement.

Another possibility would be the demilitarized zone (DMZ) dividing the Republic of Korea and the Democratic People's Republic of Korea, a vast strip of land that symbolizes the tragedy of the twentieth century, a century of war and violence.

---

243 Shakyamuni (Gautama Siddartha) (*c.* 560–480 BCE), the founder of Buddhism.
244 King Ashoka (*c.* 268–432 BCE), ruler of the Indian Maurya dynasty and the first king to unify India.
245 Mohandas (Mahatma) Gandhi (1869–1948), Indian champion of nonviolence.
246 Jawaharlal Nehru (1889–1964), first Prime Minister of independent India (1947–64).

The idea of an Asian Office of the UN in the DMZ on the Korean Peninsula may evoke a strong sense of the chasm between ideals and reality, in light of the history of and the bleak atmosphere of confrontation embodied by this place. But I feel compelled to make this proposal based on a long-term vision encompassing the half-century division of the Korean Peninsula for the sake of Asia in the twenty-first century.

Stability and Peace in the Asia-Pacific Region (2005)[247]

I would like to offer some ideas for building the foundations of trust and peace in the Asia-Pacific region. To begin, I would like to propose the establishment of a United Nations Asia-Pacific office as a new regional base. The establishment of an office for the Asia-Pacific region would mark the start of a new effort to advance human security in the region, and to make it a model for the UN's goal of building a world with fewer threats.

At present, in addition to the UN Headquarters in New York, there are the UN Offices at Geneva, Vienna and Nairobi. These three cities are home to a variety of UN offices and agencies, each with a focus on a different cluster of concerns—human rights and disarmament in Geneva, crime prevention and international trade in Vienna, and environment and human habitat in Nairobi.

In a previous proposal (1994), I spoke of the desirability of the UN having a regional base in Asia. I would like on this occasion to extend that idea to embrace the Pacific region as well, which includes such key supporters of UN activities as Canada and Australia. As many UN activities are focused on the particular needs of countries in Asia, these linkages could generate valuable synergies.

Moreover, Japan, which is both an Asian and a Pacific country, is home to the United Nations University (UNU), whose research and capacity-building activities in recent years have been focused on two areas: peace and governance; and the environment and sustainable development.

A UN Asia-Pacific office could form a hub with organic links to UNU and other institutions in the region. Its energies could be focused on the realization of human security and UN-centered efforts toward building the structures of global governance that will enable people to live secure and fulfilling lives. The Economic and Social Council (ECOSOC), which presently convenes its

---

247 From 2005 Peace Proposal, "Toward a New Era of Dialogue: Humanism Explored."

four-week substantive sessions alternately in New York and Geneva, could consider including this Asia-Pacific office in the rotation.

One possible location for such an office would be Bangkok, currently home to the United Nations Economic and Social Commission for Asia and the Pacific (UNESCAP). Another might be Okinawa in Japan or Cheju Island in South Korea. Having endured the indescribable misery of armed conflict, both could be considered "peace islands" whose people harbor strong aspirations for a world without war.

The Toda Institute for Global Peace and Policy Research has been studying the issues of human security and global governance for many years as one of its major projects. To mark its tenth anniversary, in February 2006 the institute plans to host an international conference on strengthening the UN and global governance. The Toda Institute will be carrying out an accelerated program of joint research with other institutions, including explorations of the feasibility of a UN Asia-Pacific office.

The next area I would like to address is laying the foundations in East Asia for the kind of regional integration we see in the European Union (EU) and the North American Free Trade Agreement (NAFTA).

Since the currency and economic crisis that struck East Asia in 1997, there have been growing calls for greater regional cooperation centered on the Association of Southeast Asian Nations (ASEAN). A framework for intra-regional dialogue, consisting of the ten ASEAN countries plus China, Japan and South Korea (ASEAN+3), is now well established. Against this backdrop, in November 2004 a summit of ASEAN leaders decided to hold the first East Asia Summit in Malaysia this autumn. Discussions here are also expected to include moves toward greater integration with an eye to the eventual establishment of an "East Asian community."

As someone who has called at every available opportunity for greater integration in Asia, I welcome these moves and hope that summits and other gatherings will clarify the aim of building a regional community that is open to the rest of the world and contributes to peace, stability and prosperity.

Issues such as ecological integrity, human development and disaster response strategies are amenable to intra-regional cooperation. Successful collaboration would foster trust and open the way to the formation of a regional community.

In the area of the environment, frameworks such as the Acid Deposition Monitoring Network in East Asia (EANET) and the Asia Forest Partnership

(AFP) are already in operation. Further cooperative structures should be developed to respond to the full range of environmental challenges.

In human development, public health and hygiene is a particular focus. The decade to 2015 has been designated the International Decade for Action, "Water for Life," and I hope efforts will be made through such initiatives as the Water Environment Partnership in Asia (WEPA) to safeguard and manage water resources. With the number of reported HIV infections in East Asia rising rapidly, channeling resources into combating the virus will also be critical.

Strategies for mitigating natural disasters can be an important focus for regional cooperation. The huge earthquake that devastated the historic city of Bam in southeast Iran in December 2003, the powerful earthquake that hit Niigata Prefecture in Japan last October, and the deaths of over 200,000 people in the earthquake and subsequent tsunami in the Indian Ocean in December of last year (2004)—all have highlighted the acute need for an international recovery system.

This month, a decade after an earthquake killed more than six thousand people in Kobe, Japan, the World Conference on Disaster Reduction was convened in that city. Delegates to the conference adopted the Hyogo Framework for Action for the next ten years, which sets out a list of five key objectives including to "ensure that disaster risk reduction is a national and local priority with a strong institutional basis."[248] Another outcome of the conference was an agreement to set up an international recovery platform to support the mid- to long-term recovery and reconstruction efforts of societies hit by natural disasters.

Tragically, it is impossible to entirely eliminate natural disasters. It is therefore crucial, as the Kobe conference stressed, to promote disaster reduction efforts that minimize the damage caused by disasters by putting in place early warning systems and strengthening response capacities. I hope the new international recovery platform will become functional as soon as possible and would like to see substantive progress on a full range of systems for cooperation on disaster prevention and recovery support in Asia. A priority must be to set up the kind of early warning system whose need was made painfully clear by the Indian Ocean tsunami.

248　UNISDR (United Nations International Strategy for Disaster Reduction). 2005. "Hyogo Framework for Action 2005–2015: Building the Resilience of Nations and Communities to Disasters."

As mentioned, the EU provides one model for the type of regional integration that I believe could greatly benefit East Asia. Last year saw an effective relaunch of the EU following enlargement to twenty-five member states. This coincided with the signing of the EU Constitution. Together these mark a major step toward the creation of a political community transcending traditional conceptualizations of national sovereignty.

Joseph Nye,[249] former dean of the John F. Kennedy School of Government at Harvard University, offers the following analysis: "Eight of the new members are former Communist countries that were locked behind the Iron Curtain for nearly half a century. Their attraction to the Union is a sign of the appeal—the 'soft power'—of the idea of European unification."[250]

Soft power is the diametrical opposite of the use and threat of military might to dominate and coerce, which has played a predominant role in shaping human history to date. Taking the form of dialogue and regional cooperation, grounded in a gradualist yet tenacious process of consensus-building, soft power has been the key to EU integration.

In Europe, it was France and Germany who worked to overcome a history of conflict in two world wars to build the relationship of trust and cooperation that became the driving force behind integration. In the same way, closer ties of friendship between China, Japan and South Korea can be pivotal to opening the way to the kind of united, integrated community that will make war in East Asia unthinkable.

At talks between the leaders of these three countries last November, agreement was reached on an Action Strategy on Trilateral Cooperation designed not only to strengthen cooperation in areas such as environmental protection, disaster prevention and management, but also to promote cultural and people-to-people exchanges.

In terms of concrete initiatives, the EU Erasmus program provides a model for student mobility that could profitably be emulated by China, Japan and South Korea. Erasmus consists of a series of inter-university programs that seek to realize a target of 10 percent of all students in participating countries having the experience of studying at an institution of higher education in another country.

---

249 Joseph S. Nye Jr. (1937–), American political scientist, US Assistant Secretary of Defense for International Security Affairs (1994–95).

250 Nye, Joseph S. Jr. 2004. "America Confronts Old and New Europe." *Project Syndicate*. May 18.

The experience of the EU points toward a number of issues that would have to be overcome in order to successfully build a corresponding infrastructure for student exchanges in East Asia. These include: ensuring adequate funding for exchange students, easing worries about studying in another country and resolving uncertainties about recognition of credits and qualifications.

I personally have long been an enthusiastic proponent of educational ties. Young people carry the hopes for our shared future, and I believe firmly that the connections forged by people of different countries in their youth can form the basis for lasting peace.

Under the University Mobility in Asia and the Pacific (UMAP) program, exchanges of students and teaching staff from institutions of higher education have been taking place since 1993. I believe these should be extended significantly—to eventually form a youth educational exchange program embracing all the countries of Asia. Such a program would do much to lay the foundations for long-term peaceful coexistence in the region.

There is already a considerable basis on which to build an inter-university network linking China, Japan and Korea that could act as a precursor to a more comprehensive structure. China at present ranks second behind the US in the number of exchange agreements with Japanese universities, while Korea ranks third. And Chinese exchange students at universities and technical schools in Japan are more numerous than any other nationality.

Here again Korean exchange students are the next largest in number. I was very proud when Soka University in 1975 became the first university in Japan to accept exchange students from China following the normalization of diplomatic relations.

Soka University currently has exchange agreements with ninety universities in forty-one countries and territories worldwide. These include twenty-two universities in China and five in Korea. There are also plans for Soka University to open a Beijing office by the end of 2005, in anticipation of a further expansion of educational exchanges.

For its part, the Soka Gakkai in Japan has been working to form closer ties between its youth membership and the All-China Youth Federation (ACYF), to which over 300 million of China's young people belong. Since a delegation led by China's current president, Hu Jintao[251] (then chair of the ACYF), came to Japan and signed an exchange protocol twenty years ago, exchange delegations

---

251 Hu Jintao (1942–), President of the People's Republic of China (2003–13).

have visited both countries on a regular basis. A new ten-year exchange agreement was formally signed in 2004.

In addition, this year is also Japan–Korea Friendship Year, commemorating forty years since the normalization of relations between Japan and South Korea. This offers an excellent opportunity to further develop friendly relations that in recent years have seen lively growth in cultural interaction and the movement of people.

My hope is that 2005 will mark a new start for relations between China, Japan and South Korea. Sixty years after the end of World War II, we should work to support and encourage forward-looking exchanges among the young people of our respective countries based on a willingness to confront and learn from the lessons of the past.

Toward an East Asian Union (2007)[252]

I would like to focus on Asia, a region long afflicted by conflict and tension, and put forward my thoughts on the direction of regional cooperation in the twenty-first century. I would like to preface this with a review of the origins of the Soka Gakkai and the SGI and of the history of my efforts to contribute to the peace and development of the Asia-Pacific region.

The broad underpinnings of the SGI's movement for peace are to be found in the humanistic philosophy of Nichiren Buddhism. We draw specific inspiration from Josei Toda's[253] declaration for the abolition of nuclear weapons, and, looking back over 100 years, from the book *Jinsei chirigaku* (The Geography of Human Life) authored by Tsunesaburo Makiguchi,[254] the founding president of the Soka Gakkai.

The culminating vision of this work is of a transition from the kind of ruthless competition in which the strong prey upon the weak in pursuit of material prosperity to "humanitarian competition" where states benefit themselves by benefiting others through active engagement with the international community.

---

252 From 2007 Peace Proposal, "Restoring the Human Connection: The First Step to Global Peace."

253 Josei Toda (1900–58), second president of the Soka Gakkai (1951–58).

254 Tsunesaburo Makiguchi (1871–1944), founding president of the Soka Kyoiku Gakkai (forerunner of the Soka Gakkai) (1930–44).

When *Jinsei chirigaku* was published in 1903, imperialism and colonialism were the dominant forces in the world. But Makiguchi stressed the need to create mutually enhancing, not mutually destructive, relations among peoples: "[O]ur lives rely on the world, our home is the world, and the world is our sphere of activity."[255]

Characterizing Japan as one storefront on "Pacific Avenue," he also critiqued the policies of military expansionism that Japan was pursuing in the Korean Peninsula and China. In later years, his devoted efforts, along with those of his disciple Josei Toda, would come to fruition in his major work *Soka kyoikugaku taikei* (The System of Value-Creating Pedagogy). In this work, he elaborated a philosophy of education dedicated to the realization of happiness for oneself and others—in other words, of bringing about a new era of humanitarian competition through the power of education.

November 18, 1930, the publication date of this book—a crystallization of the ideal of mentor and disciple striving together toward a common goal—became the Soka Gakkai's founding day.

Obviously, Makiguchi's stance, which gave clear precedence to the individual and humanity as a whole over the state, was diametrically opposed to that of the militarist government of the time, provoking an increasingly oppressive reaction from the authorities. Eventually, both Makiguchi and Toda were detained (in July 1943) on charges of violating the Peace Preservation Law and failure to show adequate respect to the emperor. They both, however, steadfastly refused to compromise their beliefs.

Already in his seventies at the time of his arrest, Makiguchi died in prison on November 18, 1944. Toda was finally released on July 3, 1945; the two years of imprisonment had taken a heavy toll on his health.

I chose Toda as my mentor in life and joined the Soka Gakkai after the war precisely because he was someone who had fought against fascist militarism to the end, refusing to succumb despite the harsh conditions of his imprisonment.

During the war, my family twice lost our home in air raids. My four brothers were conscripted; the eldest was killed in action in what is today Myanmar. The words he spoke to me while on leave from China—"There's nothing at all glorious about war. What the Japanese army is doing is

---

255 (trans. from) Makiguchi, Tsunesaburo. 1981–97. *Makiguchi Tsunesaburo zenshu* [The Complete Works of Tsunesaburo Makiguchi]. 10 vols. Tokyo: Daisanbunmei-sha. Vol. 1, p. 26.

horrible. Such arrogance and high-handedness! I feel terrible for the Chinese people"—still ring in my ears to this day.

These personal war experiences, together with Toda's tutelage, form the unshakable foundation of my actions for peace. After the war, Toda strove single-mindedly to rebuild the Soka Gakkai, embracing the vision bequeathed him by his mentor, Makiguchi. At the same time, he intensely longed for the peace of Asia and the happiness of its peoples, and urged young Japanese people to make it their mission to work toward the achievement of these goals.

"All the world's states, great or small, earnestly seek peace, but nonetheless are constantly under the threat of war!"[256] Toda's passionate call to young people was most powerfully expressed in the declaration for the abolition of nuclear weapons and his philosophy of global citizenship, an ideal of remarkable foresight.

Sadly, Toda never had the opportunity to travel abroad. But he exhorted me, in what would be one of his lasting instructions for my life: "There are vast continents beyond the ocean. The world is enormous. There are people afflicted with suffering. There are children trembling in the flickering shadows of war. You must travel! You must go out into the world on my behalf!"

On October 2, 1960, I embarked on my first journey overseas in the effort to contribute to world peace. This was two years after my mentor's passing and soon after I was inaugurated as third president of the Soka Gakkai. I visited destinations in North and South America, carrying Toda's portrait in the pocket of my jacket closest to my heart.

I chose Hawai'i as my first stop in light of the immense tragedy unleashed by the Japanese attack on Pearl Harbor in December 1941. I sought to engrave that historical lesson in the depths of my being and reaffirm my determination to generate an unstoppable current toward a world without war.

I visited various cities including San Francisco, the birthplace of the United Nations, and New York, where I observed the debate of the General Assembly at the UN Headquarters, and was inspired to think deeply about the central role the international body could play in creating a peaceful world.

---

256 (trans. from) Toda, Josei. 1981–90. *Toda Josei zenshu* [The Complete Works of Josei Toda]. 9 vols. Tokyo: Seikyo Shimbunsha. Vol. 1, p. 127.

In 1961, I traveled to Hong Kong, Ceylon (Sri Lanka), India, Burma (Myanmar), Thailand and Cambodia. At each site I offered sincere prayers for the victims of war and deeply reflected on the challenge of realizing lasting peace in Asia.

When I visited Bodhgaya in India, by tradition the site where Shakyamuni[257] first attained enlightenment, I keenly felt the need for an institution dedicated to multifaceted research into the philosophical and thought traditions of Asia and the rest of the world in order to lay the foundations of a world without war. In 1962, I founded the Institute of Oriental Philosophy to conduct such research and promote dialogue among different civilizations and faith traditions.

Likewise, I unveiled plans for establishing the Min-On Concert Association, which would be founded in 1963, during my stay in Thailand. This grew out of my conviction that mutual understanding among ordinary people serves as the basis for peace, and artistic and cultural exchange play a crucial role in facilitating such understanding.

During this trip through Asia, I directly sensed the dark shadows cast over the region by the deep divisions of the Cold War. Soon after this visit, the Vietnam War expanded to engulf the entire country with the start of US aerial attacks against the North in February 1965.

This was just two months after I began writing what would become a major undertaking in my life, the novel *The Human Revolution,* in Okinawa, which at that point was still under American occupation. The novel begins with the words: "Nothing is more barbarous than war. Nothing is more cruel."[258] When I heard of the escalation of the war in Vietnam, I was filled with a profound anger that this very tragedy was being repeated once more in Asia.

As the fighting intensified, tensions grew to a point where a direct confrontation between the US and China was feared. Feeling it imperative that the war be ended as soon as possible, in November 1966 I made a public call for an immediate cease-fire and a peace conference bringing together the concerned parties, and strongly urged again in August 1967 that the bombing of North Vietnam be halted.

On September 8, 1968, I issued a proposal that outlined concrete steps toward the normalization of Sino–Japanese diplomatic relations based on my

---

257 Shakyamuni (Gautama Siddartha) (*c.* 560–480 BCE), the founder of Buddhism.
258 Ikeda, Daisaku. 2004. *The Human Revolution*. Book 1. Santa Monica, California: World Tribune Press, p. 3.

belief that ending China's isolation within the international community was an absolute requirement not only for the stability of Asia but also for global peace.

My proposal was met with fierce criticism in Japan where, at the time, there was a deep-seated perception of China as an enemy nation. But it seemed clearly untenable for a country comprising some 20 percent of the world's population to be denied a legitimate seat at the UN or to lack diplomatic ties with its neighbor Japan. Here also I was inspired by my mentor, Josei Toda, who had often voiced his conviction that China is certain to play an essential role in world history and that friendship between the two countries would be of utmost importance.

Starting in the 1970s, I embarked on a process of dialogue with prominent leaders and thinkers from various countries in order to cast bridges of friendship across the fissures of an increasingly divided world.

In 1970, I met with Count Richard Coudenhove-Kalergi,[259] an early proponent of European unity, and discussed for a total of over ten hours such issues as the prospects for a Pacific civilization. In 1972 and 1973, I held a dialogue with one of the twentieth century's most prominent historians, Arnold J. Toynbee.[260] Our talks covered a broad range of topics, including the path toward global integration. He urged me, in light of my relative youth, to carry on the work of dialogue in order to help bring the whole of humanity together. I sensed that he was entrusting me with a task dear to his own heart.

Ever since, I have engaged in dialogue with leading figures from a wide variety of religious, cultural and national backgrounds, who are committed to taking action in their respective fields for the sake of our human future. To date, a total of forty-three of these dialogues have been published in book form.

In January 1973, I addressed a letter to US President Richard M. Nixon[261] urging the cessation of the Vietnam War, forwarding this to him via Henry Kissinger,[262] his National Security Adviser at the time. And later that year, I forwarded to President Nixon a proposal expressing my views on America's

---

259 Count Richard Nikolaus von Coudenhove-Kalergi (1894–1972), Austrian thinker and founder of the first Pan-European movement.
260 Arnold J. Toynbee (1889–1975), British historian.
261 Richard M. Nixon (1913–94), 37th President of the United States (1969–74).
262 Henry Kissinger (1923–), US Secretary of State (1973–77), recipient of the Nobel Prize for Peace in 1973.

role in the world. I conveyed my heartfelt respect for the brilliant spiritual heritage dating back to the country's birth, a heritage that must be made manifest in leadership for peace, human rights and coexistence if there is to be positive change in the world.

It was out of a similar conviction that I founded, in September 1993, the Boston Research Center for the 21st Century,[263] an institution dedicated to peace education and dialogue, and also Soka University of America (SUA), which opened in May 2001.

During 1974 and 1975, I visited China, the Soviet Union and the US in my capacity as a private citizen, in the hope of contributing to defusing the tensions among them. At the time there was a real danger the world would split irrevocably into three hostile blocs as relations between the US and the USSR continued to deteriorate while the Sino–Soviet confrontation escalated.

On my first visit to China in May 1974, I witnessed the people of Beijing building a vast network of underground shelters against the intensely felt threat of Soviet attack. In September the same year, I visited the Soviet Union for the first time, and met with Premier Alexei N. Kosygin.[264] I spoke of China's deep concern about the Soviet Union's intentions, and asked him straight out whether the Soviet Union was planning to attack China or not. The premier responded that the Soviet Union had no intention of either attacking or isolating China.

I brought this message with me when I next visited China in December of that year. It was also on this visit that I met with Premier Zhou Enlai,[265] and discussed with him the importance of China and Japan working together for global peace and prosperity.

During our meeting, Premier Zhou stressed that China had no wish to be a superpower. Taken together with Premier Kosygin's words, this statement convinced me that an easing of tensions between the two countries was not far off. And indeed, this proved to be the case.

In January of 1975, I visited the United States and exchanged views with Secretary of State Henry Kissinger. When I told him of Premier Zhou's wish to conclude a Sino–Japanese peace and friendship treaty, Kissinger expressed his agreement and support for the idea.

---

263   Subsequently renamed the Ikeda Center for Peace, Learning, and Dialogue.
264   Alexei N. Kosygin (1904–80), Premier of the Soviet Union (1964–80).
265   Zhou Enlai (1898–1976), Premier of the People's Republic of China (1949–76).

I met with the Japanese Minister of Finance, Masayoshi Ohira,[266] on the same day in Washington. I conveyed Kissinger's words to him and expressed my own sense of the absolute necessity of such a treaty. Ohira, who later served as Japan's prime minister, responded that he was fully committed to bringing such a treaty about. Three years later, in August 1978, the Treaty of Peace and Friendship between Japan and the People's Republic of China was officially concluded.

On my third visit to China in April 1975, I met with Vice Premier Deng Xiaoping[267] in Beijing. I also had the opportunity to confer with the Cambodian monarch in exile, Prince Norodom Sihanouk,[268] to discuss the road toward peace for his country.

It was in the midst of such dialogue-centered efforts to build peace that the Soka Gakkai International was launched on January 26, 1975, in Guam, the site of fierce fighting during World War II. Representatives from fifty-one countries and territories around the world came together to launch a people's movement for peace that today has grown into a grassroots network in 190 countries and territories.

Around the time of the SGI's founding, I began to pour my energies into educational exchanges, particularly the promotion of university exchange programs aimed at fostering leaders for the next generation. When traveling to different countries, I have always tried to make time to visit universities and educational institutions, sharing views with faculty and students.

In 1968, as heir to the vision of Presidents Makiguchi and Toda, I founded the Soka school system, followed in 1971 by Soka University. My determination was to build these schools up into centers of learning consecrated to the goal of peace, working with educators throughout the world.

In April 1974, just prior to my first visit to China, I was invited to speak at the University of California, Los Angeles, in what was for me the first such occasion. Then, in May 1975, I delivered a lecture entitled "A New Road to East–West Cultural Exchange" at Moscow State University, in which I made the following statement, which still remains my firm belief:

266 Masayoshi Ohira (1910–80), Japanese Minister of Finance (1974–76), Prime Minister of Japan (1978–80).

267 Deng Xiaoping (1904–97), Vice Premier of the People's Republic of China (1975–83).

268 Prince Norodom Sihanouk (1922–2012), twice king of Cambodia (1941–55, 1993–2004).

At no time in history has there been as great a need for a spiritual Silk Road extending all over the globe, transcending national and ideological barriers, and binding together people at the most basic level.[269]

On that occasion I received an honorary doctorate from Moscow State University. Since then, it has been my privilege to receive a total of 202 such degrees and professorships from universities and academic institutions around the world. I consider these honors more a recognition of the SGI as a whole than of myself. They are also proof that the halls of wisdom that are the world's universities can come together in a shared and earnest yearning for peace and humanism.

It is my humble hope that the path of dialogue I have forged will become the kind of Silk Road of the spirit connecting people's hearts that I called for in my Moscow State University address.

From the 1980s on, I have continued to conduct dialogues with leading figures from around the world. Particularly with the leaders of the Asian countries that suffered the atrocities of Japanese militarism during the war and still hold mixed feelings toward Japan, our dialogues have confronted the tragedies of the past and have envisioned a hope-filled future of lasting peace in Asia.

Among the political leaders and heads of state I have met in my efforts to deepen trust and friendship with the peoples of Asia are: Presidents Jiang Zemin[270] and Hu Jintao[271] of China; Prime Ministers Lee Soo-sung[272] and Shin Hyon-hwak[273] of South Korea; Presidents Corazon Aquino[274] and Fidel Ramos[275] of the Philippines; President Abdurrahman Wahid[276] of Indonesia;

---

269 Ikeda, Daisaku. 1995. *A New Humanism: The University Addresses of Daisaku Ikeda*. New York: Weatherhill, p. 68.
270 Jiang Zemin (1926–), President of the People's Republic of China (1993–2003).
271 Hu Jintao (1942–), President of the People's Republic of China (1993–2003).
272 Lee Soo-sung (1939–), Prime Minister of South Korea (1995–97).
273 Shin Hyon-hwak (1920–2007), Prime Minister of South Korea (1979–80).
274 Corazon Aquino (1933–2009), President of the Philippines (1986–92).
275 Fidel Ramos (1928–2009), President of the Philippines (1992–98).
276 Abdurrahman Wahid (1940–2009), Indonesian Muslim religious leader, President of Indonesia (1999–2001).

Sultan Azlan Shah[277] and Prime Minister Mahathir Mohamad[278] of Malaysia; President S. R. Nathan[279] and Prime Minister Lee Kuan Yew[280] of Singapore; King Bhumibol Adulyadej[281] and Prime Minister Anand Panyarachun[282] of Thailand; President Natsagiin Bagabandi[283] of Mongolia; King Birendra Bir Bikram Shah Dev[284] of Nepal; and Presidents Kocheril Raman Narayanan[285] and Ramaswamy Venkataraman[286] and Prime Ministers Rajiv Gandhi[287] and Inder Kumar Gujral[288] of India.

In addition, every year since 1983, I have set out ideas for strengthening the UN and resolving global issues in my peace proposals commemorating January 26, SGI Day, with a special focus on peace in the Asia-Pacific region.

For example, regarding the quest for peace and stability on the Korean Peninsula, although many challenges remain, over the course of time there has been progress toward realization of a number of the proposals I have made: the holding of a North–South summit, the signing of a pledge of mutual nonaggression and renunciation of war, and the holding of multilateral talks to resolve the issues surrounding North Korea's nuclear program.

In recent years in these proposals, I have called for the promotion of a joint research project to build the foundations for a shared understanding of history in Asia. I have also insisted that it is necessary to recall the spirit that prevailed at the time of the normalization of diplomatic relations between Japan and China as a way to seek an improvement in bilateral relations. My ongoing dialogues with Asia's political and cultural leaders aim to cultivate an environment conducive to the realization of such ideas.

---

277 Sultan Azlan Shah (1928–), the Raja Muda of Perak, Malaysia (1984–).
278 Mahathir bin Mohamad (1925–), Prime Minister of Malaysia (1981–2003).
279 S. R. (Sellapan Ramanathan) Nathan (1924–), President of Singapore (1999–2011).
280 Lee Kuan Yew (1923–), Prime Minister of Singapore (1959–90).
281 Bhumibol Adulyadej (1927–), King of Thailand (1946–).
282 Anand Panyarachun (1932–), Prime Minister of Thailand (1991–92).
283 Natsagiin Bagabandi (1950–), President of Mongolia (1997–2005).
284 Birendra Bir Bikram Shah Dev (1945–2001), King of Nepal (1972–2001).
285 Kocheril Raman Narayanan (1920–2005), President of India (1997–2002).
286 Ramaswamy Venkataraman (1910–2009), President of India (1987–92).
287 Rajiv Gandhi (1944–91), Prime Minister of India (1984–89).
288 Inder Kumar Gujral (1919–), Prime Minister of India (1997–98).

It was particularly gratifying to witness the China–Japan and South Korea–Japan summit talks in October 2006, the first steps toward the betterment of Sino–Japanese and Korean–Japanese relations after several years of heightened tensions.

Moreover, South Korean Minister of Foreign Affairs and Trade Ban Ki-moon[289] has just been inaugurated as UN Secretary-General, the second Asian to hold the post. I sincerely extend my best wishes for his success, and hope that under his leadership UN-centered efforts to promote global peace will advance with great vigor.

This year marks the 400th anniversary of the arrival of the first of a long series of Korean diplomatic delegations to Japan, which has been recognized by the two countries as a profoundly significant milestone in their relations. Japan and South Korea have agreed on a new program whereby cities in both countries send youth delegations to each other. Combined with the ongoing youth exchanges between China and Japan, it is anticipated this will nurture friendship among the young generations of China, Korea and Japan.

The Japan–China Joint Press Statement issued at the summit meeting in Beijing last October was the first such statement in eight years. It contains important elements that will serve as the guiding principles for relations between the two countries into the future. The following section in particular drew my attention: "[I]t is the solemn responsibility of both countries and of the bilateral relations in the new era to contribute constructively to the peace, stability, and development of Asia and the world."[290]

The spirit expressed here is deeply consonant with the vision for the future of China and Japan upon which Premier Zhou Enlai and I concurred when we met over thirty years ago.

It is now thirty-five years since the normalization of Sino–Japanese diplomatic relations, and the time has come to ensure that the progress made thus far is secure and irreversible. To this end we must continue to promote cooperation and exchange in a variety of areas and build relations of trust that will serve as the immovable foundations of peace and coexistence in East Asia.

The Joint Press Statement mentioned earlier includes, among its recommendations for the year 2007, the enhancement of friendly sentiment between

---

289 Ban Ki-moon (1944–), South Korean statesman, 8th Secretary-General of the United Nations (2007–).

290 MOFA (Ministry of Foreign Affairs of Japan). 2006. "Japan–China Joint Press Statement." October 8.

the two peoples and the active development of exchange, especially youth exchange, through the Japan–China Year of Culture and Sports. In addition, it calls on the two countries to "strengthen mutually beneficial cooperation particularly in the areas of energy, environmental protection, finance, information and communication technology, and protection of intellectual property."[291]

Here, I would like to suggest that the decade starting from 2008, the year of the Beijing Olympic Games, be designated as a decade for building Sino–Japanese friendship for the twenty-first century, with different areas of cooperation given particular focus on an annual basis; for example, by following the Japan–China Year of Culture and Sports with a year for energy cooperation, a year for environmental protection, etc.

Additionally, as part of this decade, I would like to suggest an exchange program between the diplomats of the two countries. A similar program played a crucial role in helping France and Germany overcome the bitter memories of two World Wars to become the driving force for European integration. The system by which diplomats from each country are assigned to serve in the other's Foreign Ministry has become well established and is said to have been highly effective in preventing misunderstandings and deepening diplomatic collaboration.

Japan has also had similar diplomatic exchange programs with the United States, France and Germany. Extending these programs to include Asian countries such as China and Korea would surely strengthen the foundations for a future East Asian Union.

Next, I would like to briefly consider India which, like China, is one of the emerging powers of the twenty-first century. In July of last year, on the final day of the St. Petersburg G8 Summit, an expanded conference was held with the participation of China, India, Brazil, Mexico and South Africa. There, the leaders of the five countries were invited to exchange views and opinions on the St. Petersburg Plan of Action on Global Energy Security and other outcome documents. This meeting was symbolic of the fact that the views and voices of these major developing nations have become indispensable to the summit process.

In December of 2006, Indian Prime Minister Manmohan Singh[292] visited Japan for a summit meeting, at the conclusion of which the Joint Statement Towards Japan–India Strategic and Global Partnership was released. I

---

291 Ibid.
292 Manmohan Singh (1932–), Prime Minister of India (2004–).

welcome this development and wish all success for the Japan–India Friendship Year 2007, which commemorates the fiftieth anniversary of the Cultural Agreement between the two countries.

To contribute to this process, I would like to propose that Soka University of America help organize an international conference of scholars and experts from Japan, the United States, China and India on the theme of deepening and expanding global partnership in the twenty-first century. SUA's Pacific Basin Research Center is dedicated to research on the peaceful development of the Asia-Pacific Region and would be able to contribute significantly to the success of such a conference.

Finally, I would like to make two specific proposals toward the formation of an East Asian Union. The first is for the establishment of an East Asian environment and development organization.

In January 2007, the East Asia Summit was held in the Philippines, the second such summit following the December 2005 meeting in Malaysia. Together with the ASEAN+3 (China, Korea and Japan) Summit that preceded it, this meeting is part of an ongoing process of building trust and strengthening regional relations through dialogue.

Many important issues, however, remain unresolved, and the path to integration such as through the formation of an East Asian Union seems long. In this regard, I believe pilot programs focused on specific concerns can build the structures of cooperation in a way that makes visible the contours of future regional collaboration and enhances and maintains enthusiasm and interest for this in each country.

In particular, the establishment of bodies focused on crucial issues such as the environment and energy would be desirable. There are an increasing number of voices calling for full-fledged cooperation through, for example, the ASEAN+3 Environmental Ministers Meeting held every year since 2002. The regional initiatives developed to date, such as those working to combat acid rain, should be brought together under the unified aegis of an East Asian environment and development organization. This would make possible more comprehensive and effective responses to the challenges facing the region.

Second, I would like to propose the establishment of an East Asian equivalent of the College of Europe. This center for graduate studies was established soon after the end of World War II, and has fostered the talents of young people who have played an active role in promoting integration in their respective fields. For more than fifty years, the intellectual training conducted at the College of Europe has promoted a European identity among its graduates that transcends the narrow framework of individual states. This identity has been crucial in supporting the growth and development of the European Union.

Establishing such an institution at this point in time would develop a pool of talent essential to any future regional community. There would be no need for the curriculum to be limited to regional issues and concerns. Collaborating with such bodies as the United Nations University (UNU), it could become a venue for creative in-depth exploration of the challenges to realizing systems of global governance, systems in which the UN would no doubt play a crucial role.

Envisioning a United States of Africa (2001)[293]

Africa is, along with Asia, a region of crucial importance to world peace. Since the end of the Cold War, regional and internal conflicts have broken out in various parts of Africa, ravaging people's lives and livelihoods. According to one survey, in the eleven years since the end of the Cold War, there have been 108 armed conflicts that have each claimed more than one thousand lives.[294] The majority of these tragic conflicts have occurred in Asia and Africa.[295]

As a result of prolonged conflict situations, a growing number of Africans live as refugees, as many as 6.2 million as of January 2000 according to the Office of the United Nations High Commissioner for Refugees (UNHCR).[296]

Food shortages and famine are often the tragic by-products of conflict. "The State of Food and Agriculture 2000" published by the Food and Agriculture Organization (FAO) reports that nineteen African countries suffer from famine whose primary cause is armed conflict.[297] And there has been a much more dramatic increase in such cases than for those where famine is provoked by natural disaster.

---

293 From 2001 Peace Proposal, "Creating and Sustaining a Century of Life: Challenges for a New Era."

294 Wallensteen, Peter and Margareta Sollenberg. 1999. "Armed Conflict, 1989– 98." *Journal of Peace Research.* September 1. Vol. 36. No. 5. London, Thousand Oaks, CA and New Delhi: Sage Publications, p. 593.

295 Ibid., p. 595.

296 See UNHCR (United Nations High Commissioner for Refugees). 2000. "Refugees by Numbers, 2000 edition." Table 1.

297 See FAO (Food and Agriculture Organization). 2000. "The State of Food and Agriculture 2000." Rome: FAO, pp. 72–73.

Failure to find effective remedies to the problem of persistent poverty has given rise to a misplaced sense of pessimism about the continent, intensified by so-called "aid fatigue" on the part of developed countries. Consequently, international concern for Africa has shrunk in inverse proportion to the severity of need, exacerbated by the problem of AIDS.

Africa's crisis, however, is a challenge that must be met if we are to realize peace in an increasingly globalized world. And from a basic humanitarian perspective, indifference is inexcusable. The historical realities Africa has long endured—colonial rule and arbitrary division of territory by the great powers—must be acknowledged as among the root causes of the present crisis situation. It is therefore humanity's shared responsibility to ensure that this tragic legacy is not carried forward into the future.

Africa is the birthplace of humankind. It has been a continent of hope, giving rise to a rich diversity of civilizations since ancient times which have given humanity numerous blessings in many areas, including philosophy and science.

It has long been my belief that the twenty-first century must be the century of Africa. This conviction is in part rooted in the experience of my first visit to the UN Headquarters in 1960, soon after I accepted the responsibility to serve as third president of the Soka Gakkai. There, I witnessed and was deeply impressed by the energy and vitality of the African delegates participating in the General Assembly and various committee meetings. Indeed, 1960 was an extraordinary year for Africa, with seventeen African nations winning their independence.

From that time I began to develop friendships with the political, cultural, and intellectual leaders of various African countries, hoping to contribute to the realization of a century of Africa. Moreover, as the founder of Soka University and the Min-On Concert Association, I have been actively engaged in promoting broad educational and cultural exchange at the grassroots level.

The SGI has been particularly committed to supporting refugee relief activities undertaken by the Office of UNHCR. Our fund- and awareness-raising campaigns in support of UNHCR and other bodies will continue this year, the fiftieth anniversary of the Refugee Convention.

Lasting peace in Africa, our neighbor in an interconnected world, must be an immediate concern to everyone. Over the decades, many important, constructive visions for Africa have been set forth. Ideas to bring together the nations of Africa in strong solidarity and a shared pursuit of peace and prosperity include those made by Ghana's first president Kwame Nkrumah[298] and other leaders of the Pan-Africanist movement for a United States of Africa. These cannot be dismissed as mere relics from the dawn of the post-colonial period.

A United States of Africa was one of the visions that Nigerian president Olusegun Obasanjo[299] and I discussed during our dialogue two years ago (1999). Indeed, there is a rising awareness among African countries of the importance of strengthening Pan-African solidarity.

At the summit meeting of the Organization of African Unity (OAU) held in Lomé, Togo, in July 2000, leaders from twenty-seven countries signed a proposal to create an African Union. Drawing from the experience of European integration, this African Union will have an African Parliament, a Pan-African court of justice and the continent's own central bank.

Although no agreement was reached on a timetable for its creation, it is truly significant that African countries have agreed on the common goal of an African Union. Over the course of its long history, the OAU has realized many achievements, ranging from the establishment of the Banjul Charter on Human and Peoples' Rights and the African Nuclear-Weapon-Free Zone Treaty to the recent mediation of the Ethiopia–Eritrea conflict.

It is the international community's responsibility to provide unstinting support and cooperation to the creation of an African Union and the further strengthening of continental unity. The European Union reviewed its achievements of the past half century in *Strategic Objectives for 2000–2005: "Shaping the New Europe"* as follows: "The European Union provides living proof that peace, stability, freedom and prosperity can be brought to a continent once torn apart by wars."[300] Viewed over a span of fifty to one hundred years, there is no reason to believe that what has been accomplished by the EU should not be possible for Africa also.

Envisaging a United States of Africa, President Nkrumah of Ghana stated that "it will emerge . . . as a Great Power whose greatness is indestructible because it is built not on fear, envy, and suspicion, nor won at the expense of

---

298 Kwame Nkrumah (1909–72), first President of independent Ghana (1957–66).

299 Olusegun Obasanjo (1937–), President of Nigeria (1999–2007).

300 Commission of the European Communities. 2000. *Strategic Objectives for 2000–2005: "Shaping the New Europe."* Brussels: Office for Official Publications of the European Communities. February 9, p. 3.

others, but founded on hope, trust, friendship and directed to the good of all mankind."[301]

I believe that this vision of peaceful solidarity, defined as Africa's mission by President Nkrumah, should be the guiding principle of regional integration in the twenty-first century. Competition rooted in animosity and exclusion, external pressure and coercion, breeds only fear, envy and suspicion. In contrast, the overflowing vitality of the human spirit seeking creative coexistence and autonomy cultivates hope, trust, and friendship.

This year is the United Nations International Year of Mobilization against Racism, Racial Discrimination, Xenophobia and Related Intolerance. The World Conference on this theme is to be held in September in South Africa. The SGI plans to participate in NGO forums to be held in parallel with the intergovernmental meetings, and to stress the importance of human rights education to counteract the ignorance that is the root cause of intolerance.

The destiny of Africa and indeed of all humankind in the twenty-first century hinges on the degree to which ordinary people awaken their inner capacities for strength, for wisdom, and for solidarity. I cannot stress enough the value of open dialogue in bringing forth these qualities.

Dialogue has the power to restore and revitalize our shared humanity by setting free our innate capacity for good. It is an indispensable lodestone around which people are united and trust is fostered. It was the failure to make dialogue the foundation of human society that unleashed the bitter tragedies of the twentieth century.

The year 2001 has been designated the Year of Dialogue among Civilizations. We must spread the spirit of dialogue to make it the current and flow of the twenty-first century—a century of life. In this way we can together create an era in which all people enjoy the fruits of peace and happiness and celebrate their limitless dignity and potential. Dialogue can lead to the creation of a new global civilization. The members of the SGI, as engaged and responsible citizens of their respective societies, will continue to use honest dialogue to build a people's solidarity for peace and humanity throughout the world.

---

301 Nkrumah, Kwame. 1973. *I Speak of Freedom*. London: Panaf Books Ltd., p. xii.

African Youth Partnership Plan (2008)[302]

I would now like to turn my attention to Africa, as its future is critical in building a global society that upholds human dignity.

In the quest for lasting peace and sustainable growth, the nations of Africa have, since entering the twenty-first century, embarked on a new challenge with the African Union (AU) playing the pivotal role. Founded in July 2002 as a successor to the Organization of African Unity (OAU) and comprising fifty-three countries and territories, the AU is the world's largest regional organization. Rapid progress is being made toward establishing the institutional framework that will ensure its effectiveness, with the Assembly of Heads of State and Government as its supreme organ, as well as the Pan-African Parliament, the Peace and Security Council, the Economic, Social and Cultural Council and the Court of Justice.

Over the years, I have dedicated myself to engaging in dialogue with African leaders and experts in various fields and promoting cultural and educational exchange on a people-to-people level. In this regard, I sincerely hope that the AU undertaking will bear abundant fruit to the benefit of the people of Africa.

It is my unchanging belief that an African Renaissance will herald a renaissance of the world and of humanity.

In fact, many of the important initiatives to transform vicious cycles of human tragedy in recent decades have originated in the African continent. This is seen, for example, in the work of the people of South Africa under the leadership of President Nelson Mandela[303] to dismantle apartheid and conduct the Truth and Reconciliation process, as well as in the empowerment of women and environmental protection realized by the Green Belt Movement led by Dr. Wangari Maathai[304] of Kenya. These transformative initiatives are generating interest and inspiring similar undertakings around the world. Recent years have seen the resolution of several civil wars and conflicts in Africa. There have been important transitions to civilian government, and many parts of the continent have seen improved rates of economic growth.

---

302 From 2008 Peace Proposal, "Humanizing Religion, Creating Peace."

303 Nelson Mandela (1918–), President of South Africa (1994–99), recipient of the Nobel Prize for Peace in 1993.

304 Wangari Maathai (1940–2011), Kenyan politician and environmental activist, founder of the Green Belt Movement, recipient of the Nobel Prize for Peace in 2004.

This is not to understate the seriousness of the issues Africa faces. There are ongoing conflicts such as those in the Darfur region and Somalia, as well as dire poverty and desperate refugee situations, and the fact is that in much of sub-Saharan Africa progress toward the realization of the MDGs has been woefully inadequate.

Today, African nations, which have refused to succumb under the historical burdens of the slave trade and colonialism, are striving to forge solidarity as they unleash their potential and confront their common challenges. This is an undertaking of enormous significance.

The adoption of the New Partnership for Africa's Development (NEPAD) is a concrete manifestation of such solidarity. It is a pledge by African leaders to strive for peace and security, democracy, stable economic governance and people-centered development based on a shared recognition that Africa "holds the key to its own development."[305] It is crucial that the international community actively support this ambitious project of the people of Africa.

In May 2008, the Fourth Tokyo International Conference on African Development (TICAD IV) will be held in Yokohama, Japan. This conference was initiated by Japan in 1993 and has since been held every five years in conjunction with the United Nations and other co-organizers. Participants include African heads of state and representatives of international organizations; the conference serves as a vital forum for sharing a common awareness of the problems Africa faces and for exploring solutions.

I would like to urge that discussions focus on concrete measures to ensure that the empowerment of youth is at the heart of all policy proposals. It is critical that we take measures now to break the vicious cycle of intergenerational poverty and poor living conditions. Improved conditions for young people will be the linchpin of a transition to a positive cycle of step-by-step improvements in the living conditions of people of all generations.

TICAD has promoted human resources development through ensuring access to basic education, support for learning centers and vocational training. I would like to urge that, building on these achievements, a program for African youth partnership be established as one of the pillars of TICAD, helping foster the talents of the young people who will play a critical role in creating a brighter future for Africa.

---

305 AU (African Union). 2001. "The New Partnership for Africa's Development (NEPAD)." Abuja, Nigeria: AU, p. 67.

I would also like to call for the creation of a network of and for youth, facilitating ties of exchange between the young people of Africa and the youth of Japan and countries throughout the world, as a platform for confronting the challenges faced not only in Africa but around the globe. This year, 2008, has been designated the Japan–Africa Exchange Year. I would hope that the events of the Exchange Year will become the starting point for the establishment of programs of regular exchange between Japanese and African youth and students.

CHAPTER 2

A UN to Eliminate Misery from the Earth

For a Sustainable Global Society: Learning for Empowerment and Leadership

2012 Environment Proposal (Full Text)
June 5, 2012

On behalf of Soka Gakkai International (SGI) members in 192 countries and territories around the world, I would like to offer some thoughts and proposals on the occasion of the United Nations Conference on Sustainable Development (Rio+20) to be held in Rio de Janeiro, Brazil, starting June 20.

Every year, 53,000 square kilometers of forest are lost. In many countries, water tables continue to drop, provoking chronic water shortages, and it is estimated that almost 25 percent of the planet's land area is being affected by the processes of desertification.[1] These are among the pressing issues the Rio+20 Conference must grapple with.

But as the Conference title "The Future We Want" suggests, it also represents an effort to develop a clear vision of a more ideal relationship between humankind and Earth. It is crucial that the effort to establish a vision rooted in an awareness that we are neighbors sharing this planet succeeds; and it is even more important that increasing numbers of people feel inspired to work for its realization, both individually and in solidarity with one another.

Even the most inspiring vision will become a reality only with the powerful support of civil society. It must be felt as a matter of personal commitment by large numbers of people. It must be shared, reflected in daily life and firmly established as a guideline shaping patterns of action within society.

---

1   See Brown, Lester R. 2011. *World on the Edge: How to Prevent Environmental and Economic Collapse.* New York and London: W. W. Norton & Co., pp. 36–37.

A focus on people and their daily lives will be essential to ensure that debate on the key themes of the Conference—a green economy in the context of sustainable development and poverty eradication, and the institutional framework for sustainable development—is meaningful and productive. I therefore hope that the Conference's deliberations will be underpinned by a determination to enable people to become agents of change and ensure their sustained commitment and action. The future we want can be achieved only when there is a deep and personal appreciation that we are the ones who must bring it into being.

In this proposal, I would like to focus on the kind of empowerment that brings forth the truly limitless potential we all possess. It is important that a sense of leadership be fostered within each individual, generating waves of transformation within our communities and societies. Only then can we realize the goal of a sustainable global society in which the inherent dignity of life is given paramount importance.

A human scale

Addressing the significance of the upcoming Conference, Helen Clark,[2] Administrator of the United Nations Development Programme (UNDP), made the following powerful statement:

> Sustainability is not exclusively or even primarily an environmental issue. . . . It is fundamentally about how we choose to live our lives, with an awareness that everything we do has consequences for the 7 billion of us here today, as well as for the billions more who will follow, for centuries to come.[3]

Today, there are widespread calls for a paradigm shift from the pursuit of material wealth to sustainability. To achieve this, we must of course review and revise current economic and environmental policies; but this will not be

---

2   Helen Clark (1950–), Prime Minister of New Zealand (1999–2008), Administrator of the United Nations Development Programme (UNDP) (2009–).

3   Clark, Helen. 2011. "Foreword" in "Human Development Report 2011." New York: UNDP, p. iv.

enough. Rather, we must interrogate the very nature of human civilization, from the ways in which our societies are organized to the manner in which we conduct our daily lives.

This is not to deny the reality that many societies will continue to prioritize economic growth. But I believe it is necessary for all societies to reexamine the underlying objectives and rationales for growth and be clearly aware of other priorities. I hope that the Rio+20 Conference will spur deep and earnest consideration of such questions.

The devastating earthquake that struck Japan in March last year (2011) brought these issues into stark relief. The inability of a society at the highest levels of economic and social development to contain the damage wrought by this natural disaster was revealed—not only to people in Japan but throughout the world. In the Fukushima nuclear disaster, the unintended consequences of science and technology were on full display—in the large numbers of people forced to evacuate their homes, in the grave and still unmitigated scope of radioactive contamination, and in the as-yet-unknown long-term effects on people's health.

The loss of human life, the wounding of dignity, the destruction of the familiar nature and ecology of the community—such are the cruel outcomes wrought not only by natural disaster but by armed conflict and environmental degradation. In the case, for example, of climate change, no place can be fully free from risk over the long term; the impacts will be felt by all present inhabitants of Earth and, further, by future generations.

In this sense, shifting the orientation of human civilization toward sustainability requires that the issues involved be considered on an authentically human scale, within the context and experiences of daily life. This is where we must sense the full weight of life's inalienable dignity, and reflect on what is truly important to us and what we must come together to protect.

This is why it is unacceptable to consider the pursuit of sustainability as simply a matter of adjusting policies in order to find a better balance between economic and ecological imperatives. Rather, sustainability must be understood as a challenge and undertaking requiring the commitment of all individuals. At its heart, sustainability is the work of constructing a society that accords highest priority to the dignity of life—the dignity of all members of present and future generations and the biosphere that sustains us.

The pursuit of the possible

Here I am reminded of Aurelio Peccei[4] who, by founding the Club of Rome, helped shape the 1972 United Nations Conference on the Human Environment, the earliest precursor to the Rio+20 Conference. In the dialogue we published in 1984, he declared:

> Mesmerized by our power, we do what we *can* do, not what we *ought to* do and go all the way without taking into consideration any practical *dos* and *don'ts,* or even the moral and ethical restraints that we should consider inherent in our new condition.[5]

I was struck by this statement, not least because it resonates at a deep level with the awareness expressed by the founding president of the Soka Gakkai, Tsunesaburo Makiguchi,[6] in his 1903 work, *Jinsei chirigaku* (The Geography of Human Life).[7] He sketches the following outline of the conditions prevailing in the early years of the twentieth century, when a single-minded pursuit of the possible produced a global order in which the strong preyed on the weak with little or no thought to the sacrifices entailed:

> [The Great Powers] are constantly on the lookout for any opportunity for profit; in other words, any opening that might be exploited to gain an economic foothold or political advantage. Just as in the physical atmosphere areas of high pressure flow into those of low pressure, an analogous phenomenon can be seen in international power relations.[8]

---

4   Aurelio Peccei (1908–84), Italian industrialist and cofounder of the Club of Rome.

5   Peccei, Aurelio and Daisaku Ikeda. 2009. *Before It Is Too Late.* New York: I.B.Tauris, p. 10.

6   Tsunesaburo Makiguchi (1871–1944), founding president of the Soka Kyoiku Gakkai (forerunner of the Soka Gakkai) (1930–44).

7   Makiguchi, Tsunesaburo. [1903]. *Jinsei chirigaku* [The Geography of Human Life] in *Makiguchi Tsunesaburo zenshu* [The Complete Works of Tsunesaburo Makiguchi]. Tokyo: Daisanbunmei-sha. Vols. 1–2.

8   (trans. from) Makiguchi, Tsunesaburo. 1981–97. *Makiguchi Tsunesaburo zenshu* [The Complete Works of Tsunesaburo Makiguchi]. 10 vols. Tokyo: Daisanbunmei-sha. Vol. 2, p. 400.

Almost 110 years have passed since Makiguchi wrote these words; how much have things changed in the intervening decades?

Contemporary civilization continues to be enthralled by an amoral pursuit of the possible, largely unimpeded by ethical constraints. This can be seen in the ceaseless competitive quest for armaments to intimidate others and enhance one's "prestige," as well as in global economic competition waged with utter indifference to the issues of poverty and expanding income disparities.

The spiral of desire—in which ambitions and impulses at first thought to be well under control expand in tandem with their successive attainment until they entirely escape our command—lies at the heart of many of the critical challenges facing our world: the prioritization of economic growth leading to ecological degradation, financial and economic crises brought on by overheated speculation, the ultimate inhumanity of nuclear weapons. . .

The accident at the Fukushima nuclear power plant of course originated in a natural disaster. But it also demonstrates the severe risks inherent in relying on energy generated through controlled nuclear reactions; risks that had been obscured by an unquestioning faith in the superiority and safety of the Japanese nuclear industry.

At the same time, the pursuit of the possible has been an important impetus to development, bringing such benefits as fulfilling essential needs for food, clothing and shelter, improving people's health and welfare and dramatically increasing the movement of both people and goods through advances in transportation and communication technologies.

Makiguchi did not deny the benefits of this pursuit, and in fact carefully noted the power of positive competition to hone and refine people's capacities and unleash their energy. "We find progress and development where competition is strong and powerful; where it is hampered, either by natural or human factors, we find stagnation, immobility and regression."[9]

His prime focus, however, was on the need to shift away from the kind of military, political and economic competition in which benefit is sought for oneself with no thought to the sacrifices imposed on others. He called for a new form of what he termed "humanitarian competition" in which "one protects, extends and advances the lives of others while doing the same for

---

9   Ibid. Vol. 2, p. 402.

oneself" and "one benefits and serves the interests of others while profiting oneself."[10]

Makiguchi was seeking a qualitative transformation in the nature of competition so that the energies of desire—the impulse to do something about one's current situation—are oriented toward more valuable ends, generating happiness for both self and others.

Buddhism describes this transformation in the depths of consciousness as follows: "We burn the firewood of earthly desires and behold the fire of enlightened wisdom before our eyes."[11] Rather than allowing the anger or grief we feel about our present circumstances to find outlet in acts that harm or degrade others, we must expand and elevate those feelings to become the motivation for action to counter the social ills and threats that bring suffering to ourselves and others. Buddhism teaches that such transformation enables us to live lives that illuminate society with the qualities of courage and hope.

If we were to translate Makiguchi's vision and its resonances with Buddhist philosophy into contemporary realities, we would see a transformation of military competition into a striving among countries to deploy their capacities not simply for national security but also for "human security" in areas such as controlling the spread of infectious disease and disaster prevention and mitigation. This is because the kind of competition that spurs efforts to meet and overcome shared threats will bring desirable mutual benefit to all countries.

Likewise, political competition can be transformed from a hard power struggle for hegemony into a soft power competition to develop creative policy proposals, thus gaining the respect of other countries. Examples of this might be seen in the powerful solidarity of nongovernmental organizations (NGOs) and forward-looking governments which catalyzed each other's efforts to bring about multilateral treaties banning antipersonnel mines and cluster munitions. This achievement was made possible through the pressure brought to bear on different countries to prioritize the humanitarian imperative over the pursuit of what was technologically and militarily possible, as well as the support that was generated throughout international society as a result.

---

10   Ibid. Vol. 2, p. 399.

11   (trans. from) Nichiren. 1952. *Nichiren Daishonin gosho zenshu* [The Complete Works of Nichiren Daishonin]. Ed. by Nichiko Hori. Tokyo: Soka Gakkai, p. 710.

The call to establish a green economy in the context of sustainable development and poverty eradication, one of the overarching themes of the Rio+20 Conference, could be said to correspond to a shift in economic competition toward modes in which "one benefits and serves the interests of others while profiting oneself."

There is growing support for the creation of a system in which countries can share their best practices, build technological capacity and support other countries in the application of these technologies. This is seen as an essential means of achieving a global transition to the kind of green economy that is characterized by low-carbon emissions and the efficient utilization of resources. It is my strong hope that the Conference will reach agreements about such a system whereby countries with leading-edge experience in these fields can act on the principle of humanitarian competition. The same principle can, and I earnestly hope will, be aggressively applied along the temporal axis, in the formulation "to benefit and serve the interests of the future while profiting the present."

To many people, sustainability evokes images of various constraints being imposed upon individuals and societies. But such a narrow approach will not give rise to the kind of transformative ripple effects that are required.

Although physical resources are finite, human potential is infinite, as is our capacity to create value. The real significance of sustainability is, in my view, as a dynamic concept in which there is a striving or competition to generate positive value and share it with the world and with the future.

Put simply, efforts by people, communities and societies to benefit others bring to the fore our most positive and creative aspects. Likewise, the most profound improvement to our present condition comes when we strive for a better future. It is through such repeated efforts, with constant reference to self and other, present and future, that we can protect each other's inalienable dignity and work to build a world in which all people can live in peace and happiness.

The key here is our sense of responsibility to those with whom we share the planet—our sense of responsibility toward the future.

Grounded in the local community

Although many people, confronted with news of horrific events in different parts of the world or of the dire threats to the global ecology, are pained and feel compelled to take action, the cumulative effect of the ceaseless flow of such news can be a deepening sense of powerlessness.

Arthur[12] and Joan[13] Kleinman, who have been conducting joint research in cultural anthropology at Harvard University, offer this analysis of the pitfalls of our contemporary information society: "Thus, our epoch's dominating sense that complex problems can be neither understood nor fixed works with the massive globalization of images of suffering to produce moral fatigue, exhaustion of empathy, and political despair."[14]

To avoid becoming overwhelmed by these feelings, it is crucial to be grounded—to find a standpoint from which one can sense the impact of one's actions and feel one is making concrete progress in transforming reality. This, in my view, is the role of the local community. A sense of responsibility toward the world or the future is not something that can be developed overnight, in isolation from the realities of daily living. If we cannot establish this within our immediate relationships and environment, we cannot hope to do so relative to the entire planet or the distant future.

The word "responsibility" indicates the ability or capacity to respond. It is through the persistent effort to strengthen and forge our capacity to respond to the evolving realities of the community that a sense of commitment toward all those with whom we share the planet and toward future generations is developed.

The film *A Quiet Revolution*,[15] whose production the SGI supported and which was first shown at the 2002 World Summit on Sustainable Development (WSSD) in Johannesburg, South Africa, focuses on activities undertaken by ordinary citizens around the world that illustrate this principle. Produced by the Earth Council in cooperation with the United Nations Development Programme (UNDP) and the United Nations Environment Programme (UNEP), the film introduces the efforts of people to protect their community, its children and their future. It features villagers in Neemi in Rajasthan, India, restoring ancient traditions of rainwater harvesting; people in Slovakia, tackling chemical pollution in the Zemplinska Sirava lake; and

---

12   Arthur Kleinman (1941–), American physician and anthropologist.

13   Joan Kleinman (1939–2011), American China scholar.

14   Kleinman, Arthur, Veena Das and Margaret Lock, eds. 1997. *Social Suffering*. Berkeley, Los Angeles and London: University of California Press, p. 9.

15   Earth Council. 2002. *A Quiet Revolution: The Earth Charter and Human Potential*. DVD. Costa Rica: Earth Council. http://www.sgi.org/resource-center/ngo-resources/education-for-sustainable-development/a-quiet-revolution.html (accessed April 2, 2013).

the activities of the Green Belt Movement in Kenya to combat desertification through tree planting.

To date, the SGI has organized screenings of this film in more than fifty-five countries and territories in order to promote the message that every individual has the power to change the world.

Moved to action

The Green Belt Movement featured in *A Quiet Revolution* was started by the Kenyan environmental activist Dr. Wangari Maathai.[16] It illustrates how a community-based people's movement can foster a sense of responsibility toward the future in each individual.

My meeting with Dr. Maathai, who sadly passed away last year, took place in February 2005. I am fondly reminded of the embracing smile, bright as the sun, which she broke into when I proposed the planting of a fig tree at Soka University of America in honor of her many years of effort and achievement.

To Dr. Maathai, the fig tree was a symbol of irreplaceable dignity and worth in her home community. In point of fact, it was a fig tree that motivated her to dedicate herself to a tree planting movement.

One time, returning to Kenya from the US where she was studying bio-logical science, she visited her family in Nyeri. There she was shocked to see that the natural environment around her home had undergone serious change in just a few years. With an increased focus on profit, farmers were cutting down forests to plant cash crops. Dr. Maathai discovered that even a fig tree her mother had taught her to revere as sacred had been felled in the process.

She observed that landslides had become more common in the region and that as a consequence sources of clean drinking water were now scarce. She learned that many Kenyan women were struggling daily with problems caused by environmental degradation.

Convinced that "solutions to most of our problems must come from us,"[17] she launched in her local community what would develop into the Green Belt Movement.

---

16   Wangari Maathai (1940–2011), Kenyan politician and environmental activist, founder of the Green Belt Movement, recipient of the Nobel Prize for Peace in 2004.

17   Maathai, Wangari. 2004. "Nobel Lecture." Oslo. December 10.

This movement, which Dr. Maathai described as "a testament to individuals' ability to change the course of environmental history,"[18] illustrates three points of crucial importance.

The first is the consistent emphasis on ensuring that all participants were genuinely convinced of the validity of what they were doing and were able to maintain a palpable sense of achievement as the movement developed and grew. Dr. Maathai held seminars in the communities where the movement was active and encouraged people to identify the problems facing them. She would ask them what they felt the source of the problems was, and most would blame the government. While acknowledging that was largely the case, she stressed that nothing would change as long as people attributed all responsibility to the government. She said to them: "It is your land. You own it, but you are not taking care of it. You're allowing soil erosion to take place and you could do something about it. You could plant trees."[19]

People planting trees would sometimes say, "I don't want to plant this tree, because it will not grow fast enough." Dr. Maathai would remind them that the trees people were harvesting today had not been planted by them, but by those who came before. Thus, it was necessary to plant trees now that would benefit the community in the future: "Like a seedling, with sun, good soil, and abundant rain, the roots of our future will bury themselves in the ground and a canopy of hope will reach into the sky."[20]

However lofty the purpose may be, people are not prompted to action unless they are fully convinced of its worth. It is the sincere effort to engage with individuals, carefully responding to and helping them resolve each of their questions, that leads to such conviction.

In addition to this process of continuous dialogue, the Green Belt Movement has been able to involve more and more people because its tangible results have given each participant a concrete sense of achievement. I think that here can be found the most powerful factor enabling people to participate in the movement; the joy and pride that derive from the knowledge that their actions are contributing to actual change has freed people from a sense of powerless resignation.

As Dr. Maathai stated in her Nobel Peace Prize acceptance speech:

---

18 Maathai, Wangari. 2004. *The Green Belt Movement: Sharing the Approach and the Experience*. New York: Lantern Books, p. xi.

19 Maathai, Wangari. 2008. *Unbowed: A Memoir*. London: Arrow Books, p. 173.

20 Ibid., p. 289.

Tree planting is simple, attainable and guarantees quick, successful results within a reasonable amount of time. This sustains interest and commitment.

So, together, we have planted over 30 million trees that provide fuel, food, shelter, and income to support their children's education and household needs. The activity also creates employment and improves soils and watersheds.[21]

The second point I would like to note is that the Green Belt Movement has empowered each individual, inspiring people to live with a larger sense of purpose and bringing out their limitless innate potential.

There is a tendency to regard the movement simply in terms of the number of trees it has planted. Its greater significance, however, lies in people's empowerment, as attested by Dr. Maathai's conviction that her work was not just about planting trees; it was a movement to inspire people to take responsibility for their lives and the environment, governance and the future. When she realized that she was working not only for herself but for something larger, she grew stronger.

Through the process of people planting and nurturing trees with their own hands, the movement enabled its participants, rural women in particular, to realize it was up to them to choose between maintaining and regenerating the environment or allowing its destruction to continue.

They further came to recognize, through the regular opportunities for learning and awareness-raising the movement provided, that their efforts to plant trees and keep forests from being cleared were part of a larger mission to build a society that values democracy and social conscience and observes the rule of law, human rights and the rights of women.

Rural women, who initially came to Dr. Maathai seeking access to fuel and drinking water, grew confident as they gained experience. They began to exercise leadership in their communities, eventually assuming responsibility for community-wide projects such as managing tree nurseries, collecting rainwater and securing food resources.

The transformation from empowerment to leadership experienced by these women is reminiscent of the dramatic awakening depicted in the Lotus Sutra, which expresses the essence of Buddhism: a transformation from individuals

---

21   Maathai, Wangari. 2004. "Nobel Lecture." Oslo. December 10.

seeking salvation to individuals taking action to help others free themselves from suffering.

Buddhism teaches that the means to fundamentally overcome our suffering do not exist outside ourselves. Through the process of awakening to and fully manifesting our unlimited inner potential, we are transformed in a way that enables us to lead others to happiness and security. This great inner transformation enables us to make our own suffering the impetus to improve society.

In this context it is relevant to introduce the example of a woman by the name of Srimala,[22] which appears in the Buddhist canon. Her vow is recorded as follows:

> If I see lonely people, people who have been jailed unjustly and have lost their freedom, people who are suffering from illness, disaster or poverty, I will not abandon them. I will bring them spiritual and material comfort.[23]

Srimala is said to have lived true to her vow, devoting her life to helping those mired in suffering.

When Dr. Maathai declared, "We are called to assist the Earth to heal her wounds,"[24] her words reverberate with just this kind of lifetime commitment to one's vow.

When one has such a commitment, one's actions are not predicated on fear of legal sanctions or the desire for personal benefit or financial reward. One remains determined regardless of adversity and refuses to rely on others to take action. It is a question of moving forward unflinchingly to fulfill one's mission, no matter how difficult it may be. Dr. Maathai described this as being energized by seeing the enormity of the task ahead of her.

This kind of community-based empowerment ignites courage and wisdom in individuals, inspiring them to take action and exercise leadership in order to improve their situation. As this approach to life becomes more internalized and established, people can work together to advance, however small each

---

22 Srimala, also known as Lady Shrimala or Queen Shrimala. A daughter of King Prasenajit of Kosala in India and his consort Mallika, in the time of Shakyamuni.

23 Wayman, Alex and Hideko Wayman, trans. 1974. *The Lion's Roar of Queen Srimala: A Buddhist Scripture on the Tathagata-garbha Theory.* New York: Columbia University Press, p. 65.

24 Maathai, Wangari. 2004. "Nobel Lecture." Oslo. December 10.

step may be, toward the fulfillment of their individual vow or mission. I think that this process can serve as the basis for building an expanding grassroots movement in pursuit of sustainability on a global scale.

The third point I would like to touch on is the efforts taken by Dr. Maathai to ensure the continuation of the movement; her emphasis on encouraging and educating younger generations.

Responding to a question about the way she always spoke of her initiatives in terms of "we" instead of "I," Dr. Maathai memorably replied:

> I'm very conscious of the fact that you can't do it alone. It's team-work. When you do it alone you run the risk that when you are no longer there nobody else will do it.[25]

While it is possible for a single individual to initiate a movement, the very nature of any attempt to achieve a great goal is that it will require many years and the cooperation of a large number of people.

The question of how to pass on the spirit of a movement from one generation to the next has often come up as a matter of urgency in the course of my discussions with various world figures engaged in efforts to resolve global issues. Among them was Sir Joseph Rotblat[26] who, as a founder of the Pugwash Conferences on Science and World Affairs, dedicated his life to the abolition of nuclear weapons and of war.

Dr. Rotblat had already been working tirelessly since the early days of Cold War confrontation to build a spiritual solidarity of scientists transcending borders when he supported the formation of International Student/Young Pugwash (ISYP) for a younger generation of scientists, launched in 1979. By that time he was in his seventies, but his eyes were firmly fixed on the future.

When the Russell–Einstein Manifesto warning against the perils of nuclear weapons was issued on July 9, 1955, Dr. Rotblat was the youngest of the signatories. What thoughts must have gone through his mind in the later stages of his life as he watched a stream of young scientists adopt the pledge,

---

25   Maathai, Wangari. 2004. *The Green Belt Movement: Sharing the Approach and the Experience.* New York: Lantern Books, p. 136.

26   Sir Joseph Rotblat (1908–2005), British physicist and philanthropist, founding member (1957), Secretary-General (1957–73), President (1988–97) of the Pugwash Conferences on Sciences and World Affairs.

"I will not use my education for any purpose intended to harm human beings or the environment."[27]

I have also been striving to build a global solidarity of people for a world free of nuclear arms, embracing the declaration issued in 1957 by my mentor, second Soka Gakkai president Josei Toda,[28] in which he called for the abolition of nuclear weapons. Nothing is more encouraging to me than seeing young people undertaking such initiatives as the Soka Gakkai Youth Division's drive to collect 2.27 million signatures calling for a Nuclear Weapons Convention (NWC), which were submitted to the United Nations in May 2010.

In order to involve children in tree planting, Dr. Maathai established tree nurseries in schools and consistently supported the participation of young people in environmental conservation. She wrote of her expectations for younger generations, as well as her vision for the future:

> I have always believed that, no matter how dark the cloud, there is always a thin, silver lining, and that is what we must look for. The silver lining will come, if not to us then to the next generation or the generation after that. And maybe with that generation the lining will no longer be thin.[29]

It was on June 5, 1977, that Dr. Maathai initiated the Green Belt Movement when she and a group of supporters planted seven trees in Kamukunji Park on the outskirts of Nairobi. Since that day, the movement has spread throughout Kenya and to numerous countries in Africa, with as many as 40 million trees having been planted on the continent. Since 2006, when, in partnership with UNEP and other organizations, Dr. Maathai called for a global tree planting campaign, over 12.5 billion trees have been planted throughout the world. People everywhere were saddened to learn of her passing in September last year, but the number of trees being planted continues to grow.

This is not a miracle—far from it. It was made possible by the strong determination of Dr. Maathai and others who decided to do something about the crisis unfolding around them. Their determination elicited broad support, stirring the hearts of countless people, moving them to action. There is much

---

27   Student Pugwash USA. "Student Pugwash USA's Pledge to Work for a Better World." http://www.spusa.org/pledge/Pledgebrochure.pdf (accessed April 2, 2013).

28   Josei Toda (1900–58), second president of the Soka Gakkai (1951–58).

29   Maathai, Wangari. 2008. *Unbowed: A Memoir.* London: Arrow Books, p. 290.

to learn from the example of Dr. Maathai's activism, as we join together in the quest to create a sustainable global society.

New goals

Next, I would like to offer some specific proposals for the Rio+20 Conference, concentrating on three broad areas.

1. To generate a set of shared objectives for a sustainable future. These should provide a global vision toward which humanity can strive and serve as norms guiding the actions of the individuals who share this planet.
2. To establish a new international organization through the merger of United Nations agencies in the fields of the environment and development. This will better promote efforts for a sustainable global society centered on collaboration with the different sectors of civil society.
3. To recommend to the UN General Assembly the creation of an educational framework promoting sustainability. This will raise awareness among individuals and enable people to move from empowerment to leadership within their respective communities.

Regarding the first of these, it is vital that any new set of goals should, in addition to carrying on the spirit of the UN Millennium Development Goals (MDGs) of alleviating the suffering of people forced to live in difficult and degrading conditions, be a catalyst promoting positive change among people toward the construction of a sustainable global society.

The MDGs, officially established during the Millennium Summit in 2000, were groundbreaking in their departure from prior international efforts that were focused on improving macroeconomic indicators. They stressed improving the conditions of individuals and provided clear numerical goals in concrete time frames, such as reducing by half the percentage of people living on less than one dollar a day by 2015.

At present, it is expected that the proportion of people living in extreme poverty will have fallen to below 15 percent, easily surpassing the original target, while the poorest countries have made significant progress toward the goal of universal primary education provision, and as many as 1.8 billion people have gained access to cleaner drinking water.[30]

---

30   See UN (United Nations). 2011. "The Millennium Development Goals Report 2011." New York: UN, p. 4.

But even these important improvements have not necessarily been felt by people living in the most difficult economic circumstances or those socially disadvantaged due to such factors as gender, age, disability, minority status, etc. It is vital that these disparities be addressed with even greater attention and urgency than has been the case to date.

More and more people are calling for a successor arrangement covering the period after 2015. The report of the High-level Panel on Global Sustainability established by UN Secretary-General Ban Ki-moon[31] stresses the need to establish sustainable development goals to achieve this end.

The report suggests that key issues in determining the framework for such goals should include the need for them to cover challenges to all countries rather than just developing nations, to incorporate a range of key areas that were not fully covered in the MDGs, such as climate change, biodiversity and disaster risk reduction and resilience, and to engage all stakeholders in sustainable development, including local communities, civil society and the private sector, as well as governments.[32]

This January, in my annual peace proposal issued to mark the anniversary of the founding of the SGI, I proposed that the creation of a working group to deliberate the content of these new goals be included among the agreements reached at the Rio+20 Conference. In addition to the aspects noted above, I believe that a commitment to an expansive global vision coupled with a focus on the local community should inform the process of generating sustainable development goals.

Regarding the first, a visionary commitment to the welfare of all of humankind and the global community of life should be at the heart of the new goals. Such a vision can encourage the engagement of more societies and individuals so that they strive in a humanitarian competition to make the most meaningful contribution. Core concepts that could be deployed effectively here include those I referenced earlier: human security, soft power and a green economy.

Article 26 of the Charter of the United Nations states the following objective: "to promote the establishment and maintenance of international peace and security with the least diversion for armaments of the world's human and

---

31 Ban Ki-moon (1944–), South Korean statesman, 8th Secretary-General of the United Nations (2007–).

32 See UN (United Nations). 2012. "Resilient People, Resilient Planet: A Future Worth Choosing." Report of the Secretary-General's High-level Panel on Global Sustainability. New York: United Nations, p. 72.

economic resources. . . ." The human security benefits of disarmament concern all states, and any progress here would be highly beneficial not only to governments but to all people living on Earth today, and to future generations.

Similarly, the UN has designated this year as the International Year of Sustainable Energy for All. If states with records of achievement in this field could engage in positive competition to contribute to the diffusion of these technologies, it would help establish the infrastructure by which societies struggling with poverty can protect the lives, livelihoods and dignity of their people without increasing the burden on the environment. This would in turn greatly reduce the demands placed on the global ecosphere going into the future. A similar formula could be applied to the transition to a zero-waste society through promotion of the "3 Rs" of Reduce, Reuse and Recycle.

I feel that any new set of goals should include the kinds of targets that will broadly encourage humanitarian competition, earlier defined as actions that "benefit and serve the interests of others while profiting oneself" and "benefit and serve the interests of the future while profiting the present."

The second component is a focus on the community as the site for action. This will enable more people to palpably sense the degree to which their actions are giving rise to positive change and contributing to a sustainable future.

In one sense, the MDGs were focused on reducing negative impacts on people and societies by finding ways to alleviate the suffering of poverty and remove threats to people's lives and dignity. They were also to a large degree centered on the role and efforts of states; for example, in promoting primary education and eliminating gender disparities in educational opportunities. It is vital to continue and indeed accelerate such efforts, but it is also important to establish goals that generate positive ripple effects throughout society and which can be undertaken by any and all within the context of their immediate circumstances.

Examples of the proactive engagement of local communities might include: afforestation projects or other efforts to protect the local ecology; citizen-centered efforts to create more disaster-resilient communities; linking up with other communities to increase the degree of local production and consumption; working cooperatively to make waste reduction and recycling an intrinsic part of people's lives; and encouraging the introduction of renewable energy sources in ways appropriate to each locale, thus reducing the environmental footprint.

Local authorities and communities are central to this process, and cities have particularly key roles to play. Although cities occupy no more than 2 percent of Earth's total land area, they are responsible for the consumption of approximately 75 percent of the planet's resources and a similar proportion of the pollutants released into the atmosphere and the planet's rivers, lakes and oceans.[33] The observation that the actions and policies of the world's cities will determine the fate of Earth is fully justified.

I therefore hope that the new sustainable development goals will include targets related to cities, with a number of specific indices. This could be linked with a system enhancing cities' ability to share technical knowledge, best practices and year-to-year progress toward the achievement of these goals.

Conventional intergovernmental negotiations will probably be inadequate to the task of formulating the kind of goals that relate directly to the patterns of people's lives. I therefore strongly hope that, along with ensuring the full participation of representatives of civil society in the deliberative process, the Rio+20 Conference endeavors to generate goals that will be personally taken up by individuals and inspire cooperation toward their achievement.

Institutional framework

One of the key themes of the Rio+20 Conference is the institutional framework for sustainable development.

Behind the adoption of this theme lies concern among many governments about the slow pace of UN efforts in the field of sustainability, as well as about duplication and fragmentation of the activities of related agencies, lack of funding and inadequate coordination.

While it is of course vital that these concerns be addressed with haste, I believe that institutional reform cannot be limited to these areas. Rather, I hope that the debate will aim toward the establishment of a new international organization that can respond to the realities of the twenty-first century and serve as a pioneering model for the UN system.

Concretely, I would like to propose the establishment of a "global organization for sustainable development" that would be the outcome of a bold, qualitative transformation of the current system along the following lines:

- The consolidation of relevant sections and agencies, including UNDP and UNEP;

---

33   See UNEP (United Nations Environment Programme). 2009. "Statements by Local Authorities' Major Group." Input for the discussion within the 25th UNEP Governing Council and the Global Ministerial Environment Forum on "Globalization and the environment – global crises: national chaos." February 16.

- The participation of all interested governments in deliberations related to the operation of the new organization;
- A fully collaborative relationship with civil society; and
- The active participation and involvement of youth.

One rationale for institutional consolidation is the importance of inclusivity, evidenced by the fact that "inclusive and sustainable development" headed the list of eight specific action areas for 2011 decided upon by the UN General Assembly.[34]

An approach that classifies global issues according to the nature of the threat may succeed in effecting improvement in a particular area. In light of the increasing complexity and intertwined nature of crises, however, such an approach will not succeed in fundamentally alleviating people's suffering and ensuring access to necessary social goods. We need to develop the institutional capacity to implement comprehensive responses that prioritize the actual and expressed needs of people and build the foundation for lives of dignity.

Next, regarding the need for a decision-making process that is open to the participation of all governments, at present both UNDP and UNEP are structured so that only those states that are members of the respective governing councils have a final say in decisions. In light, however, of the importance of sustainable development and the wide range of issues and sectors involved, I believe we must ensure that all states that wish to may participate in deliberations.

Today, international society faces the challenge of developing effective modes of shared action, and the establishment of a firm institutional foundation would contribute greatly to advancing this cause. Reform efforts should be guided by the goal of establishing institutional frameworks for collaborative efforts with civil society and a point of focus enabling all people to take a leadership role for the future of the planet.

The kind of institutional reform I have in mind would continue, extend and crystallize the many efforts that have been undertaken in the years since the 1972 United Nations Conference on the Human Environment in Stockholm, the first global conference on international environmental issues.

The Stockholm Conference was noteworthy for the holding, parallel to intergovernmental discussions, of an NGO Forum attended by representatives

---

34   Ban Ki-moon. 2011. "Remarks to the General Assembly on 2011 Priorities." UN News. January 14.

of civil society and for the fact that there were calls for governments to include NGO representatives in their delegations. This was an important step toward reflecting the voices of civil society—"We the peoples" in the words of the UN Charter—in the activities of an organization marked by a strong tendency to function principally as a collection of sovereign states.

This marked the beginning of a stance of openness to the active participation of civil society that came to characterize a series of world conferences organized by the UN on such global challenges as population and food over the course of the 1970s and 1980s.

The 1992 Rio Earth Summit built on this tradition and advanced it dramatically. In addition to being the first UN Conference convened as a Summit, it was structured to facilitate participation by a broad range of actors from such fields as science and industry, as well as NGOs lacking official consultative status with the UN.

Where the Stockholm Conference was attended by only two heads of government, Rio was attended by ninety-four. Further, with a total of four times the number of participating NGOs, most of them engaged in grassroots activities in developing countries, this represented a major quantitative and qualitative advance over earlier conferences. Further, starting from the Earth Summit, a growing number of states began to include NGO representatives in their delegations to international conferences.

The German environmentalist Ernst Ulrich von Weizsäcker,[35] with whom I am currently conducting a serialized dialogue, has offered the following analysis of how the Earth Summit succeeded as a "huge undertaking"[36] enlisting the involvement of great numbers of the world's people.

> Without that momentum and public pressure it would have been easy for some governments to leave everything to diplomatic routine and thereby let the conference fail, an outcome nearly assured by the deep divide between North and South over the central issues.[37]

Building on this hard-won record of achievement, the Rio+20 Conference should be seized upon as an opportunity to place collaboration between the UN and civil society at the very heart of any institutional restructuring.

---

35   Ernst Ulrich von Weizsäcker (1939–), German scientist and politician.

36   Weizsäcker, Ernst Ulrich von. 1994. *Earth Politics*. London and New Jersey: Zed Books.

37   Ibid., p. 169.

A concrete model for this can be seen in the International Labour Organization (ILO), which adopts a tripartite system of governance consisting of the representatives of governments, business and labor. Similarly, any new organization should consider some variant of this, such as a four-party system that would ensure participation of the full spectrum of civil society actors and would consist of governments, NGOs, businesses and academic and research institutions.

Presently, the UN includes such frameworks as the Global Compact for industry and business and the Academic Impact for universities and other institutions of higher education, which enable these important actors to function as partners supporting the UN's activities. Both of these can be viewed as proactive undertakings by which different actors pursue the ethical imperative—what we *ought to* do. In this sense they share the kind of orientation I am proposing regarding the establishment of a new set of goals as discussed earlier—giving rise to positive value in the local community and society and generating change on a global scale.

The earliest draft of the outcome document issued in advance of the Rio+20 Conference emphasizes that "a fundamental prerequisite for the achievement of sustainable development is broad public participation in decision-making."[38] Establishing a solid institutional framework in this field based on the principle of facilitating collaboration between the UN and civil society will provide a precedent and practical model for creating similar institutions to tackle other global issues.

The last point I would like to discuss regarding institutional reform concerns the active engagement of young people, the members of the rising generation. Last autumn, UNEP convened a conference in which 1,400 children and youth from 118 countries gathered in Indonesia and adopted the Bandung Declaration, expressing their determination to take action. "Our planet's future—our future—is in peril. . . . We cannot wait another generation, until a Rio+40, before we act."[39]

We need to create, at the earliest opportunity, a focal point for the passion and power of youth, expressed in this declaration, so that they can move the human future in a new and more hopeful direction. I would like to call for the establishment of a "committee of the future generations" as a forum in which

---

38   UN (United Nations). 2012. "The Future We Want." Zero draft of the outcome document. January 10.

39   UN (United Nations). 2011. "The Voice of Children and Youth for Rio+20." 2011 Tunza International Children and Youth Conference. Bandung Declaration. October 1.

representatives of the youth of the world can consider paths to a sustainable future and advise the new sustainability organization on its annual plans and policies. This could further serve as a crucial node for strengthening youth action networks on a global scale.

Young people not only possess the strong desire to transform the world, they inherently possess the capacity to do so on a broad and expanding scale. The degree to which the UN is successful in drawing upon the enormous potential of youth will have a determinative impact on humanity's future.

I hope that institutional reform in this field will be guided by the principles I have outlined here. And I trust that the representatives of governments gathered at this conference will be inspired by a sense of responsibility to the future to consider fundamental reforms and to reach accords that will earn the respect and gratitude of future generations.

Learning for empowerment

The final area I would like to address concerns the establishment of an educational framework promoting sustainability. This would raise awareness among individuals and enable people to move from empowerment to leadership within their respective communities. It would encourage individuals to act as protagonists within their local community and to treasure the inalienable dignity of all people and the irreplaceable value of all that surrounds us.

Concretely, I would like to propose that the Conference recommend to the UN General Assembly the initiation of an "educational program for a sustainable global society," to start in 2015 and to follow up the work of the United Nations Decade of Education for Sustainable Development (2005–14).

Ten years ago, advocating the idea of such a decade to the 2002 World Summit on Sustainable Development (WSSD) in Johannesburg, I stressed the importance of comprehensive awareness-raising comprising three steps: to learn, to reflect and to empower.

Since the start of the Decade in 2005, schools and NGOs have deployed great creativity toward improving the means and techniques of raising people's awareness, and as a result there has been welcome progress in encouraging learning and reflection. But unless this gives rise to empowerment and, beyond that, to the exercise of leadership, it will not generate real transformation.

I therefore urge that any successor framework to the Decade be focused on this goal—fostering the capacities of large numbers of people, who can be genuine change agents spreading waves of hope wherever they go.

"Seeds of Change: The Earth Charter and Human Potential," an exhibition created by the SGI and the Earth Charter Initiative which was launched at the Johannesburg Summit and has since been shown in twenty-seven countries and territories around the world, and "Seeds of Hope: Visions of sustainability, steps toward change," a renewed version of the exhibition which premiered in 2010, were both developed with the determination that they would do more than simply inform, but would serve as catalysts to encourage people to take action and exercise leadership.

This is far from easy, but as Dr. Maathai demonstrated over the course of her life, the key to moving forward in this challenge lies in educational efforts grounded in the local community. I fully share her conviction, which she expressed memorably in the following words: "Education, if it means anything, should not take people away from the land, but instill in them even more respect for it, because educated people are in a position to understand what is being lost."[40]

In a book published 100 years ago (in 1912),[41] founding Soka Gakkai president Tsunesaburo Makiguchi, who dedicated his life to the research and practice of humanistic education, similarly urged that education be rooted in the lived realities of the local community. Upholding the belief that people do not exist apart from the land and that we cannot consider anything divorced from its relationship with people, Makiguchi called for the establishment of a community studies program that would bring together and unify all academic subjects—in what would today be called a core curriculum—and would treat the human and natural environment of the local community as a living textbook.

His aim was not simply to have children gain generic knowledge of the geographic implications of mountains and rivers or understand the ecological connections among the living inhabitants of oceans and forests, or even to develop their general understanding of nature.

He showed no interest in making children learn "the kind of isolated facts such as tend to comprise courses in natural history and can be carried about

---

40   Maathai, Wangari. 2008. *Unbowed: A Memoir.* London: Arrow Books, p. 138.
41   Makiguchi, Tsunesaburo. [1912]. *Kyoju no togo chushin toshite no kyodoka kenshu* [Research into Community Studies as the Integrating Focus of School Education] in *Makiguchi Tsunesaburo zenshu* [The Complete Works of Tsunesaburo Makiguchi]. Tokyo: Daisanbunmei-sha. Vol. 3.

at will."[42] Rather, he saw the goal of his educational program as helping children "gain a distinct awareness of the complex and multifaceted forces at work within the natural and human realms in the local community and the relationships that shape the process by which we develop and grow: to enable them to observe the myriad phenomena of nature and humanity that surround them and thus become cognizant of the subtle and exquisite mutual relationships that pertain among them all."[43]

He sought to encourage children to develop in the course of daily living a sense of the indissoluble bonds between people and the land, to foster appreciation for the seen and unseen ways in which the local community makes our existence possible, and to encourage a way of life in which this sense of appreciation gives rise to concrete action.

In the earlier (1903) work *Jinsei chirigaku,* Makiguchi wrote: "The noble human qualities of compassion, goodwill, friendship, kindness, earnestness and simplicity cannot be fostered outside the context of the local community."[44]

He also wrote this about the local community:

> The knowledge and virtues that learners will require when they later become active in the larger society are all present in outline in this microcosm. If we scrupulously observe the realities that surround us, we can establish the principles which will later be necessary for understanding the world.[45]

Makiguchi saw the local community as the place where the various principles by which society and the world operate come together in directly observable form. His program of community studies was founded on this central awareness. Through it, he sought to instill in children the basic tenets of a contributive way of life—to work for the good of local and national society, and of humanity as a whole, based on a sense of the mutual interdependence of all life developed through the child's interactions with the local community.

---

42   (trans. from) Makiguchi, Tsunesaburo. 1981–97. *Makiguchi Tsunesaburo zenshu* [The Complete Works of Tsunesaburo Makiguchi]. 10 vols. Tokyo: Daisanbunmei-sha. Vol. 3, p. 59.

43   Ibid. Vol. 3, p. 66.

44   Ibid. Vol. 1, p. 25.

45   Ibid. Vol. 1, pp. 25–26.

Makiguchi did not consider the local community in the narrow sense of one's hometown or native place, but rather, more broadly as the foundation for one's present life—the place where one walks and lives, where one sees and hears and is moved by various events. Makiguchi understood our sense of belonging and rootedness as members of a local community to be the foundation for a consciousness of global citizenship:

> To know that our life extends to the entire world. The world is our home, and all the nations within it are the field of our action.[46]

Drawing from Makiguchi's insights, I would like to suggest three qualities of community-based education for a successor framework to the Decade of Education for Sustainable Development.

- It should not stop at simply providing knowledge of the natural environment, customs and history of the local community, but should encourage feelings of affection for that community and the determination to treasure it.
- It should inspire a deep sense of appreciation for the ways in which the surrounding environment, including the productive and economic activities of others living in the community, enhances our lives: it should encourage daily actions based on that sense of appreciation.
- It should enable people to consider the issues of the local community in terms of what we must protect for the sake of future generations and the kind of society we must construct on their behalf, placing this at the heart of our way of life.

This kind of education cannot be successfully promoted simply through classroom instruction, but requires the flexible and proactive involvement of the local community to create opportunities for people of all generations and all walks of life to learn together. This should involve the entire community, transforming it into a site for lifelong learning in which the concerns and aspirations of all are shared and passed from generation to generation.

---

46   Ibid. Vol. 1, p. 13.

It is also important to provide regular opportunities for children to take the lead in protecting the local environment and enhancing the sustainability of the community. They should be able to point out issues and problems that might elude the observation of adults, and to offer proposals for their resolution.

Just as Dr. Maathai was able to acutely sense the crisis facing her community through the loss of the fig tree she had treasured as a symbol of her village since childhood, we must learn to read the signs in small changes before threats escalate beyond remedy. The local community is where people can take action to halt the damage before it is too late.

One aspect of global crises is that they arise from destructive spirals that impact different localities, gaining seemingly unstoppable momentum. Conversely, unless we can respond effectively to global crises, we cannot hope to protect local communities from the dangers and threats they face. This is the significance of the local community: it is a place where people can recognize small changes as the symptoms of larger issues and can, by framing this in a greater scheme of meaning, convert a sense of distress into determination and action. By protecting our respective communities and expanding solidarity among them, we can confront even the most pressing global threats. And we can engage in the kind of patient community building that will open a broad path to the sustainable global society of the future.

Contributing to transformation

The proposals I have made here regarding shared goals for sustainability, institutional reform and promotion of an educational framework grow from my sense that our key challenge here is to foster individuals capable of being change agents spreading hope wherever they go throughout their lives.

Considering the prospects for this important Conference, I am reminded of the words of Aurelio Peccei in our dialogue *Before It Is Too Late*.

> There exists in each individual a natural endowment of qualities and abilities that have been left dormant but that can be brought out and employed to redress the deteriorating human condition. . . .
>
> [This human potential] can become the trump card up our sleeve that can help us turn the tables. The innate, vital resourcefulness and intelligence intrinsically innate in every human being, from the most talented and fortunate to the most deprived and marginal,

constitute the unequalled patrimony of our species, though now we squander and misuse it badly.[47]

It is education and learning that will turn the limitless possibilities possessed by all people—"the unequalled patrimony of our species"—into a wellspring of energy for meeting the unprecedented challenge of building a sustainable global society.

Learning can take place anywhere, wherever people come together; it is something in which we can all take part. And even when its results are not immediately apparent, it takes deep root within society and exerts an increasingly positive influence as it is passed from one generation to the next.

This is the reason the SGI's efforts to promote the resolution of global issues are always focused on the idea of empowerment—by, for and of the people.

As the titles of the exhibitions we have organized to stimulate consideration and dialogue about paths to a sustainable future—"Seeds of Change" and "Seeds of Hope"—indicate, we firmly believe that planting the seeds of a new awareness in the hearts of people is the most effective means of transforming the world. The Buddhist scriptures state: "Even a single seed, when it is planted, will grow and produce much fruit."[48]

In our activities to protect ecological integrity in various countries, we have always focused on education. This year marks the twentieth anniversary of the founding of the SGI's Amazon Ecological Conservation Center (AECC) in Manaus, Brazil. In addition to projects to restore degraded tropical rainforest, the Center also promotes environmental education, through which local residents learn to take the lead in building a sustainable future.

Through these activities and other exchanges, it has been my honor to develop a friendship with Amadeu Thiago de Mello,[49] one of Brazil's foremost poets who has worked for years to protect the Amazonian rainforest, "the lungs of the world."

I would like to offer, as a coda to this proposal, an impromptu verse that the poet shared with me when we met in Tokyo in April 1997.

---

47   Peccei, Aurelio and Daisaku Ikeda. 2009. *Before It Is Too Late*. New York: I.B.Tauris, p. 110.

48   (trans. from) Nichiren. 1952. *Nichiren Daishonin gosho zenshu* [The Complete Works of Nichiren Daishonin]. Ed. by Nichiko Hori. Tokyo: Soka Gakkai, p. 971.

49   Amadeu Thiago de Mello (1926–), Brazilian poet and activist.

I live armed with love,
to perform my work singing,
to construct a new day.
Love gives everything
without holding back.
Sharing hope,
I plant the light of new life.

Once they tried to silence
the cry of my heart's fraternity
in the peaks of the Andes
ablaze with flames.
But I rose above those flames
and continue to sing.

There are no new paths,
only new ways of walking them.

With the pain of the dispossessed,
the dark dreams
of the child who sleeps with hunger—
I have learned:
this Earth does not belong to me alone.
And I have learned, in truth,
that the most important thing
is to work, while we still have life,
to change what needs changing,
each in our way, each where we are.

Vivo armado de amor
para trabalhar cantando,
na construção da manhã.
Amor dá tudo o que tem:
reparto a minha esperança
e planto a claridade
da vida nova que vem.

Um dia, na cordilheira dos Andes ardendo em fogo,
quiseram calar o meu coração de companheiro.
Mas atravessei o incêndio e continuo a cantar.

Não tenho caminho novo,
o que tenho de novo é o jeito de caminhar.

Com a dor dos deserdados,
com o sonho escuro da criança que dorme com fome,
aprendi que o mundo não é só meu.
Mas sobretudo aprendi que, na verdade, o que importa
antes que a vida apodreça,
é trabalhar na mudança do que é preciso mudar.

Cada um na sua vez, cada qual no seu lugar.

Poverty and Human Development

The Elimination of Poverty (1996)[50]

The year 1995, which marked the fiftieth anniversary of the end of World War II, was an important turning point for our era. In many ways, it represents an invaluable opportunity to look back and evaluate the twentieth century as a whole.

Now that more than six years have passed since the end of the Cold War, we can reflect on the past with a measure of objectivity. In fact, historians and social scientists have been doing just that in recent years, and already several works dealing with recent history have been published. These works all share the common realization that any close examination of the problems that have erupted since the end of the Cold War inevitably leads to the study and assessment of the twentieth century in its entirety.

One such work is *The Age of Extremes: The Short Twentieth Century, 1914–1991* by the British historian Eric Hobsbawm,[51] published in 1994.

---

50 From 1996 Peace Proposal, "Toward the Third Millennium: The Challenge of Global Citizenship."

51 Eric Hobsbawm (1917–2012), British historian.

Hobsbawm had already dealt with the history of the nineteenth century in three previous works: *The Age of Revolution: Europe, 1789–1848, The Age of Capital: 1848–1875,* and *The Age of Empire: 1875–1914.* In *The Age of Extremes,* he defines "the long nineteenth century"[52] extending from 1789, when the French Revolution broke out, to 1914. During that time, he contends, civilization made virtually continual progress on the material, intellectual and moral levels. Hobsbawm then goes on to identify "the short twentieth century"[53] extending from the outbreak of World War I in 1914 to the collapse of the Soviet Union in 1991. According to Hobsbawm's analysis, this short twentieth century was characterized by the retreat of norms and standards that had once been taken for granted and the emergence of trends toward extremes of both productivity and destruction.

The twentieth century has indeed been incomparably more extreme than the nineteenth, both quantitatively and qualitatively. Its history chronicles one tragedy after another, including two World Wars, the Nazi Holocaust, the Soviet gulags, the plight of Palestinian and other refugees, the widespread massacres in Cambodia, *ad infinitum.* On several occasions, I have proposed various means of overcoming the horrors of what could be termed a century of war and brutality. It seems to me, however, that the real problem lies in the failure of human wisdom, by which we remain trapped in the vicissitudes of history, despite our heartfelt anguish at the misery of these events.

Former Soviet President Mikhail Gorbachev[54] echoes these sentiments in a collection of our dialogues that is currently being compiled. "The tragedy of the 20th century was that," he points out, "as a rule, people heeded counsel only after it was too late and the important chance had been missed."[55] Unless we bring to a halt the accelerating tendency toward extremes, acts of human folly will result in the self-destruction of the species.

Observing the unspeakable atrocities taking place in Rwanda, the former Yugoslavia and elsewhere in the wake of the Cold War, I feel strongly that our pain and anguish can no longer be considered a merely individual matter. If we do not squarely confront the question of what might be called the shared

---

52   Hobsbawm, Eric. 1994. *The Age of Extremes: The Short Twentieth Century, 1941–1991.* New York: Viking Penguin, p. 13.

53   Ibid., p. 56.

54   Mikhail Gorbachev (1931–), President of the Soviet Union (1990–91), recipient of the Nobel Prize for Peace in 1990.

55   Gorbachev, Mikhail and Daisaku Ikeda. 2005. *Moral Lessons of the Twentieth Century.* Trans. by Richard L. Gage. London and New York: I.B.Tauris, p. 87.

karma of humanity, we will have no way of overcoming the inhuman night-mares of the twentieth century.

We must not allow the approaching twenty-first century and the history of the third millennium to be sullied with the same kind of brutality and bloodshed that has ravaged the present era. I strongly appeal to all people to prevent the spread of fanaticism, which is so often used to justify inhuman acts. With every repetition of these tragedies, the price we have had to pay has been enormous. We must not let the bitter lessons of the twentieth century go to waste; rather, we must overcome the divisive forces that have once again emerged and, in the little time remaining in this century, place highest priority on generating the basis for a common struggle of humanity against such global problems as environmental degradation and poverty.

When we stop to consider this common struggle of humanity, I am reminded of the words of Dr. Aurelio Peccei,[56] cofounder of the Club of Rome. In our collection of dialogues entitled *Before It Is Too Late,* he states that we must "prepare responsibly and compassionately a way of life for the generations of those who will follow us."[57]

It will take many years and much effort to resolve the global problems we now face. The long-term endeavor toward their resolution can only be sustained by a strong and broad-based spirituality among people. I believe it is precisely to this motivating force that Dr. Peccei refers when he speaks of our responsibility for the future. We must carefully and prudently choose our paths of action based on a broad perception of the obligation we have to future generations of humanity and all forms of life.

In the course of our discussions, Dr. Peccei and I concluded that the true problem lies not in our ailing Earth but in the malaise of humanity itself; we also agreed on the pressing need for a "human revolution." Dr. Peccei empha-sized: "Only the human revolution can unearth our inner potential and make us feel fully what we really are and behave accordingly. . . ."[58] These words can truly be considered an expression of the ultimate goal of the "human revolution" movement that we of the SGI have undertaken on a global scale.

In 1989, the SGI sponsored the exhibition "War and Peace: From a Century of War to a Century of Hope" at the UN Headquarters in New York.

---

56   Aurelio Peccei (1908–84), Italian industrialist and cofounder of the Club of Rome.
57   Peccei, Aurelio and Daisaku Ikeda. 1984. *Before It Is Too Late.* Ed. by Richard L. Gage. Tokyo: Kodansha International Ltd., p. 129.
58   Ibid.

With hopes for the common struggle of humanity, I wrote as follows in my exhibition message:

> We cannot sit by passively. Like-minded people must unite in soli-
> darity to show proof in our time that nothing can defeat the courage
> and wisdom of the human being. Is this not the greatest heritage we
> can bequeath to the future?

Inspired by a sense of responsibility for the future, the SGI has sponsored many events over the years. As an NGO with official ties to the United Nations, we have held various exhibitions designed to raise awareness of global problems (including "Nuclear Arms: Threat to Our World," "War and Peace," and "The Amazon—Its Environment and Development"); we have supported the UN human rights education campaign with another series of exhibitions (including "Toward A Century of Humanity: An Overview of Human Rights in Today's World," "What are Children's Rights?" and an exhibition on the Holocaust entitled "The Courage to Remember"); and we have pursued various humanitarian activities throughout the world to support the efforts of the office of the UN High Commissioner for Refugees (UNHCR).

***

The United Nations has designated 1996 as the International Year for the Eradication of Poverty, and the First UN Decade for the Eradication of Poverty will begin in 1997. It is thus preparing to put its full strength into solving the perennial problem of poverty, which was one of the principal themes of the World Summit for Social Development (WSSD) held in March 1995.

In "An Agenda for Development" published in May 1994, UN Secretary-General Boutros Boutros-Ghali[59] pointed out that many of the causes for the world's conflicts can be traced to the fact that more than 1 billion people live on this planet in a condition of "absolute poverty."[60] According to the World Bank's "Social Indicators of Development 1995," 1.1 billion people cannot obtain even the minimum necessary nutrition or satisfy basic human needs.

---

59   Boutros Boutros-Ghali (1922–), Egyptian statesman and 6th UN Secretary-
      General (1992–96).
60   UNGA (United Nations General Assembly). 1994. "An Agenda for
      Development." A/48/935. Report of the Secretary-General. May 6.

With the world population estimated at about 5.8 billion people, this means that at least one out of every six people lives in extreme poverty.[61]

The problem lies not just in the magnitude of these numbers but in their ceaseless increase. The World Bank estimates that in the absence of effective countermeasures, 1.3 billion people will live in absolute poverty by the year 2000.[62] Similarly, the World Health Organization (WHO) states in its "World Health Report 1995" that "[t]he world's most ruthless killer and the greatest cause of suffering on earth is . . . extreme poverty."[63] The report goes on to warn that one-third of all the world's children suffer from malnutrition.[64]

Various efforts have been made at the national level and through the UN and concerned organizations to deal with the issue of poverty. Those efforts have proven inadequate, however, and we have made little headway toward a solution. In the post-Cold War era, we often witness conditions of poverty and want feeding the flames of confrontation, and the resulting conflicts cause deeper and more widespread destitution. This spiral of interlocking violence and poverty has devastated such countries as Somalia and Rwanda.

According to a report issued by the International Federation of Red Cross and Red Crescent Societies last year (1995), there are currently fifty-six armed conflicts raging in the world; some 16 million people have been forced to flee to foreign territory; and some 26 million have become displaced persons within their own countries.[65] Thus, with their lives, freedom and property threatened, nearly 1 percent of the world's people have been driven from their homes.

Further, the advanced industrialized nations, partly due to global economic stagnation, are increasingly showing signs of "donor fatigue" in their dealings with developing countries. In fact, the Economic and Development Review Committee of the Organisation for Economic Co-operation and Development (OECD), which coordinates the official development assistance (ODA) provided by advanced countries, announced a policy in May of last year that would reduce the future number of recipient countries and regions.

---

61 World Bank. 1995. "Social Indicators of Development 1995: World Development Indicators." Washington DC: The World Bank.

62 Ibid.

63 WHO (World Health Organization). 1995. "The World Health Report 1995: Bridging the Gaps," p. 1.

64 Ibid., p. 6.

65 International Federation of Red Cross and Red Crescent Societies. 1995. "World Disasters Report 1995." Geneva: Martinus Nijhoff Publishers, p. 7.

Some scholars claim that the current situation simply reflects the dead end that has been reached by what has been called a "systemless system." Unless an international framework can be created that will shift the focus away from bilateral assistance, which tends inevitably to be shaped by arbitrary and self-serving interests, it will be difficult to prevent the situation from worsening.

The international community must earnestly seek effective legal and institutional measures that will realize the spirit enshrined in the Universal Declaration of Human Rights, which states in its Preamble that "the advent of a world in which human beings shall enjoy freedom of speech and belief and freedom from fear and want has been proclaimed as the highest aspiration of the common people."[66]

As I have stated in the past, it is my belief that we need to shift toward a new concept of "human security," which centers not on the security of states but on the well-being of people.

Dr. Arnold J. Toynbee[67] once observed that the way to determine whether aid is offered with correct long-term goals is to ascertain whether it is designed to link material assistance with spiritual assistance.[68] As Dr. Toynbee suggests, assistance up to now has tended to focus on macroeconomic development of the recipient country. In this sense, development efforts have not been sufficiently focused on those who are suffering from poverty, or on education, health or other fields that must be accorded priority for "human development." For this reason, I feel it is imperative that we effect a fundamental reorientation of current assistance programs.

When people's basic needs are met and they are given the opportunity to establish their lives, they naturally develop their abilities and, manifesting those abilities, begin to take an active role in society. Once people are set on a path to "human development"—one which encourages self-reliance and autonomy—the societies and nations to which they belong move steadily toward stability. It is therefore critical that we achieve a transition to this type of participatory development.

The word "development" has strong utilitarian overtones. In contrast, "human development" encompasses a broader conceptual framework that includes the element of individual commitment. As such, its main aim is to

---

66   UN (United Nations). 1948. "Preamble" in "Universal Declaration of Human Rights."

67   Arnold J. Toynbee (1889–1975), British historian.

68   Peccei, Aurelio and Daisaku Ikeda. 1984. *Before It Is Too Late*. Ed. by Richard L. Gage. Tokyo: Kodansha International Ltd., p. 37.

draw forth the limitless capacities of citizens. With the UN playing a pivotal role, we must strive to create an environment that will encourage and foster the inner potentialities of each individual, as these constitute a resource that is "both renewable and expandable."[69]

Doing so will make it possible to stop armed conflicts before they begin, and to prevent the deadly spiral of violence that brings such misery to humankind. I am convinced that we must take a direct approach to the intractable problem of eradicating poverty as a first step toward correcting the distortions and imbalances that presently afflict global society.

Efforts are already being made to establish new ethical underpinnings that will support this endeavor. In January 1995, the Commission on Global Governance (an international group of twenty-six intellectuals and activists of global stature) published their final report, *Our Global Neighborhood*. The central vision of this work is the fostering of an ethic of world citizenship and the enhancement and strengthening of global civil society.[70]

Last year (1995), a series of three "United Nations Renaissance Conferences" was sponsored by the Boston Research Center for the 21st Century,[71] an SGI-affiliated peace research institute. Participants discussed the need, if the coming century is to be an era of hope, for an awakened world citizenry to unite in solidarity in bringing about fundamental changes in our thought and institutions. In particular, there was consensus that a clear vision is necessary for there to be a true transformation within society and that constructive reforms in the UN and other global institutions must arise from changes within the hearts of people.

We can say with confidence that the most pressing need of our times is for world citizens who will respond with courage and imagination to the deepening global crisis of human dignity.

As my thoughts turn to this most urgent of issues, I am reminded of the works of Karl Jaspers.[72] In the peace proposal I issued on the thirteenth anniversary of the founding of the SGI in 1988, I argued, citing historical parallels to what Jaspers called the "Axial Period,"[73] that our present age, more than

---

69   Ibid., p. 116.
70   Commission on Global Governance. 1995. *Our Global Neighborhood: The Report of the Commission on Global Governance.* New York: Oxford University Press.
71   Subsequently renamed the Ikeda Center for Peace, Learning, and Dialogue.
72   Karl Jaspers (1883–1969), German philosopher.
73   Jaspers, Karl. 1965. *The Origin and Goal of History.* Trans. by Michael Bullock. New Haven and London: Yale University Press, p. 1.

any past era, demands individuals committed to the welfare of the whole of humankind. Jaspers stated a fundamental truth when he wrote:

> We must seek the philosophical idea and the thinker in their physical reality. The truth does not hover all alone in the air of abstraction.[74]

He manifested his commitment to this credo through his unwavering involvement, broad-ranging interests and relentless examination of the essential issues of our age.

Jaspers wrote books pertaining directly to current political issues, including *Man in the Modern Age* (1931; English translation 1933) written just prior to the Nazi ascent to power, followed by *The Question of German Guilt* (1946) immediately after the collapse of the Third Reich, and *The Atomic Bomb and the Future of Man* (1961). His way of life was such that his disciple, Hannah Arendt,[75] was moved to comment as follows: "Jaspers, at least in all his writings after 1933, has always written as if to answer for himself before all of mankind."[76]

Jaspers has this to say to those who have grown idle in the midst of a false and superficial peace:

> We can enjoy the happiness of existence in the interim granted to us. But it is a last respite. Either we avert the deadly peril or prepare for the catastrophe.[77]

He then leaves us with this warning:

> Today we stand poised on the razor's edge. We have to choose: to plunge into the abyss of man's lostness, and the consequent extinction of all earthly life, or the leap to the authentic man and his boundless opportunities through self-transformation.[78]

---

74   Jaspers, Karl. 1951. *Way to Wisdom: An Introduction to Philosophy.* Trans. by Ralph Manheim. London: Victor Gollancz Ltd., p. 134.

75   Hannah Arendt (1906–75), German-born American political scientist and philosopher.

76   Arendt, Hannah. 1970. *Men in Dark Times.* San Diego, New York and London: Harcourt Brace & Company, p. 75.

77   Jaspers, Karl. 1967. *Philosophy is for Everyman.* Trans. by R. F. C. Hull and Grete Wels. New York: Harcourt, Brace and World, Inc., p. 124.

78   Ibid.

According to Jaspers, as long as this "last respite" is nothing more than a postponement, we cannot afford to turn our eyes from the harsh reality that surrounds us. The concept of "world citizen" is not a distant or disembodied one. I believe that the transformation of the self into what Jaspers calls the "authentic man" will be the first step toward world citizenship.

How can we speak of the future of humankind if we are so desolate of spirit and desensitized that we can ignore the sufferings and the threats to the dignity of those with whom we share this world?

One of the necessary attributes of a world citizen is a shift in focus toward the welfare of humankind. Unless we discipline our spirits through our day-to-day experience, however, such a conceptual shift alone will not give us the strength we need to set a new course for our times.

This is in fact one of the issues the SGI is now attempting to address through our movement for human revolution. Simply stated, this movement is dedicated to encouraging people to become aware of their own bound-less inner power and to take responsibility for the welfare of humankind. Although it may seem an indirect approach, I am convinced that this human revolution, with its first principle of inner transformation, is in fact the most certain path toward realizing a genuine global revolution.

A Global Marshall Plan (2000)[79]

The United Nations has designated its fifty-fifth General Assembly, scheduled to open in September 2000, the Millennium Assembly of the United Nations, and aims to "articulate and affirm an animating vision for the UN in the new era" and "provide an opportunity to strengthen the role of the UN in meeting the challenges of the twenty-first century."[80]

A Millennium Summit of the United Nations, attended by world leaders, is also scheduled as an integral part of this. The overall theme of the summit will be "the United Nations in the twenty-first century," with the subtopics of peace and security, including disarmament; development, including poverty eradication; human rights; and strengthening the United Nations.

***

---

79   From 2000 Peace Proposal, "Peace through Dialogue: A Time to Talk."

80   UN (United Nations). 1999. "The Millennium Assembly of the United Nations." A/RES/53/202. Resolution adopted by the General Assembly. February 12.

The eradication of poverty, one of the four specific subtopics of the Millennium Summit, is a humanitarian challenge of great urgency. One effect of globalization has been an ever-growing gap between rich and poor. While people in a few countries consume a disproportionately massive amount of resources and enjoy affluent lifestyles, fully one-quarter of the world's population subsists in extreme poverty. For these people, human dignity is under constant assault. We must eliminate these obscene imbalances if we are to fulfill our responsibilities for the new millennium.

It is not impossible to achieve that goal. According to an estimate by the United Nations Development Programme (UNDP), the costs of eradicating poverty would be about 1 percent of global income and no more than 2 to 3 percent of national income in all but the poorest countries. Cuts in military spending, with the savings channeled to poverty reduction and measures for human development, would realize a considerable alleviation of the problem.[81]

Poverty is one of the key causes of conflict, as it destabilizes societies. Poverty gives rise to conflict, which in turn further aggravates poverty. Choosing to sever this vicious circle would simultaneously lead to the eradication of one of the causes of war and resolve this global injustice. Removing the causes of war and poverty that menace human dignity will enhance enjoyment of human rights.

The 1999 Cologne Economic Summit adopted the Cologne Debt Initiative to speed up debt relief for heavily indebted poor countries (HIPCs). The initiative seeks to ensure that resources made available by debt relief will be invested in poverty alleviation and social development in areas such as education, nutrition and sanitation and health care.

I welcome this as one tangible step toward the eradication of poverty, and call for ever more bold thinking in this regard. We need a total commitment to enabling these societies to raise themselves out of poverty—a program to be implemented with determination and consistency, equivalent, perhaps, to a "Global Marshall Plan." The UN should be at the center of efforts to take the Summit's agreements further—to a deeper level—toward a global community that protects and nurtures all members of the human family.

Regarding the promotion of human development on a global level, I would also like to call for the extension of the functions of UN Houses, which are

---

81 See UNDP (United Nations Development Programme). 1997. "Human Development Report 1997: Human Development to Eradicate Poverty." New York and Oxford: Oxford University Press, p. 12.

centers to coordinate various UN programs and agencies in each country. The original purpose of the UN Houses was to improve cooperation between UN agencies engaged in development and related projects. The plan sought to bring together the various bodies active in each country into a common building called a UN House, to encourage coordination of their activities under the banner of the UN.

It is my suggestion that the role of UN Houses be broadened one step further, that they function as a UN Embassy in each country and thus play a comprehensive role as a local center for the promotion of substantive programs as well as public information activities.

Efforts at poverty eradication and human development require in particular that plans be based on a thorough understanding of unique local circumstances. By bringing together and giving a permanent standing to the avenues of communication with governments, implementation of such plans would surely become smoother.

An Earth Forum for Social Justice (2001)[82]

According to the World Bank's *World Development Report 2000/2001: Attacking Poverty,* 1.2 billion people, approximately 20 percent of the world's population, live on less than US$1 a day. And all indications are that this number is, if anything, increasing.[83]

Last year (2000), the World Bank also published an important report titled *Voices of the Poor.*[84] This is the product of a ten-year effort to collect the firsthand voices of some sixty thousand people from sixty countries. Conveying the actual realities of poverty-stricken lives, the study seeks to illuminate the underlying nature of the problem and what poor people seek.

The World Bank urges that the following points be considered in implementing policies and assistance programs:

1. Expanding economic opportunities for the poor to free themselves from poverty;

---

82 From 2001 Peace Proposal, "Creating and Sustaining a Century of Life: Challenges for a New Era."

83 See World Bank. 2000. *World Development Report 2000/2001: Attacking Poverty.* New York: Oxford University Press, p. vi.

84 World Bank. 2000. *Voices of the Poor.* 3 vols. New York: Oxford University Press.

2. Empowering people to shape decisions that affect their lives and work; and

3. Developing basic infrastructure and programs to extend assistance during disasters and emergencies.

The Nobel prize-winning economist Amartya Sen[85] echoes this view. In his book *Development as Freedom,* he maintains that people should not merely be regarded as the beneficiaries of development programs but that:

> With adequate social opportunities, individuals can effectively shape their own destiny and help each other. They need not be seen primarily as passive recipients of the benefits of cunning development programs.[86]

I completely agree with Dr. Sen that people should be seen as the agents of change. It is crucial to find out from the people themselves what is needed and reflect it in assistance and development programs rather than arbitrarily planning these in a unilateral, "top-down" manner. This is the true significance of democratization.

At the international level there should be a permanent forum where the voices of marginalized people can be heard. Currently, it is only the wealthy developed countries that have created opportunities, such as the Organisation for Economic Co-operation and Development (OECD) summits and the annual meeting of the World Economic Forum in Davos, Switzerland, to come together and discuss the direction of international politics and economics.

Here I would like to propose that what might be called an "Earth Forum" be established as a bridge between the people of the developing countries and these meetings of the world's wealthy. This could facilitate dialogue and discussion toward a global society that is truly just and equitable.

I envision that this forum would centrally involve the participation of the developing countries through their governmental and nongovernmental representatives, as well as those of international bodies, including the Secretary-General of the United Nations. Sharing and learning from the

---

85   Amartya Sen (1933–), Indian economist, recipient of the Nobel Prize in Economic Sciences in 1998.

86   Sen, Amartya. 1999. *Development as Freedom.* New York: Anchor Books-Random House, Inc., p. 11.

failures as well as the best practices of various countries and agencies, it would encourage the kind of globalization policies that will truly respect developing countries' points of view, the kind of human development that will meet the real needs of people. This forum could meet twice a year, sending representatives to summit meetings and Davos to present its findings and demands, ensuring that the views of the developing world are more adequately reflected in the agendas of these conferences.

The G8 Kyushu-Okinawa Summit 2000 was the first OECD summit that included dialogue between the leaders of developed and developing countries. This experience should be built on, and such dialogue should be made an integral part of the ongoing summit process. This kind of dialogue is vital to unite the world's people in the cause of eradicating poverty and the untold suffering it causes.

The Millennium Development Goals (2003)[87]

The Commission on Human Security (CHS) was launched in June 2001. This Commission is preparing a report on ways to promote public understanding of the concept of human security and to ensure that human security becomes a universal operational tool for policy formulation and implementation throughout international society. The Commission's report is slated for publication in June this year (2003).

A group of thirty-six researchers working in the field of human security has been discussing these issues, and the fruits of their work have been brought together as an open letter on human security to the chairs of the CHS. This report concentrates on four viewpoints: the need to focus on day-to-day insecurities; the need to focus on the most vulnerable segments of society; the need to respect diversity; and the need to encourage reciprocity. It calls for attention to be paid to the problems arising from militarism and globalization as threats to human security.[88] These are all concepts that I have stressed for many years, and I strongly endorse this research.

***

---

87   From 2003 Peace Proposal, "A Global Ethic of Coexistence: Toward a 'Life-Sized' Paradigm for Our Age."

88   Mushakoji, Kinhide, ed. and trans. 2002. "Ningen anzen hosho nitsuiteno kokaishokan" [Open Letter on Human Security]. *Sekai*. May. Tokyo: Iwanami Shoten, pp. 187–98.

According to a report by the United Nations Development Programme (UNDP), the number of people around the world who have to survive on less than US$2 a day is 2.8 billion, with 1.2 billion forced to subsist on less than US$1 a day. The number of people suffering from malnutrition is thought to exceed 800 million.[89] It is imperative that the international community take determined steps to remedy this intolerable situation.

In the United Nations Millennium Declaration, adopted three years ago (2000), the world's leaders pledged themselves to action on this subject: "We will spare no effort to free our fellow men, women and children from the abject and dehumanizing conditions of extreme poverty."[90]

The UN Millennium Project contains numerous goals to be achieved by the year 2015. These consist of eight core goals divided into eighteen[91] specific, concrete targets, including halving the proportion of people living on less than US$1 a day and halving the proportion of people living in hunger. These goals were distilled from the various international conferences held during the 1990s as well as the UN Millennium Summit in 2000. Together they are referred to as the Millennium Development Goals (MDGs).

The cooperation of all countries will be required if the Millennium Development Goals are to be achieved. Further, this will serve as a powerful symbol of the unity of the international community. However, at the present pace, thirty-three countries, between them representing more than one-fourth of the world's population, will be unable to achieve even half of the targets. UNDP has issued a report that powerfully concludes: "Without a dramatic turnaround there is a real possibility that a generation from now, world leaders will be setting the same targets again."[92]

In my peace proposal three years ago (2000), I called for the implementation of a program equivalent to a "Global Marshall Plan." The original Marshall Plan after World War II, on which this idea was based, is a successful

---

89 See UNDP (United Nations Development Programme). 2002. "Human Development Report 2002: Deepening Democracy in a Fragmented World." New York: Oxford University Press, pp. 17–21.

90 UNGA (United Nations General Assembly) 2000. "United Nations Millennium Declaration." A/RES/55/2. Resolution adopted by the General Assembly. September 8.

91 Subsequently increased to twenty-one.

92 UNGA (United Nations General Assembly). 2002. "Implementation of the United Nations Millennium Declaration." A/57/270. Report of the Secretary-General. July 31, p. 2.

example of victors giving concrete form to the power of self-control. We deeply need to work to embody this same spirit of self-control on a global scale now.

In that sense, I welcome the decision by the World Summit on Sustainable Development (WSSD) last year (2002) to create a World Solidarity Fund. This idea was included in the WSSD action plan, the Global Implementation Document, and was officially approved by the UN General Assembly in December 2002.[93] It will create the first fund to specifically target the eradication of poverty and promote social and human development. Like the Global Environment Facility (GEF, created after the 1992 Rio Earth Summit), it is significant as a fund established as the outcome of a global summit.

The UN, too, is issuing an annual Report of the Secretary-General covering progress toward achieving the MDGs. In this regard, I would like to propose that world summits be held periodically toward the year 2015 in order to ensure that the world's heads of state and government are thoroughly informed of the content of these reports and to further strengthen international cooperation in this regard. Every second year might be an appropriate timing for such meetings.

This would enable world leaders to gather together before the start of the UN General Assembly, creating a forum for them to focus on the peace and well-being of humanity in the twenty-first century. I think this would be a forward-looking, hope-filled development. Such summits would not have to be held only at the UN Headquarters in New York: In fact, I think it would be preferable that they take place in those parts of the world most severely beset by poverty and starvation.

To strengthen the frameworks of international cooperation in this way, it will be essential to have the deep-rooted support and involvement of the people of the world. The UN has launched the Millennium Campaign aiming to create an environment in which people can expand their personal awareness of the MDGs and whereby various organizations and entities can cooperate toward their achievement.

The SGI thoroughly endorses the goals of this campaign and will wholeheartedly embark on activities to spread awareness at the grassroots level, in

---

93   UNGA (United Nations General Assembly). 2002. "Environment and Sustainable Development: Implementation of Agenda 21 and the Programme for the Further Implementation of Agenda 21." A/57/532/Add.1. Report of the Second Committee. December 12.

forms such as exhibitions and seminars focusing on related issues. We are also keen to contribute to the creation of a global network of academics and researchers, especially through the activities of the Boston Research Center for the 21st Century (BRC).[94] Last year, for example, the BRC published *Subverting Greed: Religious Perspectives on the Global Economy,*[95] which explores the prospects for global economic justice.

In addition to poverty and starvation, one of the most pressing issues we face is that of water resources. At present, 40 percent of the world's population face a shortage of water, with 1.1 billion people lacking access to safe drinking water. Some 2.5 billion lack access to basic sanitation. It is estimated that more than 5 million die from water-related diseases every year, ten times the number of people killed in wars, on average, each year. UN Secretary-General Kofi Annan[96] has stated: "No single measure would do more to reduce disease and save lives in the developing world than bringing safe water and sanitation to all."[97] This is indeed an urgent task.

This year, 2003, has been designated by the UN as the International Year of Freshwater. The 3rd World Water Forum will be held in Japan in March. I feel that Japan, as the host country of this event, should play an active role in areas such as technological support and the provision of skilled personnel.

The global water problem was one of the core themes of the WSSD last year, where Japan and the United States announced a joint initiative called "Clean Water for People." In the past, Japan has been actively engaged in this field, helping provide more than 40 million people around the world with access to safe drinking water and sanitation. Making full use of this experience, I hope that Japan will demonstrate meaningful leadership in the field of water resources.

---

94   Subsequently renamed the Ikeda Center for Peace, Learning, and Dialogue.

95   Knitter, Paul F. and Chandra Muzaffar, eds. 2002. *Subverting Greed: Religious Perspectives on the Global Economy*. New York: Orbis. Published in association with the Boston Research Center for the 21st Century.

96   Kofi Annan (1938–), Ghanaian statesman, 7th Secretary-General of the United Nations (1997–2006).

97   Annan, Kofi. 2000. "We the Peoples: The Role of the United Nations in the 21st Century." New York: United Nations, p. 60.

A Global Primary Education Fund (2004)[98]

Human security is a concept that has emerged in recent years from the effort to rethink established notions of security. It is a new approach centered on security for people rather than states. It addresses not only the threats posed by direct forms of violence such as war, terrorism and crime, but also poverty and environmental pollution, violation of human rights, discrimination and lack of access to education and sanitation. These are all issues that seriously impact the safety and dignity of human beings.

In his New Year's message, UN Secretary-General Kofi Annan[99] warned that the war in Iraq had distracted the world from addressing threats that kill "millions and millions of people every year" such as extreme poverty and hunger, unsafe drinking water, environmental degradation and infectious disease. He appealed to world leaders to make 2004 "the year when we begin to turn the tide."[100]

Since the United Nations Development Programme (UNDP) first outlined the basic concept of human security in 1994, recognition of its importance has been growing steadily. The year 2001 saw the formation of the Commission on Human Security, whose report "Human Security Now: Protecting and Empowering People" was released in May 2003. Reviewing the evolution of the concept, the report defines human security as "protecting fundamental freedoms—freedoms that are the essence of life" and "protecting people from critical and pervasive threats and situations."[101]

What I find striking about the report is that it identifies empowerment, together with protection, as one of the two keys to the realization of human security. It stresses the importance of developing the innate strengths and abilities of human beings, empowering them to find their own happiness as they contribute to society:

> People's ability to act on their own behalf—and on behalf of others—is the second key to human security. Fostering that ability

---

98 From 2004 Peace Proposal, "Inner Transformation: Creating a Global Groundswell for Peace."

99 Kofi Annan (1938–), Ghanaian statesman, 7th Secretary-General of the United Nations (1997–2006).

100 UN (United Nations). 2003. "Secretary-General's Message for New Year, 2004." SG/SM/9095. Press Release. December 24.

101 Commission on Human Security. 2003. "Human Security Now: Protecting and Empowering People." New York: Commission on Human Security, p. 4.

differentiates human security from state security, from humanitarian work and even from much development work. Empowerment is important because people develop their potential as individuals and as communities.[102]

This resonates with my own conviction that the struggle to create something of new and positive value within society by taking action for the sake of others forms the indestructible foundation for peace.

As I have stressed on many occasions, I believe that education must be the focus of efforts to extend human security. In the world today, 860 million adults are said to be illiterate, and 121 million children have no access to school.[103] The Education for All campaign, spearheaded by UNESCO, aims to realize universal basic education with concrete benchmarks for achievement. Last year was also the start of the United Nations Literacy Decade (2003–12).

Literacy opens the door to knowledge, empowering people to develop their innate abilities and fulfill their potential. Raising literacy rates among women, who account for two-thirds of the illiterate, and providing girls with greater access to primary education would undoubtedly prove powerful in improving the lives not only of women but also of their families and communities.

"The State of the World's Children 2004," released by UNICEF in December 2003, warns that none of the world's development objectives can be achieved without progress in girls' education, and calls for urgent reform of international development efforts.[104] Lack of funding has caused many countries to fall behind in the drive for universal primary education, and this is an obstacle that needs to be eliminated through international cooperation.

According to estimates by the UN and the World Bank, the target of realizing primary education for all by the year 2015 could be achieved if just four days' worth of the world's annual military expenditure were diverted to education every year.[105] Universal primary education is one of the UN's eight

---

102 Ibid., p. 11.

103 See UNGA (United Nations General Assembly). 2002. "United Nations Literacy Decade: Education for All." A/RES/56/116. Resolution adopted by the General Assembly. January 18.

104 See UNICEF (United Nations Children's Fund). 2004. "The State of the World's Children 2004".

105 See Commission on Human Security. 2003. *Human Security Now*. New York: Commission on Human Security, pp. 117–18.

Millennium Development Goals. To help us move closer to achieving it, I believe there is a definite role for a "global primary education fund" as a focus for greater international funding cooperation.

A "Water for Life" Fund (2008)[106]

I would like to call attention once more to the Millennium Development Goals (MDGs), which aim to establish the social and life-supporting infrastructure that is indispensable to maintaining human dignity.

The MDGs include such concrete objectives as reducing by half the number of people suffering from poverty and hunger, and the year 2007 represented the halfway point toward the target date of 2015. According to the UN progress assessment, there is real concern that these goals will not be attained at the present pace, despite improvements in such areas as primary school enrollment in developing countries and declines in the extreme poverty rate and child mortality.

In July 2007, the leaders of the US, Canada, Japan, Ghana, Brazil, India and a number of European countries signed the Declaration on the Millennium Development Goals by Heads of State. UK Prime Minister Gordon Brown[107] took the lead in calling for this declaration; it confirms the importance of mustering the political will in both developed and developing countries to bring together "the right policies and right reforms . . . combined with sufficient resources."[108]

The UN designated the years 2005–15 as the International Decade for Action "Water for Life" and 2008 as the International Year of Sanitation. In this context, I would like to urge the creation of a global framework that brings together the right policies, the right reforms and sufficient resources to secure access to safe water and sanitary living conditions for all the world's people.

Today, more than 1 billion people are denied the right to safe water, and 2.6 billion do not have access to adequate sanitation. As a result, about 1.8 million children die every year from diarrhea and other diseases. Moreover, the burden of collecting water falls unevenly on the millions of women and

---

106 From 2008 Peace Proposal, "Humanizing Religion, Creating Peace."

107 Gordon Brown (1951–), British Prime Minister (2007–10).

108 DFID (Department for International Development). 2007. "Declaration on the Millennium Development Goals by Heads of State."

girls charged with doing this for their families every day. This in turn reinforces gender inequalities in employment and education. Chronic ill health
due to the lack of safe water and sanitation undermines productivity and
economic growth, deepening global inequalities and trapping vulnerable
people in cycles of poverty.

The United Nations Development Programme (UNDP) considers
overcoming the water and sanitation crisis to be one of the crucial human
development challenges for the first half of this century and stresses that
success here will without doubt advance progress toward achieving all the
MDGs. It is estimated that the cost of providing safe water and sanitation
to all would require the additional expenditure of around US$10 billion per
year. This amount, however, is the equivalent to a mere eight days of world
military spending. The UNDP "Human Development Report 2006" states:

> In terms of enhancing human security, as distinct from more nar-
> rowly defined notions of national security, the conversion of even
> small amounts of military spending into water and sanitation
> investments would generate very large returns.[109]

One example of an effective framework for providing financial resources to
help achieve the MDGs is the Global Fund to Fight AIDS, Tuberculosis and
Malaria, founded in 2002. The Global Fund is innovative in that it strives to
ensure the "ownership" of projects by the developing countries. Programs that
reflect the needs of different countries are supported, and financial resources
are directed to areas of greatest need through independent review processes,
rather than assigning predetermined budgets to each region and disease.

The Fund's board members represent not only governments but also the
private sector, NGOs from both developed and developing countries, as well
as patient advocacy groups. All parties have an equal voice and vote, which
ensures that their diverse views will be reflected in the decision-making
process.

In this connection, I would like to propose the establishment of a world
fund for "Water for Life" as a step toward securing the kind of funding and
focused strategies that will ensure the rapid amelioration of conditions that
continue to threaten the dignity of so many people.

---

109 UNDP (United Nations Development Programme). 2006. "Human
Development Report 2006," p. 59.

"Human security . . . is a concern with human dignity." These are the words of Dr. Mahbub ul-Haq,[110] who, in a keynote speech at an international conference organized by the Toda Institute for Global Peace and Policy Research in June 1997, emphasized that "it is easier, more humane, and less costly to deal with the new issues of human security upstream rather than face their tragic consequences downstream."[111]

Dr. Haq, who was one of the great collaborators of the Toda Institute from its inception, also pioneered the concept of human development, a core element of the Human Development, Regional Conflict, and Global Governance (HUGG2) project, which the Toda Institute initiated two years ago (2006).

Dr. Haq wrote that human security should be reflected in people's lives in concrete terms: "a child who did not die, a disease that did not spread."[112] In this sense, the effort to achieve the MDGs must be focused on not only meeting targets but also restoring the well-being of the individual who is suffering.

Eliminating the word "misery" from the human lexicon was the fervent wish of my mentor, second Soka Gakkai president Josei Toda.[113] The Toda Institute was inspired by Toda's philosophy of peace. It will continue to sponsor international conferences and research to support the achievement of the MDGs, sustainable development and other endeavors to advance human development on a global scale.

A World Food Bank and an International Solidarity Tax (2009)[114]

One of the pillars for transforming the unfolding global financial crisis into a catalyst for opening a new future for humanity is the sharing of responsibility

---

110 Mahbub ul-Haq (1934–98), Pakistani economist, adviser to the United Nations Development Programme (UNDP) (1989–95).

111 Haq, Mahbub ul-. 1999. "Global Governance for Human Security." In *Worlds Apart: Human Security and Global Governance*. Ed. by Majid Tehranian. London: I.B.Tauris, p. 80.

112 Haq, Mahbub ul-. 1995. *Reflections on Human Development*. New York: Oxford University Press, p. 116.

113 Josei Toda (1900–58), second president of the Soka Gakkai (1951–58).

114 From 2009 Peace Proposal, "Toward Humanitarian Competition: A New Current in History."

through international cooperation on global public goods, a key element of which would be the creation of a world food bank.

In my proposal last year (2008), I referred to access to safe water as an integral element of promoting human development and human security. Likewise, securing stable food supplies is essential to sustaining human life and human dignity, and must be the starting point for all our efforts to combat poverty.

Starting in the fall of 2006, a sharp rise in grain prices led to simultaneous food crises in numerous countries around the world, pushing an additional 40 million people into hunger. It is estimated that 963 million people now suffer from malnutrition worldwide.[115]

The further tragedy is that this is largely a man-made disaster resulting from market speculation and increased biofuel production. As a result of the US subprime mortgage crisis, a huge volume of speculative capital poured into the grain market, causing a sharp rise in prices. The jump in grain prices also reflected a dramatic drop in grain production for food due to increased demand for biofuels as an energy source.

To ensure secure access to food for all the world's people, we need to design a mechanism to keep a certain amount of grain in reserve at all times as a global public good. These reserves could be distributed as emergency relief during a food crisis or released onto the market to stabilize prices.

I first called for the establishment of a world food bank in 1974, worried that national interests were taking precedence over humanitarian concerns in the response to global hunger and based on my conviction that life-sustaining commodities must not be politicized. Of course, it is vital for any country to guarantee stable supplies of food for its own people, but this should not be achieved at the expense of other countries. What we need to establish is global food security.

The food crisis was one of the points discussed at the G8 Hokkaido Toyako Summit held in July 2008. In the G8 Leaders Statement on Global Food Security, they for the first time undertook to "explore options on a coordinated approach on stock management, including the pros and cons of building a 'virtual' internationally coordinated reserve system for humanitarian purposes."[116]

---

115 See FAO (Food and Agriculture Organization). 2008. "Number of Hungry People Rises to 963 Million." News Article. December 9.

116 G8 Hokkaido Toyako Summit. 2008. "G8 Leaders Statement on Global Food Security."

Prior to the G8 summit, World Bank President Robert Zoellick[117] called on the G8 leaders to study the value of establishing such a reserve system.[118] The time has come to move forward with these initiatives.

I also would like to call for the expanded use of innovative financing mechanisms such as international solidarity levies to raise funds toward overcoming poverty and improving health care and sanitation in line with the UN Millennium Development Goals (MDGs). The effort to develop innovative funding mechanisms can be thought of as a type of humanitarian competition, as various states constructively vie with one another to develop the most effective ideas and proposals.

The idea of such innovative financing mechanisms initially gained prominence at the first International Conference on Financing for Development in Monterrey, Mexico, in 2002, and since then several new mechanisms have been introduced, mainly in health-related fields.

Among already established mechanisms of this kind are the International Finance Facility for Immunization (IFFIm) to support programs that save millions of lives and the Air Ticket Levy to help provide funds for the treatment of such infectious diseases as HIV/AIDS, malaria and tuberculosis. Interest in these mechanisms has continued to grow, to the point that more than fifty countries participated in the launch of the Leading Group on Solidarity Levies to Fund Development in 2006.

Possibilities for other mechanisms such as a currency transaction tax and a carbon tax are currently being explored. It is hoped that many more states will actively become involved. Such funding is essential to the humanitarian imperatives of the twenty-first century, which demand cooperation on a global scale equivalent to the Marshall Plan of the twentieth.

There is an urgent need to energize preparatory discussions toward the Fourth UN Conference on the Least Developed Countries scheduled for 2011 and to build momentum toward the achievement of the MDGs. And we must construct tightly knit safety net systems to protect the most vulnerable members of global society beyond 2015, the target date for the MDGs.

---

117 Robert B. Zoellick (1953–), US politician, President of the World Bank (2007–12).

118 Zoellick, Robert B. 2008. "Letter to Prime Minister Yasuo Fukuda." July 1. http://siteresources.worldbank.org/NEWS/Resources/zoellick-fukuda-070108.pdf (accessed April 2, 2013).

"The bottom billion"[119]—the poorest of the poor in fifty-eight countries, who have long been left behind by global economic growth—were one focus of debate at the UN last year. The stark disparity in the value of human life and dignity, virtually predetermined by where one is born, is an unconscionable injustice in global society that must be corrected.

If we are to lay any claim to human dignity—to manifest the feelings of compassion that Jean-Jacques Rousseau[120] assures us were at the heart of even the earliest human communities—we must take steps to remedy this situation.

Nobel laureate in economics Amartya Sen[121] has astutely pointed out that "poverty must be seen as the deprivation of basic capabilities rather than merely as lowness of incomes."[122] For people in the bottom billion, what is urgently needed is the kind of support from the international community that will empower them to take steps out of difficult and often degrading circumstances.

Japan was able to make a rapid and remarkable recovery from the devastation of defeat in World War II. It is my earnest hope that Japan will put this experience to good use, demonstrating active leadership in the effort to establish, as a global common good for the twenty-first century, the right of all people to live in peace and humane conditions.

Decent Work for All and Improvement of Education for Girls (2010)[123]

The global economic crisis has had a severe impact on the lives of citizens in many countries. There is also concern that one of its outcomes will be a slowing or scaling back of international cooperative efforts to respond to the complex array of global issues that confront us, including poverty and

---

119 Collier, Paul. 2007. *The Bottom Billion: Why the Poorest Countries Are Failing and What Can Be Done About It.* New York: Oxford University Press.

120 Jean-Jacques Rousseau (1712–78), Swiss-born French philosopher.

121 Amartya Sen (1933–), Indian economist, recipient of the Nobel Prize in Economic Sciences in 1998.

122 Sen, Amartya. 1999. *Development as Freedom.* New York: Oxford University Press, p. 87.

123 From 2010 Peace Proposal, "Toward a New Era of Value Creation."

environmental destruction. We must avoid a vicious cycle in which crisis gives rise to pessimism, which in turn exacerbates crisis.

While efforts to create an international framework for reducing greenhouse gases past 2013 have stalled, this does not mean that there is a complete absence of hopeful developments. For example, the tree planting campaign initiated by the United Nations Environment Programme (UNEP) in 2006 has, as of the end of 2009, resulted in the planting of some 7.4 billion trees worldwide. This effort has seen the participation of millions of citizens, from elementary schoolchildren to heads of state; the total number of newly planted trees comes to more than one tree per inhabitant of Earth.[124]

Additionally, in 2008, UNEP launched the Climate Neutral Network, whose members seek to achieve zero net emissions of greenhouse gases. A number of national and local governments as well as corporations, NGOs, universities and educational institutions are participating in this network. As these examples demonstrate, while it may be true that intergovernmental negotiations have been largely deadlocked, continued efforts are being made to achieve breakthroughs with approaches based on new forms of international cooperation and driven by the proactive engagement of individuals and organizations.

In terms of finding a path toward the resolution of global issues, the year 2010 will be a critical one, with a number of important meetings scheduled, including the Review Conference of the Parties to the Treaty on the Non-Proliferation of Nuclear Weapons (NPT) in May and the special summit in September on the Millennium Development Goals (MDGs).

We must remember that there is always a way, a path to the peak of even the most towering and forbidding mountain. Even when a sheer rock face looms before us, we should refuse to be disheartened, but instead continue the patient search for a way forward. In this sense, what is most strongly required of us is the imagination that can appreciate the present crises as an opportunity to fundamentally transform the direction of history. By mustering the force of inner will and determination we can convert challenges into the fuel for positive change.

When the Soka Gakkai was founded in 1930, Japan and the world were shuddering under the impact of the financial panic of the previous year. People were afflicted by a deepening sense of dread and unease. Writing at

---

124 See UNEP (United Nations Environment Programme). 2009. "The Billion Tree Campaign: 7.4 Billion Trees and Counting." Press Release. December 31.

that time, the founder of the organization, Tsunesaburo Makiguchi,[125] called
for a transition from a dependent or even an independent way of life to what
he called a contributive way of life. He rejected a passive, dependent way of
life in which one is swayed by and at the mercy of one's surroundings and
the conditions of the times. He likewise rejected a way of life in which we
are capable of looking out for our own needs but remain indifferent to the
sufferings of others.

He urged, instead, a contributive way of life as described by the Buddhist
maxim that when we light a lantern for others, our own way forward is lit.
The source of illumination needed to dispel the chaos and darkness of the
age is to be found in actions that bring forth our own inner light through
committed action on behalf of others.

The second president of the Soka Gakkai, Josei Toda,[126] as heir to
Makiguchi's spirit, declared: "I wish to see the word 'misery' no longer used
to describe the world, any country, any individual."[127] He put this conviction
into practice through his efforts dedicated to peace and people's happiness and
to the construction of popular solidarity rooted in a philosophy of respect for
the sanctity of life and the dignity of the human person.

Surveying the challenges that confront contemporary global society, I am
convinced that nothing is more crucial than an essential reorientation of our
way of life based on a commitment to the welfare of all of humankind and
the entire planet, such as Makiguchi and Toda called for. Rather than stand
to one side and ponder how the future might develop, we must focus on what
each of us can do at this critical moment—the role each of us can choose to
play in changing the direction of history. We must strive to make a proactive,
contributive way of life the prevailing spirit of the new era.

***

Next, I would like to discuss steps toward the resolution of the structural distortions of global society that threaten human dignity and have been brought
to the fore by the current economic crisis.

125　Tsunesaburo Makiguchi (1871–1944), founding president of the Soka Kyoiku
　　　Gakkai (forerunner of the Soka Gakkai) (1930–44).

126　Josei Toda (1900–58), second president of the Soka Gakkai (1951–58).

127　(trans. from) Toda, Josei. 1981–90. *Toda Josei zenshu* [The Complete Works of
　　　Josei Toda]. 9 vols. Tokyo: Seikyo Shimbunsha. Vol. 3, p. 290.

Last year, there was a sharp slowdown in economic growth in developing countries; as a whole, the global economy contracted for the first time since World War II. The impact on the more vulnerable members of society has been particularly severe. There are growing concerns that new humanitarian crises may arise in different parts of the world unless targeted assistance addressing the needs of these populations is provided.

I have long stressed the crucial need for the development of international safety nets to safeguard the lives and dignity of people and to make human security a robust reality. At the same time, I have advocated the empowerment of individuals as a long-term response. Premised on this, I would here like to offer concrete proposals on employment and on empowering women.

First, I urge governments to make efforts to address unemployment and to expand employment opportunities, in particular for young people. The international community as a whole must make efforts to help stabilize employment in the developing world in accordance with the Global Jobs Pact adopted by the International Labour Organization (ILO) in June 2009.

Global unemployment in 2009 is said to have reached at least 219 million, the highest level ever on record.[128] It is important that we direct our gaze beyond this staggering figure to the innumerable individual tragedies it represents. There is a clear political obligation to continue to take measures to relieve the insecurity and poverty that afflict wide sectors of society.

Young people, in particular, can be deeply affected if they are unable to find work or abruptly lose their jobs soon after joining the workforce. In addition to financial difficulty, they can be scarred with feelings of lack of worth and of insecurity concerning the future in such a way that can even undermine the will to live. At the same time, human dignity is gravely threatened when individuals are employed under inhumane or degrading conditions, or if lack of job security makes it impossible to plan realistically for the future.

Based on the conviction that "labour is not a commodity" and that "work must be a source of dignity,"[129] the ILO has advocated the concept of decent work for all. The leaders of the G20, gathering for the Pittsburgh Summit in September 2009, fully endorsed this: "We cannot rest until the global

---

128 ILO (International Labour Organization). 2009. "ILO Communication to the G20." ILO/09/45. Press Release. September 18.

129 ILO (International Labour Organization). 2009. "ILO marks its 90th anniversary with global dialogue for decent work and a fair globalization." ILO/09/22. Press Release. April 20.

economy is restored to full health, and hard-working families the world over can find decent jobs."[130] All measures must be taken to avoid the kind of sustained and deep economic contraction that followed the 1929 financial panic, in which ordinary people were left defenseless and society was thrown into ever-deepening turmoil.

Governments must take care to avoid prematurely terminating assistance initiatives specifically formulated in the face of the current economic crisis. As the ILO warns, this could delay the restoration of the employment market for years and stunt the fledgling economic recovery. It is therefore essential that governments continue to develop well-coordinated measures to expand employment, in line with the Global Jobs Pact.

Here I would like to propose the establishment of a task force dedicated to promoting decent work and the Global Jobs Pact under the G20 umbrella, which could be done at the G20 labor ministers' meeting scheduled for later this year. In this way, the G20 should take responsibility to be the driving force for global employment recovery, taking committed action until people are able to palpably sense that the crisis has passed.

My second proposal focuses on the promotion of education for girls, which is vital for many reasons and also key to the achievement of the Millennium Development Goals (MDGs) that seek to greatly reduce the numbers of people suffering from poverty and hunger but whose attainment by the target date of 2015 is in serious doubt.

Many developing countries have been particularly hard hit by the current economic crisis, for which they bear little direct responsibility. It has not only undermined efforts to combat poverty, but also pushed people who were on the brink of poverty over the edge. Active support on the part of the developed world has become even more indispensable than ever, as expressed by UN Secretary-General Ban Ki-moon,[131] who has called for a final push toward achieving the MDGs by 2015.[132]

An MDG Summit is scheduled for September. This must be seized upon as an opportunity to renew frameworks of international cooperation and

---

130 G20. 2009. "Leaders' Statement: The Pittsburgh Summit." September 24–25.

131 Ban Ki-moon (1944–), South Korean statesman, 8th Secretary-General of the United Nations Minister (2007–).

132 See Ban, Ki-moon. 2009. "'Now Is Our Time.' Report to the General Assembly." September 23.

redouble our efforts toward an era that enables all people to enjoy their dignity and realize their full potential.

I would like to stress the importance of girls' education and its crucial impact on all aspects of human development. All the objectives of the MDGs, such as alleviating poverty and hunger, involve and affect women. In this sense, gender equality and the empowerment of women hold the key to regaining momentum toward the achievement of those goals.

Children whose mothers completed primary education have twice the chance of survival beyond age five, and are more likely to be better nourished and go to school. Thus the education received by women can be a major factor in ending the generational cycle of poverty. Further, countries that have invested in girls' education over the long term have consistently shown higher levels of economic development.

Empowering a girl through education will lead to a brighter future for herself, her family and her children, eventually permeating society as a whole with the light of hope. Education indeed has such potential.

Primary school enrollment for girls has shown remarkable improvement through efforts such as the United Nations Girls' Education Initiative led by UNICEF. Looking ahead toward 2015, we should strive to create the conditions for more girls to be able to access secondary or higher levels of education.

Here I would like to propose an internationally administered fund dedicated to realizing a better future for women, in which a portion of developing countries' debts is forgiven and the equivalent amount allocated to girls' education.

Women face many challenges and threats. Broader opportunities for education can empower them to stand up as self-reliant actors, able to break through crises and redirect their lives and societies toward the better future they envision. Planting the seeds of empowerment now will make this a reality.

One hundred years ago, when the social standing of women in Japan was extremely low, the founding president of the Soka Gakkai, Tsunesaburo Makiguchi, worked passionately to expand advanced educational opportunities for women out of the belief that it is they who will build a better society. He established a program that offered correspondence education to women who were unable to receive a secondary education after graduating from primary school, compiling learning materials and editing a related periodical. He was also instrumental in establishing a facility that offered free classes to women with limited financial resources to learn sewing and embroidery, skills that constituted a major element in Japanese girls' education at the time. It was as heir to his spirit that I created the correspondence programs at Soka University and founded Soka Women's College.

Women play a pivotal role in the SGI's global movement for peace. The exhibition "Women and a Culture of Peace" was created by the Women's Peace Committee of the Soka Gakkai in Japan in collaboration with peace scholar Elise Boulding,[133] and forums on a culture of peace have been held to help raise awareness in many local communities. The message underlying these efforts is that women are the builders of peace; this represents a translation of Makiguchi's beliefs into contemporary contexts.

At the same time, these activities share the spirit of UN Security Council Resolution 1325, adopted ten years ago in October 2000. The significance of the resolution lies above all in the fact that it was a declaration to the world at the threshold of the twenty-first century that women's involvement is essential if lasting peace is to be realized. I have recently had the privilege of exchanging views on this with former UN Under-Secretary-General Anwarul K. Chowdhury,[134] who worked tirelessly for its adoption. Ambassador Chowdhury also emphasized that women's engagement enables a culture of peace to take deeper root.

In September 2009, in a reform designed to enhance overall effectiveness, the UN General Assembly adopted a resolution to merge four agencies and offices dealing with issues concerning women—the UN Development Fund for Women, the Division for the Advancement of Women, the Office of the Special Adviser on Gender Issues and the UN International Research and Training Institute for the Advancement of Women—into a new high-profile entity dedicated to gender equality.

It is my hope that this new body will include among its core activities monitoring implementation of Resolution 1325, together with the promotion of women's empowerment, including of course education for girls.

The degree to which the spirit of Resolution 1325 has taken root is clearly reflected in women's participation in peace processes. On the one hand, the UN Peacebuilding Commission was guided by Resolution 1325 in its reconstruction work in Burundi and Sierra Leone. Worldwide, however, women

---

133 Elise Boulding (1920–2010), American peace scholar and activist.
134 Anwarul K. Chowdhury (1943–), Bangladeshi diplomat, Under-Secretary-General and High Representative of the United Nations (2002–07).

still make up less than 2 percent of the signatories of peace agreements and only 7 percent of the peace negotiators.[135]

This year marks the fifteenth anniversary of the Beijing Platform for Action, an international standard for policies related to women adopted at the Fourth World Conference on Women, as well as the tenth anniversary of Resolution 1325. It is important to make 2010 a breakthrough year, with significant progress toward the further empowerment of women on a global scale. To this end, I hope that more countries will join the Friends of 1325, an ad-hoc group of UN member states actively working for the implementation of the resolution. At this and other forums, there must be earnest debate on how best to enhance women's participation in peacebuilding processes.

Environment and Energy

An Environmental Security Council (1990)[136]

At the beginning of 1989, I proposed that the most practical way to build a new political and economic order in an increasingly multipolarized world was to allow the United Nations to play the pivotal role. The SGI has consistently stressed the need to focus on the UN and strengthen its authority in order to put in place a system of integration toward a new world order. It is extremely encouraging that the value placed on the role of the UN has grown greater than had been expected in recent years.

The ideological confrontation between the Eastern and Western blocs is practically over. The ground is being laid for the UN to use its powers more effectively and organically. In light of recent world affairs, the role of the UN is becoming increasingly important, calling for new ideas and initiatives.

When I met in December 1989 with UN Under-Secretary-General for International Economic and Social Affairs Rafiuddin Ahmed,[137]

---

135 UNIFEM (United Nations Development Fund for Women). 2009. "UNIFEM Statement at the 2009 Annual Session of the UNDP/UNFPA Executive Board." Speech by Executive Directors at UNDP/UNFPA Executive Board Meeting, 2009 Annual Session. May 28.

136 From 1990 Peace Proposal, "The Triumph of Democracy: Toward a Century of Hope."

137 Rafiuddin Ahmed (1932–), Pakistani diplomat, Under-Secretary-General for International Economic and Social Affairs of the United Nations (1987–91).

Under-Secretary-General for Human Rights Jan Mårtenson[138] and Under-Secretary-General for Disarmament Affairs Yasushi Akashi,[139] we agreed unanimously on these points.

***

I would like to propose that a permanent forum be created during the General Assembly this year whereby heads of state can meet at the UN Headquarters and discuss solutions for various problems with a focus on the United Nations. I would also hope that the Secretary-General will take the initiative to organize a UN summit meeting to be attended by the United States, the Soviet Union, China, Japan, France, the United Kingdom, West Germany, Italy, Canada, Brazil as well as representatives from the European Community.

Currently, summit meetings of the leaders of major industrialized countries are held annually. But we have entered an era when discussions and agreements exclusively among leaders of the Western bloc are no longer sufficient. There are too many pressing issues that must be solved by bringing our wisdom together, transcending the East–West and North–South boundaries.

This proposed UN summit meeting should thoroughly explore means of bringing an end to regional conflicts. Deliberations should focus on crucially important themes such as disarmament, the environment and the North–South issue—problems that require communication and mutual understanding among world leaders. Preparatory meetings would inevitably be necessary for this.

Environmental problems in particular are presenting enormous challenges throughout the world today, and we need to take bold initiatives to deal with them. In June 1992, a United Nations conference on the environment and development will be held in Brazil to discuss measures for global environmental issues, and the outcome of this conference will have a critical impact on the environment on a global scale.

In order to ensure truly effective measures, I propose that an environmental security council be created within the UN, and that it be equipped with an environment sustainment force, a powerful presence dedicated to the

---

138 Jan Mårtenson (1933–), Swedish diplomat, Under-Secretary-General for Human Rights and Director-General of United Nations Office of Geneva (1987–92).

139 Yasushi Akashi (1931–), Japanese diplomat, Under-Secretary-General for Disarmament Affairs, Under-Secretary-General for Humanitarian Affairs and Emergency Relief Coordinator (1996–97).

protection of the environment, similar to the UN Peacekeeping Force. The magnitude of our environmental problems has already outgrown the stage of mere discussion and requires drastic and fundamental measures.

If world leaders were to meet annually at a summit held in conjunction with the General Assembly and have frequent dialogue on the United Nations platform, tensions would be eased, creating a positive atmosphere in the world.

A United Nations of Environment and Development (1992)[140]

The age of Cold War confrontation, which long divided the world into the Eastern and Western blocs, has come to an end. What we must do now is to map out a clear blueprint for a new order for global society that reflects the massive changes that have taken place in the world, and bring together our wisdom in achieving that order.

Several years ago, I engaged in comprehensive discussions about the environment with Dr. Aurelio Peccei,[141] a cofounder of the Club of Rome, and these were published in a book entitled *Before It Is Too Late*.[142] After a long hiatus, the Club of Rome published last fall (September 1991) a new report entitled *The First Global Revolution*.[143] In it, the authors stress that all of humankind's wisdom must be brought together immediately if we are to survive into the twenty-first century. I agree this must be done, before it is too late.

The icy standoff between the Eastern and Western blocs has thawed. It is more crucial than ever that we earnestly tackle the many long-standing global problems such as poverty, the population explosion and environmental destruction.

This year in particular is likely to be a crucial turning point in our attempts to solve our global environmental problems. In June, heads of state from around the world and concerned NGOs will meet in Rio de Janeiro for the

---

140 From 1992 Peace Proposal, "A Renaissance of Hope and Harmony."

141 Aurelio Peccei (1908–84), Italian industrialist and cofounder of the Club of Rome.

142 Peccei, Aurelio and Daisaku Ikeda. 1984. *Before It Is Too Late*. Ed. by Richard L. Gage. Tokyo: Kodansha International Ltd.

143 King, Alexander and Bertrand Schneider. 1991. *The First Global Revolution: A Report by the Council of The Club of Rome*. New York: Pantheon Books.

United Nations Conference on Environment and Development (UNCED), the so-called Earth Summit. Although I share with others a hope for a fruitful outcome, prospects are not completely positive.

The Earth Summit marks the twentieth anniversary of the United Nations Conference on the Human Environment held in Stockholm in 1972. Many action plans were adopted at the Stockholm Conference; various treaties were adopted and new organizations created. But the situation did not improve. On the contrary, environmental destruction has become more serious and North–South tensions have intensified.

The reason for this is clear. In the past twenty years, industrialized countries have pursued material wealth above all, placing utmost precedence upon economic growth. The prosperity of one's own country comes first, putting aside concern for the Earth's environment. They have continued to provide economic assistance to developing countries, but it has not resulted in improving the livelihoods of people. Poverty and the population explosion that accompanies it have been left unaddressed. This has ultimately led to environmental destruction within developing countries. These factors have compounded into cumulative effects: global environmental destruction.

Another issue that must be addressed immediately is rapid population growth. The world's population has reached 5.4 billion, an increase of 1.6 billion in the twenty years since the Stockholm Conference. Continuing at the present rate, there will be some 10 billion people in the world by the year 2050, far more than the Earth can support. And nearly all of that growth will occur in the developing countries.

The high infant mortality rate in developing countries is a factor causing mothers to believe it is best to have as many children as possible. As a result, the rate of population growth is highest in the very regions where poverty is most extreme. It is clear that no solution will be found to the population problem unless poverty is alleviated. At the same time, people in the developing countries afflicted with poverty and population growth have also had a negative impact on the natural environment through reckless slash-and-burn agriculture and haphazard collection of wood for fuel.

Global environmental destruction, population growth and poverty are inextricably linked in this way. Humanity is facing an extremely difficult situation with the need to find a solution to these three monumental problems simultaneously and comprehensively.

Needless to say, effective assistance from developed countries is essential for developing countries to break free from poverty. Ultimately, however, success depends on the inner-motivated efforts for development on the part of developing countries. It is education that holds the key.

The difficult challenge confronting humanity today is how to rectify the developmental imbalance between the North and the South. With this awareness, the Soka Gakkai Women's Peace Committee has organized two exhibitions in support of UN activities: "What are Children's Rights?" sponsored by the United Nations Children's Fund (UNICEF) and "The Children of the World and UNICEF." They have been shown throughout Japan and sparked considerable interest.

At this moment, some 150 million young children are afflicted with starvation. As many as 40,000 young lives are lost every day because of war, poor healthcare services and natural disasters.[144] Our exhibitions have been promoted with the intent of stimulating and deepening people's awareness about these critical conditions; they are our attempt to address the extremely difficult problem of how to build, as world citizens, a solidarity of the heart between people of developed and developing countries in the context of daily living.

I feel compelled to urge once again that we take effective measures to address poverty, starvation and the population problem by the end of the 1990s before it is too late.

The plight of refugees, whose number has already swelled to some 17 million people, is another prominent problem facing the 1990s. In addition to refugees who leave their homelands and flee to nearby countries to escape the ravages of war, we are also seeing a sharp increase in the number of people pouring into developed countries to escape poverty, as well as victims of ethnic conflict who are forced to wander homeless within the confines of their own countries. These conditions are becoming a serious problem internationally. As an NGO affiliated with the United Nations, the SGI is deeply concerned about this issue and has earnestly undertaken refugee relief activities.

Measures are urgently required for each of these problems. The 1990s seem to have ushered in an era of pressing choices that demand our immediate response; choices that could determine the survival of humanity. By their

---

144 See UNICEF (United Nations Children's Fund). 1991. "The State of the World's Children 1991." Oxford: Oxford University Press, p. 3.

very nature, the global problems confronting us call for the concerted efforts of all people from both the North and the South. However, confrontation between developed and developing countries has come to the fore, causing deep concern as we head toward the Earth Summit to be held in June of this year.

The foremost goal of the Earth Summit is the concrete realization of the concept of "sustainable development," an ideal that integrates development with the protection of the environment. Sustainable development represents a balanced approach to development that ensures environmental protection, replacing the conventional approach of squandering natural resources at the expense of environmental destruction. It is a form of development that seeks to look directly to the future, protecting the interests of future generations and meeting the basic needs of the present generation. Nevertheless, there are deep and entangled disagreements between the North and the South concerning precisely how sustainable development is to be implemented.

Specifically, developing countries are raising their voices in criticism of the unbridled consumerism of the developed countries as the primary cause of the severe environmental degradation. In addition, the development policies of the North are coming under increasingly harsh criticism because they have failed to contribute to the betterment of living conditions or prevent environmental destruction in the South.

Certainly, rather than alleviating poverty, development mechanisms implemented under the initiative of developed countries have placed a huge burden of accumulated debt on developing countries. This has indeed deprived people of the ability to think about environmental conservation.

We must also reflect on the fact that the economic assistance provided thus far has not been put to effective use. It is estimated that military expenditures in developing countries have grown to as much as US$200 billion per year, and that much of the funds given to developing countries as assistance are actually used to procure weapons.[145] This must be changed immediately.

If the aid-giving countries or international organizations were to establish an assessment system, this might prevent developing countries from escalating

---

145 See UNDP (United Nations Development Programme). 1990. "Human Development Report 1990: Concept and Measurement of Human Development," p. 77. UNDP (United Nations Development Programme). 1991. "Human Development Report 1991: Financing Human Development," pp. 82–84.

their military spending. Under such a system, a comprehensive assessment would be made of the ratio of military spending to overall expenditure and the weapons procurement patterns of the recipient countries, on the basis of which a decision could be made as to whether economic assistance is appropriate. On the other hand, this would raise the question of interference in internal affairs, so a delicate balance needs to be maintained.

While bitter confrontation between the North and the South continues, developed countries are unable to agree on a coordinated plan, casting a dark cloud over the prospects for the Earth Summit.

For example, distinct differences are apparent between Western Europe and the United States concerning the Summit's primary issue: the adoption of a framework convention on climate change. Western European countries are anxious to reduce carbon dioxide emissions, a major cause of global warming. The Americans, on the other hand, have doubts concerning the mechanism of global warming and, worried about the possible impact on their economy, are less enthusiastic about restrictions.

Confrontations between the North and the South, together with these differences among the developed countries, have given rise to an extremely complex and difficult situation that some believe threatens the success of the UN conference itself.

Needless to say, the essence of our environmental problem is how we should create a society that can coexist in harmony with the natural ecosystem. It poses the fundamental question of how human beings should live, transcending the boundaries of politics, economics, science and technology. It is a multifaceted problem encompassing all fields of endeavor ranging from our values to the nature of culture in our future society.

The problem requires far more than a political or economic response within the borders of any one country. We must promote a transformation of people's consciousness on a global scale. An inner-motivated spirituality is urgently needed for us to share a sense of crisis as global citizens. This inner transformation is a task confronting humanity as a whole.

At the same time, we are also facing the urgent need to create a new international framework that is capable of responding effectively to global crises.

With the end of the Cold War, the confrontation between the United States and the Soviet Union has dissolved, revitalizing the UN in what some refer to as a United Nations Renaissance. The UN is now free from the functional paralysis it once suffered as a result of the Security Council members' indiscriminate use of their right to veto. On the other hand, the UN in its present form is not necessarily well equipped to deal with global problems such as the environmental crisis.

Over forty years have passed since the UN was established, and the circumstances surrounding the world have changed dramatically since that time. The global crises we face today were not foremost in the minds of the founders. Environmental problems were certainly not considered important.

I believe that the time has come for a fundamental reform of the United Nations. We need to create an international organization for the new era that can respond effectively to global problems. With the weight of the East–West confrontation having been removed, this is an excellent opportunity for a new departure.

Thirteen years ago, in November 1978, I called for the creation of an "Environmental United Nations."[146] I was convinced that such an organization would be absolutely necessary in the near future. It was as an extension of that proposal that I suggested the creation of an Environmental Security Council by dividing the Security Council into two bodies last year (1991). There has been encouraging support for this idea from people of conscience both in Japan and abroad.

I believe that the time is steadily becoming ripe. Some experts have suggested the division of the Security Council into several groups to deal with the environment, food and other issues. I hope that the UN leadership will show a flexible response to these suggestions, in keeping with the new requirements of the times.

I am reminded of a very interesting idea for UN reform proposed by the peace scholar Dr. Johan Galtung,[147] with whom I have exchanged opinions on several occasions in Japan. Dr. Galtung suggests that the UN be divided into upper and lower houses, a bicameral structure with the upper house retaining the present system of one nation, one vote, and the lower house reflecting actual population ratios.[148]

What interests me most in his suggestion is the complete change in thinking that this idea represents. Setting aside for the moment the question

---

146 See Ikeda, Daisaku. 1978. "Kankyo mondai wa zenjinrui tekina kadai [The Environment: A Challenge for All Humanity]." *Seikyo Shimbun.* November 19, p. 5.

147 Johan Galtung (1930–), Norwegian peace scholar.

148 See Galtung, Johan and Daisaku Ikeda. 1995. *Choose Peace.* London: Pluto Press, p. 139.

of whether or not this kind of bicameral structure is appropriate, conditions in the world today undoubtedly require dramatic reform of this kind.

At any rate, the current structure—where the Economic and Social Council works with the UN Conference on Trade and Development (UNCTAD), the UN Environment Programme (UNEP), the UN Population Fund (UNFPA) and the UN Development Programme (UNDP)—is inadequate to effectively address the global problems we face.

Here, I would like to suggest that in order to strengthen the UN, we should view it as two independent bodies: one engaging in peacekeeping activities, and the other dealing with such global problems as the environment, the economy, development, population, food and human rights. The first could be called the "United Nations of Security," and the second the "United Nations of Environment and Development."

Reform of this nature would answer much of the criticism of the current UN structure regarding the lack of organic cooperation and the wasteful overlaps in its activities. In light of the fact that 70 percent of the UN's fiscal and human resources are presently devoted to development aid and humanitarian activities in developing countries, the establishment of a United Nations of Environment and Development would respond to the needs of our time. I also propose that this new organization would have an Environment and Development Security Council, as an equivalent of the Security Council in a putative United Nations of Security.

The reason I propose the creation of a new organization rather than restructuring and strengthening the existing Economic and Social Council is that we need a powerful organization capable of making decisions for the international community. It should not be kept as a mere forum for international consultation.

The limitations of the present UN lie in its organizational structure as a collective body of sovereign states. The interests of each member state come first, making it difficult to reach voluntary decisions from the standpoint of the general good of the global community and humanity. It is essential that a United Nations of Environment and Development have a certain degree of bidding power to overcome these limitations.

The permanent and non-permanent members of an Environment and Development Security Council would be selected based on such factors as Gross National Product (GNP), population and a balanced representation of all regions of the world to ensure the Council equally reflects the views of the North and the South.

I am fully aware that many hurdles must be overcome before this idea can be actualized. Presently, the UN is hard pressed for funds. Under these circumstances, creating a new organization might seem impossible, even if it were built upon the existing foundations. When we consider the gravity of the crisis confronting our planet today, however, it is imperative that we think with a global perspective, setting aside national interests, and strengthen financial support for international organizations that are dedicated to solving this crisis.

The UN's current annual budget is approximately US$2.3 billion. This is clearly inadequate in light of the estimated US$1 trillion the world spends on defense each year and the crucial role of the UN in today's world.

It has often been pointed out the UN lacks the financial resources necessary to systematically promote the kind of sustainable development that takes environmental conservation sufficiently into account. For example, UNEP has an annual budget of just US$40 million, a meager amount considering the significance of its mission. This is only half of the budget of one of leading private environmental protection groups in the United States.

Among the developed countries, many Western societies, with the exception of Japan, are suffering from economic recession and high unemployment rates. The Commonwealth of Independent States (CIS) countries are facing an economic crisis, and are now on the receiving end of international economic aid programs. All of this might lead to the conclusion that few countries can currently afford to offer financial support to international organizations.

That is precisely why I believe now is the time, with the Cold War behind us, for us to change our approach. We have no choice but to cut our bloated military spending and reallocate the funds saved to financial support for the United Nations. It is quite clear that there are neither resources nor justification to continue such huge military investment.

It will take an enormous amount of money to fully engage in environmental conservation on a global scale, ranging from the prevention of global warming to the preservation of biodiversity. The Earth Summit secretariat recently estimated that US$125 billion per year would be required for environmental conservation over the eight years from 1993 to 2000.[149] How are we to raise such an amount annually?

---

149 See UNDPI (United Nations Department of Public Information). 1997.
     "Financing the Future." DPI/1874/SD.

The only possible answer would lie in dramatic cuts to the world's estimated US$1 trillion annual military expenditure. Specifically, I suggest that each country set aside a portion of their military expenditure and contribute it to a United Nations arms reduction fund dedicated to the conservation of the Earth's environment.

Fundraising for environmental conservation should not be left entirely to national and local governments and other public agencies. The effort should also involve environment-related NGOs, which can help raise people's awareness. They could bring their wisdom together as to how they can support the UN financially and raise funds for it.

Many NGOs from all over the world will gather at the Earth Summit in June. Expectation for NGO participation in a UN conference has never been higher. Practical issues such as those mentioned above must be thoroughly discussed on this occasion.

As an NGO affiliated with the Economic and Social Council, the SGI has consistently supported the UN, and we would like to actively contribute to the Earth Summit. Specifically, we are planning to promote an awareness-raising campaign for environmental conservation with a focus on the exhibition "Coexistence and Hope: Development and Environment" with the cooperation of the Earth Summit secretariat and the Rio de Janeiro Department of Environment.

A United Nations of Environment and Development would only be possible if governments were willing to put the interests of our planet before national interests, placing utmost precedence upon the survival of humankind and the Earth itself. Governments would have to move away from the conventional supremacy of national sovereignty and even be prepared to delegate part of their sovereignty to the international body.

The accomplishments of the European Community (EC) could be an example in this respect. The EC countries have resolved to abolish their own separate currencies and go ahead with their plan for economic and monetary union based on a single currency in the near future. They are also expected to coordinate their diplomacy and security policies to achieve political union. This constitutes a substantial limitation or delegation of sovereignty. The question is how international organizations should reflect this trend toward transnationalism.

The idea of international levies is currently attracting attention. In fact, the Earth Summit secretariat has already proposed that a tax be levied on the development or use of the oceans, the atmosphere or other international public goods to raise funds needed for global environmental conservation.

If governments implemented such a levy and gave it to the United Nations, it would not only raise funds for the conservation of the Earth's environment, but also be an important step away from the supremacy of national sovereignty. With developments in the EC raising fundamental questions about the nature of national sovereignty, we should take this opportunity to implement an international tax of this nature.

The key to overcoming the limitations of an international organization comprising sovereign states lies in utilizing the constructive power of NGOs, which has proven effective in such fields as environmental conservation, the protection of human rights and development cooperation. Our challenge is to create a new framework that ensures the participation of all major international actors, including governments and NGOs that can bring together the grassroots voices of civil society. In this respect, the charter to be written for a United Nations of Environment and Development must be based on the ideals of global democracy, mapping the path for humanity into the twenty-first century.

The United Nations will celebrate its fiftieth anniversary in 1995. Toward this juncture, let us make every effort to stir international public opinion for its fundamental reform.

The Drafting of an Earth Charter (1997)[150]

Humankind is faced on every side by inescapable dilemmas: the threat of nuclear armaments and other weapons of mass destruction, the intensification of ethnic discord, damage to the Earth's environment from the effects of global warming and destruction to the ozone layer, the widening of the economic gap between North and South, the spread of psychopathological phenomena and brutal crimes. . .

The gravity of the crisis, which casts its dark shadow over the path ahead, is multilayered, affecting not only individuals and societies, but ethnic groups and nations, as well as the ecosystem and even the survival of the Earth itself. There is no longer any doubt that this shadow is a symptom of the deadlock that grips contemporary civilization.

It is precisely because of this deadlock, I believe, that a thorough reappraisal of the history of humankind, viewed from a very broad perspective,

---

150 From 1997 Peace Proposal, "New Horizons of a Global Civilization."

is indispensable. We need to review the whole history of modern civilization as it has unfolded over the past few centuries, and take a bold new look, one millennium at a time, through a macroscopic, bird's-eye view of human history.

What is the nature of the tasks we currently face? How should we envisage the character, systems and order of the global civilization which will inevitably shape the world of the twenty-first century? Many and diverse approaches are being taken to these questions, each resonating against those around it as they build a crescendo leading into the coming century. Each and every approach leads to a specific and important statement, yet none seems to be based on a firm grasp of what the coming century will be, so that all-in-all we have not moved beyond the stage of groping in the darkness.

This is perhaps only to be expected. For the murk of uncertainty and unpredictability of our fin-de-siècle is that dark, and the scale and quality of the impasse that bears down upon us are that utterly new. These are dilemmas as never experienced or heard of in the history of humankind. To describe them with such a positive adjective as "new," however, could be misleading, for they are the source of foreboding signs that tell us in no uncertain terms that failure to find real solutions could mean the end of human history.

**

Currently I am engaged in a continuing dialogue with Hong Kong author Jin Yong,[151] who is known as the contemporary Dumas.[152] In our conversations, he expressed his hope that it would become possible for people to move back and forth between Hong Kong and Japan without visas after the return of the British colony to China. Of course, I said I was very much in favor of the idea. However, a dream is a dream, and I fear that it will be a very long time before all peoples of the world can bypass familiar frameworks and freely move back and forth from one country to another without visas.

Nevertheless, I believe that the age in which the sovereign nation-state was the strongest, virtually the only agent of decision-making power in international society will gradually fade with the passing of the twentieth century into history. We cannot afford to lose sight of this mega-trend.

---

151 Jin Yong (the pen-name of Louis Cha Leung-yung) (1924–), Hong Kong-based Chinese author and journalist.
152 Alexandre Dumas (1802–70), French novelist.

The trend is inevitable for several reasons. To cite the negative factor first, it is because none of the global problems I mentioned at the beginning of this appeal, including damage to the Earth's environment and overpopulation, can be solved within the framework of sovereign states alone. Remedies can only be found through the close and coordinated efforts of all actors in the international arena.

In terms of the positive reasons, a transnational trend is now the unarguable development in almost all realms of human activity, brought about by the tremendous strides made in information, telecommunications and transportation technology.

***

As we observe this mega-trend that is irrevocably binding the world into one, beyond all national boundaries, beyond ethnic differences, for better or for worse, we are seeing that the term "global civilization"—which, if not purely fantasy, once carried a mostly utopian ring—is now suddenly ready to take on a realistic image.

We need to know what is most essential to give this global civilization some clarity of image. If we do not endeavor to fulfill this task, even in the roughest outline, we may find that global civilization turns out to be no more than a pipe dream. This would be a most regrettable—not to mention irresponsible—legacy to leave to posterity. We must not allow ourselves to depart the twentieth century with sighs of regret and resignation.

***

I would like here to explore the means for changing the norms that are required to create a new global civilization or "human civilization," focusing on environmental issues which have emerged and are demonstrating the limits of contemporary civilization. Today, ecologists are telling us that if radical changes are not made, the Earth itself might not survive another century. The greatest threat to human existence, therefore, is our failure to deal properly with environmental problems.

People have warned for a long time that science and technology are like a two-edged sword. But their voices have been overwhelmed by the rapid succession of advances making what was once thought impossible possible. Economic growth and prosperity brought about by technological advancement have so captured people's imaginations that the progress and spread of the civilization of science and technology has known no limits and no barriers.

But now the triumph has been found to be marred, with damage to the Earth's environment inflicted by the side effects of that civilization, telling us that limitless growth is an illusion and declaring that progress may in fact turn out to be our downfall. Air pollution, water pollution, pollution of the soil, indiscriminate cutting of vast forests, desertification, damage to the Earth's protective ozone layer and the resultant effects of global warming: none of these issues can be simply left to resolve themselves.

In 1972, the Club of Rome issued the first statement recognizing these problems as tasks of global concern in its report *The Limits to Growth*.[153] That same year, the United Nations Conference on the Human Environment was held in Stockholm, known for its catch phrase, our "Only One Earth." That conference ended with the Declaration of the United Nations Conference on the Human Environment, which states that environmental problems pose a real and serious threat to the survival of humankind and calls on the international community to contribute to their solution.[154]

A great deal of research has since been conducted and numerous projects and initiatives undertaken to remedy the causes of environmental destruction, and the United Nations Conference on Environment and Development (the Earth Summit) held in Rio de Janeiro in June 1992 drew the world's close attention. This Summit was successful to a certain extent, marking the signing of a number of declarations and agreements, including the Rio Declaration on Environment and Development, Agenda 21, an action plan aimed at achieving what came to be known as "sustainable development," adoption of a set of principles for the protection of the world's forests, a United Nations Framework Convention on Climate Change and the Convention on Biological Diversity.

The Convention on Biological Diversity went into effect in December 1993 and the United Nations Convention to Combat Desertification in December 1996. The remarkable progress made in establishing restrictions on the use of chlorofluorocarbons in order to protect the Earth's ozone layer is testimony to the significance of consensus and concerted effort within international society.

This year, five years after the Rio Earth Summit, the next United Nations Special Conference on the Environment will be held to evaluate and discuss what has been done and what progress has been made in the interim.

---

153   Club of Rome. 1972. *The Limits to Growth*. London: Earth Island Ltd.
154   See UN (United Nations). 1972. "Declaration of the United Nations Conference on the Human Environment." June 16. Stockholm.

Attention is centering on the third conference of countries signatory to the UN Framework Convention on Climate Change to be held in Japan as the occasion when specific conclusions will be reached about measures on reduction of carbon dioxide emissions to be implemented in the year 2000.

Despite the steady advances being made in international society on these issues, many reports point out that they are far outpaced by the speed with which conditions of the Earth's environment are worsening. In April 1996, the United Nations Environment Programme (UNEP) issued a statement prior to celebrations of Earth Day declaring that the Earth's environment had reached a critical state in so many areas that if major changes were not made celebrations of Earth Day would soon become meaningless. The 1996 white paper published by the Worldwatch Institute stated: "The world today is faced with an enormous need for change in a period of time that is all too short." It also stressed that "if we fail, our future will spiral out of control."[155]

Indeed, it is now clear that the problems of the Earth's environment cannot be resolved merely as the extension of approaches adopted in the past. I believe that there is a growing awareness of an impending cataclysm that will drastically change current trends if efforts are not made to fundamentally reevaluate the nature of civilization.

Many and diverse efforts have been initiated to scrutinize and reexamine the ideas and values that have sustained the modern technological civilization from this viewpoint, and the field of environmental ethics is now becoming well established as an academic discipline. The theory of accountability of one generation to its successors proposed by Hans Jonas,[156] the idea that the present generation ought to limit its freedoms for the sake of coming generations, is certain to be the subject of close scrutiny from now on. The discussion unfolding on this topic involves not only a fundamental reexamination of the concept of "freedom," as it has been understood until now, but also a reevaluation of the synchronic approach to decision-making based on the interests and consent of contemporary people alone. This debate is extremely instructive in appraising not only the validity of the "science-is-superior" persuasion but the implications of the progressive view of history extolled throughout the modern and contemporary eras.

155　Brown, Lester R. et al. 1996. *State of the World 1996.* New York: W. W. Norton & Co., p. 18.

156　Hans Jonas (1903–93), German philosopher.

In addition to fairness and responsibility among generations, of course, we must also pursue social fairness in our own time, as symbolized in the North–South problem. Any efforts we make to consider sustainable development as the keynote in dealing with environmental problems will be meaningless if we do not pay careful attention to these two dimensions of fairness. As many opinion leaders have pointed out, it is the conspicuous patterns of consumption of the nations of the North that lie at the core of today's environmental crisis, and I do not believe this charge can be denied.

It is fantasy to think that the kind of conspicuous consumption of resources by the mass-producing, mass-consuming North could be sustainable much longer. More importantly, it is very shortly going to be something that global society will no longer condone. A vicious circle plagues the nations of the South, our close neighbors on this one-and-only Earth, linking poverty, population growth and environmental destruction. As many observers have pointed out, the harsh realities of the so-called PPE (poverty, population growth and environment) problem are directly attributable to the North–South disparities that have resulted from the structure of the international economy.

With regard to the polarization of the hemispheres, the yearly report of the United Nations Development Programme (UNDP) published last year, "Human Development Report 1996," warns that "If present trends continue, economic disparities between industrial and developing nations will move from inequitable to inhuman."[157]

The report describes the distortions of economic growth under five patterns—jobless growth (growth without an increase in job opportunities); ruthless growth (growth that does nothing to redress the disparity between rich and poor); voiceless growth (growth not accompanied by democratization or the advance of individuals in society); rootless growth (growth that infringes on the ethnic identity of individuals); and futureless growth (growth through wasteful consumption of resources that will be needed by future generations)—summing them up as "patterns of growth 'that perpetuate today's inequalities [and are] neither sustainable nor worth sustaining.'"[158]

Attention at last year's World Food Summit focused on the plight of the more than 800 million people who suffer from starvation or malnutrition in the world today, and the Declaration of Rome and a related action plan were

---

157 UNDP (United Nations Development Programme). 1996. "Human Development Report 1996." Oxford: Oxford University Press, p. iii.
158 Ibid., p. 4.

adopted aiming to decrease the numbers of the starving by half by the year 2015. I might add that 1997 is year one of the first United Nations Decade for the Eradication of Poverty (1997–2006).

In furthering international endeavors such as these, I believe, it is crucial to establish an environment in which the inner resources with which each and every human being is endowed can be amply displayed. Eliminating starvation and eradicating poverty cannot be achieved through stopgap measures that simply supply material goods and financial support. Alleviating these problems depends, rather, on securing empowerment for the long term, which can be achieved by creating environments in which individuals can realize their inherent potential and by establishing the conditions where self-reliance can thrive.

In many cases, the causes of the devastating conflicts occurring in various parts of the world are deeply rooted in economic problems. All of us, I believe, must recognize our responsibility, as fellow members of a global society, to contribute in any way we can to break the vicious circle mentioned above.

It hardly needs to be said that environmental problems are not simply political, economic or technological issues that can be eliminated or alleviated by merely establishing wise methods of using valuable resources. I believe a way will be found out of our difficulties if we probe much deeper, questioning and redesigning the relationships of human beings to each other, of human beings to the environment, and of human beings to society as a whole. Now is the time to transform our civilization into one based on values premised on the principle of human dignity in the true sense. It is time for a shift in the fundamental perspective of each and every person in the world.

The clues to a view of life and the world that will lay the philosophical foundations for that revolution can be found in the wisdom of Buddhism. The Buddhist canon gives us a beautiful parable of the cosmic view of history, showing how all the phenomena of the universe interrelate, producing a perfect, subtle harmony: Suspended above the palace of Indra, the Buddhist god who symbolizes the natural forces that protect and nurture life, is an enormous net. A brilliant jewel is attached to each knot in the net. Each jewel contains and reflects the image of all the other jewels in the net, which sparkles in the magnificence of its totality.

This poignant image illustrates the concept of "dependent origination" (Jp. *engi*). Dependent origination is the fundamental Buddhist doctrine that teaches the coexistence of all things in the universe, including human beings and nature, in interdependent relationships. It expounds the symbiosis of the micro-cosmos and the macro-cosmos that unite as one organism.

The idea goes far beyond the mechanistic view of the world removed from humanity that formed the background for modern science. What I would like particularly to emphasize is that Buddhism sees the relationships of all things in the universe not as a still, static image but as the dynamic pulsing of creative life.

Buddhism sums up the dynamism of life as follows: "Without life, environment cannot exist, even though life is supported by its environment"[159] "Life" here refers to the subjective life (Jp. *shoho*) and "environment" to the objective world (Jp. *eho*) that surrounds it.

The point I would like to make is that this passage conveys not a static image by simply giving two sentences showing that life and environment are the same thing. The first and second parts of the sentence cannot be reversed. By saying first "Without life, environment cannot exist" it is clear that the subjective display of human life that embraces the universe comes first. Yet that expression alone constitutes an idealism, or indulges in the Faustian arrogance of the moderns. The second part of the sentence—"even though life is supported by its environment"—is added, therefore, to remind us not to forget that human beings, too, are part of nature.

This Buddhist doctrine of the oneness of life and environment (Jp. *esho-funi*) is a dynamic, volitional concept seeing human life as the initiator of reform while referring to the impact environment in turn can have on it. It is in its relations with humanity in this fashion that environment is viewed.

The word "symbiosis" is often heard in our time, but I believe that real symbiosis can be achieved only through the well-balanced interaction of "life" and "environment," which requires firm determination to carry out reform— a resolve demonstrated in the phrase "without life, environment cannot exist"—while at the same time maintaining close consideration toward the environment as the sustenance of our lives.

For that reason I feel a strong interest in and affinity with the idea of life expressed by the Spanish philosopher José Ortega y Gasset.[160] The theme that

---

159 (trans. from) Nichiren. 1952. *Nichiren Daishonin gosho zenshu* [The Complete Works of Nichiren Daishonin]. Ed. by Nichiko Hori. Tokyo: Soka Gakkai, p. 1140.

160 José Ortega y Gasset (1883–1955), Spanish liberal philosopher and essayist.

he himself said epitomizes all of his philosophical speculation is: "I am myself plus my circumstance, and if I do not save it, I cannot save myself."[161]

Just as stated in "without life, environment cannot exist," by saying "I am myself and my environment" Ortega meant that there can be no environment that simply exists—that environment does not idealistically or conceptually exist within one. One lives within environment, and environment, moreover, is a kind of objective entity that will continue to exist even after one's death. That is why he was thoughtful enough to add "if that environment cannot be saved, I cannot be saved": like the second sentence of the above passage of the Buddhist canon, "life is supported by its environment." He placed the essential and acting "I" at the fine intersection of "I" and "environment."

Ortega's concise and profound proposition, reminiscent of Descartes'[162] "Cogito ergo sum" (I think, therefore I am), keenly expresses the crisis of modern civilization. As distinct from the Cartesian and mechanical or dualistic model of the world, it is oriented to dualistic monism or monistic dualism. His question was: When will we awaken to the realization that definitive existence in this world is not material or spiritual, but essentially a matter of perspective?

I cannot help thinking that by implication this perspective shares the same principle as the subjective and dynamic display of creative life, the principle that runs through the Buddhist doctrine of the oneness of life and the environment.

I mention these similarities because the dilemma—or perhaps I should say "trilemma" (destruction of the global environment vs. injunction to economic growth vs. the energy and resources crisis)—that confronts contemporary civilization on all sides presents such a pessimistic outlook as to cause people to lose all hope. I believe that we will not be able to muster the indomitable courage and confidence it will take to chart a firm path toward resolution of these problems without the support of a strong philosophy of action.

It is out of this conviction that I argue that we must begin with revolution within the individual heart—the human revolution—through which we can then realize a revolution in the human relationship with the environment and thereby a revolution of "global civilization." It is indeed with this awareness

---

161 Ortega y Gasset, José. 1961. *Meditations on Quixote*. New York: W. W. Norton & Company, Inc., p. 45.

162 René Descartes (1596–1650), French philosopher, mathematician and writer.

that the SGI has approached our endeavors to raise consciousness about environmental issues through exhibits and other activities.

In 1992, in conjunction with the Earth Summit, we mounted an exhibition entitled "Toward the Century of Life: The Environment and Development." That exhibit toured throughout Brazil after the summit ended. At Brazil-SGI's Amazon Ecological Research Center, we are also engaged in a joint research project on reforestation of the Amazon rainforest. Since 1993, the "Ecology and Human Life" exhibit has been touring major cities of the United States, and in 1996 we also opened an exhibition on "The Amazon—Its Environment and Development" in Bolivia.

These exhibitions have been aimed at clarifying the sources of the problems and fostering a firm determination among people to act in unison toward their solution. And, as I have declared many times, if we are ever to solve global problems of this kind, we must move beyond outmoded thinking based on national interest and seek approaches based on the interests of humankind as a whole.

Global environmental problems require that we reorient our perspective. We have to come to grips with the realization that the age has ended when we can afford to think of our concerns and responsibilities as limited by national boundary lines drawn from narrow, even arbitrary motives.

Here, I would like to present a number of proposals for the consideration of the United Nations, which will play a pivotal role in the solution of global environmental problems.

One of the achievements of the Earth Summit was the establishment in 1993 of the Commission on Sustainable Development (CSD) under the auspices of the UN Economic and Social Council. This commission will supervise the implementation of Agenda 21, the action plan adopted in order to achieve sustainable development, and will oversee and coordinate the related programs being carried out under different UN agencies.

The United Nations Environment Programme (UNEP) was established back in 1972, and the founding of the CSD will contribute immensely to the coordination of policy in this field. Already the CSD is involved in follow-up activities for implemented projects by theme. However, as symbolized by the complicated debate over finances in the UN, there are many hurdles to overcome. In addition, even if the CSD is able to achieve a well-coordinated UN environmental policy, it will take considerable executive power to ensure that it can be transmitted into action.

Part of the limitations under which the UN labors today derives from its organization founded on the assembly of sovereign nation-states. It will not be able to release itself from those limitations unless nations become able to think in terms that transcend national interests. I believe that efforts must be made on the global level to create a system for promoting cooperative relations on global issues through the kind of voluntary restraint on sovereign rights being pursued in the European Union in environmental and other areas of policy.

Although the founding of the CSD has considerably ameliorated the problems of policy coordination, certainly there is an urgent need for an organization that can wield the strong leadership required to make final decisions and clarify the distribution of responsibility among different organizations with regard to global environmental problems. There ought to be an "Environment and Development Security Council," such as I have been advocating for some time, to serve as a forum for international decision-making regarding urgent problems of this kind.

Various groups have presented plans for the reform and reorganization of the UN, and many seek changes to a system that emphasizes a response to environmental issues. I believe that expert opinion should be widely sought and the options for the form and powers of the institution broadly studied in the process of determining the proper course for UN reform.

Another matter that should be studied is a framework for broad reflection of popular opinion in the changes made to the United Nations. Finding ways to take advantage of the constructive energies of NGOs will not only help to solidify the directions of policy but contribute to the formation of the support base that is indispensable for implementation of policy.

Considering the relative diminishing status of the sovereign state touched on above, I am convinced that within the UN as well, its character as a federation of sovereign states will gradually fade, with the faces of individuals gradually taking precedence over the faces of states. In that process the network of NGOs will certainly grow stronger and larger.

If there is a broad support base on the popular level, I believe it will open the way for obtaining the financial resources needed to execute policy, a matter which is now the greatest priority. At present, while it has become possible to procure funds for environmental protection through the Global Environment Facility, the available support remains small in scale, so it has yet to function as a full-fledged world system. Meanwhile, proposals have been advanced for securing working funds through environment taxes or fees for use of common international territories (such as for use of seaways and airspace). I believe the international groundwork will be laid for realistically considering such proposals as participation on the popular level expands.

I would therefore like to propose that an assembly along the lines of the Global Forum held in parallel with the Earth Summit five years ago be created to convene once a year. This forum could play a number of roles: as the "antennae of the people" channeling information from NGOs for the benefit of discussion at the regular and special sessions of the United Nations General Assembly, to pool voices from the grassroots and to provide a certain overall direction to the outcome of discussions.

In my volume of dialogues with the pioneer of peace studies Dr. Johan Galtung,[163] he proposed the founding of a United Nations People's Assembly as a second assembly to function in parallel with the current UN General Assembly. While it may take time to realize such an assembly, I believe it will be meaningful to establish the regular functioning of a system like the above-mentioned Global Forum as an assembly which could bring to bear on decision-making in international society a certain amount of influence from the standpoint of the people.

This proposal should be considered not only in order to ensure that the UN is permeated with the spirit, symbolized by the opening lines of its Charter, that each and every individual is an important actor in the global society, but in order to enhance the United Nations as a "parliament of humanity" in fact as well as in name.

All of these proposals will be difficult to realize, but I believe that, as we grapple with the problems and continue to search for the best possible measures for resolving the global environmental crisis, the new character of the United Nations that the times demand will gradually and naturally make itself manifest.

***

A task I would like to propose is a grassroots endeavor that lays down a new set of principles, what can be called an "Earth Charter," that will provide a clear vision for the third millennium.

The Universal Declaration of Human Rights is the crystallization of the wish to guarantee human existence for all people based on the resolve not to repeat the tragedies of World War II. Likewise, an Earth Charter should be a distillation of the spirit of coexistence and the resolve not to pass down

---

163 Johan Galtung (1930–), Norwegian peace scholar.

the evils perpetrated by modern civilization to subsequent generations. Realization of such a charter will certainly involve many difficulties, but we have no choice but to break the path toward it by sharing responsibility for our common struggle against global crisis and by building trust through sustained dialogue.

The late Austregésilo de Athayde,[164] recalling his involvement in the work of formulating the Universal Declaration of Human Rights, said in his dialogue with me that the declaration—created after a process entailing much clash of doctrines, creeds, interests and ideologies—would survive forever as a milestone of hope along the arduous path of development of the human race. He also said that economic and political ties were too fragile to unite people, and that there must be a kind of bond that links people together on a dimension that is noble enough, broad enough, and strong enough to determine the fate of humanity.[165] The same kind of spirit, I believe, is required for the drafting of the Earth Charter.

I urge the establishment of such an Earth Charter with the support of people around the world as proof that human beings possess the courage and wisdom as well as unshakable solidarity to determine our own destiny. I would like to propose that the SGI, too, devote itself to that endeavor, centered on such organizations as the Boston Research Center for the 21st Century[166] in the United States.

A Global Green Fund and Renewable Energy (2002)[167]

June 2002 marks the tenth anniversary of the Earth Summit (World Conference on Environment and Development) held in Rio de Janeiro, Brazil. In August of this year, the World Summit on Sustainable Development (WSSD) will be held in Johannesburg, South Africa. Convened immediately in the wake of the Cold War and amidst greatly heightened interest in

---

164 Austregésilo de Athayde (1898–1993), Brazilian writer and journalist, President of the Brazilian Academy of Letters (1959–93).

165 Athayde, Austregésilo de and Daisaku Ikeda. 1995. *Nijuisseiki no jinken o kataru* [Human Rights in the Twenty-first Century]. Tokyo: Ushio Shuppansha, p. 129.

166 Subsequently renamed the Ikeda Center for Peace, Learning, and Dialogue.

167 From 2002 Peace Proposal, "The Humanism of the Middle Way: Dawn of a Global Civilization."

environmental issues, the Rio Earth Summit was an international gathering of unprecedented scale, attended by the representatives of 183 countries and territories. It produced important results, including the signing of treaties on climate change and biodiversity, as well as the adoption of the Agenda 21 plan of action. Then UN Secretary-General Boutros Boutros-Ghali[168] described the Rio Summit as an "epistemological break,"[169] suggesting the significance of its impact on people's awareness.

Since then, however, global environmental degradation has advanced apace as there has been little progress in implementing these agreements. Taking global warming as one example, it took nine years after the adoption of the treaty aimed at preventing climate change before agreement was finally reached in November of last year on the operational details of the Kyoto Protocol that commits signatory states to the reduction of greenhouse gases.

To be meaningful, the WSSD must bring about a transformation in behavior corresponding to the revolution in awareness of a decade ago. The WSSD will of course review the progress made over the past ten years. But even more important is the need to muster a strong new determination, to offer new proposals and ideas, unconstrained by previous thinking, and to make the conference the point of departure for decisive action for the future.

Here I would like to propose three ideas for consideration by the WSSD, ideas that I feel could help enhance international cooperation. These are:

1. The establishment of the office of UN high commissioner for the environment;
2. The phased consolidation of the secretariats overseeing the implementation of the various environmental treaties and the establishment of a global green fund; and
3. A convention for the promotion of renewable energy.

The UN High Commissioners for refugees and human rights have proven effective advocates for their respective constituencies and concerns. In the

---

168 Boutros Boutros-Ghali (1922–), Egyptian statesman, and 6th UN Secretary-General (1992–96).
169 UNGA (United Nations General Assembly). 1992. "The Proceedings of the Conference and Opening and Closing Statements." A/CONF.151/26 (Vol. IV). Report of the United Nations Conference on Environment and Development. September 28.

same manner, a high commissioner for the environment would be charged with coordinating the activities of various agencies, exercising strong and visible leadership toward the resolution of global environmental issues.

At present, in addition to the UN Environment Programme (UNEP), a number of other international agencies including the UN Development Programme (UNDP) and the World Health Organization (WHO) are all involved in activities related to the environment. These activities are conducted under the separate mandates of these organizations, and there is a strong need for improved information exchange and coordination guided by a shared vision.

The holder of this new post could enunciate such a vision. She or he should be accorded authority equivalent to an under-secretary-general with a mandate to issue international recommendations and advisories, convene meetings or panels of experts and eminent persons and draft and release reports that envisage the future.

My second proposal is designed to alleviate the problems arising from having separate secretariats for each international treaty on the environment. Bringing together and eventually consolidating these should have the effect of strengthening the linkages between their activities, as well as realizing cost reduction through streamlining of reporting and other procedures. Under many treaties, signatory states are required to report on the status of their activities to fulfill their treaty obligations, and the costs of preparing these reports could also be reduced. Monies saved through such cost-cutting measures could be pooled into a global green fund that would promote protection of the ecosystem, reforestation activities, etc.

The SGI has been engaged in research at its Amazon Ecological Research Center in Brazil aimed at the preservation and revitalization of the rainforest. Based on this experience, we are committed to working in all ways possible to resolve the global environmental crisis.

The third proposal I would like to offer would encourage the accelerated implementation of renewable energy and help smooth the transition away from today's fossil fuel-dependent society. UNEP, which has been actively engaged in this issue, has stated that "accelerating the introduction of green, 'environmentally friendly' energy, such as solar, wind and wave power, is one of the most pressing issues facing mankind in the new millennium. . . ."[170] In

---

170 UNEP (United Nations Environment Programme). 2001. "UNEP: Renewable and Sustainable Energy a Critical Issue for This Millennium." UNEP News Release 01/02. January 10.

March of last year, UNEP published a report on this subject, titled "Natural Selection: Evolving Choices for Renewable Energy Technology and Policy."[171]

Within the leadership of the advanced industrial economies there has been an increasing awareness of the importance of this issue. At the 2000 Kyushu-Okinawa Summit, the G8 Renewable Energy Task Force was established; it presented its final report at the 2001 Genoa Summit. Further, the joint Communiqué of the Genoa Summit included this statement in the section "A Legacy for the Future": "We will ensure that renewable energy sources are adequately considered in our national plans and encourage others to do so as well."[172] This was the first time that a G8 communiqué had clearly called for the promotion of renewable energy.

In Europe, concrete planning has already begun. In September 2001, the European Union Council issued a directive on the promotion of renewable energy sources that calls for doubling the share of total energy consumption produced from renewable sources by the year 2010. At the same time, developing countries have been the site of many innovative efforts led by NGOs or as part of UNDP's Sustainable Rural Energy Project, which has introduced solar energy into remote villages in Bangladesh.

In this regard, I would like to propose that a convention for the promotion of renewable energy sources be considered at the WSSD as a means of consolidating and strengthening consensus on this crucial issue in both the developed and developing worlds.

In connection with the WSSD, I would like here to make mention of the Earth Charter. This document, which elucidates the values and principles for a sustainable future, was developed through a drafting process guided by the Earth Charter Commission headed by Mikhail Gorbachev,[173] president of Green Cross International, and Maurice Strong,[174] secretary-general of the 1992 Rio Earth Summit. The final draft was completed in June 2000, and it is hoped that it will be officially acknowledged at the WSSD.

---

171 UNEP (United Nations Environment Programme). 2000. *Natural Selection: Evolving Choices for Renewable Energy Technology and Policy.* Paris: UNEP.

172 G8 Genoa Summit. 2001. "Communiqué." Article 27. July 22.

173 Mikhail Gorbachev (1931–), President of the Soviet Union (1990–91), recipient of the Nobel Prize for Peace in 1990.

174 Maurice Strong (1929–), Canadian entrepreneur, first Executive Director of the United Nations Environment Programme (UNEP) (1972–75).

Within the SGI, there has been widespread support for the goals and principles of the Earth Charter; activities to promote the Earth Charter process have been organized in many countries around the world. In addition, the SGI-affiliated peace research institute the Boston Research Center for the 21st Century[175] organized symposiums and publications that offered multifaceted input into the drafting process.

The Earth Charter is not limited in its concerns to environmental issues but contains important language related to social and economic justice, democracy, nonviolence and peace. In this sense, it is a comprehensive statement of the norms and values required for effective global governance. It may be considered a guideline for humanity in the twenty-first century. Only with a shared vision, and shared effort toward the realization of that vision, will we be able to greet a more hopeful future. For this reason, it is imperative that the Earth Charter be given the support and recognition of the international community.

Further, it is vital that there be ongoing grassroots efforts to raise awareness so that the Earth Charter may become the fulcrum for the common struggle of humankind. The SGI is determined to continue working with the Earth Council and other organizations to support the translation of the Earth Charter into various languages and the development of pamphlets, videos and other materials that will publicize its ideas.

We need a global consensus behind environmental education, especially aimed at the new generations who will bear the burden of the future. I understand that the WSSD is being promoted with poster and essay contests for young people. There is a similar need to develop materials that will introduce the message of the Earth Charter to children and young people in language that is easily accessible to them. With this in mind, the SGI is committed to the promotion of environmental education and the dissemination of environmental information through a wide variety of means and channels.

UN Decade of Education for Sustainable Development (2005)[176]

The United Nations Framework Convention on Climate Change was adopted just prior to the UN Conference on Environment and Development (Earth

---

175 Subsequently renamed the Ikeda Center for Peace, Learning, and Dialogue.
176 From 2005 Peace Proposal, "Toward a New Era of Dialogue: Humanism Explored."

Summit) held in Rio de Janeiro, Brazil, in 1992. After a long and tortuous process, the ratification by Russia in 2004 of the Kyoto Protocol will finally cause it to enter into force this February (2005).

The Kyoto Protocol stipulates at least a 5-percent reduction in emissions of carbon dioxide and other greenhouse gases by the industrialized countries party to the treaty relative to their 1990 levels.

There are, however, many crucial issues that still need to be addressed, including the United States' withdrawal, the participation of developing countries and the development of a truly effective successor framework for the period after 2013.

Climate change is a key agenda item for this year's G8 Summit of leading industrial countries to be held at Gleneagles in the United Kingdom, to which both India and China have been invited. The participation of these two countries would certainly be desirable, as would substantive efforts to encourage the US to modify its position while developing a successor framework to the Kyoto Protocol.

In parallel with negotiations for the implementation of the convention, efforts have been made in various countries to establish the legal framework for a transition to a sustainable society. The European Union, for example, has led the way since the 1990s by such measures as introducing an environmental tax to control emissions of greenhouse gases and efforts to increase the share of renewable energy sources as a replacement for fossil fuels.

In this way, the short- and medium-term questions of the global environmental crisis have become part of international political and economic discourse. But in a more essential sense, this crisis needs to be addressed from a long-term perspective as something that threatens to undermine the very foundations of human survival.

It is said that in order to halt global warming it will be necessary to reduce total emissions by half. We need to rethink our ways of life as individuals and the core values and structures of contemporary civilization. The nature of the long and difficult path to sustainability reinforces once again the importance of taking action now with a long-term perspective.

The truly difficult and frightening aspect of the environmental crisis is that, even if we are able to note and respond to specific, individual danger signals, we cannot predict the most distant effects within the context of a vast system of interconnections.

In November of last year (2004), a documentary on the environmental crisis, *Strange Days on Planet Earth,*[177] was broadcast in Japan. It traced the connections between what at first seem to be unrelated phenomena—respiratory illness in the Caribbean and African dust storms; landslides in Hawai'i and changes in the flora of South America—demonstrating that they are all interlinked parts of a global ecological crisis.

Such improbable connections and unanticipated consequences have been referred to as the "Butterfly Effect"—the chains of connection and causality whereby the fluttering of a butterfly's wings in Brazil could be the cause of a tornado in Texas. It is one of the subjects touched on in my dialogue with Professor Victor Antonovich Sadovnichy,[178] rector of Moscow State University, in the context of resource and environmental issues.[179]

If we look back over the past several years, they were marked by a series of extreme weather conditions, from the deadly heat wave that struck Europe to massive floods in India and Bangladesh, as well as the hurricanes that devastated parts of North and Central America. Many experts consider these phenomena to be related to global climate change.

Chingiz Aitmatov,[180] in his book *The Mark of Cassandra,* uses the following parable to describe the psychological state that prevails among so many people.

> Suppose that a severe structural defect has been discovered in one of the massive bridges spanning San Francisco Bay, but it can still be traveled. It is as if we are saying that so long as the bridge holds up and is passable, let's keep transporting freight over it, leaving the problem of the bridge itself for someone else to deal with in the future.[181]

---

177 *National Geographic's Strange Days on Planet Earth.* 2004. Documentary. Produced by Sea Studio Foundation for Vulcan Productions, Inc., and National Geographic Television & Film.

178 Victor Antonovich Sadovnichy (1939–), Russian mathematician, Rector of Lomonosov Moscow State University (1992–).

179 Sadovnichy, Victor A. and Daisaku Ikeda. 2004. *Gaku wa hikari* [The Light of Learning]. Tokyo: Ushio Shuppansha, p. 236.

180 Chingiz Aitmatov (1928–2008), Kyrgyz author.

181 (trans. from) Aitmatov, Chingiz. 1996. *Kassandora no rakuin* [The Mark of Cassandra]. Tokyo: Ushio Shuppansha, p. 239.

In this work, which bears the name of the Greek prophetess of doom, Aitmatov portrays the dark side of contemporary civilization. As is symbolized by the fact that the Framework Convention on Climate Change required thirteen years to become operative through the entry into force of the Kyoto Protocol, international efforts are lagging behind the rapid pace of ecological degradation; at this rate the gap will only grow greater. We need to pay earnest heed to Cassandra's prophecy (the various signals indicating changes in the global environment) and take action—at the international, national and local levels—to redirect the path of human civilization before these predictions of disaster become a reality.

***

It is for just this reason that I must emphasize the need for firm determination and action. Sustainability cannot be realized without sustained effort.

It was with this in mind that I stressed the need to learn, reflect and empower in the proposal I made to the World Summit on Sustainable Development (WSSD) held in 2002.[182] For I believe that these three steps are critical to the larger effort to promote and realize the goals of the UN Decade of Education for Sustainable Development. Concretely, the SGI has held the exhibition "Seeds of Change: The Earth Charter and Human Potential" (developed jointly by the SGI and the Earth Charter Initiative) in more than ten countries; we are further planning a new exhibition on global ethics and the Earth Charter to be held in Japan from this year.

Strategies to Prevent Global Warming (2006)[183]

In February 2005, I met with Nobel Peace laureate Prof. Wangari Maathai[184] who was visiting Japan on the occasion of the entry into force of the Kyoto Protocol. During our meeting, Professor Maathai talked about the millions

---

182 Ikeda, Daisaku. 2002. "The Challenge of Global Empowerment: Education for a Sustainable Future." Environment proposal. http://www.sgi.org/sgi-president/proposals/environmental-proposal.html (accessed April 2, 2013).

183 From 2006 Peace Proposal, "A New Era of the People: Forging a Global Network of Robust Individuals."

184 Wangari Maathai (1940–2011), Kenyan politician and environmental activist, founder of the Green Belt Movement, recipient of the Nobel Prize for Peace in 2004.

of people involved in the environmental movement worldwide, and stated that her Nobel Peace Prize served to convey a strong message that protecting the environment is crucially important for the realization of peace. Indeed, resolving the global environmental crisis is an integral part of meeting the challenge of building a peaceful world.

Professor Maathai founded the Green Belt Movement to fight against the desertification of her homeland, Kenya. Over the past thirty years, the many women involved in the movement have planted 30 million trees throughout Africa.

Desertification is a serious and growing problem, particularly in the dry and arid regions of Africa and Asia. There is strong evidence that anthropogenic climate change is exacerbating the problem and its impact. Desertification was one of the subjects of the Millennium Ecosystem Assessment conducted under the auspices of the United Nations. The livelihoods of the almost 2 billion people living in drylands worldwide are potentially at risk if global warming continues to aggravate desertification at the current pace.

It was against this background that the UN declared 2006 the International Year of Deserts and Desertification to promote international cooperation to address this challenge. While supporting the goals of the International Year, I would like to urge continued efforts to find new approaches in the response to climate change.

Climate change is an area in which, like acid rain and ozone layer depletion before it, international efforts have coalesced. The Kyoto Protocol, which finally entered into force in 2005, obliges its industrialized signatories to reduce, by 2012, their emissions of greenhouse gases by at least 5 percent compared to 1990 levels.

There is, however, scientific consensus that these measures are insufficient, and emissions need to be reduced to at least half the current level in order to control global warming. Now the primary challenge has become how to reengage the United States and bring developing countries such as China and India, whose emissions are rapidly increasing, into some framework of international cooperation. This question was raised at the G8 Summit held at Gleneagles in July 2005.

At the eleventh session of the Conference of the Parties to the 1992 Climate Change Convention, which was held in conjunction with the first Meeting of the Parties to the Kyoto Protocol in December 2005 in Montreal, Canada, a working group was created to discuss over the next two years successor frameworks to the protocol for the period after 2012. It was significant that the conference provided a venue where representatives of all countries could meet and talk. The participation of the United States and the major developing countries—although conditioned on the nonbinding nature of the talks—was enough to save the convention from collapse, which once seemed imminent.

As the country that, as host, made a significant contribution to the completion of the Kyoto Protocol, I believe Japan has a special role to play in developing a successor framework. It can no doubt be most effective in this by working with countries with strong commitment to environmental issues.

The Kyoto Protocol commits all parties to improve energy efficiency, promote afforestation and take other measures to reduce emissions and increase the removal of carbon dioxide from the atmosphere. To facilitate these efforts, it also makes use of a scheme called the Kyoto Mechanism that allows the absorption of carbon by forests acting as carbon sinks to be factored into the achievement of emission reduction targets. In addition to exerting maximum effort toward achieving its own targets, Japan should take the initiative in assisting other countries in preserving and restoring forests and the introduction of renewable energy sources.

In addition to the Kyoto Mechanism, there is the Clean Development Mechanism (CDM), which enables developed countries to invest in projects that reduce greenhouse gases in developing countries. The proposals made by developing countries at the Montreal Climate Change Conference to add forest conservation programs to those covered in the CDM merit support.

I am convinced that it is crucial to encourage developing countries to participate in the framework of emission reduction programs by offering constructive mechanisms that respond to their specific needs and demands.

It is estimated that deforestation is responsible for 10 to 20 percent of the world's total rise in greenhouse gas emissions. There is an acute need to build a global network of cooperation for forest conservation. It was with these considerations in mind that I called, in my 2002 proposal, for the adoption of an international treaty for the promotion of renewable energy and the establishment of a global green fund.

Parallel with these efforts to combat global warming, I believe Japan has an important role to play in the field of education. The UN Decade of Education for Sustainable Development (DESD) began last year. The idea, originally put forward by the SGI and other NGOs, was proposed by the Japanese government at the 2002 World Summit on Sustainable Development in Johannesburg. It was later formally adopted by the UN General Assembly.

As an advocate of the DESD, the SGI will continue to work to promote it, for example through the exhibition "Seeds of Change: The Earth Charter and Human Potential" and the documentary film *A Quiet Revolution,*[185] whose production we supported.

In October 2005, the United Nations Educational, Scientific and Cultural Organization (UNESCO) drew up the International Implementation Scheme for the DESD. It defined the overall goal as "to integrate the principles, values, and practices of sustainable development in all aspects of education and learning,"[186] and through this it aims to change patterns of behavior and thus create a more sustainable future. It also called on governments to formulate national implementation schemes and structures to promote the DESD in order to raise awareness about sustainable development.

As sponsor of the DESD, Japan has a particular responsibility to provide a model for implementation at home and abroad. This should take the form of cooperation and assistance extended to Asian and African countries where lives and livelihoods are impacted by the effects of desertification and other forms of environmental degradation.

I have stressed on many occasions that the way forward for Japan in the twenty-first century is to make environmental and humanitarian commitments its very raison d'être. These commitments come together in efforts to provide aid and assistance that will enable people and societies to advance on the path of sustainable development.

A World Environmental Organization (2008)[187]

This year will mark the sixtieth anniversary of the adoption of the Universal Declaration of Human Rights (UDHR), an expression of the shared resolve never to repeat the horrors and tragedies of World War II. The UDHR comprises a total of thirty articles that set forth civil and political rights on the one hand and economic, social and cultural rights on the other. It opens

---

185 Earth Council. 2002. *A Quiet Revolution: The Earth Charter and Human Potential.* DVD. Costa Rica: Earth Council. http://www.sgi.org/resource-center/ngo-resources/education-for-sustainable-development/a-quiet-revolution.html (accessed April 2, 2013).

186 UNESCO (United Nations Educational, Scientific and Cultural Organization). 2005. "United Nations Decade of Education for Sustainable Development (2005–2014): Draft International Implementation Scheme," p. 6.

187 From 2008 Peace Proposal, "Humanizing Religion, Creating Peace."

with the noble preamble: "Whereas recognition of the inherent dignity and of the equal and inalienable rights of all members of the human family is the foundation of freedom, justice and peace in the world. . . ."[188]

The Declaration has influenced the policymaking of governments and served as the basis for human rights-related conventions and institutions, as well as inspiring generations of human rights activists. When it was adopted, the UDHR both gave voice to a universal vision of human rights and established the goal of bringing into being a world free from fear and free from want. Together with the United Nations Charter, likewise adopted in the wake of World War II, the UDHR signaled a new departure and charted a path to new modes of peaceful coexistence for humankind.

In the twenty-first century, the "horizontal" (spatial) axis of a universality that transcends national borders as advocated in the UDHR must be complemented by the "vertical" (temporal) axis of a sense of responsibility that extends to future generations. This is especially crucial in our efforts to construct a sustainable and peaceful global society.

In October 2007, the United Nations Environment Programme's "Global Environment Outlook: Environment for Development (GEO-4)" was issued. According to this report, although air quality in some cities has improved, more than 2 million people globally are estimated to die prematurely each year due to air pollution. The Antarctic hole in the stratospheric ozone layer that gives protection from harmful ultraviolet radiation has grown to its largest extent ever. Moreover, available freshwater per person has decreased on a global scale, and at least 16,000 species have been identified as threatened with extinction.[189] Progress has been made on the relatively simpler issues, but the more complex and intractable issues have yet to be addressed with any degree of adequacy. There is an urgent need for action.

The "Fourth Assessment Report" issued by the Intergovernmental Panel on Climate Change (IPCC) in November 2007 reveals that the sharp increase in CO_2 emissions in recent years has almost doubled the pace of the warming trend for the fifty years from 1956 to 2005 compared to that for the one hundred years from 1906 to 2005.[190] If present trends continue, the Earth's

---

188 UN (United Nations). 1948. "Universal Declaration of Human Rights."
189 See UNEP (United Nations Environment Programme). 2007. "Global Environment Outlook: Environment for Development (GEO4)." Nairobi: UNEP.
190 See IPCC (Intergovernmental Panel on Climate Change). 2007. "IPCC Fourth Assessment Report: Climate Change 2007," p. 30.

surface temperatures may rise by as much as 6.4 degrees Celsius by the end of the twenty-first century.[191]

The report further warns that if global warming proceeds unchecked, the Arctic sea ice will continue to shrink, and droughts, heat waves, torrential rainfall and other extreme weather events are likely to increase in frequency.[192] These changes could seriously threaten the very foundations of human existence on Earth.

The steadily deepening sense of urgency regarding environmental issues is reflected in the fact that climate change has consistently been on the agenda at recent annual summit meetings, culminating in the High-Level Event on Climate Change held at the UN Headquarters in September 2007. Nevertheless, international society lags in its attempt to come together in coordinated action.

Ecological integrity is the shared interest and concern of all humankind, an issue that transcends national borders and priorities. Any solution will require a strong sense of individual responsibility and commitment by each of us as inhabitants sharing the same planet.

The founding president of the Soka Gakkai, the educator and geographer Tsunesaburo Makiguchi,[193] stressed that individuals should be aware of three levels of citizenship: our local roots and commitments based in our immediate community; our sense of belonging to a national community; and an appreciation of the fact that the world is ultimately the stage on which we live our lives and that we are all citizens of the world. On this basis, he urged that people transcend an excessive or exclusive attachment to national interests and develop an active awareness of their commitment to humankind as a whole.

This was the principle underlying the SGI's call in 2002 for a UN Decade of Education for Sustainable Development and our subsequent collaboration with relevant UN agencies and other NGOs toward the realization and implementation of the Decade.

We are living at a time when concerted, committed action—for the sake of the entire Earth and all humankind—is acutely needed. The United Nations is the global institution that can serve as the facilitating focus for such efforts. The UN has, for example, developed and coordinated environmental activities through the United Nations Environment Programme (UNEP), which hosts

---

191 Ibid., p. 45.
192 Ibid., p. 51.
193 Tsunesaburo Makiguchi (1871–1944), founding president of the Soka Kyoiku Gakkai (forerunner of the Soka Gakkai) (1930–44).

the secretariats of various international environmental treaties, and promotes sustainable development and environmental protection programs through a network of six regional offices.

In recognition of UNEP's solid record of achievement, there are calls for the expansion of its capacity in order to enable it to respond better to global environmental threats that continue to grow in complexity and magnitude. A common understanding was reached regarding such demands at the UNEP Governing Council/Global Ministerial Environment Forum held in Nairobi in February 2007. There, the need for a stronger institutional framework to collect and analyze scientific findings and to coordinate the drafting, adoption and implementation of environmental conventions was emphasized, and an upgrading of UNEP from programme to agency status was called for.[194]

It has long been my view that global environmental issues would constitute one of the UN's principal missions in the twenty-first century. In my 2002 peace proposal, I suggested the establishment of the office of a UN high commissioner for the environment, with a core mandate to coordinate the activities of various agencies and exercise strong leadership toward the resolution of global environmental issues. Thus I would like to join my voice to those calling for UNEP to be strengthened and upgraded to the status of a specialized agency, a world environmental organization.

The key reason I support such moves is that, at present, only those countries that serve on the UNEP Governing Council are able to participate directly in its debates and decision-making. If UNEP is accorded the status of a specialized agency, however, any country that chooses to become a member state will find a place at the table.

A similar vision underlay the call I made in 1978 for the creation of an "Environmental United Nations."[195] Developing an institutional framework that enables all states to engage with environmental issues will be of utmost importance, especially toward the widely acknowledged goal of establishing effective global environmental governance.

In this, the need to combat climate change is recognized as a paramount challenge. At the Heiligendamm Summit held in Germany in June 2007, the G8 leaders gave serious consideration to the goal of halving global greenhouse

---

194 See The International Institute for Sustainable Development – Reporting Services Division (IISD RS). 2007. "Ministerial Consultations: UNFCCC Address."

195 Ikeda, Daisaku. 1978. "The Environment: A Challenge for All Humanity." *Seikyo Shimbun.* November 19, p. 5.

gas emissions by 2050. But at present the only existing framework for reducing greenhouse gas emissions is the one based on the Kyoto Protocol, which will expire at the end of 2012. Clearly, it is vital that any new framework ensure global participation, particularly by the countries that were not included in the existing framework, if the 50-percent reduction is to be achieved.

In December 2007, the United Nations Climate Change Conference (UNCCC) was held in Bali, Indonesia, and the Bali Roadmap, which charts the course toward the creation of a post-2012 framework, was adopted. Although stopping short of setting specific emission reduction targets, it represents a degree of progress, as the United States, India and China—major sources of greenhouse gas emissions that were not part of the Kyoto Protocol framework—all agreed to participate in the process.

I would urge all parties pursuing the negotiations to be held under the Bali Roadmap to break away from the negative approach of minimizing national obligations and burdens and instead adopt a positive focus on the achievement of larger, global objectives. This kind of fundamental reorientation is essential.

Combating climate change is a challenge that demands us all to rise above the constraints of self-interest. We need to build an international framework of cooperation and solidarity against this threat. Specifically, I would ask the major emitters to take the initiative in establishing ambitious goals and implementing bold and effective policies while actively supporting the efforts of other countries. In this way, I hope they will engage in positively oriented competition aimed at making the greatest contribution to the resolution of this planetary crisis.

In a book published in 1903, Tsunesaburo Makiguchi called for "humanitarian competition" among states.[196] This was a vision of an international order in which the world's diverse states strive to positively influence each other, to coexist and flourish together rather than pursuing narrowly defined national interests at each other's expense. I feel that the work of solving the global environmental crisis provides a unique opportunity to move toward such a world. It is my earnest hope that Japan, which assumes the G8 Presidency for the Hokkaido Toyako Summit in July this year, will lead the way in fostering positive attitudes and approaches appropriate to the needs of the new era.

Regarding the most effective means of reducing greenhouse gas emissions, I would like to focus on the transformation toward a low-carbon no-waste

---

196 (trans. from) Makiguchi, Tsunesaburo. 1981–97. *Makiguchi Tsunesaburo zenshu* [The Complete Works of Tsunesaburo Makiguchi]. 10 vols. Tokyo: Daisanbunmei-sha. Vol. 2, p. 398.

society. The first step toward this must be the introduction of renewable energy and energy conservation measures. The proactive setting of goals and commitments will unleash the kinds of positive thinking that take, for example, the form of technological innovation.

The European Union has already taken important steps to encourage the use of renewable energy sources. Agreement reached at the EU Heads of States and Government meeting held in March 2007 requires EU member states to increase their use of solar and other renewable sources of energy, setting a binding target of raising the share of renewable energies in overall EU energy consumption from the current 6.5 percent to 20 percent by 2020.

Parallel to this, energy conservation and enhanced energy efficiency are critical in the transition to a low-carbon no-waste society. Japan has a wealth of experience and achievement in this field and should play an active role, collaborating closely with its neighbors, in developing East Asia into a global model of energy efficiency.

In my 2007 peace proposal, I called for the creation of an East Asia environment and development organization as a pilot model of regional cooperation and the kernel for the eventual creation of an East Asian Union. It would be desirable, as one step toward this long-term goal, for Japan to take the lead in energy conservation issues.

In addition to "top-down" reform through institutional reframing, it is crucial to encourage "bottom-up" change by broadening grassroots engagement and empowering people toward collective action. This conviction underpinned my call for a Decade of Education for Sustainable Development. I believe strongly in the power of learning. Empowerment through learning brings out the unlimited potentials of individuals and consequently creates currents, first within the respective regions, and eventually globally across borders, that can fundamentally transform the world in which we live.

The SGI supported the production of the educational film *A Quiet Revolution*[197] in collaboration with the Earth Council, UNEP and the United Nations Development Programme (UNDP) in 2001, as well as the exhibition "Seeds of Change: The Earth Charter and Human Potential," which was initially created in collaboration with the Earth Charter Initiative. These tools have been used to promote the UN Decade of Education for Sustainable

---

197 Earth Council. 2002. *A Quiet Revolution: The Earth Charter and Human Potential.* DVD. Costa Rica: Earth Council. http://www.sgi.org/resource-center/ngo-resources/education-for-sustainable-development/a-quiet-revolution.html (accessed April 2, 2013).

Development since its inception. Prior to the start of the Decade, the Boston Research Center for the 21st Century[198] supported the drafting process of the Earth Charter, a declaration of fundamental principles and values for building a just and sustainable global society.

In the area of environmental protection, SGI-Brazil founded the Amazon Ecological Research Center in 1992. The center has since been collecting and preserving seeds of tree species critical for the integrity of the Amazonian ecosystem. Meanwhile, SGI organizations in Canada, the Philippines and elsewhere have also been engaged in tree planting activities.

When I met in February 2005 with Nobel Peace laureate and founder of the Green Belt Movement Prof. Wangari Maathai,[199] our dialogue focused on the deeper meaning of planting trees. We discussed Shakyamuni,[200] who taught the profound value of tree planting 2,500 years ago, and King Ashoka,[201] the ancient Indian ruler known for his renunciation of war and his policies of non-violence, compassion and tolerance, who implemented programs to protect the environment, among them establishing mango groves and planting trees along thoroughfares. The Green Belt Movement has greatly contributed to the empowerment of women, and we concurred that "to plant trees is to plant life"—to sow and foster the seeds of the future, of a peaceful society.

Merely acquiring knowledge about environmental issues is not enough to make the Decade of Education for Sustainable Development meaningful. It is vital that individuals tangibly perceive the irreplaceable value of the ecosystem of which they are an integral part, and make a commitment to its protection. Such awareness is best developed through the kind of hands-on experience that participation in tree planting projects affords.

The Billion Trees Campaign, promoted by UNEP and originally inspired by Professor Maathai, is a striking global grassroots initiative to counter climate change. The Campaign has been a rousing success, with 1.9 billion trees planted during 2007 and a goal of planting another billion trees in 2008. This will provide vitally important opportunities for experiential learning,

---

198 Subsequently renamed the Ikeda Center for Peace, Learning, and Dialogue.

199 Wangari Maathai (1940–2011), Kenyan politician and environmental activist, founder of the Green Belt Movement, recipient of the Nobel Prize for Peace in 2004.

200 Shakyamuni (Gautama Siddartha) (c. 560–480 BCE), the founder of Buddhism.

201 King Ashoka (c. 268–432 BCE), ruler of the Indian Maurya dynasty and the first king to unify India.

and I hope linkages with the UN Decade of Education for Sustainable Development will be deepened as this program goes forward.

The success of the Decade and, more crucially, of efforts to slow and reverse ecological degradation, hinges on each individual's ability to feel this as a personal challenge and take concrete action on that basis. We need to think about and discuss what we—on the individual, family, community and workplace level—can do in our immediate environment to build a sustainable future, and work together to this end.

This approach may be thought of as an action network for a sustainable future. There is no reason for this network to be limited to environmental issues. By expanding cooperation and collaborative links with activities in such areas as poverty alleviation, human rights and peace, we can build the solid foundations of a common struggle to resolve the shared problems facing humanity. The SGI is committed to playing an ever more active role in building such an action network.

An International Sustainable Energy Agency (2009)[202]

In addition to the global economic downturn, the world is also facing the intertwined crises of climate change, environmental degradation, energy and food shortages and poverty. Viewed from a historical perspective, the current situation seems to combine some of the most alarming characteristics of both the 1930s and the early 1970s.

In the 1930s, in response to the Great Depression, efforts were made to achieve intergovernmental policy coordination to lower tariff barriers and stabilize exchange rates. However, these negotiations ended in failure, and each country turned to protectionist economic policies designed only to defend its own interests without consideration for others. This resulted in a further worsening of the global economic crisis, in a demonstration of the destructive nature of mutual mistrust described in the famous game-theory model of the "Prisoner's Dilemma." Regrettably, it was only in the wake of the horrific tragedy of World War II that the lessons of the Great Depression were applied by the international community.

In the first half of the 1970s, abrupt changes in US economic and currency policies known as the Nixon shock were followed by the oil crisis. These

---

202 From 2009 Peace Proposal, "Toward Humanitarian Competition: A New Current in History."

years also marked the emergence of a series of new global challenges. In response, the first international conferences on environmental and food issues were organized under the auspices of the United Nations, and the world's major industrialized democracies held their first summit meeting (G6) in Rambouillet, France.

Although these events marked the origins of important international cooperation frameworks that continue until the present day, it is all too evident that they have not functioned effectively in the face of conflicting national interests. This is evidenced by the fact that the problems that emerged at that time remain largely unresolved.

Today we need to act with far greater boldness and on the basis of a much broader vision than was demonstrated during the crises of past decades. In the United States, which is the epicenter of the global financial crisis, "change" was the central theme of the presidential campaign of recently inaugurated President Barack Obama.[203] In his inaugural address he stated, "[T]he world has changed, and we must change with it. . . . What is required of us now is a new era of responsibility."[204] The challenge to bring about change confronts not only the US but the entire world.

***

Global warming is having profound impacts on ecosystems everywhere. In addition to causing meteorological disasters, it has the potential to aggravate armed conflicts and the problems of poverty and hunger. It epitomizes the twenty-first-century crisis of human civilization.

United Nations Secretary-General Ban Ki-moon,[205] who has identified climate change as one of the key issues for the UN to address, has warned: "Yet, in the longer run, no one—rich or poor—can remain immune from the dangers brought by climate change."[206] None of us, in other words, can be a bystander: We must all see this issue as our own.

---

203 Barack Obama (1961–), 44th President of the United States (2009–), recipient of the Nobel Prize for Peace in 2009.

204 Obama, Barack. 2009. "President Barack Obama's Inaugural Address." January 20.

205 Ban Ki-moon (1944–), South Korean statesman, 8th Secretary-General of the United Nations (2007–).

206 Ban, Ki-moon. 2007. "Climate Change—Together We Can Win the Battle" in "Human Development Report 2007/2008. Fighting Climate Change: Human Solidarity in a Divided World," p. 23.

Climate change is both an ongoing multidimensional crisis and a threat to the future of humankind, in that it burdens future generations with immense challenges of dire consequence.

Regrettably, no conspicuous progress was made in negotiations on the reduction of greenhouse gas emissions last year. It is imperative that constructive discussions take place in the lead-up to this December, the deadline to agree upon a successor framework to the Kyoto Protocol whose first commitment period ends in 2012. It is vital that developing and emerging countries be committed participants in any new framework, in addition to renewed efforts by the developed countries.

The critical question, therefore, is in what way can we achieve a genuine sharing of action?

Energy policy is clearly an area around which international cooperation can be built. Not only is securing adequate sources of energy a critical issue for developing and emerging countries; energy issues are also key to any effort by developed countries to effect the transition to a low-carbon no-waste society. In view of the fact that nearly 60 percent of greenhouse gas emissions originate in consumption of fossil fuels, global shared action on energy policy would be a highly effective approach in combating climate change.

US President Barack Obama's economic stimulus and job creation strategy has a focus on new industries and jobs in areas such as alternative energy resource development, and might be called a "Green New Deal." In like manner, an increasing number of countries—Japan and South Korea among them—are now either considering or implementing emergency economic measures that promote investment in the energy and environmental sectors.

In my peace proposal last year (2008), I called for humanitarian competition to be at the heart of efforts to solve the global environmental crisis, urging the promotion of renewable energy measures and energy efficiency initiatives as a way to realize a transition from dependence on fossil fuels to a low-carbon no-waste society. Recent developments suggest movement in this direction.

One example is the establishment of the International Renewable Energy Agency (IRENA) with the support of more than fifty countries. The intergovernmental organization was founded in Bonn, Germany, on January 26 this year, setting in motion an international effort to promote the use of renewable energy that embraces industrialized, developing and emerging countries alike. Having called for a convention for the promotion of renewable energy sources in a proposal seven years ago, I welcome the establishment of this new international agency.

There has also been a new initiative in the area of energy efficiency. In December 2008, energy ministers from a group of countries including the G8, China, India and Brazil issued a joint statement calling for an International Partnership for Energy Efficiency Cooperation (IPEEC) to be established during 2009 with its secretariat located within the International Energy Agency (IEA).

These new initiatives need to be functioning by the end of 2012, when the first commitment period of the Kyoto Protocol ends. Going forward, they can serve as a focus for building international cooperation and play key roles in the implementation of the 1992 United Nations Framework Convention on Climate Change.

In addition to these measures, I would propose that in the future an international sustainable energy agency be created under the aegis of the UN to further the work of these two organizations—IRENA and IPEEC—so that international cooperation on energy policy may take firm and universal root throughout the global community.

Some may express concern over these initiatives, arguing that technology transfer could undermine the economic competitiveness of individual countries and that financial cooperation further adds to the burden on their taxpayers. But international cooperation toward the common goal of reversing the trend of global warming can be framed by the principle Tsunesaburo Makiguchi[207] considered central to humanitarian competition, that "by benefiting others, we benefit ourselves."[208] From this broad perspective, efforts to benefit the whole of humanity ultimately serve the national interest.

Further, this new agency could serve as a locus for bolstering solidarity, embracing input from local governments, the private sector and NGOs, for the building of a sustainable global society. Its functions could, for example, include an open registration system whereby any interested organization could freely document its activities and best practices, which would then be made available in an open database on the Internet, providing a platform for information exchange and the facilitation of partnerships.

---

207 Tsunesaburo Makiguchi (1871–1944), founding president of the Soka Kyoiku Gakkai (forerunner of the Soka Gakkai) (1930–44).

208 (trans. from) Makiguchi, Tsunesaburo. 1981–97. *Makiguchi Tsunesaburo zenshu* [The Complete Works of Tsunesaburo Makiguchi]. 10 vols. Tokyo: Daisanbunmei-sha. Vol. 2, p. 399.

The SGI-affiliated Toda Institute for Global Peace and Policy Research held a conference titled "Facing Climate Change with a Renewed Environmental Ethic" in November 2008. A focal point was the need to form a synergistic alliance among governments, the private sector and civil society based on a shared sense of responsibility to future generations. The conference also underlined the importance of gaining the broad-based support and active participation of the public in such an alliance.

Since 2002, the SGI has held the exhibition "Seeds of Change: The Earth Charter and Human Potential," developed in collaboration with the Earth Charter Initiative, in twenty countries and eight languages. The SGI has also organized environmental activities such as afforestation projects in several countries working with other like-minded organizations. While each individual environmental initiative has a great significance of its own, collaborative efforts generate important multiplier effects.

The UN Decade of Education for Sustainable Development reaches its midpoint this year, a fact that highlights the need for ordinary citizens to become even more vigorously engaged in education and awareness-raising activities.

Human Rights

Overcoming Racial Discrimination (1996)[209]

One of the biggest issues facing the international community today is to find means of resolving the conflicts and confrontations that continue to erupt throughout the world, in particular the internal conflicts that have become so prevalent, and thus achieve a genuine and lasting peace.

The United Nations designated 1995 the Year for Tolerance, providing an opportunity to raise awareness of the racial, ethnic and religious intolerance that so often sparks confrontation; however, the year also saw the occurrence of a truly tragic incident that made us all acutely aware of just how deeply rooted the problem is. This was the assassination of Israeli Prime Minister Yitzhak Rabin,[210] one of the principal proponents of Middle East peace, in

---

209 From 1996 Peace Proposal, "Toward the Third Millennium: The Challenge of Global Citizenship."

210 Yitzhak Rabin (1922–95), Israeli Prime Minister (1974–77, 1992–95), recipient of the Nobel Prize for Peace in 1994.

November. The fact that the assassin was an Israeli student belonging to an extremist Jewish group opposed to peace with the Palestinians is truly sad.

For many years I have watched the steady progress of the Middle East peace process and have considered it a hopeful sign of the advent of an "age of reconciliation." Inasmuch as I have long called for compromise in the interest of peace and welcomed the progress being made, Prime Minister Rabin's death came as an especially heavy blow.

In Bosnia, as well, the end of last year (December 1995) finally brought into sight an exit from a conflict that victimized many and produced countless tragedies over the course of more than three and a half years. It must be said, however, that it is still too early to let down our guard. The fact that the conflict was permitted to reach a stalemate despite the condemnations of international public opinion can be attributed to two things: the ease with which ethnic and religious differences came to be viewed in absolute terms, and the mistake of allowing all problems to be blamed on such differences.

It is equally disturbing to note, as demonstrated by the ominous rumblings of ethnic strife continuing in the former Soviet Union, the clearly regressive phenomena of fanaticism and intolerance that mark the history of our post-Cold War, post-Yalta system world.

The "old fissiparous nationalism"[211] to which Edward H. Carr[212] referred in his 1945 book *Nationalism and After,* has in fact revived in the wake of the Cold War and become the driving force behind various ethnic and national movements. In this context, I cannot help thinking that the concept of "national self-determination" (as set forth in the UN Charter[213] and the International Covenant on Civil and Political Rights[214]) should perhaps not be accorded the overriding value it has enjoyed and that a reassessment may be necessary. Although this right is recognized in various ways under international law, the question remains as to whether it can be applied without limits.

Of course, I do not deny the importance of ethnic or national self-determination. But if we say that the goals of peace and freedom cannot be achieved in its absence, then we are saying that most of the nations and peoples

---

211   Carr, Edward Hallett. 1945. *Nationalism and After*. London: Macmillan, p. 36.

212   Edward Hallett Carr (1892–1982), British political scientist and historian.

213   UN (United Nations). 1945. "Charter of the United Nations." Chapter 7, Article 51.

214   UN (United Nations). 1966. "International Covenant on Civil and Political Rights." Article 1.

who have not attained statehood in the full sense of the term will never be able to realize these goals. At the same time, we must note that established nation-states have not necessarily succeeded in realizing these goals, either.

It therefore seems clear to me that national self-determination cannot be viewed in absolute terms. Instead, what is needed is a calm and measured look at the factors that prevent the sought-after fruits of national self-determination—peace and freedom—from being realized. We must thoroughly examine the circumstances that permit simplistic national rhetoric to take precedence over more complex realities. Likewise, we must continually strive to see beyond the surface and think long and hard about what genuinely constitutes the best interests of the human person.

I believe that it is precisely the spirit of tolerance that nourishes the much-desired fruit of peace and freedom. If any nation proves this, it is the new South Africa led by President Nelson Mandela,[215] which continues to make efforts toward this cause. President Mandela himself has spoken of these challenges and of the grand dream of transforming South Africa from a "country in which the majority lived with little hope, to one in which they can live and work with dignity, with a sense of self-esteem and confidence in the future."[216]

More than a year and a half has passed since the people of the new South Africa took up the task of forging a "rainbow nation." This beautifully evocative phrase indicates a nation in which people of different ethnicities and cultures form a multi-hued, harmonious whole while giving free rein to the distinctive characteristics of each component group. Many issues must be resolved before the South African people can fully emerge from the shadow of long years of discrimination and abuse. It is clear, however, that they are making steady progress toward building a society of racial harmony.

As evidence of this, the UN Commission on Human Rights, which had debated the issue of apartheid since 1967, announced in February 1995 that the era of apartheid has ended in South Africa.[217] Accordingly, the

---

215 Nelson Mandela (1918–), President of South Africa (1994–99), recipient of the Nobel Prize for Peace in 1993.

216 Mandela, Nelson. 1994. "Nelson Mandela's Address to the People of Cape Town, Grand Parade, on the Occasion of His Inauguration as State President, 9 May 1994."

217 See UNHCR (United Nations Commission on Human Rights). 1995. "Implementation of the International Convention on the Suppression and Punishment of the Crime of Apartheid." E/CN. 4/RES/1995/10. Resolution adopted by UNHCR. February 17.

Commission resolved to remove the issue from its agenda. South African progress toward democratization has also been recognized by the Organization of African Unity (OAU), which has agreed to readmit South Africa as a member. Thus, South Africa is taking one step after another to reinstate itself in the international community.

I have had the opportunity to meet twice with President Mandela and once with Deputy President de Klerk.[218] In my discussions with both men, I felt strongly that the central ideas driving the move to abolish apartheid were the desire to overcome hatred and distrust and a commitment to dialogue. There is no doubt that sustained dialogue, in which each party makes every effort to understand the other's position, is the preeminent factor in preventing the slide into violence and chaos and in enabling the splendors of human tolerance to shine through.

In June 1992, then President de Klerk expressed these thoughts concerning the end of apartheid: "We desire to create a society in which all people are victors, instead of one consisting of winners and losers who oppose and threaten one another in the pursuit of self-interests."[219]

This determination not to create losers is crucial if we are to resolve the widespread civil strife that plagues our world today. So long as there are even a few losers—people who know the bitter taste of defeat—we can neither hope for a truly stable society nor expect to eliminate completely the seeds of future conflict.

I believe that education is the only tool available to us that can heal past wounds and build forward-looking societies in which everyone is a victor. In my conversations with President Mandela, we continually returned to the theme of education. At first, education may seem an indirect means of addressing these problems, but I am convinced that it is in fact the most effective means of instilling the spirit of tolerance. Only through learning can we open the spiritual windows of humanity, releasing people from the confines of ethnic or other group-based worldviews. Ethnic identity is deeply rooted in the human unconscious, and it is crucial that it be tempered through

---

218 Frederik Willem de Klerk (1936–), President of South Africa (1989–94), recipient of the Nobel Prize for Peace in 1993.

219 (trans. from) "Meiyokaicho, Minami Ahurika no Dekuraku daitoryo to kaidan" [SGI President Meets with President de Klerk of South Africa]. *Seikyo Shimbun.* June 5, 1992, p. 2.

unremitting educational efforts that encourage a more open and universal sense of humanity.

Since President Mandela assumed office, he has given national priority to educational policy. Desiring to support that effort, last year the SGI-USA youth division undertook the "Friendship through Knowledge Exchange: Books for Africa" project, through which 10,000 volumes were donated to South African universities and other educational institutions. Such support for education has not been limited to South Africa: the members of the Soka Gakkai youth division in Japan have been in the forefront of support for a UNESCO-sponsored literacy project in Asia and Africa.

These are perhaps humble contributions, but they stem from the conviction that the success of South Africa's efforts to create a "rainbow nation" are certain to give hope to other African nations and, by extension, all who suffer from ethnic division. I personally believe that South Africa's continuing struggle to champion the spirit of tolerance manifests the kind of philosophy of coexistence that our times demand. I also believe the international community should spare no effort to support this unprecedented challenge.

As I observe developments in South Africa, I am reminded that the true source of human happiness lies in the reconciliation and harmonization of different groups, not in their division and conflict. It may be only natural for people to tend to strengthen their association with groups in an attempt to assuage the uneasiness arising from a vacuum of identity. I have come to suspect, however, that "national consciousness" is largely a fiction half-intentionally created over the course of modern history.

The Bengali poet Rabindranath Tagore[220] possessed both a delicate sensibility that permitted him to directly grasp the eternal and a penetrating insight into the nature of human existence. In his work *The Religion of Man,* he reflected on the nature of ethnic conflicts, what we might call the impasse of human history:

> Our great prophets in all ages did truly realize in themselves the freedom of the soul in their consciousness of the spiritual kinship of man which is universal. And yet human races, owing to their

---

220 Rabindranath Tagore (1861–1941), Bengali poet, writer, composer, playwright, essayist and painter, recipient of the Nobel Prize for Literature in 1913.

external geographical condition, developed in their individual isolation a mentality that is obnoxiously selfish.[221]

Tagore forcefully indicts the kind of human brutality and inhumanity that can erupt at any time given the right conditions. He leaves us with the following warning:

> The vastness of the race problem with which we are faced to-day will either compel us to train ourselves to moral fitness in the place of merely external efficiency, or the complications arising out of it will fetter all our movements and drag us to our death.[222]

More than half a century has passed since this cry rose out of the soul of this great poet, and his words shine all the brighter as the regressive phenomena of world history become increasingly evident. It may be possible for opposing groups to reach some sort of an agreement concerning "external efficiencies" in the political or economic sphere. Certainly, such understandings are important; but unless we address the issue of "moral fitness" posed by Tagore, hostilities will inevitably break out again at the slightest provocation.

Tagore explained to Albert Einstein[223] the main theme running through *The Religion of Man* in the following way:

> Our religion can only have its significance in this phenomenal world comprehended by our human self. . . . [Divine reality] has found its highest place in the history of our religion owing to its human character . . . and offering an eternal background to all the ideals of perfection which have their harmony with man's own nature.[224]

The inherent role of religion can be defined as taking human hearts that are divided and connecting them through a universal human spirit. In a speech delivered at Harvard University (in September 1993), I emphasized that it

---

221 Tagore, Rabindranath. 1931. *The Religion of Man*. New York: Macmillan, p. 154.
222 Ibid., p. 156.
223 Albert Einstein (1879–1955), German-born American physicist, recipient of the Nobel Prize for Physics in 1921.
224 Tagore, Rabindranath. 1931. *The Religion of Man*. New York: Macmillan, p. 203.

is "the religious" that supports, inspires and provides the impetus for people searching for the good and the valuable in their lives; moreover, religious sentiment can offer people a means to access the inner resources that enable them to transcend themselves.[225] This was precisely what Tagore was seeking, and it also constitutes one of the conditions religion must meet if it is to contribute to a more hopeful future.

Tolerance is more than just a mental attitude; it must grow out of a sense of order and coexistence, a cosmic sensibility that issues up from the deepest wellsprings of life. As explained by the Buddhist doctrine of "dependent origination," no phenomenon in either the human or natural domains arises independently of all others. The cosmos is created through the interrelation and interdependence of all things. Tolerance that is firmly rooted in a world-view of dynamic interdependence can, I believe, be instrumental in enabling us to transcend the threat of a clash of civilizations and to realize a philosophy of coexistence that will permit us to build a world of human harmony.

In my earlier remarks on the problem of ethnicity, I emphasized that the principal criterion for appraising a given political decision must be whether or not it truly serves the best interests of people. In concrete terms, our yardstick should be to ensure individual dignity and human rights.

With the adoption of the Vienna Declaration at the World Conference on Human Rights in 1993, the universality of human rights has been accorded a new degree of recognition by the international community. Respect for those rights in all parts of the world is becoming a matter of common concern for all people.

One of the pioneers in this field was the late Austregésilo de Athayde,[226] who was involved in the drafting of the Universal Declaration of Human Rights (UDHR). Mr. Athayde maintained that human rights constitute the most sublime and inalienable value to which humankind has given birth.[227] For this very reason, he insisted that it is necessary to define human rights in terms that are eternal and universal, free from national or temporal restrictions.[228] It

---

225 See Ikeda, Daisaku. 1995. *A New Humanism: The University Addresses of Daisaku Ikeda.* New York: Weatherhill, p. 158.

226 Austregésilo de Athayde (1898–1993), Brazilian writer and journalist, President of the Brazilian Academy of Letters (1959–93).

227 See Athayde, Austregésilo de and Daisaku Ikeda. 1995. *Nijuisseiki no jinken o kataru* [Human Rights in the Twenty-First Century]. Tokyo: Ushio Shuppansha, p. 28.

228 Ibid., p. 101.

would seem that the international community is at long last making substantive efforts to establish the universality of human rights.

The UN is making various efforts to support this trend. One such effort that I have followed in particular is the attempt to encourage each country to quantify in detail the level of human development—a prerequisite for human security—and use this to identify problem areas. This is called the Human Development Index (HDI), originally formulated and continually refined under the auspices of the United Nations Development Programme (UNDP).

Stefan Zweig[229] was one thinker who cast his unwavering gaze on the endless madness and tragedy resulting from militarism. As he observed in his 1941 book *Brazil: Land of the Future*: "And so we are no longer willing to judge a country by its industrial, financial, and military strength, but rather by its peaceful way of thinking and its humane attitude."[230] I think that the HDI and Zweig's thinking are related in important ways.

When seeking to define human rights in the broadest sense, I believe that the right to live in a truly humane way can be said to constitute the essence of human security. Human rights are fundamental and must take priority over all else: without human rights, neither peace nor human happiness is possible. Because human rights represent the most sublime and inalienable value and endow people with their distinctly human character, their violation cannot be permitted, whether by states or by any other actor.

Nearly a century ago, Tsunesaburo Makiguchi,[231] the first Soka Gakkai president, clearly foresaw the trends of our era in his book *Jinsei chirigaku* (The Geography of Human Life).[232] It was a time (1903) when the reach of imperialism had extended to the entire world and when, following Japan's victory in the Sino–Japanese War and before the outbreak of the Russo–Japanese War, Japanese nationalism was on the rise. While the Japanese state was growing aggressive and jingoistic abroad, it strengthened its grip over the lives of citizens at home. This was the context in which Makiguchi, looking upon the

---

229 Stefan Zweig (1881–1942), Austrian writer.
230 Zweig, Stefan. 1941. *Brazil: Land of the Future.* Trans. by Andrew St. James. New York: The Viking Press, p. 12.
231 Tsunesaburo Makiguchi (1871–1944), founding president of the Soka Kyoiku Gakkai (forerunner of the Soka Gakkai) (1930–44).
232 Makiguchi, Tsunesaburo. [1903]. *Jinsei chirigaku* [The Geography of Human Life] in *Makiguchi Tsunesaburo zenshu* [The Complete Works of Tsunesaburo Makiguchi]. Tokyo: Daisanbunmei-sha. Vols. 1–2.

institution of the state from a global perspective of concern for humankind, set forth his vision of the new age to come. In *Jinsei chirigaku,* he emphasized that the primary mission of the state is to ensure the personal freedom of its citizens, protect individual rights and work to augment people's happiness and well-being.

Makiguchi proclaimed that the ultimate purpose of the state was not domination and control but the attainment of a more humane way of life and living. He also called for an era of "humanitarian competition," rather than competition by means of military might, political power or economic power. I feel that the validity of his foresight is being borne out by the developments of the present time.

Although the HDI may not work directly to improve the human rights situations in specific countries, it certainly provides a valuable incentive that can help usher in an era in which all states compete to attain a greater humanity. Only when the kind of humanitarian competition envisaged by Makiguchi becomes the central trend of the times can we usher in an era of universal human rights.

This year is the second year of the UN Decade for Human Rights Education. This campaign, dedicated to fostering social norms that will encourage people everywhere to respect human rights, was launched with the vigorous support of NGOs worldwide.

Until now, efforts to establish the norms and standards of human rights have been pursued principally through the adoption and promulgation of various declarations and treaties. To work toward the actual implementation of those rights in the countries and societies concerned, however, it is first necessary to create a foundation for a universal culture of human rights throughout the world. Here again, education is the key.

As I have already noted, the SGI has sought to do its part to encourage and spread awareness of human rights by sponsoring exhibitions such as "Toward A Century of Humanity: An Overview of Human Rights in Today's World" in venues around the globe. Through these efforts, we have called on people to join in the fight against discrimination.

When I consider this fight against discrimination, I always remember something I heard in 1990, in a meeting with Nelson Mandela, who at that time was vice-president of the African National Congress. I had just proposed to him various ideas for an anti-apartheid exhibition, lectures on human rights and suggestions for cultural exchange when one of his aides, Ismail

Meer,[233] made a remark that wrung my heart: "Your proposals for educational exchange mean that you recognize us as human beings, but in South Africa we are registered not as human beings but as blacks."

It should be noted that the problem of not seeing people *as people*—of judging people by preconceived labels—is hardly one restricted to apartheid-era South Africa. On the contrary, this kind of mistaken, discriminatory attitude is at the root of all denial of human rights, providing cover for the shame people feel when they defame and persecute their fellow human beings.

At least one scholar has suggested that the reason the German people could not prevent the tragedy of the Holocaust during World War II was due to an "inability to mourn"[234] or a failure of empathy. It is no coincidence that Nazi Germany, which engaged in the violation of human rights domestically, also pursued aggression internationally; these constitute two sides of the same coin, and are rooted in the same contempt for human dignity.

The same thing can be said about Japan in the 1930s and early 1940s. While the militarist government invaded the countries of Asia, committing one atrocity after another, it also increasingly curtailed popular freedoms at home, beginning with the freedom of religious belief, and sacrificed the Japanese people at the altar of its aggressive policies. We must never forget this history.

A Network of Human Rights Agencies (1998)[235]

This year marks the fiftieth anniversary of the Universal Declaration of Human Rights (UDHR). Adopted in December 1948, the Preamble to this historic document proclaims that "recognition of the inherent dignity and of the equal and inalienable rights of all members of the human family is the foundation of freedom, justice and peace in the world."[236]

This Declaration, which contains so much in a mere thirty articles, is considered "soft law," a resolution without binding force. Nonetheless it has, over

---

233 Ismail [Chota] Meer (1918–2000), South African journalist, trade unionist, attorney and political activist.

234 Mitscherlich, Alexander and Margarete Mitscherlich. 1975. *The Inability to Mourn: Principles of Collective Behavior.* New York: Grove Press, p. 23.

235 From 1998 Peace Proposal, "Humanity and the New Millennium: From Chaos to Cosmos."

236 UN (United Nations). 1948. "Universal Declaration of Human Rights."

the last fifty years, served as the international community's effective standard on questions of human rights. It has also given birth to numerous international human rights conventions, including the International Covenants on Human Rights. As of September 1997, no fewer than twenty-three multilateral human rights treaties had been drafted and adopted under UN auspices. The number of resolutions, statements and declarations dealing with human rights issues, of course, exceeds that number many times over.

The UDHR has come to occupy a unique place in international society, to the extent that it is said to carry the weight of international customary law. The extraordinary significance of this document in human history is a topic I discussed with Austregésilo de Athayde,[237] the late president of the Brazilian Academy of Letters, who played an important role in its drafting.[238]

International human rights treaties can be said to differ in a fundamental sense from other international law. It is commonly asserted that the principle of reciprocity—the principle that one country's observance of treaty conditions requires other signatory countries' reciprocal observance—does not to apply in the case of human rights conventions. In other words, since human rights conventions are aimed at securing universal human rights, they contain elements that transcend some of the limitations of agreements undertaken between states, including the generally sacrosanct principle of nonintervention in the domestic affairs of another state. In this sense, international human rights law represents a limitation and tempering of traditional concepts of national sovereignty.

Likewise, many of the concrete measures that have been adopted—from the establishment of international tribunals, various committees and commissions responsible for overseeing the implementation of treaties, to systems for reporting human rights abuses—represent important, if limited, steps toward the establishment of a supranational system of human rights protection and promotion.

However, international accords and the resulting structure of human rights law are not in themselves sufficient to bring about any tangible improvements in the lives of individuals whose rights are being infringed. The tragic reality of human rights violations and abuses can be found everywhere; the spirit of

---

237 Austregésilo de Athayde (1898–1993), Brazilian writer and journalist, President of the Brazilian Academy of Letters (1959–93).

238 Athayde, Austregésilo de and Daisaku Ikeda. 1995. *Nijuisseiki no jinken o kataru* [Human Rights in the Twenty-First Century]. Tokyo: Ushio Shuppansha.

the UDHR has yet to become a reality for people around the world in equal measure.

For many years, there has been agreement that the human rights agenda must move beyond the setting of standards; true implementation must begin. Needless to say, the path to universal implementation of human rights standards is strewn with difficulties. As one possible means of overcoming these obstacles, I would like to propose a network of human rights agencies, present in each national setting yet with a status independent of the national government, charged with implementing the human rights agreements which that state has signed.

The work of these agencies would include compiling reports on national efforts to implement international human rights treaties, fostering public awareness of human rights and working to secure redress in specific cases. The essence of this plan is to create a new framework of transnational cooperation, involving national human rights agencies, NGOs and competent UN bodies, in order to make existing human rights agreements most effective.

The idea of national human rights agencies has had advocates within the UN for some time now, and in some countries institutions independent of the national judiciary have been established in the form of ombudspersons or human rights commissions. As a means of reinforcing and accelerating this trend, I would like to take up the idea of "transgovernmentalism" advocated by Harvard Law School professor Anne-Marie Slaughter[239] as a new form of international cooperation. To this idea, I would like to add some suggestions which might enhance its participatory aspects. In essence, transgovernmentalism as proposed by Professor Slaughter is a system that transcends individual states but which differs from traditional multilateral arrangements in that it involves lateral, functional linkages between the similarly charged agencies in different states.

Professor Slaughter writes, "Disaggregating the state permits the disaggregation of sovereignty as well, ensuring that specific state institutions derive strength and status from participation in a transgovernmental order."[240] The idea of disaggregated national sovereignty holds the promise of providing what would be the critical element required for the effective functioning of

---

239 Anne-Marie Slaughter (1958–), American academic and foreign policy analyst.
240 Slaughter, Anne-Marie. 1997. "The Real New World Order." *Foreign Affairs.* September–October. New York: Council on Foreign Relations.

the network of agencies I am proposing—namely their independence and impartiality.

I do not completely agree with every aspect of Professor Slaughter's idea, however. I am concerned that she posits transgovernmentalism as the only alternative to either liberal internationalism or neo-medievalism. In my view, in developing a new global order, we should feel free to choose from a range of visions, incorporating their useful aspects in a mutually supportive manner. Still, she sets forth a number of important ideas, emphasizing, for example, the centrality of such qualities as efficacy and accountability in any international framework for the resolution of global issues.

While these may be the necessary conditions for establishing human rights agencies, they are not in themselves sufficient to ensure success. The resolution adopted by the UN General Assembly on national institutions for the promotion and protection of human rights states in its principles that they should be established in a way that ensures pluralist representation of civil society, through the participation and cooperation of NGOs.[241] As this shows, the work of NGOs, which have played a vitally important role in the area of human rights, should not be undervalued. It would be imperative for the national human rights agencies I am proposing to develop constructive partnerships with NGOs. These relationships would help assure the accountability of the agencies while enhancing their legitimacy.

It is clearly time to advance the relationship between NGOs and governments beyond the adversarial one that presently pertains, in which governments regard NGOs with disfavor and occasionally with open hostility. The time has come for mutual recognition of the respective roles of NGOs and governments and for them to work together—ideally in a relationship of creative tension—to promote human rights. However, care must be exercised to ensure that such cooperation does not leave NGOs in the position of "subcontractors," carrying out the work that governments would rather, for whatever reason, not do themselves.

I would also like to propose that the technical training programs currently conducted by the Office of the UN High Commissioner for Human Rights (OHCHR) for government employees be expanded to include the participation of those responsible for national human rights agencies and the staff

---

241 UNGA (United Nations General Assembly). 1993. "National Institutions for the Promotion and Protection of Human Rights." A/RES/48/134. Resolution adopted by General Assembly. December 20.

of the NGOs alongside whom they will be working. This would not only provide a regular venue for ongoing exchange between the three groups but would also encourage a deeper understanding of the ideals and goals of the UN and facilitate policy coordination with UN agencies.

Alongside the need for an improved institutional framework, there must be a parallel effort to create a robust culture of human rights. Simply put, this means cultivating the awareness that human rights are not something special, but norms of behavior that should be accepted and adhered to everywhere. While such an effort will take time, in the end it will be the most effective way of closing the gap between the ideal of human rights and the reality.

There are distinct signs that such an effort is finally under way. As one outcome of the World Conference on Human Rights in Vienna in June 1993, the United Nations Decade for Human Rights Education, 1995–2004, was established. Likewise, human rights education is one of the important objectives of the OHCHR, which was also established in the wake of the World Conference. Thus we see the creation of a human rights culture emerging as a common theme and concern of the international community.

In order to support this endeavor, the SGI has actively sought to promote human rights education. The exhibition "Toward a Century of Humanity: An Overview of Human Rights in Today's World," for example, was first shown at the United Nations University (UNU) in Tokyo in April 1993. It has since been shown in twenty-one cities in seven countries, including Geneva in December 1993, as one of the events commemorating the forty-fifth anniversary of the adoption of the Universal Declaration of Human Rights. The SGI has also sponsored exhibitions on children's rights, the Holocaust and other human rights issues.

We also see renewed recognition of the overarching importance of human rights within the UN itself. This is encouraging, as the UN is the natural focal point for humanity's shared efforts to secure human rights. A report released by UN Secretary-General Kofi Annan[242] in July 1997, "Renewing the United Nations: A Program for Reform," states that, "Human rights are integral to the promotion of peace and security, economic prosperity, and social equity," and that, "A major task for the United Nations, therefore, is to

---

242 Kofi Annan (1938–), Ghanaian statesman, 7th Secretary-General of the United Nations (1997–2006).

enhance its human rights program and fully integrate it into the broad range of the Organization's activities."[243]

This fresh prioritization of human rights at the UN and the positioning of the issue at the heart of the question of UN reform merits our attention. It can be thought of as an effort to rectify the many years of relative isolation of human rights concerns within the UN and to respond to the many calls for comprehensive efforts to effectively ensure the observance of human rights standards.

International support for universal human rights is clearly growing. It is now five years since the World Conference on Human Rights was held in Vienna, and an interim review is due to be conducted of the progress made toward the achievement of the goals set out at that Conference.

This year should therefore be one in which we renew our commitment to the future and launch substantive actions. Among the many proposals made by those sincerely determined not to permit this great opportunity to pass by unexploited, I am particularly struck by a plan formulated by the InterAction Council, an organization of former heads of government, among them former West German chancellor Helmut Schmidt[244] and former Costa Rican president Óscar Arias Sánchez.[245] The group proposes the adoption of a "Universal Declaration of Human Responsibilities" by the UN as a document complementing the Universal Declaration of Human Rights and as an aid in our efforts to create a better world.

Article 1 of the proposed declaration states, "Every person, regardless of gender, ethnic origin, social status, political opinion, language, age, nationality, or religion, has a responsibility to treat all people in a humane way." Running through all nineteen articles of the declaration is a determination to balance the notions of freedom and responsibility. One especially striking clause calls on us to "move away from the freedom of indifference towards the freedom of involvement."[246]

---

243 UNGA (United Nations General Assembly). 1997. "Renewing the United Nations: A Program for Reform." A/51/950. Report of the Secretary-General. July 14.

244 Helmut Schmidt (1918–), Chancellor of West Germany (1974–82).

245 Óscar Arias Sánchez (1941–), President of Costa Rica (1986–90, 2006–10), recipient of the Nobel Prize for Peace in 1987.

246 The InterAction Council. 1997. "A Universal Declaration of Human Responsibilities." September 1.

I find much to agree with in the InterAction Council's proposal. The challenge that faces us is that of establishing the kind of ethics it proposes in the midst of society's complex realities.

In this regard, I recall a response made by the late Linus Pauling[247] following an address I delivered at Claremont McKenna College in January 1993. At that time, he expressed his sense of the importance to humankind of attaining and acting in accordance with what Buddhism calls the bodhisattva life-state, to which I had referred in my address.

***

The qualities that make a bodhisattva can be described from various perspectives, but here I would mention one that is of particular relevance to human rights. The bodhisattva undertakes a vow to save others and bases all action upon this vow, which is a spontaneous and unforced expression of altruism. Nor is the vow a mere expression of determination or desire, but a defining commitment to whose realization the bodhisattva devotes her or his entire being. The bodhisattva refuses to be dissuaded or discouraged by the difficulties posed by this challenge.

The Lotus Sutra speaks of the pure white lotus rising from the waters of a muddy pond. This analogy illustrates the attainment of a pure and empowered state of life in the midst of the sometimes degrading realities of human society. In this way, the bodhisattva never tries to escape from reality, never leaves suffering people unsaved and plunges into the turbulent waters of life in the effort to help each person drowning in suffering onto the great vessel of happiness.

Another Buddhist scripture describes the vow of Srimala,[248] the daughter of King Prasenajit and a contemporary of Shakyamuni Buddha[249]:

> If I see lonely people, people who have been jailed unjustly and have
> lost their freedom, people who are suffering from illness, disaster or

---

247 Linus Pauling (1901–94), American scientist, recipient of the Nobel Prize in Chemistry in 1954 and the Nobel Prize for Peace in 1962.

248 Srimala, also known as Lady Shrimala or Queen Shrimala. A daughter of King Prasenajit of Kosala in India and his consort Mallika, in the time of Shakyamuni.

249 Shakyamuni (Gautama Siddartha) (c. 560–480 BCE), the founder of Buddhism.

poverty, I will not abandon them. I will bring them spiritual and material comfort.[250]

True to her vow, she worked throughout her life for the benefit of others, striving always to bring forth the inner goodness that exists in all people.

My point in introducing the concept of the bodhisattva is this: Human rights will only become truly universal and indivisible when they span the most basic, existential division—that of self and other. And this can only occur when both the right to and duty of humane treatment are observed, not in response to externally imposed norms, but through spontaneous action stemming from the naturally powerful desire to assist our fellows whose ability to live in a humane manner is under threat.

In this regard, I would like to introduce the words of Upendra Baxi,[251] an Indian law scholar, in his lecture "Human Rights Education: The Promise of the Third Millennium?":

> The single most critical source of human rights is the consciousness of peoples of the world who have waged the most persistent struggles for decolonization and self-determination, against racial discrimination, gender-based aggression and discrimination, denial of access to basic minimum needs, environmental degradation and destruction, systematic "benign neglect" of the disarticulated, disadvantaged and dispossessed (including the indigenous peoples of the Earth).[252]

The similarity of the concerns expressed in this remark and Srimala's bodhisattva vow is striking indeed.

Buddhism stresses the quality of our motivation, valuing that which issues spontaneously from within, as expressed in the simple phrase, "Our heart is

---

250 Wayman, Alex and Hideko Wayman, trans. 1974. *The Lion's Roar of Queen Srimala: A Buddhist Scripture on the Tathagata-garbha Theory.* New York: Columbia University Press, p. 65.

251 Upendra Baxi (1938–), Indian legal scholar, Vice Chancellor of the University of Delhi (1973–96).

252 Baxi, Upendra. 1995. "Human Rights Education: The Promise of the Third Millennium?" 8th Zakir Husain Memorial Lecture at Zakir Hussain College, New Delhi. December 19.

what matters most."[253] It teaches that the ultimate objective of Shakyamuni's life was revealed in the humanity he manifested in his behavior and actions. Thus the cultivation and perfection of a person's character is considered in the Buddhist tradition to be the true goal of religious training. Norms that are not inner-generated and do not encourage the development of individual character are ultimately weak and ineffective. Only when external norms and inner values function in a mutually supportive manner can they enable people to resist evil and live as genuine advocates and champions of human rights.

Over half a century ago, at the height of Japanese militarism, the Soka Gakkai's founding president Tsunesaburo Makiguchi[254] declared, "Rejecting evil and embracing good are two actions born of the same impulse."[255] He also said, "Only a person courageous enough to fight against evil can be a true friend of the good,"[256] and, "It is not enough to indulge passively in goodness; we must have the moral courage actively to pursue good."[257] In this way Makiguchi launched a critique of the militarist regime which trampled human rights as it carried out its wars of invasion. In the face of constant persecution, he never yielded an inch, holding firm to his beliefs up to the moment of his death in prison. I derive profound personal inspiration from the struggles that culminated in his martyrdom; I feel that it is here that we can find the spiritual wellsprings of the SGI's current activities to promote human rights.

Just twenty-three years ago I appealed to members of the newly formed SGI, saying, "Let us not seek praise or glory for ourselves, but instead dedicate our lives to sowing the seeds of the Mystic Law for peace everywhere in the world." Just as unhappiness is not something only others suffer, neither can happiness be for ourselves only. In this sense, my appeal was a cry from the depths of my heart that we should live the bodhisattva way of life: overcoming the ego, developing an extended, more inclusive sense of self—seeing ourselves in others and feeling others to be part of ourselves.

---

253 (trans. from) Nichiren. 1952. *Nichiren Daishonin gosho zenshu* [The Complete Works of Nichiren Daishonin]. Ed. by Nichiko Hori. Tokyo: Soka Gakkai, p. 1192.

254 Tsunesaburo Makiguchi (1871–1944), founding president of the Soka Kyoiku Gakkai (forerunner of the Soka Gakkai) (1930–44).

255 (trans. from) Makiguchi, Tsunesaburo. 1981–97. *Makiguchi Tsunesaburo zenshu* [The Complete Works of Tsunesaburo Makiguchi]. 10 vols. Tokyo: Daisanbunmei-sha. Vol. 9, p. 97.

256 Ibid. Vol. 6, p. 71.

257 Ibid. Vol. 6, p. 180.

As responsible citizens of their respective societies, the members of the SGI are working to advance a movement for peace, culture and education. In the immediate context of their daily lives, they act with the bodhisattva spirit, refusing to ignore or abandon those who suffer. They initiate and carry out countless acts for the benefit of others, striving to encourage this person, to relieve the anguish of that person, and to help those around them. I am proud of them and believe theirs are the kind of quiet, grassroots endeavors that will certainly help to create the human rights culture that our times demand.

It is my belief that if we can foster, in the depths of each individual human life, the kind of active, independent basis for altruistic behavior exemplified in the bodhisattva's vow, we can establish the fundamental foundation for an ethic of responsibility and commitment upon which a genuine culture of human rights can flourish. This is because the inner motivation that spurs people to act in the face of threats to human dignity is, for human rights, the most crucial supporting and sustaining force.

As was evident in the sharp division of views at the World Conference on Human Rights in 1993, the issue of the universality of human rights is not fully resolved and requires careful and sensitive treatment. As I have tried to describe through my discussion of the bodhisattva ideal, I believe that when people spontaneously undertake to live by those norms which they find most desirable, and to the extent to which they bring their actual behavior in line with those norms, human rights can transcend the limitations of an externally imposed regime and, as internalized values, become a force for the transformation of reality.

In that sense, it is vitally important that dialogue be undertaken to promote a new synthesis between the views of those who argue for the universality of rights and those who consider them embedded in cultural relativism. It is only through such dialogue that a genuinely universal understanding of human rights can be reached and the conditions created by which human rights can be implemented equally and without distinction among all the Earth's inhabitants.

Prohibition of the Use of Child Soldiers (1999)[258]

To lay the foundations for a lasting peace, we must deinstitutionalize war. We must effect a transition from a culture of war to a culture of peace. With the

---

258 From 1999 Peace Proposal, "Toward a Culture of Peace: A Cosmic View."

end of the Cold War, for the time being at any rate, the threat of an all-out nuclear conflict has been averted. Unfortunately, however, local and ethnic conflicts grow in number year by year all over the world. To cite only two examples, fighting in Kosovo and in the Democratic Republic of the Congo have already taken high tolls in dead and wounded and have resulted in refugees numbering many tens of thousands. Mercilessly swept up in a tempest of hatred and madness, once peaceful citizens now maim and kill each other.

Through the annals of history, ordinary citizens have lamented the destruction and misery of war. The cause of that lament must not be allowed to persist into the new millennium. The time has come for humanity to raise its voice in a paean to peace and the richness of life.

***

Nowhere is this victimization more extreme than in the case of child soldiers. According to a report issued in October 1998 by Olara Otunnu,[259] the Special Representative of the Secretary-General for Children and Armed Conflict, up to 300,000 children under eighteen years of age are now serving as combatants in ongoing conflicts. Every day, some 800 of them are killed or wounded, often by land mines. Between 1987 and 1997, 2 million were killed outright; another 6 million disabled or injured; and 10 million psychologically traumatized. It is also estimated that children are suffering the effects of war in approximately fifty countries.

To quote Mr. Otunnu's report: "in today's internecine conflicts, children are specifically targeted in strategies to eliminate the next generation of potential adversaries."[260] A report issued by Amnesty International in January 1999 estimates that forty-four countries enlist combatants under eighteen. Many, having already lost their families to war, have been impressed into the army and forced to fight to stay alive.

Exposure to violence affects children deeply. Forcing them into battle is a heinous violation of their rights. It perpetuates war and creates an unbreakable cycle of hatred and revenge. That is why the world community must

---

259 Olara Otunnu (1950–), Ugandan lawyer, United Nations Under-Secretary-General and Special Representative for Children and Armed Conflict (1998–2005).

260 UNGA (United Nations General Assembly). 1998. "Protection of Children Affected by Armed Conflict." A/53/482. Report of the Special Representative of the Secretary-General for Children and Armed Conflict. October 12, p. 4.

move quickly to adopt and ratify the optional protocol to the Convention on the Rights of the Child prohibiting the military recruitment of anyone under eighteen.

The Convention on the Rights of the Child (2002)[261]

I would like to make several proposals related to the UN Special Session on Children to be held this May (2002). The purpose of this meeting is to review progress toward the goals agreed upon at the 1990 World Summit for Children. Originally scheduled for last September, its postponement was forced by the terror attacks in the United States.

When societies break down, it is always children whose lives, health and best interests are sacrificed. There are some 2.1 billion children under the age of eighteen on Earth today.[262] Of these, however, fewer than one in ten live in countries where their health and growth is afforded adequate protection.

In the decade since the holding of the World Summit for Children, we have seen definite progress. It has been possible to reduce the number of children dying from preventable diseases and to increase the number able to receive basic education.

Despite such advances, and perhaps because the plan of action adopted by the 1990 Summit was not given sufficient international attention, progress has been checkered. UNICEF has responded by initiating a global movement for children, calling for participation from governments, NGOs, educational institutions and the media. The Special Session on Children is being held within this context, and, as UNICEF Executive Director Carol Bellamy[263] has stated, its purpose is to clarify the link between healthy children today and a healthy world tomorrow.[264]

Among the activities organized by the SGI in support of UNICEF has been the exhibition "Treasuring the Future: Children's Rights and Realities"

---

261 From 2002 Peace Proposal, "The Humanism of the Middle Way: Dawn of a Global Civilization."

262 See UNICEF (The United Nations Children's Fund). 2001. "The State of the World's Children," p. 97.

263 Carol Bellamy (1942–), American lawyer, UNICEF Executive Director (1995–2005).

264 See UNICEF (The United Nations Children's Fund). 2001. "A Major Month for Children." Press Release. May 11.

originally held in New York in June 1996 to commemorate the fiftieth anniversary of the founding of UNICEF. Since then, this exhibition has traveled to venues throughout the United States as well as to Cape Town, South Africa. There are plans to show an updated version in New York in conjunction with the Special Session.

I call on leaders from all countries who gather for the Special Session to make this the occasion for creating a global alliance for children, based on the vow to put children first and to always give the interests of the child the top priority.

As a first step toward this, I strongly urge the ratification by all countries of the two Optional Protocols to the Convention on the Rights of the Child (CRC). These Protocols are designed to protect children from those actions that most heinously abuse their rights—the use of children as soldiers and their sale or use in prostitution.

In addition, I hope that either at the Special Session or elsewhere in the near future consideration will be given to creating a world charter on education.

The shared commitment of 155 countries and territories throughout the world to promote literacy and other forms of basic education was first expressed in the World Declaration on Education for All adopted in Thailand in 1990. A world charter for education would develop and extend this agreement. It would encourage international cooperation to enhance the educational environment globally. It would set forth a vision for education in the twenty-first century, prioritizing the lifelong happiness of the learner as the true goal of education, putting the full resources of each society at the service of education. It would also express a moral commitment to peace education and education for global citizenship—the foundations on which human security in the twenty-first century must be built.

Human Rights Education (2004)[265]

Human rights education is a cornerstone of the drive to build a world without war.

My friend and coauthor the late Norman Cousins[266] wrote in his book *Human Options,* "A casual attitude toward human hurt and pain is the surest

---

265 From 2004 Peace Proposal, "Inner Transformation: Creating a Global Groundswell for Peace."

266 Norman Cousins (1912–90), American author, president of the World Federalist Association (1976–91).

sign of educational failure."[267] As this wise American journalist and activist warned, the price of our collective failures in the endeavor of education in the broadest sense of the term is resentment and the potential for conflict. In many societies tensions simmer below the surface, ready to erupt into outright violence, especially when exacerbated by economic downturn and rising unemployment. To successfully eliminate violent conflict from the world and build a basis for peaceful coexistence, we need to transform these underlying feelings of hostility and prejudice.

It was with this in mind that I called for a Decade for Human Rights Education for Peace to follow on from the UN Decade for Human Rights Education (1995–2004), in a message addressed to the World Conference Against Racism, Racial Discrimination, Xenophobia and Related Intolerance held in Durban, South Africa, three years ago (2001). Last August, the UN Sub-Commission on the Promotion and Protection of Human Rights issued a recommendation calling for the General Assembly to proclaim a second Decade for Human Rights Education to begin on January 1, 2005.[268] I wholeheartedly welcome this initiative and urge that implementation be focused particularly on children, who are the protagonists of the future. At the same time, I believe that the larger goal of building a global society of peace and coexistence must be kept firmly in sight.

For its part, the SGI will continue to support the activities of the UN, and work in partnership with other NGOs to do whatever we can to promote peace education and human rights education across the globe.

The year 2004 is the International Year to Commemorate the Struggle against Slavery and its Abolition. This surely makes it the ideal opportunity to learn critical lessons from the past and build the foundations for overcoming racism and intolerance. The crucial importance of human rights education is underlined by numerous examples in recent years of mass media stirring up hatred against people of a specific nationality or ethnic group and a proliferation of "hate" websites attacking people for their ethnicity, culture or creed. This is exacerbated by the rapid growth of the information society,

---

267 Cousins, Norman. 1981. *Human Options*. New York: W. W. Norton & Company, Inc., p. 30.

268 See UN ECOSOC (United Nations Economic and Social Council). 2003. "United Nations Decade for Human Rights Education." E/CN.4/Sub.2/2003/L.14. August 7.

which has fueled fears that it may become a breeding ground for conflict and hate crimes.

In December 2003, the UN convened the first World Summit on the Information Society in Geneva, Switzerland. As well as discussing the growing gap between the "haves" and "have-nots" of information, the so-called digital divide, the Summit was an important opportunity to examine many aspects of the information society, including the kinds of abuse cited above. The Declaration of Principles adopted by the Summit, while acknowledging freedom of the press and media independence as indispensable, called for the responsible use and treatment of information "in accordance with the highest ethical and professional standards."[269] It is my hope that there will be further in-depth discussion of the ethical issues surrounding emerging technologies in advance of the second information summit next year (2005) in Tunisia.

Making progress on the wide-ranging challenges of human security will require bold, innovative ideas and sustained effort. To this end, I hope that the world's diverse societies will engage in the kind of "humanitarian competition" envisaged by Tsunesaburo Makiguchi[270]—to vie with each other to make the greatest and most lasting contribution to human happiness. Here we can take inspiration from Thailand, for example, which has recently established a Ministry of Social Development and Human Security.

In this connection I would also strongly advocate the sharing of knowledge and best practices through such initiatives as organizing technical exchanges and providing skilled personnel to help realize human security on a global scale. And most importantly, I believe such activities will achieve most when not confined to the governmental level, but when sustained by grassroots understanding and action.

The UN Human Rights Council (2006)[271]

The year 2005 marked the sixtieth anniversary of the United Nations, and this provided additional momentum to the debate on UN reform. In March,

---

269 WSIS (The World Summit on the Information Society). 2003. "Declaration of Principles." WSIS-03/GENEVA/DOC/4-E. December 12, p. 8.

270 Tsunesaburo Makiguchi (1871–1944), founding president of the Soka Kyoiku Gakkai (forerunner of the Soka Gakkai) (1930–44).

271 From 2006 Peace Proposal, "A New Era of the People: Forging a Global Network of Robust Individuals."

UN Secretary-General Kofi Annan[272] issued a report "In Larger Freedom: Towards Development, Security and Human Rights for All." In it he laid out a broad vision of the UN's mission and the aims of reform: freedom from want, freedom from fear and freedom to live in dignity.

The report spells out, in stark and powerful terms, the interdependent relationship among these three freedoms: "Humanity will not enjoy security without development, it will not enjoy development without security, and it will not enjoy either without respect for human rights."[273]

For my part, I have consistently stressed that human development, human security and human rights must serve as the guiding principles for UN reform. The UN's fundamental mission is symbolized in the opening words of the Charter: "We the peoples. . . ." It must be dedicated to the welfare of all the citizens of the world and the elimination of needless suffering from the face of the Earth.

Following sustained debate of the Secretary-General's and other proposals, the High-level Plenary Meeting of the General Assembly held in September adopted the 2005 World Summit outcome document.

***

The activities of the Commission on Human Rights as currently constituted include: addressing human rights issues in specific countries as well as issues common to diverse countries and regions; debating and examining means for enhancing human rights; making recommendations through the adoption of resolutions; and publicizing abuses in order to shame those responsible into desisting.

There has been, however, a strong tendency to politicize human rights issues—a direct reflection of the diplomatic dynamics among states represented on the Commission—and the persistent impeachment of particular governments has generated stalemate. Thus there has been a long-standing recognition of the need to restore confidence in the Commission and its work.

---

272 Kofi Annan (1938–), Ghanaian statesman, 7th Secretary-General of the United Nations (1997–2006).

273 UN (United Nations). 2005. "Executive Summary" in "In Larger Freedom: Towards Development, Security and Human Rights for All."

I would like to make some suggestions regarding the functions and structures of the new Human Rights Council, which world leaders committed to establish at the Summit as a replacement for the Commission.

First, human rights education and public information should be a standing agenda item.

Examining specific abuses and seeking redress for victims are among the important tasks to be inherited from the Human Rights Commission. But in addition, sustained efforts are needed to change the social paradigms and political culture that would condone or tolerate human rights violations. This is the only way to prevent abuses from occurring and break entrenched patterns of recurrence.

The World Programme for Human Rights Education was initiated last year (2005). Making human rights education a standing agenda item of the Human Rights Council would ensure its consistent engagement with the program and encourage it to actively monitor implementation.

Second, I wish to urge that representatives of civil society have ample opportunity to participate in the work of the new Human Rights Council. It is a fact that the UN's efforts to promote human rights have been importantly sustained by the active involvement of many NGOs and other civil society organizations. As one of the functional commissions of the Economic and Social Council (ECOSOC), the Human Rights Commission has had official working relationships with NGOs in consultative status with ECOSOC. It is my earnest hope that the Human Rights Council will maintain and enhance this structure so NGOs can continue to speak at plenary meetings and engage in vigorous consultations with state and UN representatives.

Third, I wish to support calls for a consultative body of human rights experts under the Human Rights Council. Specifically, either the existing Sub-Commission on the Promotion and Protection of Human Rights may be continued, or an organ with equivalent functions be created. In addition to its investigative and research functions in support of the deliberative processes of the new Human Rights Council, the body as I envisage it should serve to reflect the views and concerns of civil society. I would also urge that any such consultative body carry forward the mechanisms, which evolved under the Sub-Commission, of special rapporteurs and working groups on specific human rights concerns, such as those of indigenous peoples, minorities, etc.

An International Conference on Human Rights Education (2008)[274]

Already some twenty years have passed since the end of the Cold War, which held international society in its grip for nearly half a century. Despite having entered the new century, the outlines of a new global framework have yet to emerge.

In October 1990, the dialogue I had conducted with two-time Nobel laureate Linus Pauling[275] was published. At the start of the dialogue, Dr. Pauling set out this hopeful view:

> I am so excited by the prospects for our world. I am filled with courage. The Soviet Union has started to move. Under the leadership of President Mikhail Gorbachev, the global tides have started to turn toward disarmament. . . . For the first time, humanity is walking a path that accords with rationality and reason. We have finally started to move toward such a world.[276]

Dr. Pauling was almost ninety at the time, and these words bring to mind the warm and gentle visage of this great champion of peace.

Regrettably, subsequent developments proved to be a bitter betrayal of Dr. Pauling's hopes. For a time in the early 1990s, the idea was trumpeted of a "new world order" led by the United States, the country at the forefront of an inevitable process of globalization. But new strains and conflicts quickly emerged, and this vision was forced into retreat. Our present situation could best be characterized as one of global disorder.

But we must not allow the wheels of history to slip backward. Whatever the difficulties, we must not abandon the search for a new global order that will serve the interests and the welfare of all humankind. Only through such committed efforts can we prevent global society from being enveloped by an ever-deepening chaos.

---

274 From 2008 Peace Proposal, "Humanizing Religion, Creating Peace."

275 Linus Pauling (1901–94), American scientist, recipient of the Nobel Prize in Chemistry in 1954 and the Nobel Prize for Peace in 1962.

276 (trans. from) Pauling, Linus and Daisaku Ikeda. 1990. *Seimei no seiki eno tankyu* [The Search for a Century of Life]. Tokyo: Yomiuri Shimbunsha, pp. 14–15.

Important initiatives are being taken in this direction. Recently (January 15–16, 2008), more than seventy-five United Nations member states and international organizations participated in the Alliance of Civilizations Forum in Madrid, Spain, with a shared belief that the maintenance of international peace and security requires the overcoming of cultural animosities. Addressing the gathering, UN Secretary-General Ban Ki-moon[277] called on the participants to further their endeavors for peace: "You may have different backgrounds and perspectives, but you share a common conviction that the Alliance of Civilizations is an important way to counter extremism and heal the divisions that threaten our world."[278]

Likewise, in a press conference held at the start of this year, French President Nicolas Sarkozy[279] advocated a "policy of civilization" (*politique de civilisation*) with an emphasis on humanity and solidarity. Stating, "You cannot organize the world of the twenty-first century with the organization of the twentieth,"[280] he proposed that the current G8 summit meeting be expanded to include China, India, South Africa, Mexico and Brazil, to create a new G13 system.

I have for some time urged that the current summit system be expanded to include China, India and other countries to form a "summit of responsible states," a step that will promote a wider sharing of global responsibility. As such, I can lend my wholehearted support to this proposal.

It was under the banner of freedom and democracy that moves to construct a "new world order" were promoted in the aftermath of the Cold War. While these values are, of course, essential, we must recognize the danger that inevitably accompanies any attempt to transplant specific institutions and practices to the soil of a different political culture. Even where they are established, any slackening of the effort to maintain and enhance freedom and democracy will allow them to regress, until we are left with forms devoid of real substance.

---

277 Ban Ki-moon (1944–), South Korean statesman, 8th Secretary-General of the United Nations (2007–).

278 Ban, Ki-moon. 2008. "Remarks at the Inauguration of the Alliance of Civilizations Forum." January 15.

279 Nicolas Sarkozy (1955–), President of France (2007–12).

280 Sarkozy, Nicolas. 2008. "Sarkozy Wants to Change UN, G8, Europe – Summary." *Trend News Agency.* January 8.

This was the thrust of the analysis I made in my 1990 peace proposal just months after the fall of the Berlin Wall in November of the previous year. I based this on my reading of Plato's *Republic,* in which he states that by supporting the insatiable pursuit of freedom, democracy nurtures a multitude of desires that gradually and insidiously "seize the citadels of the souls of youth."[281] Finally, the situation gets out of control and a strong leader is sought to restore order. From among the "idle drones," a single stinger-equipped creature is chosen. In this way, Plato stresses the logic and likelihood of a regression from democracy to tyranny.

The concerns I expressed at that time have not proven baseless. The unhinged march of finance-centered globalization has produced a world riven by disparities of an unprecedented scale, the unabashed worship of material wealth on the one hand and a corresponding sense of frustration at the absence of economic justice on the other. This structural inequity is a key factor—perhaps *the* key factor—underlying the forms of terrorism now proliferating throughout the world.

History teaches that any attempt to suppress terrorism and similar crimes through the unilateral application of force without a careful analysis of and response to the structural factors involved will only make things worse. Order that relies on force is the near neighbor of chaos.

As a Buddhist, I direct my deepest concern toward the mentality that has arisen against this backdrop—what might be described as a slide toward fundamentalism. This is not limited to the religious fundamentalism that has been the subject of so much debate, but includes ethnocentrism, chauvinism, racism and a dogmatic adherence to various ideologies, including those of the market. Such fundamentalisms flourish in conditions of chaos and disorder. What is common to all of them is that abstract principles and ideas take precedence over living human beings who in turn are forced into a subservient role.

While I will not attempt a detailed analysis here, I believe that Albert Einstein[282] expressed the essence of the issue when he stated, "principles are made for men and not men for principles."[283]

---

281 Plato. 1888. *The Republic of Plato.* Trans. by B. Jowett. Oxford: Clarendon Press, p. 268.

282 Albert Einstein (1879–1955), German-born American physicist, recipient of the Nobel Prize for Physics in 1921.

283 (qtd. in) Hermanns, William. 1983. *Einstein and the Poet: In Search of the Cosmic Man.* Brookline Village, MA: Branden Press, Inc., p. 53.

To sustain and put into practice with any consistency the worldview evoked by Einstein is not an easy task. People are quick to turn to pre-established rules that provide a ready-made answer to their questions or doubts. To borrow a metaphor from Simone Weil,[284] people and society are ceaselessly dragged down by the forces of gravity (*la pesanteur*), a seemingly inherent force in human beings that leads us to debase ourselves. The essential nature of this force is that it causes us to lose sight of the sense of self that should form the core of our humanity.

The kind of humanism I am convinced our times require is one capable of confronting and halting the slide toward fundamentalism. This is the work of restoring people and humanity to the role of central protagonist, something which ultimately can only be undertaken through a ceaseless spiritual effort to train and to temper ourselves.

***

During the final years of his life, I had the privilege of conducting a dialogue with former Brazilian Academy of Letters president Austregésilo de Athayde,[285] who played an important role in the drafting of the Universal Declaration of Human Rights (UDHR).

In our dialogue, Mr. Athayde looked back on the drafting process and made this remark:

> In drafting the Universal Declaration of Human Rights and considering a number of difficult questions we faced, there was one point to which I paid particular care; that is, to create spiritual bonds among the peoples of the world and, more specifically, to establish the universality of the spirit.[286]

Mr. Athayde thus participated in the drafting work with a firm conviction that it was essential to develop bonds that were loftier, broader and more

---

284 Simone Weil (1909–43), French philosopher and activist in the French Resistance during World War II.

285 Austregésilo de Athayde (1898–1993), Brazilian writer and journalist, President of the Brazilian Academy of Letters (1959–93).

286 (trans. from) Athayde, Austregésilo de and Daisaku Ikeda. 1995. *Nijuisseiki no jinken o kataru* [Human Rights in the Twenty-First Century]. Tokyo: Ushio Shuppansha, pp. 128–29.

enduring in order to bring the world's peoples together. Indeed, connections between countries that are contingent on the changing conditions that govern economic and political relations are too fragile and impermanent to serve as the foundation of lasting peace.

The year 2008 marks the sixtieth anniversary of the UDHR. A yearlong campaign was launched on December 10 last year, at the initiative of the Office of the UN High Commissioner for Human Rights, under the theme "Dignity and Justice for All of Us" to communicate the vision of the Declaration. To make this anniversary substantive, it is vital that governments and civil society work together to actively promote concrete programs that bring human rights education to all.

I have repeatedly stressed the importance of establishing an ongoing global framework for human rights education, as I did in my message to the World Conference against Racism, Racial Discrimination, Xenophobia and Related Intolerance held in Durban, South Africa, in August 2001. After the conclusion of the UN Decade for Human Rights Education (1995–2004), the UN launched the World Programme for Human Rights Education in January 2005. This kind of continuity is of the utmost importance.

Human rights issues must not only be debated actively among governments; we must establish a shared global culture of human rights that is rooted in the realities of daily life and based on unfailing and uncompromising respect for human dignity.

The promotion of human rights education was cited in a General Assembly resolution as one of the primary tasks of the Human Rights Council, a body established in 2006 as part of the UN reform process.[287] In September 2007, the Council determined to prepare a draft declaration on human rights education and training. Once adopted, this declaration will be added to the existing human rights standards under international law, alongside the Universal Declaration of Human Rights and the International Covenants on Human Rights. It is crucial that the drafting process take into sufficient consideration civil society's perspectives and concerns and that the resulting document be one that genuinely promotes a culture of human rights rooted in people's daily lives.

To that end I would urge the holding of an international conference specifically dedicated to the theme of human rights education to gather broad-ranging views from civil society as an integral part of the drafting

---

287 See UNGA (United Nations General Assembly). 2006. "Human Rights Council." A/RES/60/251. Resolution adopted by the General Assembly. April 3.

process. Although regional conferences and small-scale meetings of experts have been held to discuss human rights education, no full-scale international conference has yet been realized. Such a conference, focusing on civil society and held at the initiative of civil society, would be able to discuss not only the new declaration but also measures to ensure the success of the World Programme for Human Rights Education.

Building a Culture of Human Rights (2011)[288]

I would next like to discuss the challenge of building a culture of human rights.

The term "a culture of human rights" was popularized in part through the UN Decade for Human Rights Education (1995–2004), and refers to an ethos inculcated throughout society that encourages people to take the initiative to respect and protect the full spectrum of human rights and the dignity of life. This UN framework was realized largely through the work of NGOs. It has, at its foundation, the awareness that, alongside legal guarantees of human rights—and remedies in the event they are violated—it is necessary to foster a culture that prevents violations from occurring in the first place.

I am currently engaged in a serialized dialogue with the American historian Dr. Vincent Harding,[289] who was a close friend of the civil rights leader Dr. Martin Luther King Jr.[290] and has dedicated himself to the struggle for human rights for many years. I was struck by his observation, which I believe is highly germane in this context, that the term "civil rights movement" is inadequate to describe the movement that he, Dr. King and others had been involved in. He expressed his concern that subsequent generations might consider it simply a matter of past history, seeing the process as completed with the adoption of various laws banning discrimination. He asserted:

> If, instead of referring to the movement as the "civil rights move-
> ment," we spoke in terms of "the expansion of democracy," then

---

288　From 2011 Peace Proposal, "Toward a World of Dignity for All: The Triumph of the Creative Life."

289　Vincent Harding (1931–), American historian, theologian, civil rights activist and colleague of Martin Luther King Jr.

290　Martin Luther King Jr. (1929–68), American religious leader and civil rights activist, recipient of the Nobel Prize for Peace in 1964.

each new generation would recognize that they have a responsibility to expand democracy beyond the way they found it. This duty is an ongoing task that each new generation must accept.[291]

It is necessary to emphasize here that it is not because they have been codified into law that human rights have value. The spiritual wellspring that supports the law is found in the struggle to gain and realize our rights. The brilliance of human rights lies in the endless succession of courageous individuals who arise to take up the challenge of extending and expanding them as heirs to that spirit. This serves as a guideline for efforts to instill a respect for the dignity of life throughout society and resonates with the insight of Buddhism: "The Law does not spread by itself: because people propagate it, both people and the Law are respectworthy."[292]

Buddhism views all people as fundamentally equal, as they all possess life, which has ultimate value and dignity. It is through our actions that this dignity is made manifest. As Shakyamuni[293] admonished:

> Judge not by birth, but life.
> As any chips feed fire,
> mean birth may breed a sage
> noble and staunch and true.[294]

Buddhism is also a teaching that seeks to realize happiness and security for both oneself and others, as encapsulated by Shakyamuni's famous words:

> May all be well and secure,
> May all beings be happy![295]

---

291 (trans. from) Harding, Vincent and Daisaku Ikeda. 2010. *Kibo no kyoiku, heiwa no koshin* [Advancing for Peace Through Hope-filled Education]. *Daisanbunmei*. August. Tokyo: Daisanbunmei-sha, pp. 53–54.

292 (trans. from) Nichiren. 1952. *Nichiren Daishonin gosho zenshu* [The Complete Works of Nichiren Daishonin]. Ed. by Nichiko Hori. Tokyo: Soka Gakkai, p. 856.

293 Shakyamuni (Gautama Siddartha) (c. 560–480 BCE), the founder of Buddhism.

294 Chalmers, Robert, trans. 1932. *Buddha's Teachings*. Cambridge: Harvard University Press, p. 109.

295 Buddharakkhita, Acharya, trans. 1989. *Karaniya Metta Sutta*. In *Metta: The Philosophy and Practice of Universal Love (WH 365)*. Kandy: Buddhist Publication Society.

The SGI's focus on education as the means to promote human rights arises from Buddhism's emphasis on inner transformation.

In April 1993, in the lead-up to the World Conference on Human Rights that was held in Vienna in June of that year, we organized the exhibition "Toward a Century of Humanity: An Overview of Human Rights in Today's World" at the United Nations University (UNU) in Tokyo. By the end of 2004, the last year of the UN Decade for Human Rights Education, the exhibition had been viewed in forty cities around the world, contributing to awareness-raising on the popular level.

In my message to the World Conference Against Racism, Racial Discrimination, Xenophobia and Related Intolerance held in Durban, South Africa, in August 2001, and on other occasions, I have called for the continuation of a global framework for human rights education by the United Nations. I was therefore deeply gratified that the World Programme for Human Rights Education, which was launched in 2005 as the successor to the UN Decade, stressed at the outset the importance of "building a universal culture of human rights."[296] It is also significant that the promotion of human rights education and learning was established as one of the principal duties of the Human Rights Council (HRC), which began functioning in June 2006 in place of the earlier Commission on Human Rights.

In September 2007, in response to a proposal made by the governments of Switzerland and Morocco, the HRC determined to begin drafting a UN declaration on human rights education and training. Work is continuing on this now with the aim of adoption by the UN General Assembly that will convene in September (2011). This will be the first time that international standards for human rights education will be officially proclaimed by the UN, and I hope that the adoption of the declaration will be an opportunity for all stakeholders to work together to encourage a more conscious and robust culture of human rights in all countries.

To strengthen the foundations for this, I would like to offer three concrete proposals.

---

296 UNGA (United Nations General Assembly). 2005. "World Programme for Human Rights Education." A/59/525/Rev.1. Revised draft plan of action for the first phase (2005–2007) of the World Programme for Human Rights Education. March 2, p. 3.

The first regards the establishment of UN and civil society bodies that will promote human rights education. As mentioned, drafting work continues on the UN declaration on human rights education and training. In order to gain the support of as many states as possible in the UN General Assembly, and to ensure that the declaration is implemented worldwide, the consistent backing of civil society is indispensable. Likewise, because there is no specialized international agency for the World Programme for Human Rights Education, here also the active engagement of NGOs is required.

The NGO Working Group on Human Rights Education and Learning in Geneva, which is part of the network of the Conference of NGOs in Consultative Relationship with the United Nations (CoNGO), has been striving to ensure that the voices of civil society are fully reflected in UN policies related to human rights education. In March 2009, the Working Group, in collaboration with the international network Human Rights Education Associates (HREA), presented a substantive proposal to the HRC cosigned by 365 NGOs and national human rights institutions.

The SGI's representative is currently the Chair of the NGO Working Group, and the SGI, in collaboration with HREA, is working to produce a DVD, scheduled for release during 2011, that will introduce case studies of successful outcomes generated through human rights education.

Here, I would like to propose the formation of an international coalition of NGOs for human rights education. Bringing together NGOs and NGO networks, this coalition would work in close consultation with the HRC and the Office of the UN High Commissioner for Human Rights to promote human rights education on an international scale.

As collaborative relations between the UN and civil society in this field develop, the formation of a standing specialized UN agency to promote human rights education would also be worthy of consideration. In addition to securing a more adequate operational and financial basis, such an agency could be a venue for the UN, governments and civil society to deliberate on the best means of implementing the World Programme and the UN declaration within each national context, in this way bringing a culture of human rights to flower around the world.

My second proposal is for strengthening coordinated regional efforts for human rights education with a special focus on youth. At the United Nations, the year commencing on August 12, 2010, has been designated the International Year of Youth to encourage young people to "devote their energy, enthusiasm and creativity"[297] to the resolution of the problems confronting humankind.

As seen in the examples of Mahatma Gandhi[298] and Dr. Martin Luther King Jr., who both became active in their twenties, many human rights struggles have been initiated and sustained through the power and passion of youth. The importance of the role of youth in challenging seemingly intractable social realities and creating a new era cannot be overstated.

Near the end of his life, Dr. King addressed these words to young people: "When an individual is no longer a true participant, when he no longer feels a sense of responsibility to his society, the content of democracy is emptied."[299]

The same principle applies to the work of building a culture of human rights. As Dr. Harding stressed in our dialogue, a strong and unbroken intergenerational succession of people dedicated to human rights is essential. In view of the ongoing processes of globalization, it is vital that in addition to national efforts there also be strengthened and expanded endeavors for human rights education on a regional basis, including various opportunities for direct exchange.

Presently, the Council of Europe is promoting Education for Democratic Citizenship and Human Rights. Defining a citizen as "a person co-existing in a society,"[300] this campaign seeks to foster actively engaged young citizens. I believe that similar forms of transnational solidarity for human rights education could be undertaken effectively in other regions with the proactive involvement of civil society.

In my 1987 peace proposal, I called for a UN decade of education for global citizenship, focused on the four themes of environment, development, peace and human rights, to encourage awareness among young people of the challenges and responsibilities of global citizenship for the twenty-first century. In

---

297	UNGA (United Nations General Assembly). 2010. "Proclamation of 2010 as the International Year of Youth: Dialogue and Mutual Understanding." A/RES/64/134. Resolution adopted by the General Assembly. February 1, p. 1.

298	Mohandas (Mahatma) Gandhi (1869–1948), Indian champion of nonviolence.

299	King, Martin Luther Jr. 1967. *The Trumpet of Conscience*. New York: Harper & Row Publishers, p. 44.

300	O'Shea, Karen. 2003. "Education for Democratic Citizenship 2001–2004. Developing a shared understanding: A Glossary of Terms for Education for Democratic Citizenship." DGIV/EDU/CIT (2003) 29. Strasbourg: Council of Europe, p. 8.

line with this, the SGI has conducted activities in support of the UN Decade for Human Rights Education (1995–2004) and also of the International Decade for a Culture of Peace and Non-Violence for the Children of the World (2001–10).

Further, together with other NGOs, we called for the establishment of a Decade of Education for Sustainable Development and have been actively engaged in efforts to support the Decade (2005–14) since it was launched. We are committed to activities to ensure that a culture of peace takes root throughout the world and to finding paths to a sustainable future. We will continue to conduct multifaceted activities to foster in young people an enduring awareness of and commitment to human rights, specifically through providing opportunities for direct personal encounters and exchanges across national borders. Such exchanges can promote the spirit of recognizing human commonalities and respecting diversity as a source of creativity and vitality.

My third proposal regards interfaith dialogue toward the construction of a culture of human rights. A commitment to human rights cannot be fostered simply through the transmission of knowledge. This is reflected in the guidebook *ABC, Teaching Human Rights. Practical activities for primary and secondary schools* produced by the Office of the UN High Commissioner for Human Rights.

> However, even taught with the greatest skill and care, documents and history alone cannot bring human rights to life in the class-room. . . . For these documents to have more than intellectual significance, students need to approach them from the perspective of their real-life experience and grapple with them in terms of their own understanding of justice, freedom and equity.[301]

When children confront, for example, a situation of bullying among their peers, how can they be empowered not only to refuse to participate but to be part of the effort to stop it? It is only through such real-life daily struggles and challenges that a genuine sensitivity to human rights can be inculcated. This is a truth that is not limited to school education: it applies to all of us.

---

301 OHCHR (Office of the United Nations High Commissioner for Human Rights). 2003. *ABC, Teaching Human Rights. Practical activities for primary and secondary schools*. New York and Geneva: United Nations, p. 20.

The foundation for this must, I believe, be the workings of conscience, in particular an empathetic openness to the sufferings of others. It must also grow from the determination to bring out one's "best self," to behave at all times and in all situations in a manner that one can proudly affirm. And it is the original mission of religion, I am convinced, to encourage the growth and development of such an ethos.

However thoroughly the legal guarantees for human rights may be promulgated, so long as these are seen as externally imposed, the full positive impact on people's lives will not be realized. As Gandhi said: "Non-violence is not like a garment to be put on and off at will. Its seat is in the heart, and it must be an inseparable part of our very being."[302]

It is only when the norms of human rights are elevated to a personal vow—the sense that unless I hold to this I can no longer be myself—that they become a source of inexhaustible energy for social transformation. This is not to suggest, of course, that only religion can provide an ethical foundation. There are many other sources, such as the Hippocratic Oath that guides the actions of medical practitioners, that encourage people in the fulfillment of their responsibilities, and these will only increase in their importance going forward.

But as the theologian Paul Tillich[303] pointed out, religion has in its depths an orientation toward the pursuit of meaning framed by such soul-shaking questions as, "To what end do we as human beings live?" In this sense, religions have a great contribution to make. It is through the effort to identify a more noble state of life that religion can unleash the vitality that, in Tillich's words, "is the power of creating beyond oneself without losing oneself."[304]

As mentioned, the SGI movement seeks to make manifest, in both oneself and others, such a state of life through an inner transformation within each individual. This has shaped our efforts in the field of human rights education toward a focus on promoting civil society initiatives that enable individuals to embody the ideals of human rights amidst the realities of their daily lives.

The Lotus Sutra, which expounds the essence of Buddhist teachings, portrays the example of Bodhisattva Never Disparaging. Based on the conviction that the lives of all people are endowed with incomparable dignity, this

---

302 Gandhi, Mohandas K. 1960. *My Non-violence*. Ahmedabad: Navajivan Pub. House, p. 36.

303 Paul Tillich (1886–1965), German-born American theologian and philosopher.

304 Tillich, Paul. 1952. *The Courage to Be*. New Haven: Yale University Press, p. 81.

bodhisattva engaged in the practice of bowing to each person he met and reciting the following words: "I have profound reverence for you, I would never dare treat you with disparagement or arrogance."[305]

The age in which this bodhisattva lived was a benighted one, and he was subject not only to ridicule and unbridled verbal abuse but was at times attacked with staves and stones. But he refused to abandon his practice of offering obeisance to all he encountered.

When the Lotus Sutra was transmitted to China, the name of this bodhisattva was translated by Kumarajiva[306] into Chinese characters that mean "the bodhisattva who never belittled or made light of others." The spirit that was expressed in this name is at the heart of the human rights struggle undertaken by the Soka Gakkai since its founding some eighty years ago.

In its early years, the Soka Gakkai was dismissed in Japan as a gathering of the sick and the poor. But the members, taking this as a badge of the highest honor and filled with a burning conviction that striving for the sake of those who suffer constitutes the very essence of Buddhism, undertook the patient work of engaging in dialogue with people one at a time, in order to encourage and spark in them the flame of hope.

The Lotus Sutra also describes the actions of a number of other bodhisattvas, including Universal Worthy, Medicine King, Wonderful Sound and Perceiver of the World's Sounds, each of whom strives for the happiness of others on the basis of their unique characteristics.

Transposing this spirit into contemporary society, we have stressed that each person must develop her or his special capacities to the highest degree. This is the basis for mutual growth, for realizing the values of one current focus of the UN's activities is to encourage new generations to take action under the theme "Speak Up, Stop Discrimination." I believe that the world's religions should begin discussions regarding the contributions each can make, and this theme provides an excellent starting point.

When I spoke at Harvard University in 1993, I posed the following questions, from which, of course, I consider the SGI in no way exempt: Does religion make people stronger, or does it weaken them? Does it encourage what is good or what is evil in them? Are they made better and more wise—or

---

305 Watson, Burton, trans. 1993. *The Lotus Sutra*. New York: Columbia University Press, pp. 266–67.

306 Kumarajiva (c. 344–413), Buddhist scholar and translator of Buddhist scriptures into Chinese.

less—by religion?[307] These, I believe, are the criteria we must keep firmly in view.

I believe it would be valuable for the world's religions to engage in what the founding president of our organization, Tsunesaburo Makiguchi,[308] termed "humanitarian competition"—that we conduct dialogue toward the shared goal of constructing a culture of human rights and, reflecting on our respective origins and histories, mutually strive to foster in people the capacity to take the lead in this endeavor.

Culture of Peace

Overcoming the Culture of War (1999)[309]

The United Nations has designated 2000 as the International Year for the Culture of Peace. And in November 1998, the UN General Assembly designated the first ten years of the century the International Decade for a Culture of Peace and Non-Violence for the Children of the World. For some time, leading thinkers and various organizations have called for designations of this kind, including UNESCO and many of the people whom I have met in my pursuit of dialogue, such as former president of the Soviet Union Mikhail S. Gorbachev,[310] president of South Africa Nelson Mandela,[311] Argentine sculptor and human-rights champion Adolfo Pérez Esquivel[312] and Arun Gandhi[313] (the grandson of Mahatma Gandhi[314]), founder of the M. K. Gandhi Institute for Nonviolence.

---

307 Ikeda, Daisaku. 1995. *A New Humanism: The University Addresses of Daisaku Ikeda.* New York: Weatherhill, p. 157.

308 Tsunesaburo Makiguchi (1871–1944), founding president of the Soka Kyoiku Gakkai (forerunner of the Soka Gakkai) (1930–44).

309 From 1999 Peace Proposal, "Toward a Culture of Peace: A Cosmic View."

310 Mikhail Gorbachev (1931–), President of the Soviet Union (1990–91), recipient of the Nobel Prize for Peace in 1990.

311 Nelson Mandela (1918–), President of South Africa (1994–99), recipient of the Nobel Prize for Peace in 1993.

312 Adolfo Pérez Esquivel (1931–), Argentine sculptor, architect, champion of human rights and nonviolent reform in Latin America, recipient of the Nobel Prize for Peace in 1980.

313 Arun Gandhi (1934–), South African-born peace activist, founder of the M. K. Gandhi Institute for Nonviolence.

314 Mohandas (Mahatma) Gandhi (1869–1948), Indian champion of nonviolence.

The resolution making this designation states: "to save future generations from the scourge of war requires transformation towards a culture of peace."[315] The designation aims to encourage the cooperative efforts of member states, the UN and its specialized agencies and NGOs toward ensuring the happiness of children, who are always the greatest victims of war.

***

Ways of resolving international problems and conflicts peacefully must be devised if we are to break successfully with the culture of war. Too often in the past, military intervention has been considered the only way. Recent examples include possible NATO air strikes in the conflict in Kosovo, American retaliation for terrorist attacks on US embassies in Kenya and Tanzania, and British and American air strikes against Iraq for refusing to permit arms inspections. Although we cannot afford to overlook problems that pose a major threat to the international community, we must always be extremely cautious in opting for military force as a solution.

In the final analysis, since they usually leave scars that continue to fester, forcibly imposed "hard power" solutions are not real solutions at all. As Hegel[316] suggested, no matter how much we try to justify or rationalize them, as long as the opponent regards them as unfair, such measures will always lead to an intractable cycle of conflict or revenge.

Instead of resorting to hard power solutions, we must first clarify the nature of the problem and then employ dialogue—the essence of soft power—to remove, one by one, the obstacles to solution.

Deeply battle-scarred Northern Ireland is already beginning to accept this challenge. After nearly thirty years of terrorism and bloodshed, the conflict there had come to seem irremediable. Then, in April 1998, thanks to the resolute pursuit of dialogue, an historic compromise agreement was reached. Finally, fed up with the fighting and bloodshed that had cost the lives of three thousand, voters on both sides of the border endorsed the peace accord.

The newly established North/South Ministerial Council, a real political breakthrough, undertakes cross-border efforts to develop consultation and

---

315 UNGA (United Nations General Assembly). 1998. "International Decade for a Culture of Peace and Non-Violence for the Children of the World, 2001–2010." A/53/25. Resolution adopted by the General Assembly. November 19, p. 1.

316 Georg Wilhelm Friedrich Hegel (1770–1831), German philosopher.

cooperation for the entire island, both the Republic of Ireland and Northern Ireland. Transcending the framework of national borders and stressing the will of the local residents, this Council attempts to deal creatively with the psychology of group-identification that lies at the heart of the conflict. If it stays on track, it can provide a valuable model for resolving other regional conflicts. Indeed, its influence has already opened the way to a cease-fire between Spain and Basque separatists.

Issues like weapons decommissioning remain. Still, as both sides become increasingly trustful of each other, the international community must support their efforts to reach agreement. As these events in Northern Ireland have shown, even the most entrenched conflicts are not beyond resolution. The important thing is not to cast the other party in the role of enemy but to determine the nature of the problem and the cause of the disagreement. The first step toward peace is recognizing the other party's humanity.

The UN General Assembly resolution designating 2001 as the United Nations Year of Dialogue among Civilizations expresses the will of the international community when it welcomes the collective endeavor "to enhance understanding through constructive dialogue among civilizations on the threshold of the third millennium."[317]

This theme is reflected in the motto of the Toda Institute for Global Peace and Policy Research: "Dialogue of Civilizations for World Citizenship." In February 2000, the Toda Institute will be holding an international conference on the topic "Dialogue of Civilizations: A New Peace Agenda for a New Millennium" to celebrate the centennial of the birth of second Soka Gakkai president Josei Toda,[318] after whom it is named.

As founder of the institute, I am engaged in discussions with its director Prof. Majid Tehranian[319] of the University of Hawai'i in an attempt to promote dialogue between two of the world's major religious cultures, Islam and Buddhism. Professor Tehranian has written that the world today is "endowed

---

317 UNGA (United Nations General Assembly). 1998. "United Nations Year of Dialogue among Civilizations." A/RES/53/22. Resolution Adopted by the General Assembly. November 16, p. 2.

318 Josei Toda (1900–58), second president of the Soka Gakkai (1951–58).

319 Majid Tehranian (1937–2012), Iranian-born Professor of International Communication at the University of Hawai'i, Director of the Toda Institute for Global Peace and Policy Research (1996–2008).

with expanding channels of communication yet sorely in need of dialogue."[320] Undeniably, in our information-saturated society, we are being inundated by ready-made stereotypes obscuring the truth of people and situations. This is why person-to-person dialogue—always the basis of dialogue among civilizations—is more than ever in demand.

Even at the height of the Cold War, confident that we all share the same humanity, I worked hard to build bridges of friendship by frequently visiting the Soviet Union, China, and other communist countries. Similarly I have engaged in dialogue with people from many different religious, ethnic and cultural backgrounds. I am convinced that we can solve any problem as long as we keep our minds open and stand firm in our belief in our common humanity.

No one really wants war. Unfortunately, however, isolation breeds mistrust, and mistrust breeds conflict. Convinced that humanity cannot afford to isolate any country or ethnic group, I have traveled the world over and, sometimes through dialogue, sometimes through educational and cultural activities, have striven, step by step, to strengthen bonds of friendship and to build bridges of peace.

The Swiss psychologist C. G. Jung[321] emphasized that real and fundamental change in individuals can come only from direct personal interaction.[322] The effort of each individual to pursue dialogue today will lead to a culture of peace and a global community of harmonious coexistence tomorrow.

The Role of Women for Peace (2000)[323]

It is estimated that in the ten years following the end of the Cold War in 1989, more than fifty states underwent the wrenching drama of violent conflict, division or independence. These wars claimed some 4 million lives.

---

320 (trans. from) Tehranian, Majid and Daisaku Ikeda. 1998. *Nijuisseki e no sentaku* [Choices for the Twenty-first Century]. *Ushio.* October. Tokyo: Ushio Shuppansha.

321 Carl G. Jung (1875–1961), Swiss psychologist and psychiatrist, founder of analytical psychology.

322 See Jung, Carl G. 1959. *The Undiscovered Self.* Trans. by R. F. C. Hull. New York: Mentor Books, pp. 40–41.

323 From 2000 Peace Proposal, "Peace through Dialogue: A Time to Talk."

The dread reality of contemporary conflicts is that it is not unusual for 90 percent of the victims to be unarmed civilians; a horrific number of these are children. Survivors are often forced into a precarious existence as refugees or internally displaced persons. The Office of the United Nations High Commissioner for Refugees (UNHCR) estimates that some 23 million people worldwide are in need of international protection and assistance.[324]

As part of the global effort to transform the tragic legacy of the twentieth century, the United Nations has declared 2000 the International Year for the Culture of Peace, and has designated the first decade of the new century (2001–10) the International Decade for a Culture of Peace and Non-Violence for the Children of the World. In this sense, we have a truly unique opportunity to muster the will of the international community and to initiate action that will transform the age-old "culture of war" into a new culture of peace.

In its annual report, "The State of the World's Children 2000," the United Nations Children's Fund (UNICEF) reaffirms the possibility of overcoming entrenched patterns of structural violence, poverty and discrimination within a single generation, and urges our commitment to realizing this.[325]

We cannot afford to lose heart in the face of challenging realities or look on passively at problems which do not directly affect us. We must not overlook the ills of society, but instead look for ways to act, with a clear set of goals in sight.

At this moment in history, we should determine to eliminate all needless suffering from this planet that is our home. It is in our efforts to realize this goal that we will find the key to ensuring that the new century does not mimic the last, but becomes a genuine departure toward an era of peace and hope.

Humanity is charged with the task of not merely achieving a "passive peace"—the absence of war—but of transforming on a fundamental level those social structures that threaten human dignity. Only in this way can we realize the positive, active values of peace. Efforts to enhance international cooperation and the fabric of international law are, of course, necessary. Even more vital, however, are the creative efforts of individuals to develop a

---

324 See UNHCR (United Nations High Commissioner for Refugees). 1999. "UNHCR by Numbers." Geneva: Public Information Section, UNHCR. Table 1.

325 See UNICEF (The United Nations Children's Fund). 2000. "The State of the World's Children 2000."

multilayered and richly patterned culture of peace, for it is on this foundation that a new global society can be built.

The members of the SGI worldwide are actively engaged in the work of fostering a culture of peace. For example, in 1999, the youth membership of SGI-USA launched a "Victory Over Violence" campaign to help young people uncover and counteract the root causes of violence in their lives. It encourages young people to respect their own lives, respect all life and inspire hope in others. Similarly, SGI representatives participated in the NGO conferences held at The Hague in May and in Seoul in October, on both occasions organizing symposiums to explore various aspects of the culture of peace.

The SGI-affiliated Boston Research Center for the 21st Century (BRC)[326] held a series of conferences and consultations on this theme in the first part of 1999. Linking all of these dialogues was the question of how the deeply ingrained and culturally reinforced psychology of confrontation and hatred can be transformed into an even more robust psychology of peaceful and harmonious coexistence.

The SGI has long supported UNHCR's efforts to protect and rebuild the lives of refugees and displaced persons. These are the people who have suffered not only the immediate scourge of war and destruction but have also been forced by violence and fear to flee their homes. Their long-term needs must be addressed.

The youth members of the Soka Gakkai in Japan have held twenty fund- and awareness-raising campaigns, starting with that organized for Vietnamese and West African refugees in 1973. Since 1980, we have dispatched fourteen observation and information-gathering missions in order to provide up-to-date information to donors and the general public on the living conditions of refugees and the status of relief efforts. In 1999, for example, SGI representatives observed and publicized refugee repatriation efforts in war-ravaged Kosovo and camp conditions for refugees from the Democratic Republic of the Congo, Burundi and Rwanda. We intend to continue and expand such activities, which we are convinced are integral to the vital humanitarian and social mission of Buddhism.

***

326 Subsequently renamed the Ikeda Center for Peace, Learning, and Dialogue.

UNESCO, which is responsible for coordinating the activities of the International Year for the Culture of Peace, is currently taking the initiative in a worldwide awareness-raising movement called Manifesto 2000, aimed at submitting to the UN Millennium Assembly 100 million signatures to a pledge to put into practice the values, attitudes and forms of behavior which inspire the culture of peace.

The SGI supports the ideals of Manifesto 2000 and will back up the movement in various areas, including public information. To date, the SGI has supported the International Literacy Year (1990) in consonance with the goals of UNESCO, and "The World Boys and Girls Art Exhibition" has been shown in numerous countries as part of our efforts to develop an awareness of the culture of peace.

I would especially like to stress the role that women can play in creating a culture of peace. Throughout the long history of humanity, women have suffered the most whenever society has been wracked by war, violence, oppression, abuse of human rights, disease and famine.

It has been women, in spite of this, who have persevered in turning society in the direction of good, in the direction of hope and in the direction of peace. Women hold the key to opening a future filled with hope, as Mahatma Gandhi[327] emphasized:

> If by strength is meant brute strength then, indeed, is woman less brute than man. If by strength is meant moral power then woman is immeasurably man's superior. . . . If non-violence is the law of our being, the future is with women.[328]

The SGI has a number of women-focused projects such as a series of publications recording women's experiences of war, exhibitions for awareness-raising and various lecture series. An SGI-sponsored symposium entitled "Women Leading the Way to a Culture of Peace" was held at the 1999 Seoul International Conference of NGOs last October. Reviewing various problems confronting humankind from women's perspectives, the Boston Research Center for the 21st Century, the publisher of *Women's Views on the Earth Charter*,

---

327 Mohandas (Mahatma) Gandhi (1869–1948), Indian champion of nonviolence.
328 Gandhi, Mohandas K. 1980. *All Men Are Brothers: Autobiographical Reflections.* Ed. by Krishna Kripalani. New York: Continuum International Publishing Group, p. 148.

plans this year to hold a two-part event, "Creating Connections: Peace with Self, Sister and Society," to examine women's role in creating peace.

A special session of the UN General Assembly, "Women 2000: Gender Equality, Development and Peace for the Twenty-First Century," will be held in June, in which the SGI is scheduled to participate. I have great hopes that this gathering will stimulate intensive discussions on this theme.

In addition to these efforts, it is equally essential to work to create in concrete, tangible ways a culture of peace in daily life. Dr. Elise Boulding,[329] a renowned peace studies scholar, stresses that cultures of peace are to be found in each individual's process of tenaciously continuing peace-oriented behavior. She attaches particular importance to women's role in this aspect.

Peace is not something to be left to others in distant places. It is something we create day to day in our efforts to cultivate care and consideration for others, forging bonds of friendship and trust in our respective communities through our own actions and example. As we enhance our respect for the sanctity of life and human dignity through our daily behavior and steady efforts toward dialogue, the foundations for a culture of peace will deepen and strengthen, allowing a new global civilization to blossom. With women leading the way, when each and every person is aware and committed, we will be able to prevent society from relapsing into the culture of war, and foster and nurture energy toward the creation of a century of peace.

The SGI has always been committed to empowerment—of the people, by the people and for the people—a process we describe as human revolution. The essence of empowerment is to fully unleash the boundless potential inherent in every human being based on the Buddhist understanding that our own happiness is inextricably linked to the happiness of others.

It is our belief that through active engagement with others and the process of mutual support and encouragement, individual peace and happiness will be realized and the foundations for world peace will be further solidified.

It is my great joy and pride that SGI members, committed to the inconspicuous but steady practice of empowerment by encouraging friends who are suffering and bringing out their courage to live and to hope, have built a people's solidarity through their movement of peace, culture and education as good citizens of their respective countries and communities.

---

329 Elise Boulding (1920–2010), American peace scholar and activist.

I would like to affirm once again that it is the forging of personal relationships based on trust and respect that is exactly the culture of peace put into
practice. I am convinced that a culture of peace can truly be realized on a
global scale and become permanent when peace takes root in the mind of
every single person.

Planting Seeds of Peace (2004)[330]

In March of last year (2003), United Nations Under-Secretary-General
Anwarul K. Chowdhury[331] was the keynote speaker at the Soka University
and Soka Women's College commencement ceremony. On that occasion, he
compared the departure of the graduates on their careers with humanity's
departure on the adventure of world peace in the twenty-first century.

At the start of this year, I received a New Year's message from Ambassador
Chowdhury in which he stressed the importance of the home and family in
building world peace. Expressing his support for my view that a family that
interacts openly with society will produce individuals who are independent
and creative, able to face hardships, he wrote, "If the message of a culture of
peace and the values of tolerance, understanding and respect for diversity is
inculcated in the children from an early stage by their families, I believe that
in the coming decades the world will experience a distinct change for the
better in our conflict- and violence-ridden societies."

This statement takes on added significance in light of the fact that these are
the words of someone committed to working for peace from the global perspective of the United Nations. I believe it reflects Ambassador Chowdhury's
understanding that the soft power approach that touches the core of human
beings is paramount; that without cultivating the spiritual dimension the
goal of lasting peace will remain distant; and that the family—the smallest
and perhaps earliest human community—is where this crucial work must be
undertaken.

---

330 From 2004 Peace Proposal, "Inner Transformation: Creating a Global
     Groundswell for Peace."
331 Anwarul K. Chowdhury (1943–), Bangladeshi diplomat, Under-Secretary-
     General and High Representative of the United Nations (2002–07).

In a way, I believe this same understanding is reflected in the words of Katsuhiko Oku,[332] the Japanese diplomat who was killed in the line of duty in Iraq last year. In a series of articles entitled "Iraku dayori" (Letter from Iraq), he describes the severe challenges facing that country. However, he writes:

> There is hope; it is to be found in the brightly shining eyes of the children. . . . When I look at the sparkling eyes of the children of Iraq, I feel certain that things will work out for this country.[333]

In conflict-torn countries such as Iraq, the mistrust and hatred that fill the eyes of so many adults can provoke a sense of despair. But even then, the shining eyes of children seem to shed a ray of hope into situations that condense the most intractable aspects of human history. It is for this reason that we must focus with renewed determination on education in the broadest sense—all the places and occasions where young people are fostered, where their spirits are energized and enlivened.

Here I am reminded of the words of my mentor, the second president of the Soka Gakkai, Josei Toda,[334] whose limitless love for young people spurred him to make this impassioned call:

> Our struggle is one that requires that we love all living beings. Yet there are so many young people who are incapable of loving their own parents. How can they be expected to care about perfect strangers? The effort to overcome the coldness and indifference in our own lives and attain the same state of compassion as the Buddha is the essence of human revolution.[335]

Love and compassion for all living beings is the ultimate message of Buddhism. Yet the compassion that is at the core of a universal love for humankind will remain an empty, unrealized ideal unless we can take that first, immediate step—exemplified here by the simple act of loving one's

---

332 Katsuhiko Oku (1958–2003), Japanese diplomat.

333 Oku, Katsuhiko. 2003. "Iraku no yorokobu kodomotachi" [The Cheerful Children of Iraq]. "Iraku dayori" [Letter from Iraq] series. May 14. http://www. mofa.go.jp/mofaj/press/staff/iraq/20030514.html (accessed April 2, 2013).

334 Josei Toda (1900–58), second president of the Soka Gakkai (1951–58).

335 (trans. from) Toda, Josei. 1981–90. *Toda Josei zenshu* [The Complete Works of Josei Toda]. 9 vols. Tokyo: Seikyo Shimbunsha. Vol. 1, p. 58.

parents. "Dig beneath your feet, there you will find a spring." As this saying indicates, the consistent, daily effort to take that one step, while it may seem insignificant, is in fact all-encompassing.

In this context, the single step is for both parent and child to build on the foundation of their existing emotional attachments, recognizing each other as distinct and independent individuals, interacting frankly on the basis of their mutual "otherness." In this way, they can provide each other with an opportunity to forge and foster each other. This makes the home a point of departure from which we take that first step out into the community and toward public spiritedness. The path from there leads to larger values, such as a healthy love of country and a universal love for all humanity.

The spirit of the world today is in retreat and regression, almost a kind of meltdown. And this is why the global questions of peace must be rethought from the perspective of the immediate reality of our lives. At the very least, any attempt to deal with these large problems that does not take such immediate realities into full consideration will not constitute a fundamental response. I therefore believe strongly in the value of each of us initiating action, taking that first step, from where we are standing right now.

***

Last year (2003), as part of our peace education program, an exhibition on the life and ideas of Linus Pauling[336] was organized at the UNESCO Headquarters in Paris and the European Headquarters of the UN in Geneva. In February, SGI-USA will organize an exhibition entitled "Building a Culture of Peace for the Children of the World" at the UN Headquarters in New York.

Eliminating the word "misery" from the human lexicon was the fervent wish of my mentor, Josei Toda. The Toda Institute for Global Peace and Policy Research, which I founded to respond to his vision, has been deeply involved in projects to promote human security and global governance and in building a peace research network worldwide.

I am currently engaged in a dialogue with peace scholar Dr. Elise Boulding,[337] who has long advocated a culture of peace as the foundation for human life in the twenty-first century. In the course of our exchanges, Dr. Boulding has noted that human beings do not exist solely in the present; a

---

336 Linus Pauling (1901–94), American scientist, recipient of the Nobel Prize in Chemistry in 1954 and the Nobel Prize for Peace in 1962.

337 Elise Boulding (1920–2010), American peace scholar and activist.

short-term perspective makes us vulnerable to being overwhelmed by present events. To maintain hope, we must take constructive action with a long-term view.

Looking far into the future, Toda predicted that the Soka Gakkai would become a profound and inexhaustible source of hope and inspiration for all humankind. Embracing that proud mission as we look forward to the thirtieth anniversary of the founding of the SGI in 2005, we will continue to forge solidarity among the world's citizens as the basis for a robust and enduring culture of peace.

Empowerment of the people, by the people and for the people—individuals taking initiative to realize their infinite potential as they contribute to society—is the basis for the SGI's movement of human revolution.

In January 1975, when people assembled from all over the world to launch the SGI, I called on that diverse gathering: rather than seeking to bring your own lives to bloom, devote yourselves to planting the seeds of peace throughout the world. And I vowed to do the same.

My conviction remains firm today. Peace is not some abstract concept far removed from our everyday lives. It is a question of how each one of us plants and cultivates the seeds of peace in the reality of daily living, in the depths of our being, throughout our lives. I am certain that herein lies the most reliable path to lasting peace.

A Respect for Diversity and the Spirit of Dialogue (2005)[338]

In the years since the terror attacks of September 11, 2001, the world has experienced an extraordinary heightening of tensions. As governments tighten security measures to forestall the terrorist attacks that could occur at any time, the lives of many ordinary citizens are filled with a sense of fear and insecurity. There is no sign of a return to normality.

While conditions during the Cold War were in some ways similar, there is something even more unfathomable about the current threat. It is impossible to identify the potential perpetrators of terrorist acts, and there is no clear sense of what would constitute a resolution to the situation. There is a gnawing sense of vulnerability which even the most aggressive military actions or intrusive security measures are powerless to alleviate.

---

338 From 2005 Peace Proposal, "Toward a New Era of Dialogue: Humanism Explored."

The situation in Iraq likewise remains chaotic. Despite the transfer of sovereignty to a provisional government last June (2004), military clashes and terror attacks continue to occur throughout the country, and many question the chances of success for the January 30 elections for the national assembly.

Further, efforts to realize peace in the Middle East remain deadlocked. Talks on the issue of North Korea's nuclear weapons program are stalemated. Together with a large number of regional conflicts, these circumstances have prompted pessimistic voices to warn that we are in danger of repeating the war and violence that characterized the twentieth century.

In many countries the priority accorded to national security has in recent years fueled a drive to expand armaments. Increasingly, domestic security concerns are being used to justify curtailment of rights and freedoms. Meanwhile, energy and attention have been distracted from international efforts to address such global issues as poverty and ecological degradation. The resultant aggravation of threats to people's lives and dignity is another tragic outcome of terrorism and efforts to suppress it.

How can twenty-first-century humankind overcome the crises that face us?

There is, of course, no simple solution, no "magic wand" we can wave to make it all better. The way forward will be perilous as it requires finding an appropriate response to the kind of violence that rejects all attempts at engagement or dialogue.

Even so, there is no need to fall into meaningless and unproductive pessimism. All these problems are caused by human beings, which means that they must have a human solution. However long the effort takes, so long as we do not abandon the work of unknotting the tangled threads of these interrelated issues, we can be certain of finding a way forward.

The core of such efforts must be to bring forth the full potential of dialogue. So long as human history continues, we will face the perennial challenge of realizing, maintaining and strengthening peace through dialogue, of making dialogue the sure and certain path to peace. We must uphold and proclaim this conviction without cease, whatever coldly knowing smiles or cynical critiques may greet us.

***

This year marks the thirtieth anniversary of the SGI. The year 1975 was also a time of deepening conflict and division in the world. The aftershocks of the fourth Arab–Israeli War (1973) and the war in Vietnam were still being felt; the first summit of leading industrialized countries was held in that year to strengthen the unity of the Western bloc, while in the Communist bloc, the confrontation between China and the Soviet Union was escalating ominously.

I dedicated the year leading up to the founding of the SGI to intensive efforts in dialogue. My first visits to both China and the Soviet Union were made in 1974. Keenly aware of the potentially explosive tensions, I met repeatedly with the top leadership of both countries, engaging them in earnest dialogue.

In Japan at the time, the Soviet Union and its people were regarded with violent hostility. There were many who criticized my decision to travel there, asking what purpose could possibly be served by a person of religion going to a country that officially denied the value or validity of religion. But my sincere belief, as a Buddhist, was that no vision of peace was possible that didn't recognize and include the one-third of the world that was the Communist bloc. It was crucial, in my view, that a breakthrough be found as soon as possible.

On my first visit to China in May 1974, I witnessed the people of Beijing building a vast network of underground shelters against the eventuality of a Soviet attack. When I met, some three months later, with Soviet Premier Alexei N. Kosygin,[339] I conveyed to him the concerns I had encountered in China about Soviet intentions and asked him straight out if the Soviet Union was planning to attack China. The premier responded that the Soviet Union had no intention of either attacking or isolating China.

I brought this message with me when I next visited China in December of that year, conveying it to the Chinese leadership. It was also on this visit that I met Premier Zhou Enlai,[340] discussing with him the importance of enhancing and strengthening friendship between China and Japan and of working together for the betterment of the entire world.

In January of 1975, I visited the United States and presented to the United Nations a petition with more than 10 million signatures calling for the abolition of nuclear weapons gathered by the youth membership of the Soka Gakkai in Japan. I also had the opportunity to exchange views with US Secretary of State Henry Kissinger.[341]

---

339 Alexei N. Kosygin (1904–80), Premier of the Soviet Union (1964–80).
340 Zhou Enlai (1898–1976), Premier of the People's Republic of China (1949–76).
341 Henry Kissinger (1923–), US Secretary of State (1973–77), recipient of the Nobel Prize for Peace in 1973.

It was in the midst of such feverish efforts to promote dialogue that the SGI was founded thirty years ago on this day, January 26, 1975. The inaugural meeting was held on the island of Guam, site of fierce fighting in World War II, and was attended by the representatives of fifty-one countries and territories. From its inception, the SGI has sought to draw on people's energy and creativity to forge an effective grassroots movement for peace.

Since that first gathering, the members of the SGI have consistently upheld the conviction that dialogue represents the sure and certain path to peace. I have also committed myself to "human diplomacy," the kind of diplomacy that seeks to unite a divided world in the spirit of friendship and trust, and to promoting broad-based, grassroots exchanges in the cultural and educational fields.

Seeking to look beyond national and ideological differences, I have engaged in dialogue with leaders in various fields from throughout the world. I have met and shared thoughts with people of many different philosophical, cultural and religious backgrounds, including Judaism, Christianity, Islam, Hinduism and Confucianism. My consistent belief, reinforced through this experience, is that the basis for the kind of dialogue required in the twenty-first century must be humanism—one that sees good in that which unites and brings us together, evil in that which divides and sunders us.

As I review my own efforts to foster dialogue in this way, I gain a renewed sense of the urgent need to redirect the energies of dogmatism and fanaticism—the cause of so much deadly conflict—toward a more humanistic outlook. In a world rent by terrorism and retaliatory strikes, by conflicts premised on ethnic and religious differences, such an attempt may appear to some a hopeless quest. But even so I believe that we must continue to make efforts toward this goal.

***

One of the core concerns regarding the current situation in Iraq is that the conflict will become entrenched and develop into a full-scale confrontation between opposing worldviews, that it will become the spark for a clash of civilizations. To prevent a descent into such a quagmire, it is vital that we not conflate specific impulses to violence with the cultural traditions of whole civilizations. We must be constantly on guard against the stereotyped, deterministic approach to others that, in fact, constitutes the core of all extremist philosophies, the very snares of dogmatism.

In any society, in any country, in any civilization, the vast majority of people reject extremist views. And it is only a tiny minority that harbor hegemonic ambitions to impose their culture or legal system on other countries.

Five years ago, in 2000, I published a dialogue with Iranian-born Prof. Majid Tehranian[342] of the University of Hawai'i in which we discussed and compared the Buddhist and Islamic traditions. Professor Tehranian noted the persistence of widespread prejudice against Islam, the misconception that it is somehow violent or threatening. He stressed, for example, that the true meaning of *jihad* is an inner struggle waged by individuals in the quest for spiritual elevation. He also spoke of the policies of accommodation toward people of other faiths under the Ottoman Turks and the historical reality that such European cities as Sarajevo and Cordoba enjoyed religious pluralism and flourished under Muslim rule. We agreed that at the core of Islamic civilization is to be found not intolerance but an aspiring to the universal and a respect for diversity.

Starting in February, publication will begin of a serialized dialogue between myself and Prof. Nur Yalman,[343] a professor of cultural anthropology at Harvard University originally from Turkey. The realities and spirituality of Islamic society are among the topics we will cover in this dialogue, which we hope will contribute in some way to opening the path toward a global civilization based on the peaceful coexistence of all humankind.

Over the years, I have had the privilege of meeting with many distinguished individuals from throughout the Islamic world, from the Middle East, Asia and Africa. Through these encounters I have sensed a deep-seated yearning for peace, and this has reinforced my faith in the great majority of Muslims who seek harmonious coexistence.

The SGI as a whole has been actively participating in interfaith dialogue in various forums. Immediately following the September 11 terror attacks, for example, we joined representatives of the Jewish, Christian, Islamic and Buddhist faiths in a dialogue convened by the European Academy of Arts and Sciences. Further, SGI-affiliated institutes such as the Boston Research Center

---

342 Majid Tehranian (1937–2012), Iranian-born Professor of International Communication at the University of Hawai'i, Director of the Toda Institute for Global Peace and Policy Research (1996–2008).

343 Nur Yalman (1931–), Turkish academic, Professor of Social Anthropology and of Middle Eastern Studies at Harvard University.

for the 21st Century[344] and the Institute of Oriental Philosophy have been actively engaged in efforts in interfaith and cross-cultural dialogue. All these endeavors seek to contribute to the search for a path to peace, perspectives that will enable the resolution of the complex of global challenges.

The "2004 Human Development Report," issued by the UN Development Programme (UNDP), is focused on the theme of cultural liberty. It contains important insights into the nature of coercive movements that use violence or threats to force their views on others or to establish cultural domination. The report notes that the focus of such coercive movements "is not on solving real grievances but on using ostensible grievances as rallying cries."[345]

As the report makes clear, it is important that we have a keen awareness that people are not moved to extreme acts simply because they belong to a certain religion or nationality: "Movements of cultural domination also target members of their own community by denigrating and suppressing dissenting opinions and questioning integrity and loyalty (purity of faith or patriotism)."[346] In other words, such movements will even turn against those whom they claim as members of the same group, religion or nationality.

It is for this reason that unilateral military measures are not an effective response to violent and extremist movements, as they can in fact end up increasing sympathy and support for such movements among the general population. It is crucial that persistent efforts be made to remove the underlying causes of social instability, the grievances on which extremist groups feed.

Here, education holds the key.

When properly implemented (when it is not, that is, merely a tool for social control as was the case in pre-1945 militarist Japan), education is a powerful force for the positive transformation of individuals and society as a whole. Education for global citizenship can help transform humankind's long-standing culture of war into a culture of peace. It challenges us to fulfill our genuine potential as users of language (*Homo loquens*). The United Nations can serve as a powerful coordinating focus for such efforts.

344　Subsequently renamed the Ikeda Center for Peace, Learning, and Dialogue.

345　UNDP (United Nations Development Programme). 2004. "Human Development Report 2004: Cultural Liberty in Today's Diverse World." New York: Hoechstetter Printing Co., p. 75.

346　Ibid.

The World Programme for Human Rights Education, initiated in January 2005, provides a vital opportunity in this regard. The need for ongoing global efforts for human rights education has been a long-standing concern of mine; in a written statement to the World Conference Against Racism, Racial Discrimination, Xenophobia and Related Intolerance, held four years ago in Durban, South Africa, I urged that efforts be made to this end. The SGI has worked with other NGOs, UN agencies and the representatives of UN member states to encourage the adoption of this program. The United Nations Commission on Human Rights adopted a recommendation for such a program in April 2004; it was formally established by a resolution of the UN General Assembly in December of that year. The program will focus in its first three years (2005–07) on integrating human rights issues into the curricula of primary and secondary schools.

The SGI worked to support the UN Decade for Human Rights Education (1995–2004) through the international exhibition "Human Rights in Today's World: Toward a Century of Hope." Plans are currently under way for a follow-up exhibition to be held in venues throughout the world in support of the new program.

The year 2005 also marks the start of the UN Decade of Education for Sustainable Development, something which the SGI has called for and worked toward in collaboration with other members of international civil society. UNESCO, the lead agency for the promotion of the decade, describes its goal as "a world where everyone has the opportunity to benefit from education and learn the values, behavior and lifestyles required for a sustainable future and for positive societal transformation."[347]

This is obviously not limited to environmental education but has a much broader scope. It must take into consideration such global challenges as poverty alleviation and peace, while laying the foundation for our joint efforts to build a sustainable global society that we can leave as a proud legacy to future generations.

In that sense, human rights education and education for sustainable development reflect intertwined concerns and objectives. Global society should seize upon these two UN-centered initiatives as an important opportunity to

---

347 UNESCO (United Nations Educational, Scientific and Cultural Organization). 2005. "United Nations Decade of Education for Sustainable Development (2005–2014): International Implementation Scheme." Paris: UNESCO, p. 6.

set a positive direction for humanity in the twenty-first century. I call on all parties to work for their success.

A Global Society that Puts Children First (2010)[348]

In both the developed and developing worlds, it is children who are forced to pay the highest price when their societies face a crisis. With economies falling into recession and both national and family budgets hit hard by the current crisis, there are concerns over the increasing numbers of children who are denied access to adequate nutrition and health care or are forced to quit school in order to work.

I would like to suggest that schools should function as a refuge to protect children from various threats—as strongholds of human security—and become a venue for fostering children as protagonists of a new culture of peace.

In 1995, the World Health Organization (WHO) launched the Global School Health Initiative to strengthen health promotion through schools. This approach has been carried over into the FRESH (Focusing Resources on Effective School Health) framework, launched in 2000 as a partnership of WHO, UNICEF, UNESCO and the World Bank. FRESH aims to improve the learning environment by teaching life skills needed to establish lifelong healthy practices, providing nutritious school meals, etc.

School meal programs are a crucial safeguard for children's health and future, as the experience of the World Food Programme has proved over more than four decades. UNICEF has advocated child-friendly schools and the building of classrooms that can withstand earthquakes and storms so that schools serve as a refuge in times of crisis where children can recover a sense of normalcy and their hearts can begin to heal.

I would like to propose that these and other school-focused efforts and experiences be built upon and expanded into a program that makes schools centers for promoting human security and building a culture of peace.

Emphasis has been placed in recent years on empowering children as agents of change rather than simply affording them protection, as important as that is. We should create an environment that enables children, who will shape the

---

348 From 2010 Peace Proposal, "Toward a New Era of Value Creation."

next generation, to initiate waves of change, transforming and breaking the historical cycles of human suffering and tragedy.

The year 2010 will be the last year of the International Decade for a Culture of Peace and Non-Violence for the Children of the World. Global efforts to promote a culture of peace should continue beyond this year, with schools serving as focal points for this.

The Declaration and Programme of Action on a Culture of Peace, adopted by the General Assembly in 1999, calls on all relevant actors to: "Ensure that children, from an early age, benefit from education on the values, attitudes, modes of behaviour and ways of life to enable them to resolve any dispute peacefully and in a spirit of respect for human dignity and of tolerance and nondiscrimination."[349]

I would like to urge that we use this as a guideline as we foster in children the skills needed to deal with threats to life and dignity, as well as the spirit of resolving issues through dialogue rather than violence. Such efforts should involve all the places where children learn—home, school and the wider community. We must establish the means by which children develop into individuals who can be effective advocates for their own rights and dignity, as well as those of others. Children must play a key role in enabling a culture of peace to take root in society.

To further expand the reach and positive impact of a culture of peace, it is crucial that sustained efforts be made not only by the UN and governments but also by civil society. Through such efforts we must raise awareness about the constituent ideas of a culture of peace in terms of values, behaviors and ways of life.

As heirs to the spirit of Tsunesaburo Makiguchi,[350] the SGI has continued to urge that the happiness of children be the standard for measuring the success of any effort to resolve the problems confronting society.

Seeking to respond to the adoption of the Convention on the Rights of the Child in 1989, we created the exhibitions "The Children of the World and UNICEF" and "What Are Children's Rights?" which were held in locations throughout Japan. Another exhibition, "Treasuring the Future: Children's

---

349 UNGA (United Nations General Assembly). 1999. "Declaration and Programme of Action on a Culture of Peace." A/RES/53/243. Resolution adopted by the General Assembly. October 6, p. 6.

350 Tsunesaburo Makiguchi (1871–1944), founding president of the Soka Kyoiku Gakkai (forerunner of the Soka Gakkai) (1930–44).

Rights and Realities," toured the United States starting in 1996. As part of our support for the International Decade, the exhibition "Building a Culture of Peace for the Children of the World" has traveled globally since its launch in 2004, and the "Children and a Culture of Peace" exhibition has been shown in numerous cities in Japan since 2006.

Children are envoys of the future; they are humanity's shared treasure. Convinced that instilling courage and hope in their hearts is the most certain path to a peaceful world, we will continue striving to build a global society that puts children first.

CHAPTER 3

A UN for a World without War

Building Global Solidarity toward Nuclear Abolition

2009 Nuclear Abolition Proposal (Full Text)
September 8, 2009

If nuclear weapons epitomize the forces that would divide and destroy the world, they can only be overcome by the solidarity of ordinary citizens, which transforms hope into the energy to create a new era.

Albert Einstein,[1] one of the greatest physicists of the twentieth century, considered one thing the gravest mistake of his life: and that was having written to US President Franklin D. Roosevelt,[2] informing him of the risk that the Nazis would develop an atomic weapon and urging him to respond quickly to this threat.

In 1929, Einstein had declared: "I would absolutely refuse any direct or indirect war service . . . regardless of the reasons for the cause of a war."[3] His pacifist sentiments were overwhelmed, however, by the weight of military logic. What finally persuaded him, some ten years later, to respond affirmatively to a fellow scientist's suggestion that he write to Roosevelt was a deep sense of fear and anxiety at the consequences for the world if an atomic weapon were to fall into the hands of the Nazis. More than anyone, he understood the

---

1 Albert Einstein (1879–1955), German-born American physicist, recipient of the Nobel Prize for Physics in 1921.

2 Franklin D. Roosevelt (1882–1945), 32nd President of the United States (1933–45).

3 Einstein, Albert. 2005. *The New Quotable Einstein.* Ed. by Alice Calaprice. Princeton: Princeton University Press, p. 156.

potential destructiveness of nuclear weapons, and such an outcome was for him unthinkable.

The factors that originally compelled Einstein to write this letter were rendered irrelevant when the defeat of Nazi Germany removed the motivation for atomic weapons development by the Allies. Einstein's relief was short-lived, however, as atomic bombs were soon used against the cities of Hiroshima and Nagasaki in Japan.

Shocked and horrified, for the remaining decade of his life Einstein continued to urge the international community to abolish nuclear weapons.

In 1947, he wrote, in an article in the *Atlantic Monthly*: "Since the completion of the first atomic bomb nothing has been accomplished to make the world more safe from war, while much has been done to increase the destructiveness of war."[4] This article was written a year after negotiations on the Baruch Plan—a proposal for international control of atomic energy— had collapsed at the United Nations, and Britain and the Soviet Union had launched their nuclear weapons programs. Three times in this article Einstein repeated his outraged warning.

For me personally, 1947 was the year I met my mentor in life, second Soka Gakkai president Josei Toda.[5] Arrested for his resistance to the Japanese militarist government during World War II, Toda held fast to his beliefs through two years in prison, emerging after the war to spearhead a people's movement for peace.

As early as October 1949, he warned: "If an atomic war were to occur, the only path facing the peoples of the world would be one of total destruction."[6] This was immediately after the Soviet Union had announced that it had tested its first nuclear weapon, following in the footsteps of the United States.

Sixty years have passed since the world entered the era of nuclear confrontation, but no fundamental measures have been taken in response to Einstein's warning. On the contrary, the situation is becoming ever more dangerous.

Even though the threat of global nuclear war has diminished since the end of the Cold War, the number of states with nuclear arms has nearly doubled since the Treaty on the Non-Proliferation of Nuclear Weapons (NPT) entered

---

4   Einstein, Albert. 1950. *Out of My Later Years*. New York: Philosophical Library, p. 190.

5   Josei Toda (1900–58), second president of the Soka Gakkai (1951–58).

6   (trans. from) Toda, Josei. 1981–90. *Toda Josei zenshu* [The Complete Works of Josei Toda]. 9 vols. Tokyo: Seikyo Shimbunsha. Vol. 3, pp. 408–09.

into force in 1970.[7] There are still some 25,000 nuclear warheads in existence in the world. At the same time, there is rising fear that the spread of nuclear weapons technologies and materials through the black market will unleash the nightmare of nuclear terrorism.

In his speech delivered in Prague, Czech Republic, in April of this year (2009), US President Barack Obama[8] noted the moral responsibility of the United States as the only country to have actually used a nuclear weapon, and expressed his resolve to realize a world without nuclear weapons.

President Obama met with Russian President Dmitry Medvedev[9] in April and again in July, at which time they agreed on the broad outlines of a nuclear disarmament treaty to replace the Strategic Arms Reduction Treaty (START I), which expires in December.

A joint statement expressing a commitment to "creating the conditions for a world without nuclear weapons"[10] was issued at the G8 Summit in L'Aquila, Italy. Meanwhile, a special meeting of the UN Security Council on nuclear nonproliferation and disarmament will take place on September 24 during the General Assembly. These developments illustrate progress in new directions, positive new initiatives to break the existing deadlock.

In the end, will these initiatives create new currents truly capable of transforming the era? The five-year Review Conference of the Parties to the Treaty on the Non-Proliferation of Nuclear Weapons scheduled for May 2010 will be crucial.

The last Review Conference, in 2005, produced no meaningful results, stalemated by a clash between those states advocating that priority be given to disarmament and those advocating priority consideration of nonproliferation. There are now signs of compromise in an effort to avoid a repeat of this failure, such as the decision made this year at the Conference on Disarmament

---

7   UNGA (United Nations General Assembly). 1961. "Declaration on the Prohibition of the Use of Nuclear and Thermo-Nuclear Weapons." A/RES1653 (XVI). Resolution adopted by the General Assembly, New York. November 24.

8   Barack Obama (1961–), 44th President of the United States (2009–), recipient of the Nobel Prize for Peace in 2009.

9   Dmitry Medvedev (1965–), President of Russia (2008–12), Russian Prime Minister (2012–).

10   G8 Summit. 2009. "L'Aquila Statement on Non-Proliferation," p. 2.

(CD) in Geneva to begin negotiations on a Fissile Material Cut-off Treaty (FMCT).

This change in mood, however welcome, is not in itself enough to dispel the dark clouds of the nuclear age. We must face the essential reality, which transcends political or military interests: the degree to which the existence of nuclear arms destabilizes the world and threatens humankind.

Here I would like to direct attention to the words of the British historian Arnold J. Toynbee.[11] In his *A Study of History,* he addressed the nuclear weapons issue as "a challenge which we cannot evade,"[12] urging all people to respond.

In 1972–73, Toynbee and I met and conducted a dialogue which was later published in English under the title *Choose Life.* One of his remarks that made a deep impression on me was his statement that a "self-imposed veto"[13] on the possession of nuclear weapons must be adopted by the world's governments.

Elsewhere, Toynbee described the effort to respond to that challenge as follows:

> The emotional resistance to this revolutionary break with ingrained habits and to this painful renunciation of familiar institutions will have to be overcome by self-education; in the Atomic Age it cannot be broken with force. The Gordian Knot has to be untied by patient fingers instead of being cut by the sword.[14]

To date, humankind has managed to avoid the catastrophe of full-scale nuclear war. Yet today we face a growing array of destabilizing elements, and here I would like to urge the leaders of all states that either possess nuclear weapons themselves or whose national security is reliant on the nuclear weapons of other states to ask themselves these questions:

> Are nuclear weapons really necessary? Why do we need to keep them?

---

11   Arnold J. Toynbee (1889–1975), British historian.
12   Toynbee, Arnold J. 1934–61. *A Study of History.* 12 vols. London: Oxford University Press. Vol. 6, p. 320.
13   Toynbee, Arnold J. and Daisaku Ikeda. 2007. *Choose Life.* London: I.B.Tauris, p. 194.
14   Toynbee, Arnold J. 1966. *Change and Habit: The Challenge of Our Time.* London: Oxford University Press, p. 100.

What justifies our own stockpiles of nuclear weapons when we make an issue out of other states' possession of them?

Does humanity really have no choice but to live under the threat of nuclear weapons?

Learning the lessons

Next I would like to delve into some lessons of history that might shine a light on these questions, with Toynbee's concept of "self-education" as the key.

Here I would first like to revisit the dilemmas and doubts that assailed scientists as they worked on the development of the first nuclear weapons, and examine the ways in which people have thought about these weapons over the years.

Although we have become numbed to the existence of nuclear weapons, we need to remember that many of the scientists involved in their development did not welcome their arrival, expressing deep concerns and misgivings.

In December 1938, the year before the outbreak of World War II, Otto Hahn[15] discovered nuclear fission of uranium in his Berlin laboratory. Realizing the horrendous possibilities, Hahn is said to have considered throwing all his uranium into the ocean and committing suicide.

In the following year, 1939, Leo Szilárd[16] proved that a chain reaction of nuclear fission—a next key step to producing an atomic bomb—was possible. He also foresaw tragedy, later declaring, "I knew the world was headed for sorrow."[17]

In 1942, scientists at the University of Chicago produced the first controlled nuclear chain reaction in a nuclear pile, importantly advancing the Manhattan Project. And it was scientists involved in that work at the University of Chicago who drafted a petition urging President Harry S. Truman[18] not to use the atomic bomb against Japanese cities, even as the final preparations for the first atomic bomb test were under way in July 1945.

---

15   Otto Hahn (1879–1968), German chemist, recipient of the Nobel Prize in Chemistry in 1944.

16   Leo Szilárd (1898–1964), Hungarian-born American physicist.

17   (qtd. in) Lens, Sidney. 1982. *The Bomb.* New York: E. P. Dutton, p. 8.

18   Harry S. Truman (1884–1972), 33rd President of the United States (1945–53).

In January 1975, just prior to the founding of the SGI, I had the occasion to visit the University of Chicago. After meeting with the vice president and visiting the library, I was crossing the campus when I saw a monument commemorating the nuclear development project. There, I reflected about the anguish that had tormented those scientists, and deepened my resolve to help achieve the abolition of nuclear weapons. My feelings were intensified by the fact that, just a few days earlier, I had submitted to the United Nations Headquarters in New York 10 million signatures calling for nuclear abolition collected by the Soka Gakkai Youth Division in Japan.

The University of Chicago is home to the Doomsday Clock representing the current status of the threat of global nuclear war. We must heed the concerns of the pioneers of nuclear science as encapsulated in the Doomsday Clock: although they have been accorded little prominence, the personal dramas behind the history of nuclear development urgently deserve our attention.

Also demanding our attention are the various responses of political leaders to the crises that have arisen during the nuclear age; important lessons can be derived from their experience and examples.

In the years since the end of World War II, there have been a number of situations in which the use of nuclear weapons was seriously considered. The most imminent was the Cuban Missile Crisis of October 1962, which brought the United States and the Soviet Union to the brink of all-out nuclear war.

What is remarkable about the attitude of US President John F. Kennedy[19] following the crisis is that he emphasized the importance of overcoming hostility and discrimination as the prerequisite to exploring possibilities of peaceful coexistence with the Soviet Union. In his famous speech "The Strategy of Peace" in June 1963, President Kennedy referred to the Soviets' allegations against the United States:

> Yet it is sad to read these Soviet statements—to realize the extent of the gulf between us. But it is also a warning—a warning to the American people not to fall into the same trap as the Soviets, not to see only a distorted and desperate view of the other side, not to see conflict as inevitable, accommodation as impossible, and communication as nothing more than an exchange of threats.[20]

---

19 John F. Kennedy (1917–63), 35th President of the United States (1960–63).
20 Kennedy, John F. 1963. "Commencement Address at American University." June 10.

I believe that we must learn from his message—not to let our eyes become clouded by prejudice and preconceptions—if we are to untie the Gordian Knot of the nuclear age.

I was deeply convinced of this when I visited China and the Soviet Union in 1974 to meet with their top leaders in an effort to ease tensions between them. As a Buddhist who seeks a peaceful world, I believe that the people of no nation desire war, and made the determined effort to build a bridge between the two countries.

When I met with Soviet Premier Alexei N. Kosygin[21] three months after my first visit to China, we discussed the brutal Siege of Leningrad, which he had personally experienced. Then I told him that the Chinese leaders I met with had clearly stated that China would never initiate an attack against another country. China was anxious about the Soviet Union's intentions: The Chinese people were building underground bomb shelters against the threat of Soviet attack. Finally, I asked: "Is the Soviet Union going to attack China?"

Kosygin responded that the Soviet Union had no intention of either attacking or isolating China. Soon afterwards, I brought this message to the Chinese leadership. I later visited the United States, where I exchanged views with Secretary of State Henry A. Kissinger[22] on Sino–American relations and the status of the Strategic Arms Limitation Talks (SALT).

I took away two lessons from these meetings: The only way to accurately grasp the other's intention is to conduct open and frank dialogue; and, no matter how difficult the circumstances may be, dialogue can lead to a breakthrough.

Although they failed to attain their ultimate objectives, I think that the meeting between Soviet leader Mikhail Gorbachev[23] and US President Ronald Reagan[24] at Reykjavík, Iceland, in October 1986, represents a striking example of the importance of maintaining this spirit of dialogue.

---

21 Alexei N. Kosygin (1904–80), Premier of the Soviet Union (1964–80).

22 Henry Kissinger (1923–), US Secretary of State (1973–77), recipient of the Nobel Prize for Peace in 1973.

23 Mikhail Gorbachev (1931–), General Secretary of the Communist Party of the Soviet Union (1985–91), President of the Soviet Union (1990–91), recipient of the Nobel Prize for Peace in 1990.

24 Ronald Reagan (1911–2004), 40th President of the United States (1981–89).

When, at the start of the year, Gorbachev proposed a program for achieving complete nuclear abolition, Reagan responded positively. His advisers were opposed to the radical proposal, but he reassured them:

> I'm not going soft. . . . But. . . I have a dream of a world without nuclear weapons. I want our children and grandchildren particularly to be free of these terrible weapons.[25]

For his part, Gorbachev was intensely impacted by the disaster at Chernobyl that occurred four months after he made his proposal, and this strengthened his resolve to achieve nuclear abolition.

At the October summit, the two leaders engaged in a frank exchange of views, and an agreement to reduce their nuclear arsenals to zero within ten years, by 1996, was in reach. In the end, however, they failed to conclude what would have been a historic accord because they could not come to terms regarding the US missile defense plan, the Strategic Defense Initiative (SDI).

In January 2007, George P. Shultz,[26] who as Reagan's Secretary of State was a firsthand witness to the Reykjavík Summit, joined with Kissinger, William J. Perry[27] and Sam Nunn[28] to call for "A World Free of Nuclear Weapons" in an influential editorial of the same name in *The Wall Street Journal*. With the danger of nuclear proliferation escalating, the aim of the proposal was to revisit the vision of a nuclear-weapon-free world that had almost been reached at Reykjavík.[29]

I had an opportunity to hear directly from Gorbachev details of the Reykjavík Summit during a meeting in 2001. He recalled:

> We were determined to take the initiative and absolutely create a forum of dialogue regardless of the attitude on the part of the US. To be honest, to get the Soviet government to move in this direction was in itself an extremely onerous task. But the fact that the Soviet

---

25 (qtd. in) Leffler, Melvyn P. 2007. *For the Soul of Mankind*. New York: Hill and Wang, p. 388.

26 George P. Shultz (1920–), US Secretary of State (1982–89).

27 William J. Perry (1920–), US Secretary of Defense (1994–97).

28 Sam Nunn (1938–), American statesman, Co-chairman and CEO of Nuclear Threat Initiative (NTI) (2001–).

29 Shultz, George P., William J. Perry, Henry A. Kissinger and Sam Nunn. 2007. "A World Free of Nuclear Weapons." *The Wall Street Journal*. January 4.

Union called for dialogue was unprecedented, and I believe this compelled President Reagan to modify his attitude as well.[30]

I think the Reykjavík Summit demonstrated the particular importance of three qualities. These are: a shared vision based on a clear awareness of crisis; unflagging determination to take the initiative undeterred by the possibility of being rebuffed; and a sense of mutual trust sustained to the end despite the challenging negotiation process.

I urge that the world's leaders take these lessons to heart as they struggle to free humankind from the dire threat of nuclear weapons.

A prescient vision

In his Prague speech, President Obama declared: "Just as we stood for freedom in the 20th century, we must stand together for the right of people everywhere to live free from fear in the 21st century."[31]

In an earlier era, when the competition to develop larger and more deadly nuclear arsenals was escalating, my mentor Josei Toda issued his historic "Declaration Calling for the Abolition of Nuclear Weapons."[32] His declaration was rooted in the perspective of ordinary citizens, an awareness of the fearful threat nuclear weapons bring to people's lives.

Toda delivered the speech in which this declaration was issued just seven months before his death, at a time when his health was extremely precarious. It was, in fact, fifty-two years ago today, September 8, 1957, that Toda addressed a gathering of some 50,000 people, principally young people, and declared the goal of eliminating all nuclear weapons from the face of Earth to be the foremost of his instructions to his followers.

In light of present-day realities, I think that three themes of particular relevance can be extracted from this speech. These are: the need for a transformation in the consciousness of political leaders; the need for a clearly shared

---

30   (trans. from) Gorbachev, Mikhail and Daisaku Ikeda. 2001. *"Gorubachofu-shi to katarai"* [Dialogue with Gorbachev]. *Seikyo Shimbun.* November 20, pp. 2–3.

31   Obama, Barack. 2009. "The Remarks by President Barack Obama." Delivered at Hradcany Square, Prague, Czech Republic. April. 5.

32   Toda, Josei. 1981–90. *Toda Josei zenshu* [The Complete Works of Josei Toda]. 9 vols. Tokyo: Seikyo Shimbunsha. Vol. 4, pp. 564–66. (English text at http:// www.joseitoda.org/vision/declaration.)

vision toward the outlawing of nuclear weapons; and the need to establish "human security" on a global scale.

Regarding the first theme, Toda stated:

> [W]e, the citizens of the world, have an inviolable right to live. Anyone who jeopardizes that right is a devil incarnate, a fiend, a monster.[33]

This was a striking condemnation of the national egotism that underlies the urge to develop and possess nuclear weapons. With this very strong language, he sought to jolt political leaders out of their existing way of thinking and encourage a transformation in their worldview.

While we may find such expressions as "devil incarnate," "fiend" or "monster" disconcerting, Toda's main intent in the use of such language was to expose the aberrant nature of nuclear deterrence. For at the heart of deterrence theory lies a cold and inhuman readiness to sacrifice vast numbers of people in order to realize one's own security or dominance. He was, at the same time, pressing political leaders to reflect on their assumptions and attitudes.

In the same year that Toda made this statement, Bertrand Russell,[34] the British philosopher who cofounded the Pugwash Conferences on Science and World Affairs, described those who wield power over others and look down on them, as from a great height, as being "armed, like Jove, with a thunderbolt. . . ."[35]

The sixth-century Chinese Buddhist philosopher Chih-i[36] (the Great Teacher T'ien-t'ai) described those possessed by the desire to dominate others in these words: "always seeking to surpass, unable to countenance inferiority, disparaging others and overvaluing oneself."[37] Buddhism further describes

---

33   (trans. from) Toda, Josei. 1981–90. *Toda Josei zenshu* [The Complete Works of Josei Toda]. 9 vols. Tokyo: Seikyo Shimbunsha. Vol. 4, p. 565.

34   Bertrand Russell (1872–1970), British philosopher, cofounder of the Pugwash Conferences on Science and World Affairs, recipient of the Nobel Prize for Literature in 1950.

35   Russell, Bertrand. 1975. *Power: A New Social Analysis*. London: Unwin Books, p. 22.

36   Chih-i (T'ien-t'ai) (538–97), Buddhist monk, founder of the T'ien-t'ai school.

37   (trans. from) Nichiren. 1952. *Nichiren Daishonin gosho zenshu* [The Complete Works of Nichiren Daishonin]. Ed. by Nichiko Hori. Tokyo: Soka Gakkai, p. 430.

the ultimate form of the life-state that sees everything and everyone as the means to the fulfillment of one's own goals and desires as a state in which the existence of others is reduced to insignificance, where one does not feel the slightest qualm or hesitation about inflicting upon them even the most terrible suffering.

Lee Butler,[38] the retired general who from 1992 to 1994 had been in charge of the United States Strategic Command, has analyzed the psychology of the nuclear mind-set this way: "By clinging to the extreme precepts of cold war nuclear deterrence we erode the respect for life that anchors our sense of humanity. . . ."[39]

Joseph Rotblat[40] of the Pugwash Conferences gained renown as the only scientist to leave the Manhattan Project on moral grounds despite having been involved in it from its earliest stages. Rotblat worked with the delegation from the Solomon Islands preparing evidence for a public sitting leading up to the 1996 Advisory Opinion on the Legality of the Threat or Use of Nuclear Weapons by the International Court of Justice (ICJ). In his statement, he stressed:

The property of fall-out to extend the injurious action both in space and time, is a novel and unique characteristic of nuclear warfare. Not only the inhabitants of the combatant countries, but virtually the whole population of the world, and their descendants, would be victims of a nuclear war—therein lies the radical change which nuclear weapons introduce into the whole concept of warfare.[41]

---

38   George Lee Butler (1939–), Commander in chief of the United States Strategic Command (1992–94), President of Second Chance Foundation (1999–).

39   Butler, George L. 1999. "On Ridding the World of Nuclear Dangers." Acceptance speech for the Nuclear Age Peace Foundation's Distinguished Peace Leadership Award, Santa Barbara, CA. April 30.

40   Sir Joseph Rotblat (1908–2005), British physicist and philanthropist, founding member (1957), Secretary-General (1957–73) and President (1988–97) of the Pugwash Conferences on Science and World Affairs.

41   ICJ (International Court of Justice). 1995. "Public Sitting." CR 1995/32. Verbatim record in the case in Legality of the Use by a State of Nuclear Weapons in Armed Conflict and in Legality of the Threat or Use of Nuclear Weapons. November 14, pp. 72–73.

Having studied the impact of radiation on the human body, and speaking on behalf of the people who have been exposed to radioactive fallout each time the nuclear-weapon states have conducted tests, he was particularly well placed to issue this warning to the whole of humankind.

The inability of decision-makers who are in full possession of the knowledge of the catastrophic consequences of nuclear war to rethink existing nuclear policy signals a bankruptcy of imagination, a failure of empathy toward those who would experience its realities. The time has come to muster the courage necessary to part ways with the doctrine of deterrence, this negative legacy of the Cold War—to consign it to the dustbin of history.

The second theme of Toda's declaration is his assertion of the absolute inadmissibility of the use of nuclear weapons, whatever the rationale or justification. Here again, he used very strong language: "I wish to declare that anyone who ventures to use nuclear weapons, irrespective of their nationality or whether their country is victorious or defeated, should be sentenced to death without exception."[42]

As a Buddhist for whom respect for life was a core principle, Toda was adamantly opposed to the death penalty. His invocation here of capital punishment should therefore be understood as an effort to undermine and uproot the logic that would justify the use of nuclear weapons. For Toda, nuclear weapons, which fundamentally threaten humanity's right to survival, represented an "absolute evil." He was determined to counteract any attempt to justify them as a "necessary evil" whose use might be viewed as an extension of conventional warfare.

At the time, the Eastern and Western blocs were engaged in a war of words directed at each other's nuclear arsenals. Toda sought to refute the underlying fallacy of such an approach; impartial with regard to ideology, he denounced all nuclear weapons equally in the name of humankind. My mentor had at great personal cost resisted Japanese militarism during World War II, and it was his conviction that no country or people deserved to be victimized by war. He was an advocate of what he called "global nationalism" (Jp. *chikyu minzokushugi*)[43]; his call for the abolition of nuclear weapons can be understood as the logical outcome of that thinking.

---

42   (trans. from) Toda, Josei. 1981–90. *Toda Josei zenshu* [The Complete Works of Josei Toda]. 9 vols. Tokyo: Seikyo Shimbunsha. Vol. 4, p. 565.

43   Ibid., Vol. 3, p. 460.

In the years since Toda's declaration, a similarly unequivocal stance against nuclear weapons has been expressed by the international community on numerous occasions. In 1961, for example, the United Nations General Assembly adopted a resolution declaring that: "Any State using nuclear and thermo-nuclear weapons is to be considered as violating the Charter of the United Nations, as acting contrary to the laws of humanity and as committing a crime against mankind and civilization. . . ."[44] Most recently, in 2006, the Weapons of Mass Destruction Commission (the Blix Commission) offered the following view in their final report: "The Commission rejects the suggestion that nuclear weapons in the hands of some pose no threat, while in the hands of others they place the world in mortal jeopardy."[45]

So long as the notion persists that it is possible to separate "good" nuclear weapons from "bad" ones, any attempt to strengthen the nonproliferation regime will lack legitimacy and persuasiveness. Toda's declaration brings into clear relief this critical issue.

The third theme of Toda's declaration is expressed figuratively with this language:

> Although a movement calling for a ban on the testing of atomic or nuclear weapons has arisen around the world, it is my wish to go further, to attack the problem at its root. I want to expose and rip out the claws that lie hidden in the very depths of such weapons.[46]

My understanding of my mentor's declaration is that the "hidden claws" underlying nuclear weapons represent any conception of security predicated on the suffering and sacrifice of ordinary citizens. He is urging us to confront and extirpate such ways of thinking because, without this, no solution is possible.

---

44   UNGA (United Nations General Assembly). 1961. "Declaration on the Prohibition of the Use of Nuclear and Thermo-Nuclear Weapons." A/RES1653 (XVI). Resolution adopted by the General Assembly, New York. November 24.

45   WMDC (Weapons of Mass Destruction Commission). 2006. "Weapons of Terror: Freeing the World of Nuclear, Biological, and Chemical Arms." Stockholm, Sweden: WMDC, p. 60.

46   (trans. from) Toda, Josei. 1981–90. *Toda Josei zenshu* [The Complete Works of Josei Toda]. 9 vols. Tokyo: Seikyo Shimbunsha. Vol. 4, p. 565.

Any hostile nuclear exchange would produce damage not limited to the opposing country; all countries involved would necessarily suffer massive casualties. In light of this reality, any call for "national security" rings hollow if it necessitates the slaughter of the very people whose lives and safety it claims to protect.

Even when nuclear weapons are not used, weapons testing has exposed large numbers of people to radiation, causing fatal cancers and genetic diseases. Similar patterns of negative impact on human health and life have been observed around nuclear weapons facilities throughout the world.

Toda's deepest determination is perhaps expressed most fully in his statement: "I wish to see the word 'misery' no longer used to describe the world, any country, any individual."[47] His call for the abolition of nuclear weapons gives condensed expression to that determination. It is rooted in a perspective remarkably cognate with the widely advocated concept of "human security." This is an approach that sees alleviating the suffering—removing the misery—from each individual's life as a necessary foundation for stability and peace. What I find especially important is that Toda stressed the need to eliminate situations of misery and suffering equally from all levels—the personal, the national and the global.

Put differently, the destruction of any nation or state is unacceptable, even if it were to be justified as essential to the maintenance of world peace. Likewise, the sacrifice of ordinary citizens cannot be justified in the name of achieving security for the state. I believe strongly that it is the shared task of all members of the human family to clearly identify the fundamental error in such thinking and to "rip out the claws that lie hidden in the very depths" of the nuclear weapons issue.

Toda concluded with these words: "I ask those who consider themselves to be my students and disciples to be heirs to the spirit of the declaration I have made today, and to make its meaning known throughout the entire world."[48] These words, which were burned into my mind that day, have remained with me and have inspired my actions in the more than half-century that has passed since then. I have never for even a single day forgotten his stirring call to action and have worked tirelessly to create a rising tide of public opinion in favor of nuclear abolition.

---

47   Ibid. Vol. 3, p. 290.
48   Ibid. Vol. 4, p. 565.

In 1960, two years after Toda passed away, I succeeded him as the third president of the Soka Gakkai, and in October of that year, carrying a photograph of Toda in the breast pocket of my jacket, I traveled to the United States. This was the first of a long series of journeys that would, over the years, take me throughout the world. In the course of these travels, I have met with leaders of the five declared nuclear-weapon states, Secretaries-General and other officials of the United Nations, as well as numerous scholars and intellectuals. The elimination of nuclear weapons and the realization of global peace has been a consistent theme of these dialogues.

Further, I wrote proposals on the occasion of the three United Nations General Assembly Special Sessions on Disarmament (1978, 1982 and 1988) in the hope of contributing to their success. Since 1983, I have authored an annual peace proposal, released each year on January 26 to commemorate the founding of the SGI. Here also nuclear abolition has been a constant concern. In 1996, I founded the Toda Institute for Global Peace and Policy Research, which seeks to implement the vision of Josei Toda as a focal hub of a network of people-oriented peace research. The Toda Institute has taken up the abolition of nuclear weapons as one of its principal research projects, holding conferences and publishing proceedings on this theme.

As a movement of ordinary citizens, the SGI has engaged in an extensive range of activities to convey to a wide public the inhuman nature of and the danger posed by nuclear weapons.

Despite the continued existence of this threat—the shadow of violent death cast equally on the whole of humankind—it is rarely felt as a palpable reality because it is largely invisible, relegated to an unconscious realm. In our initiatives to advocate nuclear abolition, the SGI has considered that the first priority is to break down this barrier of unconscious avoidance.

To that end, we organized the exhibition "Nuclear Arms: Threat to Our World," which was launched in June 1982 in support of the United Nations World Disarmament Campaign. Since then, the SGI has organized numerous exhibitions on this theme, which have been seen by many of the world's citizens, including those of the nuclear-weapon states. In recent years, we have engaged in activities that seek to promote public awareness in support of disarmament and nonproliferation education as called for by the United Nations.

Rooted in the conviction that it is essential that the world's people commit themselves and unite globally toward a world without nuclear weapons, in 1997 and 1998, members of the SGI collected 13 million signatures for the

Abolition 2000 campaign, presenting these to the United Nations in October 1998.

In a proposal on UN reform written in August 2006, I called for a "People's Decade for Nuclear Abolition." In September 2007, on the fiftieth anniversary of Toda's declaration, the SGI launched the Decade with a new exhibition that challenges the logic of nuclear weapons from the perspective of human security. Since then, the exhibition "From a Culture of Violence to a Culture of Peace: Transforming the Human Spirit" has been seen in numerous venues around the world.

Toward the same end, we have produced as an educational tool a five-language DVD documenting the experiences of atomic bomb survivors, *Testimonies of Hiroshima and Nagasaki: Women Speak Out for Peace*.[49] We further intend to produce DVDs recording the testimony of people throughout the world whose lives have been impacted by exposure to toxic levels of radiation.

In this way, we have taken action over the past five decades to bring the underlying spirit of Toda's call for nuclear abolition to the world and to generate a groundswell of popular opinion, making it the prevailing spirit of the new era. We are determined to continue to build a global solidarity toward the goal of a world free from nuclear weapons.

A five-part plan

Based on my many years of experience in this field, it is clear to me that a new confluence of forces is emerging.

That is, in addition to movements for nuclear abolition rooted in a traditional pacifist perspective, we now hear voices calling for a world without nuclear weapons, based on a "realist" assessment of the dangers, arising from within the nuclear-weapon states. As Henry Kissinger has recently pointed out, collaboration between people rooted in these two approaches could generate powerful new momentum toward nuclear abolition.

I am convinced that a clear vision, unyielding determination and courageous action are the pivotal factors for effective collaboration, and on the basis of this I would like to make the following proposals.

---

49 SGI (Soka Gakkai International). 2009. *Testimonies of Hiroshima and Nagasaki: Women Speak Out for Peace*. DVD. Tokyo: Soka Gakkai International. http://www. peoplesdecade.org/decade/survivors/ (accessed April, 2. 2013).

I believe it is possible to lay the foundations for a world without nuclear weapons during the five-year period leading up to 2015, and to this end would suggest a five-part plan. I call on:

1. **The five declared nuclear-weapon states** to announce their commitment to a shared vision of a world without nuclear weapons at next year's NPT Review Conference and to promptly initiate concrete steps toward its achievement.
2. **The United Nations** to establish a panel of experts on nuclear abolition, strengthening collaborative relations with civil society in the disarmament process.
3. **The states parties to the NPT** to strengthen nonproliferation mechanisms and remove obstacles to the elimination of nuclear weapons by the year 2015.
4. **All states** to actively cooperate to reduce the role of nuclear weapons in national security and to advance on a global scale toward the establishment of security arrangements that are not dependent on nuclear weapons by the year 2015.
5. **The world's people** to clearly manifest their will for the outlawing of nuclear weapons and to establish, by the year 2015, the international norm that will serve as the foundation for a Nuclear Weapons Convention (NWC).

1. A shared vision

The first element is for the five declared nuclear-weapon states to announce, at the 2010 NPT Review Conference, their shared vision of a world without nuclear weapons and to promptly initiate concrete steps toward implementation.

Despite the discriminatory structure of the NPT, most non-nuclear-weapon states are parties to it; its importance was recognized in 1995 when it was extended indefinitely. This reflects the judgment on the part of the non-nuclear-weapon states that their own security interests, and the cause of global peace, are best served by the permanent relinquishment of the option of possessing nuclear weapons, a choice predicated on the promise of the nuclear-weapon states to disarm.

For too long, however, the nuclear-weapon states have been delinquent in fulfilling their disarmament obligations. This, alongside efforts on the part of some states to develop nuclear weapons, has undermined the trust necessary to obtain international cooperation on nuclear nonproliferation. Thus, the four US statesmen who jointly called for a world without nuclear weapons in editorials in *The Wall Street Journal* have warned: "Without the vision of moving toward zero, we will not find the essential cooperation required to stop our downward spiral."[50]

If, at the 2010 NPT Review Conference, the five declared nuclear-weapon states publicly pledge their commitment to realizing a world without nuclear weapons, their courageous action will be rewarded with a renewal of trust on the part of the world's people, and this in turn will prompt synergistic progress toward the twin goals of nonproliferation and disarmament.

Further, the five declared nuclear-weapon states should take the following concrete steps. They should commit to: 1) a moratorium on any further development or modernization of nuclear weapons; 2) substantively enhanced transparency regarding their nuclear capabilities; and 3) deliberations on the absolute minimum number of nuclear weapons on the path to total abolition.

Regarding the first of these commitments, I would strongly urge that, together with a shared vision of a world without nuclear weapons, the nuclear-weapon states pledge to refrain from further expansion or modernization of their nuclear arsenals. It is clear that nuclear weapons have no purpose other than to establish or perpetuate a dominant position relative to other states. An undertaking on the part of the nuclear-weapon states to freeze the arsenals in their current status would demonstrate a first and meaningful act of self-restraint. It would put a decisive end to any expansion of nuclear capabilities, and I am confident that such an act would be an important step toward overcoming the impulse to dominate others that Toda denounced as an inherent aspect of nuclear weapons.

Next, ensuring a high degree of transparency regarding nuclear capabilities is an important prerequisite to establishing a timetable toward the actual achievement of abolition. As the history of US–Soviet disarmament negotiations makes clear, it is virtually impossible to conduct constructive debate without a clear understanding of each other's actual status. It would be desirable for the nuclear-weapon states, having announced a moratorium on further development, to make full disclosure of their capabilities to the United Nations Security Council within one year.

---

50   Shultz, George P., William J. Perry, Henry A. Kissinger and Sam Nunn. 2008. "Toward a Nuclear-Free World." *The Wall Street Journal.* January 15.

It would then be necessary for each state to conduct a careful review and initiate multiparty discussions regarding what each considers the minimum essential level of nuclear warheads while moving toward total abolition. The UN Secretary-General should be a party to these talks and, once a level—for example, 100 warheads each—has been determined, this should be positioned as an intermediate goal on the path to zero.

This kind of concrete goal would provide important impetus to the vision of a world without nuclear weapons and could serve as a "base camp" in the ascent toward the summit of zero. Together, these actions would represent a good-faith effort to fulfill the "unequivocal undertaking by the nuclear-weapon States to accomplish the total elimination of their nuclear arsenals"[51] that was affirmed at the 2000 NPT Review Conference.

Immediately after the end of World War II, Einstein declared: "there is no distance ahead for proceeding little by little and delaying the necessary changes. . . ."[52]

The five declared nuclear-weapon states are, of course, at the same time, the permanent members of the UN Security Council, bearing a principal responsibility for the maintenance of international peace and security. Now is the time for them to act together to heed this warning, to feel the full weight of their responsibility and to make the "necessary changes" our world requires.

2. An expert panel

My second proposal is for the United Nations to establish a panel of experts on nuclear abolition, strengthening collaborative relations with civil society in the disarmament process.

In the early 1990s, a system was created by which different governments worked to support the dismantling and disposal of the nuclear arsenals of the newly independent states that emerged following the collapse of the Soviet Union. Further, the International Science and Technology Center (ISTC) was established, tasked with providing opportunities for scientists and engineers formerly involved in work related to weapons of mass destruction to put

51   UNODA (United Nations Office for Disarmament Affairs). 2000. "2000 Review Conference of the Parties to the Treaty on the Non-Proliferation of Nuclear Weapons." NPT/CONF.2000/28 (Part I and II), p. 14.

52   Einstein, Albert. 1954. *Ideas and Opinions*. New York: Crown Publishers, Inc., p. 117.

their talents to use toward civilian purposes. When all the nuclear-weapon states begin a disarmament process aimed at the ultimate goal of zero nuclear weapons, the demand for this type of support will far exceed that which arose in the wake of the dissolution of the Soviet Union.

The panel of experts whose formation I am proposing would build on the knowledge and experience of the Advisory Board on Disarmament Matters that currently reports to the Secretary-General. It would have, however, a specific focus on nuclear weapons and would include a wide range of specialists from both within and outside the disarmament field; it would advise the Secretary-General on the measures, including technical aspects, necessary to achieving complete nuclear abolition.

In addition to this central function, I would propose three further roles for the panel:

1. To periodically issue reports on the threat posed by nuclear weapons in order to foster international public opinion for nuclear abolition, developing this as the single greatest force for ensuring the irreversibility of the abolition process;

2. To support the development of more adequate medical treatment for those around the world who continue to suffer from the effects of exposure to radioactive materials; and

3. To research means for establishing "societal verification," that is, a system by which the ordinary citizens of each country can monitor their government's compliance with its disarmament obligations and prohibitions, reporting any violations.

In creating such a panel of experts, it would be desirable for the Secretary-General to enlist support not only from the disarmament specialists of different countries and international organizations, but also from such NGOs as the Pugwash Conferences, the International Physicians for the Prevention of Nuclear War (IPPNW), the International Association of Lawyers Against Nuclear Arms (IALANA), the International Network of Engineers and Scientists Against Proliferation (INESAP), as well as academic and peace research institutions with specialist and technical knowledge. The Toda Institute for Global Peace and Policy Research would fully support the work of such a panel, bringing to bear its research achievements to date and its wide-ranging network of peace researchers.

In 2010, Japan will host an international conference on nuclear disarmament. I strongly hope that Japan will exercise leadership toward the formation of the kind of panel I am proposing. In doing so, the Japanese government should collaborate with Norway, which has put forth a similar vision, and the UK, which is stressing the importance of research into verification related to the dismantling of nuclear weapons.

3. Removing obstacles

My third proposal regards means of strengthening nonproliferation mechanisms to remove obstacles toward the elimination of nuclear weapons. As a first condition for this, I strongly urge that as many heads of state and government as possible attend the 2010 NPT Review Conference. I would hope that all of the leaders of the states parties to the NPT would attend; I would also propose inviting the leaders of states not part of the NPT regime to attend as observers, in order to enhance the character of the Review Conference as a global summit on nuclear issues.

I would also urge that the conference establish a standing working group to engage in intensive deliberations on strengthening international cooperation for nuclear disarmament and nonproliferation during the five-year period leading up to the next Review Conference in 2015. It would further be worth considering developing, on the basis of this working group, a standing body with decision-making powers toward the fulfillment of the NPT's objectives.

In order to lay the groundwork for a world without nuclear arms, it is important to critically analyze the actual nature of the threats that have been used to justify deterrence and thus the development and possession of nuclear weapons over the years. Such efforts will bring greater clarity regarding the most effective responses to various threats.

With the end of the Cold War, it has become virtually unthinkable that any of the five declared nuclear-weapon states would use nuclear weapons against any of the others.

As a result, the justifications for the possession of nuclear weapons that continue to be put forward generally fall into the following three categories: 1) to deter the use of nuclear weapons by another state that would threaten oneself or an allied state; 2) to prevent or deter nuclear weapons development programs that can lead to nuclear proliferation; and 3) to prevent or deter nuclear terrorism by non-state actors.

The first case is one that requires careful examination and consideration, which I will attempt in my fourth proposal below. The second and third cases are widely considered by experts not to be amenable to the use or threat of use of nuclear weapons.

Regarding these types of threat, rather than increased nuclear deterrent capability, it would certainly be more effective to seek to change the behavior of other states by first changing one's own stances and policies. Through such efforts, the declared nuclear-weapon states should seek to bring nuclear powers outside the NPT regime, as well as those whose intentions are suspect, into an expanded and strengthened nonproliferation system. It is also through such efforts that international structures for preventing the spread of nuclear technologies and materials can be strengthened in order to keep such materials out of the hands of terrorists.

At this juncture, few actions would carry a greater symbolic weight, a more powerful portent of self-transformation, than the ratification of the Comprehensive Nuclear Test Ban Treaty (CTBT). President Obama has indicated that he will seek CTBT ratification by the US Senate. Success here would greatly raise the likelihood that China would also ratify. Ratification by the US and China would serve as encouragement to India and Pakistan to sign or ratify, moving the treaty closer to entry into force. Such changes would also encourage Israel and Iran, which have yet to ratify, and North Korea, which has yet to sign the CTBT, toward taking bold new steps.

If a positive reaction along these lines were to begin, it would lay the foundations for a nonproliferation regime that would comprise all states, including those which are currently outside the NPT system.

Beyond the goal of CTBT entry into force, a number of measures would have both a substantive and symbolic impact. These include the prompt conclusion of a Fissile Material Cut-off Treaty, placing the nuclear fuel cycle under international control and encouraging further ratification of the Nuclear Terrorism Convention. Also important, in my view, are the complete demilitarization of outer space as well as measures to increase energy efficiency and encourage the use of renewable energy sources.

With demand for energy increasing globally, and out of the desire to reduce greenhouse gas emissions, there has been an expansion of nuclear power generation facilities with many countries considering the adoption of nuclear energy. This has led to an inevitable heightening of concerns regarding nuclear weapons proliferation and the threat of nuclear terrorism.

UN Secretary-General Ban Ki-moon[53] has expressed his own concern regarding the risk that a "nuclear renaissance"[54] will introduce new destabilizing elements into the world. From this perspective, it seems clear that, in addition to strengthening the monitoring capacities of the International Atomic Energy Agency (IAEA), international cooperation on energy policy—such as supporting the introduction of renewable energy sources and encouraging the diffusion of energy efficiency technologies—could help strengthen the bulwarks against nuclear weapons proliferation.

Such measures should be among the priority agenda items of the standing working group I am suggesting the 2010 NPT Review Conference set up, and I hope that this working group will engage in concrete deliberations over the five-year period leading up to the next Review Conference in 2015. To this end, it is necessary that the UN Office for Disarmament Affairs, which presently functions as a secretariat for the NPT, be strengthened.

4. Nuclear-free security

My fourth proposal is for all countries to coordinate their efforts to actively reduce the role of nuclear weapons in national security strategies in order to facilitate the transition to security theory and practice that is not reliant on nuclear weapons.

In his Prague speech, President Obama announced the scaling back of the role of nuclear weapons in US security strategy and urged other countries to follow suit. While stating that this is necessary to put an end to the ways of thinking that characterized the Cold War, he reserved the right of the US to defend itself and its allies against nuclear threats.

Regarding this, one crucial fact cannot be overlooked: For sixty-four years since the unimaginable suffering unleashed by the atomic bombings of Hiroshima and Nagasaki, no political leader of any country has been able to bring him- or herself to actually use nuclear weapons.

To me, this indicates that the threshold against the use of nuclear weapons, comprising moral and other considerations, is quite high; there has been a

---

53   Ban Ki-moon (1944–), South Korean statesman, 8th Secretary-General of the United Nations (2007–).

54   Ban, Ki-moon. 2008. "The United Nations and Security in a Nuclear-Weapon-Free World." Address to the East-West Institute. New York. October 24.

steadily growing awareness among the leaders of states that nuclear weapons are essentially unusable as a means of achieving military objectives.

I believe that, more than deterrence, it is this unseen moral and practical threshold that has prevented the use of nuclear weapons over the years.

The fact is that the large majority of countries neither possess nuclear weapons nor rely on the "nuclear umbrella" of a nuclear-weapon state; and yet these countries have on the whole not been threatened with nuclear attack. By reducing regional tensions and through establishing nuclear-weapon-free zones, these states have made continuous efforts to raise even further the threshold against the use of nuclear weapons.

Thus, regarding this final justification for nuclear deterrence, first priority should be given to reducing the perception of threat. This, rather than seeking to respond with increased nuclear weaponry of one's own, represents both the most realistic and morally acceptable course of action.

Likewise, in seeking to remove nuclear weapons from the security framework, it is critical to always remember that the obligation to realize complete disarmament under Article 6 of the NPT is not limited to the nuclear-weapon states, but is equally shared by all states parties to the treaty.

Even if a nuclear-weapon state should seek to reduce the role of nuclear weapons and, through this, to achieve major disarmament, this will be complicated if its allies demand the continuance or strengthening of the nuclear umbrella. Such a demand would constitute a violation of the spirit of the NPT. How, then, is it possible to continue to justify extended deterrence as a vitally necessary security measure?

It is crucial for nuclear-weapon states and their allies to engage in careful and earnest deliberations regarding extended deterrence. Together, they should develop alternatives, starting with effective measures for reducing regional tensions. I first proposed such an approach some ten years ago and today repeat that call with renewed urgency.

In Germany, which was on the front lines of East–West Cold War confrontation, there have been calls for a rethinking of security systems that rely on nuclear weapons. In January of this year, four important political figures including former president Richard von Weizsäcker[55] and former foreign minister Hans-Dietrich Genscher[56] issued a statement that responded to the

---

55   Richard von Weizsäcker (1920–), President of the Federal Republic of Germany (1984–94).
56   Hans-Dietrich Genscher (1927–), German Foreign Minister (1974–82, 1982–92).

editorials by George Shultz and his coauthors. Stating that "[r]elics from the age of confrontation are no longer adequate for our new century," they advocate a "general non-first-use treaty between the nuclear-weapons states" and for all remaining US nuclear warheads to be withdrawn from German territory.[57]

Translating this same thinking to a different context, I am convinced that a clear demonstration of political will on the part of the United States and Japan could transform conditions in Northeast Asia, where the lingering negative impact of Cold War thinking is symbolized by the stalemate surrounding North Korea's nuclear development program.

The economist John Kenneth Galbraith[58] who, among other responsibilities, served as a key adviser to President Kennedy, in the course of our dialogue shared with me the following views regarding the respective roles and responsibilities of Japan and the United States:

> I expect special leadership from Japan in the realm of peace. No other country on the globe has had the same experience with war. . . . No other county is so aware of the meaning and effect of nuclear conflict. Perhaps this is a special responsibility of Japan and the United States. They are the two countries in the world with a history of nuclear war. Along with Japan, we should be . . . a leader in the effort to see that humankind is not again subject to this massive and relentless death.[59]

As noted earlier, the SGI has produced a DVD recording the experiences of survivors of the Hiroshima and Nagasaki bombings, making these interviews available over the Internet. To quote one of the women from Hiroshima:

> Having survived, I wondered what I should do with my life. But I came to feel that my role is to communicate the horrors of the nuclear attack and to share with people my sense of the utter folly of

---

57 Schmidt, Helmut, Richard von Weizsäcker. Egon Bahr and Hans-Dietrich Genscher. 2009. "Toward a Nuclear-Free World: A German View." *The New York Times.* January 9.

58 John Kenneth Galbraith (1908–2006), Canadian-born American economist.

59 (trans. from) Galbraith, John K. and Daisaku Ikeda. 2005. *Ningenshugi no daiseiki o* [The Great Century of Humanism]. Tokyo: Ushio Shuppansha, pp. 171–72.

human beings killing each other in war. I now feel that is the reason why I am alive.[60]

What comes across with great power and poignancy through the testimonials of these women is the earnest hope that no one else should ever have to experience the suffering they have endured. This same determination must be the foundation of any antinuclear message issued from Japan.

It is morally impermissible for Japan, the only country to have experienced the use of nuclear weapons in war, to revise its non-nuclear principles (not possessing, not producing and not permitting the introduction of nuclear weapons into its territory), much less to consider becoming a nuclear-weapon state itself. I urge Japan to reaffirm its adherence to the three non-nuclear principles and to once again declare, promptly and categorically, that it will never possess nuclear weapons.

Based on this, Japan and the US should cooperate to resolve the North Korean nuclear issue and build peace in Northeast Asia. Specifically, I call for all the countries currently engaged in the Six-Party Talks on North Korea's nuclear program—China, Japan, North Korea, Russia, South Korea and the United States—to declare Northeast Asia a nuclear non-use region.

For many years, I have urged the same countries to establish a Northeast Asia nuclear-weapon-free zone. One factor that has seriously complicated the realization of such a zone is the fact that all six countries either possess nuclear weapons or have extended deterrence agreements with a nuclear-weapon state. Thus, as a first step toward breaking out of the current stalemate, I think it is crucial to offer mutual pledges not to use nuclear weapons against each other nor to take actions that would heighten the threat posed by weapons of mass destruction, and to give that pledge institutional form.

All six countries are parties to the Biological Weapons Convention; with the exception of North Korea, all are parties to the Chemical Weapons Convention. North Korea should be encouraged to become party to this latter treaty and to fulfill its commitment, announced in the Joint Statement issued by the Six-Party Talks four years ago, "to abandoning all nuclear weapons

---

60   SGI (Soka Gakkai International). 2009. *Testimonies of Hiroshima and Nagasaki: Women Speak Out for Peace.* DVD. Tokyo: Soka Gakkai International. http://www. peoplesdecade.org/decade/survivors/ (accessed April 2, 2013).

and existing nuclear programs."[61] Concurrent with this, the other countries should pledge and support the pledge of the non-use of nuclear weapons. This would serve as the basis for the next step forward.

Should such a pledge be made and supported, it could function as a point of reference for South Asia, the Middle East and other regions where there has been no significant progress toward creating nuclear-weapon-free zones.

I am convinced that transforming the structures of confrontation in Northeast Asia and universalizing the commitment that no country or people should ever fall victim to the horrors of nuclear weapons should be the pivotal elements of US–Japanese partnership in the twenty-first century. Together, our two countries should take the lead in creating a world without nuclear weapons.

5. Outlawing nuclear weapons

The fifth proposal I would like to make is for the world's people to manifest a clear expression of their will to see the outlawing of nuclear weapons and to establish, by the year 2015, the international norm that will serve as the basis for their prohibition.

Drawing from the 1996 International Court of Justice (ICJ) Advisory Opinion on the Legality of the Threat or Use of Nuclear Weapons, in 1997 IPPNW in collaboration with two other NGOs drafted a model Nuclear Weapons Convention (NWC) that would prohibit the development, testing, production, use and threat of use of nuclear weapons. This has since been circulated as a UN document. The draft was revised in 2007 and has been submitted as a working paper to the Preparatory Committee for the 2010 NPT Review Conference.

There is a swelling chorus of calls for the establishment of a clear international norm against nuclear weapons, as evidenced by the statement made last October by Ban Ki-moon, in which he noted the importance of the draft convention. The SGI has to date supported the movement, led by the International Campaign to Abolish Nuclear Weapons (ICAN) of IPPNW, to foster public support for the adoption of an NWC; and we will continue to do so.

---

61   MFAPRC (Ministry of Foreign Affairs of the People's Republic of China). 2005. "Joint Statement of the Fourth Round of the Six-Party Talks." September 19.

What I would like to propose here is a campaign to give people, on the individual, community and national levels, the opportunity to express our desire to ban these most inhumane weapons that threaten our fundamental right to exist. This would solidify the international norm that would serve as the basis for the adoption of an NWC.

The preamble of the model NWC opens with the words: "We the people of the Earth. . . ."[62] As this makes clear, this convention is not envisaged merely as an agreement among states, but is to be adopted in the name of each individual inhabitant of Earth, as an expression of the shared desire for peaceful coexistence.

The path to the adoption of an NWC is likely to be a difficult one. But, rather than be paralyzed by this difficulty, we should take action now to generate overwhelming popular support for the prohibition of nuclear weapons, such that calls for the adoption of an NWC become impossible to ignore.

In this connection, I would like to cite the very cogent comments of Rebecca Johnson[63] of the Acronym Institute for Disarmament Diplomacy in her article titled "Security Assurances for Everyone":

> [T]he process of stigmatising and outlawing the use of nuclear weapons offers opportunities for courageous leaders to take unilateral steps that build towards creating a multilateral norm. This is an important initiative that non-nuclear weapon states—and indeed citizens and public movements—can declare support for, and help to build up a strong ethical norm and create a breathing space for nuclear disarmament initiatives to take hold.[64]

Specifically, I would like to propose initiating a movement in support of a "declaration for nuclear abolition by the world's people" that could be jointly

---

62 ICAN (International Campaign to Abolish Nuclear Weapons). 2007. "Securing Our Survival (SOS): The Case for a Nuclear Weapons Convention." Cambridge, Massachusetts: International Physicians for the Prevention of Nuclear War, p. 46.

63 Rebecca Johnson (1954–), British expert on nuclear disarmament and nonproliferation, Executive Director of the Acronym Institute for Disarmament Diplomacy (1995–).

64 Johnson, Rebecca. 2009. "Security Assurances for Everyone: A New Approach to Deterring the Use of Nuclear Weapons." *Disarmament Diplomacy*. No. 90. Bradford, West Yorkshire: Acronym Institute.

supported by individuals, organizations, spiritual and religious groups, universities and research institutions, as well as agencies within the UN system.

If we are to put the era of nuclear terror behind us, we must struggle against the real "enemy." That enemy is not nuclear weapons *per se*, nor is it the states that possess or develop them. The real enemy that we must confront is the ways of thinking that justify nuclear weapons; the readiness to annihilate others when they are seen as a threat or as a hindrance to the realization of our objectives.

This is the new consciousness we must all share, and it was to this that my mentor Josei Toda referred when he spoke of declawing the threat hidden in the very depths of nuclear weapons and urged that the spirit of his declaration be made known throughout the world. He was expressing his conviction that the sharing of this kind of awareness could serve as the basis for a transnational solidarity among the world's people. He further believed that a revolutionary change in the consciousness of individuals, spreading throughout the world, is the only force deep and radical enough to bring an end to the nuclear age.

When the ICJ was deliberating its Advisory Opinion in 1996, it received some 4 million "declarations of public conscience" in more than forty languages, along with evidence of the widespread rejection by the public of nuclear weapons, and the ICJ considered these in the process of reaching its conclusion.

The SGI intends to consult widely with civil society and national representatives in determining the final content and form a new declaration should take. We would like to see this submitted to the UN General Assembly by the year 2015 in order to further momentum for NWC negotiations and as an important reference document for the drafting of the NWC's preamble.

Gathering support for this declaration will be a core program for the SGI's People's Decade for Nuclear Abolition. We are determined to work with a wide range of individuals and organizations to foster global popular solidarity for the complete and final elimination of nuclear weapons from the face of Earth.

Building global solidarity

In conclusion, I would like to suggest that the real significance of achieving a world free of nuclear weapons is by no means limited to their physical elimination. Rather, it involves transforming the very nature of states and interstate relations.

Albert Einstein insisted that we should tackle the issue of nuclear weapons in the same manner we would "if an epidemic of bubonic plague were threatening the entire world." Under such circumstances, Einstein argued, states would "hardly raise serious objections but rather agree speedily on the measures to be taken" and certainly would "never think of trying to handle the matter in such a way that their own nation would be spared whereas the next one would be decimated."[65]

In this scenario, what would need to be done—from a moral and ethical as well as a practical and realist perspective—is urgently clear. It would be patently unacceptable for any state to pursue its own security without regard for others.

Just over 100 years ago, Tsunesaburo Makiguchi,[66] the founding president of the Soka Gakkai, proposed a new mode of competition, "humanitarian competition"—in which "by benefiting others, we benefit ourselves"[67]—as a means of overcoming conflict among nations. He called on each state to engage in a positive rivalry to contribute to the world through humane action, in order to spread the spirit of peaceful coexistence and build a truly global society.

The five proposals I have presented here are all rooted in Makiguchi's concept of humanitarian competition, which shares a basic orientation with the idea of a "joint enterprise" to change the "disposition of the states possessing nuclear weapons"[68] advocated by George Shultz and his coauthors. Such a change in the disposition of nuclear-weapon states is crucial to creating the conditions in which it will be possible to redirect the vast financial and human resources that have been poured into nuclear weapon development and maintenance toward the work of meeting such global challenges as ecological protection and poverty alleviation.

---

65 Einstein, Albert. 1950. *Out of My Later Years*. New York: Philosophical Library, p. 204.

66 Tsunesaburo Makiguchi (1871–1944), founding president of the Soka Kyoiku Gakkai (forerunner of the Soka Gakkai) (1930–44).

67 (trans. from) Makiguchi, Tsunesaburo. 1981–97. *Makiguchi Tsunesaburo zenshu* [The Complete Works of Tsunesaburo Makiguchi]. 10 vols. Tokyo: Daisanbunmei-sha. Vol. 2, p. 399.

68 Shultz, George P., William J. Perry, Henry A. Kissinger and Sam Nunn. 2007. "A World Free of Nuclear Weapons." *The Wall Street Journal*. January 4.

Martin Luther King Jr.[69] was no doubt expressing a similar vision when he stated: "[W]e must transform the dynamics of the world power struggle from the negative nuclear arms race which no one can win to a positive contest to harness man's creative genius for the purpose of making peace and prosperity a reality for all of the nations of the world."[70]

Powerful support by civil society is indispensable to realizing the epochal challenge of building a global society. In this regard, it is timely and welcome that the 62nd Annual Conference of NGOs affiliated with the UN's Department of Public Information to be convened in Mexico City this month will, for the first time in the history of this conference, take up disarmament as its central theme.

Let us abandon the habit of studiously ignoring the menace posed to Earth by nuclear weapons and instead demonstrate—clearly and through the power of people—that a world without nuclear weapons can indeed be realized in our lifetimes.

Raising one's voice or taking action is something we all can do. All that is required are the natural feelings shared by people everywhere: the desire to live in peace, the wish to protect those we love, the determination to spare the world's children needless suffering.

I remember Linus Pauling,[71] whose achievements are engraved in the history of science and of peace in the twentieth century, telling me of the role his wife played in motivating his actions: "I felt compelled to earn and keep her respect."[72] I am convinced that such human bonds are shared by all people and can serve as the essential sustenance for action.

The members of the SGI in 192 countries and territories around the world have been working to build solidarity with and among our fellow citizens. Our efforts are based on the belief that it is dialogue, first and foremost, that opens one heart to another. However slow this process may appear, we are convinced that it is the most certain path to world peace.

---

69   Martin Luther King Jr. (1929–68), American religious leader and civil rights activist, recipient of the Nobel Prize for Peace in 1964.

70   King, Martin L., Jr. 1964. "The Quest for Peace and Justice." Nobel Lecture. December 11.

71   Linus Pauling (1901–94), American scientist, recipient of the Nobel Prize in Chemistry in 1954 and the Nobel Prize for Peace in 1962.

72   Pauling, Linus and Daisaku Ikeda. 2009. *A Lifelong Quest for Peace.* London: I.B.Tauris, p. 66.

The Buddhist concept "three thousand realms in a single moment of life" (Jp. *ichinen sanzen*) teaches that there exists in each of us an unlimited power or capacity. Thus a change in the deepest levels of an individual's consciousness and commitment can give rise to waves of transformation in one's surroundings and society, eventually spurring nations and even the entire world to change. Bringing forth this unlimited potential from within each individual and channeling it toward the quest for peace is at the heart of the SGI's endeavors.

Within each human being lies the potential to change one's circumstances—whether in a positive or a negative direction. For example, Einstein's famous mass-energy formula was originally just an equation in the field of physics. However, human beings discovered in it a blueprint for weapons of unprecedented cruelty. This blueprint was developed by governments around the world, devoting all their might to creating weapons of ultimate destruction. From that day forth, humankind has found itself mired in the dangers of the nuclear age.

It is time for us to apply Einstein's same equation to tap the infinite potential that exists in the depths of each person's heart and unleash the courage and action of ordinary people to create an indomitable force for peace. In the final analysis, this is the only way to put an end to the nuclear nightmares of our age.

In this work, no one has a more crucial role to play than young people.

Even the most brilliant ideal will be no more than a dream if it remains locked up in one's heart. To bring it into being as a lived reality requires that we confront and triumph over feelings of powerlessness and resignation. What is needed is the courage to initiate action.

It is the passion of youth that spreads the flames of courage throughout society. This courage, transmitted from one person to the next, can melt the daunting walls of difficulty and open the horizons on a new era in human history.

Based on the proud determination to make the struggle for nuclear abolition the foundation for a world without war, and convinced that participation in this unprecedented undertaking is the greatest gift we can offer the future, I call on people of goodwill everywhere to work together toward the realization of a world finally free from the menace of nuclear weapons.

Control of Conventional Weapons

The UN Register of Conventional Arms (1995)[73]

Although an international regulatory framework is being constructed for weapons of mass destruction (atomic, biological and chemical weapons), there are almost no regulations for conventional weapons.

Any attempt to usher in an era without war can only end as an empty fantasy in a world overflowing with weaponry. We are confronted with the formidable task of reducing and dismantling the armaments industry that churned out huge numbers of weapons during the Cold War. Nevertheless, the United States and Russia are making little progress in efforts to convert munitions factories to civilian use, primarily because of a lack of capital. Weapons manufacturers that can no longer rely on the patronage of their own governments are now concentrating their efforts on exporting their products to developing countries.

In 1991, the United Nations General Assembly adopted the UN Register of Conventional Arms, a registration system for the transfer of weapons that was jointly proposed by Japan and the European Community (EC). Implementation began in 1992, but the resolution is nonbinding so arms export reports are submitted voluntarily at the discretion of the member countries. Unless reports are made mandatory as quickly as possible, the system will be ineffectual in controlling arms exports.

The Iran–Iraq War lasted eight long years because the combatants had access to weapons supplied by other countries. Arms exports also strengthened Iraq's military to the point of igniting the Gulf War. I believe the advanced industrialized countries are primarily responsible for the failure of the international community to make any progress in regulating arms deals.

The fact that the five permanent members of the UN Security Council are responsible for more than 80 percent of worldwide arms exports[74] can only be described as abnormal. Certainly, it seriously undermines the credibility of these countries as guardians of international security. It may be difficult to

---

73   From 1995 Peace Proposal, "Creating a Century without War through Human Solidarity."

74   See Grimmett, Richard F. 1994. "Conventional Arms Transfer to the Third World, 1986–1993." Washington DC: Congressional Research Service, Library of Congress, p. 62.

make the Register of Conventional Arms mandatory immediately, but the five major exporters should at least reach concrete agreement among themselves concerning a framework for regulating weapons exports. I believe Japan should take the international initiative on this issue because of its official policy forbidding the export of weapons.

In September 1994, I had the pleasure of talking with Dr. Óscar Arias Sánchez,[75] the former President of Costa Rica, who has played a leading role in promoting peace in Central America. Dr. Arias praised the exhibition "Nuclear Arms: Threat to Our World," an SGI-sponsored exhibition that has toured many countries, and expressed his wish to bring it to Costa Rica, a neutral country which constitutionally abolished its army in 1949. He also talked about his vision for a "Global Demilitarization Fund," which would collect the excess funds generated by disarmament and use them to conquer poverty and promote education in Third World countries. I myself have long advocated a similar idea and completely agree with his proposal.

At our meeting, Dr. Arias also proposed that Third World countries follow a three-point policy of demilitarization, disarmament and dismantling of the military, and expressed his approval of the demilitarization of Costa Rica's neighbor, Panama. This is the first time in history that two nations have existed side-by-side without armies. We have no reason, therefore, to be pessimistic about our current situation. Based on a number of factors, war has come to be seen as futile, and there is a widespread realization that it is not worthwhile to take up arms.

Of course, these developments apply primarily to developed nations, and there are some who believe that armed conflict will continue in the former Communist bloc and the poor countries of the Third World. Certainly, when we encounter such abominable words as "ethnic cleansing," we cannot but question whether the human race has made any progress at all.

Nevertheless, under the watchful eye of international opinion, it is gradually becoming impossible to stage an outright war of aggression. If we maintain our faith in the future of humankind and consciously work to close the gap between North and South, I am confident that we will find our way to a brighter future. In this effort, I believe the resources and contributions of nongovernmental organizations (NGOs) will be in greater demand than ever. These organizations are creating an international civil society on a global scale

---

75　Óscar Arias Sánchez (1941–), President of Costa Rica (1986–90, 2006–10), recipient of the Nobel Prize for Peace in 1987.

by working in fields that transcend national and ethnic boundaries, such as human rights, humanitarian aid and peace education.

Guidelines for Arms Transfers (1999)[76]

One of the factors required for the deinstitutionalization of war is to reduce the international traffic in arms.

The arms trade intensifies and protracts warfare. Lamentably, far from decreasing, the international arms trade increases year after year. According to *The Military Balance 1998/99,* the annual report of the International Institute for Strategic Studies, arms transactions rose by 12 percent in 1997. The increase was especially great in the Middle East and East Asia. Total arms transfers amounted to US$34.6 billion in 1997.[77] Other research confirms that areas experiencing regional conflict continue to be the major export market for the arms trade. There is even a thriving market for second-hand weapons in Africa, scene of numerous regional and internal conflicts.

In his April 1998 report "The Causes of Conflict and the Promotion of Durable Peace and Sustainable Development in Africa," United Nations Secretary-General Kofi Annan[78] expressed grave concern about this issue. He requested governments of member states to adopt legislation making the violation of a Security Council arms embargo a criminal offense under their national laws. In addition, he requested the Security Council to bring to light the covert operations of international arms dealers.[79]

To profit from warfare and carnage in other countries, to use it to enhance one's own national influence and prestige, to callously sacrifice human life for one's private gain. . . The arms trade is evil. Murderous and morally unforgivable, it is an assault on humanity and human security. It epitomizes the worst that humanity is capable of.

---

76   From 1999 Peace Proposal, "Toward a Culture of Peace: A Cosmic View."

77   See IISS (The International Institute for Strategic Studies). 1998. *The Military Balance 1998/99.* London: The International Institute for Strategic Studies.

78   Kofi Annan (1938–), Ghanaian statesman, 7th Secretary-General of the United Nations (1997–2006).

79   See UNGA (United Nations General Assembly). 1998. "The Causes of Conflict and the Promotion of Durable Peace and Sustainable Development in Africa." A/52/871 – S/1998/318. Report of the Secretary-General. April 13.

When one country in a region strengthens its military might through arms imports, this heightens regional tensions and instabilities by inciting its neighbors to acquire new weapons systems of their own. Likewise, increasing supplies of arms to the factions in an internal conflict prolongs and intensifies the fighting.

Breaking this vicious circle requires a two-pronged approach. The first step is to reduce demand through efforts to defuse suspicions and build mutual confidence, and the second is to block the supply of weapons flowing into conflict areas.

About half the UN member states now report arms transfers under the UN Register of Conventional Arms initiated in 1992. Significantly, although the system is voluntary, the major arms exporters—the five permanent members of the Security Council and Germany—submit reports. As these six countries account for more than 85 percent of total arms transfers, their information gives a good idea of the overall situation.

To further promote transparency, I propose that a treaty be negotiated that would expand this system to cover more kinds of armament and make reporting mandatory for all UN member states. If implemented, such a treaty would promote world stability by generating trust among member states and by providing an early warning system about sudden arms buildups.

I have two other proposals to make relative to inhibiting the arms trade. First, we must restrict illicit arms transactions. As is mentioned in Secretary-General Annan's report, anyone providing arms or covert aid to conflicting parties—especially if such aid violates a UN Security Council arms embargo—should be strictly punished under national law. We should also seek consensus within the international community to expand the competence of the International Criminal Court (ICC) to cover the crime of illegal arms trafficking.

Second, major arms-exporting nations should take the initiative in drawing up guidelines to limit the trade. Talks to this end that started after the Gulf War of 1991 among the five permanent members of the Security Council have now broken down. To get them back on track, I suggest that a G9 (G8 plus China) meeting be held this year to address this topic. I suggest using the G9 as the proper setting since it includes Germany, a major arms exporter, and because it would give Japan and Canada the chance to mediate.

Organizations such as the United Nations Children's Fund (UNICEF) and various NGOs jointly urged the 1998 G8 Summit to support a UN resolution calling for a treaty restricting arms transfers. The difficulty involved in concluding a treaty only shows how important it is for the major arms exporters to draw up voluntary guidelines. Implementing these guidelines will enhance trust and encourage restraint on the part of other arms exporters.

An Arms Trade Treaty (2007)[80]

The final disarmament issue I wish to discuss here is that of controlling the international transfer of conventional weapons, which take countless lives in civil wars and regional conflicts around the world. These are, for all intents and purposes, weapons of mass destruction.

Currently there are around 640 million small arms and light weapons in circulation worldwide, with some 8 million more manufactured every year. The proliferation of such weapons fuels human rights violations and armed conflicts, killing more than 1,000 people every day.[81]

The Control Arms campaign was launched by a group of NGOs in October 2003. It has gained momentum to the point that support among governments produced a resolution by the United Nations General Assembly in December 2006 that paves the way for an arms trade treaty.[82] Such a treaty would define the legal limits of the international transfer of arms, and would prevent the movement not only of small arms but of all conventional weapons that fall outside those limits.

The UN Secretary-General will seek the views of member states on an arms trade treaty and report back to the General Assembly within the year. A group of governmental experts will then be set up to discuss the issue in greater depth and will submit a more detailed report to the General Assembly in 2008.

For the past thirteen years, I have called repeatedly for the strengthening of international frameworks regulating the arms trade toward the larger goal of the deinstitutionalization of war. It is my fervent hope that such a

---

80   From 2007 Peace Proposal, "Restoring the Human Connection: The First Step to Global Peace."

81   See Amnesty International. 2006. "Almost One in Three People Affected by Gun Crime." POL 30/020/2006. Press Release. June 18.

82   See UNGA (United Nations General Assembly). 2006. "Towards an Arms Trade Treaty: Establishing Common International Standards for the Import, Export and Transfer of Conventional Arms." A/RES/61/89. Resolution adopted by the General Assembly. December 18.

treaty be concluded as soon as possible. When that happens, it will be the second disarmament treaty, following the Convention on the Prohibition of Anti-Personnel Mines, in which NGOs have played a leadership role. I have no doubt that this would also do much to reenergize negotiations in other disarmament-related fields.

Control of Small Arms (2005)[83]

I would like to call for the earliest possible conclusion of multilateral legal controls on the arms trade. In my 1999 proposal, I stressed the urgency of restricting the trade in arms to prevent the flow of weapons into regions with ongoing conflict or heightened confrontation and tension, as one element in the process to deinstitutionalize war.

There is a rising global chorus of voices calling for such curbs. The Control Arms campaign was launched in October 2003 to advocate legally binding controls on the arms trade at all levels. Three NGOs—Amnesty International, Oxfam and the International Action Network on Small Arms—are working together to promote this campaign, appealing to governments to conclude a treaty that would limit transfers of small arms by next year (2006).

Today, there are over 600 million small arms in the world, and more than 500,000 people are killed with conventional weapons every year. The United Nations held the first Conference on the Illicit Trade in Small Arms and Light Weapons in All Its Aspects in 2001, and adopted a program of action to "prevent, combat and eradicate" this trade.[84]

In addition to such measures against the illegal arms trade, a regulatory structure must be put in place as soon as possible to cover authorized arms exports in light of their scale—a staggering annual value totaling US$21 billion[85]—and impact.

---

83   From 2005 Peace Proposal, "Toward a New Era of Dialogue: Humanism Explored."

84   UN (United Nations). 2001. "Programme of Action to Prevent, Combat and Eradicate the Illicit Trade in Small Arms and Light Weapons in All Its Aspects" A/CONF.192/15. Adopted at the United Nations Conference. July 9–20.

85   See Amnesty International. 2003. "Amnesty International, Oxfam, IANSA Control Arms Campaign Media Briefing: Key Facts and Figures." POL 30/018/2003. October 8.

Exporting weapons into regions of heightened tension, whether legally or illegally, flouts any move toward conflict prevention. By feeding local and regional arms races, it also has a seriously negative impact on human security, diverting budget resources to military expenditures and away from basic services such as education, health care and sanitation desperately needed by impoverished people.

According to the Control Arms campaign, the five permanent members of the UN Security Council account for 88 percent of the world's exports of conventional weapons.[86] In the last four years, the United States, the United Kingdom and France earned more income from arms exports to Africa, Asia, the Middle East and Latin America than they provided in aid.

It is imperative that humanity deinstitutionalize war in the twenty-first century. The first step toward this must be to learn to resist the temptation to exploit war and civil strife in other countries for the sake of one's own influence and profit.

Earlier in this proposal, I touched on the participation of China and India in the deliberations on climate change to be held during the G8 Summit in Gleneagles this year. In the same spirit, I would like to propose that a guideline for strengthening controls on small arms be discussed in the context of a G10 framework.

Last year, I was fortunate to meet with former president Kocheril Raman Narayanan[87] of India. One of the topics we discussed was the increasing importance of China and India in the world. Today, it would be virtually impossible to consider solutions for global challenges without their involvement.

I emphasized the significance of both countries for the twenty-first century in my proposal four years ago (2001). It is my conviction that the spiritual heritage in which both Chinese and Indian civilizations are rooted, when brought to full blossom as soft power in the contemporary world, can make great contributions to creating peace in Asia and the world.

My proposal in 1998 that the G8 Summit meetings should evolve into a "summit of responsible states" through the added participation of China and India was also based on this idea. Although full development into a G10 summit may take some time, I would urge that the small arms issue be discussed during the Gleneagles Summit this year and that negotiations on a treaty involving the major powers be initiated promptly as we work toward

---

86   Ibid.
87   Kocheril Raman Narayanan (1920–2005), President of India (1997–2002).

the second Conference on the Illicit Trade in Small Arms and Light Weapons in All Its Aspects scheduled for next year.

Prohibition of Land Mines (1997)[88]

Support for disarmament and nuclear weapons abolition has increased since the end of the Cold War, and quite a number of efforts are being made in this direction throughout international society. In 1996, these efforts bore fruit in the realization of several landmark events.

In the field of disarmament, the Chemical Weapons Convention (CWC), which had been signed in 1993, will finally go into effect this April (1997). This Convention is thorough enough to be considered a genuine disarmament treaty because it outlaws existing chemical weapons as well as the production of chemical weapons of any kind from now onward. It not only orders the abolition of all chemical weapons including those that are obsolete or abandoned in other countries' territory, but the demolition of facilities for the production of chemical weapons in order to ensure the cessation of their manufacture.

The important aspect of this treaty is that it is binding on all signatory nations, thereby resolving the inequities that were an issue with regard to the Treaty on the Non-Proliferation of Nuclear Weapons (NPT). Also, in order to prevent violations, the treaty approves a system for inspections of related industrial facilities as well as a challenge inspection procedure following a request from a third party. These features make it an extremely good model for disarmament treaties to be drawn up in the future.

How effective such an epoch-making treaty will prove to be, however, depends on the attitude of the twenty countries that possess or are believed to possess chemical weapons. Particularly regarding the countries which hold most of the chemical weapons in the world but have yet to ratify the treaty, international society must unite in urging them to sign the treaty as soon as possible.

I believe that the success of this treaty, with its highly reliable and broad-ranging verification systems, is an extremely important landmark in the movement toward disarmament of other kinds of weapons as well. As each signatory nation conscientiously performs its responsibilities under the treaty and trust is restored through the transparency attained under its verification

---

88   From 1997 Peace Proposal, "New Horizons of a Global Civilization."

procedures, the number of signatory nations will increase until it becomes established as an effective international institution. If success can be achieved even in this single area of chemical weapons, I believe it will have a great impact on endeavors in other areas of disarmament where a consensus has been reached but little real progress made, such as in the case of the Biological Weapons Convention (BWC), whose effectiveness, despite the fact that it came into force in 1975, has been drastically lowered because it does not include verification or inspection clauses.

Another such example is the problem of the proposed treaty restricting the use of antipersonnel land mines, which saw some progress in 1996. In a Review Conference on the Convention on Certain Conventional Weapons (CCW) held last May, a new agreement was reached on the complete revision of the protocols on the tightening of restrictions on antipersonnel land mines. However, a grace period of a maximum nine years before the restraints would come into effect was approved and, since the introduction of an inspection system was put off for future discussion, some have voiced fears that it may end up being no more than a "moral law" that carries no real clout.

In order to attain the goal of total abolition of antipersonnel mines being sought by the various United Nations agencies and by NGOs, I propose that, apart from the CCW—which requires agreement on a ban by all signatory nations—we should work toward a separate framework aimed at the enactment of a ban on antipersonnel land mines. [. . .]

According to studies by the International Red Cross, some 800 lives are lost each month and countless people are gravely injured by the 100 million live land mines that remain strewn about different parts of the world.[89] The vast majority of the victims of land mines are civilians, especially children. The perils of undetonated land mines remain long after the horrors of war are over. I strongly urge that international society move as quickly as possible toward the total abolition of land mines, which imperil the lives and activities of innocent people every day.

---

89   See ICRC (International Committee of the Red Cross). 1994. "Report of the ICRC for the Review Conference of the 1980 UN Conventions on Prohibitions or Restrictions on the Use of Certain Conventional Weapons Which May be Deemed to be Excessively Injurious or to Have Indiscriminate Effects." Article. No. 299. April 30.

An International Treaty Banning the Use, Production and Stockpiling of Cluster Munitions (2008)[90]

My next proposal toward building the infrastructures of peace is to call for the early signing of a treaty banning so-called "cluster bombs." These weapons spread numerous submunitions over a wide area. They indiscriminately kill and maim people in the target area, and the bomblets that remain unexploded put lives at risk for years after a conflict has ended, causing serious hindrance to reconstruction.

As many as 440 million submunitions have already been used in twenty-four countries and territories, killing and injuring an estimated 100,000 people. Some seventy-three countries still continue to stockpile cluster bombs.[91]

The Cluster Munition Coalition, a network of civil society organizations calling for the conclusion of an international treaty banning the use, production and stockpiling of cluster munitions, was formed in 2003. The movement has gained momentum, and in February 2007 a conference attended by more than forty governments and representatives of civil society was held in Oslo, Norway, to frame a new treaty to ban cluster munitions. From this conference, an initiative called the Oslo Process was launched, which, like the Ottawa Process that produced the 1997 treaty banning land mines, brings NGOs and interested states together in shared action.

Discussions are under way within the framework of the United Nations Convention on Certain Conventional Weapons (CCW) to address the issue of cluster bombs, but they have as yet failed to make any significant progress. Thus, while it is of course desirable that as many states as possible eventually become parties, priority must be placed on getting a treaty signed and in place by the end of this year as called for in the Oslo Process. And just as the Ottawa Treaty has over the past decade attained the weight of an international humanitarian norm that discourages even non-signatory states from using land mines, a similar consensus must be built in global society against cluster bombs.

---

90   From 2008 Peace Proposal, "Humanizing Religion, Creating Peace."

91   See Handicap International. 2007. "Circle of Impact: The Fatal Footprint of Cluster Munitions on People and Communities." Brussels: Handicap International ASBL-VZW.

The success of such efforts with strong civil society support will have a definite and positive impact on momentum toward disarmament in other fields.

The Deinstitutionalization of War

A Universal Declaration Renouncing War (1984)[92]

When we look at the condition of the world today, it is growing increasingly confused and chaotic, with little prospect of a new international order. Rather, it is fraught with volatility, further aggravating instability. Far from achieving any order, our planet has entered a new era of nuclear instability: underpinned by anxiety and fear, the nuclear arms race fundamentally precludes the possibility of stability. Indeed, instability is inevitable.

The discontinuation of negotiations on the limitation of intermediate-range nuclear forces and the indefinite suspension of the US–Soviet Strategic Arms Reduction Talks (START) have intensified the fear of nuclear war around the world. If the two countries reach no consensus this year and the new race in deploying intermediate-range nuclear missiles in Europe continues, tensions involving nuclear weapons will certainly escalate.

The hands of the Doomsday Clock pictured in the American scientific journal *The Bulletin of the Atomic Scientists*[93] stand at three minutes before a figurative midnight symbolizing the moment at which nuclear war will break out, ushering in the end of the world. It is not surprising that this is the worst crisis since the end of 1953 when the hands of the Doomsday Clock were at two minutes to midnight following the hydrogen bomb tests conducted by the Soviet Union and the United States. In this sense, this year marks a critical crossroads for the world between being able to open a way for disarmament or moving on toward further military expansion, depending on the actions of the United States and the Soviet Union.

The television film *The Day After*,[94] which depicted the horror of nuclear catastrophe, transfixed 100 million viewers in the United States and aroused

---

92   From 1984 Peace Proposal, "A World Without War."

93   *Bulletin of the Atomic Scientists.* 1984. Vol. 40, No. 1. January 1984. Chicago: Educational Foundation for Nuclear Science, Inc.

94   *The Day After.* 1983. Television film broadcast by ABC, directed by Nicholas Meyer.

a tremendous response in Japan last year (1983). Part of it was also broadcast on state-run television in the Soviet Union. Earlier this year, meanwhile, a Soviet scientist announced the partial results of research warning that a full-scale nuclear war between the United States and the Soviet Union would kill 1.1 billion people instantly and that survivors would be reduced to utter misery, jeopardizing the continued existence of the human species itself. These predictions coincide with a description of nuclear war by the American science writer Jonathan Schell[95] in his book *The Fate of the Earth*.[96]

In the face of the threat of nuclear war, differences of ideology and social systems are completely irrelevant. Nevertheless, the absurd arms race persists because the utterly outdated worship of nuclear deterrence is still very much alive today.

Bertrand Russell[97] called nuclear weapons an absolute evil,[98] and I fully agree. The evil does not lie only in their colossal destructive and lethal power. The worship of nuclear deterrence depending on this power originates in and exacerbates distrust among human beings. Indeed, the growth in the cult of nuclear weapons is inversely proportional to the ability of human beings to trust each other.

This is why I believe nuclear stability and nuclear equilibrium to be essentially impossible. Buddhism teaches the oneness of life and its environment (Jp. *esho funi*). In light of this principle, it is impossible to create peace in a constant state of insecurity under the threat of nuclear weapons. I have commented from this perspective on several occasions.

What lies behind nuclear deterrence is the modern worldview that places utmost precedence on efficiency. One scholar keenly summarized the slogan of the efficiency doctrine as "maximum effect, efficiency and convenience." The scientific and material accomplishments brought about by the efficiency doctrine cannot be entirely denied. But we must not overlook the inevitable tendency of such a mind-set and worldview to reduce human beings to mere things.

---

95   Jonathan Schell (1943–), American writer and editor.

96   Schell, Jonathan. 1982. *The Fate of the Earth*. New York: Alfred A. Knopf.

97   Bertrand Russell (1872–1970), British philosopher, cofounder of the Pugwash Conferences on Science and World Affairs, recipient of the Nobel Prize for Literature in 1950.

98   (qtd. in) Yukawa, Hideki. 1981. "The absolute evil." *The Bulletin of the Atomic Scientists*. January. Vol. 37. Issue 1, p. 37.

At the height of the theory of nuclear deterrence, terms such as "assured destruction," "damage limitation" and "cost versus benefit ratio" were frequently used. They represent a mercilessly grotesque vocabulary of the efficiency doctrine in that they regard human beings as things and take the price of massive death for granted. This way of thinking is far from extinct in the minds of strategists who have recently been discussing nuclear preemptive strikes and nuclear arms control; we must remember that it is capable of returning in different forms on any occasion.

I have consistently warned that it is politicians and scientists, the elite of the nuclear civilization and establishment, who succumb most easily to efficiency-oriented ideas.

Another name for the modern doctrine of efficiency is reductionism. Modern science has made remarkable progress based on the analysis and reduction of objects to their simplest elements, and numerous benefits have been derived as a result. On the other hand, the overwhelming emphasis placed on fragmented elements means that a holistic view that includes our spiritual world has been neglected. I feel that this harmful aspect has deeply affected the conventional procedures of disarmament negotiations.

The START and intermediate-range nuclear forces negotiations seem to have reached an impasse, with the latter especially apparently lost in a maze. Undeniably, a major reason here is an overemphasis on the elements at the expense of a view of the whole picture.

For those who emphasize nuclear stability and nuclear equilibrium, it may be reasonable to precisely categorize nuclear weapons by their type and capability and negotiate on each item. Such negotiations may be necessary, but it should be remembered that there is a pitfall in their reasoning: the more detailed the categories, the more they lose sight of the overall picture, failing to see the wood for the trees. Even if discussions on the capabilities of particular weapons led to some decisions, little progress would be made on the whole issue. I think that this constitutes a blind spot in the current nuclear disarmament negotiations.

Furthermore, nuclear weapons are not the only type of weapon that should be the subject of disarmament. In light of the true nature of conventional weapons—they have been used in all wars since World War II; their current destructive power is immense; and they are inseparable from nuclear weapons in actual armaments—it is clear that including conventional weapons in the disarmament process is a challenge shared by all people of the world.

Since the end of World War II, there have been some 300 regional conflicts, many of which are ongoing. Among the various causes, conflicts arising primarily from ethnic and religious factors tend to become prolonged.

Needless to say, most modern wars have been initiated by states. With some exceptions, they have been mainly waged between sovereign states for national gain and pride, and this has not changed today. At this very moment, there are people in various parts of the world afflicted with suffering due to senseless wars among states. We must face this grim reality once again.

How should we seek the solution? In our search for a path to peace toward the twenty-first century, we need to examine the causes of wars that have taken place since the end of World War II, how to prevent them and how to create and maintain world peace. Moreover, it will be necessary to build a mechanism for concrete steps to sustain peace. The intellectual abilities of humanity must be brought together toward this goal.

Obviously, this is an enormous endeavor which I cannot discuss thoroughly here. With the intensifying tensions between the United States and the Soviet Union and the crises or conflicts they provoke in various parts of the world, I feel compelled to urge that we now need a radical shift to a global perspective.

***

I am deeply concerned about the arms race that has recently begun in outer space, in particular when I view the vast universe from the standpoint of peace and disarmament. There have been reports of the creation of an anti-missile defense shield and the development of anti-satellite weapons designed to destroy satellites for military purposes in outer space. Toward the twenty-first century, nothing could be more dangerous than a US–Soviet arms race in outer space. I believe that the colossal spending on armaments should instead be channeled into our shared efforts to preserve the planet Earth.

To this end, it is extremely urgent that a treaty be concluded between the United States and the Soviet Union prohibiting the deployment of weapons and the use of armed force in outer space as well as the armed targeting of Earth from outer space. I urge that the people of the world develop an awareness of the stark reality of the arms race in outer space and call for such a treaty through the power of international public opinion.

Next year (1985) has been designated International Youth Year, and 1986 the International Year of Peace. The Third Special Session of the UN General Assembly devoted to Disarmament (SSOD-III) is scheduled to be convened by 1988. In order to sustain such a dynamic momentum for peace into the twenty-first century, I would like to stress here the crucial importance of deepening and strengthening our resolve to renounce war while at the same time striving for disarmament.

In my conversations with former NASA astronaut Gerald P. Carr[99] in October 1983, I emphasized the renunciation of war and he wholeheartedly agreed. Unless we rid the world of war, the abolition of weapons remains no more than just a dream. Negotiations on disarmament that have taken place thus far lack real substance, with the parties in fact engaging in further military buildup in case of war. It is as if they were kicking each other in the shins while shaking hands, which is of course ultimately futile.

What is truly needed now is to bring together the will of humanity to renounce war without being trapped by the technicalities of the disarmament process. The stronger the will becomes, the more conspicuous the futility of military expansion will be, further advancing disarmament.

The renunciation of war has never in history been as urgently needed as in this nuclear age, even though to some it remains utterly unrealistic. With the threat of nuclear weapons broadly perceived at the grassroots level worldwide, the absurdity of war has never been so strongly felt as today.

In December 1948, the United Nations unanimously adopted the Universal Declaration of Human Rights at its Third General Assembly. This was a document of great significance as a model of a guarantee of human rights for the world, stipulating in detail basic individual freedoms and economic, social and cultural basic rights. In 1966, the UN adopted and opened for signature the International Covenant on Civil and Political Rights and the International Covenant on Economic, Social and Cultural Rights as legally binding treaties based on the Declaration.

I propose that the UN adopt a "Universal Declaration Renouncing War," following the steps of these predecessors. I believe that this would serve as a valuable breakthrough toward realizing lasting peace. Adoption of such a declaration may be a lengthy process, so I suggest that as a first step NGOs work to prepare the groundwork.

Discussions among states tend to focus on tactics and strategies, making it difficult to reflect the sincere desire of the people for a world without war.

---

99   Gerald P. Carr (1932–), American astronaut, commander of Skylab 4 (1973–74).

NGOs, on the other hand, would be able to reflect the people's sentiments more accurately in their work.

It is essential above all for the people of the world to take the initiative to create a current toward the renunciation of war wherever they can. Considerable results can be achieved if such currents expand continuously toward the International Year of Peace and become the keynote spirit of the SSOD-III. This would serve as a global network of the people to ensure the renunciation of war.

I have great hope in the power of young people as the leading advocates of these currents for a world without war. Toward International Youth Year, I hope that young people from NGOs will join forces for peace and disarmament, and particularly to abolish war from the world.

A UN Decade for Peace and Disarmament (1988)[100]

At the end of last year (December 1987), we witnessed one of the most profound directional changes in the march of political events since World War II. This was the signing of the Intermediate-Range Nuclear Forces (INF) Treaty, designed to abolish intermediate- and shorter-range nuclear forces, at the US–Soviet summit held in Washington DC.

Last year also marked the thirtieth anniversary of the "Declaration Calling for the Abolition of Nuclear Weapons" issued by my mentor, second Soka Gakkai president Josei Toda.[101] In this declaration, he keenly identified the demonic nature of nuclear weapons and entrusted their abolition to members of the younger generation.

I have stressed for more than a decade the urgent need for US–Soviet summit meetings aimed at the abolition of nuclear weapons. The historic signing last year of the INF Treaty was a truly significant change in the course of history for our time.

Obviously, the elimination of intermediate- and shorter-range nuclear weapons will not immediately move the world toward peace and disarmament: we will have to keep a close watch on the course of US–Soviet relations in the years to come. Nevertheless, it is undeniable that the people of the

---

100 From 1988 Peace Proposal, "Cultural Understanding and Disarmament: The Building Blocks of World Peace."
101 Josei Toda (1900–58), second president of the Soka Gakkai (1951–58).

world perceived in the US–Soviet dialogue last year a sign of hope unlike anything we have seen thus far.

In his message to the world issued following the signing ceremony of the INF Treaty, US President Ronald Reagan[102] described the circumstances leading up to the historic agreement by quoting the great Russian writer Leo Tolstoy's[103] observation: "The strongest of all warriors are those two—time and patience."[104]

In turn, Mikhail S. Gorbachev,[105] General Secretary of the Central Committee of the Communist Party of the Soviet Union, speaking of his own determination to reduce nuclear armaments, borrowed a line from the American poet and philosopher Ralph Waldo Emerson[106]: "The reward of a thing well done is to have done it."[107]

I saw the inclusion in the two leaders' speeches of the words of Tolstoy and Emerson—two of the authors I have most loved since my youth—as signaling a change in their patterns of thinking, their dialogue moving beyond mere exchange of diplomatic rhetoric. Additional signs of such change may be seen in President Reagan's statement that "for the first time in history the language of arms control was replaced by arms reduction . . . this required a dramatic shift in thinking,"[108] and in General Secretary Gorbachev's comment about the triumph of common sense.

***

At the end of May this year, the Third Special Session of the UN General Assembly devoted to Disarmament (SSOD-III) will be held. Over the years, I have taken various opportunities to present proposals for disarmament,

---

102 Ronald Wilson Reagan (1911–2004), 40th President of the United States (1981–89).

103 Leo Tolstoy (1828–1910), Russian writer.

104 Reagan, Ronald Wilson. 1987. "Address to the American and Soviet Peoples on the Soviet–United States Summit Meeting, December 8, 1987."

105 Mikhail Gorbachev (1931–), General Secretary of the Communist Party of the Soviet Union (1985–91), President of the Soviet Union (1990–91) and recipient of the Nobel Prize for Peace in 1990.

106 Ralph Waldo Emerson (1803–82), American author.

107 Shanker, Thom. 1987. "Battle Turns Gentle with Proverbs Galore." *Chicago Tribune*. December 9.

108 Reagan, Ronald Wilson. 1987. "Remarks at the Signing of the INF Treaty with Soviet Premier Gorbachev." December 8.

including the abolition of nuclear weapons, and for ways to create a world without war.

On the occasions of the First Special Session on Disarmament (SSOD-I) held in 1978 and of the Second Special Session on Disarmament (SSOD-II) in 1982, I submitted concrete proposals for disarmament and nuclear abolition. In these proposals, I have repeatedly stressed the role of the United Nations. I believe that we have no choice at the moment but to improve and strengthen functions of the UN centered on security in our quest for a new, peaceful world order.

Appraisals of the past two Special Sessions on Disarmament vary. Criticism was made of the SSOD-II that not to mention nuclear weapons, not a single gun was eliminated as a result.

Though concrete evidence of disarmament is important, I would like to place value on the fact that the Special Sessions helped heighten significantly global awareness of the threat of nuclear war and create a surge in international public opinion supporting the abolition of nuclear weapons. It is undeniable that the momentum of public opinion had both a direct and an indirect impact in ultimately bringing about the historic signing of the INF Treaty in December of last year.

The timely convening of the SSOD-III this year will certainly play an important role. In my annual proposal last year, I suggested that this year, during which the SSOD-III is scheduled, be designated an "International Year of Disarmament" by a consensus of the United Nations. It was my hope that 1988 would be made the year of a real breakthrough in developing a global current of disarmament toward the twenty-first century.

I urge that we take the signing of the INF Treaty as an excellent opportunity to make an "International Year of Disarmament" a reality as soon as possible, and also launch a "United Nations Decade of Peace and Disarmament."

In 1969, the UN adopted a resolution designating the 1970s as a Disarmament Decade,[109] based on the proposal of Secretary-General U Thant.[110] However, it failed to produce satisfactory results, as the final document approved at the SSOD-I in 1978 admits: "The Disarmament Decade

---

109 UNGA (United Nations General Assembly). 1969. "Question of General and Complete Disarmament." A/RES/2602 (XXIV). Resolution adopted on the report of the First Committee. December 16.

110 U Thant (1909–74), Burmese diplomat, 3rd Secretary-General of the United Nations (1961–71).

solemnly declared in 1969 by the United Nations is coming to an end. Unfortunately, the objectives established on the occasion by the General Assembly appear to be as far away today as they were then, or even further because the arms race is not diminishing but increasing and outstrips by far the efforts to curb it."[111]

The UN then decided to make the 1980s a Second Disarmament Decade, but we must say that little progress has been made on disarmament. Therefore, I believe that it would be of great significance to launch a new "Decade of Peace and Disarmament" to finally initiate practical steps toward disarmament, the most fervent desire of humanity.

The prospects for the world economy are extremely uncertain, with numerous factors of instability. There is no positive outlook. Many agree that increases in military expenditure against this background only obstruct the healthy development of the world economy as a whole.

The next decade is absolutely crucial as it leads up to the twenty-first century. It is my hope to make this year a first year of disarmament when the power of the people brings about a dramatic shift from arms expansion to arms reduction. With growing global interdependence, the prospects for the global economy will improve if countries move toward disarmament together. It is out of my wish to see the UN take the initiative in global efforts for disarmament that I propose that it declare a "Decade of Peace and Disarmament." The SSOD-III provides an excellent opportunity for this.

Needless to say, the UN is a forum of discussions for sovereign states. But we cannot afford to leave the question of arms reduction to deliberations among governments alone. What truly matters is to develop an upsurge in international public opinion supporting peace and disarmament on the grassroots level. Herein lies the importance of the role played by NGOs. A key to ensuring the success of the SSOD-III lies in building an international network of such public opinion.

In cooperation with the UN, the SGI has held the exhibition "Nuclear Arms: Threat to Our World" in various parts of the world in support of the World Disarmament Campaign adopted at the SSOD-II in 1982.

---

111 UNGA (United Nations General Assembly). 1978. "Final Document of the Tenth Special Session of the General Assembly." A/RES/S-10/2. Resolution adopted on the Report of the Ad Hoc Committee of the Tenth Special Session, p. 15.

Shown in a total of eighteen cities in fifteen countries around the world—at the United Nations Headquarters in New York, Geneva, Vienna, Paris, Stockholm, Helsinki, Oslo, Bergen, West Berlin, Athens, Belgrade, Zagreb, New Delhi, Montreal, Toronto, Beijing, Moscow and Bangkok—this exhibition has drawn considerable attention and interest, and is highly praised as a practical tool for education on peace and nuclear abolition.

For six years the "Nuclear Arms: Threat to Our World" exhibition has played a significant role in developing public opinion calling for nuclear abolition on a global scale. I suggest that it be upgraded into a new campaign calling for comprehensive disarmament and a peaceful world that better reflects today's realities on the occasion of the SSOD-III. I would urge that this initiative be taken by youth members of the Soka Gakkai.

A major challenge in nuclear arms reduction this year is a proposed 50-percent cut in strategic nuclear weapons. This will be the central focus of discussion at the US–Soviet summit scheduled to be held in Moscow sometime between now and June. I sincerely hope that the SSOD-III will serve as a catalyst for some real progress in the direction of a total ban on nuclear tests, a goal I have long advocated, as well as in negotiations for prohibiting chemical weapons.

Although we should not be overly optimistic, there is a likelihood of phased nuclear reductions toward total abolition. If the US–Soviet relationship shifts from confrontation to a new state of peaceful coexistence, world tensions will become drastically relaxed.

Nevertheless, nuclear arms reduction is not enough to realize a truly peaceful world. We must face the fact that since the end of World War II, there have been a total of more than 150 wars and armed conflicts in the world, producing greater casualties than those which took place during World War II itself. Conventional weapons have been used in all of these wars and conflicts. It is predicted that the development of conventional weapons making full use of advanced technology will only intensify.

Sadly, the logic of power still prevails in the realm of international politics. What is crucially needed now is the rallying of wisdom and public opinion from around the world in order to create a new order for a peaceful and stable international community. The world has entered a period of immense transition. It would not be an overstatement to say that the transition is of a scale unprecedented in human history.

The German philosopher Karl Jaspers[112] called the period between 800 and 200 BCE the Axial Age, emphasizing how important that time was in the history of humankind.[113] It was a period of history that saw the advent of a large number of giants in religion, thought and philosophy who shine brilliantly in world history: Shakyamuni,[114] Confucius,[115] Lao Tzu,[116] Deutero-Isaiah,[117] Heraclitus,[118] Plato,[119] Archimedes[120] and others.

According to Jaspers, it is what was realized, created and contemplated during the Axial Age that has sustained humanity until today.[121] He characterized the age as one in which human beings became aware of their existence as a whole, of themselves as human beings and their own limitations, and defined the sweeping change in human existence as "spiritualization."[122]

I feel that a period of massive transition has arrived today, a "second axial age." What characterizes this period is the presence of nuclear weapons with their destructive capacity to annihilate humanity in an instant and a crisis that could lead the entire Earth to total devastation. We have no choice but to think from a global point of view beyond national boundaries, a drastic paradigm shift. If the Axial Age was a period of consciousness as an individual, a second axial age of today may be one of consciousness as individuals of the same species, an age in which individuals need to have an awareness as fellow members of humanity.

The reason I stress that we are at a great turning point in human history is because there is an intense struggle in various areas of international politics between the awareness of individuals as members of the human race and the logic of sovereign states. With the advent of nuclear weapons, war as

112 Karl Jaspers (1883–1969), German philosopher.
113 Jaspers, Karl. 1953. *The Origin and Goal of History.* Trans. by Michael Bullock. New Haven, Connecticut: Yale University Press, p. 7.
114 Shakyamuni (Gautama Siddartha) (*c.* 560–480 BCE), the founder of Buddhism.
115 Confucius (*c.* 551–479 BCE), Chinese philosopher.
116 Lao Tzu (Laozi) (flourished 6th century BCE), Chinese Daoist philosopher.
117 Deutero-Isaiah (flourished 6th century BCE), Hebrew prophet.
118 Heraclitus (*c.* 540–480 BCE), Greek philosopher.
119 Plato (*c.* 428–347 BCE), Greek philosopher, student of Socrates and teacher of Aristotle.
120 Archimedes (*c.* 290–212 BCE), Greek mathematician.
121 Jaspers, Karl. 1953. *The Origin and Goal of History.* Trans. by Michael Bullock. New Haven, Connecticut: Yale University Press, p. 2.
122 Ibid., p. 3.

a sovereign right could well lead to the extinction of humanity. We face an urgent demand for a paradigm shift to move beyond national borders, from national interests to the interests of humanity, from national sovereignty to human sovereignty. I am convinced that this new, surging tide of history is already irreversible.

The question is how to introduce a new set of guiding principles in the arena of international politics and build a new international order to make this tide more firm and constant.

Here, I would like to present a plan for the United Nations, the parliament of humanity. As I observe recent developments in international politics, I find signs of a gradual change in how national sovereignty is perceived, which has traditionally been considered to be of an absolute nature.

For example, clauses on verification and inspection are included in the INF Treaty between the United States and the Soviet Union. The inspection and verification stipulated there are the strictest in the history of US–Soviet disarmament negotiations. The two countries have agreed upon complying with strict on-site inspection, which can involve a degree of interference with national sovereignty. It is proof that they now acknowledge that the nuclear problem will not be solved as long as precedence is placed upon national pride and egoism.

Another encouraging sign is that US and Soviet experts recently visited each other's nuclear-testing sites to improve verification capabilities, thereby finding a way toward negotiations on phased limitations on nuclear testing. If these trends develop further, they could possibly break through the hard wall of the notion that state sovereignty is absolute.

The time when it was taken for granted that sovereign states could unconditionally resort to armed force and war to protect their interests is over. The ravages of modern war are exponentially greater than their predecessors. It is absolutely necessary to impose some kind of restriction on the arbitrary exercise of sovereign power and armed force.

In 1928, the Kellogg-Briand Pact (General Treaty for the Renunciation of War as an Instrument of National Policy) was concluded in Paris. The treaty outlawed war as a means of settling international disputes, denied war as an instrument of national policy, and rejected the justification and legitimacy of war as an institution. Jurists consider that the Kellogg-Briand Pact ushered in an era in which the norm that war is not only immoral but also a violation of international law has become irrefutable.

It would be easy to find fault with the Pact. But subsequent developments in history show that the environment and conditions of the world at that time were not ripe for it to be truly effective.

In my proposal for 1984, I urged that a "Universal Declaration Renouncing War" be drafted as soon as possible. I also proposed that it be adopted by the UN, though I was fully aware that such a proposal would be criticized as being premature. It is my earnest hope that some restrictions be imposed on the right to war that has been taken for granted as an attribute of state sovereignty.

Sixty years have passed since the signing of the Kellogg-Briand Pact in Paris. The times have changed greatly, and I would not be the only one who feels that conditions in the world have never been as ripe as today to accept the concept of the renunciation of war.

The final document approved at the SSOD-I stated that "[t]he time has therefore come to put an end to this situation, to abandon the use of force in international relations and to seek security in disarmament."[123] It is of tremendous significance that the document was unanimously adopted by the member states.

Times are changing gradually but undeniably. It is imperative that we boldly change our ways of thinking and bring together the power of the people to take the first step forward to open a new era of peace.

This year marks the fortieth anniversary of the adoption of the Universal Declaration of Human Rights by the third session of UN General Assembly. To make it legally binding and mandatory for states to implement it, the UN drafted the International Covenants on Human Rights.

Following this precedent, I propose that the United Nations adopt a Universal Declaration Renouncing War and subsequently draw up International Covenants on the Renunciation of War to be signed by each state. Ideally, this would lead to the establishment of regional pacts for Europe, Asia, the Americas and Africa, each reflecting local conditions.

A global renunciation of war may seem to some a mere fantasy. But we must remind ourselves that it was only a quarter-century ago that US and Soviet representatives seriously discussed the possibility of complete disarmament on the floor of the UN General Assembly. At the Fourteenth

---

123 UNGA (United Nations General Assembly). 1978. "Final Document of the Tenth Special Session of the General Assembly." A/RES/S-10/2. Resolution adopted on the Report of the Ad Hoc Committee of the Tenth Special Session, p. 3.

General Assembly in 1959, Soviet Premier Nikita Khrushchev[124] proposed the complete elimination of all weapons. The proposal included a detailed program for general and complete disarmament. In the same year, an eighty-two-nation joint draft resolution on general and complete disarmament was adopted unanimously at the UN General Assembly.

In September 1961, the United States and the Soviet Union agreed on the McCloy-Zorin Accords, or The Agreed Principles for Disarmament Negotiations. The two countries introduced this proposal to the UN General Assembly, and it was passed unanimously in December of the same year.

In his first address at the General Assembly in September 1961, US President John F. Kennedy[125] presented a new plan for eliminating arms, known as the United States Program for General and Complete Disarmament in a Peaceful World.[126] In 1962, the United States and the Soviet Union submitted a full-fledged draft treaty on general and complete disarmament to the newly established Conference of the Eighteen-Nation Committee on Disarmament, and the deliberations focused on it.

What actually ensued, however, was an intense arms race between the two countries.

Now that the world is entering a new era of arms reduction, let us return afresh to the original spirit of disarmament. I sincerely hope that the International Covenants on Human Rights and putative International Covenants on the Renunciation of War will be made the two main pillars to sustain humanity toward the twenty-first century. I believe that they should serve as guiding principles as we plan a new order for the world.

An International Conference for a World without War (1990)[127]

Agreements on disarmament in the Strategic Arms Reduction Talks (START) and the Negotiations on Conventional Armed Forces in Europe (CFE) are

---

124 Nikita Khrushchev (1894–1971), Premier of the Soviet Union (1958–64).

125 John F. Kennedy (1917–63), 35th President of the United States (1960–63).

126 Department of State. 1961. "Freedom from War: The United States Program for General and Complete Disarmament in a Peaceful World." Publication 7277. Disarmament Series 5.

127 From 1990 Peace Proposal, "The Triumph of Democracy: Toward a Century of Hope."

expected to be concluded by the end of this year (1990). Enormous amounts of money and human resources have been devoted to building up arms, but world leaders are at last awakening to the sobering fact that this poses serious obstacles to healthy economic growth.

It is still too early, however, to become completely optimistic. While considerable progress may be made in reducing the world's arsenal of nuclear arms, there is as yet no indication that they will be abolished altogether. Reduction of conventional weapons is even more difficult. Although the mind-sets of political leaders are changing and nations are depending less on military might in the conduct of international relations, there is still no effective mechanism for preventing regional conflict.

In order to make a peaceful transition from the old, postwar world order to a new one and to make the twenty-first century a century of hope, we must take bold and dynamic steps. With the United States and the Soviet Union still possessing massive nuclear arsenals, it has been pointed out that we need to think in terms of "common security" for the survival of humankind.[128] Common security aims to build a global security mechanism that will ensure the survival of both one's own and the other sides. In more constructive terms, it means to build a system for achieving a world without war.

Our nuclear situation is such that a nation's exercise of its sovereign right could directly result in total annihilation. Thus I have repeatedly stressed that we have no choice but to transcend national boundaries and make a paradigm shift from national interests to the interests of humanity and from national sovereignty to the sovereignty of humanity.

The problem is how to transform the notion of absolute national sovereignty into a relative one. It does not mean, however, the dissolution of nation-states and an immediate shift to a world federation. Such a scenario will be far too unrealistic for quite some time to come.

A more realistic approach might be to explore ways for the nations of the world to introduce the renunciation of the right of belligerency, as found in the 1946 Constitution of Japan, while maintaining their national entities. This would help abolish the institution of war instigated in the name of state sovereignty.

The roles states play in protecting the freedom and human rights of citizens and providing welfare services continue to be essential. These aspects of

---

128 See Independent Commission on Disarmament and Security Issues. 1982. "Common Security: A Blueprint for Survival." New York: Simon and Schuster.

state sovereignty that hold positive humanistic values must be maintained. The right of self-determination of peoples must also be respected. The right to wage war, however, must be denied constitutionally. If this single principle spread throughout the world, it would open up the possibility of institution-alizing the renunciation of war.

Prof. Norman Cousins[129] of the University of California, Los Angeles, and I have fully agreed on this point in our recent series of discussions on world peace. Professor Cousins has for many years led a movement to strengthen the United Nations as president of the World Federalist Association.

Humanity plunged itself into two World Wars, and, with deep remorse, vowed never to go to war again. It was from this experience that the spirit of the United Nations Charter was born. Sadly, the postwar years witnessed the escalation of a Cold War, in stark contrast to people's desire for lasting peace. The United States and the Soviet Union became locked in an arms race to a point where the continued existence of humanity was threatened.

Now, the Cold War regime has ended, and a new age seems to have arrived upon us. I believe that it is time to go back to the original spirit of the United Nations Charter and start building a new global community upholding the renunciation of war for the survival of humankind.

I suggest that we approach this endeavor in units of ten years. The decade of the 1990s would be a time of preparation for a "Conference for a World without War" to be held at the UN Headquarters in the year 2001. It should be a major peace conference attended by both political leaders and private citizens.

The support and strength of international public opinion is essential if the movement for a world free from war is to become a global current. This requires grassroots efforts to introduce the renunciation of the right of belligerency in the constitution of each country. The key lies in bringing together the power of the people beyond national boundaries, as was seen in the changes that took place in Eastern European countries. This could be an international campaign for a world without war promoted by UN-registered NGOs.

The international showings of the "War and Peace" exhibition organized by the SGI constitute one effort to underpin such a campaign. The SGI will

---

129   Norman Cousins (1912–90), American author, president of the World Federalist Association (1976–91).

promote the new campaign for a world without war in addition to supporting the UN's international campaigns for disarmament and human rights.

At the proposed Conference for a World without War in 2001, I hope that a "Universal Declaration Renouncing War," for which we of the SGI have been calling, will be adopted, and a concrete blueprint for an international covenant and agreement for a world without war will be discussed.

Efforts on the political level must be accompanied by initiatives in civil society. Toward this end, I propose the creation of an international wise men's conference championing the United Nations. This body would investigate ways to strengthen and reform the UN through bringing together the wisdom of civil society in order to institutionalize the renunciation of war throughout the world.

A UN Peace Summit (1994)[130]

The greatest hope for many of us when the Cold War ended was that we could stop wasting money on military expenditures. In reality, there has been no noticeable progress in arms reduction, and it seems that reducing the amount invested in the military and spending the money instead for peaceful purposes, the so-called "peace dividend," is becoming no more than a dream. It is particularly worrying that Asia has become the world's largest purchaser of arms.

In the five years from 1987 through 1991, the five countries of the United States, the Soviet Union, France, the United Kingdom and China were responsible for 86 percent of global weapons exports[131]—weapons that make international disputes more difficult to resolve. It is ironic that all five permanent members of the UN Security Council, who are charged with maintaining international peace, are at the same time the world's top weapon exporters.

By buying these arms, Third World countries are simply making an already tough economic situation worse and doubtless preventing improvement in the lives of their own citizens. It is grievous that the end of the Cold War has not resulted in a positive contribution to their situations. We must change

---

130 From 1994 Peace Proposal, "Light of the Global Spirit: A New Dawn in Human History."

131 See Congress of the US, Congressional Budget Office (CBO). 1992. *Limiting Conventional Arms Exports to the Middle East.* Washington, DC: CBO, p. 12.

this reality so that the money which ought to be paid for food, medical care and education is no longer diverted to arms procurement.

There is no quick and simple solution to this problem. The first step is for the arms-exporting nations to take the initiative in promoting disarmament and refrain from exporting large quantities of weapons. In 1991, on the basis of a proposal presented by the European Commission (EC) and Japan, the UN General Assembly established a registration system for the transfer of weapons. However, no one is obligated to use this system, and we can only hope that each country will register voluntarily. Such an inadequate system cannot possibly control arms exports. This is an area where Japan, which has not been involved in arms exports in the postwar period, is perfectly suited to help establish systematic control of such exports, thereby applying a brake on worldwide weapons traffic.

To stop Third World countries from buying weapons, the leverage of official economic assistance should be brought into play. Weapons purchases could be closely monitored, and any country that bought large amounts of weapons could be denied foreign aid. This would prove very effective if established as an international institution.

Next year, 1995, will be a highly symbolic year for world peace. It will mark both the fiftieth anniversary of the founding of the United Nations and the fiftieth anniversary of the dropping of atomic bombs on Hiroshima and Nagasaki. Also, in the spring of next year, a Review Conference will convene to determine whether the Treaty on the Non-Proliferation of Nuclear Weapons (NPT) should be extended indefinitely or for a specified period. In the midst of all this, however, it seems to me that interest in nuclear disarmament has weakened in recent years.

Although the end of the Cold War alleviated the threat posed by the fierce nuclear arms race between the two former superpowers, there is still a grave concern about the threat represented by the huge existing nuclear arsenals. Nuclear proliferation continues to be a major problem, as symbolized by the current dispute over nuclear inspections in North Korea. But the essential challenge for all humanity is to reduce the huge arsenals of the nuclear powers as quickly as possible and to eventually find a way to eliminate them altogether. I believe that we should try to make 1995 a turning point in our efforts to solve the myriad problems associated with nuclear weapons.

We must first finalize the Comprehensive Nuclear Test Ban Treaty (CTBT) to ban all nuclear testing. At the NPT Review Conference to be held next year, we must ensure that the nuclear powers strongly reaffirm the ultimate goal of total abolition of nuclear weapons. The uncertain question concerning the abolition of nuclear weapons in Ukraine has fortunately been resolved, but nevertheless, even if the United States and Russia are able to significantly reduce their stockpiles, we will still need an international nuclear monitoring system if we hope to get that level down to zero, and some sort of organization must therefore be established for that purpose.

The end of the Cold War has rendered the idea of nuclear deterrence meaningless, and I believe this is precisely the time we should pursue the path of total abolition. We will need to expand the Conference on Disarmament (CD) into a new UN Disarmament Agency that can also address such issues as the disposal of nuclear waste.

I call on all people concerned to seriously consider how they should approach these peace-related challenges during the watershed year of 1995, when the UN celebrates its fiftieth anniversary. Japan in particular should take this historic opportunity to take leadership in the work of peace as it has advocated the abolition of nuclear weapons throughout the postwar years, based on its own experiences at Hiroshima and Nagasaki. For example, we could work to convene a UN peace summit in 1995 that would gather the world's leaders at the UN to build consensus toward total disarmament.

An international nuclear monitoring system or total disarmament may seem like unrealistic dreams. Yet soon after World War II (June 1946), the United States itself presented the Baruch Plan to the United Nations Atomic Energy Commission (UNAEC), which was a plan for an international nuclear monitoring system. Also, in 1952, it proposed a comprehensive disarmament plan that, on the basis of the UN Charter, was designed to build a world without war by outlawing war as a means of settling disputes.

It is up to us people to build a world without war. The fate of the twenty-first century hinges on whether we give up the idea as being impossible, or continue to work at this difficult task.

Toda Institute for Global Peace and Policy Research (1996)[132]

We are now entering a great period of transition between the end of one century and the beginning of another, and people in all parts of the world are experiencing the confusion that characteristically accompanies

---

132 From 1996 Peace Proposal, "Toward the Third Millennium: The Challenge of Global Citizenship."

such transitions. Perhaps our expectations that governments will create a new order have been excessive. What is in fact needed is an alternative concept of grassroots power that will build a new world order from the ground up.

Since the beginning of the 1990s, the United Nations has organized world conferences and otherwise backed serious efforts to address a variety of global issues, including those of the environment, indigenous peoples, human rights, the family, population, social development and the status of women. A recurring theme in the process is that the task of building a society in which all members can live with true human dignity cannot be left to governments alone. There is growing recognition that the active engagement of the world's people must be sought and that the emergence of a new global civil society can be an important element in the resolution of the problems we presently face.

In the peace proposal I wrote two years ago (1994), I proposed that the Boston Research Center for the 21st Century[133] conduct research on reforming and strengthening the UN as it marked the fiftieth anniversary of its founding. I am delighted to write that the center's research was completed in the form of a report entitled "A People's Response to Our Global Neighborhood,"[134] which was delivered to the UN Headquarters in October last year (1995).

This project is especially significant because it was achieved through open dialogue, with people examining UN issues in a personal context. The important point here is that the results were achieved through dialogue that brought together the collective wisdom of specialists and ordinary citizens. I believe that the new world order for peace will come into being as the power of this kind of popular solidarity grows to take on global proportions.

With this in mind, the SGI resolved last year to establish the Toda Institute for Global Peace and Policy Research, which will open this spring. Last year marked the fiftieth anniversary of second Soka Gakkai president Josei Toda's[135] release from prison, where he was wrongfully incarcerated by Japan's military authorities during World War II. The institute will base its

---

133 Subsequently renamed the Ikeda Center for Peace, Learning, and Dialogue.

134 Boston Research Center for the 21st Century. 1995. "A People's Response to Our Global Neighborhood: Dialogues on the Report of the Commission on Global Governance." Boston, Massachusetts: Boston Research Center for the 21st Century.

135 Josei Toda (1900–58), second president of the Soka Gakkai (1951–58).

work on his concepts of peace, including the abolition of nuclear weapons, protection of the right of existence (the right to human dignity) and global citizenship. Thus, it will endeavor to contribute to world peace in ways that meet the needs of our times.

The Toda Institute will seek the cooperation of leading researchers throughout the world to grapple with various global problems and propose solutions. One of its most important characteristics, however, will be the links it will forge between researchers and activists, through which it will attempt to contribute to the formation and enhancement of a global movement of people's power. In this way, the Toda Institute will embody the new concept of a people's research institute.

Hitherto, the energy and efforts of researchers and activists have tended to be fragmented and uncoordinated. What we hope to do is promote greater solidarity through the common dimension of the world's people, thereby directing these energies more effectively toward the solution of the world's problems. To achieve this, it will be necessary to publish and make available the results of the institute's research efforts worldwide. In cooperation with academic and research institutions as well as NGOs, the institute will set to work on creating a new global network of citizens, scholars and activists.

Many specific research topics are slated for study, including security, development, human rights and the environment, as these interact with cultural, religious and ethnic factors. However, in view of the fact that Toda himself issued a "Declaration Calling for the Abolition of Nuclear Weapons" in 1957 and enjoined the younger generation to work toward the abolition of nuclear weapons, highest priority will be accorded to projects dealing with the issue of nuclear weapons and disarmament.

***

In view of the fact that we have now put the fiftieth anniversary of the end of World War II behind us, I hope the institute will work to map out a long-term grand design for a world without war. It is my understanding that the Fourth United Nations Special Session on Disarmament (SSOD-IV) is scheduled for 1997. With this in mind, I hope the institute will take up a topic I have consistently emphasized—how to construct a global, cooperative system that renounces war—and that it will play a central role in bringing together the world's intellectual resources to formulate alternatives for a brighter human future.

One specific direction that should be explored is transforming the nuclear-weapon-free zones now spreading throughout the world and designating them "war-free zones." If this is achieved, we will be well on our way to realizing a world in which no rational positing of a need for nuclear weapons is possible. If, on the other hand, this is beyond our reach, then the ultimate abolition of nuclear weapons will probably remain elusive.

At the end of 1995, I enjoyed a second discussion with Dr. Óscar Arias Sánchez,[136] the former president of Costa Rica and recipient of the Nobel Peace Prize. As we exchanged opinions concerning war and peace, Dr. Arias emphasized that military expenditures should be cut back and the funds spent instead to promote education and culture. In fact, his ideal is to eliminate all armaments worldwide. After World War II, the Marshall Plan was carried out to rebuild Europe. Dr. Arias contends that a new, global Marshall Plan is now necessary so that resources can be invested in "human development" rather than arms.

While it might be easy to dismiss such talk as mere idealism, Dr. Arias' assertions are persuasive in that Costa Rica's Constitution, adopted in 1949, actually succeeded in abolishing that country's armed forces. Some might say that this achievement was only feasible because Costa Rica is a small country. Nevertheless, the elimination of armaments on a larger scale is not completely impossible, as evidenced by the abolition of slavery, apartheid and other inhuman institutions when people have finally recognized that they serve no use and bring only harm.

At the urging of Dr. Arias, Costa Rica's neighbor, Panama, revised its Constitution in October 1994 to remove the legal basis for its armed forces. Although many problems remain, Haiti, too, has begun to dismantle its army and move in the direction of abolishing its military.

I am in wholehearted agreement with Dr. Arias' proposal that we inculcate in younger generations a "culture of peace" to supplant a "culture of war." The Toda Institute should conduct the kind of comprehensive research that will show the way toward worldwide disarmament and demilitarization, reflecting the will of the world's people.

Although the third millennium will begin in approximately five years, this does not mean that a new era will come about naturally, without conscious effort. Such renewal ultimately depends upon the human will to open the

---

136　Óscar Arias Sánchez (1941–), President of Costa Rica (1986–90, 2006–10), recipient of the Nobel Prize for Peace in 1987.

door to a new age. Human beings have an innate ability to create new options and to make informed choices. The challenges before us may be difficult, but inasmuch as we ourselves have created them, it is clear that we also have the capability to resolve them. As Dr. Arnold J. Toynbee[137] pointed out, the most potent historical forces are unleashed when people resolve to confront serious challenges.[138] We find ourselves enmeshed in deepening crisis not because we lack the necessary capacities, but because we do not adequately recognize our possession of them.

One of my close friends, the late Norman Cousins,[139] once warned:

> [T]he main characteristic of pessimism, like cynicism, is that it sets the stage for its own omens. It shuns hope for the future in the act of denying it. It narrows the field of vision, obscuring the relationship between the necessary and the possible.[140]

In this way, he keenly admonished anyone who, without making any particular effort, would simply give up. Let us etch these words in our hearts and remain faithful optimists as we work together to take up the challenge of doing what is required of us.

Disarmament Education

World Disarmament Campaign (1983)[141]

According to a report released earlier this year by a well-known think-tank in Washington DC, the next two or three years will determine whether the East–West nuclear arms race intensifies or we move toward disarmament in the long term. This is because the nuclear powers are rushing to develop a

---

137 Arnold J. Toynbee (1889–1975), British historian.

138 (qtd. in) Cousins, Norman. 1981. *Human Options*. New York: W. W. Norton & Co., p. 51.

139 Norman Cousins (1912–90), American author, President of the World Federalist Association (1976–91).

140 Cousins, Norman. 1981. *Human Options*. New York: W. W. Norton & Co., p. 48.

141 From 1983 Peace Proposal, "New Proposals for Peace and Disarmament."

series of new strategic nuclear weapons and are aiming to decide on nuclear weapons policies during the first half of the 1980s.

In fact, American Pershing II missiles and cruise missiles are scheduled to be deployed in Europe around December of this year (1983). If the plan is executed, it will certainly aggravate tensions between the East and West in Europe. This would also affect other parts of the world. For example, the Soviet Union has recently revealed plans to move part of its intermediate-range SS20 nuclear missiles to Siberia, apparently to counteract the deployment of American nuclear arms in the Far East.

At the recent Japan–US summit meeting that took place earlier this year, the decision was made to further strengthen the military alliance between the two countries. This is undeniably increasing tensions in Asia. The Japanese people are deeply concerned over whether Japan is moving toward peace or military buildup.

This is a critical situation that could possibly lead to global destruction, robbing humankind of its right to live. Undoubtedly, we are at a crucial crossroads between moving toward peace on the one hand and intensified tensions on a global scale on the other.

We must also remember that the arms race is deeply built into the economic, political and social structures. It is well known that today's military mechanisms constitute the military-industrial complex. With government bureaucracy and the academic establishment added, this is called the military-industrial-bureaucratic-academic complex.

The strengthening of the militaristic alliance among these vested interests is becoming increasingly conspicuous recently. The network of those who seek to maintain and expand their positions through military buildup is becoming unprecedentedly powerful. Therefore, achieving disarmament requires sustained effort based on a long-term vision.

I once described the threat of nuclear war as a catastrophe facing European-led modern civilization as a whole. Although this might seem to be an overly generalized expression, I think that the reign of force using nuclear weapons as the *ultima ratio* represents the culmination of the subjugation of people by machines and political mechanisms that have gradually evolved throughout modern history.

On the surface, it seems that a few elite policymakers control the ruling structures, backed by military power with immense destructive potential. But is it they who are truly in control? In reality, they are the ones at the mercy of the devilish nature hidden in the structures that govern nuclear weapons.

Buddhism describes this devilish nature as fundamental darkness. Shrouded by this darkness, human beings risk being ousted from their role as protagonists in all realms of society.

There are individuals who go so far beyond the theory of nuclear deterrence as to discuss the practicalities of a limited nuclear war. I see a total disregard of human beings in their psyche. Under the control of the devilish nature of nuclear weapons, there is absolutely no room in this callous estimation of casualties in the hundreds of thousands and even millions to take into consideration the suffering of the individual destroyed by such a war. In this kind of mind-set, nuclear weapons are the protagonist, with human beings reduced to a miserable secondary presence.

This kind of devilish nature is not limited to nuclear arms: it is inherent in all weaponry. The true horror of nuclear weapons lies in the fact that they have magnified the monstrous quality of the devilish nature to extremity.

Carl von Clausewitz[142] famously described war as "a mere continuation of politics by other means."[143] The assumption here was that war was well under human control. The emergence of nuclear weapons has completely overturned this rather optimistic assumption.

In that sense, nuclear weapons embody the failure of modern civilization itself. Their advent was a fateful event for human history. The fact that power structures underpinned by nuclear weapons are dominated by the elite few is the epitome of the defeat of humanity, the domination of human beings by their own creation. It would not be an overstatement to say that this signifies the death of human dignity.

Faced with the fateful advent of nuclear arms, we are urged to place the leading role on the stage of human history back into the hands of human beings, and ordinary people in particular. Therefore, I would like to reconfirm here the unchanging guiding principle of the SGI to eternally stand on the side of ordinary people.

The surge of global activism against nuclear weapons and for disarmament beginning in 1981 is of historical significance in that regard. It is ordinary citizens who are engaged in this antinuclear movement, and its spread beyond national boundaries made us conscious of the emergence of a new era of the people. The development of a new awareness that citizens are the protagonists

---

142 Carl von Clausewitz (1780–1831), Prussian general and military thinker.

143 Clausewitz, Carl von. 1982. *On War.* Trans. by J. J. Graham. New York: Penguin Books, p. 119.

in the effort to ensure peace in the face of nuclear weapons as humanity's common enemy opened new horizons in peace activism. For the first time in history, civil activism has evolved into an organized entity that is equally powerful as governments and international organizations.

I have been eagerly awaiting the arrival of such an era for over a decade. In my own capacity as a private citizen, I have exerted myself to develop currents of lasting peace by visiting more than forty countries to engage in dialogue with leaders of various fields and by promoting exchanges among the people. It was my resolve to realize the arrival of that era as soon as possible.

The change has only begun. The wall of obstacles presented by state and political power still remains daunting. The challenge now is for ordinary people to break through this formidable wall and open a way for lasting peace for humanity.

I believe that there is no need to be pessimistic over the current situation. Despair and resignation do not provide a vision for the future. I agree with Karl Jaspers[144] who, toward the end of his life, said that "[n]o situation is absolutely hopeless."[145] We need to move forward with the hope and confidence that we are the ones who will open the door to the twenty-first century.

American sociologist Prof. Robert N. Bellah[146] of the University of California, Berkeley, also stressed this point during his recent dialogue with me. He stated that to merely emphasize the tragic consequences of nuclear weapons and nuclear war and stir fear in people would only deprive people of a sense of hope for the future and push young people into egotism. He believed that peace movements in our time should be able to encourage people to transform human society and inspire hope that humanity can realize their deepest aspirations. He also stated that, as an embodiment of such movements, he holds great expectations for the various activities for peace promoted by the SGI.

The role of NGOs will certainly become greater in bringing together the voices of people calling for peace. Their work aims to realize peace and the well-being of humanity from a transnational standpoint, beyond the narrow confines of national interests. The SGI is one such NGO, actively engaged in

---

144 Karl Jaspers (1883–1969), German philosopher.
145 Jaspers, Karl. 1961. *The Future of Mankind.* Chicago, Illinois: University of Chicago, p. 167.
146 Robert N. Bellah (1927–), American sociologist, Elliott Professor of Sociology, Emeritus, at the University of California, Berkeley.

activities for peace as an NGO working with the United Nations Department of Public Information (UNDPI).

In addition to the civil solidarity and people's activism led by NGOs, there is a need for a global network to give them a theoretical direction, possibly comprising universities, research institutions and local governments exploring ways to create peace. The time has come for us to seriously consider building a multidimensional international network dedicated to creating peace.

Obviously, this will take a long time. It is an endeavor to find solutions not only for the problem of nuclear weapons but for the global problems that are crucial to human survival to create a new order for peace.

In the proposal for disarmament and nuclear abolition I submitted to the Second Special Session of the UN General Assembly on Disarmament (SSOD-II) in 1982, I urged non-nuclear states to unite in the creation of a global network of peace to counter the United States and the Soviet Union.[147] The achievement of this aim requires a multidimensional approach. Starting this year, the SGI will take initial steps toward building an international network dedicated to creating peace, strengthening cooperation with Soka University. As part of our efforts in this connection, we will work with Soka University to organize a conference in the form of a peace summit of experts this fall, inviting renowned scholars, peace activists and experts in UN circles.

We will continue to support the UN from this global perspective this year. One aspect of that support will be cooperation with the World Disarmament Campaign. The exhibition "Nuclear Arms: Threat to Our World," launched last year at the UN Headquarters in New York, received considerable attention, contributing to the surge of public opinion opposing nuclear weapons and supporting disarmament around the world.

Secretary-General Javier Pérez de Cuéllar[148] expressed his wish to have materials and documents on atomic bombs permanently displayed at a total of sixty-eight United Nations offices including the sixty-three Offices of Public Information, the Headquarters in New York and the Offices at Geneva and

---

147 Ikeda, Daisaku. 1982. "Gunshuku oyobi kakuheiki haizetsu eno teigen" [Proposal for Disarmament and the Abolition of Nuclear Weapons]. *Seikyo Shimbun.* June 5, p. 3.

148 Javier Pérez de Cuéllar (1920–), Peruvian diplomat, 5th UN Secretary-General (1982–91), Prime Minister of Peru (2000–01).

Vienna. The UN has officially decided to do this. It is said that "Nuclear Arms: Threat to Our World" served as a catalyst for this.

In my ten-point proposal to the First Special Session devoted to Disarmament (SSOD-I) in 1978, I suggested that documents, photographs and films depicting the tragedy and cruelty of war, the destructive power of nuclear weapons, the realities of the Hiroshima and Nagasaki bombings and the present state of nuclear weapons be collected and displayed for all visitors to the United Nations. I also proposed that the UN establish a Peace Museum as a center dedicated to promoting the use of these materials throughout the world.[149] I appreciate and welcome the direction that the UN has taken toward this.

Currently, the world's existing nuclear warheads have more than a million times the destructive power of the bombs dropped on Hiroshima and Nagasaki. The greater the magnitude of destruction or numerical units of force, the more difficult it becomes for us to comprehend the extent of these weapons' destructive capability. Thus it is all the more essential today to call on people to remember the horror of Hiroshima and Nagasaki. Toward this end, we will continue international showings of "Nuclear Arms: Threat to Our World" this year to help shape public opinion against nuclear weapons and for disarmament.

"Nuclear Arms: Threat to Our World" Exhibition (1985)[150]

On the occasion of its tenth anniversary, I would like to take this opportunity to share the basic guiding principles of the SGI:

1. The members of the SGI shall contribute to the prosperity of their respective societies and countries as good citizens, respecting their individual cultures, customs and laws.

2. The members of the SGI shall aim for the realization of lasting peace and the development of humanistic culture and education based on Nichiren Buddhism, which expounds the fundamental sanctity of life.

---

149 Ikeda, Daisaku. 1978. "Zensekai shuno kaigi kaisai nado jukomoku no teisho [Ten Proposals Addressed Mainly to the World Summit Meeting]." *Seikyo Shimbun.* May 23, p. 1.

150 From 1985 Peace Proposal, "New Waves of Peace toward the Twenty-first Century."

3. The members of the SGI shall contribute to the well-being of humankind and the prosperity of the world while denying war and violence of
any kind. Toward this end, they shall aim to abolish nuclear weapons
and realize a world without war as the ultimate goals, supporting the
spirit of the Charter of the United Nations and the United Nations'
efforts to maintain world peace.

In order to actualize a world without war, there is no other way than to
bring together the collective strength of the people. Since 1982, the youth
members of the Soka Gakkai, in collaboration with the United Nations and
the cities of Hiroshima and Nagasaki, have taken the initiative to sponsor an
exhibition entitled "Nuclear Arms: Threat to Our World." In doing so, we
hope to help bring together the will of the people who oppose nuclear war and
wish to abolish nuclear weapons.

We have shown the exhibition in European cities since 1983—Geneva,
Vienna and Paris in 1983; Stockholm, Helsinki and Bergen in 1984; and
West Berlin this year—because we believe that easing of tensions in Europe
is urgently needed to ensure peace for the entire world. The exhibition has
attracted considerable attention in each venue. Fully aware of its significance,
I have given it my utmost support.

Hoping to bring together the wisdom of as many people as possible, I have
made sure that a Soka Gakkai delegation engages in exchanges with individuals working for peace and disarmament in various fields by organizing
disarmament seminars and other events concurrently with the exhibition. Last
year (1984), for example, this effort resulted in exchanges with Swedish Prime
Minister Olof Palme,[151] the chair of the Palme Commission.

This exhibition was first shown at the UN Headquarters in New York
on the occasion of the Second Special Session of the General Assembly on
Disarmament (SSOD-II) in June 1982. It has traveled to other countries in
response to requests from various cities around the world. It is scheduled to
be shown in China, the Soviet Union and other countries as part of our effort
to support the United Nations World Disarmament Campaign.

The exhibition has been highly regarded by the people of the countries where it was shown, UN personnel, experts and peace activists. UN

---

151 Sven Olof Palme (1927–86), Prime Minister of Sweden (1969–76, 1982–86),
Chair of the Independent Commission on Disarmament and Security Issues.

Secretary-General Javier Pérez de Cuéllar[152] informed me that he wished every ambassador, minister and diplomat attending the SSOD-II would see the entire exhibition. I hope that it will help create a broad surge of public opinion supporting nuclear disarmament toward the Third Special Session on Disarmament.

The significance of the exhibition does not lie in merely consolidating public opinion toward nuclear abolition. Today, the efforts of private organizations are becoming exponentially important for world peace. The importance of the role played by NGOs cannot be emphasized too much.

The exhibition could be considered a valuable example of successful cooperation for world peace between the UN and an NGO. I think it is also significant in that it reflects the will for peace shared by ordinary people everywhere, which is in complete accordance with the ideals of the Charter of the United Nations. The SGI will further develop the scope of its activities as an NGO beyond this exhibition to address various global issues.

I made proposals to the First and Second Special Sessions devoted to Disarmament (SSOD-I and SSOD-II) because the abolition of nuclear weapons is my fervent hope as a representative of a religious movement. It is also a reflection of my desire to support and protect the UN as the leader of the SGI as an NGO.

The Spirit of the "Declaration Calling for the Abolition of Nuclear Weapons" (1987)[153]

This year marks the thirtieth anniversary of the "Declaration Calling for the Abolition of Nuclear Weapons"[154] issued by second Soka Gakkai president Josei Toda[155] on September 8, 1957.

---

152 Javier Pérez de Cuéllar (1920–), Peruvian diplomat, 5th UN Secretary-General (1982–91), Prime Minister of Peru (2000–01).

153 From 1987 Peace Proposal, "Spreading the Brilliance of Peace toward the Century of the People."

154 Toda, Josei. 1981–90. *Toda Josei zenshu* [The Complete Works of Josei Toda]. 9 vols. Tokyo: Seikyo Shimbunsha. Vol. 4, pp. 564–66. (English text at http://www.joseitoda.org/vision/declaration.)

155 Josei Toda (1900–58), second president of the Soka Gakkai (1951–58).

In it, he declared the use of nuclear weapons to be an absolute evil and entrusted to the youth members of the Soka Gakkai the task of carrying out an antinuclear campaign, condemning any threat to humanity's right to life as "a devil incarnate, a fiend, a monster." Toda said that anyone who would use nuclear weapons was a devil incarnate in the Buddhist sense of a "robber of life" and denounced any attempt to justify the possession of nuclear weapons from the profound standpoint of Buddhism.

To review the world situation at the time, in January 1956, the year before Toda made his declaration, John Foster Dulles,[156] then United States secretary of state, announced a "brinkmanship" policy approving the role of atomic weapons in the West's defense against attack. In May of the same year, the United Kingdom conducted nuclear-explosion tests and the US exploded the first airborne hydrogen bomb over Bikini Atoll.

Confrontation between the United States and the Soviet Union became increasingly apparent in October 1956, when President Dwight D. Eisenhower[157] responded to the call by Soviet Premier Nikolay A. Bulganin[158] for a halt to nuclear testing by declaring it an attempt to interfere in the internal affairs of the United States. In May the following year (1957), the Soviet Union conducted a nuclear test and the UK tested its first hydrogen bomb on Christmas Island. During this period, the US conducted a series of such tests in Nevada.

At the same time, however, the antinuclear movement was gaining considerable momentum. The chemist and peace activist Linus Pauling[159] announced in June 1957 that he had collected 2,000 signatures of American scientists in a plea for the cessation of nuclear tests. The World Peace Council issued the Colombo Appeal calling for the immediate and unconditional halt of nuclear tests in the same month.

In August, however, the Soviet Union announced successful testing of an intercontinental ballistic missile (ICBM). In December, the US successfully launched an ICBM, the Atlas. With these developments, the nuclear arms race between the two nations grew increasingly intense.

---

156 John Foster Dulles (1888–1959), US Secretary of State (1953–59).

157 Dwight D. Eisenhower (1890–1969), 34th President of the United States (1953–61).

158 Nikolai Alekasandrovich Bulganin (1895–1975), Soviet Premier (1955–58).

159 Linus Pauling (1901–94), American scientist, recipient of the Nobel Prize in Chemistry in 1954 and the Nobel Prize for Peace in 1962.

Against this background of severe tensions between the East and West with enormous emphasis on nuclear weapons, Toda, who had a penetrating insight into the depths of this global crisis, perceived nuclear weapons as an absolute evil that threatened the human right to existence and emphasized the importance of spreading this message worldwide.

Why did he make the "Declaration Calling for the Abolition of Nuclear Weapons" his most important final instruction and bequest to youth? I would like to emphasize that this is where his profound insight and keen foresight lie.

Nuclear weapons are an absolute evil precisely because they are weapons of annihilation, of an apocalyptic nature that cannot and must not be considered an extension of conventional weapons. They require a completely different approach and way of thinking.

Surprisingly, few people were aware of this at the time. Many perceived the lethal and destructive powers of nuclear weapons as a mere extension of conventional weapons. Even in Japan, a nation that has suffered atomic bombing, phrases such as "clean nuclear bombs" and "nuclear experiments for peace" were unabashedly used without being questioned. People like Albert Einstein,[160] who stated, "the unleashed power of the atom has changed everything except our way of thinking,"[161] were in the minority.

Toda's philosophy had the powerful potential to fundamentally overturn traditional ways of thinking at the time. This is why his declaration continues to shine more brilliantly with time, while right- and left-wing ideological peace theories have faded, failing to withstand the test of time.

The American journalist Jonathan Schell[162] has the following to say about the nature of the threat of extinction that nuclear arms pose:

> Extinction is more terrible—is the more radical nothingness—because extinction ends death just as surely as it ends birth and life. Death is only death; extinction is the death of death.[163]

---

160 Albert Einstein (1879–1955), German-born American physicist, recipient of the Nobel Prize for Physics in 1921.

161 (qtd. in) *New York Times*. 1946. "Atomic Education Urged by Einstein." May 25, p. 13.

162 Jonathan Schell (1943–), American writer and editor.

163 Schell, Jonathan. 1982. *The Fate of the Earth*. New York: Alfred A. Knopf, p. 119.

"The death of death" exquisitely describes the deadly and apocalyptic nature of nuclear weapons. The landscape resulting from a full-scale nuclear war would be total bleakness, with corpse piled upon corpse, a world of noth-ingness. It is a world devoid of all meaning, where even the word nothing ceases to exist.

I would like to urge on this occasion marking the thirtieth anniversary of Toda's declaration that we continue to cry out its message, revealing the devilish nature of these weapons of annihilation, until his philosophy becomes the prevailing spirit of our time.

After Toda's passing, the Soka Gakkai carried out his instructions, devel-oping an extensive antiwar and antinuclear movement both in Japan and overseas. For example, in the period up to September 1974, we collected 10 million signatures calling for the abolition of war and nuclear weapons. In January of the following year, I visited the United Nations Headquarters in New York and personally delivered the petition to Kurt Waldheim,[164] Secretary-General at the time.

Our antinuclear weapons campaign is part of our movement toward a world completely free from war. In connection with this work, the youth and women of the Soka Gakkai have compiled ninety-six volumes of antiwar pub-lications, selected parts of which have been published in English, German, French and Romanian.

In 1982, we sent a delegation to the Second Special Session of the United Nations General Assembly devoted to Disarmament (SSOD-II). Building upon the antiwar and antinuclear exhibitions that had been shown in Japan, we held an exhibition entitled "Nuclear Arms: Threat to Our World" at the UN Headquarters and sponsored a symposium and panel discussion attended by survivors of the atomic bombings of Hiroshima and Nagasaki. On this occasion, my ten-point proposal for disarmament and the abolition of nuclear weapons was handed to UN Secretary-General Javier Pérez de Cuéllar.[165]

In coordination with the World Disarmament Campaign launched at the SSOD-II, we organized a worldwide tour of "Nuclear Arms: Threat to Our World," working together with the UN and the cities of Hiroshima and Nagasaki, and the exhibition attracted considerable attention. I am pleased

---

164 Kurt Waldheim (1918–2007), Austrian diplomat and statesman, 4th UN Secretary-General (1972–81), President of Austria (1986–92).

165 Javier Pérez de Cuéllar (1920–), Peruvian diplomat, 5th UN Secretary-General (1982–91), Prime Minister of Peru (2000–01).

that our youth division members have passionately taken the initiative in promoting it in an effort to carry out the spirit of Toda's declaration.

After being shown at the UN Headquarters, the exhibition traveled to Geneva, Vienna, Paris, Stockholm, Helsinki, Oslo, Bergen, West Berlin, Athens, Belgrade, Zagreb, New Delhi, Montreal and Toronto. In October of last year (1986), it was shown in Beijing, giving added impetus to the UN International Year of Peace. In June of this year, it is scheduled to open in Moscow, Russia, which will be the seventeenth city and fourteenth country in which it will have been seen. Furthermore, we hope to show it in Southeast Asia next year (1988).

I emphasize the significance of showing such an exhibition because I keenly feel the need to build up and bring together the will of the people of the world who, above all else, desire peace and the abolition of nuclear weapons. The issue of nuclear disarmament will determine the fate of all humanity. We cannot afford to stand by and watch where the discussions between the United States and the Soviet Union might go.

The time has come to develop a global network of public opinion to urge the two superpowers toward peace. It is my earnest hope that such a great surge of international public opinion against nuclear weapons will have an impact on the Third Special Session of the General Assembly devoted to Disarmament (SSOD-III).

A World Citizens' Charter (1988)[166]

Last year (1987), as a private citizen supporting the United Nations, I put forward a specific proposal for the establishment of a "UN Decade of Education for World Citizenship." It is of urgent necessity to educate as many people as possible to become world citizens in order to achieve lasting peace.

Such an educational program would cover comprehensively the most important themes humankind must grapple with today—the environment, development, peace and human rights. Each one of these topics requires citizens to have a global perspective that goes beyond the confines of national entities. The four themes are interrelated and must be studied together, as they all factor into the ultimate goal of securing peace for humanity.

---

166 From 1988 Peace Proposal, "Cultural Understanding and Disarmament: The Building Blocks of World Peace."

I would also suggest that a "World Citizens' Charter" be created as a basis for education for world citizenship. It would be a charter for comprehensive peace education dealing with the topics mentioned above. While people's awareness that they belong to one world is becoming widespread, that world is still mired in constant conflicts stemming from ethnic and religious confrontation.

The preamble of a "World Citizens' Charter" would embrace all people as citizens of the world from a universal point of view, calling on them to pursue peace and happiness for humanity—comparing cultural, religious, linguistic and other differences among peoples to the diversity in the species of vegetation rooted in the common soil of the Earth.

Needless to say, the standpoints of world citizenship and ethnic independence do not contradict each other. In today's world, it is fully possible to deepen one's own ethnic and cultural identities and to work toward a community of humanity with a global perspective at the same time.

President Richard von Weizsäcker[167] of West Germany has said that a person's humanistic attitude becomes truly convincing when he or she is a world citizen who is not without roots; tolerance blossoms, not where people become a rootless, universal amalgamation, but where they are aware of where they stand.[168] His argument that openness to the world and patriotism are not mutually opposed and his belief that an orientation toward world citizenship has become quite a common form of self-identification among Europeans are insightful.

From the standpoint of advocating human rights, I consider the Universal Declaration of Human Rights and the International Covenants on Human Rights to be of great significance. They are, however, the results of negotiations among sovereign states and lack a focus on the valuable role of NGOs and the threat of nuclear weapons and environmental destruction to people's right to life. They need to sufficiently reflect this focus.

---

167 Richard von Weizsäcker (1920–), President of the Federal Republic of Germany (1984–94).

168 See Bundesministerium der Finanzen (Federal Ministry of Finance). 1987. *Bulletin des Presse- und Informationsamtes der Bundesregierung* [Bulletin of the Press and Information Office of the Federal Government]. Bonn: Deutscher Bundes-Verlag, p. 1024.

The history of human rights shows that, as Karel Vasak[169] of UNESCO has pointed out, the first generation of human rights called for civil and political rights, and the second for economic, social and cultural rights. Today, the third generation of human rights is called for. They are, according to Vasak, "the right to development, the right to a healthy and ecologically balanced environment, the right to peace, and the right to ownership of the common heritage of mankind."[170]

The rights spelled out in the Universal Declaration of Human Rights are those demanded by the first and second generations of human rights; the rights to be called for in a "World Citizens' Charter" would encompass the third generation. The solid essence that runs through them would be the substantiation of the dignity of life rooted in our right to life.

The Preamble of the Charter of the United Nations speaks of "fundamental human rights" and "the dignity and worth of the human person."[171] The Preamble of the Universal Declaration of Human Rights deals with "the inherent dignity and the equal and inalienable rights of all members of the human family."[172] A "World Citizens' Charter" would clarify and further substantiate the dignity and worth of the individual as the sanctity of life from the standpoint of world citizenship. Thus, it would supplement and reinforce the Charter of the United Nations, the Universal Declaration of Human Rights and the UNESCO Constitution in such a way as to meet the needs of our era. This could be considered a product of efforts to open a way for the adoption of a "Universal Declaration Renouncing War."

For these reasons I urge that the Third Special Session of the UN General Assembly devoted to Disarmament (SSOD-III) be used as an opportunity to bring together the wisdom and sagacity of NGOs in a creative effort to bring a "World Citizens' Charter" to reality.

As humanity approaches the final years of the twentieth century, we should not be swayed by the many passing phenomena on the surface of history.

---

169 Karel Vasak (1929–), Czech-born French jurist, director of UNESCO's Division of Human Rights and Peace (1976–1980).

170 Vasak, Karel. 1977. "A 30-Year Struggle: The Sustained Efforts to Give Force of Law to the Universal Declaration of Human Rights" in *The UNESCO Courier.* Paris: UNESCO, p. 29.

171 UN (United Nations). 1945. "Preamble," in the "Charter of the United Nations."

172 UN (United Nations). 1948. "Preamble" in "Universal Declaration of Human Rights."

Rather, we should focus on the undercurrents that truly determine its course, the mighty currents of the will of the people. It is clear that the people are eagerly awaiting a world without war, a world of lasting peace.

A Special Session on Education (1990)[173]

To make the twenty-first century a century of hope, it is essential for humanity to continue the work of creating a global community without war. Equally essential is the development of human resources. We must renew our commitment to the work of education to bring out the inherent potential of people everywhere.

I applaud the accomplishments of the United Nations Educational, Scientific and Cultural Organization (UNESCO) and its efforts on the educational issues facing the world. The preamble of the Constitution of UNESCO emphasizes the importance of the education of humanity for justice, liberty and peace.[174] Based on this ideal, UNESCO has sponsored the World Congress on Disarmament Education.

UNESCO has made significant contributions to the promotion of disarmament and peace education amid the heightening of international tensions. But I believe that its work should no longer be confined to the areas of disarmament and peace. It is time for the United Nations as a whole to start working on global educational challenges in a way that truly serves the needs of the new era.

Here, I propose that the UN hold a first Special Session on Education.

There are two main reasons why I believe the UN needs to take the initiative in addressing educational issues on a global scope.

First, we are facing problems that must be resolved on a global scale, such as poverty, hunger, the population explosion and environmental destruction. They cannot be solved separately as isolated problems, but require a comprehensive solution from the standpoint of humanity as a whole. They call for a global consensus, and the role of education in forming this is crucial.

---

173 From 1990 Peace Proposal, "The Triumph of Democracy: Toward a Century of Hope."

174 UNESCO (United Nations Educational, Scientific and Cultural Organization). 1945. "Constitution of the United Nations Educational, Scientific and Cultural Organization."

The UN designated this year (1990) as the International Literacy Year. The world is still full of people who cannot read or write. Figures show that approximately 900 million people, or 30 percent of the world population of the age fifteen and over, are illiterate. The majority of these people are in Third World countries.

I recognize the importance of the UNESCO action plan aimed at eradicating illiteracy by the year 2000. But the real challenge goes far beyond the scope of learning how to read and write. We must find ways to bring forth the innate potential of the people who have been denied access to education and even the basic knowledge needed for survival, and enable them to join in the work of building a global community.

This is an extremely difficult and time-consuming endeavor that needs to be undertaken with much patience. Conventional top-down methods of development have not necessarily been able to generate sufficient momentum to solve educational problems. We need to powerfully advocate a bottom-up method of inner development by the people in order to elevate the strength of the entire global community toward the twenty-first century.

I believe in the inherent potential that the people possess. At the same time, education is essential if they are to awaken to it. We need individuals dedicated to undertaking this endeavor now. The true power of education is being put to test on a global scale.

World military expenditures have continued to expand during the postwar years. With the recognition that East–West tensions have reached the lowest level since the end of World War II, both the United States and the Soviet Union are moving in the direction of defense budget cuts. Much attention is currently being paid to the reallocation of a peace dividend from decreased military spending to the development of domestic economies.

According to a UN report, the additional expenditures needed to achieve the goal of ensuring all people of the world have access to food, water, basic health care and education are equivalent to approximately 5 percent of the world's annual military spending throughout the 1990s.

If a mere 5 percent cut is all that is needed, this is certainly a viable goal in light of expected progress in disarmament. I would like to propose that the UN collect part of the amount saved by the decrease in military spending as a contribution to an education development fund to be used effectively for the Third World.

In Japan, Japan Overseas Cooperation Volunteers (JOCV) is actively providing assistance to developing countries. Here, I propose the creation of a "UN Educational Cooperation Volunteers," an international cooperation organization modeled after the JOCV but with the focus on education. It would be entirely possible to bring together human resources from different countries with financing by an education development fund.

The second reason I believe a Special Session on Education is necessary is the need to promote education for global citizenship. I have proposed that the 1990s be designated a UN Decade of Education for World Citizenship. This would involve a comprehensive program covering the most urgent challenges for humanity: the environment, development, peace and human rights.

An awareness of things from a global perspective is becoming more widespread. But conflicts caused by racial, ethnic and religious confrontations are still rampant throughout the world. I urge that a Special Session on Education be held as soon as possible, enabling the UN to launch a full-fledged campaign for education for world citizenship and to encourage people to think globally and see the Earth as our shared home.

Disarmament and Nonproliferation Education (2005)[175]

In 2001, United Nations Secretary-General Kofi Annan[176] appointed a working group of governmental experts from ten countries. The product of their deliberations, the "United Nations Study on Disarmament and Non-Proliferation Education," was submitted and adopted at the fifty-seventh session of the General Assembly in 2002.[177]

The importance of disarmament education gained prominence at the First Special Session of the United Nations General Assembly devoted to Disarmament (SSOD-I) in 1978. In a ten-point proposal written on the occasion of that session, I called for the promotion of disarmament education at the grassroots level, highlighting the significance of activities to inform the general public in a concrete and compelling manner of the atrocity of war and the horrors of nuclear weapons.

---

175 From 2005 Peace Proposal, "Toward a New Era of Dialogue: Humanism Explored."

176 Kofi Annan (1938–), Ghanaian statesman, 7th Secretary-General of the United Nations (1997–2006).

177 UNGA (United Nations General Assembly). 2002. "United Nations Study on Disarmament and Non-Proliferation Education." A/57/124. Report of the Secretary-General. August 30.

In 1982, the UN launched a ten-year World Disarmament Campaign. Leading up to it, the SGI launched the exhibition "Nuclear Arms: Threat to Our World" in June of the same year at the UN Headquarters in New York in collaboration with the UN Department of Public Information (UNDPI) and the cities of Hiroshima and Nagasaki. The exhibition toured the world, visiting nuclear powers and countries of different social systems and ideologies, and was seen by an estimated 1.2 million people.

After the Cold War ended, we continued to organize exhibitions such as "War and Peace: From a Century of War to a Century of Hope" and an updated antinuclear exhibition, "Nuclear Arms: Threat to Humanity," bringing people together in their shared yearning for peace and generating momentum toward a world without war.

In 1998, the exhibition "Linus Pauling and the Twentieth Century" was launched. It introduces the life and ideas of Dr. Pauling[178] and pays homage to his contribution to peace and humanitarian causes. It has been shown in the United States, Japan and several European countries, and visited by more than a million people. The Pauling exhibition has been very well received. Jayantha Dhanapala,[179] then UN Under-Secretary-General for disarmament affairs, commented that the exhibit's concept of disarmament education concurs with that of the UN reflected in a resolution of the General Assembly in 2000. It was also mentioned in the UN Secretary-General's report on disarmament and nonproliferation education submitted to the General Assembly last year (2004).[180]

It is precisely because emerging threats such as terrorism have increased instability in the world that the international community must make a united effort to set our world securely on a path toward peace. Disarmament and nonproliferation education can play a vital role in this.

In his foreword to the report mentioned above, Secretary-General Annan noted, "It is striking for someone of my generation to think that an entire new

---

178 Linus Pauling (1901–94), American scientist, recipient of the Nobel Prize in Chemistry in 1954 and the Nobel Prize for Peace in 1962.

179 Jayantha Dhanapala (1938–), Sri Lankan diplomat, UN Under-Secretary-General for Disarmament Affairs (1998–2003), President of the Pugwash Conferences on Science and World Affairs (2007–).

180 UNGA (United Nations General Assembly). 2004. "Disarmament and Nonproliferation Education." A/59/178. Report of the Secretary-General. July 23, p. 18.

generation of human beings is coming to maturity without an ever present terror of nuclear catastrophe."[181] He went on to warn against the dangers of allowing ignorance and complacency about disarmament issues to take root among the younger generation.

Indeed, should this happen, no amount of treaty language will be enough to solidify a genuine trend toward peace. In that sense, I think that we need to actively incorporate disarmament and nonproliferation into school education.

One of the recommendations in the Secretary-General's 2004 report calls for participatory lesson plans based on "case studies that encourage students to think critically and to undertake specific follow-up actions to bring about positive global change."[182] It also recommends adding peace studies programs to college and university curricula.

Complementing school education are efforts to raise awareness in every part of society. For our part, the SGI will persevere in activities to promote disarmament and nonproliferation education. In this, we draw courage from the "Declaration Calling for the Abolition of Nuclear Weapons" issued by the Soka Gakkai's second president, Josei Toda,[183] which he declared was foremost among his instructions to his successors.[184]

Grassroots Education for Disarmament (2006)[185]

I would like to stress the importance of disarmament education as a means of transforming the paradigms of society to move from a culture of war characterized by conflict and confrontation to a culture of peace based on cooperation and creative coexistence.

---

181 UNGA (United Nations General Assembly). 2002. "United Nations Study on Disarmament and Non-Proliferation Education." A/57/124. Report of the Secretary-General. August 30, p. 4.

182 UNGA (United Nations General Assembly). 2004. "Disarmament and Non-proliferation Education." A/59/178. Report of the Secretary-General. July 23, p. 26.

183 Josei Toda (1900–58), second president of the Soka Gakkai (1951–58).

184 Toda, Josei. 1981–90. *Toda Josei zenshu* [The Complete Works of Josei Toda]. 9 vols. Tokyo: Seikyo Shimbunsha. Vol. 4, pp. 564–66. (English text at http://www.joseitoda.org/vision/declaration.)

185 From 2006 Peace Proposal, "A New Era of the People: Forging a Global Network of Robust Individuals."

Last year (2005), the world twice missed the opportunity to mark the sixtieth anniversary of the atomic bombing of Hiroshima and Nagasaki with positive progress on nuclear disarmament: first, in the lack of results from the Nuclear Non-Proliferation Treaty (NPT) Review Conference in May, and then in the failure to make any mention of nuclear weapons in the outcome document of the World Summit at the United Nations General Assembly in September.

Amidst fiercely divided opinion over the relative merits of nuclear disarmament versus nonproliferation, the Review Conference achieved no substantive progress; in fact the Conference could not even agree upon a chairman's summary, let alone a consensus document. This conflict of opinion persisted at the World Summit, with the result that all references to nuclear disarmament and nonproliferation were deleted from the outcome document.

This twofold failure is all the more tragic in light of the following three disturbing trends identified by the International Atomic Energy Agency (IAEA) Director General Mohamed ElBaradei[186]—the emergence of a nuclear black market, the determined efforts by more countries to acquire technology to produce the fissile material usable in nuclear weapons, and the clear desire of terrorists to acquire weapons of mass destruction.[187] The danger posed by nuclear weapons has cast deep shadows over the international community, highlighting the fact that the world's disarmament efforts stand at an absolutely critical juncture.

This can be attributed in part to a lack of political will, but also significant is the absence of a strong groundswell of world opinion calling for disarmament. While there is an urgent need to bolster the international legal framework, for example by resuscitating the NPT regime, at the same time the public must raise their voices. In concrete terms this will require a fundamental change in people's attitudes, which can be realized through peace and disarmament education. In recent years the UN has come to recognize this, and in 2002 the General Assembly adopted an expert report on the issue, "The United Nations Study on Disarmament and Non-Proliferation Education."[188]

---

186 Mohamed ElBaradei (1942–), Egyptian lawyer and government official, Director General of the International Atomic Energy Agency (IAEA) (1997–2009).

187 ElBaradei, Mohamed. 2005. "Statements of the Director General: Seven Steps to Raise World Security." *Financial Times*. February 2, p. 13.

188 UNGA (United Nations General Assembly). 2001. "General and Complete Disarmament." A/RES/55/33. Resolution adopted by the General Assembly. January 12, p. 8.

In my view, the crucial need is for a radical change in ideas and a search for new approaches. Rallying public opinion to the cause of disarmament requires not just experts or those already involved in the peace movement, but people from all walks of life. Rather than concentrating on the technical and physical facts of disarmament, there needs to be a revolutionary transformation in the way people think about peace, so that it is felt as an immediate and personal reality.

Peace is not simply the absence of war. A truly peaceful society is one in which everyone can maximize their potential and build fulfilling lives free from threats to their dignity. As a practical initiative, I believe we must fully integrate disarmament education, in this expanded sense I have described, into the International Decade for a Culture of Peace and Non-Violence for the Children of the World (2001–10), and develop activities to this end throughout civil society.

The basis for these initiatives must be a shift in our frame of reference from national to human sovereignty. Disarmament education needs to be a grassroots movement that helps to raise world citizens who are firmly committed to the interests of humankind and the planet and to strengthen the solidarity among them. In this sense, disseminating knowledge and information about disarmament should not be an end in itself: Our greatest priority should be changing people's mind-set and behavior so that they are grounded in a culture of peace.

For our part, the SGI has sponsored exhibitions such as "Building a Culture of Peace for the Children of the World," and last year we opened Culture of Peace Resource Centers within our SGI-USA centers in New York and Los Angeles to support this effort. Next year, to mark the fiftieth anniversary of the call made by Josei Toda,[189] second president of the Soka Gakkai, for the abolition of nuclear weapons, we will promote peace activities at the community level throughout the world as we seek to transform the global culture from one of war to one of peace.

A transformation in the inner life of a single individual can spur and encourage similar changes in others, and as this extends into society, it generates a powerful vortex for peace that can steadily shape the direction of events. The collective impact of "ordinary citizens," awakened and empowered, can propel humankind toward the twin goals of genuine disarmament and a flourishing culture of peace.

---

189 Josei Toda (1900–58), second president of the Soka Gakkai (1951–58).

It was one of my great pleasures to have met and held in-depth discussions with Dr. Joseph Rotblat,[190] emeritus president of the Pugwash Conferences on Science and World Affairs, who sadly passed away last year. I will never forget one of the remarks he shared with me on ridding the world of nuclear weapons, ridding the world of war:

> When a small stone is thrown into a pond, the ripples travel widely out from the center. Though the ripples may become less powerful, they still do not completely disappear. Every person has the power to create ripples that can change society. If these efforts are concentrated and channeled through NGOs, inevitably the power to influence society will grow. . . . If we unite, we can change the world. It might take some time, but viewed from a long-term perspective, the people will be victorious in the end.

This solidarity of awakened citizens for which Dr. Rotblat had such great hopes is what drives the SGI's movement of Buddhist humanism in 190 countries and territories. The next five years to 2010 are a critical opportunity; with courage and hope we look forward to working with like-minded people around the world to build the foundations of a global society of peace and creative coexistence.

Nuclear Disarmament

A Peace Summit of Nuclear Powers (1987)[191]

At the summit meeting held in Reykjavík, Iceland, last year (1986), US President Ronald Reagan[192] made a bold proposal to eliminate all strategic nuclear missiles within ten years. In response, General Secretary of the Central

---

190 Sir Joseph Rotblat (1908–2005), British physicist and philanthropist, founding member (1957), Secretary-General (1957–73) and President (1988–97) of the Pugwash Conferences on Science and World Affairs.

191 From 1987 Peace Proposal, "Spreading the Brilliance of Peace toward the Century of the People."

192 Ronald Reagan (1911–2004), 40th President of the United States (1981–89).

Committee of the Communist Party of the Soviet Union Mikhail Gorbachev[193] proposed the elimination of all nuclear weapons including strategic bombers and cruise missiles. The two leaders approached agreement but, unfortunately, failed in the end to realize it because of their disagreement over restrictions on the United States Strategic Defense Initiative (SDI).

Although this turn of events showed how deep-rooted the conflicts of opinion were over SDI, the fact remains that the United States and the Soviet Union came very close to agreeing on the ultimate goal of the abolition of nuclear weapons. The top leaders of the two nations have never come so close to a successful disarmament treaty since the end of World War II. There still remain many hurdles to be overcome before a final agreement can be reached. But what the Reykjavík meeting impressed on me was, rather than its negative aspects, the fact that disarmament negotiations are indeed possible.

I have consistently stressed the need for US–Soviet summit meetings. I feel compelled to take this opportunity to urge once again that the leaders of the two countries meet as soon as possible to engage in dialogue to boldly break through the current deadlock.

Last September (1986), I met with Dr. Henry A. Kissinger,[194] former US Secretary of State, in Tokyo. He said that the significance of the US–Soviet summit meeting lies in the fact that it reflected the desire of the people of both countries as well as of all peoples around the world, and particularly in that it would serve as a means to advance the prospects for peace.

I agree with his view. I have long believed that if the United States and the Soviet Union were to reach a groundbreaking nuclear disarmament agreement, the next step would be to hold a peace summit meeting among the nuclear powers: the United States, the United Kingdom, France, the Soviet Union, China and India.

I am fully aware that the current situation does not hold out entirely optimistic prospects. After the failure of the Reykjavík Summit, the Strategic Arms Limitation Treaty II (SALT II) was virtually ignored, and the Soviet Union unilaterally announced its intention to resume nuclear testing, overshadowing relations between the United States and the Soviet Union. The

---

193 Mikhail Gorbachev (1931–), General Secretary of the Communist Party of the Soviet Union (1985–91), President of the Soviet Union (1990–91), recipient of the Nobel Prize for Peace in 1990.

194 Henry Kissinger (1923–), US Secretary of State (1973–77), recipient of the Nobel Prize for Peace in 1973.

most serious problem is that there is a deep-seated sense of distrust between the two nations. Such distrust, however, does not have to be permanent.

In an address delivered in June 1963 at the American University in Washington DC, President John F. Kennedy[195] stated:

> History teaches us that enmities between nations, as between individuals, do not last forever. However fixed our likes and dislikes may seem, the tide of time and events will often bring surprising changes in the relations between nations and neighbors.[196]

I completely agree. We may remind ourselves that relations between the United States and China, once considered mortal enemies, underwent a dramatic change only recently.

In order to reduce hostilities and bring about a dynamic transformation in relations among nations, we need to continue tenacious efforts on the grassroots level. Even a drastic reduction of nuclear weapons would not solve all the problems facing us. The important thing is to turn back the tide of militarization that is engulfing the world and strengthen the currents of global disarmament and detente. The resources made available by these efforts should then be redirected toward the solution of such complex global problems as environmental destruction, the population explosion, hunger and the refugee crisis.

The world's annual arms expenditure continues to increase year by year and is estimated to stand at US$900 billion today. It is now widely recognized that the vast sums spent on military expansion bear heavily on the economy and obstruct its sustained growth in nations around the world. This problem affects not only the United States and the Soviet Union; Third World countries are shackled by it as well.

Humanity has bitter experience of the price of militarization. During the Great Depression of the 1930s, military expansion was adopted as a strategy to reduce unemployment and stimulate the economy. The expansion in armaments during World War II is believed to have helped the US overcome the Great Depression. But increased militarization on the part of one nation will always set up a chain reaction in which other nations follow suit. And this

---

195 John F. Kennedy (1917–63), 35th President of the United States (1960–63).
196 Kennedy, John F. 1963. "Commencement Address at American University." June 10.

in turn can lead to territorial conflicts and even world war. We must remind ourselves of this bitter lesson of history.

The myth that increased military expenditure stimulates the economy and has positive effects still persists today. As we all know, there has recently been a rapid military buildup in the US in seeming disregard of its experience during the Vietnam War. Many experts point out that this is bearing heavily on the American economy and causing a fiscal deficit and other negative effects.

Authoritative studies have revealed that increased military spending hinders the sound growth of the world economy as a whole. One such is the analytical research headed by Prof. Akira Onishi[197] at the Soka University Institute of Applied Economics and its world-economy model.[198]

Analysis based on this model has shown the impact of the US and Soviet arms race on their own economies and on the world economy. According to this model, if we assume the two superpowers fail to reach agreement on nuclear arms reduction and tensions continue to grow, with the US military budget rising at an annual rate of 2 percent from 1986 onward, the nation's real Gross National Product (GNP) will have grown by no more than 0.5 percent by the year 2000. Long-term interest rates will have risen by 3 percent, the fiscal deficit will have grown by 7.4 percent, and the trade deficit will have increased by 2.4 percent: there are considerable negative impacts.

On the other hand, if we assume that progress is made in nuclear reduction negotiations between the US and the Soviet Union, resulting in global disarmament and the US defense budget being frozen at 1986 levels, growth in real GNP of 12.9 percent may be expected in the US by the year 2000. These figures show how much the domestic economy would benefit by merely freezing military spending at present levels, with half of the extra money that would have been spent on military purposes directed toward domestic economic development and the other half toward official development aid to developing countries.

---

197 Akira Onishi (1929–), Professor of Economics at Soka University, Tokyo (1971–2002).

198 See Onishi, Akira. 1986. "Impacts of the Arms Race and Global Disarmament on the World Economy, 1986–2000, Using the FUGI (Future of Global Independence) Model." Paper prepared for the Conference on the Global Human Family Looking at the 21st Century. Seoul, Korea. September.

Similar calculations show that if the Soviet military budget were frozen at the current level, the nation could expect 9.9 percent growth in real GNP by the year 2000—an encouraging prediction. Especially noteworthy is the projection that arms reductions could lead to increased official development aid, substantially raising real GNP in developing countries.

This world model takes into account the workings of the US–Soviet arms race. The US increases its military budget in response to increases in Soviet spending from the previous year, only to have the Soviet Union respond in the same manner. A continued US–Soviet arms race can only expand military spending, perpetuating a scenario of mutual retaliation. The model also shows that the situation could dramatically improve if tensions were to be reduced.

These studies clearly indicate that the world is now standing at a crossroads between the destructive path of continued military buildup and the bold shift to disarmament to better people's lives. Choosing the former to expand armaments of massive lethal force including nuclear weapons can only lead to economic exhaustion.

A sensible aversion to the arbitrary increase of defense budgets is beginning to spread among US citizens. Demand for disarmament would also exist naturally among Soviet citizens, whose economy is suffering from chronic stagnation.

The nations of the world are becoming increasingly interdependent. If they work together in a concerted effort toward disarmament—making détente an irreversible process throughout the world—the outlook for the twenty-first century would be much brighter.

Four years ago (1983), I stressed in my peace proposal the need for international consensus on a determination not to expand our already huge military expenditures any more, including expenditures on conventional weapons. In this connection, I urged that an international conference on the freezing of military spending be held immediately.

Many developed countries continue to export weapons to developing countries, which are struggling with enormous accumulated deficits. Restrictions need to be imposed on arms exports to developing countries to solve this situation. In addition to placing a freeze on military expenditures, countries could take the funds freed as a result of progress toward disarmament and redirect them to enhancing and promoting the well-being of humanity. For example, they could be pooled to set up a development fund for the welfare and better livelihood of the people in developing countries, or to create an educational fund for promoting peace education in countries around the world.

These were some of the ideas behind my proposal for such an international conference.

The relationship between disarmament and the stability and prosperity of the world economy is one of the central themes the SGI has focused on. In "Nuclear Arms: Threat to Our World," an exhibition we organized and launched in 1982, one of the three pillars was the issue of disarmament and development.

Based on the belief that peace and human rights are inseparable in today's world, we have supported the activities of the Office of the United Nations High Commissioner for Refugees (UNHCR) and have been actively promoting refugee relief efforts through the initiatives of the Soka Gakkai Youth Peace Conference. We will continue our firm involvement in these activities to protect basic human rights and human dignity.

It is predicted that the refugee problem could become even graver in the future. It is essential that we develop a global early warning system to alert on possible refugee crises, as well as promoting comprehensive policies for development and refugee relief. It would be most appropriate to allocate the funds made available by disarmament to efforts to eradicate global problems such as hunger and poverty.

The Third Special Session of the General Assembly devoted to Disarmament (SSOD–III) is scheduled to be held next year (1988). It is our earnest hope to use this as an opportunity to achieve a breakthrough for establishing a global wave of disarmament toward the twenty-first century.

To develop a surge of public opinion throughout the world toward this end, I propose that next year be designated an "International Year of Disarmament" by the consensus of the United Nations. I urge that Japan, with its constitution upholding the renunciation of war, take the initiative in this endeavor.

Reform of the Conference on Disarmament (2002)[199]

Encouraging disarmament is an important systemic means to help prevent the escalation and spread of conflict. In recent years, there has been a heightened sense of the need to create a truly effective nonproliferation regime for nuclear, chemical and biological weapons of mass destruction—whose possible use

---

199 From 2002 Peace Proposal, "The Humanism of the Middle Way: Dawn of a Global Civilization."

by terrorists has become a matter of grave concern. As one means to create a breakthrough toward thoroughgoing and effective disarmament efforts, I strongly urge reform of the rules by which the Geneva-based Conference on Disarmament (CD) operates.

Since the CD evolved from the Ten-Nation Committee on Disarmament established in 1960, it has undergone various changes in nomenclature and constituent membership. But throughout, it has, as the sole multilateral body for disarmament negotiations, contributed to the realization of a number of important disarmament conventions, among them the Treaty on the Non-Proliferation of Nuclear Weapons (NPT), the Biological Weapons Convention (BWC) and the Chemical Weapons Convention (CWC). Since the adoption of the 1996 Comprehensive Nuclear Test Ban Treaty (CTBT), however, the CD has failed to produce any concrete results, and at present is unable even to agree on an agenda for the next round of disarmament negotiations.

In order to get beyond this deadlock, I would like to propose a change in the consensus rule, which requires unanimous agreement among all partici-pants to a negotiation. This rule is the single most distinctive feature of the CD; at the same time, because it gives each country an effective veto, it is the single greatest factor in its present deadlocked state.

As one reform measure, in August of last year, Japan informally proposed the partial introduction of a majority vote, whereby procedural issues could be decided by a two-thirds majority. If it is felt that "majority rules" voting is not appropriate for deciding substantive security issues, the alternative of "consensus minus one"—used by the World Trade Organization (WTO), in which the consensus of the whole is recognized as overriding a single dis-senting vote—might be considered. Unless some action is taken to reform the procedures by which the CD operates, it runs the risk of becoming irrelevant. Some measures must be taken to keep negotiations from bogging down even before they have begun. Procedures that facilitate agreement on the broad outlines of negotiating themes, with details worked out in subsequent talks, will prove far more productive.

Any effort in this direction, because it represents a major change in the standing traditions of the CD, is certain to raise objections. But the time has come, in my view, to give serious attention to the kinds of reform that will reprioritize concrete progress toward disarmament.

It is essential to reenergize efforts in the field of nuclear disarmament. Since September 11, 2001, there has been increasing anxiety about the pos-sible use of nuclear weapons by terrorists. Nobel Peace laureate Sir Joseph

Rotblat[200] of the Pugwash Conferences is among those to have expressed his concern.

The International Atomic Energy Agency (IAEA) has adopted a resolution urging that effective steps be taken to prevent the illicit use of nuclear material and to protect various nuclear facilities against terrorist attack. At the UN, there is ongoing debate on an international convention for the suppression of acts of nuclear terrorism. It is important to raise international public opinion in support of the earliest possible adoption of such a treaty.

But the nuclear threat is not limited to terrorism. Indeed, preventing the further spread of nuclear weapons and making further progress toward nuclear disarmament is literally a life-or-death issue for humankind in the twenty-first century.

In December 2001, the United States and Russia fulfilled their obligations under the Strategic Arms Reduction Treaty I (START I) by reducing the number of nuclear warheads to 6,000 each. However, no concrete schedule for further nuclear disarmament has been established. In 2000, the sixth Review Conference of the Treaty on the Non-Proliferation of Nuclear Weapons (NPT) unanimously adopted a final declaration that included an "unequivocal undertaking by the nuclear-weapon States to accomplish the total elimination of their nuclear arsenals."[201] It was not possible, however, to reach agreement on concrete steps toward this goal or set a time limit by which it must be achieved.

The efforts of the New Agenda Coalition, led by a group of seven non-nuclear-weapon states and supported by a network of NGOs, were crucial in pushing the nuclear-weapon states to make this "unequivocal undertaking."[202] In order to keep moving forward, we must further strengthen the network of global popular opinion to press the nuclear-weapon states to implement this commitment in good faith.

---

200 Sir Joseph Rotblat (1908–2005), British physicist and philanthropist, founding member (1957), Secretary-General (1957–73) and President (1988–97) of the Pugwash Conferences on Science and World Affairs.

201 UN (United Nations). 2000. "2000 Review Conference of the Parties to the Treaty on the Non-Proliferation of Nuclear Weapons: Final Document." NPT/CONF.2000/28 (Parts I and II). Vol. I, p. 14.

202 Ibid.

In 1957, the second president of the Soka Gakkai, Josei Toda,[203] called for the abolition of all nuclear weapons. His call was based on the Buddhist appreciation for the sanctity of life, from which perspective nuclear weapons must be condemned as an absolute evil. As heirs to this spirit, the SGI has worked to spread and strengthen popular solidarity for nuclear abolition. These activities have included the international traveling exhibition "Nuclear Arms: Threat to Our World" and support for the Abolition 2000 signature campaign. The members of the SGI are determined to continue and accelerate their efforts toward the adoption of a treaty for a comprehensive ban on all nuclear weapons.

A UN Special Session on Nuclear Disarmament (2003)[204]

Together with the Treaty on the Non-Proliferation of Nuclear Weapons (NPT), the other core element of nuclear arms limitation is the Comprehensive Nuclear Test Ban Treaty (CTBT). Regrettably, the CTBT has still not entered into force more than six years after it was adopted in 1996.

A proposal has been floated whereby the treaty would provisionally enter into force when a certain number of states have ratified it, at which point the system of international monitoring of nuclear tests would begin.[205] To prevent any further loss of momentum toward nuclear disarmament, I believe this proposal should be given all possible consideration.

Heading toward the 2005 NPT Review Conference, one issue that is essential in ensuring the nonproliferation of nuclear weapons is the control of ballistic missiles. I would like to call for the International Code of Conduct against Ballistic Missile Proliferation (ICOC), adopted in November 2002, to be given legally binding status.

At the same time as strengthening the formal framework for nuclear arms nonproliferation, I would also like to strongly advocate to the nuclear-weapon states that they make specific efforts to open the path toward the reduction and elimination of nuclear arms. [. . .]

---

203 Josei Toda (1900–58), second president of the Soka Gakkai (1951–58).

204 From 2003 Peace Proposal, "A Global Ethic of Coexistence: Toward a 'Life-Sized' Paradigm for Our Age."

205 See Miyamoto, Yuji. 2002. "Beikoku no 'ikkokushugi' to Nihon no kakugunshuku seisaku" [American Unilateralism and Japanese Nuclear Disarmament Policy]. *Ronza*. April, pp. 120–29.

In view of the fact that 2005 marks the sixtieth anniversary of the dropping of atomic bombs on Hiroshima and Nagasaki, I propose that a special session of the UN General Assembly, attended by the world's heads of state and government, be dedicated to the cause of nuclear abolition.

Not since the Third UN Special Session devoted to Disarmament (SSOD-III) fifteen years ago has there been an opportunity for a truly global discussion of the problem of nuclear abolition. In May of last year (2002), the US–Russia Strategic Offensive Reductions Treaty (the Moscow Treaty) was agreed upon as the replacement for the Anti-Ballistic Missile (ABM) Treaty. This bilateral agreement is now the only international framework for disarmament; there is no broader multilateral treaty in existence that would promote concrete reductions in the world's nuclear arsenals.

Surely it is time for us to take earnest and concrete steps to realize a world without nuclear weapons in this new century. We must confront head-on this issue on which the fate of all humanity hangs.

I have for some time been calling for the adoption of a treaty for the comprehensive ban of all nuclear weapons. As a first step toward this, I would like to urge the nuclear-weapon states to use such a special session to make progress toward negotiating a nuclear disarmament treaty. This would be a fulfillment of the "unequivocal undertaking by the nuclear-weapon States to accomplish the total elimination of their nuclear arsenals leading to nuclear disarmament"[206] made in the final document of the 2000 NPT Review Conference three years ago.

Further, I would encourage this special session to discuss the establishment at the UN of a new specialized agency dedicated to ensuring the strict and effective implementation of the nuclear disarmament pledged in Article VI of the NPT back in 1968: "Each of the Parties to the Treaty undertakes to pursue negotiations in good faith on effective measures relating to cessation of the nuclear arms race at an early date and to nuclear disarmament, and on a treaty on general and complete disarmament under strict and effective international control."[207]

---

206 UN (United Nations). 2000. "2000 Review Conference of the Parties to the Treaty on the Non-Proliferation of Nuclear Weapons: Final Document." NPT/CONF.2000/28 (Parts I and II). Vol. I, p. 14.

207 UN (United Nations). 1968. "Treaty on the Non-Proliferation of Nuclear Weapons (NPT)." Article VI.

The Toda Institute for Global Peace and Policy Research is a body that takes its inspiration from the dedication to peace of Josei Toda,[208] second president of the Soka Gakkai, who declared that nuclear weapons are an absolute evil, threatening the right to life of all humanity. During the lead-up to the NPT Review Conference in 2005, the Toda Institute will be involved in a research project, in cooperation with other research institutes from around the world, in support of nuclear disarmament and the abolition of nuclear weapons.

An International Nuclear Disarmament Agency (2005)[209]

This year (2005) is the sixtieth anniversary of the atomic bombings of Hiroshima and Nagasaki, the only times nuclear weapons have been used in war. It is also the fiftieth anniversary of the Russell–Einstein Manifesto, an international appeal for nuclear abolition.

Only one of the eleven signatories to this manifesto is still alive—Nobel Peace laureate and emeritus president of the Pugwash Conferences on Science and World Affairs, Dr. Joseph Rotblat.[210] Preparations are currently under way for the publication of a serialized dialogue between Dr. Rotblat and myself. In our conversations, he expressed deep concern over the lack of any substantial progress in nuclear disarmament. He also deplored new nuclear development programs initiated by the nuclear powers despite the "unequivocal undertaking by the nuclear-weapon States to accomplish the total elimination of their nuclear arsenals leading to nuclear disarmament" made in the Final Document of the 2000 Review Conference of the Parties to the Treaty on the Non-Proliferation of Nuclear Weapons (NPT).[211]

Addressing the fifty-fourth Pugwash Conference in October 2004, Dr. Rotblat warned that "the proliferation of nuclear weapons cannot be stopped while the Nuclear Weapons States arrogate to themselves the possession of

---

208 Josei Toda (1900–58), second president of the Soka Gakkai (1951–58).

209 From 2005 Peace Proposal, "Toward a New Era of Dialogue: Humanism Explored."

210 Sir Joseph Rotblat (1908–2005), British physicist and philanthropist, founding member (1957), Secretary-General (1957–73) and President (1988–97) of the Pugwash Conferences on Science and World Affairs.

211 UN (United Nations). 2000. "2000 Review Conference of the Parties to the Treaty on the Non-Proliferation of Nuclear Weapons: Final Document." NPT/CONF.2000/28 (Parts I and II). Vol. I, p. 14.

nuclear weapons and refuse to enter into comprehensive negotiations towards elimination. . . ."[212]

I fully concur. Even if the undertaking in the Final Document is not legally binding, it reflects the consensus of the states party to the NPT, and acts that disregard it risk undermining the very foundation of the NPT framework and accelerating trends toward nuclear proliferation.

The 2005 NPT Review Conference is scheduled for May this year. I strongly urge the five declared nuclear-weapon states, which are also the permanent members of the UN Security Council, to promptly begin building the framework for disarmament, reminding themselves of the course of events that led to the indefinite extension of the NPT ten years ago.

Over recent years, nonproliferation issues have been continuously taken up as a critical challenge at summit meetings. The G8 Action Plan on Nonproliferation, aimed at preventing illicit diversion of nuclear materials and technology, was adopted at the Sea Island Summit in 2004.[213]

Effective measures to reduce arms made in good faith by the nuclear powers are essential in order for efforts such as the G8 Action Plan and the US-led Proliferation Security Initiative to be seen by the international community as convincing and credible, and to inspire the broad-based cooperation needed if they are to succeed.

For many years, negotiations on reduction of nuclear stockpiles took the form of bilateral talks between the US and the Soviet Union or Russia. With the recent stagnation of this process, however, I think we need to step away from this approach and begin a new multilateral disarmament process.

The fact that for a long while we have had no prospect of reducing or eliminating nuclear arsenals heightens the danger of proliferation—not only of nuclear arms but of other weapons of mass destruction—with a resultant increase in military tensions.

Nuclear nonproliferation and nuclear disarmament are inseparable; when they are advanced in tandem, our world will make important strides toward peace and stability. Just as nuclear nonproliferation efforts are monitored by the International Atomic Energy Agency (IAEA), I believe we need an international nuclear disarmament agency, a specialized agency to oversee

---

212 Rotblat, Sir Joseph. 2004. "Response by Professor Sir Joseph Rotblat." Speech at 54th Pugwash Conference on Science and World Affairs. Seoul. October 4–9.
213 G8. 2004. "G8 Action Plan on Nonproliferation." June 9.

fulfillment of the "unequivocal undertaking by the nuclear-weapon States to achieve the total elimination of their nuclear arsenals" referred to above.

Progress on negotiating the Fissile Material Cut-off Treaty (FMCT) at the Conference on Disarmament has been at a standstill for many years now. We need to revive this process, urging India and Pakistan—which came to possess nuclear weapons outside the NPT—as well as Israel to join, thus engaging them in international regimes for the control of weapons-grade nuclear materials.

Toward Nuclear-Free Security (2007)[214]

The nuclear weapons test conducted last year (2006) by North Korea, together with its ongoing missile development program, has been perceived as a severe threat by neighboring countries, including Japan. Despite global condemnation expressed in repeated United Nations resolutions, North Korea has shown little inclination to abandon its nuclear development program. Although the stalemated Six-Party Talks evidenced some signs of progress since the start of this year, it is impossible to view the prospects with unreserved optimism.

Uncertainties regarding the nuclear intentions of Iran, meanwhile, are made all the more disturbing by surrounding regional conflicts and the unforeseeable results if a nuclear arms race were set off. And there is profound concern about the prospect that nuclear weapons might fall into the hands of terrorists through illicit international supplier networks, unleashing destruction on an unimaginable scale.

It is the regrettable reality that we have entered the twenty-first century burdened by the existence of 27,000 nuclear warheads. Thus, while it is only natural that world opinion urge North Korea and Iran to refrain from developing nuclear weapons, to focus criticism solely on these countries lacks balance. Much of the responsibility for the current situation must be laid at the feet of the states already possessing nuclear weapons.

The Treaty on the Non-Proliferation of Nuclear Weapons (NPT) obliges the nuclear-weapon states to take good faith measures toward nuclear disarmament. However, no progress in this direction can be discerned, and there are even concerns that the NPT will become a dead letter. It is therefore vital

---

214 From 2007 Peace Proposal, "Restoring the Human Connection: The First Step to Global Peace."

that these states take the lead in reaffirming their commitment to the spirit of the NPT, as well as the related Comprehensive Nuclear Test Ban Treaty (CTBT).

Every five years, a Review Conference is held among the states party to the NPT. However, the 2005 Conference held in New York was effectively paralyzed by the sharply conflicting positions of the nuclear-weapon and non-nuclear-weapon states.

"The current crisis is the worst that I have seen in the entire history of the treaty,"[215] Dr. Joseph Rotblat[216] told me in our dialogue, and he urged the nuclear-weapon states in particular to reengage in good faith in the NPT process. His words demand our attention, coming as they do from a man who dedicated his entire adult life to nuclear disarmament and who was the last surviving signatory of the Russell–Einstein Manifesto.

We can never lose sight of the fact that any effective movement toward general nuclear disarmament must be predicated on the good-faith efforts of those who already possess these weapons. Without such actions on the part of the nuclear-weapon states, there is little to deter those who would ignore the outrage of the international community and seek to acquire nuclear weapons for the prestige they are thought to confer.

Albert Einstein[217] declared in 1946, "The unleashed power of the atom has changed everything except our way of thinking. . . ."[218] Indeed, we need a fundamental reconfiguration of our worldview, to one based on a vision of and commitment to the human future, if we are to move away from nuclear proliferation and toward disarmament.

Einstein was clearly a visionary, and there are those who would argue that his words, while prophetic, are difficult to apply to reality. However, it would seem that even those widely regarded as realists have begun to recognize the need for the kind of paradigm shift that Einstein called for. Evidence for this can be seen in the editorial "A World Free of Nuclear Weapons" recently

---

215 Rotblat, Joseph and Daisaku Ikeda. 2006. *A Quest for Global Peace: Rotblat and Ikeda on War, Ethics and the Nuclear Threat.* London: I.B.Tauris, p. 15.

216 Sir Joseph Rotblat (1908–2005), British physicist and philanthropist, founding member (1957), Secretary-General (1957–73) and President (1988–97) of the Pugwash Conferences on Science and World Affairs.

217 Albert Einstein (1879–1955), German-born American physicist, recipient of the Nobel Prize for Physics in 1921.

218 (qtd. in) *New York Times.* 1946. "Atomic Education Urged by Einstein." May 25. p. 13.

carried in *The Wall Street Journal,* coauthored by George P. Shultz,[219] William J. Perry,[220] Henry A. Kissinger[221] and Sam Nunn[222]:

> Nuclear weapons today present tremendous dangers, but also an historic opportunity. US leadership will be required to take the world to the next stage—to a solid consensus for reversing reliance on nuclear weapons globally as a vital contribution to preventing their proliferation into potentially dangerous hands, and ultimately ending them as a threat to the world.[223]

Without the kind of shift alluded to in this editorial, it will be difficult to extract ourselves from the quagmire logic of deterrence, which is rooted in mistrust, suspicion and fear.

The challenging politics of nuclear disarmament are indeed, to borrow the words of Max Weber,[224] a process of "slow, strong drilling through hard boards, with a combination of passion and a sense of judgment."[225] But the energy released by a reconfiguration in our fundamental way of thinking can fuel the persistent exertion required.

***

Against this backdrop, at the Symposium on International Safeguards held in Vienna last October (2006), International Atomic Energy Agency (IAEA) Director General Mohamed ElBaradei[226] stressed that, without a new international or multinational approach to the fuel cycle, between twenty and

---

219 George P. Shultz (1920–), US Secretary of State (1982–89).

220 William J. Perry (1920–), US Secretary of Defense (1994–97).

221 Henry A. Kissinger (1923–), US Secretary of State (1973–77), recipient of the Nobel Prize for Peace in 1973.

222 Sam Nunn (1938–), American statesman, Co-chairman and CEO of Nuclear Threat Initiative (NTI) (2001–).

223 Shultz, George P., William J. Perry, Henry A. Kissinger and Sam Nunn. 2007. "A World Free of Nuclear Weapons." *The Wall Street Journal.* January 4, A. 15, Eastern edition.

224 Max Weber (1864–1920), German sociologist.

225 Weber, Max. 1930. *The Protestant Ethic and the Spirit of Capitalism.* Trans. by Talcott Parsons. London: George Allen and Unwin, p. 369.

226 Mohamed ElBaradei (1942–), Egyptian lawyer and government official, Director General of the International Atomic Energy Agency (IAEA) (1997–2009).

thirty more nations, what he called "virtual nuclear weapon States," would emerge with "the capacity to develop nuclear weapons in a very short span of time."[227] Unless measures are taken to counter this alarming trend, the NPT will be further undermined and the nuclear weapons crisis will continue to escalate.

I would therefore like to propose a strengthening of the structures within which members of the international community can identify a shared sense of purpose and work in concert to fulfill their responsibilities. This would not require a totally new framework. What I am calling for is a recasting—on the basis of a new conceptual outlook—of the obligations set out under the NPT which, with 189 signatories, constitutes the world's most universally accepted arms control agreement.

The Preamble to the NPT opens with the words: "Considering the devastation that would be visited upon all mankind by a nuclear war and the consequent need to make every effort to avert the danger of such a war and to take measures to safeguard the security of peoples. . . ."[228] To this end, I wish to stress the importance of all nations, regardless of whether or not they possess nuclear weapons, working as equals to achieve "the security of peoples" without a reliance on nuclear weapons. We must advance together toward the ultimate goal of banning nuclear weapons through a treaty similar to those already in place outlawing chemical and biological weapons.

In the light of this clarified shared sense of purpose, the respective responsibilities for the achievement of nuclear-free security become clear: for the nuclear-weapon states to actively pursue nuclear disarmament, and for the non-nuclear-weapon states to work together to prevent nuclear proliferation.

The report "Weapons of Terror" released last June by the Weapons of Mass Destruction Commission, an independent group of international experts chaired by former IAEA Director General Hans Blix[229] (widely referred to as the Blix Commission), offered a number of suggestions as to how such security could be achieved.

---

227 ElBaradei, Mohamed. 2006. "Addressing Verification Challenges." Statement of the IAEA Director General at Symposium on International Safeguards. October 16.

228 UN (United Nations). 1968. "Treaty on the Non-Proliferation of Nuclear Weapons (NPT)."

229 Hans Blix (1928–), Swedish diplomat, Director General of the International Atomic Energy Agency (IAEA) (1981–2007).

The report stresses the following:

> So long as any state has nuclear weapons, others will want them.
> So long as any such weapons remain, there is a risk that they will
> one day be used, by design or accident. And any such use would
> be catastrophic. . . . The Commission rejects the suggestion that
> nuclear weapons in the hands of some pose no threat, while in the
> hands of others they place the world in mortal jeopardy.[230]

This rejection of the notion of deterrence mired in fear and suspicion
coincides with the thinking behind the unequivocal condemnation of nuclear
weapons as an absolute evil expressed by second Soka Gakkai president Josei
Toda.[231]

Obviously, the issues surrounding the nuclear development programs of
North Korea and Iran need to be addressed individually and with all speed.
At the same time, preventing the reemergence of such issues in the future
will require a change in awareness across the whole of the international community. To facilitate this, I advocate the early convening of a world summit
or a special session of the UN General Assembly to initiate debate and seek
consensus toward the goal of global nuclear-free security.

The first tasks of such a gathering would be to bolster the international
frameworks for each of the three pillars of the NPT—to prevent the spread of
nuclear weapons, foster nuclear disarmament and promote cooperation in the
peaceful uses of nuclear energy—and to adopt a declaration in which all countries would pledge to fulfill their shared responsibility for the achievement
of nuclear-free security for all. Such a declaration should serve as the starting
point for the nations of the world to earnestly strive toward the ultimate
NPT objective of "the cessation of the manufacture of nuclear weapons, the
liquidation of all their existing stockpiles, and the elimination from national
arsenals of nuclear weapons and the means of their delivery"[232]—in other
words, toward the abolition and outlawing of nuclear weapons.

---

230 WMDC (Weapons of Mass Destruction Commission). 2006. "Weapons of
     Terror: Freeing the World of Nuclear, Biological, and Chemical Arms."
     Stockholm, Sweden: WMDC, p. 60.
231 Josei Toda (1900–58), second president of the Soka Gakkai (1951–58).
232 UN (United Nations). 1968. "Treaty on the Non-Proliferation of Nuclear
     Weapons (NPT)."

I would here like to make some specific suggestions and proposals to support the transition to nuclear-free security. The first group concerns the need to boost momentum toward nuclear disarmament.

At present, under the Moscow Treaty on Strategic Offensive Reductions signed by the United States and Russia on May 29, 2002, the two countries each pledge to reduce their stockpile of strategic nuclear warheads to a level of 1,700–2,200 by the end of the year 2012. However, this treaty does not include a provision for the complete elimination of all warhead stockpiles.

As the next step, therefore, I appeal strongly to the United States and Russia to reduce their strategic missile stockpiles to a few hundred warheads, and conclude a new bilateral treaty in which they commit to the complete elimination of these stockpiles, thus positioning themselves as leaders of the global effort toward nuclear disarmament.

Furthermore, they should work, in accordance with their obligation for nuclear disarmament set out in Article VI of the NPT, for the adoption of a new nuclear disarmament treaty that would include all states possessing nuclear weapons, whether signatories to the NPT or not.

Since last September, the United States and Russia have been discussing the outlines of a follow-up inspection and verification regime to take the place of the Strategic Arms Reduction Treaty (START I) set to expire in 2009. Likewise, the British nuclear weapon systems will reach the end of their service life in the mid-2020s, and there was debate last year on the question of renewing these systems. I believe such turning points should provide an opportunity for forward-looking steps toward nuclear disarmament on the part of all the nuclear-weapon states—not for upgrading nuclear arsenals or developing new weapons.

To this end, I would like to propose the formation within the UN of an international nuclear disarmament agency to coordinate negotiations for a nuclear disarmament treaty. This body should have powers of inspection to ensure that, once in effect, such a treaty is properly implemented.

Momentum in this direction is already building. For the last two years, the Article VI Forum—consisting of states and NGOs advocating nuclear disarmament—has been calling for negotiations to fulfill the obligation of nuclear disarmament stipulated in Article VI of the NPT, and to examine the legal, political and technical elements required for a nuclear-weapon-free world.

To encourage such initiatives, I would like to repeat the call I made in my UN proposal last year (2006) for the declaration of a decade of action by the world's people for nuclear abolition. In particular, I urge Japan, a nation that has experienced the nightmare of nuclear attack, to stand at the forefront of efforts to make such a decade come about, coalescing international society around the cause of nuclear disarmament and abolition, and thus contributing to a transformation in the direction of human history.

The need for widespread popular engagement with disarmament issues is stressed in the Blix Commission report, which notes:

> WMD [weapons of mass destruction] constitute challenges not just for governments and international organizations. Research communities, nongovernmental organizations, civil society, businesses, the media and the general public share ownership of the WMD challenges. They must all be allowed and encouraged to contribute to solutions.[233]

In my view, this is where young people can play a leading role. For our part, the SGI will continue to work with other NGOs and with UN programs and agencies in promoting disarmament education, harnessing the power and passion of youth to energize and expand the network of citizens seeking to rid the world of nuclear weapons.

In addition, to mark the fiftieth anniversary of Josei Toda's "Declaration Calling for the Abolition of Nuclear Weapons,"[234] the Toda Institute for Global Peace and Policy Research, which I founded to give institutional form to his vision, is planning an international conference on nuclear abolition to be held in San Francisco in September. The findings of this conference will be compiled into a report for distribution to the UN and national governments, in the hope that this will stimulate further discussion on the path toward nuclear-free security.

My second group of proposals concerns measures to prevent the further spread of nuclear weapons. We must first work to ensure that the Comprehensive Nuclear Test Ban Treaty (CTBT) enter into force at the earliest possible stage. Since its adoption by the General Assembly in 1996, the

---

233 WMDC (Weapons of Mass Destruction Commission). 2006. "Weapons of Terror: Freeing the World of Nuclear, Biological, and Chemical Arms." Stockholm, Sweden: WMDC, p. 29.

234 Toda, Josei. 1981–90. *Toda Josei zenshu* [The Complete Works of Josei Toda]. 9 vols. Tokyo: Seikyo Shimbunsha. Vol. 4, pp. 564–66. (English text at http://www.joseitoda.org/vision/declaration.)

CTBT has remained in limbo because some countries whose ratification is required for it to enter into force, including the United States, have failed to do so. As a result, doubts have been cast on the ultimate practicability of the CTBT.

However, its moral force alone has had a definite inhibiting effect, as indicated by the absence of nuclear testing in the past few years. Not only have the five permanent members of the UN Security Council, all nuclear-weapon states, declared moratoriums on nuclear testing, but so have India and Pakistan as well. As a result, until North Korea conducted its test last October, there had been no testing of nuclear weapons during the eight-year period from 1998.

Even if entry into force is not an immediate prospect, surely we should be looking for ways to move the CTBT toward full operation, such as bringing it into force provisionally upon ratification by a specified number of nations.

We also need a stronger institutional framework to prevent the diversion of programs for the peaceful use of atomic energy into the development of nuclear weapons.

Last September, the IAEA held a Special Event on Assurances of Nuclear Supply and Non-Proliferation, coinciding with its annual General Conference in Vienna. The meeting examined proposals for multilateral cooperation under IAEA auspices to guarantee a supply of nuclear fuel for peaceful applications. The IAEA will now start work formulating recommendations for such a scheme, aiming for adoption at the meeting of the Board of Governors. I strongly urge states to look beyond their narrow interests to reach consensus on the most effective system for preventing further proliferation of nuclear weapon development capabilities.

I also call for debate at summits and other forums on "no first use" pledges by nuclear-weapon states and further formalization of negative security assurances, by which such states pledge to neither launch nor threaten to launch nuclear strikes against non-nuclear-weapon states. Such measures could help transform the international climate regarding the desirability of nuclear weapons, reducing the number of potential nuclear aspirants. Negative security assurances are particularly vital to securing the effectiveness and integrity of nuclear-weapon-free zones (NWFZs).

Last September, five nations—Kazakhstan, Kyrgyzstan, Tajikistan, Turkmenistan and Uzbekistan—signed the Central Asia Nuclear-Weapon-Free Zone Treaty. The treaty prohibits the development, production or possession of nuclear weapons within the region, and is the world's sixth treaty establishing an NWFZ, following agreements covering the Antarctic, Latin America, the South Pacific, Southeast Asia and Africa.

Of special note is the important supporting role played by the UN leading up to the signing of this treaty. It is to be hoped that the UN can build on this to offer support for similar treaty negotiations in the future, especially in cases where discussions limited solely to the states concerned face difficulties. This must be part of our shared search for modalities of nuclear-free security, and at the same time will delegitimize the possession or threatened possession of nuclear weapons as an extension of state diplomacy.

There are several historical precedents to demonstrate that the development or even possession of nuclear weapons is neither fixed nor irreversible. Canada, for example, took part in the Manhattan Project, but courageously relinquished the option to produce nuclear weapons; Brazil and Argentina abandoned their nuclear weapon development programs; and South Africa dismantled its nuclear weapons and joined the ranks of the non-nuclear-weapon states.

Then there is the example of Ukraine, which inherited a massive stockpile of nuclear weapons on the breakup of the Soviet Union, yet chose to give up these weapons in exchange for security guarantees and economic assistance from the US, Russia and elsewhere. Ukraine's experience has been cited as one model for tackling the problem of nuclear weapon development by North Korea.

Ultimately, however, I believe that the only way to resolve the outstanding problem surrounding the nuclear programs of North Korea and Iran is, through processes of dialogue, to rid the regions in question entirely of nuclear weapons: in other words, for Northeast Asia and the Middle East to become nuclear-weapon-free zones. Otherwise, even if countries abandon their nuclear weapon development programs, there will always be the danger these will be restarted due to a change in the international climate or a turnaround in national policy.

I would next like to discuss the question of the complete demilitarization of space, a pressing issue for the long-term prospects for world peace.

Principles governing the peaceful use of space are set down in the Outer Space Treaty. However, while this treaty does prohibit all military use of the moon and other celestial bodies, it does not clearly define the limits on the use of other parts of space, and in recent years there have been growing calls to extend and enhance its scope to respond to advances in military technology.

This year marks forty years since the Outer Space Treaty entered into force: What better opportunity to launch an intensive review and debate on the scope and content of the treaty?

The Blix Commission recommends a complete ban on the deployment of weapons in outer space, universal adherence to the Outer Space Treaty, expansion of the scope of the treaty and a ban on testing of space weapons.

For my part, I urge that a broad-based panel be formed to discuss the demilitarization of space under the auspices of the UN Secretary-General, charged with devising specific measures and drawing broad international attention to the issue.

Regional Nuclear Disarmament

Expansion of Nuclear-Weapon-Free Zones (1995)[235]

To chart a firm course toward a world without war, we must address the problem of weapons, including nuclear weapons. Especially this year, which marks the fiftieth anniversary of the bombing of Hiroshima and Nagasaki, we should renew our commitment to moving forward toward the realization of humanity's earnest desire for the abolition of nuclear arms.

Recently, we have at long last begun to see some positive developments on the horizon with regard to the nuclear problem. One is the decision by Ukraine to formally sign the Treaty on the Non-Proliferation of Nuclear Weapons (NPT). Another is the long-awaited implementation of the First Strategic Arms Reduction Treaty (START I) between the United States and the former Soviet Union. Also, the United States and Russia are expected to ratify the START II Treaty and proceed with nuclear dismantlement once the treaty goes into effect. Finally, the United Nations General Assembly's formal adoption of the nuclear disarmament resolution, which takes the unprecedented step of calling for the total abolition of nuclear weapons, marks another significant development.

This spring (1995), the UN will meet to reevaluate the NPT, which came into effect twenty-five years ago. The treaty's purpose was twofold: to prevent

---

235 From 1995 Peace Proposal, "Creating a Century without War through Human Solidarity."

the spread of nuclear weapons to countries that do not currently possess them (horizontal proliferation) and to prevent existing nuclear powers from expanding their arsenals (vertical proliferation).

The existing nuclear powers have been slow to reduce their stockpiles, however, and for this reason, many of the non-nuclear signatories have expressed reluctance to approve an indefinite extension of the treaty. In their view, things should not be allowed to become fixed in their present state. Article VI of the treaty requires all signatories to adopt effective measures to achieve nuclear arms reduction and to pursue complete overall disarmament in good faith. At the upcoming meeting, the nuclear powers should clarify how they plan to do away with their nuclear weapons, and commit themselves to implementing those plans.

One important step toward a phased ban on nuclear weapons is the expansion of nuclear-weapon-free zones (NWFZs). Generally, such zones are defined by the following two restrictions: 1) no country within the zone can engage in testing, manufacturing or acquiring nuclear weapons; and 2) no country outside the zone is allowed to test, deploy or use nuclear weapons, or to make nuclear threats, within the zone. To date, nuclear-weapon-free zones have been established in Latin America and the Caribbean (under the Treaty for the Prohibition of Nuclear Weapons in Latin America, Tlatelolco) and in the South Pacific (under the South Pacific Nuclear Free Zone Treaty, Rarotonga). Other areas that could potentially become nuclear-weapon-free zones include the member nations of the Association of Southeast Asian Nations (ASEAN) and of the Organization of African Unity (OAU).

Nuclear-weapon-free zones require two parallel agreements: one among nations within the zone, and one with nations outside. Without the latter, no zone can be meaningfully realized. It is crucial that we have an international framework to gain accession of outside powers to such agreements.

Currently, the NPT is the most workable framework we have. Article VII stipulates the following: "Nothing in this Treaty affects the right of any group of States to conclude regional treaties in order to assure the total absence of nuclear weapons in their respective territories."[236] This approach is too passive, however, and the provision should be amended to promote the expansion of nuclear-weapon-free zones.

---

236 UN (United Nations). 1968. "Treaty on the Non-Proliferation of Nuclear Weapons (NPT)." Article VII.

Another international framework is bilateral agreements, but a shift should be made toward multilateral negotiations that will seek to place nuclear weapons under the supervision of the United Nations. Our final goal should be to conclude a treaty that bans nuclear weapons.

Bilateral negotiations inevitably get hung up on the concept of deterrence, which makes it extremely difficult to attain ultimate abolition. Even if both parties agree to reduce the number of weapons in their stockpiles, such accords are unable to halt qualitative improvement through technological development. Thus, in substantive terms, the magnitude of the threat and the destructive power involved are not reduced at all. I believe that nuclear weapons should be dealt with in the same way as biological and chemical weapons, with treaties that forbid their manufacture, possession and use.

Denuclearization of the Middle East and Northeast Asia (1997)[237]

International society, as we have seen, is very gradually moving in the direction of disarmament. Some important steps forward were made in 1996 in the area of nuclear weapons.

One of these was the signing of the Comprehensive Nuclear Test Ban Treaty (CTBT) banning tests and other detonations of nuclear weapons. Its adoption—by an overwhelming majority in the United Nations General Assembly in September 1996 after an arduous process of deliberation—has been criticized because it permits testing by computer simulation not accompanied by nuclear explosions, thereby allowing possessor countries to maintain and improve their nuclear weapons capabilities. But I believe it is still quite significant as a clear indication that nuclear testing is banned by international law, compared with the complete lack of any kind of constraint that prevailed before.

Nevertheless, no clear date has yet been set for the entry into force of the CTBT. In order for it to come into effect, it is required that forty-four nations stipulated as possessing or suspected of possessing nuclear weapons ratify the treaty. These include a few countries that have yet to indicate they will sign, which means the treaty could hang in limbo for some time.

237   From 1997 Peace Proposal, "New Horizons of a Global Civilization."

It is the common understanding in international society that signatories to a treaty should not engage in actions in violation of its intent or purposes (see, for example, Article 18 of the Vienna Convention on the Law of Treaties[238]) even before it goes into effect. I therefore believe that the CTBT, which has been signed by most of the requisite countries, including the five major nuclear powers, already serves a substantial restraining role in international society.

In that sense, it is important to take further steps toward disarmament building on the lessons learned through the problems that were not over-come in the CTBT, particularly in the area of consensus building toward a conscious commitment to disarmament among the nuclear nations. Ways must be found to overcome the matter of "quality," where the CTBT fell short, by setting in place firmer measures to put a stop to the main-tenance and improvement of nuclear arms capabilities by nuclear nations. In order to address the problem of "quantity," efforts have to be made to ensure the actual reduction of the numbers of existing nuclear weapons. One focus should be the early signing of the Fissile Material Cut-off Treaty (FMCT) that would prohibit the production of radioactive material used to manufacture nuclear weapons. Talks on this treaty are expected to be difficult, but because agreement is indispensable in order to prevent the further proliferation of nuclear weapons that is the basic premise of nuclear disarmament, the nuclear-weapon states are duty-bound to work toward an early consensus.

Another area of effort is to create the environment for actual reduction of nuclear arms. The Strategic Arms Reduction Treaty negotiations between the United States and Russia are bogged down by the latter's unwillingness to ratify START II. I urge the two countries to break through this prolonged stalemate in talks so that they can proceed to plans for implementing START II, and immediately proceed with START III talks to lay the groundwork for the next stage of disarmament negotiations among all the nuclear powers—including the United Kingdom, France, and China.

Efforts have been going on for a long time among the non-nuclear-weapon states to establish nuclear-weapon-free zones. In addition to the Tlatelolco Treaty in Latin America and the Rarotonga Treaty in the Southern Pacific region, the Southeast Asia Nuclear-Weapon-Free Zone Treaty (the Bangkok

---

238 UN (United Nations). 1969. "Vienna Convention on the Law of Treaties."

Treaty) was signed in December 1995, and in April 1996 the Pelindaba Treaty was signed in Africa. If the Antarctic Treaty is included, these treaties realize the establishment of nuclear-weapon-free zones stretching over the entire terrestrial area of the southern hemisphere and large portions of the southern part of the northern hemisphere.

As demonstrated by the documents adopted at the Review Conference held for reexamination and extension of the Treaty on the Non-Proliferation of Nuclear Weapons (NPT) in 1995, global and regional peace and security can be strengthened through the establishment of nuclear-weapon-free zones, and I believe it is important to encourage this concept in other areas such as the Middle East and Northeast Asia in order to expand nuclear-weapon-free zones even further.

At the same time, in order to make effective the nuclear-weapon-free zones that have been set up already, the guarantees and cooperation of the nuclear-weapon states are indispensable. The signing of a supplementary protocol to the Rarotonga Treaty in March last year by the United States, United Kingdom and France created a structure for the cooperation of all the five major nuclear powers. In the same way, it is hoped that the nuclear-weapon states will show readiness to pledge such cooperation for the other treaties as well.

I believe it is also urgent to conclude treaties guaranteeing the non-nuclear-weapon states that they will not be subject to nuclear attack and prohibiting the preemptive use of nuclear arms. Given the success in concluding the NPT and the CTBT, it is all the more important that the nuclear-weapon states show their commitment by taking the initiative in furthering negotiations toward the conclusion of such treaties. At the very least it will be a significant step toward eliminating the inequality between the nuclear haves and have-nots.

Indeed, the voices of those who seek a world without nuclear arms have risen to the point where the members of the nuclear club must listen. They can no longer afford to act only with their own interest in mind.

In July 1996, the International Court of Justice (ICJ) issued its Advisory Opinion on the Legality of the Threat or Use of Nuclear Weapons. The efforts of NGOs in the adoption of the December 1994 UN General Assembly resolution seeking this opinion are now widely recognized. While the opinion avoided judgment regarding the use of nuclear arms for self-defense, its statement that "the threat or use of nuclear weapons would generally be contrary to the rules of international law applicable in armed conflict, and in particular the principles and rules of humanitarian law,"[239] is significant indeed. The ICJ opinion also stressed the justices' unanimous opinion that the nuclear nations are obligated to work conscientiously toward nuclear disarmament. It is notable that this point was made as an expression of opinion of the Court itself, not in response to a question from the UN General Assembly.

I believe that the vigorous debate around the world that has unfolded concerning the illegality of nuclear weapons as a result of this statement is truly momentous. Even though, like resolutions adopted by the UN General Assembly, the ICJ's Advisory Opinion does not hold legal binding power, I believe it will have a strong moral and political impact in the creation of a consensus in international society aimed at the abolition of nuclear arms. Indeed, in the debate in the UN General Assembly concerning adoption of the CTBT, a number of countries cited the ICJ's Advisory Opinion, suggesting that it has contributed to a new rationale upon which to pursue the goal of disarmament. [. . .]

As these developments show, the world is steadily moving in the direction of a nuclear-weapon-free world. In order to strengthen that trend, I urgently call on people to discard the kind of thinking that calls the existence of nuclear arms a "necessary evil" for the sake of protecting the "national interest," and embrace the conviction that "the interests of humankind" take precedence over all, making use of nuclear weapons an "absolute evil," whatever the reason.

Departure from the Nuclear Umbrella (1999)[240]

The international community has already adopted treaties and conventions banning such weapons of mass destruction as biological and chemical weapons as well as antipersonnel land mines. As of yet, however, no international disarmament regime is in place for restricting small arms such as automatic rifles and small-caliber artillery on the one hand or, on the other end of the scale, nuclear weapons.

There are too many small arms everywhere. Following up on the proposal I made last year (1998), I again urge the creation of suitable restrictions. Some progress has been made in this area. In December 1998, the UN General

---

239 ICJ (International Court of Justice). 1996. "Legality of the Threat or Use of Nuclear Weapons, Advisory Opinion." *I.C.J. Reports. 1996.* July 8, p. 264.
240 From 1999 Peace Proposal, "Toward a Culture of Peace: A Cosmic View."

Assembly passed a resolution urging that an international conference to restrict the availability of small arms be held by 2001.

But little progress has been made in nuclear disarmament. Nearly ten years have passed since the end of the Cold War, but more than 30,000 nuclear warheads still exist on the face of the Earth. No progress has been made either in the ratification of the Strategic Arms Reduction Treaty (START) between the United States and Russia or in negotiations to reduce other kinds of nuclear armament.

Since the indefinite extension of the Treaty on the Non-Proliferation of Nuclear Weapons (NPT) in 1995, the only additional progress has been the August 1998 decision by the Geneva Conference on Disarmament (CD) to begin negotiating a treaty cutting off production of weapons-grade fissile materials.

In May 1998, India and Pakistan shocked the international community by conducting nuclear tests, thereby signaling their decision to develop their own nuclear arms. In doing so, they rocked the regime founded on the Comprehensive Nuclear Test Ban Treaty (CTBT) and the NPT to its foundations. The international community's failure to convince India and Pakistan to refrain from such testing exposes the limitations of a one-sided deterrence doctrine that can be used only by the nuclear-weapon states. There is now a clear danger that other countries may rush to join the nuclear club.

The US has recently announced its intention of using a civilian nuclear energy plant to produce tritium for the military. Tritium is one of the materials used in nuclear warheads. By taking this step, the US has abandoned its once hard-and-fast principle of separating military from civilian uses of nuclear energy. This, it must be said, demonstrates the arrogance of nuclear-weapon states and casts doubts on the sincerity of US disarmament rhetoric.

Against this background, in June 1998, eight non-nuclear-weapon states—Brazil, Egypt, Ireland, Mexico, New Zealand, Slovenia, South Africa and Sweden—issued a joint declaration calling on the five nuclear powers and the nuclear-capable powers like India, Pakistan and Israel, to undertake disarmament and nonproliferation measures. These same eight non-nuclear-weapon states submitted to the UN General Assembly a draft resolution entitled "Toward a Nuclear-Weapon-Free World: Time for a New Agenda," which was adopted in December 1998.[241] This resolution makes more concrete proposals

---

241 UNGA (United Nations General Assembly). "General and complete disarmament." A/RES/53/77. Resolution adopted by the General Assembly.

than anything yet adopted by the United Nations. For example, it emphasizes the nuclear powers' responsibilities in the area of disarmament and calls for the elimination of all nonstrategic nuclear weapons, the lifting of the state of war-readiness and the issuance of a "no first use" pledge.

The eight countries—often referred to as the New Agenda Coalition—have renounced the possession of nuclear weapons and reliance on the defensive umbrellas of nuclear powers. For this reason, their agenda has earned the support of many other non-nuclear-weapon states. In particular, Sweden, Brazil and South Africa have the experience of having abandoned nuclear weapons development programs. The coalition's proposal is rooted in the realistic assessment expressed in the words of Fernando Henrique Cardoso,[242] president of Brazil:

> We do not want an atomic bomb. It only generates tension and distrust in our region and it would annul the integration process which we are permanently strengthening for the well-being of our people.[243]

In July 1998, six South American countries—Argentina, Bolivia, Brazil, Chile, Paraguay and Uruguay—signed a protocol renouncing the right of belligerency within their region and outlawing weapons of mass destruction. They agreed never to resort to military force to resolve tensions such as border disputes. They renounced the possession of or research on nuclear, biological and chemical weapons and promised to expel militaristic or totalitarian states from the South American common market (MERCOSUR).

By forming "a zone of peace," these countries are taking steps to increase trust and confidence within their region, thus reducing the temptation for any of them to go nuclear or to place themselves under the "umbrella" of a nuclear-weapon state. This is in keeping with the point I made earlier when I said that generating regional trust is the surest way to halt weapons proliferation.

Nuclear-weapon-free zones have been established in Latin America, the South Pacific, Africa and Southeast Asia, demonstrating the way a growing number of regions are renouncing their reliance on nuclear weapons.

---

242 Fernando Henrique Cardoso (1931–), President of Brazil (1995–2003).
243 (trans. from) Cardoso, Fernando Henrique Cardoso. Quoted in 1998. *Yomiuri Shimbun*. September 2.

The time has come for countries like Canada, Norway, the Netherlands and Japan, which have strongly advocated nuclear disarmament, to declare their departure from the nuclear umbrella and to support the New Agenda Coalition, which already enjoys popular support such as that which NGOs have mustered behind the Middle Powers Initiative. I believe that if popular movements and governments supportive of disarmament join together—as they did in the Ottawa Process responsible for the realization of the land mine treaty—great strides can be made toward ridding the world of nuclear weapons.

In 1957, in his declaration against nuclear weapons, Josei Toda[244] described them as an absolute evil that deprives humanity of its right to exist. Since that time, the Soka Gakkai has consistently worked for the abolition of nuclear weapons. In 1997 and 1998, thanks mainly to the efforts of our youth membership, we combined efforts with NGOs like the Nuclear Age Peace Foundation in collecting signatures for the Abolition 2000 petition.

A model Nuclear Weapons Convention (NWC) has already been drafted, setting forth step-by-step, verifiable methods for prohibiting and eliminating nuclear weapons. It is my sincere hope that this draft convention, now an official UN document, will serve together with the proposals of the New Agenda Coalition as the basis for evolving an Ottawa Process for nuclear weapons abolition.

Disarmament negotiations must not be left entirely in the hands of the nuclear-weapon states. It is vitally important for all such plans to reflect the popular will and the views of the non-nuclear-weapon states. To support such efforts, the Toda Institute for Peace and Policy Research has conducted international conferences dealing with concrete policies and schedules for nuclear abolition.

The criticism may be advanced that no mechanism for the process can be meaningful without the participation of all the nuclear-weapon states. On the other hand, only some of the nuclear-weapon states were involved in the initial stages of formulating the NPT, but consistent effort eventually resulted in the participation of all five nuclear powers plus states thought to be nuclear-capable, as well as those which had tested but later renounced nuclear weapons. As this process suggests, taking the initiative in working on

---

244 Josei Toda (1900–58), second president of the Soka Gakkai (1951–58).

a treaty can encourage nuclear-weapon states and their allies to free themselves from their dependence.

The American philosopher Ralph Waldo Emerson[245] wrote: "It is really a thought that built this portentous war-establishment, and a thought shall also melt it away."[246] If we make Josei Toda's assertion that nuclear weapons are an absolute evil the guiding principle of our age, we shall overturn the idea that they are, as a deterrent, a necessary evil. The SGI will cooperate with other NGOs to achieve this aim and to make the twenty-first century a century free from nuclear arms.

Building Trust through Denuclearization (2003)[247]

The American scientific periodical *Bulletin of the Atomic Scientists* announced last year (2002) that the minute hand of the "Doomsday Clock" it publishes had advanced to seven minutes to midnight. The periodical cited numerous reasons for this, including: the abrogation of the Anti-Ballistic Missile (ABM) Treaty, which has until now been the foundation of nuclear arms limitation between the US and Russia; the conflict between India and Pakistan, both nuclear-weapon states; increasing concerns about the control and management of fissile materials; and the existence of terrorist groups aiming to acquire nuclear weapons.[248]

Recently, the situation has been aggravated as North Korea has announced not only that it is reactivating nuclear facilities but also that it is withdrawing from the Treaty on the Non-Proliferation of Nuclear Weapons (NPT).

If these conditions continue, not only would the framework of nuclear nonproliferation, revolving around the NPT, be shaken to its roots, but there would also inevitably be the prospect of unstoppable military escalation. Serious shadows would be cast over the prospects for control of other weapons of mass destruction such as chemical and biological arms.

---

245 Ralph Waldo Emerson (1803–82), American author.

246 Emerson, Ralph. 1929. *The Complete Writings of Ralph Waldo Emerson*. New York: Wm. H. Wise & Co. Vol. 2, p. 1129.

247 From 2003 Peace Proposal, "A Global Ethic of Coexistence: Toward a 'Life-Sized' Paradigm for Our Age."

248 The University of Chicago News Office. 2002. *"Bulletin of Atomic Scientists moves 'Doomsday Clock' two minutes closer to midnight."* A statement from the Board of Directors of the *Bulletin of the Atomic Scientists*. February 27.

The report of the first session of the Preparatory Committee for the 2005 NPT Review Conference held last April called for the promotion of measures to ensure that the Comprehensive Nuclear Test Ban Treaty (CTBT) enters into force, for Cuba, Israel, India and Pakistan to accede unconditionally to the NPT, and for North Korea to observe the safeguards of the International Atomic Energy Agency.[249]

Of the four named countries, Cuba, in October 2002, announced its intention to join the NPT and ratify the Treaty of Tlatelolco (the Treaty for the Prohibition of Nuclear Weapons in Latin America and the Caribbean). It is vital to the cause of peace that the other three countries (India, Israel and Pakistan) accede to the NPT with all haste and that North Korea renew its participation. Realistically, this can only happen if the international community works together to support and encourage effective confidence-building efforts in the regions concerned.

Regarding the question of North Korea's nuclear weapons development program, it is strongly to be hoped that North Korea will follow the path taken by Cuba—namely, to press ahead with participation in a regional non-nuclear framework as a guarantee of regional security, while remaining within the NPT framework.

I have consistently called for the creation of a nuclear-weapon-free zone in Northeast Asia. In this region, we can already look to the 1992 joint declaration of a nuclear-weapon-free Korean Peninsula and Mongolia's declaration of nuclear-weapon-free status of the same year, as well as Japan's three non-nuclear principles (not possessing, not producing and not permitting the introduction of nuclear weapons into Japan).

Based on such declarations, I think we should now seek a UN-sponsored Northeast Asia peace conference, with North Korean participation, to investigate the future establishment of a nuclear-weapon-free zone in this region and to pursue regional confidence-building initiatives. At present, the only regional security framework in which North Korea participates is the ASEAN Regional Forum. I think there would be considerable significance in a discussion focusing specifically on Northeast Asia that includes broader UN participation.

---

249 UN (United Nations). 2002. "Preparatory Committee for the 2005 Review Conference of the Parties to the Treaty on the Non-Proliferation of Nuclear Weapons." NPT/CONF.2005/PC.I/21. Report of the Preparatory Committee on its first session. April 8–19, pp. 12–16.

By the end of the twentieth century, almost all of the southern hemisphere was covered by nuclear-weapon-free agreements. These agreements have aimed to ensure the security of individual countries not through the possession of nuclear arms but through the fact of not possessing them. They have contributed not only to the benefit of each country involved but also to the security of the entire planet. This surely is powerful evidence that such measures are a realistic political option.

This being the case, I would like to strongly propose that one of the challenges the international community should embrace in the twenty-first century is to extend such nuclear-weapon-free initiatives to cover the northern hemisphere as well.

Proposals for the creation of nuclear-weapon-free zones (NWFZs) in Central Asia and the Middle East have already been laid out. I believe that the time has come for us to embark on specific measures in this regard in Northeast Asia as well.

Even if time were needed before such a nuclear-weapon-free zone could be declared, an option available to North Korea is to emulate Mongolia in declaring its nuclear-weapon-free status. The declaration by Mongolia was welcomed by the UN General Assembly. The five nuclear-weapon states in 1995 reaffirmed their Negative Security Assurance (that non-nuclear-weapon states party to the NPT would not be subject to nuclear attack) with regard to Mongolia. If North Korea could be assured a similar response, I believe the path toward the declaration of nuclear-weapon-free status would be cleared.

Denuclearization of the Arctic (2008)[250]

At the height of Cold War tensions, seeking to reduce these tensions and prevent further escalation of the arms race, I called for summit meetings between the leaders of the superpowers and engaged in citizen diplomacy to encourage dialogue and exchange. At a time when, in addition to the US–Soviet confrontation, tensions between China and the Soviet Union were at a critical level (1974–75), I traveled to all three countries in a private capacity, meeting, among others, with Chinese Premier Zhou Enlai,[251] Soviet Premier

---

250 From 2008 Peace Proposal, "Humanizing Religion, Creating Peace."
251 Zhou Enlai (1898–1976), Premier of the People's Republic of China (1949–76).

Alexei Kosygin[252] and US Secretary of State Henry Kissinger.[253] Through such efforts, I hoped to build bridges that would lead to improved relations.

In this I was driven by the determination to prevent at all costs full-scale nuclear warfare, which would have catastrophic effects for the entire human race, and to put an end to the wars that were dividing the world and inflicting massive suffering upon people. With the end of the Cold War, while the threat of full-scale nuclear warfare has receded, we now face new and emerging dangers in the form of nuclear proliferation.

In my 2007 peace proposal, I called for a transition to a system of security that is not reliant on nuclear weapons, and to this end urged the establishment of an international nuclear disarmament agency to ensure the good-faith fulfillment of existing legal commitments to nuclear disarmament.

Equally essential to nuclear abolition is establishing consensus within the international community regarding the fundamental illegality of nuclear weapons. As one element of this, I would like to focus on the call issued in August 2007 by the Canadian Pugwash Group for the establishment of an Arctic Nuclear-Weapon-Free Zone (NWFZ).[254] The SGI, as an advocate of a nuclear-weapon-free world, lends support to this call, in the spirit of Josei Toda's[255] 1957 "Declaration Calling for the Abolition of Nuclear Weapons."[256]

The Arctic Ocean occupied a position of strategic geopolitical importance during the Cold War, with nuclear-powered submarines of the Eastern and Western blocs traveling under the icecap carrying their ominous cargo of ballistic missiles.

If, as a result of global warming, the polar icecap recedes or even disappears during the summer months, this could open the way for an increased militarization of the Arctic region. It could also spark an international scramble to develop transportation, seabed and other resources, causing a clash of interests between the countries concerned. For this reason, there is an urgent need to prohibit military activity in the region, build a legal regime to conserve it as

---

252 Alexei N. Kosygin (1904–80), Premier of the Soviet Union (1964–80).

253 Henry Kissinger (1923–), US Secretary of State (1973–77), recipient of the Nobel Prize for Peace in 1973.

254 The Canadian Pugwash Group. 2007. "Canadian Pugwash Call for an Arctic Nuclear Weapon-Free Zone." Report. August 24.

255 Josei Toda (1900–58), second president of the Soka Gakkai (1951–58).

256 Toda, Josei. 1981–90. *Toda Josei zenshu* [The Complete Works of Josei Toda]. 9 vols. Tokyo: Seikyo Shimbunsha. Vol. 4, pp. 564–66. (English text at http://www.joseitoda.org/vision/declaration.)

a common heritage of humankind, and establish an Arctic Nuclear-Weapon-Free Zone (NWFZ).

The Antarctic Treaty of 1959 banned all military activity on the world's southernmost continent, specifically outlawing nuclear explosions and disposal of radioactive waste south of sixty degrees south latitude. Since then, a total of five regional treaties prohibiting the development, manufacture, possession, transportation, receipt, testing and use of nuclear weapons have been signed, and NWFZs have expanded to include Latin America and the Caribbean, the South Pacific, Southeast Asia, Africa and Central Asia.

The NWFZs, covering most of the landmass of the southern hemisphere, serve as a curb against nuclear proliferation in the respective regions. Furthermore, they help strengthen momentum toward the outlawing of nuclear weapons. Together with Mongolia, which declared its nuclear-weapon-free status in 2000, well over 100 countries—more than half the governments on Earth—have become signatories to these agreements, thus expressing their view that the development and use of nuclear weapons is or should be illegal under international law.

I would hope to see further moves toward the creation of other NWFZs, as this will solidify the trend toward making the illegality of nuclear weapons the shared norm of humankind, leading ultimately to an international treaty for the comprehensive prohibition of nuclear weapons, banning their development, acquisition, possession and use.

As a step toward this, I would like to call for the establishment of a treaty prohibiting military use of and denuclearizing the Arctic region under the aegis of the United Nations. In this endeavor Japan, as a country that directly experienced the horrors of nuclear war and which upholds as core national policy the three non-nuclear principles of not possessing, developing or allowing nuclear weapons onto its national territory, should take the initiative, working with other states and civil society partners seeking a nuclear-free world.

I believe that a similar approach would be effective in terms of nuclear nonproliferation in Northeast Asia. All efforts should continue through the Six-Party Talks toward the complete dismantling of North Korea's nuclear weapons program.

At the same time, Japan should reaffirm its uncompromising commitment to its own non-nuclear policies, and should deploy its full diplomatic resources toward the more encompassing goal of establishing a nuclear-weapon-free zone covering the whole of Northeast Asia.

Prohibition of Nuclear Weapons

People's Power and International Laws for Peace (1997)[257]

This year (1997) marks the fortieth year since Josei Toda[258] made his landmark declaration denouncing the satanic nature of nuclear weapons and pronouncing them to be an "absolute evil."

In September 1957, rallying from the fatal illness from which he was suffering, Toda summoned his remaining strength to appeal to the young. He challenged the mounting threat of nuclear arms that portend the advent of "the death of death," and issued his heroic cry for the right to existence for all people of the world.

> We, the citizens of the world, have an inviolable right to live. Anyone who jeopardizes that right is a devil incarnate, a fiend, a monster. . . . Even if a country should conquer the world through the use of nuclear weapons, the conquerors must be viewed as devils, as evil incarnate. I believe that it is the mission of every member of the youth division in Japan to disseminate this idea throughout the globe.[259]

As is clear from the passage cited above, Toda's idea was an unconditional ban on the use of nuclear arms. Striving to make his will reality, I have stressed the urgency of specific steps to be taken to achieve a treaty banning the development, possession and use of nuclear weapons. His declaration against nuclear arms—independent of all ideological or national interests and rising above all political arguments such as nuclear deterrence and limited nuclear war—shines with eternal radiance.

The declaration is imbued with his ardent wish to establish the right to live in peace as a fundamental right for every human being. He earnestly wished that people would not only be kept from the tragedies of nuclear destruction and the sacrifice of human life it entails, but also would never again suffer from war.

---

257 From 1997 Peace Proposal, "New Horizons of a Global Civilization."

258 Josei Toda (1900–58), second president of the Soka Gakkai (1951–58).

259 (trans. from) Toda, Josei. 1981–90. *Toda Josei zenshu* [The Complete Works of Josei Toda]. 9 vols. Tokyo: Seikyo Shimbunsha. Vol. 4, pp. 564–66. (English text at http://www.joseitoda.org/vision/declaration.)

Toda's declaration—the crystallization of his earnest wish "to see the word 'misery' no longer used to describe the world, any country, any individual"[260]—embodies a foresight that shares much with the central concepts of human security increasingly being called for today.

What I would like to stress here is that his declaration—as he expressed it, to "rip out the claws that lie hidden in the very depths of such weapons"[261]— was intended to urge those of us of the younger generations to wage an uncompromising fight with the evil part of human life, the invisible enemy responsible for the existence of nuclear arms.

The abolition of nuclear weapons is more than a question simply of their physical riddance. Even if all nuclear arsenals are removed, a serious question will remain as to how to deal with the knowledge of nuclear arms production that has been acquired by humankind. This is why I say that the only real solution to the issue of nuclear arms is to struggle incessantly against that evil within life that threatens the survival of humanity. And this is why Josei Toda entrusted younger generations with the task of disseminating the idea of the dignity of all life as the overarching ethos of our times.

Nichiren,[262] the thirteenth-century Buddhist sage whose teachings the members of the SGI follow, stated, "Life is the foremost of all treasures."[263] This respect for life is the essential inspiration of Toda's declaration. Herein lies the reason SGI members aspire for the inner revolution of all individuals—the human revolution—that will establish respect for all life as the basic norm of human society.

Life is the world's supreme treasure. There is no value that is worth preserving at the sacrifice of life. The human revolution movement is the basis upon which the SGI has held various exhibitions (such as "Nuclear Arms: Threat to Our World" and "War and Peace") designed to raise awareness of nuclear and other global issues, and through these activities we have worked to expand a network of solidarity among people worldwide. Our efforts are inspired by the conviction that we cannot sit by and overlook the crises occurring everywhere on the Earth.

---

260 Ibid. Vol. 3, p. 290.
261 Ibid. Vol. 4, p. 565.
262 Nichiren (1222–82), Buddhist monk, founder of Nichiren Buddhism.
263 Nichiren. 1999–2006. *The Writings of Nichiren Daishonin*. 2 vols. Ed. and trans. by The Gosho Translation Committee. Tokyo: Soka Gakkai. Vol. 1, p. 1125.

The initiative in building a world without nuclear arms and a world without war lies in the hands of each and every individual. We have to embrace that conviction and be cognizant of our responsibility in that task.

Realistic measures for eliminating nuclear weapons are included in a very provocative report compiled in August 1996 by a group of specialists called the Canberra Commission on the Elimination of Nuclear Weapons. Based on plans of this kind, I believe we should move on to the next step, which is to mobilize global public opinion and pool the wisdom of people from around the world in the endeavor to achieve consensus on more detailed procedures, as well as a specific timetable, for the eradication of nuclear weapons.

In February 1996, the Toda Institute for Global Peace and Policy Research was founded, an organization originating in Josei Toda's philosophy of peace. I am eager, knowing that this year is the fortieth anniversary of his nuclear disarmament declaration, to see the Toda Institute launch its research program with nuclear disarmament as its top priority.

Concerted efforts on the popular level should be encouraged to formulate and then implement constructive plans for a better world—alternatives that will reorient the world toward peace based on the interests of humanity. I believe that expanding such popular solidarity worldwide is the only feasible path toward constructing a world free from nuclear arms and the cataclysm of nuclear war.

In my peace proposal two years ago (1995), I commented on the importance of strengthening and establishing international law for peace as the correct course for international society toward the twenty-first century. I discussed the necessity of expanding international law for peace by augmenting current international humanitarian law and establishing a system that will have binding force. Toward that goal, I urged a close link between the United Nations and the development of international law for peace in facilitating the laying down of rules for peaceful relationships among countries.

There have recently been signs of that development, as symbolized by the conclusion of the Comprehensive Nuclear Test Ban Treaty (CTBT) and the Advisory Opinion of the International Court of Justice (ICJ) concerning the legality of the threat or use of nuclear weapons. These developments are the product of popular movements worldwide. I believe, therefore, that it is not enough to set up international laws and systems based on government-level dialogue among countries. Individual commitment to building a new order for peace as propelled from the grassroots is indispensable to the establishment of genuine international law for peace.

International laws have been effective only in settling problems *ex post facto*. Much, much more must be done, considering that the ultimate objective of international law is to achieve peace in its broadest sense. Moreover, such global issues as the environment and nuclear arms were not taken into consideration at the time of the founding of the UN, as is clear from the wording of the UN Charter.

The concept of peace today is not limited to the state of no war, but is becoming more focused on "human security" in the broader sense. I would like to urge that aggressive efforts transcending the limitations of international society and institutionalizing peace as the foundation for the new millennium begin through initiatives at the grassroots.

A Nuclear Weapons Convention (2000)[264]

The "New Diplomacy," collaborative efforts between civil society and governments committed to fundamental reform, has emerged as an important new force in the world. In a sense this corresponds to the creative synergy between inner, spiritual reform and external, institutional reform. Its greatest success to date is the adoption of the Landmine Ban Convention (the Convention on the Prohibition of the Use, Stockpiling, Production and Transfer of Anti-Personnel Mines and on their Destruction) in 1997.

This was reaffirmed in one of the Ten Fundamental Principles which emerged from The Hague Appeal for Peace (HAP) Conference held in May 1999, which declares that "all states should integrate the New Diplomacy, which is the partnership of governments, international organizations and civil society."[265] The Conference initiated new campaigns including the International Action Network on Small Arms (IANSA) and the Global Ratification Campaign for the International Criminal Court (ICC), and called for an end to the use of child soldiers. I have discussed these issues in my past proposals, and the SGI will give active support and cooperation to these campaigns.

It is particularly critical to sever the intergenerational perpetuation of the culture of war by stopping the use of child soldiers. It is a welcome and great advance that a draft optional protocol to the Convention on the Rights of the

---

264　From 2000 Peace Proposal, "Peace through Dialogue: A Time to Talk."

265　The Hague Appeal for Peace. 1999. "Ten Fundamental Principles." Conference Press Release. May 14.

Child on the involvement of children in armed conflicts, which ensures that persons who have not attained the age of eighteen years are neither voluntarily nor compulsorily recruited into the armed forces, was finally adopted in January 2000.

In addition to these campaigns, I believe that one of the challenges to be addressed under the framework of the New Diplomacy is the promotion of nuclear disarmament.

***

One notable recent development has been the campaign for enactment of a treaty banning nuclear weapons advocated by the New Agenda Coalition (NAC), a group of states actively seeking nuclear disarmament, and the Middle Powers Initiative (MPI), a coalition of NGOs. Both groups were launched in 1998. The MPI was an outgrowth of the Abolition 2000 campaign, a global network of NGOs for the abolition of nuclear weapons.

Since the NAC was formed with eight states, more and more countries have supported its goals, and it is now the core of a new movement for the promotion of nuclear disarmament. For example, sixty states sponsored the draft resolution calling for a new agenda toward a nuclear-weapon-free world submitted to the UN General Assembly in December 1999. The NAC's immediate priority is to reinforce nuclear disarmament within the framework of the Treaty on the Non-Proliferation of Nuclear Weapons (NPT).

But if the NPT Review Conference, slated for April–May 2000, achieves no positive results, the NAC will shift its focus to the enactment of a treaty banning nuclear weapons.

To move beyond this impasse, it is essential that the nuclear-weapon states and their allies fundamentally rethink their reliance on nuclear weapons. Ultimately, nuclear disarmament cannot be significantly advanced unless the deterrence mentality is overcome. In 1986, Mikhail Gorbachev,[266] then Soviet general secretary, was already declaring that no country could find real security in military power, either for defense or for deterrence.[267] It must be

---

266 Mikhail Gorbachev (1931–), General Secretary of the Communist Party of the Soviet Union (1985–91), President of the Soviet Union (1990–91), recipient of the Nobel Prize for Peace in 1990.

267 See Gorbachev, Mikhail. 1986. *Political Report of the CPSU Central Committee to the 27th Congress of the Communist Party of the Soviet Union.* Moscow: Novosti Press Agency Publishing House, p. 79.

recognized that security based on deterrence is rooted in mutual distrust; it will always be accompanied by an arms race, making it inherently unstable and dangerous.

In fact, a majority of citizens support the abolition of nuclear weapons, even in nuclear-weapon states like the United States and the United Kingdom and their allies. This was discovered in opinion surveys conducted by NGOs using research agencies in countries participating in the Abolition 2000 campaign.[268] The nuclear-weapon states cite their citizens' support as part of their justification for the possession of nuclear weapons, but the findings of this research disprove their assertions.

It has been pointed out that nuclear-weapon states and states aspiring to join the nuclear weapons club seek in nuclear weapons a confirmation of their national prestige, in addition to national security. Therefore, a starting point for achieving change is to interrogate these perspectives and the power mentality from which this definition of prestige springs.

In that sense, the efforts of the NAC and the MPI—utilizing the strengths of soft power and seeking to fundamentally change people's attitudes—exactly meet the demands of our time. As such campaigns gain ever-greater support from the people, a new superpower of trust and solidarity will be born, replacing nuclear-dependent superpowers driven by deterrence and threat.

This common goal—the enactment of a treaty for the prohibition of nuclear weapons—can only be achieved by strengthening the solidarity of citizens.

In *Jinsei chirigaku* (The Geography of Human Life),[269] published at the beginning of the twentieth century, Tsunesaburo Makiguchi,[270] the first president of the Soka Gakkai, described shifts in modes of national competition—from military, to political, to economic. Moving from the descriptive to the predictive, he set out a vision of what he termed "humanitarian competition," which represents a profound qualitative transformation of competition itself, toward a model that recognizes our interrelatedness and

---

268 Abolition 2000. 1999. "Recent Public Opinion Polls Indicate Overwhelming Support for Nuclear Weapons Abolition."

269 Makiguchi, Tsunesaburo. [1903]. *Jinsei chirigaku* [The Geography of Human Life] in *Makiguchi Tsunesaburo zenshu* [The Complete Works of Tsunesaburo Makiguchi]. Tokyo: Daisanbunmei-sha. Vols. 1–2.

270 Tsunesaburo Makiguchi (1871–1944), founding president of the Soka Kyoiku Gakkai (forerunner of the Soka Gakkai) (1930–44).

emphasizes the cooperative aspects of living. He envisaged a time in which people and countries would compete—in the original sense of the word of "striving together"—to make the greatest contribution to human happiness and well-being.

From this context, he stated that the ultimate goal of a state lies in the accomplishment of humanitarianism, and asserted that nations should always adhere to noncoercive, intangible (i.e., nonmilitary, noneconomic) means to strive to expand their sphere of influence. In this sense, Makiguchi could be said to have identified with foresight and wisdom what we now know as soft power, the ability to win naturally the hearts and minds of people.

As a Buddhist, I feel compelled to stress the deeper significance of nuclear weapons and the need for their elimination. It is more than a matter of disarmament. It is a question of fundamentally overcoming the worst negative legacy of the twentieth century—distrust, hatred and the debasement of humanity—which was the final outcome of a barbaric, hegemonic struggle between nations. It requires that we face head-on the limitless capacity of the human heart to generate both good and evil, creation and destruction.

This year marks the birth centennial of my mentor, Josei Toda,[271] the second president of the Soka Gakkai. In his "Declaration Calling for the Abolition of Nuclear Weapons"[272] in September 1957, he condemned nuclear weapons as an "absolute evil" that deprives humanity of its right to exist. From a profound understanding of the innermost processes of the human heart, he keenly discerned the true nature of nuclear weapons and declared his determination to transform the demonic aspects of humanity that gave birth to them.

As heir to Toda's vision, the SGI has constantly sought ways to spread this message throughout the world. Initiated in the midst of the Cold War, the SGI's touring exhibition "Nuclear Arms: Threat to Our World" has been shown in twenty-five cities in sixteen countries around the world, including nuclear-weapon states such as the United States, the former Soviet Union and China. SGI members have collected more than 13 million signatures in support of Abolition 2000.

---

271 Josei Toda (1900–58), second president of the Soka Gakkai (1951–58).

272 Toda, Josei. 1981–90. *Toda Josei zenshu* [The Complete Works of Josei Toda]. 9 vols. Tokyo: Seikyo Shimbunsha. Vol. 4, pp. 564–66. (English text at http://www.joseitoda.org/vision/declaration.)

These campaigns are entirely based on a conviction that there is no other way to achieve this daunting task—the abolition of nuclear weapons—than to build people's solidarity, transcending national and ethnic differences. They are also an expression of a resolute determination never to yield to the power of nuclear weapons, but rather to consistently challenge the gnawing sense of resignation and powerlessness they engender, which corrodes the human spirit.

Outlawing Nuclear Weapons (2009)[273]

I would like to discuss the creation of international frameworks that facilitate the sharing of efforts for peace toward the abolition of nuclear arms. I would first like to urge the United States and Russia, which between them account for 95 percent of the world's nuclear arsenal, to immediately resume bilateral talks on nuclear disarmament.

We must always bear in mind the fact that the Treaty on the Non-Proliferation of Nuclear Weapons (NPT) does not give the five nuclear-weapon states the right to retain their "special" status indefinitely.

Regarding the significance of Article VI of the NPT, which sets out the obligation for good faith negotiations leading to nuclear disarmament, I would like to quote remarks made last year by Judge Mohammed Bedjaoui,[274] who served as the presiding judge on the International Court of Justice (ICJ) when the court issued its Advisory Opinion on the Legality of the Threat or Use of Nuclear Weapons in 1996.

> Good faith is a fundamental principle of international law, without which all international law would collapse.[275]

> Good faith requires each state party to take, individually and in concert with every other state, whether or not party to the NPT, all positive measures likely to bring the international community closer to the purpose of the NPT, nuclear disarmament.[276]

---

273 From 2009 Peace Proposal, "Toward Humanitarian Competition: A New Current in History."

274 Mohammed Bedjaoui (1929–), Algerian diplomat and jurist, President of the International Court of Justice (ICJ) (1994–97).

275 Bedjaoui, Mohammed. 2008. "Steps Toward a Nuclear Weapons Convention: Exploring and Developing Legal and Political Aspects," p. 17.

276 Ibid., p. 20.

The credibility of the NPT depends ultimately on the good faith actions of the nuclear-weapon states. And thus, to use the words of Judge Bedjaoui, "A manifestly unjustified breaking off of negotiations is radically incompatible with good faith."[277]

For two consecutive years, former secretary of state Henry Kissinger[278] and other prominent US political figures have been calling for a world free of nuclear weapons, and there has been increasingly active discussion within the nuclear-weapon states themselves regarding nuclear disarmament.

During his presidential campaign last year, then-Senator Barack Obama[279] stated: "[W]e need to work with Russia to take US and Russian ballistic missiles off hair-trigger alert; to dramatically reduce the stockpiles of our nuclear weapons and material. . . ."[280]

As for Russia, President Dmitry Medvedev[281] has stressed the "exceptional importance"[282] his government places on concluding a new, legally binding Russian–American agreement to replace the START I (Strategic Arms Reduction Treaty) that expires in December 2009. Prime Minister Vladimir Putin[283] also expressed his support for nuclear disarmament by stating: "We should close this Pandora's Box."[284]

We cannot afford to waste this momentum. I call for the prompt holding of a US–Russia summit to discuss bold new nuclear arms reductions. If the two nations could reach a basic agreement, this would clearly demonstrate to the world their commitment to disarmament ahead of the 2010 NPT Review Conference.

---

277 Ibid., p. 21.

278 Henry Kissinger (1923–), US Secretary of State (1973–77), recipient of the Nobel Prize for Peace in 1973.

279 Barack Obama (1961–), 44th President of the United States (2009–), recipient of the Nobel Prize for Peace in 2009.

280 Obama, Barack. 2008. "A New Strategy for a New World." Speech delivered in Washington DC. July 15.

281 Dmitry Medvedev (1965–), President of Russia (2008–12), Russian Prime Minister (2012–).

282 Medvedev, Dmitry. 2008. "Speech at World Policy Conference." Speech delivered in Evian, France. October 8.

283 Vladimir Putin (1952–), President of Russia (1999–2008, 2012–), Russian Prime Minister (1999, 2008–12).

284 Beeston, Richard. 2008. "Britain Must Not Be Haven for Opponents, Says Putin." *The Times.* September 12, p. 9.

In concrete terms, the two countries need to conclude a new nuclear disarmament treaty that will make far deeper cuts than those realized by START I—working, for example, from proposals floated by the Russians in 2000 for mutual reductions in strategic arsenals to around the 1,000-warhead level.

In addition, the two countries should make immediate efforts to address long-pending issues such as US ratification of the Comprehensive Nuclear Test Ban Treaty (CTBT) and the initiation of talks on a Fissile Material Cut-off Treaty (FMCT).

Then, building on a US–Russia consensus, a five-state summit for nuclear disarmament, including the other nuclear-weapon states and the UN Secretary-General, should be convened regularly to start drawing up a roadmap of specific measures to fulfill their disarmament obligations under Article VI of the NPT.

Only when the nuclear-weapon states firmly set into motion good faith efforts toward disarmament will it be possible to obtain commitments from countries outside of the NPT framework on freezing nuclear weapon development programs and embarking on disarmament.

A parallel challenge that needs to be pursued is that of a Nuclear Weapons Convention (NWC), which would comprehensively prohibit the development, testing, manufacture, possession, transfer, use and threat of use of nuclear weapons. A model Nuclear Weapons Convention was drafted through the initiative of NGOs and submitted to the UN by Costa Rica in 1997; a revised version was circulated as a UN document in 2007. Last year, UN Secretary-General Ban Ki-moon[285] added his voice, urging governments to consider an NWC.

The policy of deterrence, to which the nuclear-weapon states continue to cling, has served as a justification for other states to seek nuclear weapons capability; it is vital to establish international norms that prohibit nuclear arms with no exception for any state.

My mentor Josei Toda,[286] the second president of the Soka Gakkai, condemned anyone who would use nuclear weapons, irrespective of nationality, in his "Declaration Calling for the Abolition of Nuclear Weapons"[287] issued

---

285   Ban Ki-moon (1944–), South Korean statesman, 8th Secretary-General of the United Nations (2007–).

286   Josei Toda (1900–58), second president of the Soka Gakkai (1951–58).

287   Toda, Josei. 1981–90. *Toda Josei zenshu* [The Complete Works of Josei Toda]. 9 vols. Tokyo: Seikyo Shimbunsha. Vol. 4, pp. 564–66. (English text at http://www.joseitoda.org/vision/declaration.)

in September 1957, the year before his passing. He perceived the national egoism that underlies the drive to possess nuclear weapons as a dire threat to the future of humankind.

Concerns have been voiced that it will be difficult to obtain the participation of the nuclear-weapon states in an NWC, and that without this it would lack all substance. There is room for hope, however, as some governments, India and the United Kingdom among them, have now officially acknowledged, although with various conditions and reservations, the need to eliminate nuclear weapons.

Despite the fact that it has yet to enter into force, the CTBT has led even states not party to the treaty to announce a moratorium on nuclear testing. Likewise, an NWC could function as an international norm exerting substantial influence on the behavior of the nuclear-weapon states.

Even if the nuclear-weapon states find it impossible to enter into immediate negotiations for an NWC, they can take actions on a regional basis that demonstrate a good faith adherence to the trend toward the outlawing of nuclear weapons. To this end, they could, for example, complete ratification of all outstanding protocols to nuclear-weapon-free zone (NWFZ) Treaties and start addressing the establishment of an Arctic NWFZ, as I called for in my 2008 peace proposal.

Public support for nuclear abolition is gathering momentum. A poll conducted last year in twenty-one countries, including the nuclear-weapon states, showed that on average 76 percent of respondents favored an international agreement to eliminate all nuclear weapons.[288]

Drawing on the experience of the initiatives taken by civil society in the campaigns for the Mine Ban Treaty and the Convention on Cluster Munitions, which opened a new chapter in the history of disarmament treaties, the calls for an NWC provide the opportunity for the people of the world to join in solidarity to lay siege to the very concept of nuclear weapons.

It was a surge in international public opinion against cluster munitions, a singularly inhuman class of weapon, that led to the adoption of the convention banning them within an exceptionally short period of time last year. Nuclear arms are the most inhumane of all weapons; once again, the humanitarian imperative must prevail over the militarist principle.

---

288 World Public Opinion. 2008. "Publics around the World Favor International Agreement To Eliminate All Nuclear Weapons." December 9.

With former US President Jimmy Carter[289] and former Soviet leader Mikhail Gorbachev[290] among its signatories, Global Zero, a campaign to eliminate nuclear weapons worldwide, was launched in Paris in December 2008. Rooted in the awareness that the broad-based mobilization of international public opinion is essential if a world free of nuclear weapons is to be realized, the campaign is planning to convene a World Summit in January 2010, bringing together political and civil society leaders.

As a long-time advocate of disarmament summitry, I hope for a successful outcome. The Global Zero World Summit and the NPT Review Conference to be held next year can serve as a springboard for negotiations toward an NWC.

When I conducted a dialogue with the British historian Dr. Arnold J. Toynbee,[291] I was deeply impressed by his statement that the crucial elements required for the resolution of the nuclear issue are powerful initiatives on the part of people and a "self-imposed veto"[292] on the possession of nuclear weapons on the part of governments.

An NWC would express and embody this self-imposed veto. Nuclear weapons epitomize an absolute evil that threatens humankind's right to live; they are incompatible with the interests not only of national security but of human security—the pursuit of peace and dignity for all people on Earth. This conviction must form the foundation for a Nuclear Weapons Convention.

I am convinced that such steps are indispensable to bringing to meaningful fruition the global sharing of efforts for peace—a commitment never to build one's peace and security upon the terror and misery of others.

There is continuing concern about the nuclear programs of Iran and North Korea, and I believe that we must make tenacious efforts to reduce tensions and build confidence in their respective regions in order to put an end to the destructive spirals of threat and mistrust.

With Josei Toda's declaration as our guiding principle, members of the SGI have consistently engaged in efforts to encourage people to see the problem of

---

289 Jimmy Carter (1924–), 39th President of the United States (1977–81).

290 Mikhail Gorbachev (1931–), General Secretary of the Communist Party of the Soviet Union (1985–91), President of the Soviet Union (1990–91), recipient of the Nobel Prize for Peace in 1990.

291 Arnold J. Toynbee (1889–1975), British historian.

292 Toynbee, Arnold J. and Daisaku Ikeda. 2007. *Choose Life*. London: I.B.Tauris, p. 194.

nuclear weapons as their own. In 2007, which marked the fiftieth anniversary of his declaration, we launched the exhibition "From a Culture of Violence to a Culture of Peace: Transforming the Human Spirit" as one concrete step to promote a People's Decade for Nuclear Abolition. Toward the same end, the Soka Gakkai Women's Peace Committee has produced a five-language DVD documenting the experiences of atomic bomb survivors, *Testimonies of Hiroshima and Nagasaki: Women Speak Out for Peace.*[293]

The year 2010 will mark the 110th anniversary of the birth of Josei Toda; an NWC would give concrete expression to his call for nuclear abolition. Working closely with other NGOs such as International Physicians for the Prevention of Nuclear War (IPPNW), who have launched the International Campaign to Abolish Nuclear Weapons (ICAN), we are determined to galvanize global public opinion toward the adoption of an NWC, with particular emphasis on activities initiated by women and young people.

The Threat or Use of Nuclear Weapons as a War Crime (2010)[294]

In the proposal I wrote in September 2009, I offered a five-part plan for laying the foundation for a world free from nuclear weapons, including the promotion of various disarmament efforts and making the transition to security arrangements that are not reliant on nuclear weapons. At the same time, I reaffirmed my long-standing conviction that if we are to put the era of nuclear terror behind us, we must struggle against the real "enemy." That enemy is not nuclear weapons *per se,* nor is it the states that possess or develop them. The real enemy that we must confront is the ways of thinking that justify nuclear weapons—the readiness to annihilate others when they are seen as a threat or as a hindrance to the realization of our objectives.

My proposals should be considered as a series of steps to overcome and transform the thinking that justifies nuclear weapons and to strengthen the momentum toward their abolition.

---

293 SGI (Soka Gakkai International). 2009. *Testimonies of Hiroshima and Nagasaki: Women Speak Out for Peace.* DVD. Tokyo: Soka Gakkai International. http://www. peoplesdecade.org/decade/survivors/ (accessed April 2, 2013).

294 From 2010 Peace Proposal, "Toward a New Era of Value Creation."

The first of these is to work, based on the existing Treaty on the Non-Proliferation of Nuclear Weapons (NPT) system, to expand the frameworks defining a clear legal obligation not to use nuclear weapons, in this way laying the institutional foundations for reducing their role in national security.

The second is to include the threat or use of nuclear weapons among the war crimes falling under the jurisdiction of the International Criminal Court (ICC), further clarifying the norm that nuclear weapons are indeed weapons that must never be used.

The third is to create a system, based on the United Nations Charter, for the General Assembly and the Security Council to work together for the complete elimination of nuclear weapons.

None of these proposals will be easy to implement, but all of them build on existing institutional foundations. They are by no means unreachable goals. It is my earnest wish that the NPT Review Conference to be held in May will initiate movement toward these goals and that they can be implemented within five years. Such efforts should culminate in a nuclear abolition summit in 2015—held in Hiroshima and Nagasaki, seventy years after the nuclear attacks that devastated these two cities—which would effectively signal the end of the era of nuclear weapons.

To date, the establishment of nuclear-weapon-free zones (NWFZs) has represented an effort to fill the gap in the legal framework left by the absence of any treaty or convention providing a blanket prohibition against the use of nuclear weapons. In 2009, NWFZ treaties entered into force in Central Asia and Africa. These followed similar agreements covering Latin America and the Caribbean, the South Pacific and Southeast Asia. The decision by so many governments to eliminate nuclear weapons from so many regions around the world is truly significant.

Although the Preamble to the NPT, which entered into force forty years ago, calls on signatories to "make every effort to avert the danger of such a war and to take measures to safeguard the security of peoples,"[295] it is clear that the nuclear-weapon states have not fulfilled that obligation.

The NPT does not, of course, accord these countries an open-ended right to possess nuclear weapons. Despite this, their continued adherence to the doctrine of nuclear deterrence has had the effect of encouraging both "vertical proliferation" (expanded and enhanced nuclear arsenals within nuclear-weapon

---

295 UN (United Nations). 1968. "Treaty on the Non-Proliferation of Nuclear Weapons (NPT)."

states) and "horizontal proliferation" (the spread of nuclear technologies to other states and entities). The real-world effect has been to shake and undermine the foundations of the NPT regime itself.

The time has come for the nuclear-weapon states to develop a shared vision of a world without nuclear weapons and to break free from the spell of deterrence—the illusory belief that security can somehow be realized through threats of mutual destruction and a balance of terror. A new kind of thinking is needed, one based on working together to reduce threats and creating ever-expanding circles of physical and psychological security until these embrace the entire world.

As evidence of the nuclear-weapon states' genuine resolve to move beyond deterrence, I urge them to undertake the following three commitments at the 2010 NPT Review Conference and to work to fully implement them by 2015.

1. To reach a legally binding agreement to extend negative security assurances—the undertaking not to use nuclear weapons against any of the non-nuclear-weapon states fulfilling their obligations under the NPT.
2. To initiate negotiation on a treaty codifying the promise not to use nuclear weapons against each other.
3. Where nuclear-weapon-free zones have yet to be established, and as a bridging measure toward their establishment, to take steps to declare them nuclear non-use regions.

I have no intention of underestimating the difficulties that lie in the way of realizing these commitments, especially the second and third. But it is important to stress that these are political decisions that the nuclear-weapon states can take now while maintaining their current status as possessors of nuclear weapons.

Regarding pledges of mutual non-use, even an agreement limited to the United States and Russia would be a watershed event that would produce a major reduction in perceived threats, from which alliance partners would equally benefit. It would also provide an opening for reviewing the extraterritorial deployment of warheads and missile defense programs as steps toward the gradual dismantling of the nuclear umbrella.

As demonstrated in the final report of the International Commission on Nuclear Non-proliferation and Disarmament, a joint initiative of the Australian and Japanese governments, issued in December 2009, there are increasing calls from within countries living under a nuclear umbrella for a review of traditional nuclear doctrine.[296]

Among the benefits of establishing declared nuclear non-use regions would be to encourage progress toward global denuclearization and a comprehensive system to prevent the proliferation of all weapons of mass destruction and forestall the dire possibility of nuclear terrorism. The aim would be to transform the confrontational stance prevailing in certain regions—including those where the nuclear-weapon states or their allies are present—of meeting threat with threat. What should be encouraged instead is the approach of mutual threat reduction exemplified by the Cooperative Threat Reduction (CTR) Program instituted between the United States and the states of the former Soviet Union in the wake of the Cold War.

Regrettably, the NPT in its current form does not include provisions for reducing threats and offering mutual assurances that can enhance confidence. If progress can be made on negotiations toward these goals on a regional basis, it will make even more salient the physical and psychological security offered by participation in disarmament frameworks, as opposed to the further deepening of isolation on the outside. This will in turn reduce motivations to develop or acquire nuclear weapons.

If, through these systems, expanding circles of physical and psychological security can be created to encompass not only countries relying on the nuclear umbrellas of nuclear-weapon states, but also North Korea and Iran, as well as countries such as India, Pakistan and Israel that are currently not part of the NPT framework, this would represent a major breakthrough toward the goal of global denuclearization.

The list of treaties that should ideally be ratified by countries within a declared nuclear non-use region would include: the Comprehensive Nuclear Test Ban Treaty (CTBT), the Nuclear Terrorism Convention, the Convention on the Physical Protection of Nuclear Material, the Biological Weapons Convention and the Chemical Weapons Convention. Looking forward, the Fissile Material Cut-off Treaty should be added to this list when it is finalized.

In these efforts, a multilayered approach is required. As US President John F. Kennedy[297] stated:

---

296   Evans, Gareth and Yoriko Kawaguchi. 2009. "Eliminating Nuclear Threats: A Practical Agenda for Global Policymakers." Canberra and Tokyo: International Commission on Nuclear Non-proliferation and Disarmament.

297   John F. Kennedy (1917–63), 35th President of the United States (1960–63).

There is no single, simple key to this peace—no grand or magic formula to be adopted by one or two powers. Genuine peace must be the product of many nations, the sum of many acts.[298]

In the proposal I issued last September, I called for all the countries currently engaged in the Six-Party Talks on North Korea's nuclear program— China, Japan, North Korea, Russia, South Korea and the United States—to declare Northeast Asia a nuclear non-use region as a step toward the denuclearization of the region including, of course, the abandonment of North Korea's nuclear weapons program. I strongly hope that discussions will be initiated toward the establishment of such systems in regions like the Middle East and South Asia where tensions have long run high.

My second proposal regards establishing norms that make explicit the illegality of the use of nuclear weapons.

To date, treaties have been established comprehensively banning the development and manufacture, possession and stockpiling, transfer or acquisition of biological and chemical weapons of mass destruction. The 1925 Geneva Protocol prohibiting the use of these weapons was adopted in light of the enormous suffering wrought by the use of poison gas in World War I and represented an important step toward these comprehensive bans.

The Protocol notes the condemnation of the use of chemical weapons by international public opinion, declaring its prohibition to be "universally accepted as a part of International Law, binding alike the conscience and the practice of nations."[299] The Protocol stipulates a similar prohibition on the use of biological weapons.

Today, the thought of the possession, much less the use, of chemical or biological weapons by any state inspires widespread revulsion in the international community; the dishonor associated with them has become firmly established. We need to give concrete form to a similar recognition regarding nuclear weapons, which are undoubtedly the most inhumane of all.

At the annual conference of United Nations Department of Public Information (DPI) NGOs held in September 2009 in Mexico City, which

---

298 Kennedy, John F. 1963. "Commencement Address at American University, June 10, 1963."

299 ICRC (International Committee of the Red Cross). 1925. "Protocol for the Prohibition of the Use of Asphyxiating, Poisonous or Other Gases, and of Bacteriological Methods of Warfare." Geneva. June 17.

SGI representatives attended, UN Secretary-General Ban Ki-moon[300] stated that "nuclear weapons are immoral and should not be accorded any military value."[301]

The time has come for those in positions of leadership to acknowledge that nuclear weapons are abhorrent and militarily useless. As the course of events leading up to the comprehensive bans on chemical and biological weapons demonstrates, the first step toward bringing the era of nuclear weapons to a decisive close must be the establishment of norms prohibiting their use.

More than half a century ago, in September 1957, my mentor Josei Toda[302] issued a declaration condemning nuclear weapons as an absolute evil never to be used under any circumstance.[303] In the years that followed, the UN General Assembly adopted a series of resolutions declaring their use a crime against humanity and civilization. And yet, a clear legal norm in this regard has yet to be established.

In 1996, the International Court of Justice (ICJ) issued an Advisory Opinion on the Legality of the Threat or Use of Nuclear Weapons: "the threat or use of nuclear weapons would generally be contrary to . . . the principles and rules of humanitarian law."[304] The court, however, refrained from offering its opinion regarding the legality of the threat or use of nuclear weapons "in an extreme circumstance of self-defense, in which the very survival of a State would be at stake."[305] So long as this critical question remains unresolved, it will be possible to develop justifications for the use of nuclear weapons, and this is why we must clearly establish the norms that will render nuclear weapons truly unusable.

---

300 Ban Ki-moon (1944–), South Korean statesman, 8th Secretary-General of the United Nations (2007–).

301 Ban, Ki-moon. 2009. "For Peace and Development: Disarm Now!" Opening address to the sixty-second Annual DPI/NGO Conference. Mexico City. September 9.

302 Josei Toda (1900–58), second president of the Soka Gakkai (1951–58).

303 Toda, Josei. 1981–90. *Toda Josei zenshu* [The Complete Works of Josei Toda]. 9 vols. Tokyo: Seikyo Shimbunsha. Vol. 4, pp. 564–66. (English text at http://www.joseitoda.org/vision/declaration.)

304 ICJ (International Court of Justice). 1996. "Legality of the Threat or Use of Nuclear Weapons, Advisory Opinion." *I.C.J. Reports.* July 8, p. 245.

305 Ibid., p. 266.

Judge Christopher Weeramantry,[306] president of the International Association of Lawyers Against Nuclear Arms, was one of the judges participating in the case. He issued a separate opinion expressing his view that "the use or threat of use of nuclear weapons is illegal *in any circumstances whatsoever*."[307] In his book *Universalising International Law,* he emphasizes that reflecting the voices and views of ordinary citizens contributes to making international law more universal and points out the importance of "[t]he views of peoples as constituting *opinio juris*."[308]

Looking back on the history of nuclear weapons, we can see that when situations of crisis and extreme danger arose they were averted and breakthroughs were achieved, and the idea that nuclear weapons can be used was steadily eroded. This was realized through the synergistic interaction of the practical and moral restraint exercised by political leaders and the growing weight of international public opinion that any repetition of the horrors of nuclear weapons use must be avoided at all costs. For example, the first restriction on nuclear weapons development, the 1963 Partial Test Ban Treaty, was adopted through the efforts of United States and Soviet leaders who had together peered into the abyss of nuclear war during the Cuban Missile Crisis and against the backdrop of the citizens movement to "ban the bomb" led by Linus Pauling[309] and other scientists.

Likewise, the 1987 Intermediate-Range Nuclear Forces (INF) Treaty, the first agreement to actually reduce the number of nuclear weapons, was adopted through a series of US–Soviet summit meetings and had as its backdrop the shock of the Chernobyl nuclear reactor disaster. Another crucial factor behind this redirection of policy was the vocal public opposition to the deployment of tactical nuclear weapons in Europe in the 1980s.

While these steps may represent only limited progress in and of themselves, they reflect the steadily deepening awareness within international society that nuclear weapons must never be used and that steps must be taken to contain

---

306 Christopher Weeramantry (1926–), Sri Lankan jurist, Vice-president of the International Court of Justice (ICJ) (1997–2000), President of the International Association of Lawyers Against Nuclear Arms.

307 ICJ (International Court of Justice). 1996. "Dissenting Opinion of Judge Weeramantry." *I.C.J. Reports.* July 8, p. 433.

308 Weeramantry, Christopher. 2004. *Universalising International Law.* Leiden, Boston: M. Nijhoff Publishers, p. 115.

309 Linus Pauling (1901–94), American scientist, recipient of the Nobel Prize in Chemistry in 1954 and the Nobel Prize for Peace in 1962.

the threat they pose. This fact is all the more striking if we recall that in the immediate aftermath of World War II nuclear weapons were considered to be no more than extremely destructive conventional weapons whose eventual use was widely considered inevitable.

No matter how great the divide between our ideals and reality may be, there is no need to give up hope or accept this with resignation. Instead, the ordinary citizens of the world need to come together to create a new reality. The prohibitions on land mines and cluster weapons that have been realized in recent years are the fruit of such solidarity.

Last year I called for a movement in support of a "declaration for nuclear abolition by the world's people" that could be jointly promoted by individuals, organizations, spiritual and religious groups, universities and research institutions, as well as agencies within the UN system.

In conjunction with this, I call on this occasion for a movement to amend the Statute of the ICC to define the use of nuclear weapons as a war crime.

We should embrace the goal of making the prohibition of nuclear weapons the shared norm and aspiration of all humankind by 2015, the seventieth anniversary of the atomic bombing of Hiroshima and Nagasaki. We must use the establishment of this norm to clear the way toward the complete abolition of nuclear weapons—the fervent desire of the survivors of the nuclear attacks and people the world over.

Many states participating in the negotiations leading up to the establishment of the ICC in 1998 urged that the use of nuclear weapons be included as a war crime falling under the jurisdiction of the court. However, this was not reflected in the final language of the Rome Statute as it was adopted. I urged reconsideration of this in the peace proposal I wrote the following year (1999).

In November 2009, at the eighth session of the Assembly of States Parties to the Rome Statute of the ICC, Mexico proposed this amendment to the Statute, and a working group has been established to consider this, together with other revisions. I welcome this development and the important opportunities it presents.

The states that are not party to the ICC, especially nuclear-weapon states, should be invited to participate in the debates on this question as observers. What is important is for the representatives of as many governments as possible to confront, through a process of earnest debate, the inhumane nature of nuclear weapons and the intolerable threat they pose. The objective of the proposed revision is obviously not to punish the actual use of nuclear weapons but to establish a clear norm that such use is always and under any circumstance unacceptable.

For the members of the SGI, the declaration made by second Soka Gakkai president Josei Toda calling for the prohibition of nuclear weapons remains our enduring source of inspiration. Drawing from this, we have, for the past half-century, continued to stress the horrors of nuclear weapons, raising public awareness and generating support for their abolition. In September 2007, on the fiftieth anniversary of Toda's declaration, the SGI launched the People's Decade for Nuclear Abolition; we have also been working with the International Campaign to Abolish Nuclear Weapons (ICAN) promoted by International Physicians for the Prevention of Nuclear War (IPPNW) to encourage adoption of a Nuclear Weapons Convention (NWC) comprehensively banning these weapons. I am convinced that amending the Statute of the ICC to make the use of nuclear weapons a war crime would spark further momentum toward the adoption of an NWC.

From the start of 2010, the members of the Soka Gakkai in Japan, in particular the youth membership, have been engaged in grassroots dialogue to deepen awareness among their peers of the nuclear issue; they have also been collecting signatures in support of an NWC to be presented to the NPT Review Conference in May. It is the essential nature of youth to remain undeterred by any difficulty, to resist the overwhelming currents of reality and to live committed to the realization of the highest ideals. If the key to the prohibition of nuclear weapons lies in mustering an overwhelming expression of popular will, it is in the solidarity of young people dedicated to this cause that the energy to transform the age will be found.

To date, the exhibition "From a Culture of Violence to a Culture of Peace: Transforming the Human Spirit" created by the SGI in 2007 has been held in fifty cities in twenty-two countries. We have also produced a five-language DVD documenting the experiences of atomic bomb survivors, *Testimonies of Hiroshima and Nagasaki: Women Speak Out for Peace*.[310] Determined to fulfill the mission bequeathed to us by Josei Toda, we will continue to use these educational tools as vehicles for creating an irresistible tide of popular energy for the prohibition and abolition of nuclear weapons.

---

310 SGI (Soka Gakkai International). 2009. *Testimonies of Hiroshima and Nagasaki: Women Speak Out for Peace.* DVD. Tokyo: Soka Gakkai International. http://www. peoplesdecade.org/decade/survivors/ (accessed April 2, 2013).

The third major theme I would like to discuss regards collaborative efforts by the UN General Assembly and the Security Council for nuclear abolition, based on the United Nations Charter.

Presently, the United States and Russia are engaged in negotiations toward a new nuclear disarmament treaty to replace the Strategic Arms Reduction Treaty (START I), which technically expired last year. Even the most ambitious reductions being negotiated between the two countries, however, would still leave an enormous number of nuclear warheads on Earth.

In order to effectively advance nuclear weapons reductions, it is essential to expand the nuclear disarmament framework beyond these two countries, to include all states that possess nuclear weapons. To this end, I would like to propose a process for developing and implementing a roadmap toward a world free of nuclear weapons based on the United Nations Charter, which all the relevant governments are pledged to uphold.

Article 11 of the UN Charter states that the General Assembly "may consider the general principles of co-operation in the maintenance of international peace and security, including the principles governing disarmament and the regulation of armaments, and may make recommendations with regard to such principles to the Members or to the Security Council or to both."[311]

Further, Article 26 clearly states that the Security Council has responsibility for formulating plans for a system for the regulation of armaments in order to "promote the establishment and maintenance of international peace and security with the least diversion for armaments of the world's human and economic resources. . . ."[312]

To date, the General Assembly has, based on Article 11, engaged actively in questions of disarmament. In contrast, the Security Council has failed to fulfill this role, leaving Article 26 essentially dormant for all these years. This is one of the reasons why the Security Council Summit on Nuclear Non-Proliferation and Nuclear Disarmament held last September was so significant. In order to fulfill the commitment made at that time to "create the conditions for a world without nuclear weapons,"[313] the Security Council—whose five permanent members are all nuclear-weapon states—should take

---

311 UN (United Nations). 1945. "Charter of the United Nations." Article 11.
312 Ibid. Article 26.
313 UN (United Nations). 2009. "Maintenance of International Peace and Security: Nuclear Non-proliferation and Nuclear Disarmament." S/RES/1887. Resolution adopted by the Security Council at its 6191st meeting. September 24, p. 1.

the lead in establishing a venue for multilateral disarmament negotiations through, for example, a series of summit meetings with the participation of the UN Secretary-General.

One action that could be taken by the General Assembly would be to build on the accumulated record of resolutions dedicated to the goal of nuclear weapons abolition. The General Assembly could start issuing, on an annual basis, recommendations to the Security Council urging it to fulfill its responsibility by achieving a specified minimum reduction of nuclear weapons. To strengthen the moral authority of this recommendation, it could be accompanied by reports by states on actions they have taken proactively toward reducing tensions and promoting disarmament.

It goes without saying that ultimate responsibility for abolishing nuclear weapons lies with the nuclear-weapon states. But there is no need for the non-nuclear-weapon states to wait passively for arms reduction negotiations to be completed. They can, through their own actions, generate pressure for abolition in order to bring about its more speedy realization. Such efforts would clearly be in line with the path set out by the ICJ's Advisory Opinion that "any realistic search for general and complete disarmament, especially nuclear disarmament, necessitates the co-operation of all States."[314]

Further, the General Assembly, by expressing through these resolutions the will of international society for nuclear disarmament, can encourage ambitious efforts by various countries to reduce tensions. This could in turn become, in the words of Costa Rica's 2008 call for the Security Council to establish a system for the regulation of armaments based on Article 26, a means "to overcome the vicious armaments race that seems to be gaining momentum in several regions of the world, competing with the prioritization of social expenditure and the international agreed development goals, including the Millennium Development Goals, and negatively affecting human security."[315]

In an era when all societies must come together to respond to the common challenges facing humankind, such as poverty and environmental destruction,

---

314 ICJ (International Court of Justice). 1996. "Legality of the Threat or Use of Nuclear Weapons, Advisory Opinion." *I.C.J. Reports.* July 8, p. 266.

315 UN (United Nations). 2008. "Strengthening Collective Security through General Regulation and Reduction of Armaments: The Safest Road to Peace and Development." S/2008/697. Concept paper presented by Costa Rica. November 19, p. 4.

military spending has absorbed far too much of the world's limited human and economic resources.

Nuclear weapons, in particular, are a fundamental evil that cannot resolve in any way the complex of global issues, but only exacerbate them.

Jayantha Dhanapala,[316] president of the Pugwash Conferences on Science and World Affairs, and Patricia Lewis,[317] deputy director of the Center for Nonproliferation Studies at the Monterey Institute of International Studies, are both internationally renowned experts on disarmament issues. In a jointly written preface to a United Nations Institute for Disarmament Research (UNIDIR) report, they urge that in any discussion of disarmament, whether it concerns small arms or weapons of mass destruction, the human security aspect must be given first priority.

> We need to mainstream disarmament to put it back in its rightful place: at the core of our thinking on people-centered security. Disarmament is humanitarian action.[318]

Based on this principle, I strongly urge that all efforts be made to fully implement Article 26 of the United Nations Charter so that the Security Council fulfills its disarmament obligations, strengthening impetus toward nuclear abolition and the demilitarization of our planet.

As a country that experienced nuclear attack, Japan has for more than a decade sponsored General Assembly resolutions calling for the abolition of nuclear weapons. Japan also espouses the three non-nuclear principles (not possessing, not producing and not permitting the introduction of nuclear weapons into its territory) as well as three principles regarding weapons exports. Japan should pledge its firm adherence to these two sets of principles as it takes the lead in mustering global public opinion for nuclear abolition.

---

316 Jayantha Dhanapala (1938–), Sri Lankan diplomat, UN Under-Secretary-General for Disarmament Affairs (1998–2003), President of the Pugwash Conferences on Science and World Affairs (2007–).

317 Patricia Lewis (1957–), British and Irish nuclear physicist, deputy director and scientist-in-residence at the James Martin Center for Nonproliferation Studies at the Monterey Institute of International Studies (2008–12).

318 UNIDIR (United Nations Institute for Disarmament Research). 2001. "Preface" in "Disarmament as Humanitarian Action." UNIDIR/2001/23. A discussion on the occasion of the 20th anniversary of the UNIDIR. New York: United Nations Publication, p. viii.

In November of last year, Japan and the United States issued a joint state-ment declaring their intent to work actively to create the conditions for the achievement of the total elimination of nuclear weapons.[319] Japan will serve as a member of the Security Council this year, and should take this opportunity to strongly encourage the United States and other nuclear-weapon states to make progress on disarmament. In this and other ways, Japan has a unique duty and responsibility to work for the realization of a nuclear-weapon-free world.

A Nuclear Disarmament Summit (2011)[320]

Following the end of the Cold War, advancing global economic integration brought such issues as poverty and environmental destruction to the fore and heightened demand for international responses. But in the first years of the twenty-first century, the world has experienced a number of profound shocks—from the terror attacks of September 11, 2001, to the recent financial crisis—and attempts to engage with these issues have not only slowed, but at times appear to have regressed.

The degree of achievement of the Millennium Development Goals (MDGs) adopted by the United Nations in 2000 is symbolic of this. Every year, more than 8 million people die as a direct or indirect result of extreme poverty, and the lives and dignity of more than a billion are subject to daily threats and affronts.[321]

The MDGs were adopted as a means of ameliorating such conditions. But with the deceleration of the global economy, the pace of international assistance has slowed. With the important exception of the goal of halving the number of people living in extreme poverty, the prospects for achieving the other MDGs by 2015 are highly questionable.

In a similar way, efforts to slow global warming would appear to have hit a wall. The sixteenth session of the Conference of the Parties (COP 16) to the United Nations Framework Convention on Climate Change (UNFCCC)

---

319 MOFA (Ministry of Foreign Affairs of Japan). 2009. "Japan–US Joint Statement toward a World without Nuclear Weapons." November 13.

320 From 2011 Peace Proposal, "Toward a World of Dignity for All: The Triumph of the Creative Life."

321 UN (United Nations). 2005. "Everyone's a Delegate." Ad campaign for the 2005 World Summit.

held in Mexico in December of last year (2010) ended without adopting a framework for reducing greenhouse gas emissions beyond 2012, the end of the first commitment period of the Kyoto Protocol.

The response to both these pressing issues is clearly inadequate, and this would appear to reflect inherent limitations in intergovernmental negotiation and deliberative processes. Even when there is widespread recognition of a problem, until it is seen as threatening the vital interests of a society, it is hard to muster the political will to introduce concrete measures either independently or in coordination with other states.

If we remember that the policy responses and aid that are so frequently postponed and delayed in fact represent a lifeline for many people, a necessary safety net for future generations, such a lack of action cannot be justified. It is therefore vital to ensure that responses to global challenges are not overshadowed by the clash of national interests.

We must keep a clear focus on those whose lives are directly impacted by these threats. It is no longer enough simply to sound the warning: the time has come for action and solidarity. In achieving this reorientation, the UN can play a pivotal role, an awareness reflected in the theme chosen for the 2010 General Assembly debate: the central role of the UN in global governance.

This echoes the approach of Dag Hammarskjöld,[322] the second Secretary-General of the United Nations, who sought ways to enable the UN to take the initiative in response to crises not limited to its role as a site for reconciling competing national interests. In doing so, Hammarskjöld referenced Bergson's concept of creative evolution and urged that the UN as "a living organism"[323] needed to be able to grow continuously to respond to the changing demands placed on it. His vision remains valid to this day.

Fulfilling Hammarskjöld's vision requires, I believe, a strengthening and solidifying of the UN's collaborative endeavors with civil society, and in particular with NGOs. This is because the vital energy of the UN

---

322 Dag Hammarskjöld (1905–61), Swedish economist and statesman, 2nd UN Secretary-General (1953–61), posthumous recipient of the Nobel Prize for Peace in 1961.

323 Hammarskjöld, Dag. 1974. "Introduction to the Fourteenth Annual Report: New York, August 20, 1959." In Cordier and Foote, eds. *Public Papers of the Secretaries-General of the United Nations. Volume IV: Dag Hammarskjöld 1958–1960*. New York and London: Columbia University Press, pp. 448–49.

as an institution resides, to quote the Preamble of its Charter, in "We the peoples ..." and most particularly in each individual inhabitant of Earth.

In this regard, I think it is worth citing the new vision of leadership that was at the heart of the proposals put forward in the Final Report of the Commission on Global Governance, *Our Global Neighborhood,* on the UN's fiftieth anniversary in 1995: "By leadership we do not mean only people at the highest national and international levels. We mean enlightenment at every level."[324]

The commission called for "courageous, long-term leadership"[325] from NGOs, small-scale community groups, the private sector and business, scientists and specialists, the worlds of education, the media and religion.

Where there is an absence of international political leadership, civil society should step in to fill the gap, providing the energy and vision needed to move the world in a new and better direction. I believe that we need a paradigm shift, a recognition that the essence of leadership is found in ordinary individuals—whoever and wherever they may be—fulfilling the role that is theirs alone to play. This in turn is the fulcrum which, in the words of Archimedes,[326] enables us to move the world.

When each of us makes our irreplaceable contribution and we develop multiple overlapping networks of solidarity, only then will we have truly learned the bitter lessons of the twentieth century, an age deeply stained by violence and war. Only then can we begin to construct a new era founded on respect for the inherent value and dignity of life.

Based on this conviction, I would like to explore the means by which the enlightened actions and solidarity of ordinary people can, through initiatives centered on the United Nations, work for the realization of two pressing challenges of the second decade of this century: prohibiting and abolishing nuclear weapons and building a culture of human rights.

The 2010 Review Conference of the Parties to the Treaty on the Non-Proliferation of Nuclear Weapons (NPT), held last May (2010), was propelled by an urgent determination not to repeat the experience of the 2005 Review

---

324   UN (United Nations). 1995. *Our Global Neighborhood: Report of the Commission on Global Governance.* Oxford and New York: Oxford University Press, p. 355.

325   Ibid., p. 356.

326   Archimedes (*c.* 290–212 BCE), Greek mathematician.

Conference, which was deeply divided and ended without reaching any substantive agreement.

The Final Document issued by the 2010 Conference contained three points that I consider to be of particular importance. It reaffirmed that the only absolute guarantee against the threat posed by nuclear weapons is their total elimination; it sought compliance with international humanitarian law in light of the catastrophic consequences of any use of nuclear weapons; and it called for special efforts to establish the necessary framework to achieve and maintain a world without nuclear weapons, making reference in this regard to a Nuclear Weapons Convention (NWC).

These are all ideas that have long been stressed by the survivors of the atomic bombings and by NGOs. It is thus genuinely significant that they should be so clearly stated in an official document issued by the parties to the NPT, which embraces the largest number of signatories of any treaty concerning nuclear weapons. It is crucial that we make the consensus reflected in this document a foundation for collaborative initiatives toward a world free of nuclear weapons.

Here I would like to propose three challenges to be undertaken in the name of "We the peoples . . .":

1. Recognizing that abolition is the only absolute guarantee against the threat of nuclear weapons, we will establish the structures through which states possessing nuclear weapons can rapidly advance disarmament toward the goal of complete elimination.

2. Finding impermissible any action on the part of any country that runs counter to the goal of a world free of nuclear weapons, we will establish the means to prohibit and prevent all nuclear weapons development or modernization.

3. Based on the awareness that nuclear weapons are the ultimate inhumane weapon capable of bringing catastrophic consequences to humankind, we will establish at an early date a Nuclear Weapons Convention comprehensively prohibiting them.

Each of these three challenges requires a change in attitude on the part of states. Even more crucially, they require the passionate commitment and action of awakened citizens who alone can create a new direction and current in history.

Regarding the first, the promotion of nuclear disarmament toward the goal of complete elimination, it is necessary to establish an ongoing framework for dialogue and negotiation at the UN with the participation of all states possessing nuclear weapons.

The New Strategic Arms Reduction Treaty (START) that was signed by Presidents Barack Obama[327] and Dmitry Medvedev[328] last April has now been ratified by the legislatures of both countries and awaits only the formal exchange of the instruments of ratification. While this treaty only effects a limited reduction for specific types of weapons, the fact is that between them the United States and Russia possess more than 90 percent of the world's stockpiles of nuclear weapons, and such actions to fulfill their disarmament responsibilities should be applauded. The Obama Administration's stated intention to follow this up with negotiations for the reduction of short-range tactical nuclear weapons is a welcome development.

I would further hope that, in line with the view expressed in the Preamble to the New START, this process will be expanded into a multilateral approach that will include all states possessing nuclear weapons.[329] At the same time, I urge a fundamental revision of the framework for nuclear disarmament, such that the goal of the multilateral negotiations is not confined to arms control but aims toward a clear vision of nuclear weapons abolition.

In order to create an environment for such negotiations, it is necessary to thoroughly challenge the theory of deterrence upon which nuclear weapons possession is predicated: the assumption that the maintenance of security is realized through a balance of terror. To this end, it is necessary to disentangle the association of nuclear weapons possession and security, and to reaffirm the simple truth that the real desire of states and their citizens is security, not nuclear weapons.

When he visited Hiroshima last August, UN Secretary-General Ban Ki-moon[330] praised the success of the 2009 UN Security Council Summit

---

327 Barack Obama (1961–), 44th President of the United States (2009–), recipient of the Nobel Prize for Peace in 2009.

328 Dmitry Medvedev (1965–), President of Russia (2008–12), Russian Prime Minister (2012–).

329 See US Department of State. 2010. "Treaty between The United States of America and the Russian Federation on Measures for the Further Reduction and Limitation of Strategic Offensive Arms (New START)." April 8.

330 Ban Ki-moon (1944–), South Korean statesman, 8th Secretary-General of the United Nations (2007–).

on nuclear nonproliferation and disarmament. He called for the regular convening of such summits, starting this year, as a means of generating political
momentum toward a world without nuclear weapons.

Over the years, I have also called for the regular holding of such summits
and therefore offer my full support to the Secretary-General's proposal. In
addition, I would like to propose that these summits not be limited to the
members of the Security Council, but that participation be opened to states
that have chosen to relinquish their nuclear weapons or programs, and that
specialists in the field and representatives of NGOs should have the opportunity to voice their opinions.

The judges participating in the 1996 International Court of Justice (ICJ)
Advisory Opinion on the Legality of the Threat or Use of Nuclear Weapons
unanimously concurred that Article VI of the NPT obligates nuclear-weapon
states not only to engage in nuclear disarmament negotiations in good faith,
but to achieve nuclear disarmament as a result of such negotiations.

Former President of the ICJ Mohammed Bedjaoui,[331] who presided over
the deliberations for the Advisory Opinion, has emphasized that all states
parties to the NPT have the right to demand that the nuclear-weapon states
fulfill their obligations and may invoke Article VI of the NPT in the event
such obligations are not fulfilled.

During the proceedings, the ICJ was presented with some 4 million
"declarations of public conscience" as affirmation of the general public's
condemnation of nuclear weapons. As this shows, any process or deliberation
that deals directly with the fate of humankind must be earnestly attentive to
the voices of civil society.

In April last year, a meeting of the InterAction Council of former heads of
state and government was held in Hiroshima. Participants visited the Peace
Memorial Museum and heard the testimony of A-bomb survivors. They
issued a communiqué that stressed the importance of world leaders, especially
those of nuclear-weapon states, visiting Hiroshima.[332] This is an idea that I
have been stressing for many years: if government leaders together witnessed
the realities of the atomic bombings, this would most certainly solidify their
resolve to free the world of nuclear weapons.

---

331 Mohammed Bedjaoui (1929–), Algerian diplomat and jurist, President of the
International Court of Justice (ICJ) (1994–97).
332 InterAction Council. 2010. "Final Communiqué: 29th Annual Plenary
Meeting." May 29–31.

Regarding the second challenge, prohibiting and preventing nuclear weapons development, the entry into force of the Comprehensive Nuclear Test Ban Treaty (CTBT), which prohibits all nuclear test explosions, is the prime focus. Since the CTBT was adopted in 1996, it has been signed by 182 countries and ratified by 153. The conditions for it to become legally binding as international law, however, are stringent: all 44 countries that possess nuclear technology must ratify, and this has yet to happen.

I believe that non-nuclear-weapon states and civil society organizations should work together to encourage those countries that have yet to do so to ratify. In addition to the prohibition of nuclear testing, the entry into force of the CTBT will be significant in the following three contexts:

1. By covering those countries that are not states parties to the NPT regime, it will effectively be universal;
2. It will express the will of international society to prohibit nuclear testing in perpetuity, thus strengthening the psychological foundations for nuclear weapons abolition; and
3. The existence of a global system of compliance monitoring, verification and inspection, administered by a treaty organization (the CTBTO), will provide an institutional model for a Nuclear Weapons Convention. It will thus help make an NWC a more realistic prospect in people's minds.

Following Indonesia's indication of its readiness to ratify the CTBT, eight "Annex 2" countries have yet to sign and/or ratify. In order to secure the necessary assent of these remaining states, the Conference on Facilitating the Entry into Force of the Comprehensive Nuclear-Test-Ban Treaty in New York in 2009 unanimously adopted a declaration encouraging bilateral, regional and multilateral initiatives. Building on this, I would like to propose that interlocking agreements of mutual obligation be established to secure the signing and/or ratification of the outstanding states within a fixed period. The UN could play an important role in mediating such agreements.

This could take the form, for example, of a bilateral commitment to sign by India and Pakistan and a tripartite agreement for mutual ratification by Egypt, Iran and Israel. In Northeast Asia, negotiations could be pursued through the Six-Party Talks for an agreement by which the United States and China ratify the CTBT, a zone is established in which all parties pledge the non-use of nuclear weapons, and North Korea abandons its nuclear weapons programs and signs and ratifies the CTBT.

Tensions on the Korean Peninsula heightened greatly last year with the sinking of the South Korean warship *Cheonan* and the North Korean shelling of Yeonpyeong Island. There is an urgent need to use all available diplomatic means to defuse the situation. But the long-term peace and stability of the region clearly hinges on an early resolution of the North Korean nuclear issue.

In a similar manner, enduring regional stability in the Middle East is unthinkable without denuclearization. It is, however, far from certain that the international conference on establishing a zone free of weapons of mass destruction in the Middle East agreed to by last year's NPT Review Conference will in fact be held as scheduled in 2012, much less that it will produce a successful outcome.

This underlines the need for further efforts to create the conditions for dialogue. One preparatory step for this conference could be informal talks, for example toward a moratorium on any expansion of stockpiles of weapons of mass destruction including nuclear weapons. The important thing is to sit at the same table and begin discussions, because this will provide the opportunity to develop a greater awareness of how one's own policies present or are perceived by others as a threat.

The obstacles on the path to a Middle East conference make the support of the international community all the more vital. I would particularly hope that Japan, as a country that has experienced the use of nuclear weapons in war and which has actively worked for the entry into force of the CTBT, will push for the denuclearization of Northeast Asia and toward creating conditions propitious to negotiations for a Middle East free of all weapons of mass destruction including nuclear weapons.

For its part, the SGI will continue to organize showings of our exhibition "From a Culture of Violence to a Culture of Peace: Transforming the Human Spirit" in different venues around the world, including the Middle East, in order to build international public opinion for the early entry into force of the CTBT and the expansion of nuclear-weapon-free zones.

In this context, I call for the adoption of agreements prohibiting the development of new nuclear weapons or their qualitative enhancement. This issue was initially brought up as a focus of debate at last year's NPT Review Conference, but then shunted aside because of opposition by the nuclear-weapon states. The refusal to address this issue, however, threatens to undermine the fundamentals of both the NPT and CTBT regimes.

The United States has expanded its budget for the modernization of nuclear weapons and facilities and in September 2010 resumed subcritical nuclear testing. Such actions not only complicate prospects for the CTBT, but run counter to the goal of a world free of nuclear weapons.

In this connection, I would urge that the five permanent members of the UN Security Council follow up on their 2008 joint declaration to maintain their moratorium on nuclear testing by declaring the cessation of any and all modernization of nuclear weapons.

The third undertaking I would like to discuss is the establishment of a Nuclear Weapons Convention comprehensively outlawing these weapons of indiscriminate slaughter. This would in fact be a kind of world law—drawing its ultimate authority and legitimacy from the expressed will of the world's peoples.

The Final Declaration of last year's NPT Review Conference "expresses . . . deep concern at the catastrophic humanitarian consequences of any use of nuclear weapons and reaffirms the need for all States at all times to comply with applicable international law, including international humanitarian law."[333]

This statement builds on the points made in the 1996 ICJ Advisory Opinion, and is groundbreaking in that it suggests the ultimate illegality of nuclear weapons. This is because the uncompromising application of the principle that inhumane weapons may never be used will eliminate the possibility of considering nuclear weapons as somehow equivalent to other weapons, to be used as circumstances require. This exceptional nature of nuclear weapons was also stressed by the ICJ, whose Advisory Opinion requires that we "take account of the unique characteristics of nuclear weapons, and in particular their destructive capacity, their capacity to cause untold human suffering, and their ability to cause damage to generations to come."[334]

These weapons are fundamentally incompatible with the principles of international humanitarian law, whoever possesses them or whatever reasons they give for doing so. This is the awareness we must foster and spread.

---

333 UN (United Nations). 2010. "2010 Review Conference of the Parties to the Treaty on the Non-Proliferation of Nuclear Weapons." NPT/CONF.2010/50 (Vol. I). Final Document, p. 19.

334 ICJ (International Court of Justice). 1996. "Legality of the Threat or Use of Nuclear Weapons, Advisory Opinion." I.C.J. Reports. July 8, p. 244.

More than half a century ago, in 1957, my mentor and second Soka Gakkai president Josei Toda[335] made a declaration in which he condemned nuclear weapons as an absolute evil and called for their prohibition.[336] In doing so, he was seeking to undermine the logic of any argument that would justify their possession or use. Toda recognized that it is ordinary people who are the ultimate victims of war, and in this sense the distinction between friend and enemy nation is meaningless.

As noted, Toda had fearlessly resisted Japanese militarism during World War II. He stated that his deepest desire was "to see the word 'misery' no longer used to describe the world, any country, any individual."[337] He understood that war waged using nuclear weapons would inevitably wreak unspeakable havoc and misery on the citizens of every country, everywhere in the world.

He made his declaration at the height of the Cold War, a time when the world was sharply divided into East/West blocs. At the time, any critique of nuclear weapons tended to be focused solely on those in the possession of the opposing bloc. Toda, however, saw beyond these differences of ideology and political system. As a Buddhist, he remained unflinchingly committed to the universal value of the dignity of life and condemned nuclear weapons as an affront to humanity's inalienable right to live.

Today we stand at a watershed moment. We have before us the potential to bring the era of nuclear weapons to an end through a treaty that comprehensively bans them. We must not allow this historic opportunity to pass.

It is truly significant that in its Final Statement the NPT Review Conference made a reference, albeit indirect, to an NWC. This creates an opening that should be pursued in order to create a world free from nuclear weapons. To that end, I would like to propose the early convening of an NWC preparatory conference through the joint initiative of states and NGOs that seek the prohibition of nuclear weapons. Even if governmental participation is limited at first, priority should be given to creating a venue for treaty negotiations. The work of the conference should focus on developing a clear

---

335 Josei Toda (1900–58), second president of the Soka Gakkai (1951–58).

336 Toda, Josei. 1981–90. *Toda Josei zenshu* [The Complete Works of Josei Toda]. 9 vols. Tokyo: Seikyo Shimbunsha. Vol. 4, pp. 564–66. (English text at http://www.joseitoda.org/vision/declaration.)

337 (trans. from) Toda, Josei. 1981–90. *Toda Josei zenshu* [The Complete Works of Josei Toda]. 9 vols. Tokyo: Seikyo Shimbunsha. Vol. 3, p. 290.

prohibitory norm that acknowledges no exceptions and a clear timeline for implementation. Through repeated convening of this conference and as more governments and NGOs join in, the way will be opened for the early start of official negotiations.

Last year, Malaysia and Costa Rica put forward a resolution in the UN General Assembly seeking the start of negotiations on a Nuclear Weapons Convention. This passed with the support of more than 130 states, including China, India, Pakistan and North Korea. These signs of an emerging consensus, however, are not in themselves enough to bring an NWC to fruition and realize the goal of a world without nuclear weapons.

If global civil society can raise its voice and increase its presence, bringing about a tectonic shift in international public opinion, this would be a force that no government could ignore. It is necessary to begin a process that will crystallize the will of the world's people in a concrete and binding legal form. This is the clear goal toward which we should move.

The law that would emerge from such a process would carry the mandate of each of the world's citizens both in terms of its establishment and of ensuring compliance. In this sense an NWC would represent a qualitative transformation in international law, which traditionally regulates relations among states, and would in fact be a kind of world or global law.

To date, those calling for nuclear weapons prohibition or abolition have approached the issue from two distinct perspectives. The first focuses on the inhumane nature of nuclear weapons, the second on the practical dangers they pose, particularly through new forms of proliferation and buildup.

The NPT Review Conference incorporated both perspectives, and we should acknowledge the legitimacy of both sets of concerns as we seek to expand momentum toward a world without nuclear weapons.

But what is important now is that more and more people awaken to a sense of personal outrage at the continued existence of nuclear weapons and thus become moved to exercise proactive and transformative leadership. I would therefore like to propose the following as a focus for popular solidarity in the rejection of nuclear weapons:

1. No country and no leader has the right to use nuclear weapons, which can instantly rob untold numbers of citizens of their lives and futures.
2. Security arrangements cannot be based on the foundation of nuclear weapons. Even if they are not used, nuclear weapons have through their development and testing caused grave damage to people's health

and the natural environment and, by their very existence, act as a continual spur to military escalation and proliferation.

3. We reject, as undermining the ability of humankind to coexist in peace, the mind-set that places no limits on the actions that can be taken in the name of protecting one's own security and interests and those of one's country—a way of thinking embodied in the possession of nuclear weapons.

These three statements express the humanitarian principle in its broadest sense—that is, the refusal to seek one's own happiness at the expense of others—as well as the goal of human security, which is to protect the dignity of life in all circumstances.

In light of these principles, it is clear that nuclear weapons represent an absolute evil. This is the message that the SGI has been striving to bring to as wide an audience as possible, most recently through the exhibition "From a Culture of Violence to a Culture of Peace: Transforming the Human Spirit."

The threat posed by nuclear weapons is neither immediately visible nor consistently palpable within the realities of daily life, and there is a tendency to consider this threat as merely a relic of the tragic past.

In order to break down the walls of apathy, it is not enough simply to make people aware of the inhumane nature of nuclear weapons or the threat they pose. We need to recognize the irrationality and inhumanity of living in a world overshadowed by nuclear weapons, wrenched and distorted by the structural violence they embody.

In this sense, I am in full agreement with the sentiment expressed by President of the Pugwash Conferences on Science and World Affairs and former UN Under-Secretary-General for Disarmament Affairs Jayantha Dhanapala[338]:

Disarmament is preeminently a humanitarian endeavour for the protection of the human rights of people and their survival. We have to see the campaign for nuclear disarmament as analogous to

---

338 Jayantha Dhanapala (1938–), Sri Lankan diplomat, UN Under-Secretary-General for Disarmament Affairs (1998–2003), President of the Pugwash Conferences on Science and World Affairs (2007–).

the campaigns such as those against slavery, for gender equality and for the abolition of child labour.[339]

The crucial thing is to arouse the awareness that, as a matter of human conscience, we can never permit the people of any country to fall victim to nuclear weapons, and for each individual to express their refusal to continue living in the shadow of the threat they pose. We must each make a personal decision and determination to build a new world free of nuclear weapons. The accumulated weight of such choices made by individual citizens can be the basis and foundation for a Nuclear Weapons Convention.

For our part, the SGI initiated the People's Decade of Action for Nuclear Abolition in 2007, the fiftieth anniversary of Josei Toda's call for nuclear abolition mentioned earlier. To promote the Decade, we have organized exhibitions and seminars and have collaborated with the International Campaign to Abolish Nuclear Weapons (ICAN) organized by International Physicians for the Prevention of Nuclear War (IPPNW). We have also initiated a joint project with the Inter Press Service (IPS) news agency to support in-depth coverage of nuclear issues.

In 2010, the youth members of the Soka Gakkai in Japan collected more than 2.2 million signatures calling for an NWC, presenting these to representatives of the President of the NPT Review Conference and the UN Secretary-General, while youth and student members of the SGI in eight countries conducted a survey of the views of their peers regarding nuclear weapons. Both of these undertakings have reaffirmed to UN officials and disarmament experts how engaged young people are with these issues.

The time is indeed ripe for global civil society to take united action. The SGI will continue to promote the People's Decade, with a particular focus on efforts to bring a Nuclear Weapons Convention into being. With our youth members in the lead, we are determined to build momentum toward 2015, the seventieth anniversary of the atomic bombings of Hiroshima and Nagasaki, and toward a world free of nuclear weapons.

---

339 Global Security Institute. 2002. "2002 Global Security Institute Annual Report: An In-depth Presentation of GSI's Achievements in 2002," p. 22.

CHAPTER 4

Empowerment for Future Change

Human Security and Sustainability: Sharing Reverence for the Dignity of Life

2012 Peace Proposal (Full Text)
January 26, 2012

Motivated by the quest for a global society of peace and coexistence, I have, every year since 1983, issued a peace proposal commemorating January 26, the day the Soka Gakkai International (SGI) was founded in 1975. The present proposal will thus be the thirtieth such proposal.

The members of the SGI throughout the world are committed to the work of constructing—through a movement for peace, education and culture— a global society in which the dignity of each person shines and all people can live in security. The spiritual foundations for this effort are found in the philosophy of Buddhism which reverences the inherent value and dignity of life. Specifically, we are inspired by the fervent desire expressed by second Soka Gakkai president Josei Toda[1]: "I wish to see the word 'misery' no longer used to describe the world, any country, any individual."[2]

Sadly, the planet continues to be wracked by violent conflict and civil unrest; people around the world face unacceptable threats to their lives and dignity in the form of poverty, hunger and environmental destruction, while the suffering caused by human rights violations and discrimination remains widespread. Further, there has been the wrenching spectacle of natural disasters that instantly rob people of their lives, disrupting and undermining the foundations of entire societies.

---

1   Josei Toda (1900–58), second president of the Soka Gakkai (1951–58).
2   (trans. from) Toda, Josei. 1981–90. *Toda Josei zenshu* [The Complete Works of Josei Toda]. 9 vols. Tokyo: Seikyo Shimbunsha. Vol. 3, p. 290.

Recent years have seen a series of major natural disasters, from the Indian Ocean earthquake and tsunami in 2004 to the massive earthquake in Haiti in 2010, exacting a horrific toll in human life. Japan was struck by a devastating earthquake and tsunami in March last year, while earthquakes also hit New Zealand and Turkey; Thailand and the Philippines experienced deadly flooding; and severe drought afflicted Somalia and much of East Africa.

I offer my heartfelt sympathies to all those affected by these disasters, my prayers for the repose of the deceased and moral support to those who are struggling to reconstruct their lives and communities.

There is also the fact, noted by the Japanese physicist Torahiko Terada[3] who issued repeated calls for more effective measures against earthquakes and tsunami, that the more civilization advances, the more intense the impact of nature's violent forces becomes.

The partial meltdown at the Fukushima Nuclear Power Plant provoked by the March 11, 2011, Tohoku earthquake and tsunami is symbolic of this. The resulting release of radiation contaminated a broad area not limited to Japanese national territory, forcing large numbers of people from their homes. It is not known when people will be able to return, and there are concerns about the impact on children's health as well as on food and agricultural products.

The compound impact of this natural and human disaster has been without precedent. It calls into question contemporary society's reliance on nuclear energy and, more broadly, the scale and pace of scientific-technological development.

The human security perspective

The economist Amartya Sen[4] has long been vocal in his warnings about the threats that can descend on communities without warning. His experience, as a young boy, of the severe famine that struck his native Bengal was formative and has inspired a lifetime of socio-economic research driven by a strong concern about the issues of poverty and inequality. He has called for the promotion, on a global scale, of the methods and approaches of "human

---

3   Torahiko Terada (1878–1935), Japanese scientist and author.
4   Amartya Sen (1933–), Indian economist, recipient of the Nobel Prize in Economic Sciences in 1998.

security" that focus on protecting the lives, livelihoods and dignity of people. In particular, he singles out "the dangers of sudden deprivation":

> The insecurities that threaten human survival or the safety of daily life, or imperil the natural dignity of men and women, or expose human beings to the uncertainty of disease and pestilence, or subject vulnerable people to abrupt penury related to economic downturns demand that special attention be paid to the dangers of sudden deprivation.[5]

Professor Sen calls attention to the fact that a genuinely secure and stable society cannot be realized without alleviating and, to the degree possible, eliminating sources of threat and insecurity to "the vital core of all human lives."[6]

Natural disaster is not the only form unanticipated threats can take: they can also arise from economic crises that create widening insecurity in people's lives and rapid environmental degradation brought about by climate change. All of these have the potential to impact both developed and developing countries.

The 2003 report of the Commission on Human Security, which Professor Sen cochaired with Dr. Sadako Ogata,[7] states:

> When people experience repeated crises and unpreventable disasters that cause them to fall—whether from extreme poverty, personal injury or bankruptcy, or society-wide shocks or disasters—the human security perspective is that there should be hands to catch them.[8]

In September of last year, World Bank President Robert Zoellick[9] warned that the world had entered a new phase of economic danger, and there is

---

5   CHS (Commission on Human Security). 2003. "Human Security Now: The Report of the Commission on Human Security." New York: CHS, p. 8.

6   Ibid., p. 4.

7   Sadako Ogata (1927–), Japanese diplomat, United Nations High Commissioner for Refugees (1991–2001).

8   CHS (Commission on Human Security). 2003. "Human Security Now: The Report of the Commission on Human Security." New York: CHS, p. 78.

9   Robert B. Zoellick (1953–), US politician, President of the World Bank (2007–12).

indeed concern that the chain reaction of economic crises will continue to spread from one country to the next. The global economy, which has been stagnant since the financial crisis of 2008, has more recently been struck by a widening sovereign debt crisis in Europe that first surfaced in Greece. Last summer, the credit rating for the United States' sovereign debt was downgraded for the first time ever. Together, these events have contributed to increasingly unstable financial markets and a further slowing of economic activity.

According to a recent International Labour Organization (ILO) report, global unemployment stands at nearly 200 million worldwide.[10] In many countries, people's living standards are under increasing threat. The impact of unemployment has been particularly severe on younger workers who, in some countries, may be two to three times more likely to be unemployed than the members of other age groups.[11] Even when they are able to find work, it is often part-time or irregular and thus poorly paid. Such insecurity is becoming a fact of life for young people around the world.

In past proposals, I have sought to address the distortions in global society that have resulted in a "living gap" and a "dignity gap." By this I mean the impermissible inequality in the value accorded to people's life and dignity based on nothing more than the society into which they were born and the circumstances in which they were raised.

In addition to these structural issues, people's lives, livelihoods and dignity can also be grievously undermined by the "dangers of sudden deprivation" such as those brought about by natural disasters or economic crises, and it is also crucial that we confront these. This is the area I would like to focus on and explore in this proposal.

The agony of loss

It is the nature of disastrous events to destroy in an instant those things that are most precious, necessary and irreplaceable to human life. Nothing is more devastating than the loss of people who have been an integral part of our

---

10   See ILO (International Labour Organization). 2012. "Global Employment Trends 2012: Preventing a Deeper Jobs Crisis." Geneva: ILO, p. 9.

11   See ILO (International Labour Organization). 2011. "Global Employment Trends for Youth: 2011 Update." Geneva: ILO, p. 2.

lives—the parent who raised us, the partner who shared our joys and sorrows, the treasured child or grandchild, the close friend or neighbor.

Buddhism refers to this as the inevitable suffering of being parted from those we love. No one is exempt from the stabbing pain that this provokes.

I am reminded of the following episode from the life of the American philosopher Ralph Waldo Emerson,[12] whose works I have loved since I was young. In his journal, Emerson recorded the death of his five-year-old son with these simple words: "Yesterday night at 15 minutes after eight my little Waldo ended his life."[13]

It had been Emerson's constant practice since his youth to keep a journal for philosophical and literary reflection. This poignant recording of the painful fact would seem to be all that he was able to muster in that moment.

The perhaps even more telling indicator of the depth of Emerson's grief is to be found in the subsequent two-day silence that is finally broken by this entry:

> The sun went up in the morning sky with all his light, but the landscape was dishonored by this loss. For this boy in whose remembrance I have both slept & awaked so oft, decorated for me the morning star, & the evening cloud. . . .[14]

Buddhism has always been centrally concerned with the mysteries of life and death. In 1276, Nichiren,[15] the founder of the school of Buddhism practiced by the members of the SGI, addressed a letter to a female believer who, after the death of her husband, had also lost her son in an unforeseen tragedy.

In it, he expresses the feelings that he imagines must fill the heart of this grieving mother, knowing that she must be wondering why her son had died, not her.

> Why did they not take you instead of your son? Why did they let you survive only to be tormented by such grief?[16]

---

12   Ralph Waldo Emerson (1803–82), American author.

13   Emerson, Ralph Waldo. 1960–82. *The Journals and Miscellaneous Notebooks of Ralph Waldo Emerson*. 16 vols. Cambridge, Massachusetts: Belknap Press / Harvard University Press. Vol. 8, p. 163.

14   Ibid.

15   Nichiren (1222–82), Buddhist monk, founder of Nichiren Buddhism.

16   Nichiren. 1999–2006. *The Writings of Nichiren Daishonin*. 2 vols. Ed. and trans. by The Gosho Translation Committee. Tokyo: Soka Gakkai. Vol. 1, p. 662.

Through his words, he seeks to enter into and share her suffering.

> I am certain you must feel that you would not hesitate to plunge into
> fire yourself, or to smash your own skull if, by so doing, you could
> see your son again. In imagining your grief, my tears do not cease.[17]

Disasters inflict on large numbers of people the suffering of the loss of friends and family members, unexpectedly and without warning. Society as a whole must be prepared to offer the kind of long-term support that is essential in such cases.

Tragically, disasters may also result in the destruction of the homes that were the basis for people's daily lives and the shredding of the bonds of community. A home is much more than simply a vessel containing the processes of life; it is inscribed with the history of a family, filled with the emotions and sensations of daily living. It encloses a special kind of time linking past to present and present to future; its loss ruptures the history of our lives.

Further, when entire communities are devastated, as in the case of the tsunami that accompanied the massive earthquake that struck Japan last March, there is an instantaneous severing of connections to people and place. The intensity of this loss grows in proportion to our affection for and attachment to the community. Even when people are able to find new places to live, they are forced to adjust to life in a new environment often without the support of the human connections and relationships developed over the years.

When I think of the agonies suffered by the evacuees, I am reminded of the words of the French author Antoine de Saint-Exupéry[18]:

> For nothing, in truth, can replace that companion. Old friends cannot
> be created out of hand. Nothing can match the treasure of common
> memories, of trials endured together, of quarrels and reconciliations
> and generous emotions. It is idle, having planted an acorn in the
> morning, to expect that afternoon to sit in the shade of the oak.[19]

---

17   Ibid.

18   Antoine Marie Jean-Baptiste Roger, Comte de Saint Exupéry (1900–44), French aristocrat, writer, poet and pioneering aviator.

19   Saint-Exupéry, Antoine de. 1992. *Wind, Sand and Stars*. Trans. by Lewis Galantiére. Orlando, Austin, New York, San Diego and London: Harcourt, Inc., p. 27.

The sense expressed here of the precious bonds of friendship and the sadness provoked by their loss pertains equally, I believe, to the loss of one's accustomed home, hometown or community. This is a reality we should always bear in mind.

Likewise, the sudden destruction of places of employment robs people of their livelihoods and thus the sense of purpose and dignity that so many derive from work.

I am currently engaged in a dialogue with Prof. Stuart Rees[20] of the Sydney Peace Foundation in Australia on the theme of peace with justice. One facet of this theme is the problem of unemployment and the unacceptable threat it poses to human dignity.

As Professor Rees has written:

> [Unemployed] people are being denied the profound human sense of self-worth that comes from work; either in the sense of earning one's keep, having the satisfaction of achieving something, or making a contribution to society.[21]

The globally renowned immunologist Tomio Tada,[22] who, at the age of sixty-seven, suffered a debilitating stroke, later described the shock he experienced when he realized he would have to abandon the work he had been engaged in.

> From that day, everything changed: my life, my goal in living, my joys, my sadness—everything was different from before.[23]

> As I thought about it, I was overwhelmed by an unbearable sense of loss, which gnawed at me mercilessly. I had to abandon everything.[24]

---

20 Stuart Rees (1939–), British-born Australian academic and author, founder of the Sydney Peace Foundation.

21 Rees, Stuart, Gordon Rodley and Frank Stilwell. 1993. *Beyond the Market: Alternatives to Economic Rationalism*. Leichhardt: Pluto Press Australia, p. 222.

22 Tomio Tada (1934–2010), Japanese immunologist, President of the International Union of Immunological Societies (IUIS) (1994–97).

23 (trans. from) Tada, Tomio. 2007. *Kamokunaru kyojin* [The Quiet Giant]. Tokyo: Shueisha, p. 10.

24 Ibid., p. 29.

Work and employment serve as a form of proof that one is necessary to society. Even if it does not bring particular recognition or fame, work can be a source of fulfillment and pride, realized through the steady pursuit of the role that is ours and ours alone to play. For people who have lost their homes and possessions in a disaster and are dealing with the strains of life as evacuees, the loss of work not only represents a severing of the economic lifeline but can further undermine the spiritual grounding necessary to move forward.

For this reason I believe that we all share the responsibility to support people in rebuilding their lives, enabling them to regain a sense of hope, and in particular, for those who have been compelled to change their place of residence or work, to rediscover places where they can feel a sense of belonging.

The lessons of history

What do we do to contain tragedy, whether it arises from natural disasters or from the complex of global issues? Clearly, we need to develop new sources of vision and concrete responses if we are to prevent a widening scope of suffering and see the word "misery" no longer used to describe the world.

Here, I think the words of Arnold J. Toynbee,[25] one of the great historians of the twentieth century, are relevant: "Our experience in the past gives us the only light on the future that is accessible to us."[26]

This year will mark forty years since I visited Dr. Toynbee's home in London at his invitation, engaging in extensive dialogue. One theme to which he continued to return in both our conversations and his writings was the "lessons of history." Fundamental to Dr. Toynbee's view of history is what he described as "the philosophical contemporaneity of all civilizations."[27]

His thinking on this point was importantly shaped by an experience he had shortly after the outbreak of World War I, while lecturing on Thucydides' account of the fifth-century BCE Peloponnesian War. Toynbee describes this as follows:

---

25   Arnold J. Toynbee (1889–1975), British historian.

26   Toynbee, Arnold J. 1966. *Change and Habit: The Challenge of Our Time.* New York and London: Oxford University Press, p. 3.

27   Toynbee, Arnold J. 1960. *Civilization on Trial: and The World and the West.* New York: Meridian Books, p. 19.

I suddenly realized that the experiences we had just had were like those of Thucydides at the beginning of the Peloponnesian War. I felt that his being separated from us by twenty-three centuries was really irrelevant. His total experience lay in our future.[28]

With this penetrating understanding, Toynbee was able to read lessons from the millennia of human history that are directly relevant to the aporia of our present-day world. In the published record of our dialogue, he states: "We must not be defeatist, passive or aloof in our reaction to the current evils that threaten mankind's survival."[29] I will never forget the impression these words made on me.

In the same way, I feel it is relevant to reference the treatise "On Establishing the Correct Teaching for the Peace of the Land" (Jp. *Rissho ankoku ron*), authored by Nichiren, as a framework for thinking about contemporary conditions. Nichiren addressed this treatise to Hojo Tokiyori,[30] who wielded ultimate political authority within the Kamakura shogunate, in 1260.

The work opens with this lamentation:

In recent years, there have been unusual disturbances in the heavens, strange occurrences on earth, famine and pestilence, all affecting every corner of the empire and spreading throughout the land. Oxen and horses lie dead in the streets, and the bones of the stricken crowd the highways.[31]

Indeed, the Japan of his day had been hit by a succession of disasters that had taken the lives of great numbers of people, giving rise to unimaginable misery. Nichiren was motivated to pen this work by the unquenchable urge to find some way of alleviating the people's suffering.

---

28 Toynbee, Arnold J. and Philip Toynbee. 1963. *Comparing Notes: A Dialogue Across a Generation*. London: Weidenfeld and Nicolson, p. 19.

29 Toynbee, Arnold J. and Daisaku Ikeda. 2007. *Choose Life*. London and New York: I.B.Tauris.

30 Hojo Tokiyori (1227–63), the fifth regent of the Kamakura shogunate (1246–56).

31 Nichiren. 1999–2006. *The Writings of Nichiren Daishonin*. 2 vols. Ed. and trans. by The Gosho Translation Committee. Tokyo: Soka Gakkai. Vol. 1, p. 6.

The role of the state

Rereading this text in light of present-day conditions and the imperatives of human security, there are three aspects that strike me as being especially relevant.

The first is the philosophical stance that the highest priority of the state must be the well-being and security of ordinary people.

The ideas set out in "On Establishing" form the core of Nichiren's Buddhist philosophy, as attested to by the fact that over the course of his life he hand-copied the text again and again. When we review the extant texts copied in Nichiren's own hand, an important fact comes to light. In addition to the standard Chinese characters for "land" or "country," which consist of a framing square—representing walls or borders—enclosing either the symbol for the king or a weapon, Nichiren uses a character in which the symbol for the common people is enclosed by the surrounding borders or walls. He uses this character—expressive of the idea that it is the people and their lives, not political authority or military force, that form the basis of the state—in the vast majority of cases. It could be said Nichiren's philosophy is condensed into this choice and use of Chinese characters.

On another occasion, he wrote that those in power must be "the hands and feet of the people."[32] That is, they must serve the interests of the common people, protecting their livelihoods and happiness.

By authoring and presenting "On Establishing" to the de facto political leader of his time, Nichiren sought to remonstrate with that leader based on his conviction that a correct understanding of Buddhist philosophy could dispel the darkness and confusion enveloping society. This was, needless to say, an extremely dangerous undertaking, and Nichiren was in fact subjected to two exiles and numerous attempts on his life despite having committed no secular crime.

Some 750 years after this text was written, it remains strikingly relevant, especially in terms of the human security concerns that now attract such attention. On this point, it is appropriate to quote the report of the Commission on Human Security again:

---

32   (trans. from) Nichiren. 1952. *Nichiren Daishonin gosho zenshu* [The Complete Works of Nichiren Daishonin]. Ed. by Nichiko Hori. Tokyo: Soka Gakkai, p. 171.

The state remains the fundamental purveyor of security. Yet it often fails to fulfill security obligations—and at times has even become a source of threat to its own people. That is why attention must now shift from the security of the state to the security of the people—to human security.[33]

In this regard, we need to ask what is the purpose of a state's existence, however successful it may be in economic or military terms, if it fails to make efforts to alleviate the suffering of its citizens and support their pursuit of a life with dignity.

Disasters and crises bring to the surface the fault lines in society that might otherwise remain hidden. They reveal the particular vulnerabilities of the aged, women, children, people with disabilities and those marginalized by economic disparities.

This has certainly been the case in the aftermath of the earthquake that struck Japan last March. When we consider the terrible burden of suffering borne by all people in the afflicted regions, but most especially by these vulnerable populations, it is impossible not to be dismayed by the very slow political response.

Recognizing our interconnectedness

The second aspect of Nichiren's treatise that I would like to consider is his call for the establishment of a worldview rooted in a vital sense of our interconnectedness. To quote a key passage: "If you care anything about your personal security, you should first of all pray for order and tranquillity throughout the four quarters of the land, should you not?"[34] This is how he expresses the idea that just as we cannot experience happiness and security in isolation— enjoying them even as others suffer from their want—we likewise cannot live insulated against the miseries and threats that afflict others.

As the problem of climate change demonstrates, in an increasingly interdependent world what may now appear as only a localized, if dire, impact in fact contains the potential to pose threats on a global scale. Likewise those threats

---

33   CHS (Commission on Human Security). 2003. "Human Security Now: The Report of the Commission on Human Security." New York: CHS, p. 2.

34   Nichiren. 1999–2006. *The Writings of Nichiren Daishonin.* 2 Vols. Ed. and trans. by The Gosho Translation Committee. Tokyo: Soka Gakkai. Vol. 1, p. 24.

whose effects may seem relatively small now can, if not dealt with, develop into problems of intractable gravity for future generations.

The importance of considering the temporal and spatial dimensions of threats was touched on in a report submitted to the United Nations General Assembly by UN Secretary-General Ban Ki-moon[35] in 2010:

> [B]y understanding how particular constellations of threats to individuals and communities translate into broader intra- and inter-State security breaches, human security seeks to prevent and mitigate the occurrence of future threats.[36]

Herein lies the significance of the Buddhist view that unless there is peace and security in "the four quarters of the land"—society as a whole—our individual or personal security will prove illusory.

This way of thinking is rooted in the Buddhist teaching of "dependent origination" (deep or existential interdependence). The words of Spanish philosopher José Ortega y Gasset[37] that I have referenced on numerous occasions in these proposals, "I am myself plus my circumstance, and if I do not save it, I cannot save myself," address the same point, as does his admonition to "save . . . the phenomena; that is to say to look for the meaning of what surrounds us."[38]

Whenever tragedies occur, people from throughout the world typically respond with earnest expressions of concern and material support. Such manifestations of empathy and solidarity are an incalculable source of courage, a bright light of hope for the victims of the disaster.

Nichiren is also recorded as saying: "the varied sufferings that all living beings undergo—all these are Nichiren's own sufferings."[39] And in "On Establishing" he describes a way of life in which we resonate viscerally with the pain of others and work tirelessly for its alleviation.

---

35 Ban Ki-moon (1944–), South Korean statesman, 8th Secretary-General of the United Nations (2007–).

36 UNGA (United Nations General Assembly). 2010. "Human Security." A/64/701. Report of the Secretary-General. March 8, p. 7.

37 José Ortega y Gasset (1883–1955), Spanish philosopher.

38 Ortega y Gasset, José. 2000. *Meditations on Quixote*. Trans. by Evelyn Rugg and Diego Marín. Urbana and Chicago: University of Illinois Press, p. 45.

39 Nichiren. 2004. *The Record of the Orally Transmitted Teachings*. Trans. by Burton Watson. Tokyo: Soka Gakkai, p. 138.

While Nichiren speaks of "the four quarters of the land" and "the nation," the scope of his concern is expansive in terms of space and time. This can be seen in his repeated use of such terms as "Jambudvipa" (a word from traditional Buddhist cosmology meaning the entire world) and his references to "the boundless future."

Today, these two vectors might be expressed as the determination not to ignore tragedy wherever it occurs and to prevent the negative legacies of the present from being visited on future generations. The former could also be thought of as awareness of our responsibilities as global citizens and the latter as a commitment to sustainability.

As people, we share this one planet which we will eventually pass on to our children. A clear and vital awareness of the full dimensions of life's interconnectedness must be the basis for all our actions.

A focus on empowerment

The third aspect of Nichiren's treatise that I would like to touch on is his focus on what today would be termed empowerment, specifically his insight that the greatest empowerment is realized when, through dialogue, we advance from a shared awareness and concern about a difficult situation to a shared pledge or vow to achieve its resolution.

Like many Buddhist texts or scriptures, "On Establishing" takes the form of dialogue—an exchange of questions and responses—in this case between a visitor representing secular authority and a host representing the perspectives of Buddhism. At the opening of the text, a traveler stops at the abode of the host where they discuss and express their deep distress at the unbroken succession of disasters that has struck the land. It is this sharing of concern and the determination somehow to bring the situation under control that enables them to see beyond the differences of their respective positions and commence the dialogue.

As the dialogue develops, the host and the guest both present their views based on their earnestly held convictions. The host, responding to the anger and confusion expressed at points by the guest, scrupulously explains and resolves each of his doubts. Through the dramatic encounter and confrontation of soul with soul, the guest is finally and fully convinced of the correctness of the host's assertions. He gives voice to the shared vow that has emerged from their initial sharing of concern: "But it is not enough that I alone should accept and have faith in your words—we must see to it that others as well are warned of their errors."[40]

The conclusion finally reached through this process of dialogue is a powerful recognition of the need to believe in the limitless possibilities of the individual human being—the message of the Lotus Sutra which constitutes the essence of Buddhist teachings. It is faith in the proposition that all people possess infinite potential, the capacity to bring forth their unique and essential dignity.

An awakening to this dignity can spark the flame of hope in a person sunk in the depths of anguish. That person in turn can ignite hope in another, and the resulting momentum of human renewal has the power to drive away the dark confusion that shrouds society.

Here again, the words of the Commission on Human Security resonate with the ideas expressed in this ancient text. For example, human security must "build on people's strengths and aspirations"[41]; one key is "People's ability to act on their own behalf—and on behalf of others."[42]

> The primary question of every human security activity should not
> be: What can we do? It should be: How does this activity build on
> the efforts and capabilities of those directly affected?[43]

Describing the chaos and confusion of his time, Nichiren deplored the fact that the people had become disempowered. Repeated calamities had taken their toll on people's morale, and many indeed seemed to have lost the will to live. Further, the prevailing ethos of society was one that encouraged people to avoid confronting realities and to seek tranquillity solely in the realm of the inner life.

Nichiren considered teachings that encourage resignation or escapism as a path to salvation to be the "one evil" that clouds people's vision, blinding them to the limitless potential they in fact possess. For Nichiren, the only

---

40   Nichiren. 1999–2006. *The Writings of Nichiren Daishonin*. 2 vols. Ed. and trans. by The Gosho Translation Committee. Tokyo: Soka Gakkai. Vol. 1, p. 26.

41   CHS (Commission on Human Security). 2003. "Human Security Now: The Report of the Commission on Human Security." New York: CHS, p. 4.

42   Ibid., p. 11.

43   Ibid., pp. 11–12.

viable path through the deadlock facing society is for people to believe in each other's possibilities and to work together to bring forth those capabilities.

In this connection, I am reminded of an episode recounted by the Austrian philosopher Ivan Illich,[44] who urged that we must never fear being a "candle in the dark."[45] He describes his friendship with a Catholic bishop, Hélder Câmara,[46] who was struggling against the inhumane brutalities of the Brazilian military junta in the early 1960s. Câmara attempted to engage in dialogue with a general who would later become known as one of Brazil's cruelest torturers. This ended in failure, and after the general left, Câmara fell into a lengthy silence. Finally, he turned to Illich and said:

> You must *never* give up. As long as a person is alive, somewhere beneath the ashes there is a little bit of remaining fire, and all our task is . . . You must blow . . . carefully, very carefully blow . . . and blow . . . you'll see if it lights up. You mustn't worry whether it takes fire again or not. All you have to do is blow.[47]

On one level, Câmara's words "You must *never* give up" represent his attempt to restore his own determination; at the same time, they reverberate with the importance of offering wholehearted encouragement to those who stand at the precipice of despair.

The spirit of empowerment is found in the act of carefully fanning the "little bit of remaining fire" in the human soul of both those who support us and oppose us. I believe that this patient faith and effort is the driving force behind the human rights struggles of Mahatma Gandhi[48] and Dr. Martin Luther King Jr.,[49] as well as those who led the popular revolutions of Eastern Europe that brought the Cold War to an end, and, more recently, the movement for democracy widely referred to as the "Arab Spring."

---

44 Ivan Illich (1926–2002), Austrian philosopher and Roman Catholic priest.
45 Cayley, David. 1992. *Ivan Illich in Conversation*. Toronto: House of Anansi Press, Inc., p. 147.
46 Hélder Pessoa Câmara (1909–99), Brazilian writer, thinker and Roman Catholic archbishop.
47 Cayley, David. 1992. *Ivan Illich in Conversation*. Toronto: House of Anansi Press, Inc., p. 148.
48 Mohandas (Mahatma) Gandhi (1869–1948), Indian champion of nonviolence.
49 Martin Luther King Jr. (1929–68), American religious leader and civil rights activist, recipient of the Nobel Prize for Peace in 1964.

During the dark years of Cold War confrontation, I visited communist countries such as the USSR and China to promote exchanges aimed at relaxing tensions and fostering mutual understanding. I have also striven to engage in dialogue with political and intellectual leaders from the world's various cultures and religions. These efforts to foster friendship across borders have been driven by the conviction that the only lasting basis for building a global society of peaceful coexistence lies in the transformation of each individual heart. This can be achieved only through the kind of dialogue and interaction that stirs each of us to the depths of our being.

The recovery of the heart

Of the three aspects of Nichiren's treatise that I have discussed, I believe that this last, empowerment, is of particular relevance to the restoration of people's sense of mental equilibrium and health, "the recovery of the heart." This kind of mental and spiritual reconstruction is among the most difficult and time-consuming challenges we face.

Earlier I made reference to the Commission on Human Security's assertion that human security must "build on people's strengths and aspirations." This challenge is difficult, if not impossible, for individuals to initiate in isolation, much less to sustain to the point where one's entire life is illuminated by the light of hope. This is why, to speak metaphorically, people need the safety ropes of heart-to-heart connections and the pitons of encouragement if they are to continue their ascent up life's precipitous cliffs.

This is illustrated by the lives of three historical figures I referenced earlier: Emerson, Saint-Exupéry and Tada.

Emerson's life was marked not only by the tragedy of the loss of his son but also the earlier deaths of his first wife and two of his siblings. He was later able to reflect that these many losses had come to assume "the aspect of a guide or genius,"[50] providing him with the impetus to make positive changes to his way of living.

In like manner, Saint-Exupéry would later write:

> What saves a man is to take a step. Then another step. It is always the same step, but you have to take it. . . . Only the unknown

---

50   Emerson, Ralph Waldo. 1971–2011. *The Collected Works of Ralph Waldo Emerson*. 9 vols. Cambridge, Massachusetts: Belknap Press / Harvard University Press. Vol. 2, p. 73.

frightens men. But once a man has faced the unknown, that terror becomes the known.[51]

The immunologist Tomio Tada eventually was able to return to writing, and, echoing Dante's *Divine Comedy,* penned these words: "If I am in a hellish condition, then let me write my Inferno." He also said, "I do not know what awaits me, but I know it will represent proof that I have lived."[52] In this way, he was able to regain a sense of purpose in life.

Underlying each of these dramas of recovery from tragedy, there was undoubtedly the support and assistance of others.

When the philosopher William James[53] undertook an investigation of the survivors of the earthquake that devastated San Francisco in 1906, he noted that when people were able to share their experiences, there was a perceptible difference in their sense of suffering and loss. Even if such sharing does not immediately translate into the ability to move forward, it can encourage people steeped in pain to look to the future.

To this end, we must learn to attend to the words that flow from another's soul, to allow our heart to shudder with another's grief and to patiently blow the breath of life on the small ember that lies hidden in another's heart.

As the German philosopher Karl Jaspers[54] noted, the vast body of teachings left by Shakyamuni—the sutras that are known as the storehouse of 80,000 teachings—is for the most part the record of words spoken to individuals and small groups. For Shakyamuni believed that "to speak to all is to speak to each individual."[55] His teachings were thus expounded in response to the specific worries and sufferings of individuals.

Calling out to others as "friend," Shakyamuni strove to enter into their hearts and minds, to clarify the essential nature of their suffering and to help them awaken to the means to overcome it. As the parable of the man shot by a poisonous arrow demonstrates, the wisdom of Buddhism does not expend

---

51 Saint-Exupéry, Antoine de. 1992. *Wind, Sand and Stars.* Trans. by Lewis Galantiére. Orlando, Austin, New York, San Diego and London: Harcourt, Inc., pp. 38–39.

52 (trans. from) Tada, Tomio. 2007. *Kamokunaru kyojin* [The Quiet Giant]. Tokyo: Shueisha, p. 48.

53 William James (1842–1910), American philosopher and psychologist.

54 Karl Jaspers (1883–1969), German philosopher.

55 Jaspers, Karl. 1962. *Socrates, Buddha, Confucius, Jesus: The Paradigmatic Individuals.* Trans. by Ralph Manheim. San Diego, New York and London: Harcourt Brace & Co., p. 35.

itself on metaphysical concepts or abstract, philosophical debates. Rather, it issues inexhaustibly from the deep desire to alleviate the suffering of each unique individual.

This can also be seen in Nichiren's teachings. In the letters he addressed to his followers he embraces each of them, lamenting their difficulties as if they were his own. His words speak to us today, offering us important guidelines for living, precisely because they are the crystallization of his compassionate prayer and determination to help his followers live their lives undefeated by such trials.

With the people

Today, members of the SGI throughout the world continue the work of fostering heart-to-heart bonds with their fellow citizens through the practice of one-to-one dialogue, constructing networks of mutual encouragement. In times of emergency, such as natural disasters, we have made our facilities available to evacuees, transported and distributed relief supplies, assisted in cleanup efforts and engaged in various other relief activities. Individual members have continued to support and encourage their neighbors even as they themselves endure the impacts of these disasters.

Such acts are a spontaneous expression of concern and the irrepressible desire to help. They are a natural extension of day-to-day religious activities that are based on the sharing of others' joys and sorrows, and the deep commitment to the kind of happiness that is only experienced when shared by self and others.

During the Office of the United Nations High Commissioner for Refugees (UNHCR) annual consultations with nongovernmental organizations (NGOs) in Geneva in June 2011, a session was devoted to the role of faith-based organizations (FBOs). This demonstrates the growing focus on the contribution made by FBOs to help those impacted by the threats arising in society.

Drawing on the experience of the earthquake and tsunami in Japan, an SGI representative addressed the session as follows: "Even in a complex and insecure environment, it is empowerment of the surviving victims that makes humanitarian relief effective and sustainable with their self-help and participation, and FBOs are in a strong position to contribute in this way."[56]

---

56 SGI (Soka Gakkai International). 2011. "Soka Gakkai's Relief and Post-Disaster Recovery Support Activities Following the Great East Japan Earthquake on March 11, 2011." June 28. http://www.sgi.org/assets/pdf/Mr.-Kawai's-presentation-at-UNHCR.pdf (accessed April 2, 2013).

As an example of this kind of empowerment, I am reminded of an episode described by Dr. Martin Luther King, Jr., of one elderly woman participating in the Montgomery Bus Boycott, refusing to ride the racially segregated buses. A man in a car who was also supporting the boycott stopped beside her and invited her to ride with him. But she refused, stating: "I'm not walking for myself. I'm walking for my children and my grandchildren."[57]

In the aftermath of disasters, there are countless people who, despite being physically and emotionally wounded themselves, are prompted to take action out of their desire to do whatever they can to help friends, loved ones and people they see in distress.

Buddhism teaches that whatever our individual circumstances, we can always discover the capacity to help others; it also assures us that those who have suffered the most have the right to the greatest happiness.

The Buddhist scriptures state, "The treasure towers are none other than all living beings."[58] This means that the magnificent treasure tower of cosmic scale that is described in the Lotus Sutra is nothing other than the original essence of each individual human being. A person who has awakened to this primordial dignity gains possession of an indestructible state of mind. This is a sense of dignity that cannot be undermined by any threat or tribulation. As the sutras state, "a mad elephant can only destroy your body; it cannot destroy your mind."[59]

As more and more people develop this conviction, extending a helping hand to those mired in suffering and together taking the first steps in the process of recovery, countless treasure towers rise up, setting in full motion the reconstruction of the community. This principle lies at the heart of our beliefs in the SGI, and forms the foundation for our activities.

As we have seen following the disasters of recent years, there are many examples throughout the world of networks of mutual support in the community and voluntary activities, involving individuals from every walk of life, springing up when local authorities have been overwhelmed. I believe this same impulse underlies the outpouring of aid and encouragement offered by people in other countries.

---

57   King, Martin Luther, Jr. 2010. *Stride Toward Freedom: The Montgomery Story.* Boston: Beacon Press, pp. 63–64.

58   Nichiren. 2004. *The Record of the Orally Transmitted Teachings.* Trans. by Burton Watson. Tokyo: Soka Gakkai, p. 230.

59   Nichiren. 1999–2006. *The Writings of Nichiren Daishonin.* 2 vols. Ed. and trans. by The Gosho Translation Committee. Tokyo: Soka Gakkai. Vol. 2, p. 135.

The actions of people at such times of disaster demonstrate the importance of constantly nourishing bonds of support and of instilling an ethos of mutual aid. This is the best way to strengthen the capacity of societies to respond to the "dangers of sudden deprivation."

Dr. Wangari Maathai,[60] the Nobel Peace Prize laureate who passed away last year, developed the Green Belt Movement in Kenya and other parts of Africa as a means of empowering people in the face of the threat of environmental destruction. The movement repeatedly met with obstruction and harassment, with many of the newly planted trees being damaged and destroyed. "Yet the trees, like us, survived," Dr. Maathai wrote. "The rains would come and the sun would shine and before you knew it the trees would be throwing new leaves and shoots into the air."[61] The encouragement to be gleaned from her words is unforgettable.

She maintained that the Green Belt Movement succeeded in bringing out the energies of people because it was "structured to avoid the urge to work *for* rather than *with* them."[62]

I believe that this spirit of working with rather than for others is the key to generating the kind of self-reinforcing cycles of empowerment of which I have been speaking. This process, driven and directed by the people themselves, can dispel the darkness of despair and cause a sun burnished with hope for the future to climb above the horizon.

A clear future vision

Next, I would like to discuss concrete proposals to tackle various threats that seriously impact people's lives, livelihoods and dignity.

But first, it is useful to note two perspectives stressed by Dr. Elise Boulding,[63] one of the earliest proponents of cultures of peace. The first is the

---

60 Wangari Maathai (1940–2011), Kenyan politician and environmental activist, founder of the Green Belt Movement, recipient of the Nobel Prize for Peace in 2004.

61 Maathai, Wangari. 2008. *Unbowed: A Memoir*. London: Arrow Books, p. 207.

62 Maathai, Wangari. 2003. *The Green Belt Movement: Sharing the Approach and the Experience*. New York: Lantern Books, p. 72.

63 Elise Boulding (1920–2010), American peace scholar and activist.

importance of taking action with a clear vision of the future one wants to see. The second is the value of thinking in terms of a time frame she called the "two-hundred-year present."[64]

Concerning the first point, Dr. Boulding shared the following episode with me. In the 1960s, at a meeting of academics studying the economic aspects of disarmament, she asked what a totally disarmed world would look like. To her surprise, their response was that they had no idea and thought that their job was to just explain and convince others that disarmament was possible. "How could they give themselves wholeheartedly to a movement the outcome of which they could not imagine?"[65]

I think this is an essential question. No matter how important peace and disarmament might be, if the movement to achieve them does not have a clearly defined vision pulsing at its depths, it will not generate the power needed to surmount the barriers and obstacles that reality presents. Dr. Boulding understood that a shared vision brings people together and enables them to "give themselves wholeheartedly."

Her other perspective, the concept of a 200-year present, means to live our lives conscious of a time frame spanning 100 years before today and another 100 years after today. Dr. Boulding stressed, "We do not live in the present only. If the present moment were all, its occurrences would crush us."[66] But if we think of ourselves as existing in a greater time frame, we can participate in the lifetimes of a multitude of people, from infants born this year to elderly people celebrating their 100th birthday. In this way, Dr. Boulding emphasized the importance of living with a vision of the larger community of which we are part.

This idea enables us to turn our thoughts to those who have experienced various forms of suffering and, at the same time, inspires in us a sense of responsibility to create a future in which these same sufferings will not be visited upon generations to come.

Bearing in mind these perspectives offered by Dr. Boulding, I would propose the values of humanitarianism, human rights and sustainability as

---

64   Boulding, Elise and Daisaku Ikeda. 2010. *Into Full Flower: Making Peace Cultures Happen*. Cambridge, Massachusetts: Dialogue Path Press, p. 113.

65   Ibid., p. 92.

66   Ibid., p. 113.

the core elements of any future vision to be shared by humankind. Concretely this is a vision of:

- A world that, refusing to overlook human tragedy wherever it occurs, unites in solidarity to overcome threats;
- A world that, based on the empowerment of individuals, gives priority to securing the dignity and right of all people to live in peace;
- A world that, remembering the lessons of the past, does not allow unborn generations to inherit the negative legacies of human history and directs all its energies to transforming those legacies.

This vision has underpinned my peace proposals since 1983.

In dealing with any kind of intractable problem, the approach of working back from a clear vision constitutes a kind of Ariadne's thread to help us find our way out of the maze, and also serves as the source of alternative approaches that will generate change.

On this basis, I will focus here on three major challenges—natural disasters, environmental degradation and poverty, and nuclear weapons—each of which presents future generations with threats and burdens that will only become greater the more we delay our response.

A rights-based approach

Regarding disaster risk reduction, I propose the strengthening of international frameworks to support disaster-affected populations, specifically by applying a rights-based approach and regularizing the involvement of the Office of the United Nations High Commissioner for Refugees (UNHCR).

At present, UN efforts to promote international cooperation to reduce the damage caused by disasters from a preventive perspective are centered on the International Strategy for Disaster Reduction (UNISDR). At the same time, however, given the unforeseeable nature of disasters, it is essential to be prepared to support those whose lives are impacted when they do occur.

Here I would like to advocate that, together with the humanitarian imperative, human rights be given a central stress in all relief efforts. This approach should focus on the right of those affected by disasters to live with dignity.

Specifically, I propose that relief activities for people impacted or displaced by disasters, which until now have been handled on a case-by-case basis by UNHCR, be officially included in UNHCR's mandate.

Throughout its history, UNHCR has expanded the range of beneficiaries and scope of its activities: In addition to its original mandate of refugee protection, it is now responsible for relief aid to internally displaced persons and war-affected populations, as well as the protection of asylum seekers and stateless persons. Article Nine of the UNHCR Mandate stipulates that it will engage in additional activities as the General Assembly may determine; subsequent UN General Assembly resolutions have provided the legal basis for these activities.

It is reported that the lives of approximately 160 million people are impacted by natural disasters in the world today, with 100,000 losing their lives every year. Compared to the 1970s, both the incidence of disaster and the number of people affected have approximately tripled. Most of the casualties are concentrated in developing countries, and the vicious cycle of disaster and poverty is a challenge we must respond to.[67]

UN High Commissioner for Refugees António Guterres[68] has observed: "Any new approach must be rights-based, since experience during the 2004 Indian Ocean tsunami and other recent disasters have confirmed that such emergencies generate new threats to the human rights of affected populations."[69]

As this indicates, there is an increasing focus on the protection of the dignity of those affected by disaster throughout the relief and recovery process. There remains, however, a tendency to regard a certain degree of deterioration in health and living conditions as inevitable. But the importance to victims of fully protecting each of their rights—including the implications for survival—is only accentuated in a disaster situation.

Steps should be taken to enable UNHCR to be consistently involved in disaster relief assistance. A structure should be established that allows UNHCR to conduct relief activities along with other international organizations, rooted in the principles of humanitarianism and a culture of human rights, and to make every effort to protect people's lives and dignity. We need to create a culture of human rights that champions the dignity of those afflicted by disasters, threats and social injustice.

---

67   Japan, Cabinet Office. Director General for Disaster Management. 2011. "Disaster Management in Japan." Tokyo: Japan, Cabinet Office, p. 41.

68   António Guterres (1949–), Portuguese politician, United Nations High Commissioner for Refugees (2005–).

69   Guterres, António. 2008. "Climate Change, Natural Disasters and Human Displacement: a UNHCR Perspective." October 23, p. 7.

The UN General Assembly adopted in December 2011 a historic new Declaration on Human Rights Education and Training that sets out the principles and goals by which international society should foster a culture of human rights. The Declaration, the drafting of which began in 2007 following a decision of the UN Human Rights Council, reflects the voices of civil society through the contributions of the NGO Working Group on Human Rights Education & Learning of the Conference of NGOs in Consultative Relationship with the United Nations and other civil society organizations.

As the chair of the NGO Working Group and in order to implement the spirit of the Declaration, the SGI is collaborating with Human Rights Education Associates (HREA) to coproduce an educational DVD in partnership with the Office of the UN High Commissioner for Human Rights (OHCHR).

Ensuring that the spirit of the Declaration becomes widely accepted on a global scale will result in the relief activities conducted by national and local governments having a consistent focus on human rights. The central challenge of the international community in the twenty-first century is to create a culture of human rights, and the SGI is committed to working to strengthen civil society's contribution to this process.

In this regard, I would also like to propose a greater emphasis on the role women play in all the processes from disaster risk reduction to relief and reconstruction as a priority objective of international society.

The gender perspective

In responding to disasters and other dangers of sudden deprivation, it is essential to pay close attention to the situation of each individual. At the same time, it is absolutely vital that people be empowered to transform their own circumstances, and it is here that a focus on women is indispensable.

Studies suggest that women are more likely than men to die in natural disasters, and this tendency increases with the scale of the disaster.[70] When disaster strikes, not only do women bear a disproportionate burden of the resulting deprivations, but their human rights and dignity are often exposed

---

70   See Neumayer, Eric and Thomas Plümper. 2007. "The Gendered Nature of Natural Disasters: The Impact of Catastrophic Events on the Gender Gap in Life Expectancy, 1981–2002." *Annals of the Association of American Geographers*. Vol. 97, Issue 3, p. 552.

to grievous threats. Clearly there is a need to afford greater recognition to women's special capacities to contribute to disaster mitigation and reconstruction, and reflect this in disaster response plans.

The Hyogo Framework for Action 2005–2015 adopted at the World Conference on Disaster Reduction in 2005 contained the following statement: "A gender perspective should be integrated into all disaster risk management policies, plans and decision-making processes."[71] Unfortunately, as the 2011 Global Assessment Report on Disaster Risk Reduction pointed out, progress in this regard remains inadequate. This needs to change, and to this end I think we need an unambiguous and legally binding mandate.

Here we can look to the example of Resolution 1325, adopted by the UN Security Council in October 2000, which reaffirms the importance of the equal participation and full involvement of women in all efforts to maintain and promote peace and security. This conveyed a powerful message to the international community.

Today, more than ten years after its adoption, full implementation still remains a challenge, and further support is required. But the existence of Resolution 1325 is of great significance because it has become a point of reference in the promotion of various initiatives throughout the world.

Former UN Under-Secretary-General Anwarul K. Chowdhury,[72] who played an indispensable role in the adoption of Resolution 1325, emphasized in our dialogue: "A culture of peace can take stronger root with the involvement of women. . . . We must not forget that there is no peaceful world in the true sense of the word when women are left behind."[73] Likewise, women can play a crucially important role in the areas of disaster reduction and recovery.

In the wake of the devastation caused by the Haiti earthquake in January 2010, there is growing acknowledgment within the UN system of the need to extend the scope of Resolution 1325 to natural disasters.

---

71 ISDR (International Strategy for Disaster Reduction). 2005. "Hyogo Framework for Action 2005–2015: Building the Resilience of Nations and Communities to Disasters." Adopted by the World Conference on Disaster Reduction, Kobe, Hyogo, Japan. January 18–22, p. 4.

72 Anwarul K. Chowdhury (1943–), Bangladeshi diplomat, Under-Secretary-General and High Representative of the United Nations (2002–07).

73 Chowdhury, Anwarul K. and Daisaku Ikeda. 2011. *Atarashiki chikyu shakai no sozo e—Heiwa no bunka to Kokuren o kataru* [Creating a New Global Society—A Discourse on the United Nations and a Culture of Peace]. Tokyo: Ushio Shuppansha, pp. 340–41.

Thus, I would like to propose either that the concept of peacebuilding in Resolution 1325 be explicitly expanded to include disaster risk reduction and recovery, or that a new resolution be adopted with a focus on the role women play in these areas.

I urge that Japan, which served as the host country when the Hyogo Framework for Action was adopted and has experienced major earthquakes in Kobe, Tohoku and other areas in the recent past, take the initiative and strive to act as a model for other countries by promptly improving the domestic environment for gender-conscious disaster prevention efforts.

Michelle Bachelet,[74] the former Chilean president and the first executive director of UN Women, which was created two years ago, has stressed the resilience and potential of women:

> I have seen myself what women, often in the toughest circumstances, can achieve for their families and societies if they are given the opportunity. The strength, industry and wisdom of women remain humanity's greatest untapped resource. We simply cannot afford to wait another 100 years to unlock this potential.[75]

Indeed, women must be empowered as effective change agents in the fields of disaster risk reduction, recovery and reconstruction, in line with similar recognition of their potential roles in conflict prevention, resolution and peacebuilding. It is intolerable to allow them to continue to bear the brunt of disaster situations.

The SGI has consistently engaged in efforts to raise awareness about the centrality of women to a culture of peace, and is committed to fostering a greater consciousness at the grassroots level regarding women's potential contributions in disaster-related issues.

---

74   Verónica Michelle Bachelet Jeria (1951–), President of Chile (2006–10), Executive Director of UN Women (2010–13).

75   Bachelet, Michelle. 2011. "International Women's Day 2011: Time to Make the Promise of Equality a Reality." Message from UN Women Executive Director Michelle Bachelet on the occasion of International Women's Day. March 8.

For a global sustainable society

The next areas of concern I would like to discuss are the environment and sustainable development.

The United Nations Conference on Sustainable Development (UNCSD) (Rio+20) is slated to be held in Rio de Janeiro, Brazil, this June. Commemorating the twentieth anniversary of the 1992 Earth Summit, it will review developments over the past two decades and focus on two themes: a green economy in the context of sustainable development and poverty eradication, and the institutional framework for sustainable development.

There is still considerable fluidity and debate concerning the definition of a "green economy." I think, however, that it is important that we avoid a too-narrow definition of this concept, for example as simply representing a compromise between competing concerns of economic growth and environmental protection, or as nothing more than a new tool for the generation of employment opportunities.

Last October, the United Nations Environment Programme (UNEP) organized a conference of young people in Bandung, Indonesia, which adopted a declaration positioning the green economy as: "The only integrated framework that is truly sustainable, placing human well-being, social equity and environmental protection on equal footing."[76] I am deeply inspired by the expansive vision and powerful sense of responsibility toward the future expressed by these young people.

Here I would like to call for the adoption of a set of common goals for a sustainable future as a follow-up to the UN Millennium Development Goals (MDGs), which cover the period until 2015. The "zero draft" of the Rio+20 Conference, a condensed compilation of the many statements and views submitted to the conference organizers, refers to the necessity of Sustainable Development Goals (SDGs). I hope that all parties will engage in in-depth deliberation on this topic based on a comprehensive view of the interlinked challenges facing humankind.

To date, international society has worked toward the achievement of the MDGs, which include such targets as reducing the number of people suffering the effects of poverty and hunger. The MDGs have helped drive efforts

---

76   UNEP (United Nations Environment Programme). 2011. "Young People Representing Half the Planet Campaign to Make Rio+20 a Green Economy Hit." UNEP News. October 1.

from various perspectives and disciplines to ameliorate the living gap and dignity gap that I referred to earlier. Presently, there are many calls for a new set of goals for the period from 2015 onward.

I welcome the attempt to establish such goals and would hope to see them inherit the spirit of the MDGs of alleviating the distortions in our global society generated by poverty and income disparities. They should also address the full range of human security issues that no country can avoid and in this way would bring people together in a shared enterprise of humanity in the twenty-first century.

To this end, I propose that the Rio+20 Conference establish a working group to consider such goals and to initiate the process of dialogue. In pursuing this work, the two key concepts are human security and sustainability.

How, then, are we to understand sustainability? In simplest terms, I think it could be described as follows: a way of life in which we refrain from seeking our own happiness at the expense of others; a determination not to pass on our local community and the planet as a whole to the next generation in a more dirty or damaged condition than it was when we entered it; a society in which the future is not sacrificed to the passing needs of the present, but where optimal choices and decisions are pursued with the interests of our children and grandchildren in mind.

The pursuit of these ideals need not be accompanied by a sense of obligation to obey externally imposed rules, or as a stifling burden of responsibility. Rather, it can be a natural sharing of the desire expressed by the economist John Kenneth Galbraith[77] in our written dialogue to create "a century in which people can say, 'I enjoy living in this world.'"[78]

I was motivated by very similar sentiments when I wrote in my 2008 proposal that the effort to achieve the MDGs must be focused on not only meeting targets but also restoring the smiles to the faces of those who presently suffer.

We should remember that there is no need to create from scratch the ethics necessary for the realization of this vision. They are expressed in many religious and cultural traditions that voice truths that contemporary society has all but lost sight of. The indigenous Iroquois people of North America, for example, exhort us: "Have always in view not only the present but also

---

77   John Kenneth Galbraith (1908–2006), Canadian-born American economist.

78   Galbraith, John Kenneth and Daisaku Ikeda. 2005. *Ningenshugi no dai seiki o* [Toward Creating an Age of Humanism]. Tokyo: Ushio Shuppansha, p. 67.

the coming generations, even those whose faces are yet beneath the surface of the ground. . . ."[79]

Likewise, in the Buddhist scriptures we find Shakyamuni's famous words:

> The seen and the unseen,
> Those living near and far away,
> Those born and those to-be-born—
> May all beings be at ease.[80]

In clarifying the underlying ethos for any new set of goals to be adopted, we should work consciously through educational and awareness-raising efforts to ensure that they are not heteronomous rules but take on the character of a vow rooted in the kind of appreciation of life expressed in these statements.

It will further be necessary to carefully consider such concrete issues as poverty and income disparities, dealing with a variety of unforeseen threats such as natural disasters, halting the destruction of human and natural environments and protecting biodiversity.

In pursuing these deliberations we must bring together the world's full resources of wisdom on the question of the kind of lifestyles and society that will most effectively protect the lives, livelihoods and dignity of people living on Earth today and into the future.

A new energy future

The United Nations has designated this year as the International Year of Sustainable Energy for All, highlighting the importance of sustainability as an essential focus for thinking about energy issues. In this context, we must consider the present and future prospects for nuclear power generation.

The accident at the Fukushima Nuclear Power Plant that accompanied the devastating earthquake and tsunami which struck Japan last March ranks

---

79 "The Constitution of the Iroquois Nations." 1996. Compiled by Glenn Welker, prepared by Gerald Murphy. Cleveland: National Public Telecomputing Network. http://www.indigenouspeople.net/iroqcon.htm (accessed April 2, 2013).

80 The Amaravati Sangha, trans. 1994–2012. *Karaniya Metta Sutta* [The Buddha's Words on Loving-Kindness]. http://www.accesstoinsight.org/tipitaka/kn/snp/snp.1.08.amar.html (accessed April 2, 2013).

with the 1979 Three Mile Island accident and the 1986 Chernobyl disaster in terms of scope and severity. The situation has yet to be brought fully under control, and there are no clear plans or prospects regarding how and where to store the soil and waste products that have been exposed to radioactive contamination. This represents an ongoing threat that continues to disrupt many people's lives.

There are estimates that it will take as much as forty years to remove all of the fuel and other radioactive materials from the reactor and fully disassemble and safely decommission the facility. There are also outstanding questions regarding the most feasible means of restoring the environment around the stricken nuclear facility in those areas heavily contaminated by radioactive pollutants. The long-term effects on human health are also unclear, and together these impose an irremediable burden on present and future generations.

For more than three decades, I have been expressing great concern about the truly imponderable implications of a major accident at a nuclear power plant. The negative legacy even from the normal and accident-free operation of such facilities—in the form of the necessary disposal of radioactive waste materials—could last hundreds or even thousands of years. Even today, no real solution to the problem of how to store these highly radioactive waste products has yet been found.

UN Secretary-General Ban Ki-moon has aptly pointed out,

> As we are painfully learning once again, nuclear accidents respect no borders. They pose a direct threat to human health and the environment. . . . Because the impact is transnational, these issues must be debated globally.[81]

Indeed, the problems posed by nuclear power generation are of such a scale that they cannot be effectively addressed within the confines of any one country's national energy policy. For Japan—located in a geographic zone that typically experiences about 10 percent of the world's earthquakes and where tsunami and the devastation they wreak are an undeniable aspect of our historical experience—it seems impossible to be sanguine about the prospects for effective accident prevention.

---

81   Ban, Ki-moon. 2011. "A Visit to Chernobyl." *International Herald Tribune*. April 25.

I therefore urge a rapid transition to an energy policy that is not reliant on nuclear power. Japan should collaborate with other countries that are at the forefront of efforts to introduce renewable energy sources and undertake joint development projects to achieve substantial cost reductions in these technologies. Japan should also take on, as its mission, efforts to promote the kind of technological innovation that will facilitate the introduction of new energy sources in developing countries that currently struggle with this issue.

In effecting this transition, it is necessary that adequate measures be taken to foster alternative industrial bases in communities that have been economically dependent on nuclear power generating facilities and have contributed to the national power supply.

Nuclear power presents many challenges to international society, and it is urgent that all states collaborate toward their resolution. Last April, on the twenty-fifth anniversary of the Chernobyl disaster, Secretary-General Ban Ki-moon wrote an opinion piece in which he stated: "Henceforth, we must treat the issue of nuclear safety as seriously as we do nuclear weapons."[82]

In point of fact, the damage to both human health and the natural environment from exposure to radioactivity is exactly the same for an equivalent dose whatever the source—the actual use of nuclear weapons, the release of radioactivity accompanying the development, production and testing of these weapons, or an accident at a nuclear power plant.

In the more than half-century since the first nuclear power station began operating in the Soviet Union in 1954, not only have many reactors reached the end of their projected lifespan, but the total volume of radioactive waste products continues to increase without cease and at a pace directly proportional to the number of operational nuclear power plants.

To date, the International Atomic Energy Agency (IAEA) has been at the heart of efforts in the fields of research and development for the "peaceful" use of nuclear energy, providing assistance in the operation of nuclear power plants and facilitating the exchange of scientific and technological know-how, as well as preventing the diversion of materials and technologies to military purposes. The global situation surrounding nuclear power generation—brought into sharper focus by the Fukushima accident—makes it imperative that, in addition to these responsibilities, the IAEA take the lead in promoting international cooperation regarding the back end of the nuclear fuel cycle.

---

82   Ibid.

In addition to the further strengthening of international cooperation for the management of radioactive waste products, the IAEA must play a central role in developing more effective responses to nuclear power plant accidents and for the decommissioning of obsolescent nuclear reactors.

Outlawing nuclear weapons

I would now like to suggest concrete ideas for achieving the prohibition and abolition of nuclear weapons.

The Fukushima nuclear accident in certain senses was reminiscent of the radioactive pollution unleashed by the nuclear weapons tests conducted by the nuclear-weapon states starting in the 1950s. This year marks the fifty-fifth anniversary of the declaration issued by second Soka Gakkai president Josei Toda calling for the prohibition of nuclear weapons. This declaration had as its background the increasingly fierce competition among nuclear-weapon states to develop ever larger and more powerful nuclear weapons.

In the declaration, Toda stated:

> Although a movement calling for a ban on the testing of nuclear weapons has arisen around the world, it is my wish to go further, to attack the problem at its root. I want to expose and rip out the claws that lie hidden in the very depths of such weapons.[83]

Here, he was expressing his conviction that, while the prohibition of nuclear weapons testing was of course essential, a deeper and more fundamental resolution of the issue would not be realized so long as national security doctrines that take for granted the suffering and sacrifice of large numbers of ordinary citizens remain unchallenged.

Prior to this declaration, Toda had already proposed the idea of *chikyu minzokushugi*,[84] which could be translated as "global nationalism" or the "underlying unity of the world's peoples" and corresponds to what today we

---

83   (trans. from) Toda, Josei. 1981–90. *Toda Josei zenshu* [The Complete Works of Josei Toda]. 9 vols. Tokyo: Seikyo Shimbunsha. Vol. 4, p. 565.

84   Toda, Josei. 1981–90. *Toda Josei zenshu* [The Complete Works of Josei Toda]. 9 vols. Tokyo: Seikyo Shimbunsha. Vol. 3, p. 460.

would call "global citizenship." This embodied his rejection of the idea that it was acceptable for any country, nation or people to be sacrificed to war. He sought, through the solidarity of ordinary citizens, to achieve the abolition of war.

This was the motivation behind his declaration, which was made in September 1957—just six months before his passing. By focusing on nuclear weapons, exposing and ripping out the "claws" that lie hidden within them, he sought to remove what he considered to be the "one evil" that served as the crucial impediment to progress on this front. Further, he declared his hope that this would be carried out by members of the younger generation.

Even when nuclear weapons are not used in an actual attack, the processes by which they are produced, tested and maintained result in grievous damage and suffering to both humans and the natural environment. This was demonstrated by the enormous harm wreaked by the US test of a hydrogen bomb at Bikini Atoll in March 1954, three years before Toda made his declaration. Even the cessation of testing would not fully resolve these issues. This is because the decision to possess nuclear weapons in itself manifests the readiness to sacrifice the lives of large numbers of people and the health of the global environment in the name of national security. In this way of thinking, anything can be justified in the name of military necessity.

Nuclear weapons represent the quintessential embodiment of this mindset. Buddhism uses the term "fundamental darkness of life" to describe the ultimate source of such deluded impulses as greed, anger and foolishness, from which war and other calamities spring. It is from this benighted aspect of human nature that contempt and hatred of others as well as a cruel and callous attitude toward life arises. Unless this impulse to disrespect and disregard life is overcome, the underlying human psychology that gives rise to the misery and suffering of war will remain unchanged, even if the actual use of nuclear weapons is somehow avoided.

This is the issue that Toda sought to address: nuclear weapons can never be accepted as a necessary evil but must be rejected, prohibited and extirpated as an absolute evil.

In point of fact, the perspective of military necessity was one that the International Court of Justice (ICJ) was unable to resolve in its groundbreaking Advisory Opinion on the Legality of the Threat or Use of Nuclear Weapons, issued in 1996. While finding that threat or use of nuclear weapons would generally be seen as illegal under international humanitarian law, the ICJ decided that it was unable to render a definitive judgment "in an extreme circumstance of self-defence, in which the very survival of a State would be at stake."[85]

The agreement reached by unanimous consent by the parties to the 2010 Nuclear Non-Proliferation Treaty (NPT) Review Conference can be understood as filling this legal lacuna and reinforcing the argument for the illegality of nuclear weapons.

To quote the final outcome document of the Conference: "The Conference expresses its deep concern at the catastrophic humanitarian consequences of any use of nuclear weapons, and affirms the need for all States at all times to comply with applicable international law, including international humanitarian law."[86] The phrase "all States at all times" indicates a legal obligation to which no exceptions are countenanced.

In my proposal for nuclear weapons abolition issued in September 2009, I called for a movement that would manifest the will of the world's people for the outlawing of nuclear weapons. This, I argued, would establish and clarify by 2015 the international norm that will serve as the foundation for a Nuclear Weapons Convention (NWC) formally banning these weapons of mass destruction.

The agreement reached by the 2010 NPT Review Conference provides a critical opening for this effort. We must with all haste begin the work of making this legally binding in the form of a treaty.

In general, the process by which new international norms come into being proceeds along the following three stages:

1. The limitations of the current norm become clear, and calls are made for a new approach.
2. Recognition of this necessity spreads, and momentum develops into a cascade of governments supporting the new norm.
3. The new norm is widely accepted within international society, formalized and given institutional expression as a legally binding instrument.

---

85 ICJ (International Court of Justice). 1996. "The Legality of the Threat or Use of Nuclear Weapons, Advisory Opinion." *I.C.J. Reports 1996*. July 8, p. 266.

86 UNGA (United Nations General Assembly). 2010. "Human Security." A/64/701. Report of the Secretary-General. March 8, p. 19.

I believe that with regard to the prohibition of nuclear weapons we are now positioned at a tipping point, the beginning of the second stage, just before the start of the cascade. I am encouraged to take this view by the following recent developments:

- The civil society initiative to draft a model NWC in 1997 has been followed up by a revised draft issued in 2007, demonstrating that the process of reviewing the legal measures necessary to achieve the prohibition and abolition of nuclear weapons is well under way.
- Since 1996, Malaysia and other countries have annually proposed a UN General Assembly resolution calling for the start of negotiations on an NWC. Support for this resolution has continued to grow; last year 130 member states supported it, including China, India, Pakistan, North Korea and Iran.
- In 2008, UN Secretary-General Ban Ki-moon proposed negotiations on an NWC or a framework of separate, mutually reinforcing instruments.
- The 2010 NPT Review Conference noted this proposal in the final outcome document that it adopted with the unanimous consent of all participants.
- The Inter-Parliamentary Union (IPU), to which 159 countries, including Russia, the United Kingdom, France and China, belong, has also unanimously expressed its support for this proposal.
- Mayors for Peace, with a membership of more than 5,100 cities and municipalities around the world, is actively seeking the early start of negotiations toward an NWC. Likewise, the InterAction Council, a group composed of former heads of state and government, has called for the conclusion of an NWC.
- In September 2009, the United Nations Security Council held a special summit session in which it adopted Security Council Resolution 1887 pledging efforts to create the conditions for a world without nuclear weapons.
- The worsening budgetary situation in different countries as a result of the ongoing economic crisis has prompted a serious rethinking of military expenditures, including in nuclear-weapon states where the costs of these armaments are finally being debated.

While it is clear that none of these developments, in itself, represents a decisive breakthrough, I believe that collectively they constitute a consistent and irreversible momentum toward the goal of a world finally free of nuclear weapons. The leading role played by civil society in developing a draft Nuclear Weapons Convention and in actively seeking the start of negotiations through petition drives and other activities clearly demonstrates that the spiritual wellspring and normative source for such a treaty exist as a vital presence in the hearts and minds of the world's ordinary citizens.

What is required now is to take this living, breathing awareness—the determination that the tragedy wrought by nuclear weapons must never be repeated and that humanity and nuclear weapons cannot coexist—and give it concrete form as a binding legal agreement expressing the shared conscience of humankind.

Expanding the antinuclear constituency

Efforts are needed to initiate the cascade toward the realization of an NWC. To this end, I am convinced that, in addition to the spirit of international humanitarian law, the perspectives and motivations of human rights and sustainability must be enlisted to focus and bring to bear the attention and will of the world's people—young people above all—toward the goal of a world without nuclear weapons. This is because a focus on human rights and sustainability makes clear the unacceptable burden placed on both present and future generations by the maintenance of security policies based on nuclear weapons, whether or not they are actually used.

The International Covenant on Civil and Political Rights (1966) is one of the foundational documents guaranteeing human rights globally. In 1984, the Human Rights Committee—mandated with oversight of the implementation of the Covenant—issued a General Comment which included the following statement:

> It is evident that the designing, testing, manufacture, possession and deployment of nuclear weapons are among the greatest threats to the right to life which confront mankind today. . . .

> Furthermore, the very existence and gravity of this threat generates a climate of suspicion and fear between States, which is in itself antagonistic to the promotion of universal respect for and observance

of human rights and fundamental freedoms in accordance with the Charter of the United Nations and the International Covenant on Human Rights.[87]

So long as nuclear weapons continue to exist, so will the temptation to threaten others with overwhelming military force. This generates a vicious cycle in which threat gives rise to insecurity, propelling further expansion of military capacity and in fact encouraging the proliferation of nuclear weapons. The destabilizing impact on our world has been incalculable.

We are forced to consider just how much enhancement and expansion of educational opportunities and human welfare would have been made possible if the vast expenditures of material and human resources on nuclear and conventional weapons systems had been directed to purposes that protect human lives, livelihoods and dignity.

The nature of the world in which we live was incisively critiqued by Bertrand Russell,[88] the philosopher renowned for, among other things, his collaboration with Albert Einstein[89] on a 1955 statement calling for the abolition of war and the elimination of nuclear weapons:

> Our world has sprouted a weird concept of security and a warped sense of morality. Weapons are sheltered like treasures while children are exposed to incineration.[90]

In the proposal I wrote in 2010, I called for the pursuit of disarmament as a humanitarian imperative, in order to implement the spirit of Article 26 of the UN Charter. In doing so, I was motivated by the urgent desire to reverse the kind of cruelties and absurdities Russell denounced.

---

87 UNHRC (United Nations Human Rights Committee). 1984. "CCPR General Comment No. 14: Article 6 (Right to Life) Nuclear Weapons and the Right to Life." Adopted at the Twenty-third Session of the Human Rights Committee. November 9.

88 Bertrand Russell (1872–1970), British philosopher, cofounder of the Pugwash Conferences on Science and World Affairs, recipient of the Nobel Prize for Literature in 1950.

89 Albert Einstein (1879–1955), German-born American physicist, recipient of the Nobel Prize for Physics in 1921.

90 (qtd. in) Abrams, Irwin. 2008. *The Words of Peace: Selections from the Speeches of the Winners of the Nobel Peace Prize.* New York: Newmarket Press, p. 81.

In addition, Jakob Kellenberger,[91] President of the International Committee of the Red Cross, issued this warning from the perspective of sustainability in April 2010: "Nuclear weapons are unique in their destructive power, in the unspeakable human suffering they cause, in the impossibility of controlling their effects in space and time, in the risks of escalation they create, and in the threat they pose to the environment, to future generations, and indeed to the survival of humanity."[92]

This is an urgent warning about the inhumanity of nuclear weapons and the threat they pose to sustainability. Together with the resolution adopted by the Council of Delegates of the International Red Cross and Red Crescent Movement in November 2011 calling for the elimination of nuclear weapons, it is a message that the nuclear-weapon states must heed.

Our world continues to be threatened by more than 20,000 nuclear warheads. This represents the capacity to kill or grievously injure all people living on Earth as well as their progeny, and to destroy the global ecosystem many times over. We are impelled to ask what it is, exactly, that is being protected by this unimaginable destructive capacity. If even some small portion of the population of one of the combatant nations were to survive, what would await them could hardly be termed a future.

By adding the perspectives of human rights and sustainability—universal issues affecting every living person—to already established concerns framed by international humanitarian law, we can greatly expand the active constituencies working for the realization of a world without nuclear weapons.

In particular, I hope that such a focus will spark a shift in thinking in the nuclear-weapon states and in countries whose populations have lived under the "extended deterrence" proffered by those states. It is critical that the citizens of these states come to understand how the continuation of the policies of nuclear weapons possession and deterrence represents a grave violation of their human rights and a threat to the prospects for a sustainable future.

We must take action to initiate concrete negotiations that will culminate in the realization of an NWC. One way to do this would be to present it as

---

91   Jakob Kellenberger (1944–), Swiss diplomat, President of the International Committee of the Red Cross (ICRC) (2010–).

92   Kellenberger, Jakob. 2010. "Bringing the Era of Nuclear Weapons to an End." Statement by Jakob Kellenberger, President of the ICRC, to the Geneva Diplomatic Corps, Geneva. April 20.

a basic treaty establishing the legal framework of a world without nuclear weapons with a set of associated protocols. The basic treaty would allow signatory states to clearly commit to the goal of a world without nuclear weapons in light of the imperatives of international humanitarian law, human rights and sustainability, and to pledge to refrain from any action that would run counter to the achievement of this goal or undermine this principle. Separate protocols could enumerate prohibited activities such as development and production, use or threat of use, and establish procedures for decommissioning and verification.

The key point of this proposal is to establish a framework within which all countries can work toward this shared global enterprise of humanity—the abolition of nuclear weapons—in conditions of physical and psychological security.

I believe that this formula could open a path for states to look beyond their current nuclear status and advance toward a common goal of a world without nuclear weapons. This treaty would make it easier for the states that are party to it to reduce confrontation and take concrete steps toward mutual threat reduction with a view to achieving their agreed-upon goal.

The framework I am proposing would provide a road map for a structural transition from mutual threat to mutual assurance. Even in the event that the protocols moving the treaty to the next stage of implementation are not ratified immediately, it would be possible to avert the kind of situation that prevails in the world today, marked by a severe lack of transparency and the threat of virtually unrestrained proliferation. In its place would be established a nuclear weapons moratorium based on a clear overall forward vision and legal norm.

It is vital that preparations for this begin as soon as possible. NGOs and forward-looking governments should establish a group that I would provisionally call the "Action Group for a Nuclear Weapons Convention" to embark on this venture. The SGI is ready to take an active role in this.

While moving forward with the drafting process for this framework treaty and developing the plans for the protocols, it will be crucially important to move global public opinion—propelled by the power and passion of young people—in order to garner the support of an expanding number of governments.

I would like to see either the release—or better yet, the signing—of an agreed-upon draft of the basic framework treaty for the prohibition and abolition of nuclear weapons by 2015, and I propose Hiroshima and Nagasaki as the venue for this.

I have for some time urged that a nuclear abolition summit to mark the effective end of the nuclear era be convened in Hiroshima and Nagasaki on the seventieth anniversary of the bombings of those cities, with the participation of national leaders and the representatives of global civil society. And I have noted that the NPT Review Conference, scheduled to be held in 2015, provides a good opportunity for such a summit.

To date, the NPT Review Conferences have all been held in New York or Geneva, and there are logistical and other difficulties involved in such a change of venue. But whether it takes the form of a nuclear abolition summit or of the holding of the NPT Review Conference, I am convinced that the effect of organizing such a meeting at the sites of the actual atomic bombings would help renew the pledge of all participants—starting with the attending heads of state and government—to achieve a world free from the threat of nuclear weapons and would solidify and make irreversible momentum toward that goal.

In recent years, former US Secretary of Defense William J. Perry[93] has, along with former Secretary of State Henry A. Kissinger[94] and other leaders, made repeated calls for a world without nuclear weapons. He has described the impact of his visit to the Atomic Bomb Dome and Hiroshima Peace Memorial Museum as follows:

> The horrific images of the aftermath of the atomic bombings are now seared in my mind. I believed, of course, that I fully understood the horrors of nuclear weapons. But to see and to in fact feel the misery created by these weapons through these images intensified my understanding of the enormous power and tragedy that can be unleashed by these weapons. The experience strengthened my resolve that these weapons must never be used again anywhere on Earth.[95]

---

93   William J. Perry (1920–), US Secretary of Defense (1994–97).

94   Henry A. Kissinger (1923–), US Secretary of State (1973–77), recipient of the Nobel Prize for Peace in 1973.

95   Perry, William J. 2011. *Kakunaki sekai o motomete* [In Search of a Non-nuclear World]. Trans. by Tsuyoshi Sunohara. Tokyo: Nihon Keizai Shuppansha, p. 175.

Everyone who visits Hiroshima will react differently, but I have no doubt that everyone will be moved in some significant way.

In the final analysis the only way that we can move past the present impasse in which proliferation continues unabated and the nightmare scenario of actual use remains a possibility is for large numbers of people throughout the world to understand that this is an issue that impinges directly on their own lives and dignity and that of their children and grandchildren.

In 2007, commemorating the fiftieth anniversary of the "Declaration Calling for the Abolition of Nuclear Weapons" by my mentor Josei Toda, the SGI launched a "People's Decade for Nuclear Abolition" with the aim of gathering and focusing the voices of the world's people. The antinuclear weapons exhibition "From a Culture of Violence to a Culture of Peace: Transforming the Human Spirit," which was created as part of this campaign, has to date been held in more than 220 cities throughout the world.

In addition, the SGI is collaborating with the International Campaign to Abolish Nuclear Weapons (ICAN) organized by the International Physicians for the Prevention of Nuclear War (IPPNW) to generate global popular solidarity for the adoption of an NWC, as well as working with Inter Press Service (IPS) on a joint international media project to promote the search for proposals and ideas toward a world without nuclear weapons.

The Toda Institute for Global Peace and Policy Research, which I founded in 1996, will be initiating a new research project in support of the global movement for the expansion of nuclear-weapon-free zones (NWFZs) as a regional approach toward the realization of a world without nuclear weapons.

The words of my mentor, spoken more than half a century ago, continue to reverberate in my heart: "I ask those who consider themselves to be my students and disciples to be heirs to the spirit of the declaration I have made today, and to make its meaning known throughout the entire world."[96]

Working alongside the youth of the SGI, I am determined to fulfill my vow to my mentor to enable the world's people to achieve, through their own efforts, a world without nuclear weapons. To this end, in taking on this unprecedented challenge, we are committed to working with all those who share this goal and aspiration.

---

96 (trans. from) Toda, Josei. 1981–90. *Toda Josei zenshu* [The Complete Works of Josei Toda]. 9 vols. Tokyo: Seikyo Shimbunsha. Vol. 4, p. 565.

A shared vow

In this proposal, I have examined such challenges as disaster prevention and mitigation, protection of the integrity of the global environment and poverty alleviation, as well as abolition of nuclear weapons, and have offered concrete ideas for their resolution. None of these problems will be solved overnight or without great effort, but I am convinced that, if we focus and bring to bear the energy and attention of the world's "ordinary citizens"—each of whom harbors within themselves truly limitless potential—a path forward is certain to open.

Sixty years ago my mentor issued a call for all the world's inhabitants to regard themselves as global citizens; five years later, he issued the declaration I have referenced here, insisting on the prohibition and abolition of all nuclear weapons. It was his consistent conviction that we must act today in ways that will serve the interests of humanity living 100 or 200 years from now.

His impassioned words, shared with and entrusted to me as his disciple, have served as a source of inexhaustible inspiration, as a vow that I share and remain determined to fulfill.

> You need not only to make concrete proposals for the peace of humankind, but to take the lead in working toward their implementation. Even when such proposals are not fully or immediately accepted, they can serve as a 'spark' from which a movement for peace will eventually spread like wildfire. Theorizing that is not grounded in reality will always remain a futile exercise. Concrete proposals provide a framework for the transformation of reality and can serve to protect the interests of humanity.

The peace proposals I have continued to author every year for the past thirty years represent my efforts to fulfill my personal vow to my mentor.

I am convinced that there is no greater force for the resolution of the difficult issues grappled with in this and all my proposals than a deepening sense of solidarity among the people of the world. To this end, I and my fellow SGI members in 192 countries and territories are engaged, day in and day out, in efforts to spark, through dialogue, the light and flame of courage and hope.

The struggle for peace, like the struggle for human rights and humanity, is not one in which, having reached the peak of the mountain, the final goal comes into view. Rather, it should be thought of as the work of generating an uninterrupted and unstoppable flow of commitment connecting and passed on from one generation to the next. This is the conviction that has supported our efforts to help build a better future for all.

Burning with this conviction, we will continue to promote a movement of empowerment that is of, for and by the people, laying the foundations for a global society of peace and harmonious coexistence.

Compassion, Wisdom and Courage: Building a Global Society of Peace and Creative Coexistence

2013 Peace Proposal (Full Text)
January 26, 2013

Commemorating the anniversary of the founding of the Soka Gakkai International (SGI), I would like to explore the prospects for constructing a global society of peace and creative coexistence looking toward the year 2030.

It has been sixty-five years since the adoption of the Universal Declaration of Human Rights. Since its founding, the United Nations has, through this and other resolutions of the General Assembly and various world conferences, clarified key themes that should guide and propel international cooperation. These include the following concepts: "sustainable development" as a response to the challenges of poverty, environmental degradation and economic instability; a "culture of peace" as a response to the challenges of conflict and structural violence; and "human security," the subject of a resolution adopted by the General Assembly in September of last year.

Together, these efforts to establish conceptual frameworks highlight both the issues in our present-day world that we cannot afford to ignore and the areas demanding priority action.

A concrete illustration of this is the Millennium Development Goals (MDGs), established in the year 2000 by the United Nations. The objective of reducing by half the proportion of the world's population suffering from extreme poverty has been realized well ahead of the target date of 2015; the goal of halving the proportion of people without constant access to improved drinking water has been achieved; and that of eliminating gender disparity in primary education is close to realization.

At the same time, there are a number of targets whose achievement by 2015 is in question at the present pace of progress. And of course, even the attainment of all the targets will still leave far too many people in conditions that threaten their lives and dignity. Clearly, further acceleration of efforts will be required.

This record of achievement nonetheless demonstrates that we can indeed change the world when people share a common awareness of the issues at hand and we set clear target dates for progress, giving focus and direction to people's efforts.

Following the United Nations Conference on Sustainable Development (Rio+20) in June 2012, efforts are now under way to define a set of Sustainable Development Goals (SDGs) as a follow-up to the MDGs, and in December 2012 a working group was established to carry out this task. The debate about these goals should serve as an opportunity to bring together diverse perspectives from which to consider what needs to be achieved toward the anticipated target date of 2030 and draw the outlines of a new global society.

A Faustian Quest

> [E]verything, dear Friend, nowadays is *ultra*, everything perpetually transcendent in thought as in action. . . . Young people are excited much too early, and then carried away in the whirl of the time. *Wealth* and *rapidity* are what the world admires, and what everyone strives to attain.[97]

While these might sound like the words of a contemporary intellectual, this incisive critique of civilization is in fact that of the German literary master Johann Wolfgang von Goethe.[98]

I am currently engaged in a dialogue with Dr. Manfred Osten[99] of the Goethe Society, headquartered in Weimar, Germany, about the life and

---

97   Goethe, Johann Wolfgang von and Carl Friedrich Zelter. 1887. *Goethe's Letters to Zelter: With Extracts from Those of Zelter to Goethe*. Trans. by Arthur Duke Coleridge. London: George Bell and Sons, p. 246.

98   Johann Wolfgang von Goethe (1749–1832), German writer, artist and politician.

99   Manfred Osten (1938–), German poet and cultural historian, member of the advisory board of the Goethe Society in Weimar, Germany.

thought of the great German writer. Dr. Osten focuses on the way that Goethe examines this pathology of civilization in his masterpiece *Faust,* where he portrays the human folly that drives us in a ceaseless quest for the "magic mantle" (the fastest means of transportation), the "quick dagger" (the quickest weapons) and "fast money," which are deployed to fulfill a succession of desires but lead ultimately to our downfall.[100]

Dr. Osten refers to these items, which Mephistopheles supplies to Faust in response to his requests, as "the tools of demonic rapidity."[101] Their names and forms, he says, differ from those of the beginning of the twenty-first century but their content is the same. He goes on to ask whether we have the capacity to recognize ourselves as contemporaries of Dr. Faust, and indeed I think we cannot afford to ignore the similarities between our age and that which Goethe described. Without calling on the assistance of any Mephistopheles, we have created a tragic situation where that which should be valued and treasured is ground underfoot with hardly a thought. The pathology that Goethe exposed has reached a crescendo in our present age.

We see it in nuclear weapons, whose use would "defend" the possessor nation at the price of humanity's extinction; in a society where free market competition is glorified at the cost of widening disparities and the conscious neglect of its most vulnerable members; in the unabated pace of ecological destruction driven by the prioritization of economic growth; in a global food crisis brought about by commodity speculation. . .

The MDGs were established with the aim of reducing suffering to the greatest degree possible. But unless we face head-on the underlying ailments of human civilization, we may find that any progress will be short-lived and could be wiped out as new challenges arise. This makes it all the more important that we heed Goethe's admonition: "It is not enough to take steps which may some day lead to a goal; each step must be itself a goal and a step likewise."[102]

---

100 Osten, Manfred. 2005. "Kasoku suru jikan aruiwa ningen no jikohakai" [Acceleration of Time or Self-destruction of the Human Being]. Trans. by Tatsuya Yamazaki. Public Lecture at the IOP European Centre. *The Journal of Oriental Studies* Vol. 44, No. 1. Tokyo: The Institute of Oriental Philosophy, p. 165.

101 (trans. from) Osten, Manfred. 2004. *"Alles veloziferisch" oder Goethes Entdeckung der Langsamkeit* ["Alles veloziferisch" or Goethe's Discovery of Slowness]. Frankfurt: Insel, p. 31.

102 Goethe, Johann Wolfgang von. 1901. *Conversations with Eckermann: Being Appreciations and Criticisms on Many Subjects.* Trans. by John Oxenford. Washington and London: M. W. Dunne, p. 18.

In other words, our efforts to improve the human condition must be more than mere stopgap measures; they must enable people struggling in the face of dire threats to recover the hope and strength needed to lead lives of dignity. Steadily bringing such efforts to fruition, we must take on the larger challenge of transforming the currents of history from destruction to construction, from confrontation to coexistence, from divisiveness to solidarity.

We need a new spiritual framework that will bring into greater clarity those things we cannot afford to ignore, while ensuring that all that we do contributes to the larger objective of a global society of peace and creative coexistence. This will also facilitate the process of establishing the new Sustainable Development Goals.

I would like to propose that respect for life's inherent dignity provides just such a framework.

The determination to share the joys and sufferings of others

If we picture a global society of peace and creative coexistence as an edifice, the ideals of human rights and human security are key pillars that hold it up, while the foundation on which these rest is respect for the dignity of life. If this foundation remains no more than an abstract conceptualization, the entire structure will be unstable and could collapse in the event of a severe challenge or crisis.

To ensure that respect for life's dignity is a meaningful and robust support for other endeavors, individuals throughout the world must feel and experience it clearly and palpably as a way of life. To this end, I would like to propose the following three commitments as guidelines for action:

- The determination to share the joys and sufferings of others
- Faith in the limitless possibilities of life
- The vow to defend and celebrate diversity

Regarding the first of these—the importance of sharing the joys and sufferings of others—I am reminded of the dialogue I conducted with the British historian Arnold J. Toynbee[103] some forty years ago on humanity's prospects in the twenty-first century. In the final stages of this dialogue, we discussed

---

103 Arnold J. Toynbee (1889–1975), British historian.

the dignity of life. "Dignity," Dr. Toynbee stressed, "is irreplaceable."[104] It is the unique and irreplaceable nature of each being that gives such immense weight and value to the dignity of life.

He went on to say, "A human being . . . also loses his own dignity if he does not respect the dignity of other people."[105] This perspective, which places the dignity of life within the context of human connections and interrelatedness, is key.

One pressing threat to the dignity of far too many people in our world today—and one that urgently demands a cooperative response on the part of the international community—is poverty.

As I noted earlier, a number of the MDG targets have already been met. But the fact that many of these targets are expressed as a reduction of the proportion of people living in conditions of misery means that, unless the pace of progress is accelerated, there will still be approximately 1 billion people in extreme poverty and more than 600 million without access to safe drinking water in 2015, the MDG target date. Further, there are regional disparities in the pace of poverty reduction, with progress in sub-Saharan Africa, in particular, lagging behind other regions such as South Asia or Latin America, which are also yet to reduce by half the number of people living in extreme poverty in line with the MDG targets.

In June of this year, the 5th Tokyo International Conference on African Development (TICAD V) will be held in Yokohama, Japan. One underlying theme of the conference is inclusive and resilient societies. I hope that it will motivate greater international solidarity toward the creation of an "African century," spreading the values of peace and coexistence from Africa to the world so that all people may live lives of dignity.

Poverty is not a problem limited to the developing world. Even affluent societies contain both poverty and social and economic disparities.

British researchers Richard Wilkinson and Kate Pickett have been studying the effects of inequality, noting that when compounded with economic deprivation it has a corrosive effect on both individual relationships and society as a whole. In their work *The Spirit Level: Why More Equal Societies Almost Always Do Better,* they note that not only do economic disparities aggravate health and social problems but "[w]ith greater inequality, people

---

104 Toynbee, Arnold J. and Daisaku Ikeda. 2007. *Choose Life.* London and New York: I.B.Tauris, p. 341.

105 Ibid.

are less caring of one another, there is less mutuality in relationships, people have to fend for themselves and get what they can—so, inevitably, there is less trust."[106] Further, because "[i]nequality seems to make countries socially dysfunctional across a wide range of outcomes,"[107] it is not just the poor but people at almost all income levels who fare badly in more unequal societies.

Economic deprivation makes virtually all the events of daily life into potential sources of distress. This is compounded when people feel that their very existence is disregarded, that they are alienated and deprived of a meaningful role and place within society. For people who are struggling to improve their lives in the midst of such difficult conditions, cold and unfeeling reactions—whether from within their immediate surroundings or from society as a whole—deepen the sense of isolation and self-doubt, deeply wounding their dignity.

This is why in recent years, in addition to economic measures to deal with the problem of poverty, there has been a growing emphasis on the need for a socially inclusive approach focused on the restoration of a sense of connection with others and of purpose in life.

Buddhism as a response to human suffering

In ancient India, Buddhism arose in response to the universal question of how to confront the realities of human suffering and engage with people ensnared in that suffering.

The founder of Buddhism, Gautama Buddha or Shakyamuni,[108] was of royal birth, which guaranteed him a life of earthly comforts. Tradition has it that his determination as a young man to abandon those comforts and seek truth through monastic practice was inspired by the "four encounters" with people afflicted by the pains of aging, illness and death.

But his purpose was never simply to reflect passively on life's evanescence and the inevitability of suffering. Later in life, he described his feelings at that time in this way: "In their foolishness, common mortals—even though they themselves will age and cannot avoid aging—when they see others aging and falling into decline, ponder it, are distressed by it, and feel shame and

---

106 Wilkinson, Richard G. and Kate Pickett. 2009. *The Spirit Level: Why More Equal Societies Almost Always Do Better*. London: Allen Lane, p. 56.

107 Ibid., p. 174.

108 Shakyamuni (Gautama Siddartha) (c. 560–480 BCE), the founder of Buddhism.

hate—all without ever thinking of it as their own problem,"[109] and he noted that the same holds true in our attitudes toward illness and death as well.

Shakyamuni's concern was always with the inner arrogance that allows us to objectify and isolate people confronting such sufferings as aging and illness. He was thus incapable of turning a blind eye to people suffering alone from illness or the aged cut off from the world.

There is an episode from his life that illustrates this.

One day, Shakyamuni encountered a monk who was stricken by illness. He asked him, "Why are you suffering, and why are you alone?" The monk replied that he was lazy by nature and unable to endure the hardships associated with providing medical care to others. Thus there was no one to tend to him. At which Shakyamuni responded, "Good man, I will look after you." Shakyamuni took the stricken monk outdoors, changed his soiled bedding, washed him and dressed him in new clothes. He then firmly encouraged him to always be diligent in his religious practice. The monk was immediately restored to a state of physical and mental well-being and joy.

In my view, it was not just Shakyamuni's unexpected and devoted care that affected the monk in this way. Rather, the fact that Shakyamuni encouraged him using the same strict yet warm language that he used with other disciples in good health revived the flame of dignity that was so close to being extinguished in this man's life.

This story as I have outlined it so far is based on an account in *The Great Tang Dynasty Record of the Western Regions*.[110] However, when we compare this to the version transmitted in other sutras, a further aspect of Shakyamuni's motivation comes to light.

After having tended to the sick monk, Shakyamuni is said to have gathered together the other monks and asked them what they knew about his condition. As it turned out, they had been aware of his illness and the gravity of his condition, and yet none among them had made any effort to provide care.

The Buddha's disciples explained themselves in terms almost identical to those of the ailing monk: he had never attended to any of them in their time of illness.

---

109 (trans. from) Nakamura, Hajime. 1992. *Gotama Budda 1* [Gautama Buddha Vol. 1]. Tokyo: Shunjusha, p. 156.

110 Xuanzang. 1996. *The Great Tang Dynasty Record of the Western Regions*. Trans. by Li Rongxi. Berkeley: Numata Center for Buddhist Translation and Research.

This corresponds to the logic of personal responsibility as it is often used in contemporary settings to negate the need to care for others. For the ailing monk, this attitude fostered feelings of resignation, and for the other disciples it manifested itself as an arrogant justification of their disinterest. This logic atrophied his spirit and clouded theirs.

"Whoever would tend to me, should tend to the sick." With these words, Shakyamuni sought to dispel the delusions clouding the minds of his disciples and spur them to a correct understanding.

In other words, practicing the Buddha's way means to actively share the joys and sufferings of others—never turning one's back on those who are troubled and in distress, being moved by others' experiences as if they were one's own. Through such efforts, not only do those directly afflicted by suffering regain their sense of dignity, but so too do those who empathetically embrace that suffering.

The inherent dignity of life does not manifest in isolation. Rather, it is through our active engagement with others that their unique and irreplaceable nature becomes evident. At the same time, the determination to protect that dignity against all incursions adorns and brings forth the luster of our own lives.

By asserting an essential equality between himself and an ailing monk, the Buddha sought to awaken people to the fact that the value of human life is undiminished by illness or age: he refused to acknowledge such distinctions and discriminations. In this sense, to regard the sufferings of others due to illness or age as evidence of defeat or failure in life is not only an error in judgment but undermines the dignity of all concerned.

The philosophical foundation of the SGI is the teachings of Nichiren,[111] who emphasized the supremacy of the Lotus Sutra which, he stated, marks the epitome of Shakyamuni's enlightenment. In the Lotus Sutra, a massive jeweled tower arises from within the earth to symbolize the dignity and value of life. Nichiren compared the four sides of the treasure tower to the "four aspects" of birth, aging, sickness and death,[112] asserting that we can confront the stark realities of aging, illness and even death in such a way that we remain undefeated by the suffering that accompanies them. We can make

---

111   Nichiren (1222–82), Buddhist monk, founder of Nichiren Buddhism.
112   Nichiren. 1952. *Nichiren Daishonin gosho zenshu* [The Complete Works of Nichiren Daishonin]. Ed. by Nichiko Hori. Tokyo: Soka Gakkai, p. 740.

these experiences—normally only seen in a negative light—the impetus for a more richly dignified and valuable way of living.

The dignity of life is not something separate from the inevitable trials of human existence, and we must engage actively with others, sharing their suffering and exerting ourselves to the last measure of our strength, if we are to open a path toward authentic happiness for both ourselves and others. Inspired by these teachings, SGI members—often derided in our early years in Japan as "a gathering of the sick and poor"—have advanced with pride in our tradition of mutual support and encouragement among people afflicted by various forms of suffering.

Today, this spirit is particularly relevant as so many people around the world are being impacted by the experience of sudden deprivation, exemplified by the devastation wrought by natural disasters and economic crises. These can rob people of all that they treasure in just moments, saddling them with an unbearable burden of pain. This makes it particularly important that they not be left isolated and forgotten.

As can be seen in the massive earthquakes that struck Haiti (2010) and northeastern Japan (2011), reconstruction efforts in the wake of disaster are long-term and often lag far behind expectations. The struggles of individuals to rebuild their lives and regain some sense of inner wholeness are difficult and ongoing. This is why it is so important that we not forget these suffering people, and that society as a whole support reconstruction, fostering the kinds of overlapping connections and bonds that enable people to live with hope.

The determination to continue to encourage people until smiles return to their faces—never abandoning them and sharing every trial and joy— empowers us to meet and overcome life's successive challenges and guides us through the seemingly capricious obstacles life throws at us.

It is through persistent efforts to defend that which is irreplaceable and to bring forth our own and others' dignity that the inequalities of society can be rectified and the unshakable basis of social inclusion established.

Faith in the limitless possibilities of life

The second commitment and guideline for action I would like to discuss is faith in the limitless possibilities of life.

In September of last year, the SGI, Human Rights Education Associates (HREA) and the Office of the United Nations High Commissioner for Human Rights (OHCHR) launched a jointly produced DVD, *A Path to Dignity: The*

Power of Human Rights Education,[113] in order to promote among a wider public the ideals and principles of the United Nations Declaration on Human Rights Education and Training, which was adopted by the UN General Assembly in December 2011.

The documentary, which is also available for online viewing, portrays human rights education in practice in three different settings. While the specific issues in each case differ, together they convey the message that it is possible to change society and that change starts with the inner transformation of individual human beings.

As a nongovernmental organization (NGO) accredited to the United Nations, the SGI has long promoted human rights education as one of our core activities. Underlying these initiatives is a conviction rooted in Buddhist philosophy. When Shakyamuni insisted, "Do not ask about descent, but ask about conduct," he was critiquing the worldview of his time that held that the circumstances of our birth in the present life are determined by karma accumulated in past lives. At the same time, through the analogy "from [any] wood, it is true, fire is born . . ."[114] he was asserting that all people inherently possess a life-state of ultimate dignity and that they are in this sense fundamentally equal and endowed with limitless possibilities.

A fatalistic outlook on life deprives those who discriminate against others of all opportunity to reflect on or question their actions, much less to actually be moved by the promptings of conscience. It creates the conditions in which a tragic disregard for human rights can pervade society: disempowering the victims of discrimination, blunting their awareness of their own irreplaceable worth and feeding resignation and a sense of futility.

The view that present circumstances are irrevocably determined by past causes undermines respect for life's dignity, both for perpetrators and victims of discrimination. Thus Shakyamuni could not leave it unchallenged.

In saying that we must focus on people's conduct rather than their birth, Shakyamuni was explaining that the relationship between cause and effect is not immutable but that our actions and attitudes in the present moment

---

113 SGI (Soka Gakkai International). 2012. *A Path to Dignity: The Power of Human Rights Education.* DVD. Tokyo: Soka Gakkai International. http://www.path-to-dignity.org/ (accessed April 2, 2013).

114 Müller, Friedrich Max, trans. 2005. *The Sutta-nipata.* In *The Sacred Books of the East,* Vol. 10, part 2. Massachusetts: Elibron. 4:9:462.

become new causes that can give rise to entirely new outcomes. It is for this reason that the true worth of a person is seen in their actions in this moment.

Further, the Buddhist teaching of "dependent origination" emphasizes our interdependence, the fact that all things exist within a fabric of mutual influence. The moment-by-moment flux of overlapping causes and effects propagates through this web of interdependence, influencing others and our surroundings. Thus our actions in this moment have the power not only to transform ourselves but to create a new and cascading series of positive reactions and outcomes. It is this magnificent capacity of life—existing within all people regardless of their condition—that Shakyamuni was trying to convey with the phrase "from [any] wood, it is true, fire is born. . . ."

This same principle is expressed in the Lotus Sutra through a number of skillfully woven parables, and what is of particular note is that these are told not by Shakyamuni himself but in the voices of various disciples. Examples of these include the parable of the wealthy man and his poor son told by voice-hearers such as Subhuti[115] and the parable of the jewel in the robe by arhats such as Kaundinya.[116]

The first of these describes a man who after a life of wandering and great misfortune unknowingly returns to the home of his wealthy father where he finds work. In the latter, a man lives out his life in ignorance of the jewel of immense value that has been sewn into the hem of his robe by a friend.

These parables are told by the Buddha's disciples to express the overflowing joy and determination they feel on encountering the core of Shakyamuni's teachings, which is that all people equally possess the Buddha nature and are thus capable of manifesting the profound and boundless wisdom of the Buddha. The Lotus Sutra portrays this drama of the inner life both in its depiction of the disciples' transformation from awakening to joyful determination and through the parables they themselves employ to describe the experience.

Buddhism thus stresses that humanity can advance one step at a time through our ceaseless efforts to inspire each other and to understand that, just as Shakyamuni's awakening sparked an awakening in his disciples, what is possible for one is possible for all. This is the philosophical basis underlying the SGI's efforts in human rights education, which emphasize the process

---

115 Subhuti, one of Shakyamuni's ten major disciples.
116 Kaundinya, one of the five ascetics who heard Shakyamuni Buddha's first sermon and thereupon converted to his teachings.

by which individual empowerment develops into leadership for the sake of others.

One of the case studies introduced in the DVD *A Path to Dignity* is that of a Turkish woman who was compelled to marry against her wishes when she was young and became the victim of her husband's violence. When she determined to divorce her husband, she found herself physically threatened not only by him but also by members of her own family. She was able to seek refuge with a women's organization where her awareness of her rights was awakened. She determined to start living a new life, declaring: "I feel strong . . . very much so. If I could help other women, then I would be even happier. That's what I want, to be an example."

This is truly an invaluable instance of human rights education in practice. In the smile of this woman who has regained the strength to live, we see the warmth of hope and the power of self-confidence that arise from becoming fully aware of one's own dignity.

Few people have expressed this idea of the warmth of hope more aptly than the American philosopher Milton Mayeroff.[117] Mayeroff was the proponent of the theory of caring, which like empowerment is based on a focused attentiveness to others.

> There is hope that the other will grow through my caring . . . it is akin, in some ways, to the hope that accompanies the coming of spring. . . . Such hope is not an expression of the insufficiency of the present in comparison with the sufficiency of a hoped-for future; it is rather an expression of the plenitude of the present, a present alive with a sense of the possible.[118]

What is important here is that hope is not relegated to the status of a kind of promissory note for the future. Rather, we find hope within the sense of plenitude and sufficiency of life in this moment.

What matters is not how our lives have been to this point: the instant that we awaken to our original worth and determine to change present realities, we start to shine with the light of hope.

---

117 Milton Mayeroff (1925–79), American philosopher.
118 Mayeroff, Milton. 1974. *On Caring*. New York: Barnes & Noble Books, pp. 18–19.

Throughout his life, Nichiren took pride in the fact that he was "born poor and lowly to a chandala family,"[119] and always stood with people who were victimized by various social evils. He described the dynamic and transformative functioning of life as analogous to "fire being produced by a stone taken from the bottom of a river, or a lantern lighting up a place that has been dark for a hundred, a thousand, or ten thousand years."[120]

Visions that can only be realized in the far-distant future—however grand and lofty—will not propel the kind of ceaseless spiritual struggle that is required to nurture possibilities and bring them to fruition. Nor do they provide concrete opportunities for people to change their surroundings through the transformation they achieve in their own lives. Only when hope is experienced on an immediate day-to-day level as "the coming of spring" can we succeed in patiently cultivating with joy and with pride the seeds of possibility. Only then can we have a positive impact on those around us through our own inner transformation and work in a sustained way for the betterment of society.

Such a perspective is, I believe, valuable not only for the challenges of constructing a culture of human rights, but also for realizing a sustainable society. We need to generate the kind of upward spiral by which we improve current conditions while working toward a better future. This is a point I stressed in the proposal I submitted to the Rio+20 Summit last June.[121] The success of our efforts toward the year 2030 will depend on how deeply the movement to empower people—and beyond empowerment, to enable them to exercise leadership—takes root in communities around the world. More than anything, it is vital that our lives in this moment be filled with the warmth of hope. For it is then that each step we take to make the world a better place will, as Goethe urged, "be itself a goal and a step."

The vow to defend and celebrate diversity

The third commitment and guideline for action is the vow to defend and celebrate diversity.

---

119 Nichiren. 1999–2006. *The Writings of Nichiren Daishonin*. 2 vols. Ed. and trans. by The Gosho Translation Committee. Tokyo: Soka Gakkai. Vol. 1, p. 303.

120 Ibid. Vol. 1, p. 923.

121 Ikeda, Daisaku. 2012. "The Challenge of Global Empowerment: Education for a Sustainable Future." Environment Proposal.

For many years, I have conducted dialogues with people from a wide range of ethnic, cultural and religious backgrounds. Through this experience, I have grown ever more deeply convinced that diversity is not simply something that must be respected: it presents us all with an opportunity to engage in self-reflection in a way that can make our lives more richly meaningful.

Today, the twin trends of globalization and the increasing penetration of information and communications technology have expanded the opportunities for people of different backgrounds to interact, communicating their thoughts and ideas instantaneously. At the same time, however, we see a flattening or homogenization driven primarily by economic processes that erodes the uniqueness of individual cultures. Further, greater cross-border movement of people has often resulted in cultural frictions that may be exacerbated by the deliberate incitement of hatred and mistrust. Differences and distinctions that could enrich our lives instead become the target of attack or are seen as a barrier that separates people. All too often this escalates into violent conflict or gives rise to other conditions that threaten people's lives and dignity.

The Seville Statement on Violence, written by a group of international scientists and adopted by UNESCO in 1989, affirmed: "It is scientifically incorrect to say that war or any other violent behaviour is genetically programmed into our human nature . . . [or] that war is caused by 'instinct' or any single motivation."[122]

I completely agree with this statement. And yet, the fact remains that numerous impediments must be overcome if we are to break the cycles of conflict and violence. To this end we need to start by asking ourselves what it is that drives people to war and destruction.

Shakyamuni believed that conflict arises from the fundamental darkness or delusion that prevents us from recognizing in the lives of others the same irreplaceable value that we sense in our own. Living in ancient India, Shakyamuni often witnessed such violent confrontations as tribal conflicts over water and other resources and power struggles between states.

He identified what he considered to be the essence of the problem: "I perceived a single, invisible arrow piercing the hearts of the people."[123] That is, because people's hearts are penetrated by the unseen arrow of fundamental

---

122 UNESCO (United Nations Educational, Scientific and Cultural Organization). 1986. "Seville Statement on Violence, Spain, 1986."

123 (trans. from) Nakamura, Hajime. 1984. *Budda no kotoba* [Words of Buddha]. Tokyo: Iwanami Shoten, p. 203.

delusion, they cannot free themselves from attachment to an egocentric worldview.

For example, Shakyamuni saw that two tribal groups in conflict were afflicted by the same desperation, "like fish, writhing in shallow water."[124] And yet their minds were clouded, and they could not recognize that the other group shared their concerns over the lack of water or the constant fear of being attacked and overrun.

It was to overcome this that Shakyamuni declared:

> All tremble at violence; life is dear to all. Putting oneself in the place of another, one should not kill nor cause another to kill.[125]

There are two key points here. The first is that Shakyamuni always focused on a process of inner reflection by which we attempt to put ourselves in the place of others and feel their anguish as our own, rather than obedience to external rules as the basis for self-control. The second point is that he did not consider it enough that we ourselves refrain from the taking of life, but insisted that we should also not cause others to kill. In this, he is urging us to cultivate, through wholehearted dialogue, the goodness that exists within the lives of others and to join with them in a mutual vow against violence and the taking of life.

The Buddhist scriptures contain the following episode in which the demoness Kishimojin (Skt. Hariti) was spurred to transform her way of life as a result of Shakyamuni entering into dialogue with her and encouraging her to reflect on her actions.

Kishimojin is portrayed as a demoness with a huge number of children—several hundred or even several thousand—and was said to kill other people's babies to feed her own children. The people appealed to Shakyamuni, asking him to put an end to her evil deeds. In response, Shakyamuni found Kishimojin's youngest child, whom she particularly treasured, and hid him. For seven days, Kishimojin searched desperately for her child. Finally, at her wits' end, she asked Shakyamuni for help, having heard that he had the capacity to know all things.

---

124 Saddhatissa, Hammalava, trans. 1994. *The Sutta-nipāta*. Richmond: Curzon Press. 4:2:936.

125 Buddharakkhita, trans. 1996. *The Dhammapada: The Buddha's Path of Wisdom*. Kandy: Buddhist Publication Society. 10:130:2.

Shakyamuni responded to her pleas by saying:

> I've heard you have an uncountable number of children. So why are
> you so distressed to lose just one of them? Most families have only
> one, three, or perhaps five children. You have been robbing those
> children of life.[126]

Hearing his words, Kishimojin realized that she had inflicted the pain she
now felt on untold numbers of other parents. After promising Shakyamuni she
would give up her evil ways, she was reunited with her youngest child. From
that point on, Kishimojin made the protection of all children her mission; in
the Lotus Sutra, she pledges, along with a number of other fierce deities, to
protect those who work for the happiness of all people. Nichiren states that
whereas she had been an evil demon, she came to act as a benevolent demon.[127]

What is important in this story is that while retaining her distinctive form
as a demon, Kishimojin was able to completely transform her way of life.
Shifting the center of gravity of her self-awareness to her identity as a mother,
she was able to put herself in the place of another, and for the first time she
keenly felt the suffering of her victims. As a result, she determined that
she would neither cause nor permit them to experience the kind of anguish
she had felt.

The plurality of our identities

The economist Amartya Sen[128] has been a leading advocate of the idea that
"the plurality of our identities" can play a key role in helping people resist the
tug of mass psychology and the incitements to violence that provoke conflict.
In his early years, Dr. Sen witnessed many people lose their lives (during the
communal strife that accompanied the end of British rule in India) simply

---

126 (trans. from) Iwano, Shinyu, ed. 1930–65. *Kokuyaku issaikyo Indo senjutsubu* [The
     Japanese Translation of the Buddhist Scriptures: Works Composed in India].
     155 vols. Tokyo: Daito Shuppansha. Vol. 29/30, p. 162.
127 Nichiren. 1952. *Nichiren Daishonin gosho zenshu* [The Complete Works of
     Nichiren Daishonin]. Ed. by Nichiko Hori. Tokyo: Soka Gakkai, p. 778.
128 Amartya Sen (1933–), Indian economist, recipient of the Nobel Prize in
     Economic Sciences in 1998.

because of religious difference. This pained him deeply and inspired him to research ways to prevent such tragedies. He warns us that:

> The insistence, if only implicitly, on a choiceless singularity of human identity not only diminishes us all, it also makes the world much more flammable. . . . Rather, the main hope of harmony in our troubled world lies in the plurality of our identities, which cut across each other and work against sharp divisions around one single hardened line of vehement division that allegedly cannot be resisted.[129]

The members of any ethnic group or faith tradition are, of course, not monolithic in their identity: the environments in which they were raised and their occupations and interests as individuals differ, as do their convictions and ways of life. It is because of this diversity of identity that, while very real differences in ethnicity or religion may exist, there is always the possibility of finding in one-to-one human interchanges points of confluence and mutual resonance. As Dr. Sen points out, this can enable us to cross over hardened lines of vehement division and establish multiple overlapping bonds of empathy and friendship.

This is why, when engaging in dialogues with partners who hail from different cultural and religious backgrounds, in addition to entering into wide-ranging explorations of possible responses to global issues and the prospects for the human future, I make a point of asking about that person's family, their memories of youth, or the events that motivated them to pursue their present path. I try to bring into view the individual convictions and motivations—the richness of character—that can be obscured behind the labels of ethnicity or creed. It is always my hope that the interaction of our lives will generate melodies that will lead us in the direction of a more genuinely humane world. As those harmonies develop, our differences become the leitmotifs that prompt each of us toward the revelation of our best self.

In a manner that is consonant with Dr. Sen's concern with human plurality, the German-American political philosopher Hannah Arendt[130] wrote the following words expressing a central aspect of her thinking: "However much

---

129 Sen, Amartya. 2007. *Identity and Violence: The Illusion of Destiny*. London: Penguin Books, p. 16.

130 Hannah Arendt (1906–75), German-born American political scientist and philosopher.

we are affected by the things of the world, however deeply they may stir and stimulate us, they become human for us only when we can discuss them with our fellows."[131] Arendt goes on to clarify that she is using the word "fellows" to indicate "friendship" rather than "fraternity"—in particular, friendship between people whose views of the truth differ. It is precisely because of such differences that the world is humanized through dialogue and the rich diversity of human life shines with its greatest glory.

This, above all, is the kind of friendship, predicated on heart-to-heart exchange, that forestalls the further fissuring of societies in which difference all too often functions as a marker for exclusion. We must strive to uphold this friendship as the very mark of our humanity, if we are to prevent the sense of empathetic connection with others from being swept away by a culture of war, a maelstrom of hatred and violence.

With the Seville Statement as one core source of inspiration, the United Nations has been promoting a culture of peace as a way of transforming humankind's deep-rooted proclivity to war. One aspect of this was the International Decade for a Culture of Peace and Non-Violence for the Children of the World (2001–10), in support of which the SGI organized various exhibitions and other programs promoting public education and dialogue—efforts that continue to this day.

To help a culture of peace take root the world over, it is necessary to patiently counteract any incidence of hatred and confrontation that may arise. We are, by virtue of being human, endowed with the tools that we need for this pursuit: the tuning fork of self-reflection with which to imagine the pain of others as if it were our own; the bridge of dialogue over which to reach out to anyone, anywhere; and the shovel and hoe of friendship with which to cultivate even the most barren and desolate of wastelands.

A friendship with the power to develop a vibrant culture of peace will have at its heart the ability to take mutual joy in our existence as people living together on this planet, as well as a vow to protect, at all costs and despite whatever differences, the dignity that is inherent in each of our lives. As Nichiren put it, "Joy means delight shared by oneself and others."[132]

---

131 Arendt, Hannah. 1970. *Men in Dark Times*. New York: Houghton Mifflin Harcourt, pp. 24–25.

132 (trans. from) Nichiren. 1952. *Nichiren Daishonin gosho zenshu* [The Complete Works of Nichiren Daishonin]. Ed. by Nichiko Hori. Tokyo: Soka Gakkai, p. 761.

Here I have considered three commitments or guidelines for action for constructing a civilization founded upon respect for the dignity of life. These can also be thought of in terms of three qualities that I suggested should be essential elements of global citizenship in a lecture I delivered at Teachers College, Columbia University, in 1996[133]:

- The compassion that never abandons others to suffer alone
- The wisdom to perceive the equality and possibilities of life
- The courage to make our differences the impetus for the elevation of our humanity

I believe that the challenge of constructing a global society of peace and creative coexistence begins with the recognition that all people inherently possess these qualities. I also believe that the social mission of religion in the twenty-first century must be to encourage the flowering of these capacities. It must bring people together in an ethos of reverence for life's dignity and worth.

Nuclear weapons: the ultimate negation of the dignity of life

I would now like to address and offer concrete proposals on two particular challenges facing our world: the prohibition and abolition of nuclear weapons and the establishment of a culture of human rights.

Regarding the first of these, nuclear weapons are the contemporary embodiment of Goethe's "quick dagger."

The French philosopher Paul Virilio[134] has explored the question of speed in relation to the different problems of contemporary civilization in a manner similar to that of Goethe's probing of the human psychology that drives the quest for a quick dagger. In *Speed and Politics* he writes: "The danger of the nuclear weapon, and of the arms system it implies, is . . . not so much that it will explode, but that it exists and is imploding in our minds."[135]

---

133 Ikeda, Daisaku. 2010. *A New Humanism: The University Addresses of Daisaku Ikeda*. London and New York: I.B.Tauris, pp. 52–61.

134 Paul Virilio (1932–), French philosopher and cultural theorist.

135 Virilio, Paul. 2006. *Speed and Politics: An Essay on Dromology*. Trans. by Mark Polizzotti. Los Angeles: Semiotext(e), p. 166.

The destruction wrought by a nuclear explosion would of course be massive and irreparable, but Virilio's point is to stress the abnormality of living under the threat of nuclear confrontation, and the spiritual impact of this even when these weapons are not used. This is an important perspective. Without it, essential aspects of our situation will be obscured. For example, as Virilio points out, "as a continuation of total war by other means, nuclear deterrence marked the end of the distinction between wartime and peacetime . . . ."[136]

More than half a century ago, as Cold War competition to develop ever more destructive nuclear weapons was intensifying, my mentor second Soka Gakkai president Josei Toda[137] issued a declaration calling for their abolition. In it, he stressed that possession of nuclear weapons represents an outright negation of the dignity of life and declared that this was impermissible under any circumstances. He called for a thoroughgoing repudiation of such ways of thinking:

> Although a movement calling for a ban on the testing of atomic or nuclear weapons has arisen around the world, it is my wish to go further, to attack the problem at its root. I want to expose and rip out the claws that lie hidden in the very depths of such weapons.[138]

In other words, while acknowledging the importance of efforts to ban nuclear testing, he stressed that the fundamental answer to this problem requires that we challenge the root thinking that enables and justifies possession of these weapons of mass destruction.

Nuclear weapons do not distinguish between combatants and noncombatants; they destroy whole cities, killing vast numbers of people instantaneously. Their impact on the natural environment is severe, and the aftereffects of radiation exposure inflict long-term suffering on people. The bombings of Hiroshima and Nagasaki made evident the indescribably inhumane nature of these weapons.

What is it, then, that is used to justify their continued possession?

---

136 Virilio, Paul. 2002. *Ground Zero*. Trans. by Chris Turner. London and New York: Verso, p. 52.

137 Josei Toda (1900–58), second president of the Soka Gakkai (1951–58).

138 (trans. from) Toda, Josei. 1981–90. *Toda Josei zenshu* [The Complete Works of Josei Toda]. 9 vols. Tokyo: Seikyo Shimbunsha. Vol. 4, p. 565. (English text at http://www.joseitoda.org/vision/declaration.)

It is, I believe, the same psychology that brought humanity to the point of total war. To restate this using the frameworks I explored earlier in this proposal, it is the way of thinking that monolithically identifies everyone on the opposing side, regardless of individual differences, as the enemy. This denies the possibility of any other way of relating to them, leaving only the option of a violent severing of all ties. Is this not an ultimate disavowal of the dignity of life?

Nothing here is mediated by what Arendt termed "the readiness to share the world with other men," which she contrasted with the cruel coldness of the misanthrope who "regards nobody as worthy of rejoicing with him in the world and nature and the cosmos."[139] This is a life-state dominated by the impulse to dismiss and destroy the lives of others—what Buddhism refers to as our fundamental darkness.

It is for this reason that Toda's determination to "rip out the claws that lie hidden in the very depths of such weapons" and to protect the right of the world's people to live was expressed in these striking terms: "I propose that humankind applies, in every case, the death penalty to anyone responsible for using nuclear weapons, even if that person is on the winning side."[140]

Toda had, as a Buddhist, often declared his opposition to the death penalty, so his seeming call for this ultimate punishment must be understood as an expression of his sense of the absolute unacceptability of the use of nuclear weapons under any circumstances. Further, this was a clear refutation of the logic of nuclear weapons possession, under which states pursue their security interests by in effect holding the world's peoples hostage.

When Toda made this declaration in 1957, the world was divided into the opposing camps of East and West, with both sides trading diatribes about the arsenal possessed by the other. In contrast, Toda denounced nuclear weapons as the central evil of contemporary civilization, and he did so in the name of the world's peoples, unswayed by the distortions of ideology or national interest.

Since that time, the number of countries possessing nuclear weapons has continued to increase, and the work of preventing their further proliferation

---

139 Arendt, Hannah. 1970. *Men in Dark Times*. New York: Houghton Mifflin Harcourt, p. 25.

140 (trans. from) Toda, Josei. 1981–90. *Toda Josei zenshu* [The Complete Works of Josei Toda]. 9 vols. Tokyo: Seikyo Shimbunsha. Vol. 4, p. 565. (English text at http://www.joseitoda.org/vision/declaration.)

has naturally been seen as an urgent task. Nonetheless, I think it is crucial that we attend to the core problem of nuclear weapons—their underlying inhumanity—that my mentor so starkly exposed.

As UN Secretary-General Ban Ki-moon[141] has pointed out:

> The possession of nuclear weapons by some encourages their acquisition by others. This leads to nuclear proliferation and the spread of the contagious doctrine of nuclear deterrence.[142]

Unless we confront the fundamental source of that contagion, moves to prevent proliferation will be neither convincing nor effective.

Outlawing nuclear weapons as inhumane

Since the 2010 Review Conference of the Parties to the Treaty on the Non-Proliferation of Nuclear Weapons (NPT), there has been a growing, if still nascent, movement to outlaw nuclear weapons based on the premise that they are inhumane.

The Final Document of the Review Conference notes a "deep concern at the catastrophic humanitarian consequences of any use of nuclear weapons" and reaffirms "the need for all States at all times to comply with applicable international law, including international humanitarian law."[143]

This groundbreaking statement was followed by a resolution by the Council of Delegates of the International Red Cross and Red Crescent Movement in November 2011, strongly appealing to all states "to pursue in good faith and conclude with urgency and determination negotiations to prohibit the use of and completely eliminate nuclear weapons through a legally binding international agreement."[144]

---

141 Ban Ki-moon (1944–), South Korean statesman, 8th Secretary-General of the United Nations (2007–).
142 Ban, Ki-moon. 2010. "Remarks at Dialogue with Waseda University Students." Tokyo, August 4.
143 UNGA (United Nations General Assembly). 2010. "2010 Review Conference of the Parties to the Treaty on the Non-Proliferation of Nuclear Weapons." NPT/CONF.2010/50 (Vol. I). Final Document, p. 19.
144 ICRC (International Red Cross and Red Crescent). 2011. "Council of Delegates 2011: Resolution 1: Working towards the Elimination of Nuclear Weapons." November 26.

Then, at the first session of the Preparatory Committee for the 2015 NPT Review Conference held in May 2012, sixteen countries led by Norway and Switzerland issued a joint statement on the humanitarian dimension of nuclear disarmament, stating that "it is of great concern that, even after the end of the Cold War, the threat of nuclear annihilation remains part of the 21st century international security environment," and stressing that "it is of utmost importance that these weapons never be used again, under any circumstances. . . . All States must intensify their efforts to outlaw nuclear weapons and achieve a world free of nuclear weapons."[145] In October 2012, this statement, with minor revisions, was presented to the First Committee of the UN General Assembly by thirty-five member and observer states.

In March of this year, an international conference on the humanitarian impact of nuclear weapons will be held in Oslo, Norway. Its purpose is to examine from a scientific standpoint the immediate and long-term effects of any use of nuclear weapons and the difficulty of humanitarian relief efforts in response to such use. Finally, in September of this year, the General Assembly will hold a high-level meeting on nuclear disarmament.

In my proposal last year, I called for the establishment of an action group for a Nuclear Weapons Convention (NWC), composed of NGOs and forward-looking governments. It is my strong hope that, through these conferences, a growing core of NGOs and governments supporting the above-mentioned statements will develop, and that they will, if at all possible before year's end, initiate the process of drafting a treaty to outlaw nuclear weapons on the basis of their inhumane nature.

A key factor here will be the stance taken by those countries which have relied on the extended deterrence of nuclear-weapon states, the so-called nuclear umbrella.

The signatories to the statements referenced above include not only countries belonging to nuclear-weapon-free zones (NWFZs) and neutral countries, but also Norway and Denmark, which are members of NATO and thus come under that organization's nuclear umbrella. And yet these two countries have not only signed these statements but have played a key role in their drafting.

---

145 UNODA (United Nations Office for Disarmament Affairs). 2012. "Joint Statement on the Humanitarian Dimension of Nuclear Disarmament." Delivered at Preparatory Committee for the 2015 Nuclear Non-Proliferation Treaty Review Conference. May 2.

Japan, which likewise comes under the extended deterrence of its ally, the United States of America, should join with other countries seeking the prohibition of nuclear weapons as inhumane and work for the earliest realization of a world free from the threat of these weapons.

Rather than accepting that the continuing existence of nuclear weapons makes reliance on extended deterrence inevitable, Japan, as a country that has experienced nuclear attack, should promote the idea that there is no distinguishing between "good" and "bad" nuclear weapons depending on who possesses them, and should play a leading role in achieving an NWC.

Earlier, I referred to Shakyamuni's admonition: "Putting oneself in the place of another, one should not kill nor cause another to kill." The survivors of the nuclear attacks on Hiroshima and Nagasaki have continued to give voice to the dual pledge that no country be victimized by nuclear attack and that no country engage in one. In like manner, Japan should stand at the forefront of efforts to forever prevent the tragedy brought about by the use of nuclear weapons.

Further, having made clear its determination to shift toward security arrangements that are not reliant on nuclear weapons, Japan should undertake the kind of confidence-building measures that are a necessary predicate to the establishment of a Northeast Asian NWFZ. In particular, Japan should make proactive contributions to the reduction of regional tensions and to shrinking the role of nuclear weapons so as to create the conditions for their global abolition.

For an expanded nuclear summit in 2015

There have recently been signs, even within the nuclear-weapon states, of changing attitudes regarding the utility of these weapons.

In a speech at Hankuk University in Seoul, Republic of Korea, on March 26, 2012, US President Barack Obama[146] stated: "My administration's nuclear posture recognizes that the massive nuclear arsenal we inherited from the Cold War is poorly suited to today's threats, including nuclear terrorism."[147]

---

146 Barack Obama (1961–), 44th President of the United States (2009–), recipient of the Nobel Prize for Peace in 2009.

147 Obama, Barack. 2012. "Remarks by President Obama at Hankuk University." March 26. http://www.whitehouse.gov/the-press-office/2012/03/26/remarks-president-obama-hankuk-university (accessed April 2, 2013).

A statement adopted at the NATO Summit in May 2012 noted: "The circumstances in which any use of nuclear weapons might have to be contemplated are extremely remote."[148]

Both of these statements assume the continuance of a policy of deterrence so long as nuclear weapons exist. And yet they both point to the lessened centrality of nuclear weapons in national security thinking.

The logic of nuclear weapons possession is also being challenged from a number of other perspectives. In numerous countries around the world, more and more voices question the wisdom of the continued possession of nuclear weapons in light of the enormous financial burdens entailed. For example, in the United Kingdom, which is still feeling the effects of the global economic crisis, the planned update of the aging submarine-launched Trident nuclear weapons system has become a focus of fiscal policy debate.

It is estimated that annual aggregate expenditure on nuclear weapons globally is around US$105 billion.[149] This makes clear the enormity of the burden placed on societies simply by the continued possession of these weapons. If these financial resources were redirected domestically to health, social welfare and education programs or to development aid for other countries, the positive impact on people's lives and dignity would be incalculable.

In April of 2012, important new research on the effects of nuclear war on the environment was announced in the report "Nuclear Famine." Issued by International Physicians for the Prevention of Nuclear War (IPPNW) and Physicians for Social Responsibility (PSR), this report predicts that even a relatively small-scale nuclear exchange could cause major climate change and that the impact on countries far-distant from the combatant nations would result in famine affecting more than a billion people.[150]

Originally inspired by second Soka Gakkai president Josei Toda's 1957 antinuclear weapons declaration, the SGI has for decades worked consistently for the prohibition and abolition of nuclear weapons. Most recently, in

148 NATO (North Atlantic Treaty Organization). 2012. "Deterrence and Defence Posture Review." Press Release. May 20.

149 See Rizvi, Haider. 2012. "Govts Boost Nukes While Cutting Aid, Social Services." Inter Press Service. July 27.

150 Helfand, Ira. 2012. "Nuclear Famine: A Billion People at Risk—Global Impact of Limited Nuclear War on Agriculture, Food Supplies, and Human Nutrition." Somerville, MA and Washington, DC: IPPNW (International Physicians for the Prevention of Nuclear War) / PSR (Physicians for Social Responsibility).

collaboration with the International Campaign to Abolish Nuclear Weapons (ICAN), we have developed a new exhibition entitled "Everything You Treasure—For a World Free from Nuclear Weapons."

Initiatives to resolve the nuclear weapons issue from a political or military perspective remain deadlocked, so this exhibition, which premiered in Hiroshima last August, seeks to reexamine the issue from multiple perspectives including, of course, the inhumane nature of nuclear weapons as well as human security, environmental protection, economic development, human rights, gender equity and the social responsibility of science.

One aim of this exhibition is to engage the interests of individual viewers to help them draw the connection between nuclear weapons and their personal concerns, and in this way expand and extend solidarity for a world free from nuclear weapons.

The SGI's efforts to grapple with the nuclear weapons issue are based on the recognition that the very existence of these weapons represents the ultimate negation of the dignity of life. It is necessary to challenge the underlying inhumanity of the idea that the needs of states can justify the sacrifice of untold numbers of human lives and disruption of the global ecology. At the same time, we feel that nuclear weapons serve as a prism through which to bring into sharper focus ecological integrity, economic development and human rights—issues that our contemporary world cannot afford to ignore. This in turn helps us identify the elements that will shape the contours of a new, sustainable society, one in which all people can live in dignity.

Toward this end, I would like to make three concrete proposals.

First, to make disarmament a key theme of the Sustainable Development Goals: Specifically, I propose that halving world military expenditures relative to 2010 levels and abolishing nuclear weapons and all other weapons judged inhumane under international law be included as targets for achievement by the year 2030. In the proposal I issued on the occasion of the Rio+20 Conference in June last year, I urged that targets related to the green economy, renewable energy and disaster prevention and mitigation be included in the SDGs, and I believe that disarmament targets should also be taken into consideration.

The International Peace Bureau (IPB), the Institute for Policy Studies (IPS) and other civil society organizations are currently advocating the global reduction of military spending, and the SGI supports this out of the awareness that disarmament is humanitarian action.

Second, to initiate the negotiation process for a Nuclear Weapons Convention, with the goal of agreement on an initial draft by 2015: To this end, we must engage in active and multifaceted debate—centered on the inhumane nature of nuclear weapons—to broadly shape international public opinion.

Third, to hold an expanded summit for a nuclear-weapon-free world: The G8 Summit in 2015, the seventieth anniversary of the atomic bombings of Hiroshima and Nagasaki, would be an appropriate opportunity for such a summit, which should include the additional participation of representatives of the United Nations and non-G8 states in possession of nuclear weapons, as well as members of the five existing NWFZs and those states which have taken a lead in calling for nuclear abolition. If possible, Germany and Japan, which are the scheduled G8 host countries for 2015 and 2016 respectively, should agree to reverse that order, enabling the convening of this meeting in Hiroshima or Nagasaki.

In past peace proposals, I have urged that the 2015 NPT Review Conference be held in Hiroshima and Nagasaki as a vehicle for realizing a nuclear abolition summit. I still hope that such a meeting can be held. Nevertheless, the logistical issues involved in bringing together the representatives of almost 190 countries may dictate that the meeting be held at the UN Headquarters in New York as is customary. In that event, the G8 Summit scheduled to be held several months after the NPT Review Conference would provide an excellent opportunity for an expanded group of world leaders to grapple with this critical issue.

In this regard, I am encouraged by the following words from President Obama's speech in Korea that I referenced earlier:

> But I believe the United States has a unique responsibility to act—indeed, we have a moral obligation. I say this as President of the only nation ever to use nuclear weapons.

This, of course, restates the conviction he first expressed in his April 2009 Prague speech. President Obama then went on to say:

> Most of all, I say it as a father, who wants my two young daughters to grow up in a world where everything they know and love can't be instantly wiped out.[151]

---

151 Obama, Barack. 2012. "Remarks by President Obama at Hankuk University." March 26. http://www.whitehouse.gov/the-press-office/2012/03/26/remarks-president-obama-hankuk-university (accessed April 2, 2013).

These words express a yearning for the world as it should be, a yearning that cannot be subsumed even after all political elements and security requirements have been taken fully into consideration. It is the statement of a single human being rising above the differences of national interest or ideological stance. Such a way of thinking can help us "untie" the Gordian Knot that has too long bound together the ideas of national security and nuclear weapons possession.

There is no place more conducive to considering the full significance of life in the nuclear age than Hiroshima and Nagasaki. This was seen when the G8 Summit of Lower House Speakers was convened in Hiroshima in 2008. The kind of expanded summit I am calling for would inherit that spirit and solidify momentum toward a world free from nuclear weapons. It would become the launching point for a larger effort for global disarmament aiming toward the year 2030.

Fostering a culture of human rights

Next, I would like to discuss the challenge of fostering a culture of human rights.

Just as the first resolution to be adopted by the United Nations General Assembly in 1946 dealt with the prohibition and abolition of nuclear weapons, the protection of human rights has been one of the major objectives of the UN since its founding.

In view of the fact that there were only very limited references to human rights in the initial draft of the UN Charter, many participants at the United Nations Conference on International Organization held in San Francisco in 1945—including NGOs—called for the inclusion of clear provisions regarding human rights. As a result, "promoting and encouraging respect for human rights" was defined in Article 1 of the Charter as one of the principal purposes of the new organization, and this became the sole theme for which the establishment of a specialized commission was stipulated.

The following year, in 1946, the Commission on Human Rights, the predecessor of the current Human Rights Council, was established; two years later, in 1948, the Universal Declaration of Human Rights was adopted. Eleanor Roosevelt,[152] the first chair of the Commission who played a crucial role in its drafting and adoption, stated, "This Universal Declaration

---

152 Eleanor Roosevelt (1884–1962), First Lady of the United States (1933–45), Chairperson of the United Nations Commission on Human Rights (1946–47).

of Human Rights may well become the international Magna Carta of all men everywhere."[153] As she anticipated, the Declaration has influenced the domestic human rights provisions of many countries, as well as serving as the philosophical basis for various international human rights treaties, and has continued to inspire human rights activists to this day.

In the sixty-five years since the adoption of the Declaration, progress has been made in defining human rights standards, in developing institutions to guarantee them and in providing remedies for human rights violations. Today, building on these achievements, there is a growing emphasis within the international community on fostering a culture of human rights.

The concept of a culture of human rights aims to promote an ethos throughout society in which people mutually treasure human dignity. In this way, it seeks to encourage each individual to make conscious efforts to strengthen the guarantees of human rights.

This accords with the principles I have stressed throughout this proposal. In order to create a society that upholds the dignity of life, a sense of the irreplaceable value of each individual must live in the heart of every one of us; at the same time, this must be the foundation of the human bonds that sustain society.

The UN has been promoting a culture of human rights through its World Programme for Human Rights Education launched in 2005. To further enhance such efforts, I would like to propose that promotion of human rights be a central element of the Sustainable Development Goals for the year 2030, alongside disarmament as discussed above. Regarding this point, I fully support the statement of UN High Commissioner for Human Rights Navanethem Pillay[154] reflecting on the outcome of the Rio+20 Summit: "we must ensure that . . . the SDG framework is a human rights framework."[155]

With this in mind, I would like to propose the inclusion of the following two specific targets. The first is implementing a Social Protection Floor (SPF) in every country to ensure that those who are suffering from extreme poverty are able to regain a sense of dignity.

---

153 Roosevelt, Eleanor. 1948. "Address to the United Nations General Assembly on the Adoption of the Universal Declaration of Human Rights." December 9.

154 Navanethem Pillay (1941–), South African jurist, United Nations High Commissioner for Human Rights (2008–).

155 OHCHR (Office of the United Nations High Commissioner for Human Rights). 2012. "Rio+20 Outcome: Human Rights Emerge as New Pillar of Sustainable Development." June 23.

Although the right to an adequate standard of living is included in the Universal Declaration of Human Rights, an unacceptably large proportion of the world's population lacks access to the minimum social protections needed to live in a humane way. To address the impact of the global economic crisis on employment, health care and education, the United Nations launched the Global Initiative for a Universal Social Protection Floor (SPF-1) in 2009.

Government policy has traditionally focused on the provision of social safety nets, but there will always be people who slip through such nets. In response, the concept has emerged of a floor that catches all people and supports them so they are able to lead dignified lives.

Providing a Social Protection Floor for people throughout the world would be a significant challenge. However, according to estimates made by the relevant UN agencies, it should be possible for countries at every stage of economic development to cover the necessary costs for a basic framework of minimum income and livelihood guarantees. In fact, some thirty developing countries have already started implementing such plans.

The Human Rights Council has taken up the issue of extreme poverty and human rights, and in September of last year it adopted a series of principles to act as guidelines for the international community. These include "agency and autonomy" and "participation and empowerment." The Council calls for states to "adopt a comprehensive national strategy to reduce poverty and social exclusion" and to "ensure that public policies accord due priority to persons living in extreme poverty."[156]

In the words of the Bangladeshi economist and founder of the Grameen Bank Muhammad Yunus,[157] "Because poverty denies people any semblance of control over their destiny, it is the ultimate denial of human rights."[158] Poverty must be addressed with a sense of urgency as something that undermines the very foundation of human rights and dignity.

Of particular concern is the situation of young people. According to the International Labour Organization (ILO), some 12 percent of global youth are

---

156 UNGA (United Nations General Assembly). 2012. "Final Draft of the Guiding Principles on Extreme Poverty and Human Rights, Submitted by the Special Rapporteur on Extreme Poverty and Human Rights, Magdalena Sepúlveda Carmona." A/HRC/21/39. July 18.

157 Muhammad Yunus (1940–), Bangladeshi economist, founder of Grameen Bank.

158 Yunus, Muhammad. 2007. *Creating a World Without Poverty: Social Business and the Future*. New York: PublicAffairs, p. 104.

unemployed,[159] and even among those with employment, over 200 million young people find themselves compelled to work for less than US$2 a day. The ILO warns, "Unless immediate and vigorous action is taken, the global community confronts the grim legacy of a lost generation."[160]

A society that deprives young people of hope cannot expect to achieve sustainability or build a culture of human rights. The effort to secure a Social Protection Floor should be undertaken with this awareness firmly in mind.

The second target I propose for inclusion in the SDGs regards the promotion of human rights education and training.

Throughout this proposal, I have stressed that interactions with other people and the support of society as a whole can provide a sense of connection and help people regain hope and dignity, no matter how challenging their present circumstances may be. In the context of human rights, efforts to raise awareness through human rights education and training could serve as such a catalyst, alongside legal systems of guarantees and remedies.

The documentary *A Path to Dignity* which I mentioned earlier illustrates how human rights education catalyzed both those impacted by human rights violations and potential perpetrators.

One case study introduces the story of a boy who himself had suffered discrimination. Through a human rights education program at his school, he was empowered to speak out against things he felt were not right. One day, he learned that a girl in his neighborhood had been engaged to marry against her will. Her parents claimed they had to arrange the wedding because they were poor, but he insisted that it was wrong and that she should be allowed to get an education. As a result of the boy's determined insistence, the wedding was called off and the girl was able to remain in school.

In Australia, all echelons of the Victoria Police Force received training in human rights, leading to a variety of reforms in their procedures for investigation, arrest and custody. As a result, complaints about human rights violations decreased, and police officers were able to gain greater trust from local citizens.

---

159 See ILO (International Labour Organization). 2012. "Global Employment Trends for Youth 2012." Geneva: ILO, p. 43.

160 ILO (International Labour Organization). 2012. "The Youth Employment Crisis: A Call for Action." Resolution and conclusions of the 101st Session of the International Labour Conference. Geneva: ILO, p. 3.

The examples in this documentary demonstrate how a personal awakening to the dignity of life—both one's own and others'—instills a palpable sense of human rights in the mind of the individual and thus lays the foundation for a broader culture of human rights.

Some years ago, I conducted a dialogue with the American historian Dr. Vincent Harding,[161] who fought alongside Dr. Martin Luther King Jr.[162] in the US Civil Rights Movement of the 1950s and 1960s. He emphasized that the goal of Dr. King's struggle was not simply to eliminate injustice and oppression but to create a new reality.[163] I believe this is also an essential element in building a culture of human rights.

To this end, I would like to propose that regional centers for human rights education and training be established along the lines of the Regional Centres of Expertise operating in collaboration with the United Nations University to promote the UN Decade of Education for Sustainable Development. Worldwide, there are currently 101 such centers, bringing together stakeholders such as universities, NGOs, local community groups and individuals.

A similar system for human rights education could involve not only communities with demonstrated best practices in human rights, but also those that are striving to improve conditions despite severely problematic histories of human rights abuse. Communities that have endured great pain and suffering have a unique potential to convey a powerful message, serving as a source of hope and encouragement to other communities struggling with similar problems. They can also facilitate the creation of a culture of human rights, as people come to perceive human rights as a tangible reality.

The rights of the child

Today's children will inevitably play a crucial role in the work of building a culture of human rights. To protect them and improve the conditions under which they live, it is crucial that all countries ratify the Convention on the

---

161 Vincent Harding (1931–), American historian, theologian, civil rights activist and colleague of Martin Luther King Jr.

162 Martin Luther King Jr. (1929–68), American religious leader and civil rights activist, recipient of the Nobel Prize for Peace in 1964.

163 (trans. from) Harding, Vincent and Daisaku Ikeda. 2013. *Kibo no kyoiku, heiwa no koshin* [Advancing for Peace Through Hopeful Education]. Tokyo: Daisanbunmei-sha, p. 172.

Rights of the Child and its Optional Protocols and pass the domestic legislation needed to fulfill the treaty obligations.

This Convention was adopted in 1989 and is today the most universal of all human rights conventions adopted by the United Nations, having been ratified by 193 countries so far. In order to prevent serious violations, two Optional Protocols—on the involvement of children under the age of eighteen in armed conflict, and on the sale of children, child prostitution and child pornography—were adopted in 2000, and a third Optional Protocol permitting children to submit complaints regarding violations of their rights was adopted in December 2011.

In reality, however, it is not uncommon for the rights spelled out in this Convention to be ignored and violated due to inadequate enactment of related domestic legislation, failure to ratify the Optional Protocols and a lack of public awareness.

I am particularly struck by the words of Ishmael Beah,[164] who, having survived the traumatic experience of life as a child soldier during civil conflict in his home country of Sierra Leone, is now a powerful advocate for children's rights.

At the age of sixteen, Mr. Beah attended a conference at the United Nations where, for the first time, he learned about the Convention on the Rights of the Child. He describes this eye-opening experience as follows: "I remember how this knowledge—particularly for those of us from war-torn countries—rekindled the value of our lives and our humanity."[165]

He goes on to emphasize:

> My life has also been enriched by articles 12 and 13, which guarantee children and youth the right to express their views fully in matters affecting them, and "to seek, receive and impart important information" of all kinds and by all media. These articles have helped many children become active participants in finding solutions to problems that affect them.[166]

---

164 Ishmael Beah (1980–), Sierra Leonean author and activist.

165 UNICEF (United Nations Children's Fund). 2009. "The State of the World's Children: Celebrating 20 Years of the Convention on the Rights of the Child." New York: UNICEF, p. 46.

166 Ibid., p. 47.

I urge that all countries uphold the Convention, always prioritizing the best interest of the child. The Convention can serve as an inspiration for the members of the younger generation to awaken to their own dignity and, as epitomized by Mr. Beah's experience, as a source of the hope needed to live.

A generation brought up in a society imbued with this ethos will be a transformative presence in that society and will surely foster this spirit in subsequent generations. The Preamble of the Geneva Declaration of the Rights of the Child of 1924, a key historical precedent and inspiration for the Convention, states, "mankind owes to the Child the best that it has to give."[167]

Ensuring that this noble vow is passed on from one generation to the next will make a culture of human rights the central axis around which human society revolves.

Lasting friendship between China and Japan

Lastly, I would like to share, from both a short- and a long-term perspective, some thoughts on ways to improve the currently strained relations between China and Japan. I am motivated by my conviction that this is indispensable to building a global society of peace and coexistence.

Last year marked the significant juncture of the fortieth anniversary of the restoration of Sino–Japanese diplomatic ties. However, a number of events and exchange programs celebrating the anniversary were canceled or postponed due to escalating tensions and frictions. Relations between the two countries have deteriorated to a post-World War II low, and economic relations have also chilled significantly.

I, however, am not at all pessimistic about the future of Sino–Japanese relations. In the words of the traditional Chinese maxim, "drops of water can pierce even a rock." In just this way, friendship between Japan and China has been nurtured in the postwar period by the devoted efforts of pioneers who, even before the normalization of diplomatic relations, worked tenaciously to break through the obstacles that stood between the two countries. These bonds of friendship have been steadily cultivated and strengthened through countless exchanges over the years, and they will not be easily broken.

---

167 UN (United Nations). 1924. "Geneva Declaration of the Rights of the Child." Declaration adopted by League of Nations. September 26.

When I called for the normalization of Sino–Japanese diplomatic relations in September 1968, it was almost unthinkable in Japan to even mention the possibility of friendship with China. In that sense, the situation was even more severe than it is today. But it was my belief that Japan had no future without friendly relations with its neighbors, and that stable and harmonious ties with China were essential for Asia and the world to advance along the great path to peace.

In 1972, diplomatic relations were finally normalized. Six years after I made that initial call, in December 1974, I was able to visit Beijing and meet with Chinese Premier Zhou Enlai[168] and Vice Premier Deng Xiaoping.[169] Through these discussions, I learned that they viewed both the Japanese and the Chinese people as victims of the Japanese militarist regime. This further deepened my determination to develop an indestructible friendship between our two peoples in order to prevent war between us from ever happening again.

Ever since, I have been passionately devoted to promoting friendship exchanges, with a special focus on members of the younger generation. In 1975, I served as personal guarantor when Soka University welcomed the first six government-financed exchange students from the People's Republic of China to study in Japan. Now, nearly forty years later, 100,000 Chinese students are studying here, and 15,000 Japanese students are pursuing their studies in China.

Over the years, China and Japan have created a history of exchanges in cultural, educational and many other fields, including, for example, a total of 349 sister-city arrangements. We have also developed a tradition of mutual support in times of hardship such as the 2008 earthquake in Sichuan and the 2011 earthquake in northeastern Japan. Despite occasional periods of tension, the current of friendship between the two countries has grown steadily stronger over the years.

This current is the accumulation of friendships developed through innumerable face-to-face interactions and exchanges, each of which makes its own small yet invaluable contribution. For this reason, it will not easily run dry no matter what trial or obstacle it encounters. And we must ensure that never happens.

---

168 Zhou Enlai (1898–1976), Premier of the People's Republic of China (1949–76).

169 Deng Xiaoping (1904–97), Vice Premier of the People's Republic of China (1975–80, 1980–83).

In a lecture I delivered at Peking University in May 1990, I urged, "No matter what issues might come between us, the bonds of friendship must never be broken."[170] Now more than ever we need to reaffirm that conviction.

The political and economic arenas are always impacted by the ebb and flow of the times. Indeed, times of tranquillity are perhaps the exception rather than the rule. This is why, when faced with a crisis, it is important to adamantly uphold the two central pledges in the Treaty of Peace and Friendship between Japan and the People's Republic of China (1978): To refrain from the use or threat of force, and not to seek regional hegemony.

So long as we uphold these principles, we will without fail find ways to overcome the present crisis. Even more than when things are going well, it is times of adversity that present opportunities to deepen understanding and strengthen ties. I strongly encourage Japan and China to reconfirm their commitment to uphold the two pledges of the Treaty of Peace and Friendship and promptly set up a high-level forum for dialogue aimed at preventing any further deterioration of relations.

The first order of business for such a forum should be to institute a moratorium on all actions that could be construed as provocative. This should be followed by a scrupulous analysis of the steps by which the confrontation evolved—how actions were perceived and what reactions were provoked. This would facilitate the development of guidelines for more effective responses to future crises. Doubtless, some sharp differences of opinion would be expressed, but unless we are prepared to face each other on those terms, hopes for the restoration of friendly relations between the two countries—for greater stability in Asia and for a peaceful world—will continue to elude us.

Immediately after the end of the Cold War, I met for the first time with then Soviet President Mikhail Gorbachev,[171] in July 1990. I opened our conversation by saying: "I have come to have an argument with you. Let's make sparks fly, and talk about everything honestly and openly, for the sake of humanity and for the sake of Japan–Soviet relations!" I expressed myself in this way to convey my hopes of having a real and frank discussion instead

---

170 Ikeda, Daisaku. 2010. *A New Humanism: The University Addresses of Daisaku Ikeda*. London and New York: I.B.Tauris, p. 17.

171 Mikhail Gorbachev (1931–), General Secretary of the Communist Party of the Soviet Union (1985–91), President of the Soviet Union (1990–91), recipient of the Nobel Prize for Peace in 1990.

of a merely formal meeting, at a time when the prospects for Japan–Soviet relations were uncertain.

The more difficult the situation appears to be, the more important it is to engage in dialogue based on a commitment to peace and creative coexistence. Heated and earnest dialogue can reveal the emotions—the fears, concerns and aspirations—that underlie the positions and assertions of each side.

In this context, I propose that China and Japan institute the practice of holding regular summit meetings.

This month marks the fiftieth anniversary of the signing of the Élysée Treaty by France and Germany. The treaty helped the two countries overcome their history of war and bloodshed, with relations becoming significantly closer due to the provisions for regular meetings of Heads of State and Government at least twice a year and for ministerial-level meetings at least once every three months in the fields of foreign affairs, defense and education. I believe that the current crisis between Japan and China presents a unique opportunity to establish a similar framework, creating an environment that enables their leaders to conduct face-to-face dialogue under any circumstances.

Further, I suggest that Japan and China together launch an organization for environmental cooperation in East Asia. This could be an interim goal to be achieved by 2015 and would lay the foundations of a new partnership focused on peace and creative coexistence and joint action for the sake of humanity.

Amelioration of environmental conditions would benefit both countries. This new organization would create opportunities for young people from China and Japan to work together toward a common goal. It would also establish a pattern of contributing together to the peace and stability of East Asia and the creation of a sustainable global society.

When I called for the normalization of diplomatic relations back in September 1968, I urged the young people of both countries to come together in friendship to build a better world. The foundation for this, I believe, has now been laid in a quiet, uncelebrated way through the exchanges and inter-actions that have been conducted to date.

Now, I believe, the focus should turn to something more visible and durable. The time has come to take a medium- to long-term perspective and develop more concrete models of cooperation across a range of new fields. I am convinced that it is through such sustained and determined efforts that the bonds of friendship between China and Japan will develop into something indestructible, something that will be passed down with pride from generation to generation.

A robust solidarity

In this proposal, I have shared my vision and some suggestions for action that I see as vital toward building a global society of peace and coexistence in the years leading to 2030. The key to realizing these goals ultimately lies in the solidarity of ordinary citizens.

In *Soka kyoikugaku taikei* (The System of Value-Creating Pedagogy), the first president of the Soka Gakkai, Tsunesaburo Makiguchi,[172] made the following observation regarding why, with rare exceptions, the efforts of people who take a stand to correct social ills end in failure:

> Throughout history, people of goodwill have met with severe persecutions. Other good-hearted people may secretly sympathize with their plight but, lacking the capacity to do anything about it, remain bystanders while the former go down to defeat. Because narrow self-preservation is at the heart of these bystanders' way of life, they remain mere constituent elements of society. They cannot serve as its binding power or prevent its disintegration.[173]

Makiguchi founded the Soka Gakkai together with my mentor, Josei Toda, in order to break this tragic pattern of human history. Transcending the narrow imperatives of self-preservation, they stood up to create a robust solidarity of people who take action to protect the dignity of all people's lives. Today, this solidarity has spread to 192 countries and territories around the globe.

The year 2030 will be a major milestone in the effort to promote international cooperation for sustainable development. At the same time, it will mark the 100th anniversary of the founding of the Soka Gakkai. Looking ahead to that significant year, we will continue to strengthen and deepen solidarity among the world's people, working with all those who share the vision of a global society of peace and creative coexistence.

---

172 Tsunesaburo Makiguchi (1871–1944), founding president of the Soka Kyoiku Gakkai (forerunner of the Soka Gakkai) (1930–44).

173 (trans. from) Makiguchi, Tsunesaburo. 1981–97. *Makiguchi Tsunesaburo zenshu* [The Complete Works of Tsunesaburo Makiguchi]. 10 vols. Tokyo: Daisanbunmei-sha. Vol. 6, p. 68.

Afterword

Dr. Olivier Urbain

This book consists of excerpts from the peace proposals that have been published annually for thirty years by the Japanese Buddhist leader Daisaku Ikeda, President of the Soka Gakkai International (SGI) and the founder of the Toda Institute for Global Peace and Policy Research. These peace proposals have explored, discussed and presented solutions to global problems through reforms conducive to the enhancement of the United Nations' effectiveness.

Since its establishment in 1996, the Toda Institute has promoted projects on Human Security and Global Governance with the motto: "Dialogue of Civilizations for Global Citizenship." Since I became its director in 2008, I have overseen such projects as well as taking on the challenge of establishing a new endeavor, namely the study of Ikeda's approach toward the creation of peace through his philosophy and actions. One can mention for example his many visits to the Soviet Union and China during the Cold War era, or his meetings and dialogues with political leaders in order to find ways to release tensions and open paths for cultural and educational exchanges. During these visits and dialogues he has continuously emphasized the importance of the mission and role of the UN, thus expanding the layers of support from the viewpoint of civil society.

As the first result of this study, I published *Daisaku Ikeda's Philosophy of Peace: Dialogue, Transformation and Global Citizenship* in 2010. Looking at Ikeda's extensive writings, which include lectures at universities and research centers, articles in newspapers and magazines, speeches, essays, novels and poems, I focused on two important pillars. The first was built on around fifty books of published dialogues with world leaders and scholars which include British historian Arnold J. Toynbee, scientist Linus Pauling, former Soviet president Mikhail Gorbachev, economist John Kenneth Galbraith and former

Pugwash president Sir Joseph Rotblat, to name a few. The second pillar I focused on was based on Ikeda's peace proposals that have been published on SGI Day (January 26) every year. These proposals focus on the issues and tasks of the time; they express Ikeda's perspective as he looks for insight into the causes and backgrounds of such issues from a philosophical and civilizational point of view, and they present concrete solutions. He has been writing these proposals annually since 1983 without a break.

In addition to excerpts from the peace proposals classified by themes, this book also includes the complete text of individual proposals presented on specific occasions. They are the United Nations Proposal (2006), Nuclear Abolition Proposal (2009), Environment Proposal (2012), and the two most recent peace proposals (2012 and 2013).

Although Ikeda published his first annual peace proposal in 1983, in fact, as a religious leader, he had started to present solutions, visions and proposals for global issues more than a decade earlier. In 1966, he made a proposal for an immediate cease-fire of the Vietnam War; in 1968 came his Proposal for the Normalization of Sino–Japanese Relations; in 1973 he wrote a Proposal for an Educational UN; in 1974 he proposed the establishment of a World Food Bank; and in 1978 he made a Proposal for an Environmental UN. In 1978, Ikeda submitted a proposal with a ten-step plan toward nuclear disarmament to the first UN Special Session on Disarmament, and repeated the same effort in 1982 to the second UN Special Session on Disarmament.

It is obvious to me that his peace proposals started in 1983 as a continuation of these efforts for peace. As the reader can see in the table of contents of this book, he discusses a wide range of issues that continue to torment people worldwide and are priority tasks of the United Nations, such as nuclear and conventional disarmament, regional conflict, poverty, development, human rights, the environment and energy.

Why has a religious leader relentlessly continued to work for the building of world peace and the search for solutions to global issues? Based on Ikeda's own words expressed in dialogues, I consider that there are three main factors in his background that play an important role in answering this question. First is his experience of war during his youth. Ikeda was born in 1928 in Japan, and experienced the bombing of Tokyo, more than once running for safety; his family twice losing their home in air raids, and the loss of his eldest brother who was killed in action in what is today Myanmar. Ikeda says he cannot forget the words his brother spoke bitterly while on leave from China, "There is nothing at all glorious about war. What the Japanese army is doing is horrible. Such arrogance and high-handedness! I feel terrible for the Chinese people."[1] This was said during a time when war tended to be spoken about in terms of people's bravery and heroism. Even though he was still young, Ikeda etched his brother's words into his heart. Those were the words of truth that most people in Japan at the time would hesitate to speak, but his brother said them without hiding his fury. Another wartime incident engraved in Ikeda's memory was when an American B-29 was shot down by antiaircraft fire. The young pilot parachuted to the ground and was attacked by some people who had crowded around him, both military police and civilians. Ikeda was saddened to hear that a youth of about the same age as him had been hurt and told the story to his mother, who said with genuine sympathy: "How terrible. His mother must be so very worried about him."[2]

I believe that through these experiences, Ikeda developed a conviction that whatever our nationality may be, it is ordinary people just like ourselves who suffer and get hurt by war. Later (1964), when he began writing the novel *The Human Revolution,* he started it with the following words, "Nothing is more barbarous than war. Nothing is more cruel."[3] I feel that the first reason why Ikeda has worked so hard in writing peace proposals every year to build a world without war must lie in his sincere desire as a human being who has experienced the cruelty of war.

The second reason, I think, is to be found in the philosophy that Ikeda puts faith in, based on the spirit of empathy found in engaged Buddhism. Empathy here has something in common with the shared pain shown by his mother and brother. The French philosopher Simone Weil said, "And this same compassion is able, without hindrance, to cross frontiers, extend itself over all countries in misfortune, over all countries without exception; for all peoples are subjected to the wretchedness of our human condition. Whereas pride in national glory is by its nature exclusive, non-transferable, compassion is by nature universal. . . ."[4] Referring to this quote, Ikeda once said, "As a Buddhist, I agree from the bottom of my heart. The great Buddhist

1   Ikeda, Daisaku. 2007. *Restoring the Human Connection: The First Step to Global Peace.* Peace Proposal.

2   Ikeda, Daisaku. 2012. "My Mother." http://www.ikedaquotes.org/stories/my-mother (accessed April 2, 2013).

3   Ikeda, Daisaku. 2004. *The Human Revolution.* Book 1. Santa Monica, California: World Tribune Press, p. 3.

4   Weil, Simone. 2001. *The Need for Roots: Prelude to a Declaration of Duties Towards Mankind.* London: Routledge, p. 172.

teachings, which are said to include more than eighty thousand teachings, are the crystallization of the most humane heart and actions. Especially the 'compassion' which originates from empathy can be called the main pillar of Mahayana Buddhism. . . . The Lotus Sutra expresses warm empathy toward the weak and suffering, using various parables. There, strong empathy toward the weak, poor and sick is flowing ceaselessly as the basis of Buddhism."[5]

Ikeda emphasizes that—contrary to some of the representations of Buddhism prevailing among Western cultures, which assert that the goal of Buddhism lies only in self-perfection through meditation—Buddhist practice is actually grounded in reality. Without denying the idea of "self-perfection," Buddhism seeks to encourage people to immerse themselves into the real world full of suffering, and to unite with others and take action through the free blossoming of creative energy. Ikeda considers the existence of the United Nations to be a core component for building a better world, and has supported it throughout the years. At a meeting with UN Under-Secretaries-General Rafiuddin Ahmed and Jan Martenson in 1989, Ikeda stated that "The Buddhist philosophy which teaches peace, equality and compassion is in keeping with the spirit of the UN. Therefore, to support the UN is for us inevitable. Otherwise, we would be betraying our mission as Buddhist practitioners."[6] In this sense, Ikeda's support of the United Nations is not based on idealism or naive expectations. It is an expression of his compelling wish for peace as a person who is rooted in his religious background, as symbolized in words such as "inevitable" and "mission."

Thirdly, it is the vow and determination that he made to his mentor, Josei Toda, the second president of the Soka Gakkai. The SGI, a lay Buddhist organization which today has spread to 192 countries and territories, has its roots in the Soka Kyoiku Gakkai (Value-Creating Education Society, the forerunner of the Soka Gakkai) that was established in Japan in 1930. Its first president, Tsunesaburo Makiguchi, promoted "humanitarian competition" which seeks happiness for self and others rather than the type of competition where the strong victimize the weak, as illustrated by Japanese imperialism at that time. This is discussed in his book *The Geography of Human Life* (1903) published in

---

5   (trans. from) Ikeda, Daisaku. 1989. "Gendai bunmei to bukkyo." [Contemporary Civilization and Buddhism]. *Seikyo Shimbun*. June 11, p. 3.

6   (trans. from) Ikeda, Daisaku. 1989. During a meeting with UN Under-Secretaries-General Rafiuddin Ahmed and Jan Martenson on December 5, 1989 for one hour in Tokyo. *Seikyo Shimbun*. December 6, p. 1.

the early twentieth century.[7] Moreover, he was an educator who sought education for the happiness of children, rather than education for national interests, as seen in his great work, *The System of Value-Creating Pedagogy* (1930–34).[8] Second Soka Gakkai president Josei Toda was also an educator, and supported efforts toward a theorization of the Soka educational system. He promoted the idea of global citizenship (1952), affirming that no country or ethnic group should be isolated or victimized. He also made a declaration against nuclear weapons in 1957, one year before his death. Both men were imprisoned by the Japanese military government during the war because neither one gave in to the government's pressure to cease their religious practice. Because of this, the elderly Makiguchi passed away in prison, and Toda's imprisonment for more than two years severely damaged his health.

Ikeda met Toda when he was nineteen years old (1947). He was deeply impressed by Toda's conviction and determination to build solidarity among people seeking peace in postwar Japan, and took faith in the same religion as his mentor. For ten years until Toda's passing, Ikeda worked hard, next to Toda, and developed the conviction and determination to "rid the world of misery."[9] Toda once said to Ikeda: "You need not only to make concrete proposals for the peace of humankind, but to take the lead in working toward their implementation. Even when such proposals are not fully or immediately accepted, they can serve as a 'spark' from which a movement for peace will eventually spread like wildfire. Theorizing that is not grounded in reality will always remain a futile exercise. Concrete proposals provide a framework for the transformation of reality and can serve to protect the interests of humanity."[10] Becoming the "fulcrum of Archimedes," the desire of people who wish for positive change will create a power to move the heavy walls of reality, when alternative possibilities for problem solving are presented.

---

7   Makiguchi, Tsunesaburo. [1903]. *Jinsei chirigaku* [The Geography of Human Life] in *Makiguchi Tsunesaburo zenshu* [The Complete Works of Tsunesaburo Makiguchi]. Tokyo: Daisanbunmei-sha. Vols. 1–2.

8   Makiguchi, Tsunesaburo. [1930–34]. *Soka kyoikugaku taikei* [The System of Value-Creating Pedagogy] in *Makiguchi Tsunesaburo zenshu* [The Complete Works of Tsunesaburo Makiguchi]. Tokyo: Daisanbunmei-sha. Vols. 5–6.

9   Toda, Josei. 2012. "Global Citizenship." http://www.joseitoda.org/vision/global (accessed April 2, 2013).

10 Ikeda, Daisaku. 2012. *Human Security and Sustainability: Sharing Reverence for the Dignity of Life*. Peace Proposal.

I believe that Ikeda's message has more power than mere political opinion because it is based on the harsh experience of war, a sense of mission from a Buddhist perspective, and his pledge to his mentor Josei Toda. In his 2012 peace proposal, Ikeda states, "The peace proposals I have continued to author every year for the past thirty years represent my efforts to fulfill my personal vow to my mentor."[11] The Toda Institute was established by Ikeda to embody a people's research institute, rather than a national or private organization, with a mission to "attempt to contribute to the formation and enhancement of a global movement of people's power," as mentioned in the 1996 peace proposal. Since then, this institute, named after Josei Toda, has expanded its networks to hundreds of scholars on all continents, based on its motto of global citizenship.

Just as with the creation of the institute, several events became a reality as Ikeda's proposals became a driving force to start a new move in international society or encouraged and enhanced efforts at the UN. For example, Ikeda proposed in 1983 that an early summit meeting between the US and the Soviet Union should take place "in order to stop nuclear competition." Prior to making this proposal, Ikeda visited the Soviet Union and met with Prime Minister Nikolai Tikhonov in May 1981. There he mentioned that Soviet and US leaders should meet and discuss issues in a neutral place such as Switzerland, away from Moscow.

In his 1985 peace proposal, Ikeda repeated that the leaders should meet as soon as possible. This was realized at the Geneva and Reykjavík summits that took place in November 1985 and October 1986, respectively. Negotiations continued, and in 1987 the Intermediate-Range Nuclear Forces Treaty (INF) was signed at the meeting of President Mikhail Gorbachev and President Ronald Reagan in Washington. It was the first treaty to reduce nuclear weapons.

In recent years, other examples of ideas that became a reality and that had been expressed in Ikeda's proposals were the "UN Decade of Education for Sustainable Development," through the efforts of the SGI and other NGOs to raise awareness, which started in 2005, and the "World Programme for Human Rights Education."

---

11   Ibid.

Responding to Ikeda's strong advocacy for and promotion of Education for Sustainable Development in 2002, the SGI initiated the proposal for the establishment of a UN Decade of Education for Sustainable Development in consultation with other NGOs in Japan on the occasion of the World Summit for Sustainable Development in 2002. After Ikeda's ideas were incorporated in the actual action plan of the summit, the proposal was eventually adopted by the 57th UN General Assembly, and the decade started in 2005.

In response to Ikeda's message to the World Conference against Racism held in 2001 in Durban, South Africa, the SGI and other NGOs made a presentation at a roundtable on Education for Human Rights and Peace at the NGO Forum held in parallel with that conference. Further, Mr. Ikeda called for a global framework for human rights education to continue after the UN Decade in the 2002 and 2004 peace proposals. Focusing on influencing global policymaking at the former UN Commission on Human Rights, the organizations continued networking, contributing to the process of the 59th UN General Assembly's adoption on December 10, 2004, of the resolution that proclaimed the World Programme for Human Rights Education as a successor to the UN Decade for Human Rights Education.

I believe that the uniqueness of Ikeda's proposals lies in the fact that he has continuously advocated the importance of solidarity among people to solve global issues, based on his belief and endless trust in the power of awakened people and on a solid optimism that problems that were created by people can be solved by people.

In this sense, the words of Pugwash President Sir Joseph Rotblat resonate with messages by Ikeda throughout his peace proposals. Rotblat said, "I believe that people have the power to influence society. No effort is a waste. When a small stone is thrown into a pond, the ripples travel widely out from the center. . . . Every person has the power to create ripples that can change society. If these efforts are concentrated and channeled through NGOs, inevitably the power to influence society will grow."[12]

As editor of this book, I hope that it will be useful in helping to strengthen the solidarity of people who seek solutions to global problems and in inspiring those who wish to enhance the UN's effectiveness. I would like

---

12   Rotblat, Joseph and Daisaku Ikeda. 2007. *A Quest for Global Peace: Rotblat and Ikeda on War, Ethics and the Nuclear Threat*. London: I.B.Tauris, p. 114.

to express my deepest appreciation to SGI President Daisaku Ikeda who has generously agreed to the publication of this volume, and to former UN Under-Secretary-General Ambassador Anwarul K. Chowdhury who proposed the idea for this book and wrote the foreword.

October 24, 2013
Commemorating UN Day
Olivier Urbain
Director, Toda Institute for Global Peace and Policy Research

Index